VERSION 4.1

Using ACCPAC® for Windows®

Small Business Series™

Erik J. Genzer
John P. McMurray

Password ADMIN

BJ

Toronto

Canadian Cataloguing in Publication Data

Genzer, Erik
Using ACCPAC for Windows Small Business series, version 4.1

ISBN 0-201-83042-6

1. ACCPAC for Windows (Computer file). 2. Small business – Accounting – Computer programs. I. McMurray, John, 1942– . II. Title.

HF5679.G464 2001 657'.9042'02855369 C00-931839-9

0-201-83042-6

Vice President, Editorial Director: Michael Young
Acquisitions Editor: Samantha Scully
Marketing Manager: James Buchanan
Associate Editor: Veronica Tomaiuolo
Production Editor: Marisa D'Andrea
Copy Editor: Laurel Sparrow
Production Coordinator: Patricia Ciardullo
Page Layout: Nelson Gonzalez
Art Director: Mary Opper
Cover Design: Anthony Leung
Cover Image: Digital Vision, Ltd.

2 3 4 5 05 04 03 02

Printed and bound in Canada.

The pages in this book open easily and lie flat, a result of the Otabind bookbinding process. Otabind combines advanced adhesive technology and a free-floating cover to achieve books that last longer and are bound to stay open.

CONTENTS

ACKNOWLEDGMENTS

Our thanks go to Samantha Scully, Veronica Tomaiuolo, and Marisa D'Andrea at Pearson Education Canada for the many hours of work they have committed to bring this book to publication. Our gratitude to Bruce Hazelton of Sheridan College for the long hours he spent reviewing the material.

We would like to extend our appreciation to our many students and colleagues at Sheridan College who have contributed to the evolution of our instructional materials over the years.

Finally, we would like to thank our families for their patience and support while we were absorbed with the development of this project.

Erik Genzer
John McMurray
Sheridan College

UNIT 1

INTRODUCTION

CHAPTER 1

USING ACCPAC FOR WINDOWS 4.1

ACCPAC for Windows Small Business Series V4.1 is the most recent version of the industry-leading ACCPAC for Windows accounting software. While it shares the look and feel of ACCPAC for Windows Corporate Series, it does not contain all of its features and functions. Because of this, a working knowledge of ACCPAC for Windows Small Business Series is a genuine asset to accounting students. *Using ACCPAC for Windows Small Business Series, Version 4.1* provides one of the easiest and most effective ways to acquire this knowledge. This book presents practical, hands-on experience organized for individual learning.

Using ACCPAC for Windows Small Business Series, Version 4.1 is a modular, skills-oriented, individualized learning package designed for students with a fundamental knowledge of accounting principles and a basic understanding of Windows operations. It applies the concepts and practices learned in an introductory accounting course to the real world of computerized accounting through the use of a simulation called Devine Designs Inc. End-of-chapter simulations that use the student's name reinforce the same skills he or she has just developed in a particular section. These simulations make excellent hand-in assignments.

This book focuses on the most frequently used accounting modules, and is presented in six logical units:

- Introduction
- System Manager
- General Ledger
- Bank and Tax Services
- Accounts Receivable
- Accounts Payable

Within each unit, chapters are specifically designed as learning modules. They provide step-by-step instructions for students to perform actual accounting tasks and apply them in the *ACCPAC Small Business Series* environment. Throughout the book, printed reports and screen images are provided as key visuals for students, so that data entry errors can be corrected before proceeding to further steps. It is strongly recommended that chapters are covered in the order presented, since the material introduced and the data entered in one chapter is then used in following chapters.

ACCPAC for Windows Small Business Software

ACCPAC's modules are designed to be used individually, or as integrated groups that work together. This flexibility, along with the comprehensive capabilities of each module, has made ACCPAC one of the most popular accounting systems available.

This book details how to install and operate the System Manager, General Ledger, Bank and Tax Services, Accounts Receivable, and Accounts Payable modules.

System Manager

The System Manager is the hub of your accounting system: it controls access to all *ACCPAC for Windows Small Business Series* accounting modules. The System Manager also includes tools that ensure data integrity, as well as complete processing of data entries. Most of the functions are divided between Administrative Services and Common Services. Administrative Services allows you to manage security, check data integrity, and activate other modules for a company. Common Services contains tools used by all modules. The System Manager must be installed first.

General Ledger

The General Ledger is central to the operation of an integrated *ACCPAC for Windows Small Business Series* accounting system. It is a batch-oriented system; transactions entered into the General Ledger are saved in groups called Transaction Batches. Each of these batches can be printed; this allows you to check entries against source documents and make any corrections before posting to the General Ledger. Numerous unposted batches can be in use at any time. Batches of transactions from other *ACCPAC for Windows Small Business Series* modules can be transferred to the General Ledger, printed, and then posted.

Bank and Tax Services

Bank and Tax Services integrates with Accounts Receivable and Accounts Payable. Bank Services tracks checks and deposits, allows you to reverse checks, and keeps an audit trail of all payments and deposits. Tax Services allows you to manage the taxes incurred by a company's sale or purchase of goods and services. These services are normally activated after the Chart of Accounts has been set up in the General Ledger.

Accounts Receivable

Accounts Receivable allows you to manage customer accounts and track important sales information and outstanding balances. You can easily record invoices, apply cash against outstanding invoices, and create recurring charges for quick invoicing of monthly charges. Printing the Posting Journals provides a complete audit trail. Accounts Receivable is fully integrated with Bank Services for complete bank reconciliation, as well as with Tax Services for the recording of sales tax liabilities.

Accounts Payable

Accounts Payable performs all of the record-keeping functions of an organization's purchasing and bill-paying processes. It allows rapid entry of vendor invoices, flexible cash disbursement, and full check reconciliation. Printing Posting Journals and Check Registers provides a complete audit trail. Accounts Payable is fully integrated with Bank Services and Tax Services.

Using This Book

This book follows the accounting cycle for Devine Designs Inc., a start-up Web design company. Each chapter is designed as a learning module that covers a specific set of related functions (using transactions that involve Devine Designs Inc.). Step-by-step instructions are provided for completing each task. Several end-of-chapter cases are available for you to reinforce the knowledge gained in each completed chapter. The parts and chapters should be worked through in order, as concepts and data from one chapter are used in subsequent chapters.

As you work through each chapter, read the descriptions and instructions carefully. If you miss an instruction, the program may appear to work improperly. Watch the "On Screen Display" as you make selections or enter data. Try to understand the system of icons, data entry windows, and messages. Too often, people using a learning package just click the mouse or press keys as instructed, without really paying attention to what each keystroke does.

When you make a mistake, do not get discouraged—making mistakes often provides the best opportunity for learning a software package. Try to trace the error to its source and then correct or adjust it.

Remember to back up your data frequently. When you work with the General Ledger, Accounts Receivable, and Accounts Payable, you should back up your data files after each chapter. If you are working on a network, ask your network administrator about back-up procedures and file locations.

The four Murphballs & Co. cases allow you to practice the skills learned in each of the four main units: General Ledger, Bank and Tax Services, Accounts Receivable, and Accounts Payable. These cases can be handed in as major assignments for a course on *ACCPAC Small Business Series.*

A Note to Instructors

The database structure created by ACCPAC is quite large. If you are working in a networked environment, ***your students need at least 40 megabytes of storage space.*** Regular back-ups will require another 40 megabytes. If the student has insufficient data storage space available, many different types of error messages will appear. The best place for a student to store data files is either on a separate Zip drive, or on the hard drive of a laptop computer linked to the network.

As an instructor, you should first work through the book and cases in the same environment used by the students. This way, if there are problems concerning insufficient memory, you will be aware of them before receiving questions from students. Preparing the material on your home computer may not be the most efficient approach.

It is recommended that your students follow the topics in the order presented. However, if the focus is on Accounts Payable or Accounts Receivable, you can omit the General Ledger. If you do this, the General Ledger account numbers must be entered directly; the finder cannot be used.

We recommend that you personally complete all of the chapters that your students will be doing. This hands-on experience will enable you to provide even more valuable assistance to your students.

Students will make mistakes; they will often have extra batches, and batches in a different order from that shown in the book. Do not be concerned; use the mistakes as an opportunity to reinforce your students' learning in both the accounting practice and the use of ACCPAC.

UNIT 2

SYSTEM MANAGER

CHAPTER 2

INSTALLATION

In this chapter, you will install the ACCPAC System Manager. If you are installing ACCPAC on a network, contact your network administrator and refer to the ACCPAC System Manager Administrator Guide.

Before installing the System Manager or an accounting application, you need an activation code from ACCPAC International. If you do not have an activation code, you can request one via the Internet (http://www.accpac.com/products/finance/accdocs/support/activation_form.asp). ACCPAC International will e-mail or fax the required information to you quickly. You need a specific activation code for each application.

System Requirements

The minimum recommended hardware that you need to run ACCPAC is:

- a personal computer with a 133 MHZ Pentium processor and 32 megabytes RAM;
- a VGA (or higher resolution) monitor, a mouse, and a 220-column printer (a laser printer is recommended);
- Microsoft Windows 95 or Windows NT 3.5, or higher; and
- a CD-ROM drive for software installation.

Installing the System Manager

Using Add/Remove Programs

❑ Display the Windows Desktop on your screen, and close all other programs.
❑ Insert the Pervasive ACCPAC System Manager 4.1 CD-ROM.

The System Manager Installation window (Figure 2-1) should appear if you are using Windows 95, 98, or NT, and Autorun is turned on. If this window does not appear, use Run on the Start menu and run the SETUP.EXE program from the CD drive root directory.

❑ Click: **Install ACCPAC (32-bit)**

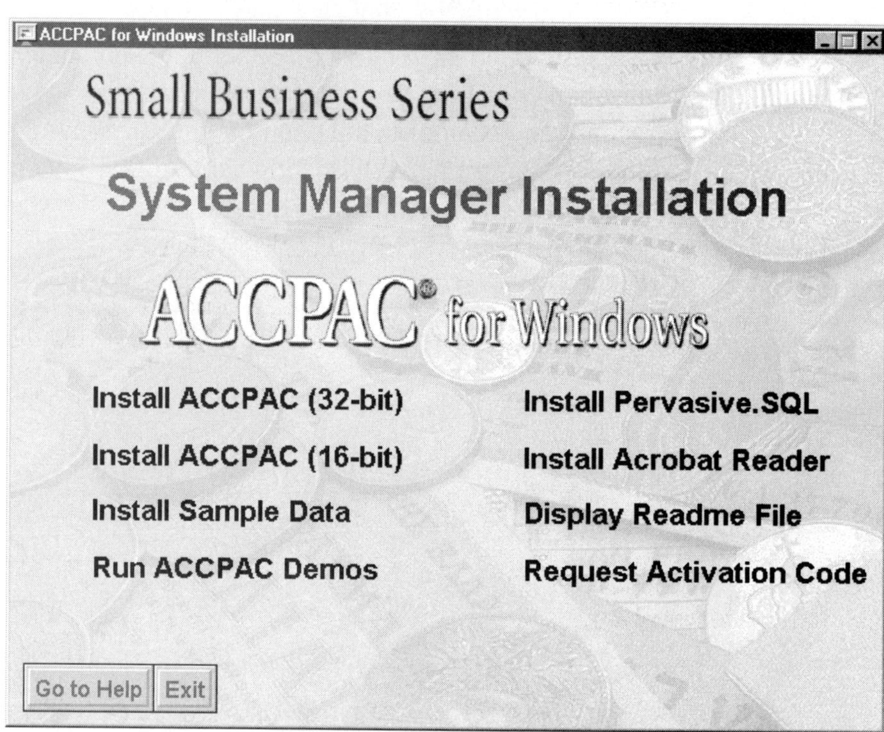

FIGURE 2-1
System Manager Installation Window

ACCPAC for Windows will load the installation software and then display a series of dialog boxes that enable you to enter the information needed to install the System Manager.

WELCOME

The ACCPAC System Manager Welcome window, shown in Figure 2-2, should be displayed on your screen.

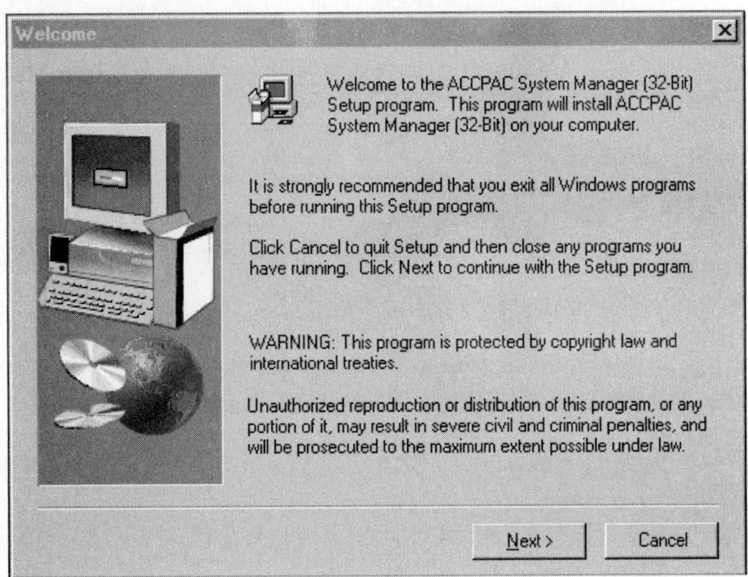

FIGURE 2-2
Welcome Window

Before running the ACCPAC System Manager Setup program, close all other Windows programs. If necessary, click **Cancel**, exit any other Windows programs, and then start installation over again.

❑ Click: **Next** [Next >]

SOFTWARE LICENSE AGREEMENT

The next window, shwon in Figure 2-3, displays a copy of the licensing agreement for installing and using ACCPAC. Use the scroll bar to view the whole agreement.

FIGURE 2-3
Software License Agreement Window

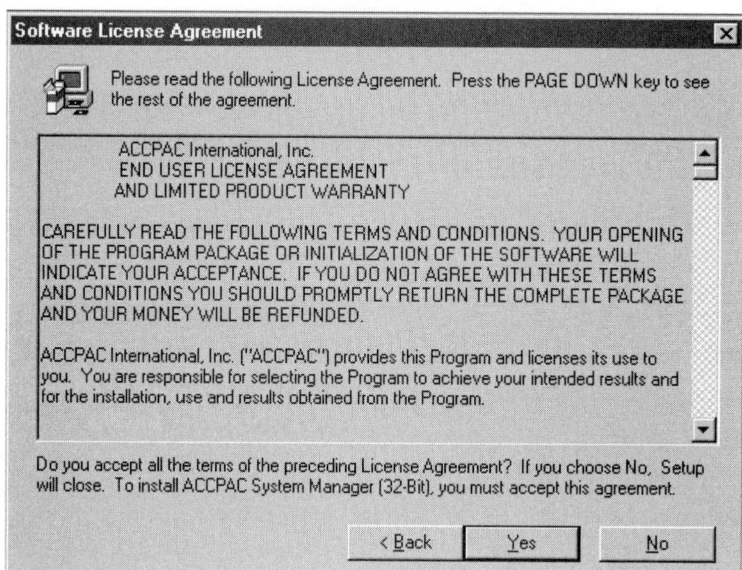

❑ Click: **Yes** [Yes] to accept the terms of the license agreement

DIRECTORIES

The ACCPAC for Windows Directories window, Figure 2-4, should appear. This window is used to enter the paths, or storage locations, that will be used by ACCPAC.

FIGURE 2-4
ACCPAC for Windows Directories Window

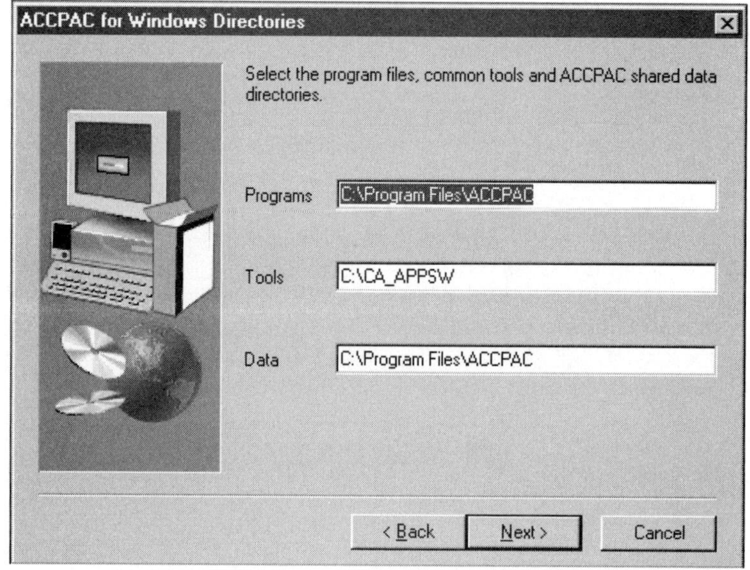

WARNING

If you want to install the System Manager to a different drive or directory, change the default pathname. If you later change the default pathname for this program, you must also edit the PLUSWIN.INI file in your Windows directory.

Programs

The Programs text box identifies where you want to install the System Manager and accounting application program files. The default directory is C:\ProgramFiles\ACCPAC.

Tools

Many of the software applications available from ACCPAC International use the same programs to perform identical tasks. These programs are called common tools and are stored in the same directory or folder on your hard drive. The default directory is C:\CA_APPSW. If these common tools have already been saved to another directory, type the pathname for that directory in the text box.

Data

The Data directory is the parent directory for the Company, Site, and User directories that ACCPAC uses to store your data. If you are installing the System Manager on a network, ask the network manager for the proper directory for the shared files.

❑ Click: **Next** [Next >] to continue

ACTIVATION

The first Activation window is shown in Figure 2-5.

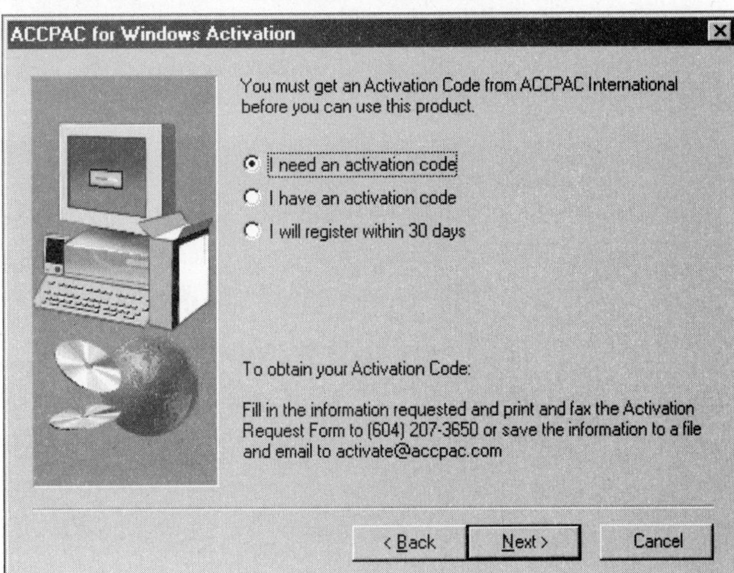

FIGURE 2-5 ACCPAC Activation Window 1

If you have an activation code,

❑ Select: **the option button** for "I have an activation code"

❑ Click: **Next** [Next >] to display the second Activation window, Figure 2–6

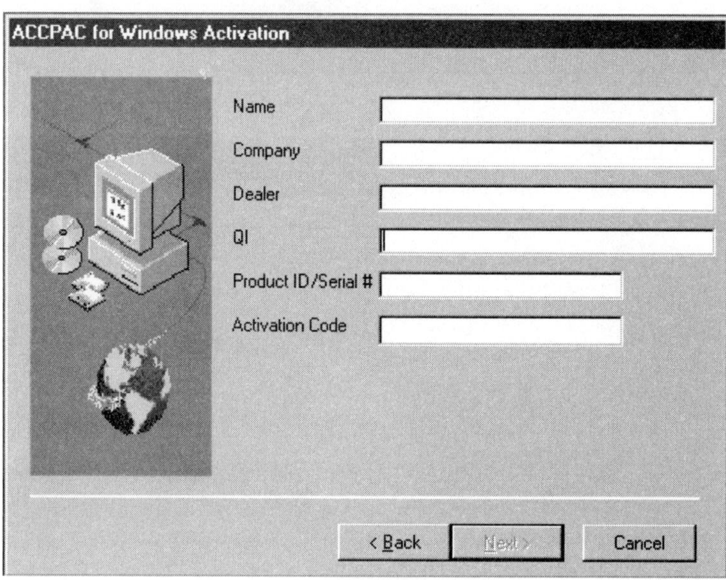

FIGURE 2-6
ACCPAC Activation Window 2

You must fill in the text boxes with the exact information supplied by ACCPAC International in response to your activation code request.

❑ Type: **your name** in the Name text box
❑ Press: **Tab** [Tab]
❑ Type: the **company name** in the Company text box
❑ Press: **Tab** [Tab]
❑ Type: the **name of the software vendor** in the Dealer text box
❑ Press: **Tab** [Tab]
❑ Type: the **name of the qualified installer** in the QI text box
❑ Press: **Tab** [Tab]
❑ Type: the **Product ID number** in the Product ID/Serial # text box
❑ Press: **Tab** [Tab]
❑ Type: the **Activation Code** in the Activation Code text box

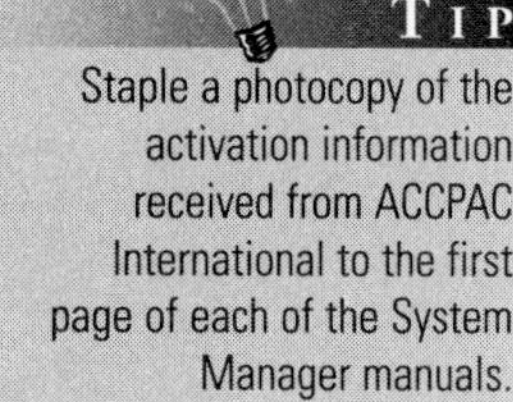

TIP
Staple a photocopy of the activation information received from ACCPAC International to the first page of each of the System Manager manuals.

As you enter the Activation Code, the **Next** button will become active. Check that you have entered the information exactly as it appears on the form you received from ACCPAC International.

❑ Click: **Next** [Next >]

SELECT COMPONENTS

The Select Components Window (Figure 2-7) allows you to select the components of the System Manager to be installed.

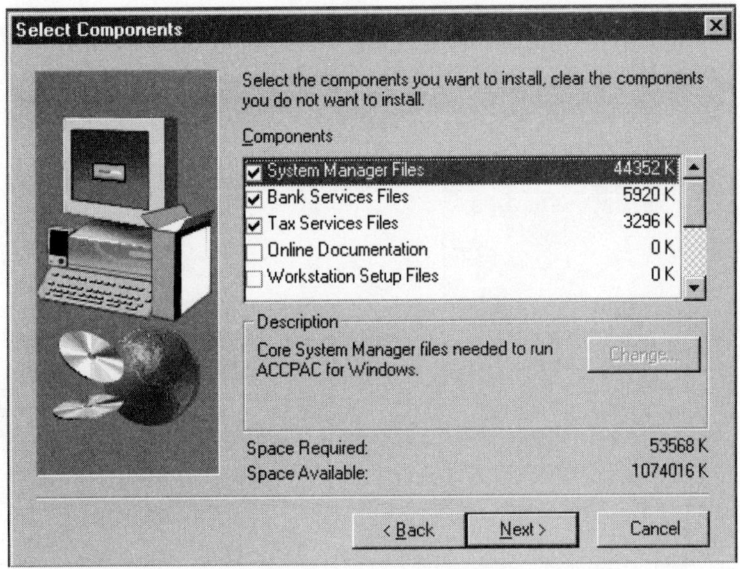

FIGURE 2-7 Select Components Window

Each selected component is indicated by a check mark in the box to the left of the component name. The hard drive storage space required for each component is shown at the right.

WARNING

If you are installing on a network, check the component selection with your network manager.

To install the System Manager on a non-networked personal computer, make certain that the Workstation Setup Files component is not selected.

The System Manager Files, Bank Services Files, and Tax Services Files should be indicated by a check mark. If one of these is not selected, click on it.

❑ Click: **Next** [Next >]

Ensure that the Pervasive.SQL 2000 Workstation check box is selected as shown in Figure 2-8.

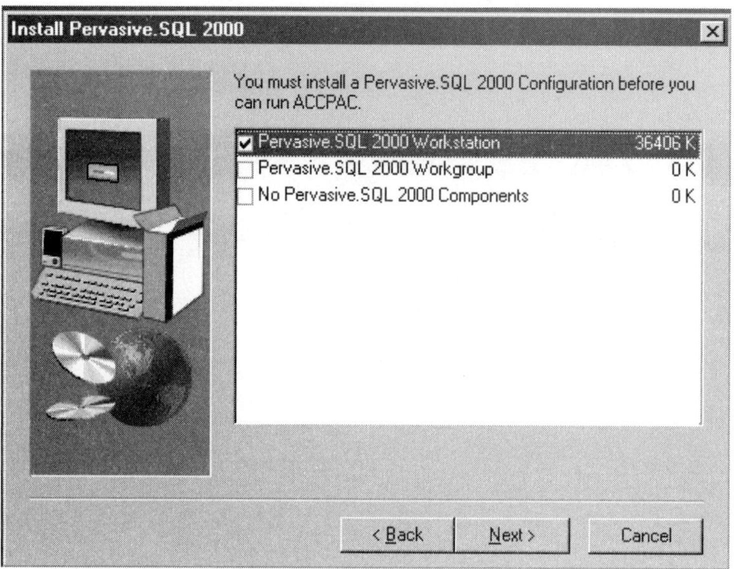

Figure 2-8 Install Pervasive.SQL 2000 Window

❑ Click: **Next** [Next >]

Program Folder

The Select Program Folder window, Figure 2-9, is used to add program icons to a folder in the Windows Start menu.

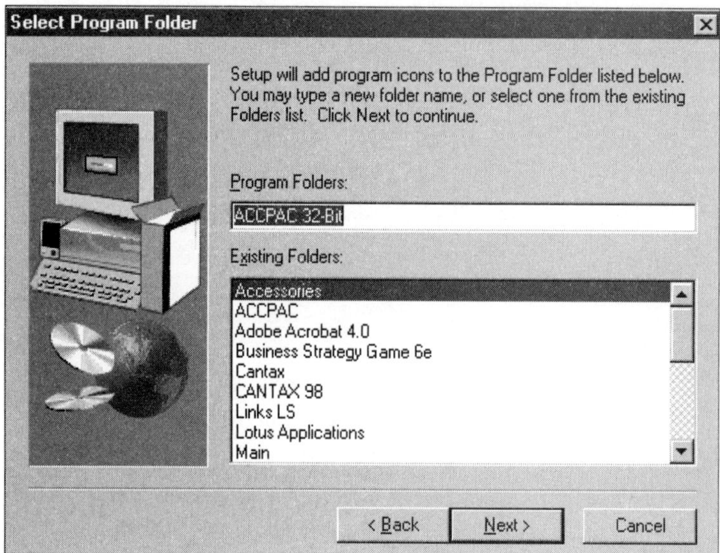

Figure 2-9 Select Program Folder Window

The Program Folder text box displays ACCPAC 32-bit as the default. The scroll box lists the existing folders. If necessary, change the default in the Program Folder text box.

❑ Click: **Next** Next >

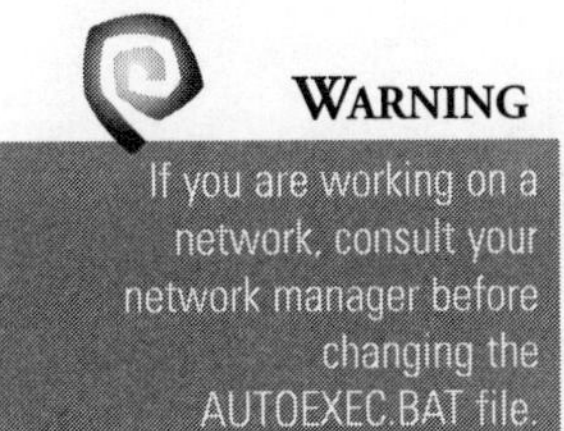

CHANGING THE AUTOEXEC.BAT FILE

ACCPAC will check the AUTOEXEC.BAT file to ensure that it contains the path to the common tools directory. If you are installing your first ACCPAC application, the AUTOEXEC.BAT file can be changed automatically (and this is preferable) or you can enter the changes manually.

❑ Click: **Next** Next >

Before you can use the ACCPAC applications that you have installed, restart your computer. This will be done after the section README.

COPYING FILES

Before copying files to your hard drive, ACCPAC displays the Start Copying Files window, Figure 2-10.

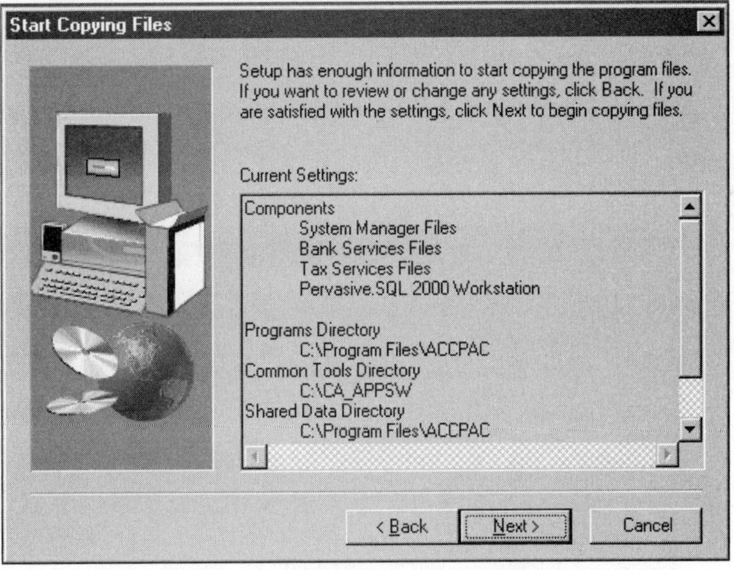

FIGURE 2-10 Start Copying Files Window

Carefully review the components to be installed and the directories to be used.

If there is not enough disk space for installation, click on **Cancel**. You can then remove applications that you do not use, or delete data or document files that you no longer need. Remember that you also require storage space for the data files that you will create as you work with ACCPAC. In some cases, it may be necessary to install additional hard drive storage capacity.

❑ Click: **Next** [Next >]

ACCPAC will display information on the progress of copying files from the CD-ROM.

If Pervasive.SQL 2000 has not been installed on your computer, Figure 2-11 will be displayed.

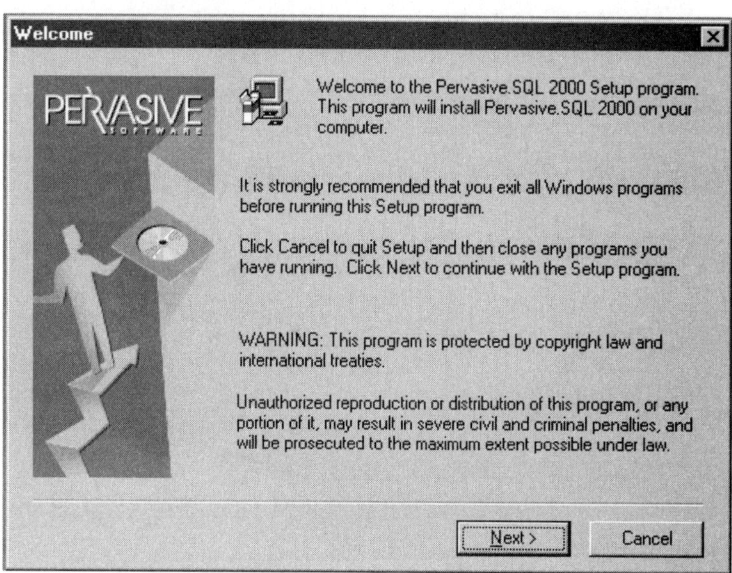

FIGURE 2-11 Pervasive Software Welcome Window

❑ Click: **Next** [Next >] to install Pervasive.SQL 2000

If you see the question as shown in Figure 2-12, it will be necessary to click **yes** and then confirm the installation by clicking **yes** on the Confirmation and License Agreement windows.

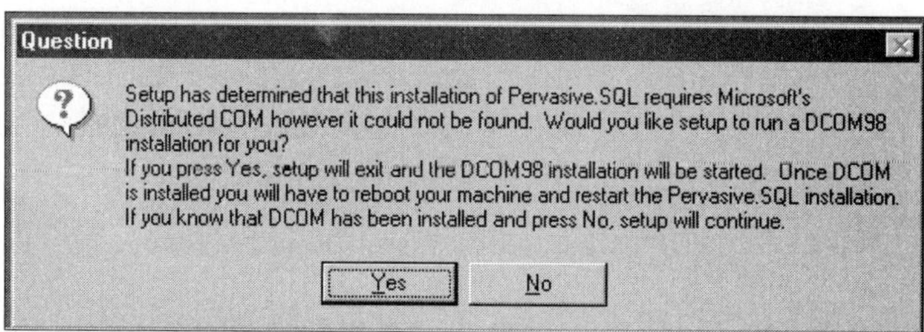

FIGURE 2-12 DCOM98 Question Window

❑ Click: **Yes** [Yes]

❑ Click: **Yes** [Yes] when you see the confirmation allowing installation of DCOM98 for Windows 95 and Windows 98.

If ACCPAC has modified your AUTOEXEC.BAT, it will display a message similar to that shown in Figure 2-13.

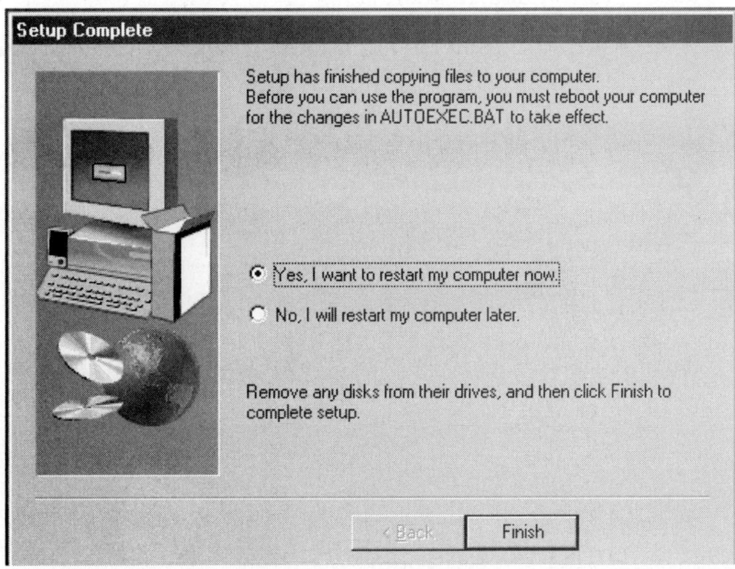

FIGURE 2-13
Setup Complete Window

- ❑ Select: the radio button for **No, I will restart my computer later.**
- ❑ Click: **Finish** [Finish]

You will then have to restart the installation and progress through the screen for installing Pervasive.SQL 2000, as shown in Figure 2-11. After clicking **Next** the Setup Type window (Figure 2-14) should be displayed.

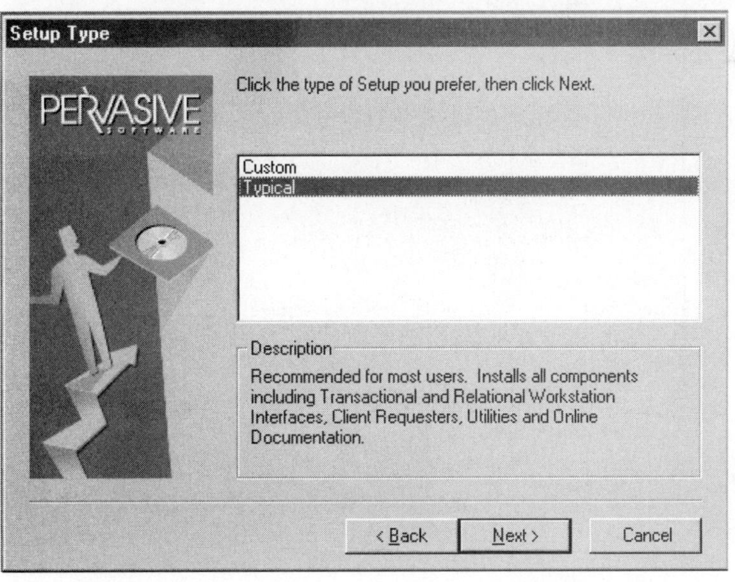

FIGURE 2-14
Setup Type Window

- ❑ Select: **Typical**
- ❑ Click: **Next** [Next >]

The Next window displays the default installation directory for Pervasive.SQL.

❑ Click: **Next** [Next >]

After Pervasive.SQL has been installed, a window will appear that allows you to test the installation. Skip this test.

❑ Click: **Skip**

❑ Click: **Yes** [Yes]

You are then asked, "Would you like to view the ReadMe file?" This is not necessary.

❑ Click: **No** [No]

The System Manager Installation window (Figure 2-1) should be displayed again.

❑ Click: **Exit** [Exit]

README

After all the System Manager files have been copied, ACCPAC will ask if you want to view the System Manager README file (Figure 2-15).

FIGURE 2-15 Setup Complete Window

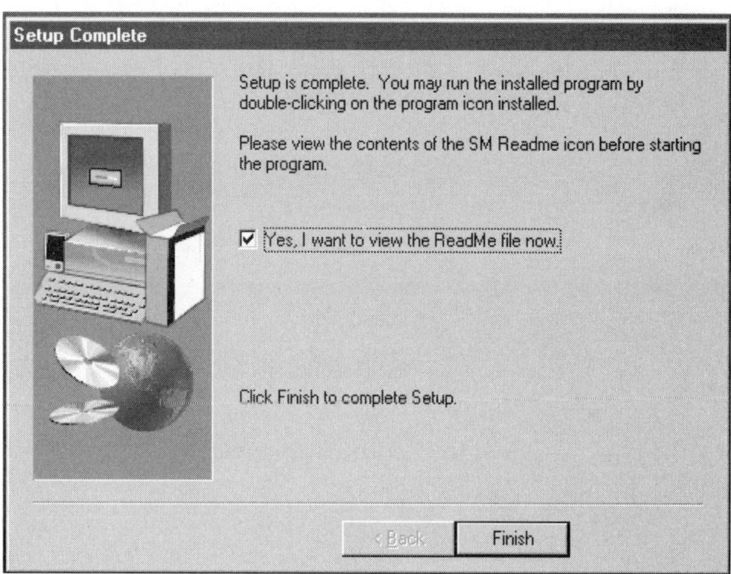

TIP Print the README file and staple a copy of it in your manual. Cut up a second copy of the printout and tape it to the related pages in your manuals.

Most software manufacturers include README files on disk to inform users of changes that have not yet been added to their printed manuals. Whenever you install a new or upgraded software package, print and read the README file and follow any additional installation steps described. Then make the necessary changes in the manual.

❑ Click: **Finish** [Finish] to view the README file in WordPad

❑ Click: the **Printer** icon to print out the README file

❑ Close: the **WordPad** window

If you are asked if you wish to save changes to the README file, click **No**.

Review the printout carefully and follow any special instructions required for installation.

- ❑ Remove: the System Manager CD-ROM and store it in a safe location.

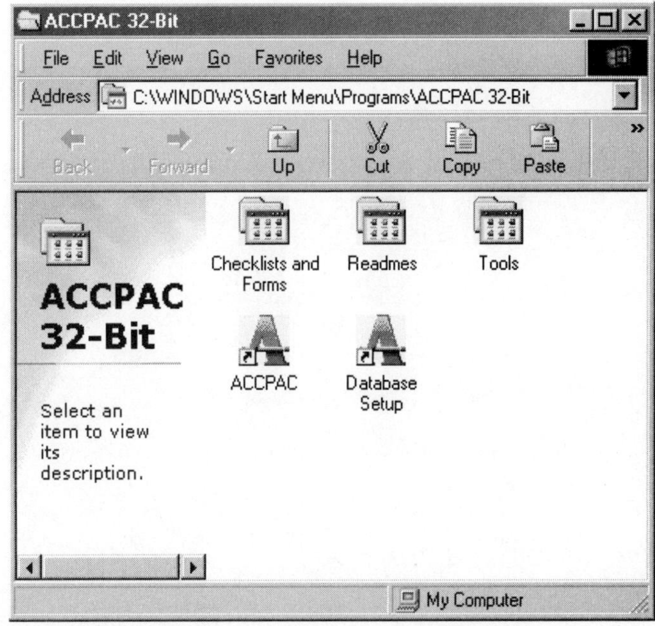

FIGURE 2-16 ACCPAC 32-bit Window

- ❑ Drag and Drop the ACCPAC and Database Setup icons from the program window to your desktop.
- ❑ Close: the **ACCPAC** programs window

RESTARTING YOUR COMPUTER

If the AUTOEXEC.BAT file has been changed, restart your computer.

- ❑ Click: **Start**
- ❑ Click: the **Restart the Computer?** option button
- ❑ Click: **Yes**

CHAPTER 3

DATABASES

WARNING

When installing ACCPAC for Windows on a network, contact your network administrator and refer to the ACCPAC for Windows System Manager Administrator Guide.

In this chapter, you will create the two kinds of databases that you need in order to use ACCPAC for Windows Small Business Series accounting applications with the simulations in this book.

SIMULATIONS

In order to make realistic entries, two simulations are used throughout this book. Devine Designs Inc. is the name of the simulation that you will use as you follow the step-by-step instructions and complete the Your Turn sections in the main parts of the chapters. In the exercises at the ends of many chapters, you will use a simulation that parallels Devine Designs Inc. but uses your name as the company name. You should work through the chapters and exercises in order, as concepts and data from one chapter are used in subsequent chapters.

Devine Designs Inc. is a company that was created on May 1, 2009, by Leslie Lee, John Paul, and Eric Jans. Leslie studied multimedia design, John was a business major, and Eric was a computer science student. During their graduating year, the three friends discussed combining their skills upon graduation to form a company in the multimedia and Internet fields. In their last semester, all three took a course in entrepreneurial studies. In this course, they developed a business plan for what eventually would become Devine Designs Inc. Immediately after finishing their courses, the three friends each contributed $500 for the initial capital of the company.

On May 1, 2009, Devine Designs Inc. was incorporated at a cost of $725 (check number 0001). The plan was for each partner to take a job for 10 months, gaining experience and contacts, while saving money to invest in the company. By March 2010, they had each saved enough money to enable them to quit their jobs and activate Devine Designs Inc., which they did on April 1. During March, the three friends investigated office rentals, used office furniture sales, computer and office equipment leasing, Internet service providers, and potential clients. The company will operate for the month of April using the ACCPAC System Manager and General Ledger. On April 30, 2010, the end of the company's fiscal year, the books will be closed. This simulation is designed so that you can work through the full accounting cycle without having to enter twelve months' work.

In May 2010, Devine Designs will add both Accounts Receivable and Accounts Payable to the ACCPAC for Windows Small Business Series accounting system.

Types of Databases

Databases are organized collections of information. ACCPAC for Windows Small Business Series uses two types of databases: system databases and company databases.

System Database

A system database stores currency and security information that can be used by more than one company database. You would create more than one system database if you kept records for companies that use different currencies or that have different security classifications. The system database must be established before you can create company databases that use this information.

Company Database

A company database contains information that is common to all ACCPAC for Windows Small Business Series accounting applications used by one company. This common information includes the company name, address, options, and fiscal calendar. You must create a company database for each company's accounting records. When you create the company database, you must specify which system database the company uses.

SIGN-ON

WARNING

The Database Setup utility cannot be used if ACCPAC for Windows Small Business Series accounting applications are active. Before using Database Setup, close any open application windows and exit ACCPAC for Windows.

You use similar Sign-on procedures each time you start to work with ACCPAC.

❑ Start: **Windows**

❑ DClick: **Database Setup** 

Your screen should now display the Sign-on dialog box shown in Figure 3-1.

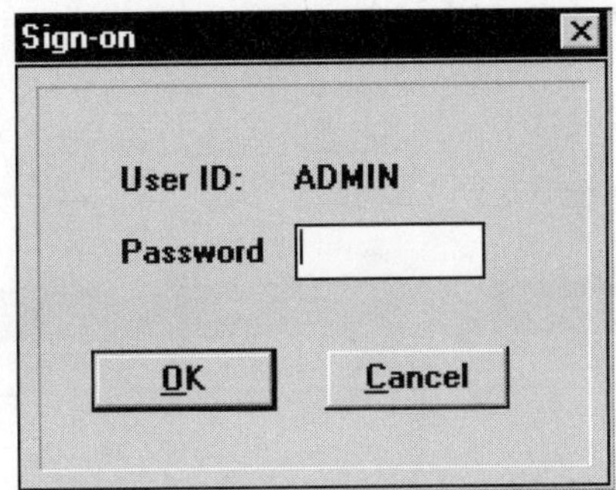

FIGURE 3-1 Sign-on Dialog Box

The User ID displayed is ADMIN, which stands for system administrator. This User ID cannot be changed as ACCPAC for Windows allows only the system administrator to create or maintain databases. Access to these functions is controlled by a password.

❑ Type: **Fred** in the text box

Note that as you type the actual letters are not displayed. This protects the security of the password being entered.

❑ Click: **OK**

A warning message, as shown in Figure 3-2, will be displayed.

FIGURE 3-2 Warning

❑ Click: **OK** to return to the Sign-on dialog box

The default system administrator password supplied with the System Manager software is ADMIN. In order to protect your accounting records, it is important that other users do not have access to the system administrator password. After you have created your databases and activated your accounting applications, change this password. Passwords should be changed regularly to protect the security of your data.

❑ Type: **ADMIN**

You can use upper- or lower-case letters as the password is not case sensitive.

❑ Click: **OK** [OK]

CREATING A SYSTEM DATABASE

A Database Setup window similar to that shown in Figure 3-3 will be displayed. Any databases that have been created will be listed.

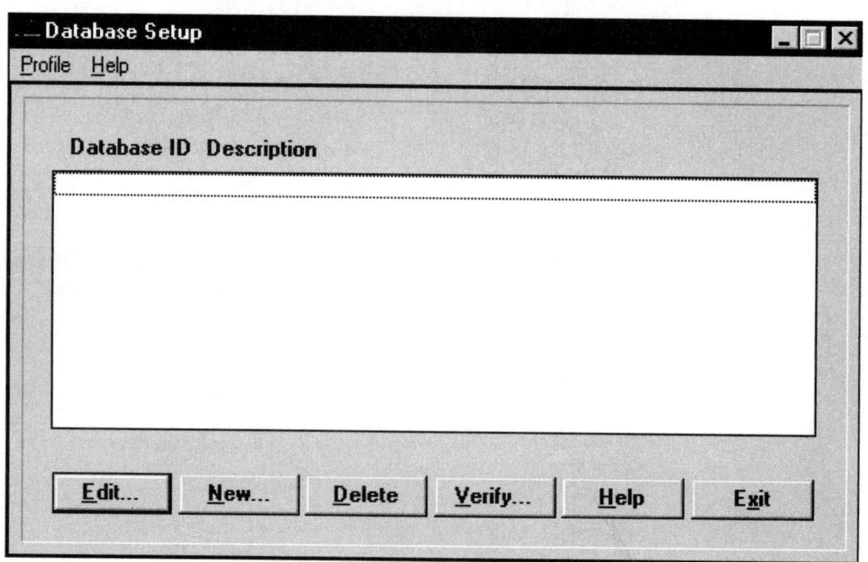

FIGURE 3-3
Database Setup Window

ACCPAC for Windows Small Business Series provides two methods for using this window. A menu bar located just below the Database Setup title bar provides access to the same functions as do the buttons at the bottom of the window. In this simulation, you will use the buttons on the active window.

❑ Click: **New...** [New...] to display the New Database dialog box as shown in Figure 3-4

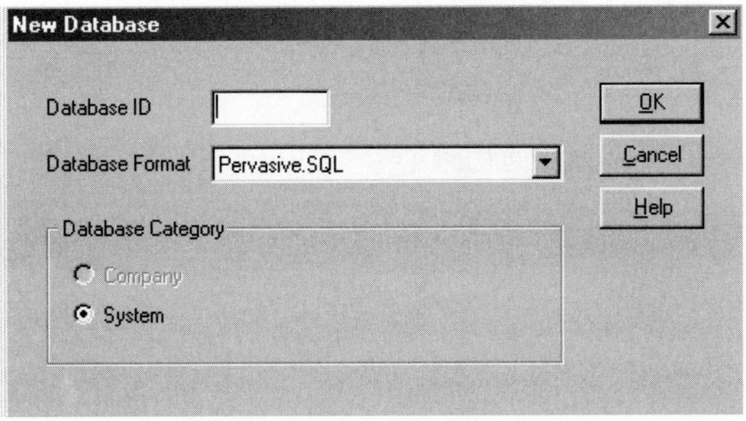

FIGURE 3-4
New Database Dialog Box

If this is the first database to be created, the option button beside System will be on and the insertion point will be in the Database ID text box.

In the Database ID text box, type a unique code for the system database that you are creating. This code can consist of up to six letters or numbers. Enter a meaningful code, as it will be displayed in the title bar of all windows that contain data common to the entire system.

❑ Click: the **Database ID** text box

Devine Designs will use the first three letters from each word in the company name as the system database identification.

❑ Type: **DEVDES**
❑ Press: **Tab** [Tab]

The next data entry area identifies the database format or structure to be used. The default format, **Pervasive.SQL**, matches the database software installed with the System Manager. Do not change this default format.

The option button to the left of System in the Database Category box should contain a black circle, indicating that the new database will be a system database. If necessary, click on this option button to turn it on.

❑ Click: **OK** [OK]

The Edit Pervasive.SQL Database Profile window, Figure 3-5, will appear.

The Description text box allows you to enter a 30-character description for the system database. The Database ID, DEVDES, should be displayed and highlighted in this text box.

❑ Type: **Multimedia Companies** in the Description text box
❑ Press: **Tab** [Tab] to move to the Default Directory text box

FIGURE 3-5
Edit Pervasive.SQL Database Profile Dialog Box

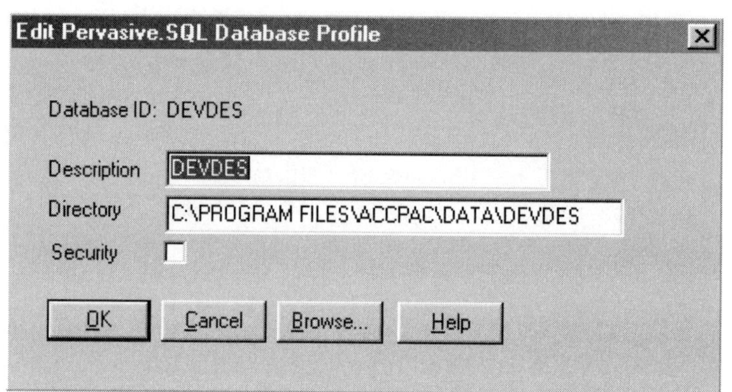

WARNING

If you are working with a networked application, consult your network administrator before changing this default directory.

The default directory is C:\PROGRAM FILES\ACCPAC\DATA\DEVDES. ACCPAC for Windows created the ACCPAC directory when you installed the System Manager. A default subdirectory, DATA, was also created. The default for the Database Setup utility is to create a subdirectory in DATA using the Database ID that you entered. You would use the default directory if you are *not* working with a networked application.

If you are working on a network, type the name of the network directory in the Directory text box.

To store the files for the new database in another location, type the full pathname in the directory text box.

If you wish to limit access to the system data to authorized users, click the Security check box. Devine Designs will not limit access at this time. Ensure that this check box has not been activated.

❑ Click: **OK** [OK] to create the system database

ACCPAC will display a confirmation request (Figure 3-6) for the creation of a directory for storing the new system database.

FIGURE 3-6
Confirmation Dialog Box

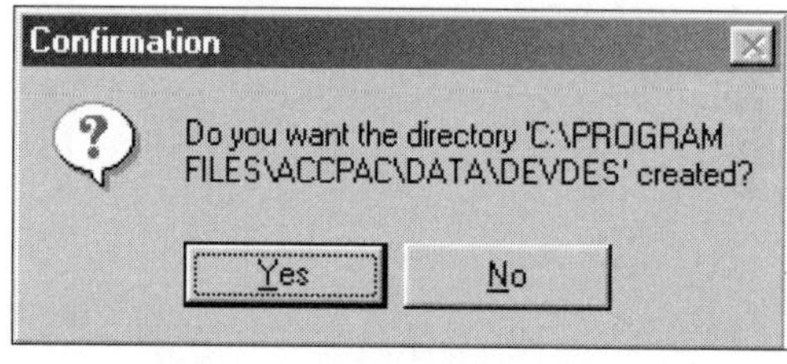

❑ Click: **Yes** [Yes]

After the new system database has been created, the Database Setup window will be displayed showing the new Database ID and Description.

Creating a Company Database

At any time after you have created a system database, you can create company databases that link to it. You must create a separate company database for each company for which you maintain accounting records.

❑ Click: **New...**

In the New Database dialog box that appears (Figure 3-7), the option button beside Company will be on and the code DEVDES will be displayed in the System Database ID list box.

FIGURE 3-7
New Database
Dialog Box

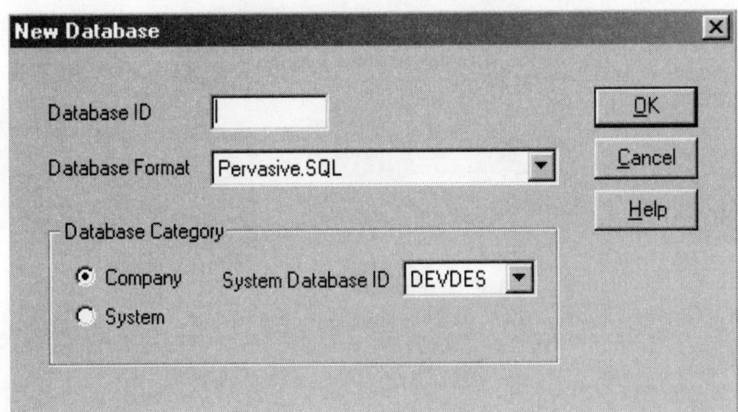

❑ Click: the **Database ID** text box
❑ Type: **DEVINE** as the ID for Devine Designs Inc.

Confirm that the option button beside Company is on, that the Database Format is Pervasive.SQL, and that the System Database ID is DEVDES.

❑ Click: **OK**

The Edit Pervasive.SQL Database Profile window will appear. The new company database ID and its related system database ID will be displayed on the first line, as shown in Figure 3-8.

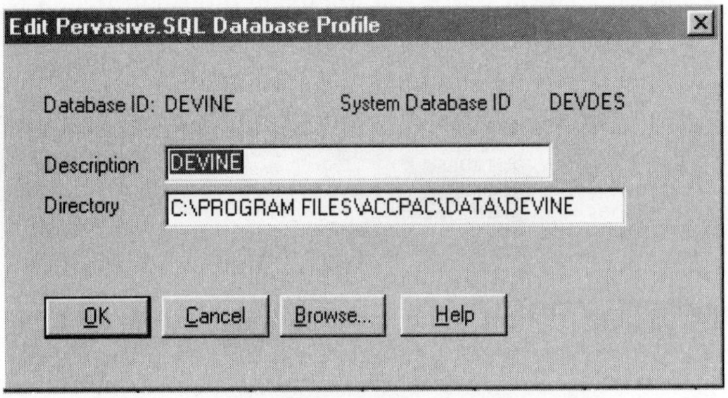

FIGURE 3-8
Edit Pervasive.SQL
Database Profile
Dialog Box

- ❑ Type: **Devine Designs Inc.** in the Description text box
- ❑ Press: **Tab** [Tab]

WARNING

If you are working in a networked environment, consult your network administrator for the proper storage location for your files. Then enter the path for that location in the Directory text box and click OK.

The default directory is C:\PROGRAM FILES\ACCPAC\DATA\DEVINE. To store the company data files in a different location, type the pathname for that location. Store the data files for each company in a separate directory.

- ❑ Click: **OK** [OK] to accept the default directory

If ACCPAC for Windows does not find the directory that you specified, you will be asked to confirm that you want the new directory created (Figure 3-9).

FIGURE 3-9 Confirmation Dialog Box

- ❑ Click: **Yes** [Yes]

After the company database has been created, the Database Setup window will appear with the ID and description for the new company database.

EDITING A DATABASE PROFILE

After a database has been created, the system administrator can edit, or change, the database profile. You can change security, the description, or the location of the company data files. If you change the location of the files, copy the files to the new location before you edit the database profile. When the database profile is edited, the database itself is not changed.

For the companies that you will use in this simulation, it has been decided to limit access to the company data files. The security check box for the system database must be activated.

- ❑ Click: **DEVDES** to highlight the line for the Multimedia Companies system database
- ❑ Click: **Edit** [Edit...]
- ❑ Click: the **Security** check box
- ❑ Click: **OK** [OK]

It has also been decided to add your name to the company database description. This will better identify your printouts if you are using a networked printer.

- ❑ Click: **DEVINE** to highlight the line for the company database for Devine Designs Inc.
- ❑ Click: **Edit** [Edit...]
- ❑ Type: **DDI** followed by your last name

If there is not enough space remaining to enter your complete last name, type as many characters as possible.

- ❑ Click: **OK** [OK]

Deleting a Database

You may wish to delete a database for a company for which you no longer maintain accounting records. Deleting the database frees up space on your hard drive. Use the Database Setup window to delete the company database profile, and then use Windows Explorer to delete the database files and remove the directory. Before deleting a system database, delete all company databases that refer to it.

- ❑ Click: **DEVINE** to highlight the line for the company database for Devine Designs Inc.
- ❑ Click: **Delete** [Delete]

As a safety measure, ACCPAC requires confirmation (Figure 3-10) before the database is deleted.

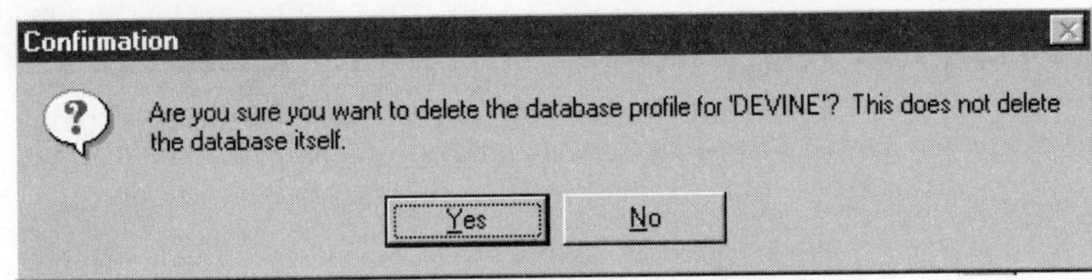

Figure 3-10 Confirmation Dialog Box

If you choose Yes, the database profile will be deleted.

- ❑ Click: **No** [No] to return to the Database Setup window without deleting the database profile

VERIFYING A DATABASE

Before you copy your data files to a backup system, or if you have any problems accessing data, have ACCPAC for Windows verify your database. This process checks the data dictionary entries for your data files.

❑ Click: **Verify** Verify... to display the Verify Database window similar to that shown in Figure 3-11

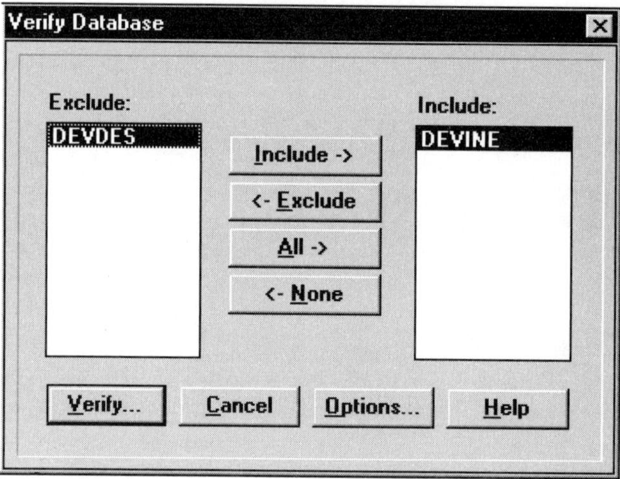

FIGURE 3-11 Verify Database Dialog Box

You can move databases between the Include and Exclude lists by clicking on the database ID and clicking on the Include or Exclude button.

TIP If the log file already exists, ACCPAC will ask for confirmation that you want to overwrite it. If this message appears on your screen, click **Yes** to continue.

❑ Click: **All** All -> to include all databases

❑ Click: **Verify** Verify...

The verify process records any errors it finds in an error log file and displays the file in a window on the screen.

When verification has been completed, a Verification complete message listing the number of errors found will appear, as shown in Figure 3-12. There should be no errors.

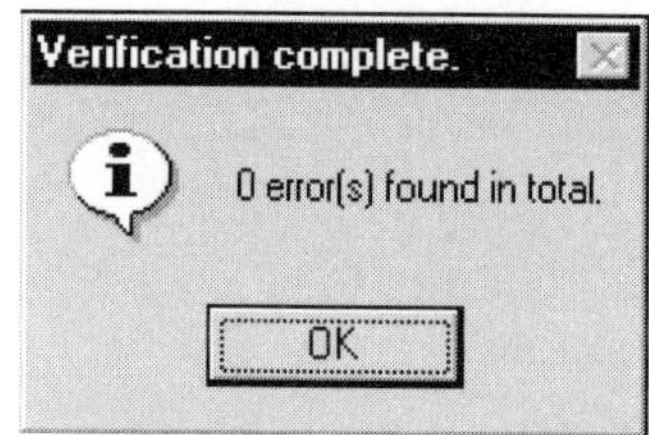

FIGURE 3-12 Verification Complete Message

- ❑ Click: **OK** to view the Verify-Log window

If there are errors, look up each error message in the manuals that came with your software and follow the instructions provided.

FIGURE 3-13
Verify - Log
Window

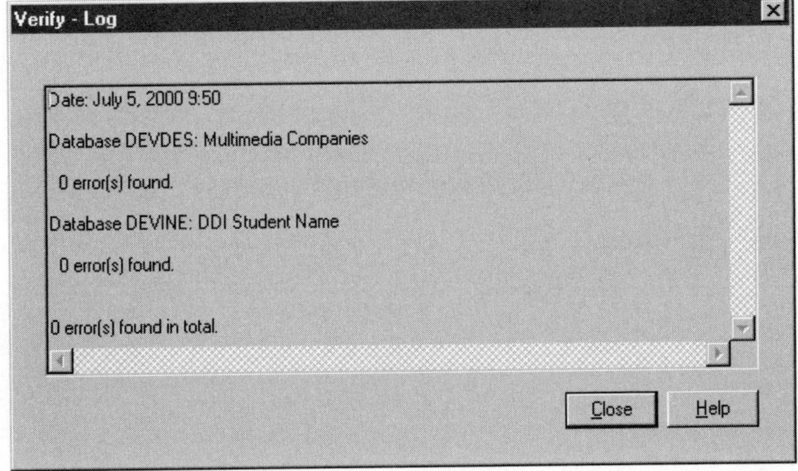

- ❑ Click: **Close** to return to the Verify Database window
- ❑ Click: **Cancel** to return to the Database Setup window
- ❑ Click: **Exit**

REVIEW QUESTIONS

1. Describe the purpose of the system database.
2. Describe the purpose of the company database.
3. Can you use the same company database for multiple companies?

EXERCISE

As you worked through this chapter, you created a system database and a company database for Devine Designs Inc. Your task in this exercise is to create an affiliated company in a nearby town. Because the two companies will be similar, you can use the DEVDES system database, but you must create a new company database.

- ❑ Create the new company database. Use **EXERCO** as the database name.
- ❑ Edit the company database profile to display your full name in the description.
- ❑ Verify the company database to ensure that the data files have been created properly.
- ❑ Exit: **ACCPAC**

CHAPTER 4

COMPANY SIGN-ON AND PROFILE

In the last chapter, you created the basic system and company database structures. In this chapter, you will activate the Administrative Services for the system database and the Common Services for the company database. You will then create the company profile for Devine Designs Inc.

When you sign on to a company, ACCPAC for Windows Small Business Series verifies that the Administrative and Common Services for the company have been activated. If the company database is the first one to use the system database, you will have to activate these services for the system database. If this is the first time that the company database has been used, you will also be prompted to activate common services for the company database. After activation, you must use the common services to create the company profile. You can then activate the accounting applications that you wish to use to record accounting data for the company.

SIGNING ON TO A NEW COMPANY

- ❑ Start: **Windows**
- ❑ Start: **ACCPAC**

ACCPAC will briefly display a copyright and ownership identification window and then display an Open Company dialog box, as shown in Figure 4-1.

FIGURE 4-1 Open Company Dialog Box

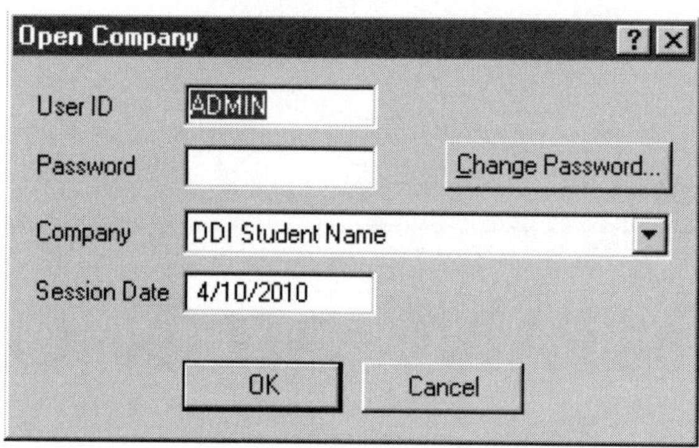

The User ID text box should display and highlight either the default User ID, ADMIN, or the last User ID.

- ❑ If necessary, type **ADMIN** in the User ID text box.
- ❑ Press: **Tab** [Tab]
- ❑ Type: **ADMIN**, the default password for the system administrator

Now select the company database that you wish to work with. If only one company database has been created, the description for that database will be displayed in the company text box. If more than one company database has been created, select the company you wish to work with from the list box.

- ❑ Click: the **list tool** for the Company text box
- ❑ Select: **DDI** followed by your name from the Company list box
- ❑ Press: **Tab** [Tab] to advance to the Session Date text box

The Session Date is usually the actual date that you are working with ACCPAC for Windows, or the date that you wish to record as the processing date. The Devine Design Inc. simulation will use session dates between April 2010 and June 2010 in order to be compatible with the educational version of ACCPAC. In this portion of the Devine Designs Inc. simulation, you will use April 1, 2010 as the Session Date.

- ❑ Type: **040110** in the Session Date field
- ❑ Click: **OK** [OK]

If you make an error or enter an invalid password, a warning message will appear. Click **OK** to return to the Open Company dialog box and then enter the proper password.

Activating Administrative Services

If Administrative Services have not been activated for the system database, ACCPAC will display the following window, shown in Figure 4-2.

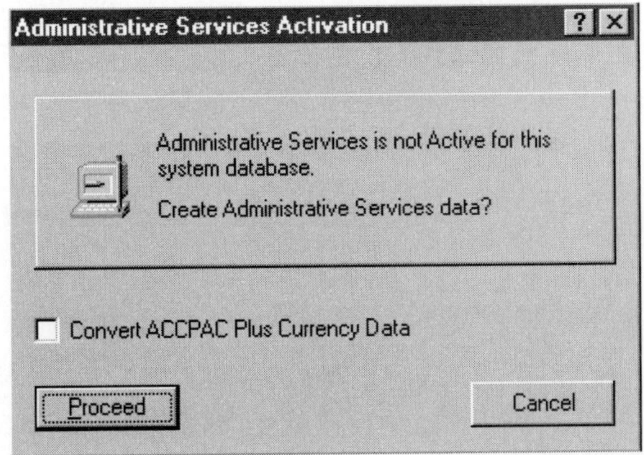

FIGURE 4-2 Administrative Services Activation Window

- ❑ Click: **Proceed** to continue with activation

As activation proceeds, messages will be displayed telling which tables are being created, and that currency codes and rate types are being loaded.

Activating Common Services

The next dialog box (Figure 4-3) allows you to activate Common Services for the company.

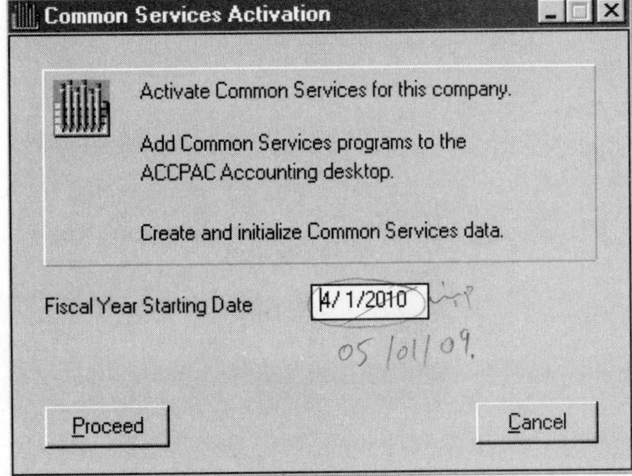

FIGURE 4-3 Common Services Activation Window

Fiscal Year Starting Date

The date displayed in the Fiscal Year Starting Date field is the date entered on the Sign-on dialog box as the Session Date. Type the starting date for the company's current fiscal year in this field. In this portion of the Devine Designs Inc. simulation, you are using April 1, 2010 as the current or processing date. The fiscal year started on May 1, 2009.

- ❑ Select: the **date** in Fiscal Year Starting Date text box
- ❑ Type: **050109**
- ❑ Click: **Proceed** Proceed

ACCPAC for Windows will activate Common Services and create the company's fiscal calendar based on the date that you entered.

Creating the Company Profile

The Company Profile window appears automatically after you have signed on to a new company and activated Common Services. This window contains a notebook, as shown in Figure 4-4.

FIGURE 4-4
Address Page

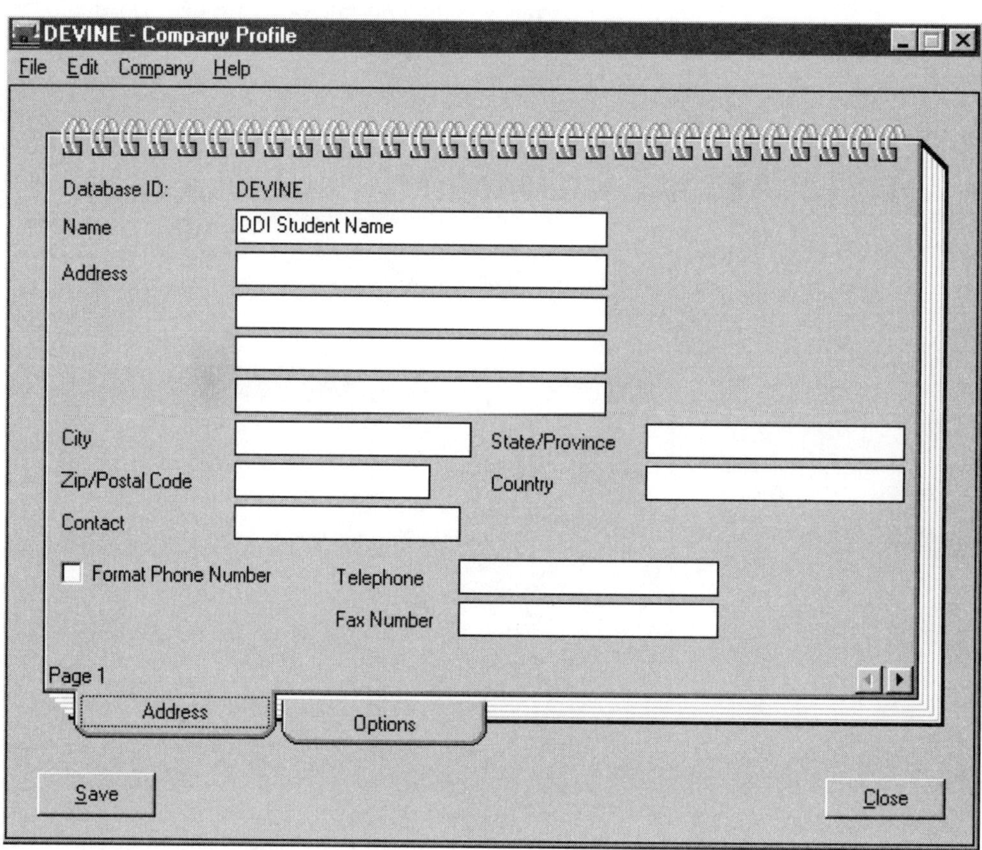

Note that the OK button at the lower left corner of the window is not active.

Address Page

The Address page of the Common Services Activation notebook includes text boxes for the company name, address, phone and fax numbers, and a contact name.

Name

The information that you entered for the description when you created and edited the company database is automatically transferred to the Name text box on the Address page. This text box should contain DDI followed by your last name. If you want to change this information, click inside the text box and enter the changes.

Address

There are four text boxes into which you can enter the company's address. This gives you sufficient space to specify a unit number in an industrial plaza, or a building and department number in a large industrial complex. Devine Designs Inc. is located in unit 14 of a commercial plaza at 286 Main St.

- ❑ Click: the first **Address** text box
- ❑ Type: **286 Main St.**
- ❑ Press: **Tab** [Tab] to advance to the next text box
- ❑ Type: **Unit 14**
- ❑ Press: **Tab** [Tab] three times to move the insertion point down to the City text box
- ❑ Type: **Georgetown**
- ❑ Press: **Tab** [Tab] to move the insertion point to the State/Province text box
- ❑ Type: **your province or state**
- ❑ Press: **Tab** [Tab] to move to the Zip/Postal Code text box

This field will hold sufficient characters to allow the entry of most international postal codes.

- ❑ Type: **your Zip or Postal Code**
- ❑ Press: **Tab** [Tab] to move to the Country text box
- ❑ Type: **your country**

Contact

- ❑ Press: **Tab** [Tab] to move to the Contact text box

The contact text box is used by firms that maintain accounting records for more than one company or one division of a company in separate databases. Use this text box to record the name of the person at the company most often contacted for general information.

- ❑ Type: **Fred Brown**

Phone and Fax

The telephone and fax number text boxes can be formatted to show a three-digit area code in brackets, followed by a three-digit exchange number, a dash, and the last four digits of the number.

- ❑ Click: the **Format Phone Number** check box
- ❑ Click: the **Telephone** text box
- ❑ Type: **5555551212**
- ❑ Press: **Tab** [Tab] to move to the Fax Number text box
- ❑ Type: **5555551313**

Review the information that you have entered. If there are any errors, click on the text box containing the error and make the necessary corrections.

OPTIONS PAGE

- ❑ Click: the **Options** tab at the bottom of the notebook page shown in Figure 4-5

FIGURE 4-5
Options Page

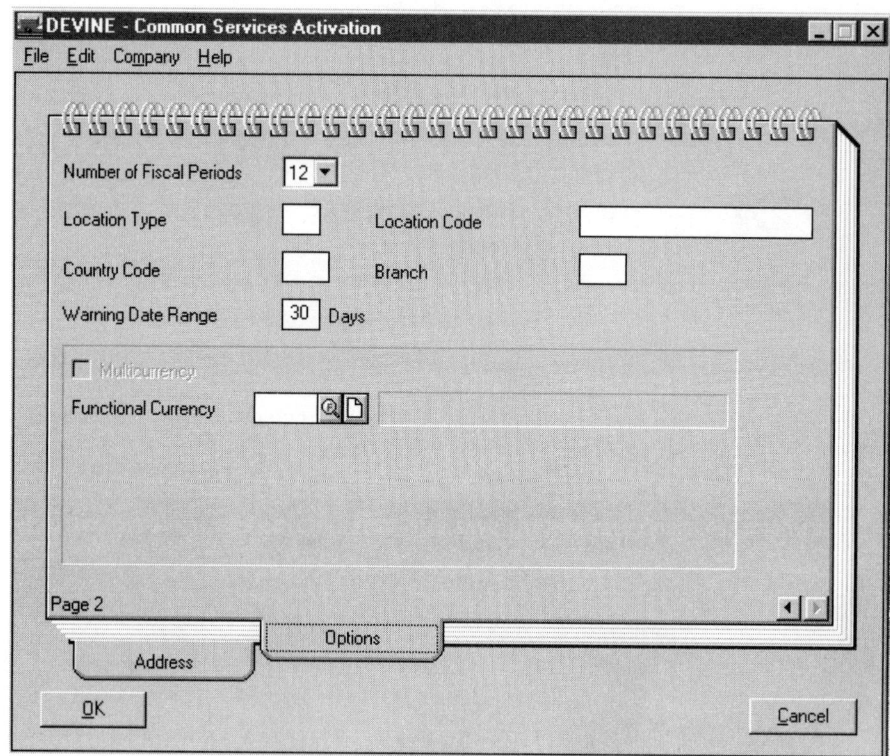

Fiscal Periods

If you change the number of fiscal periods after you have processed accounting information, you will not be able to make comparisons between years that have different numbers of fiscal periods.

You may choose either a twelve- or thirteen-period fiscal year. Select twelve periods if the company's fiscal year is divided into calendar months. Some companies use a thirteen-period fiscal year because that allows 28 days per period for comparison of the activity of identical periods. If you choose a thirteen-period fiscal year, you must specify which quarter will contain four periods. ACCPAC will automatically display a data entry field for this information if you choose thirteen periods.

❑ Select: **12** from the Number of Fiscal Periods list box

This information is used by ACCPAC to fill out fiscal period starting, ending, and report dates on the Fiscal Calendar window. If your fiscal periods vary in length, edit the dates in the Fiscal Calendar window after the company profile has been created.

Location Information

Four optional fields are provided for location information. You could use the location type and code fields for recording value added tax or sales tax information. Devine Designs Inc. has decided to record its GST (Goods and Services Tax) registration number in the location code field.

❑ Click: the **Location Code** text box
❑ Type: **R1245367908**

The Country Code and Branch text boxes can be used to identify different parts of the company for which separate accounting records must be maintained. Devine Designs Inc. has decided not to use these options.

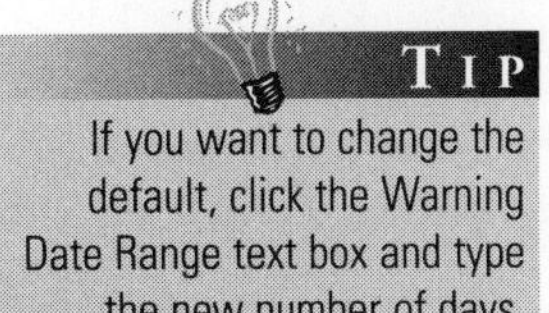

If you want to change the default, click the Warning Date Range text box and type the new number of days. Then press the tab key to complete the entry and move to the next text box.

Warning Date Range

This option helps prevent the accidental entry of incorrect dates as you record accounting transactions. You enter a number of days. If a session date is entered that is more than this number of days after the previous session date, a warning message will be displayed. Thirty (30) days is displayed as a default. Devine Designs will use the 30-days default.

Functional Currency

The Functional Currency field is used to record the code that identifies the currency which the company uses in reports. You must select a functional currency as you are creating the company profile. The functional currency cannot be changed after you save the company profile.

❑ Click: **Finder** for the Functional Currency text box

A window displaying the currency codes supplied with ACCPAC will open, as shown in Figure 4–6.

FIGURE 4-6
Finder – Currency Codes

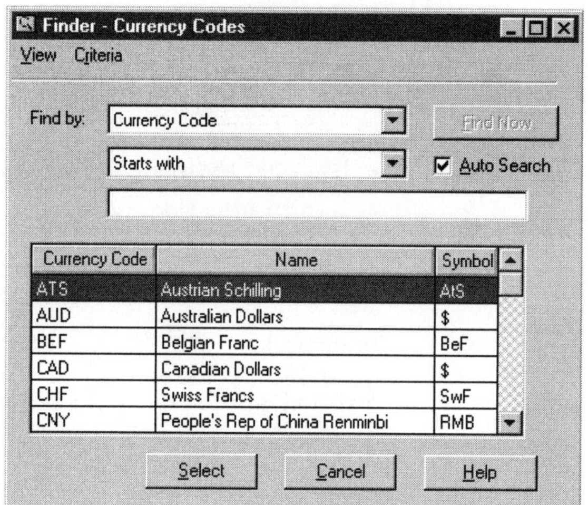

WARNING

If you are not using the educational version, ACCPAC will display an additional check box for multicurrency. Do not activate this check box.

Devine Designs will use "CAD Canadian Dollars" as the functional currency. You would select "AUD Australian Dollars" or "USD U.S. Dollars" if you were working in Australia or in the United States.

❑ Select: The **currency** for your country

The currency code and its description will be transferred to the Options page. Review the information on the Options page. If there is an error, click the field and make the necessary correction.

❑ Click: **Select** [Select]

❑ Click: **OK** [OK]

COMPANY DESKTOP

After a few seconds, the display will change to the company desktop (Figure 4-7). If you are using a version of Microsoft Internet Explorer earlier than version 4.0, the company desktop will look different, but the functions will be the same.

The Company Desktop has menu and tool bars at the top. You can use either of these to access all desktop functions.

The left portion of the menu display shows the folder structure for Devine Designs Inc.

The right portion of the main display shows the Administrative Services and Common Services icons as large icons. You can change the appearance of icons in this area of the screen using the View menu or the display icons on the Tool bar.

FIGURE 4-7
Company Desktop

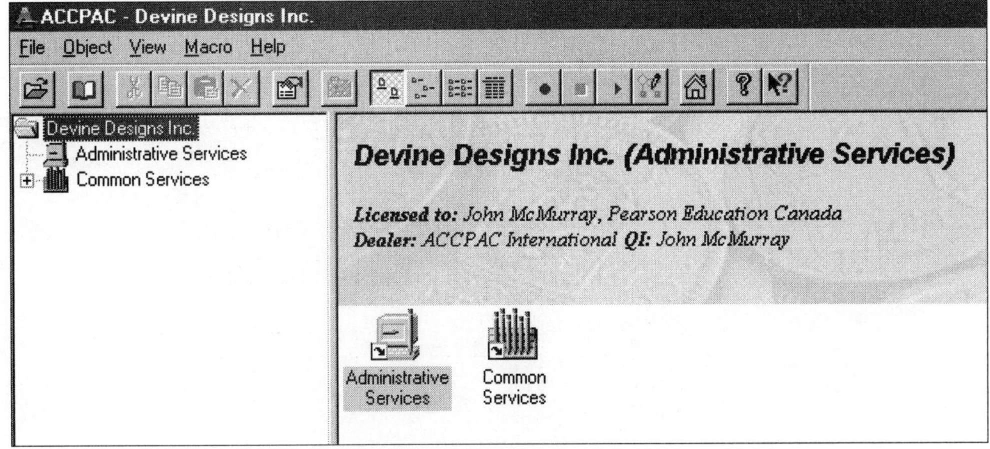

PRINTING THE COMPANY PROFILE

- ❑ DClick: **Common Services**
- ❑ DClick: **Company Profile**

The Company Profile notebook should be displayed

- ❑ Select: **File** on the menu bar
- ❑ Select: **Print** from the File menu

The Print dialog box in Figure 4-8 should display your default printer and the default settings for the report that you are going to print. You can change these settings using the setup button.

FIGURE 4-8
Print Dialog Box

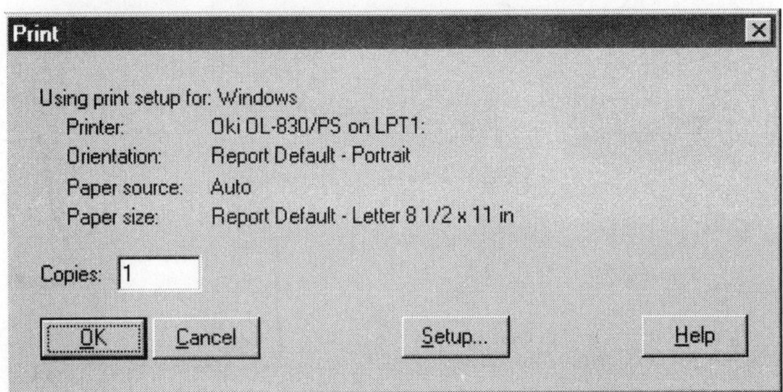

- ❑ Change the number of copies to **2**
- ❑ Click: **OK**

The Company Profile is shown in Figure 4-9.

FIGURE 4-9
Company Profile
(Scan Printout)

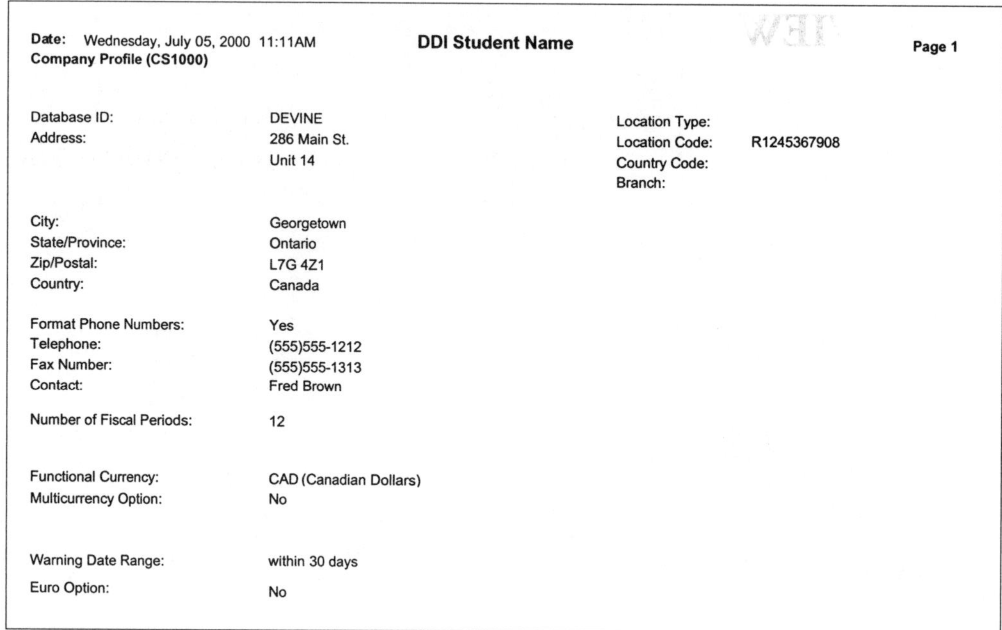

Date: Wednesday, July 05, 2000 11:11AM
Company Profile (CS1000)

DDI Student Name

Page 1

Database ID:	DEVINE	Location Type:	
Address:	286 Main St.	Location Code:	R1245367908
	Unit 14	Country Code:	
		Branch:	
City:	Georgetown		
State/Province:	Ontario		
Zip/Postal:	L7G 4Z1		
Country:	Canada		
Format Phone Numbers:	Yes		
Telephone:	(555)555-1212		
Fax Number:	(555)555-1313		
Contact:	Fred Brown		
Number of Fiscal Periods:	12		
Functional Currency:	CAD (Canadian Dollars)		
Multicurrency Option:	No		
Warning Date Range:	within 30 days		
Euro Option:	No		

❑ Close: the **Company Profile notebook**
❑ Close: the **Company Desktop**

ACCPAC will ask you to confirm that you wish to exit the program, as shown in Figure 4–10.

FIGURE 4-10
Confirmation Window

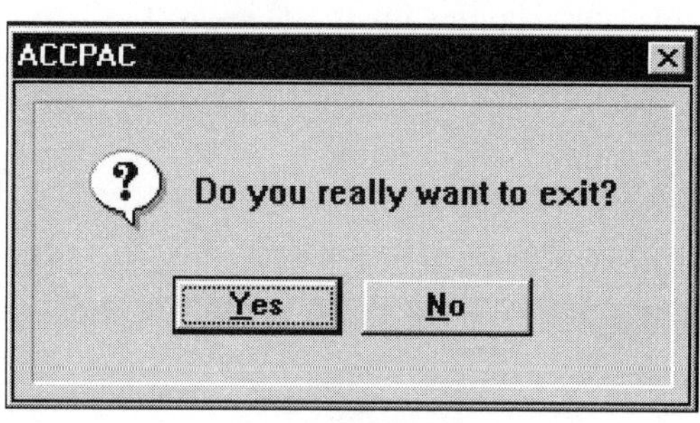

❑ Click: **Yes** [Yes]

REVIEW QUESTIONS

1. What are the two pages found in the Common Services Activation area?
2. When you click on the Options page of the Common Services Activation area, you have a number of choices. The first is the number of fiscal periods. Describe the fiscal periods that are available to you.

EXERCISE

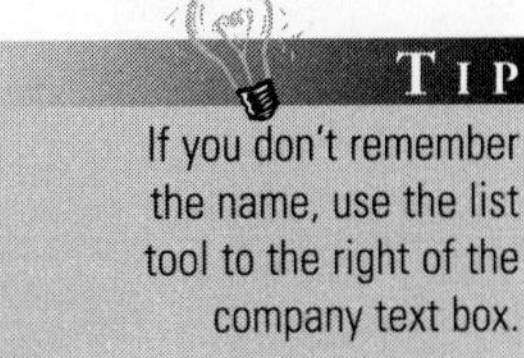

If you don't remember the name, use the list tool to the right of the company text box.

- ❑ Open EXERCO using 040110 as the Session Date.
- ❑ Activate the Common Services for your company. Remember to enter 050109 as the Fiscal Year Staring Date.
- ❑ Create your company profile using the following information:

Address page

Name:	*Your Name* Co. Ltd.
Address:	Use your company or school's address.
City:	Use the name of the city or town where you are located.
State/Province:	Use the name of the state or province where you are located.
Zip/Postal Code:	Use your company's or school's Zip/Postal code.
Contact:	Your real name
Country:	Use the name of the country where you are located.
Telephone:	Create numbers with the same area code and format where you are located.
Fax Number:	Create numbers with the same area code and format where you are located.

Options page

Number of Fiscal Periods:	12
Location Code:	2
Country Code:	Enter 3 letters identifying your country.
Branch:	2

In the interests of consistency and simplicity in an environment where the purpose is to learn the software, not to deal with different currencies, you will be limited to choosing Canadian dollars to simplify the simulation.

Functional Currency: Select Canadian dollars

- ❑ Print: Your company profile
- ❑ Exit: **ACCPAC**

CHAPTER 5

ADMINISTRATIVE SERVICES

In this chapter, you will assume the role of the system administrator as you complete the following activities for Devine Designs Inc.:

- entering a user record,
- setting up security,
- assigning user authorizations.

GETTING READY

❑ Start: **Windows**
❑ Start: **ACCPAC**

ACCPAC will briefly display a copyright and ownership identification window, and then display the Open Company dialog box, as shown in Figure 5-1.

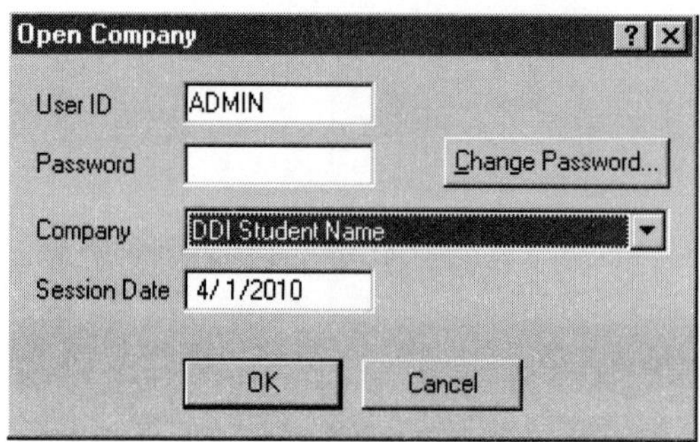

FIGURE 5-1
Open Company Dialog Box

- ❑ Type: **ADMIN** in the User ID text box
- ❑ Type: **ADMIN** in the Password text box
- ❑ Select: **DDI Your Name** from the Company list box
- ❑ Type: **040110** in the Session Date text box
- ❑ Click: **OK** [OK]

The company desktop will appear. The Administrative Services icon will only be displayed for the system administrator and those users who have been given the authority to check data integrity. The Common Services icon or window will be displayed for all users.

USING HELP

ACCPAC includes a large number of Help screens that provide information about the program and its operation.

- ❑ Click: **Help** on the menu bar

The Help menu is divided into four sections, as shown in Figure 5-2.

FIGURE 5-2
Help Menu

The top section of the Help menu allows you to access the Contents of the ACCPAC Help screens or information on Using Help. You can also access ACCPAC on the Web, as shown in Figure 5-3. Clicking any of the Web topics will open your browser and take you to the URL for the topic selected.

- ❑ Highlight: **ACCPAC on the Web**

FIGURE 5-3
ACCPAC on the Web Menu

The third section of the Help menu, System Information, displays information on the installation of ACCPAC for the current company database, and Users displays information on the users currently signed in to ACCPAC. The lower section of the menu, About ACCPAC, can be used to confirm the licensing of ACCPAC.

ACCPAC HELP CONTENTS

The Help menu provides two ways of accessing information about the operation of ACCPAC.

❑ Click: **Help Topics** on the Help menu
❑ Click: **Contents**

The ACCPAC for Windows System Help window, similar to that shown in Figure 5-4, will open.

FIGURE 5-4
ACCPAC Help Topics

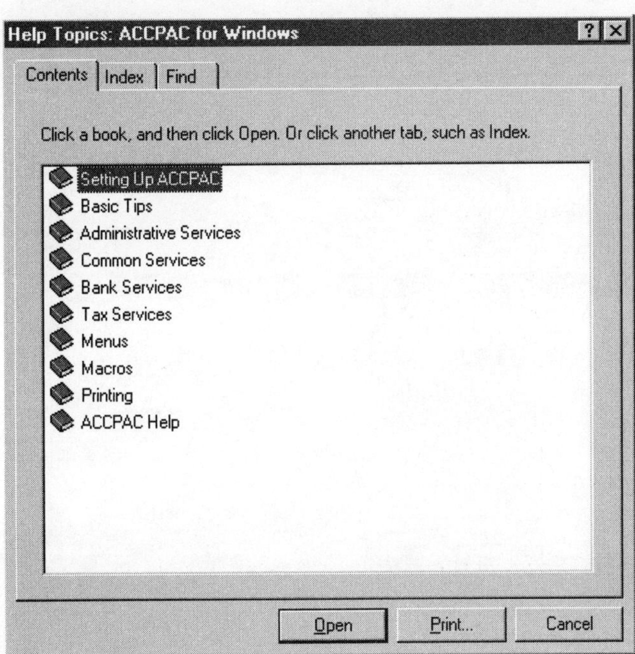

Help information is grouped in topics, each of which is represented by a book followed by the topic heading. You can expand the listing for a topic by clicking on the book at the left of the topic name.

- ❑ DClick: **Setting Up ACCPAC**

The file folder opens and displays its contents below the topic heading. To show further information, click on the underlined topic.

- ❑ DClick: **Steps to follow**

You can view the information on the screen, as shown in Figure 5-5. If all the information is not displayed in the open window, you can maximize the window or use the scroll bars to scan the text. You can explore any underlined topic by clicking on that topic. To go back to a previous topic, click on the Back button.

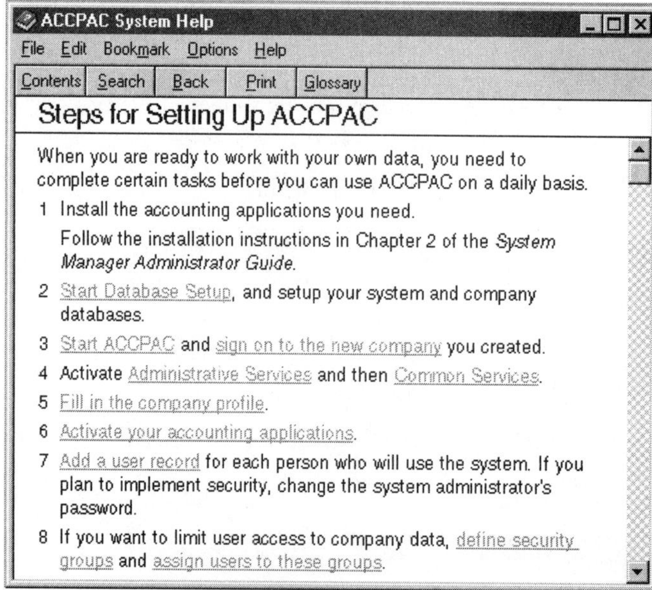

FIGURE 5-5 Steps for Setting Up ACCPAC

You can also print a copy of the information.

- ❑ Click: **Print**

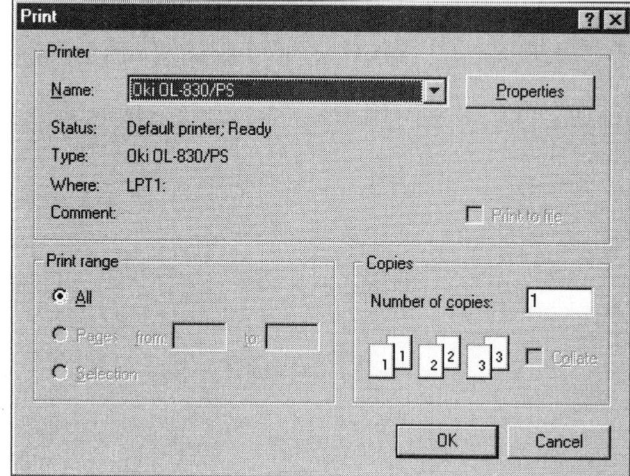

FIGURE 5-6 Print Dialog Box

The Print dialog box in Figure 5-6 allows you to select the printer to be used, the pages to be printed, and the number of copies to be printed.

❑ Click: **OK** [OK] on the Print dialog box

Review the printout. Note that you have already completed steps 1 through 5 for setting up ACCPAC for Windows. In this chapter, you will complete steps 6 through 9.

SEARCH

A second way to get information is to use the Search mode.

❑ Click: **Index** in the Help Topics window

The Search Index page dialog box, as shown in Figure 5-7, has two sections. The first section is a text entry box where you type a word related to the topic on which you want information. The second section lists items that match the word that you entered.

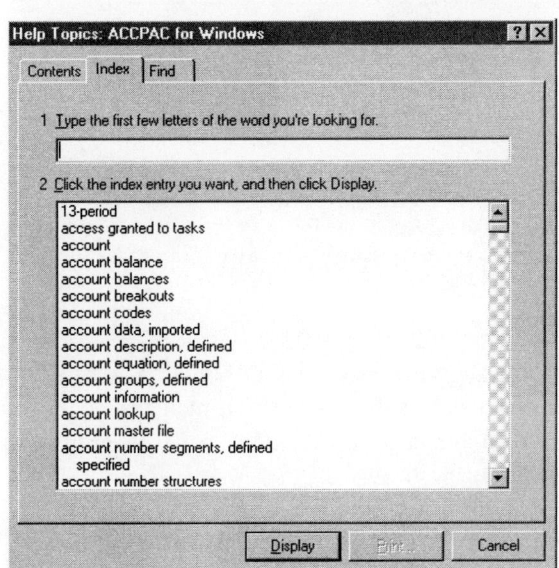

FIGURE 5-7
Index Page

❑ Type: **company profile** in the text box

Note that as you type, the list box contents change to match the entry in the text box. Select an item from the list box by clicking on the item once so that it is highlighted and then click the Display button.

❑ Click: **company desktop, creating**

❑ Click: **Display** [Display]

The topic is displayed in a new window.

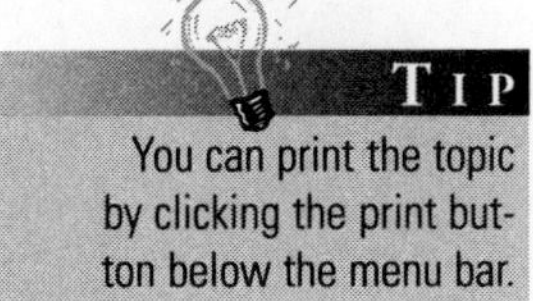

TIP
You can print the topic by clicking the print button below the menu bar.

To use the Find page, ACCPAC first creates a database of all the keywords in the help files. As this database requires a large amount of disk storage, Devine Designs Inc. has decided not to use the Find page.

❑ Close: all **Help Topics** windows

ADMINISTRATIVE SERVICES

The Administrative Services icon will only be displayed for the system administrator and those users who have been given the authority to check data integrity. The Administrative Services option activates data and checks data integrity, identifies restart records for incomplete processing, and maintains user information such as user records, security groups, and user authorizations.

❑ DClick: the **Administrative Services icon** on the Company Desktop

The six icons for Administrative Services are shown in Figure 5–8. In this chapter, you will use the Users, Security Groups, and User Authorizations icons. Data Integrity should be checked before you back up your data files. You will use the Data Activation icon later to activate accounting applications and other services. Restart Maintenance should only be used by a qualified systems administrator.

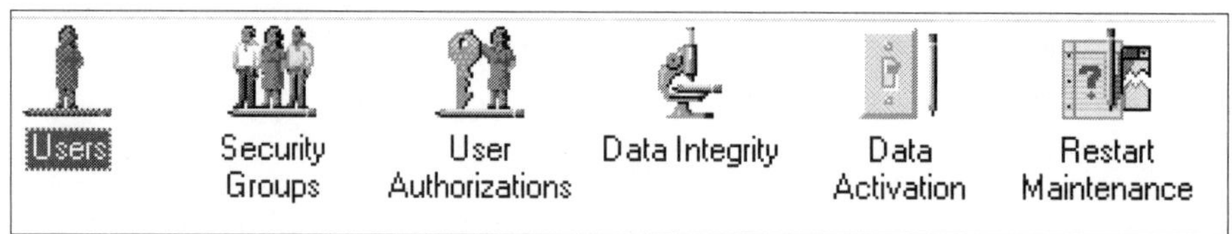

FIGURE 5-8 Administrative Services Icons

USERS

Users are people allowed to use ACCPAC with a company's data. Use this option if you need to add new users to the system. You may also change information for existing users, or delete users no longer using ACCPAC, such as employees who leave your company.

❑ DClick: the **Users** icon [Users] in the Administrative Services window

The Users window will open and display a Users dialog box, similar to that shown in Figure 5-9.

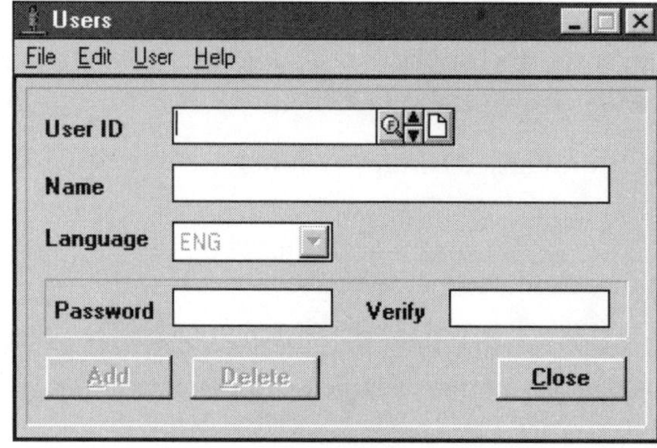

FIGURE 5-9 Users Dialog Box

❑ Click: the **Finder** for the User ID text box

FIGURE 5-10
Finder - Users

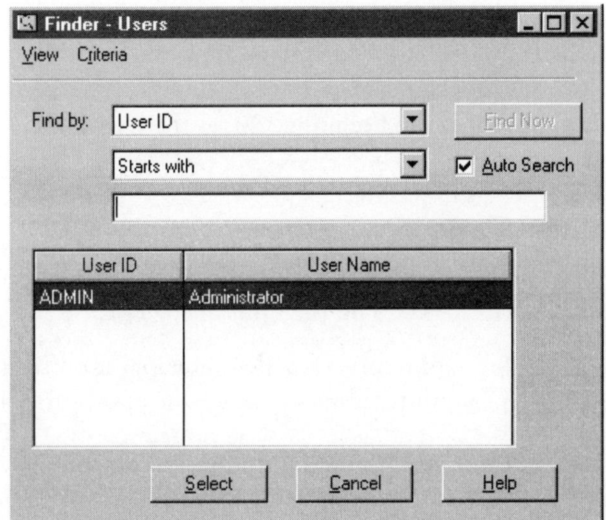

❑ DClick: **ADMIN** in the User ID column of the Finder for Users (Figure 5-10)

ACCPAC will transfer the information for the User ID ADMIN to the Users dialog box.

TIP
If you wish to change the Administrator's password, you can do so now by typing the new password in both the Password and Verify text boxes.

❑ Click: behind the word Administrator in the Name text box of the Users dialog box

❑ Type: **-John Paul** after the title Administrator

❑ Press: **Tab** Tab

Note that the Save button has now become active.

❑ Click: **Save** Save

You will now add another user using this window.

❑ Click: the **New Document** button for the User ID text box

All of the information for the Administrator will vanish. The cursor will appear at the beginning of the User ID line, ready for you to create another name.

❑ Type: **JANS** in the User ID text box

❑ Press: **Tab** Tab

❑ Type: **Eric Jans** in the Name text box

❑ Press: **Tab** Tab to move the insertion point to the Language text box

❑ Press: **Tab** Tab to accept the default, ENG

❑ Type: **Sahara** in the Password text box

❑ Press: **Tab** Tab

❑ Type: **Sahara** again in the Verify text box

❑ Press: **Tab** Tab

You do not have to use the upper and lower cases in the same manner in creating the password. If you were to repeat the password using all upper case, ACCPAC for Windows would accept it.

- ❑ Click: **Add** [Add]
- ❑ Add a user for Leslie Lee using LEE as the User ID and Leslie as her password.

You should keep a paper record of the authorized users.

- ❑ Select: **File** [File] on the menu bar
- ❑ Select: **Print** from the file menu
- ❑ Click: **OK** [OK] on the Print dialog box

Note that the password information does not appear on the printed users report. If necessary, the system administrator can change the password if the user forgets it

- ❑ Click: **Close** [Close] to return to the Company Desktop

Adding a Security Group

A security group is a group of users who are allowed to use the same ACCPAC functions. You can use security groups to restrict user access to data and applications. Security groups are part of the system database. All companies that link to a system database share the same security groups.

Use the Security Groups icon when you want to create new security groups, change information on existing groups, or delete groups that you no longer need. You will now add a security group for senior managers who will be given access to almost all ACCPAC functions.

- ❑ DClick: the **Security Groups** icon [Security Groups] in the Administrative Services window

Your screen should now display the Security Groups dialog box for the DEVDES system database, as shown in Figure 5-11.

The first step is to identify the ACCPAC application that you want the senior managers to use.

- ❑ Click: the **list tool** for the Application list box

The list box displays the names of all the ACCPAC applications that have been installed, even if they have not been activated.

- ❑ Click: **Administrative Services V4.1** in the list box
- ❑ Click: the **New Document** icon for the Group ID text box

Figure 5-11 DEVDES Security Groups Dialog Box

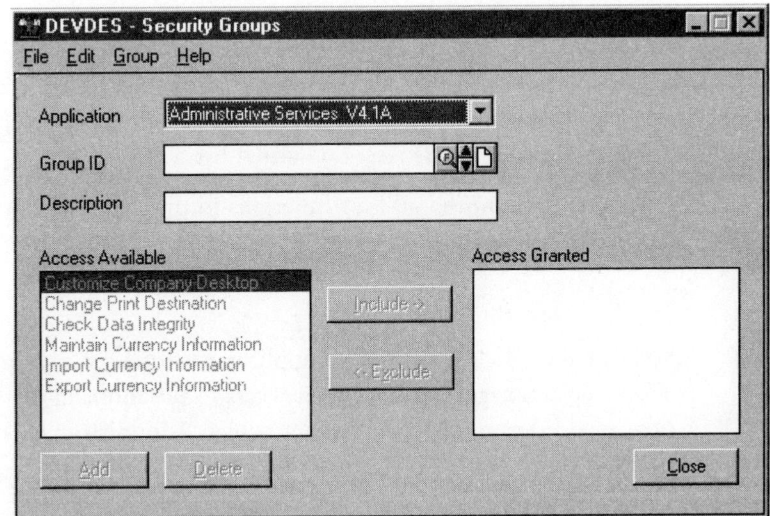

The insertion point will now appear in the Group ID box. You must type a unique Group ID and Description for each security group within an application. The Group ID may not be longer than 8 characters.

- ❑ Type: **MGT**
- ❑ Press: **Tab** [Tab] to move to the Description text box

Note that the Add, Include, and Exclude buttons and the list in the Access Available box are now active. The insertion point should be in the Description text box. The Description may be 30 characters long.

- ❑ Type: **Senior Managers**
- ❑ Press: **Tab** [Tab]

You will now identify those functions that the senior managers will be allowed to use. Do this for each application activated for the system database. This will allow the senior managers to perform these functions for any company database linked to this system database. Select the name of the task from the Access Available list, then click the Include button. Repeat this step for each task that you want the group to access.

Six functions are listed in the Access Available list box for Administrative services. Authorize the senior managers to use the following:

- Customize Company Desktop
- Change Print Destination
- Check Data Integrity
- Maintain Currency Information

- ❑ Click: **Customize Company Desktop** in the Access Available list box
- ❑ Click: **Include** [Include ->]

The line Customize Company Desktop will move to the Access Granted list box and will be deleted from the Access Available list box.

- ❑ Click: **Change Print Destination**
- ❑ Click: **Include** [Include ->]
- ❑ Repeat this process to move Check Data Integrity and Maintain Currency Information to the Access Granted list box.

Once you have moved all four functions to the Access Granted box, add the Security Group to the system database.

- ❑ Click: **Add** [Add]

You can also add access to other applications for a security group using the same name. The senior managers will be given access to functions in the Common Services application in addition to those they can access in Administrative Services.

- ❑ Click: the **list tool** for the Application text box
- ❑ Click: **Common Services V4.1A**

The Common Services functions will appear in very light type in the Access Available list box.

- ❑ Click: the **New Document** icon for the Group ID text box

The insertion point will now appear in the Group ID text box. Type a unique Group ID and Description for each security group within an application. The Group ID may not be longer than 8 characters.

- ❑ Type: **MGT**
- ❑ Press: **Tab** [Tab]

Note that the Add, Include, and Exclude buttons and the Access Available box are now Active. The insertion point will move to the Description text box. The Description may be 30 characters long.

- ❑ Type: **Senior Managers**
- ❑ Press: **Tab** [Tab]
- ❑ Select: **Maintain Company Information**
- ❑ Click: **Include** [Include ->]
- ❑ Repeat this process, giving the senior managers access to the Maintain Fiscal Calendar and Common Inquiry functions.
- ❑ Click: **Add** [Add]
- ❑ Print: the Security Groups Report using the File menu
- ❑ Click: **Close** [Close] to return to the Administrative Services window

User Authorization

Once you have created the Security Groups, you may assign users to them. Only the System Administrator has access to this window. You may assign the same user to different groups within the system database.

❑ DClick: the **User Authorizations** icon in the Administrative Services window

A User Authorizations window, similar to that shown in Figure 5-12, should appear on your screen.

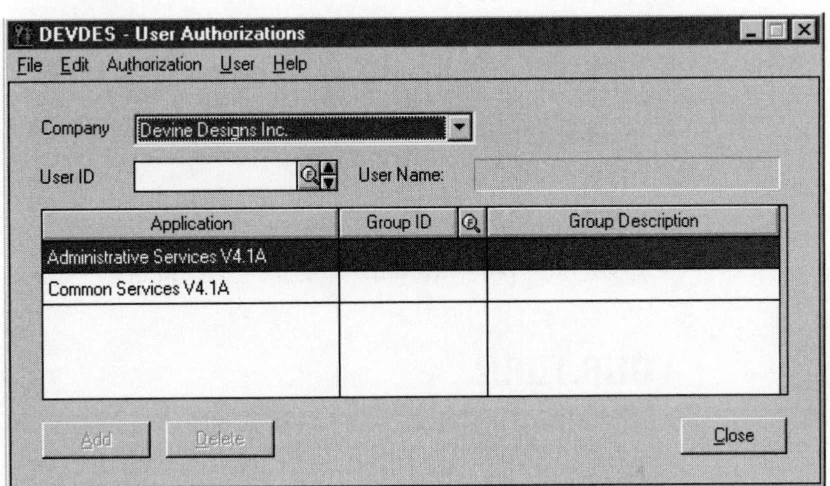

FIGURE 5-12
User Authorizations Dialog Box

First, select the name of a company from the company list.

❑ Click: the **list tool** beside the Company list box
❑ Select: the line for **DDI** followed by your name

Next, you select the user identification.

❑ Click: the **Finder** for the User ID list box, Figure 5-13
❑ Click: the line with **JANS** as the user ID and Eric Jans as the user name
❑ Click: **Select**

A list of installed applications is displayed in the lower part of the User Authorizations window. You next choose the security group for each application that you want the user to belong to.

❑ Click: **Administrative Services V4.1A**
❑ Click: the **Finder** for the Group ID text box
❑ Click: **MGT**
❑ Click: **Select**

FIGURE 5-13
Finder - Users

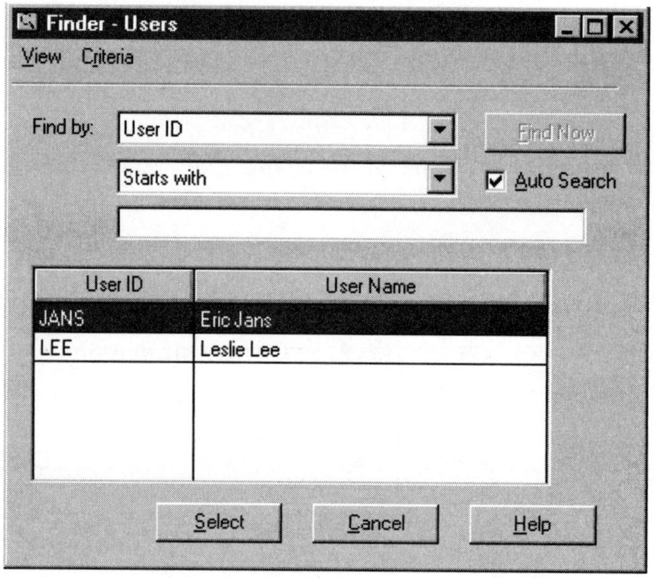

- ❑ Repeat this process for Common Services
- ❑ Click: **Add** [Add]

YOUR TURN

- ❑ Add the same user authorizations for Leslie Lee.
- ❑ Print the User Authorization Report using the File menu
- ❑ Click: **Close** [Close] to return to the Administrative Services window

You must repeat this process for each user in the company. All of the users in the same group can perform the tasks that have been defined for the group.

If you need to edit a user's authorization, you can do so by following the same steps. First, select the user ID and make the changes. Once the changes have been completed, choose Save to save them. If you want to delete a user's authorization group, select the user ID and choose Delete.

- ❑ Exit: **ACCPAC**

REVIEW QUESTIONS

1. List the six icons that appear in the Administrative Services window.
2. On whose screen does the Administrative Services appear?

3. Define the term "Security Group."
4. What functions do you access when you click on the User Authorizations icon?

EXERCISE

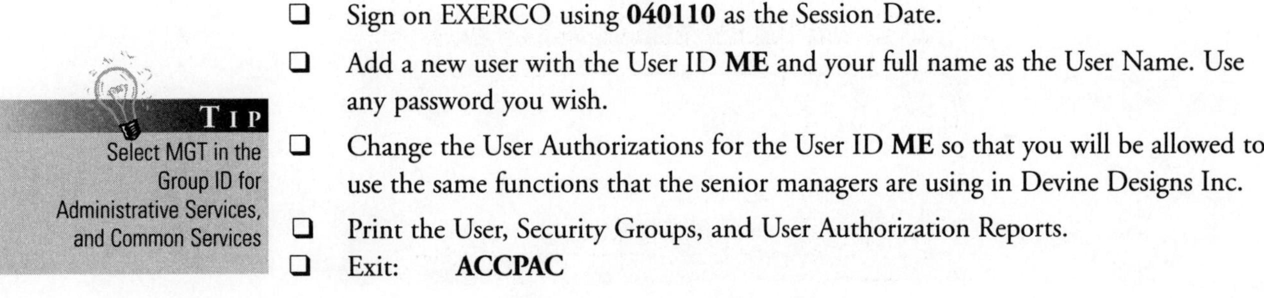

- ❑ Sign on EXERCO using **040110** as the Session Date.
- ❑ Add a new user with the User ID **ME** and your full name as the User Name. Use any password you wish.
- ❑ Change the User Authorizations for the User ID **ME** so that you will be allowed to use the same functions that the senior managers are using in Devine Designs Inc.
- ❑ Print the User, Security Groups, and User Authorization Reports.
- ❑ Exit: **ACCPAC**

CHAPTER 6

Common Services

In this chapter, you will use Common Services to set up the company profile, fiscal calendar, and currency codes. The Optional Tables will not be used. In a later chapter, you will use Common Services as you set up Tax and Bank Services.

Getting Ready

- ❑ Start: **Windows**
- ❑ Start: **ACCPAC**
- ❑ Sign-on to DDI Student Name as the system administrator.
- ❑ Type: **ADMIN** in the Password text box
- ❑ Type: **040110** in the Session Date text box
- ❑ Click: **OK** [OK]

Common Services

When you open the Common Services window, as many as four icons appear for the services you are authorized to use. The system administrator has access to all four functions, as shown in Figure 6-1. Tax and Bank Services will be activated after the General Ledger Chart of Accounts has been created.

If necessary,

❑ Open: the **Common Services** window on the company desktop

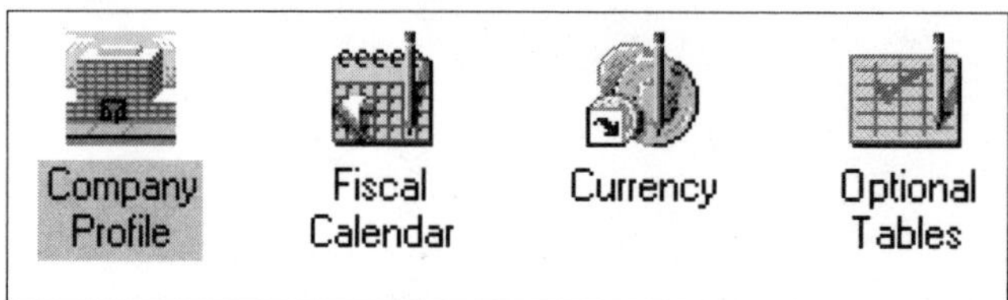

FIGURE 6-1
Common Services Icons

The **Currency** icon in the ACCPAC Small Business Series allows you to format the appearance of the functional currency. Devine Designs Inc. will use the default settings.

OPTIONAL TABLES

The **Optional Tables** icon allows you to add optional tables for your company. You can also edit existing tables or delete tables you no longer need. Devine Designs Inc. will use the tables as supplied with ACCPAC.

EDITING THE COMPANY PROFILE

The Company Profile is a two-page notebook that is used to maintain the company address and various options. You used this notebook when you created the company profile for Devine Designs Inc. in Chapter 4, Company Sign-on and Profile. Use this option if you want to change any of the information previously recorded. Upon review of the company profile, it has been decided that your name should be put in as the contact person.

❑ DClick: the **Company Profile** icon 

The Company Profile window will appear as displayed in Figure 6-2.

FIGURE 6-2
Company Profile Notebook - Address Page

DEVINE - Company Profile

File Edit Company Help

Database ID: DEVINE

Name: DDI Student Name

Address: 286 Main St.
Unit 14

City: Georgetown
State/Province: Prov.

Zip/Postal Code: L5L 6F3
Country: Country

Contact: Fred Bown

Format Phone Number
Telephone: (555) 555-1212
Fax Number: (555) 555-1313

Page 1

Address | Options

Save | Close

The company profile information is contained on two pages of a notebook. If the Address Page is not displayed on your monitor, click the Address tab at the bottom left of the notebook.

- ❑ Click and Drag to highlight the name recorded in the Contact text box.
- ❑ Type: **Your Name**
- ❑ Press: **Tab** [Tab]

Pressing the tab key completes the entry to the text box and activates the save button.

- ❑ Click: **Save** [Save]

If you accidentally click Close, ACCPAC for Windows displays a warning message, as shown in Figure 6-3.

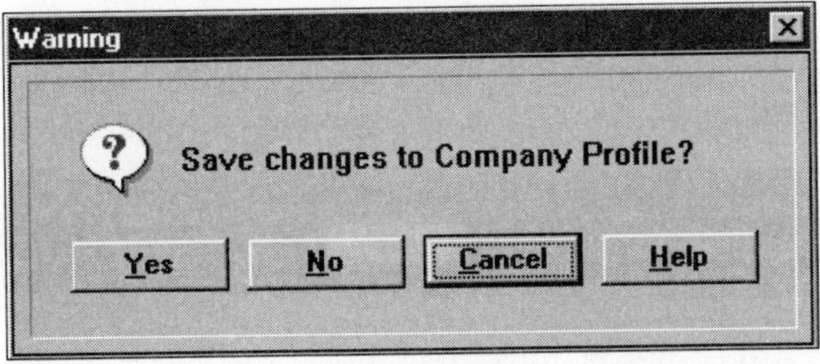

FIGURE 6–3
Warning Message

If you see this message, click **Yes** to save the changes and to return to the Common Services window. Then double click the Company Profile icon.

PRINTING THE COMPANY PROFILE

You can print a copy of the Company Profile to document the changes that you have made.

❑ Click: **File** [File] on the menu bar of the Company Profile window

❑ Click: **Print** [Print] on the File menu

The Print dialog box, shown in Figure 6-4, specifies the printer, report orientation, and paper size. If you wish to change any of these settings, click on the Setup button and enter your changes. If more than one copy is specified in the Copies text box, change the number shown to 1.

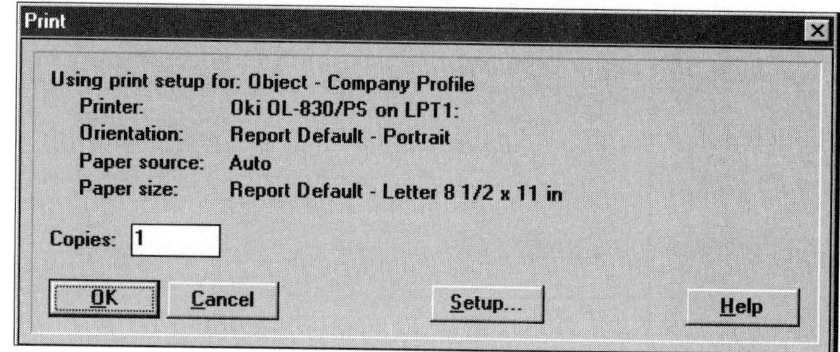

FIGURE 6–4
Print Dialog Box

❑ Click: **OK** [OK] on the Print dialog box

Review the printed company profile. If there are errors, make the necessary changes and print the company profile again.

❑ Click: **Close** [Close] to return to Common Services

FISCAL CALENDAR

The Fiscal Calendar is used to maintain the fiscal calendar for each company. The Fiscal Calendar is shared by all accounting applications used by a company. You can use this window to restrict posting to a period or to change the information for a new fiscal year, as you will do later in the Devine Designs Inc. simulation.

❑ DClick: the **Fiscal Calendar** icon 

ACCPAC uses two special fiscal periods in addition to the standard 12- or 13-period fiscal year, as shown in Figure 6-5.

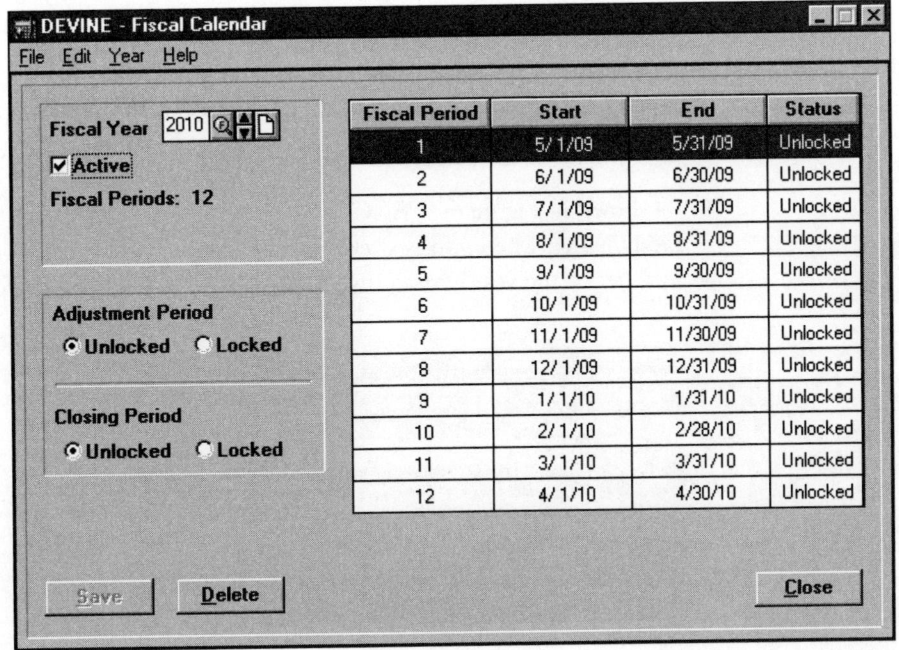

FIGURE 6–5 Fiscal Calendar Dialog Box

Adjustment Period

Period 14 is used to record and post adjustments that occur after the end of the fiscal year. Such adjustments may be the result of the auditors restating depreciation expense, bad debt expense, or additional income tax expense. Since these adjustments do not reflect the day-to-day operations of the last period, they are posted to a special period that is always the last day of the fiscal year. This feature ensures that these special adjustments that may reflect information for the full fiscal year do not distort the result of the last period.

Closing Period

Period 15 is the closing period in which revenue and expense accounts are closed at year end. The date for this period is also the last day of the fiscal year.

Status

You may prevent the posting of transactions to certain fiscal periods by changing the status of those periods from Unlocked to Locked. Devine Designs Inc. will change the status of fiscal periods 2 to 11 from Unlocked to Locked. Later, you will record transactions incorporating the company in fiscal period 1, and current transactions in fiscal period 12.

Editing the Fiscal Calendar

To edit a fiscal year, first select the year you want to edit.

❑ Click: the **Finder** icon for Fiscal Year

As shown in Figure 6-6, ACCPAC for Windows created one fiscal year for Devine Designs Inc. when you first created the company. The fiscal year is identified by the number of the year containing the last fiscal period. The current fiscal year is 2010.

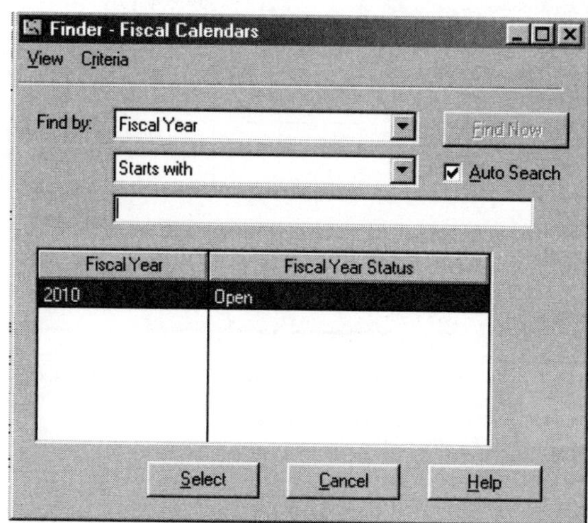

Figure 6–6 Finder - Fiscal Calendars

❑ Click: the line starting **2010**

❑ Click: **Select** Select

To change the status of a fiscal period, double click the status column for that period.

❑ DClick: the **Status** column for Fiscal Period 2 to change the Status to Locked

❑ Change the status of periods 3 through 11 to Locked.

To change the status of the adjustment or closing period, click the Locked or Unlocked option button.

❑ Click: the **Locked** option button for the Adjustment Period

❑ Click: the **Locked** option button for the Closing Period

Review the changes that you have made. If necessary, make corrections.

❑ Click: **Save** Save to save these changes to the fiscal period calendar

Printing the Fiscal Calendar

You can print a copy of the Fiscal Calendar to document the changes that you have made.

❑ Click: **File** [File] on the menu bar
❑ Click: **Print** on the File menu
❑ Click: **OK** [OK] on the Print dialog box

Compare your printout to that shown in Figure 6-7. If necessary, correct any errors and save the Fiscal Calendar again. Reprint the Fiscal Calendar to confirm that the errors have been corrected.

FIGURE 6–7
Fiscal Calendar

Date: Thursday, July 13, 2000 10:57AM **DDI Student Name** **Page 1**
Fiscal Calendar (CS2000)

Fiscal Year [2010]
Active [Yes]
Fiscal Periods [12]

Adjustment Period [Locked]
Closing Period [Locked]

Period	Period Start	Period End	Status
1	5/1/2009	5/31/2009	Unlocked
2	6/1/2009	6/30/2009	Locked
3	7/1/2009	7/31/2009	Locked
4	8/1/2009	8/31/2009	Locked
5	9/1/2009	9/30/2009	Locked
6	10/1/2009	10/31/2009	Locked
7	11/1/2009	11/30/2009	Locked
8	12/1/2009	12/31/2009	Locked
9	1/1/2010	1/31/2010	Locked
10	2/1/2010	2/28/2010	Locked
11	3/1/2010	3/31/2010	Locked
12	4/1/2010	4/30/2010	Unlocked

❑ Click: **Close** [Close] to return to **Common Services**
❑ Close: the **Company Desktop**

You should back up your data files. If you used the default settings, your data is stored in the following folders:

C:\\Program Files\ACCPAC\Company

C:\\Program Files\ACCPAC\Data

C:\\Program Files\ACCPAC\User

If you are working on a network, check with your network administrator for the data location and backup procedures information.

REVIEW QUESTIONS

1. List the four icons that appear (at this stage) in the Common Services window.
2. What is the purpose of the Report Designer?
3. What is the Company Profile?
4. What is the purpose of the Fiscal Calendar option?
5. Explain the purposes of the 14th and 15th periods.

EXERCISE

- ❑ Sign on to EXERCO using **040110** as the Session Date.
- ❑ Print the Company Profile.
- ❑ Lock fiscal periods 1 through 11 for 2010.
- ❑ Lock the adjustment and closing periods.
- ❑ Print the Fiscal Period Calendar.
- ❑ Back up the data files for your company.
- ❑ Exit: **ACCPAC**

UNIT 3

GENERAL LEDGER

CHAPTER 7

SETTING UP THE GENERAL LEDGER

WARNING

If you have not completed Part I, System Manager, you cannot set up the General Ledger. If necessary, go back to Chapter 2 and complete the step-by-step instructions in Chapters 2 through 6.

In this chapter, you will install the General Ledger and create the files for Devine Designs Inc. so that you can enter the Chart of Accounts information in the next chapter.

Before you can create the General Ledger, you must have installed the System Manager, created both a system and a company database, and chosen some company-wide selections from Common Services. Before you can create the ACCPAC for Windows Small Business Series General Ledger, you must know how the General Ledger is structured and what options will be chosen.

INSTALLING THE GENERAL LEDGER

WARNING

If you are installing the accounting application on a network, refer to the System Manager Administrator Guide and ask your network manager for help.

In this section, you will install the ACCPAC for Windows Small Business Series General Ledger. You can install other ACCPAC accounting applications following these same steps.

- ❑ Start: Windows
- ❑ DClick: the **My Computer** icon

- ❑ DClick: the **Control Panel** icon on the My Computer window
- ❑ DClick: the **Add/Remove Programs** icon on the Control Panel window

The upper portion of the Install/Uninstall page is used to install programs. As a program is installed, Windows monitors the installation and saves the information necessary for removing the program. The lower portion of the page is used to uninstall or remove programs.

- ❑ Click: **Install** [Install...]

The Install Program window reminds you to insert the first installation floppy disk or CD-ROM.

- ❑ Insert the ACCPAC for Windows Small Business Series General Ledger CD-ROM.

The General Ledger Instruction Window will appear as displayed in Figure 7–1.

FIGURE 7-1
ACCPAC for Windows Installation

- ❑ DClick: **Install ACCPAC (32-bit)**

WARNING

We will assume that your CD-ROM drive is drive D. If not, you will have to modify the drive designations accordingly.

The Welcome window will remind you to close all other Windows programs before running the General Ledger Setup Program. If necessary, click **Cancel**, exit any other Windows programs, and start Installation again.

- ❑ Click: **Next** [Next >]

The next window displayed contains a copy of the licensing agreement for installing and using ACCPAC. Use the scroll bar to view the whole agreement.

- ❑ Click: **Yes** [Yes] to accept the terms of the license agreement

WARNING

You must have an Activation Code to complete installation of the system manager. If you do not, click **Cancel** and complete the form at www.accpac.com/products/activfm.htm.

If you have an activation code,

- ❑ Select: the radio button for "I have an activation code"
- ❑ Click: **Next** [Next >] to display the second Activation window

You must fill in the text boxes with the exact information supplied by ACCPAC International in response to your activation code request. The name and company text boxes will display the information that you entered as you installed the System Manager.

If necessary,

- ❑ Type: the **name of the software vendor** in the Dealer text box
- ❑ Press: **Tab** [Tab]
- ❑ Type: the **name of the qualified installer** in the QI text box
- ❑ Press: **Tab** [Tab]
- ❑ Type: the **Product ID number** in the Product ID/Serial # text box
- ❑ Press: **Tab** [Tab]
- ❑ Type: the **Activation Code** in the Activation Code text box

TIP

Staple a copy of the activation information received from ACCPAC International on the first page of each of the General Ledger manuals.

As you enter the Activation Code, the **Next** button becomes active. Check that you have entered the information exactly as on the form you received from ACCPAC International.

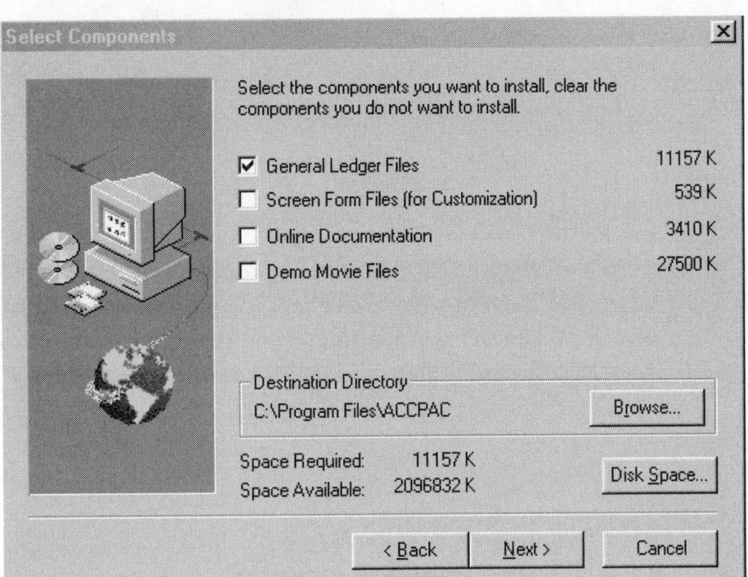

FIGURE 7-2 Select Components Window

WARNING

If you are installing the System Manager in a networked environment, ask the network manager for the proper location for installing the General Ledger.

The Select Components window (Figure 7-2) identifies the different options you can install and shows the default directory C:\Program Files\ACCPAC. If you installed the system manager to a different drive or directory, click **Browse** and select the appropriate location for the files.

- ❑ Click: **Next** [Next >]

The Select Program Folder window is used to add program icons to a folder in the Windows Start menu. The Program Folder text box displays ACCPAC 32-bit as the default. The scroll box lists the existing folders. If necessary, change the default in the Program Folder text box.

❑ Click: **Next** [Next >] to accept the default ACCPAC folder, ACCPAC 32-Bit

Before copying files to your hard drive, ACCPAC displays the Start Copying Files window, as shown in Figure 7-3.

FIGURE 7-3
Start Copying Files Window

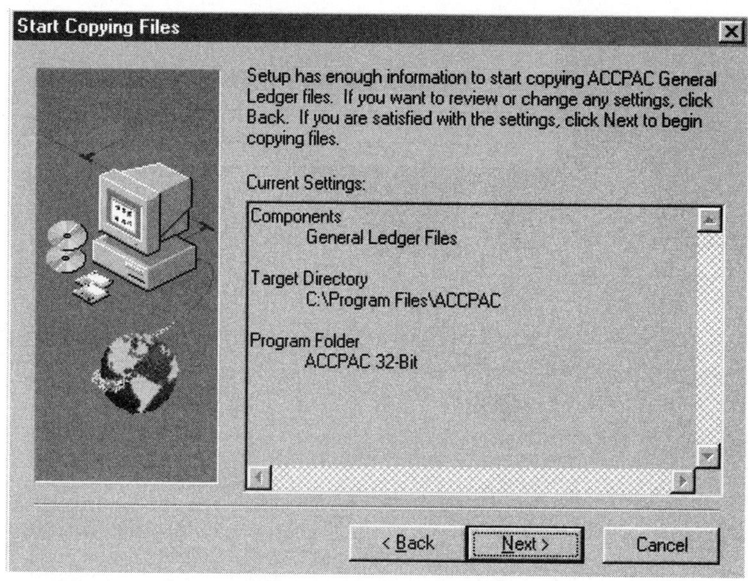

Carefully review the components to be installed and the directories to be used.

❑ Click: **Next** [Next >]

After all the General Ledger files have been copied, ACCPAC will ask if you want to view the System Manager README file. Most software manufacturers include README files on disk to inform users of changes that have not yet been added to their printed manuals. Whenever you install a new or upgraded software package, print and read the README file and follow any additional installation steps as described. Then make the necessary changes in the manual.

❑ Click: **Finish** [Finish] to view the README file in WordPad

To print the information,

❑ Click: the **Printer** icon
❑ Close: the **WordPad** window

If you are asked if you wish to save changes to the README file, click **No.**

❑ Close: the **ACCPAC 32-Bit** window
❑ Close: the **General Ledger Installation** window

The Install Program from Floppy Disk or CD ROM window will appear again.

- ❑ Click: **Exit** [Exit]
- ❑ Remove the CD-ROM and store it carefully.

ACTIVATING GENERAL LEDGER

Activation is the process of creating or upgrading company data to work with a new version of an ACCPAC accounting application. You must close all other ACCPAC program windows before you can activate data. You also must sign on with system administrator privileges to be able to activate data.

On Monday, April 12, 2010, Eric will set up the General Ledger for Devine Designs Inc. He will sign on as the system administrator.

- ❑ Start: **Windows 95/98**
- ❑ Start: **ACCPAC**
- ❑ Type: **ADMIN** in the User ID text box
- ❑ Type: **ADMIN** in the Password Text Box
- ❑ Select: **Devine Designs Inc.** in the Company List box
- ❑ Type: **041210** in the Session Date text box
- ❑ Click: **OK** [OK]

Your Company Desktop should appear.

- ❑ Select: **Administrative Services**
- ❑ DClick: the **Data Activation** icon [Data Activation] in the Administrative Services window

ACCPAC for Windows will display the following Warning message (Figure 7-4).

FIGURE 7-4
Warning Message

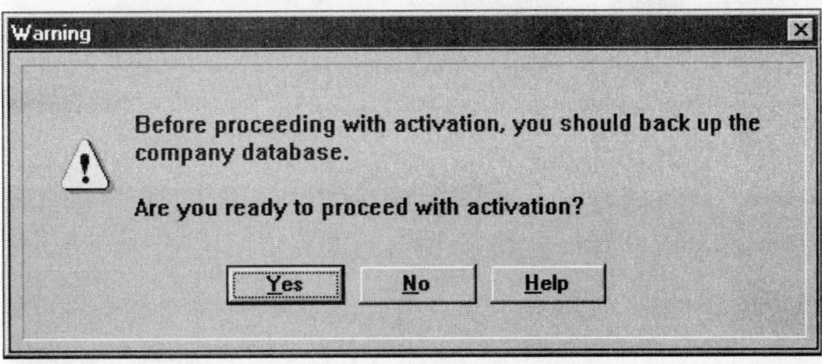

If you have not backed up your company database, you would click the **No** button, exit from ACCPAC for Windows, and back up your company database. Devine Designs Inc. will back up the company database later after more information has been added to it.

❑ Click: **Yes** [Yes] to proceed with activation

Applications that have been installed but not activated for the company database that you are using are listed in the Applications box. To activate an application, first highlight it on the list and then click **Activate**, as shown in Figure 7-5.

FIGURE 7-5
Data Activation Dialog Box

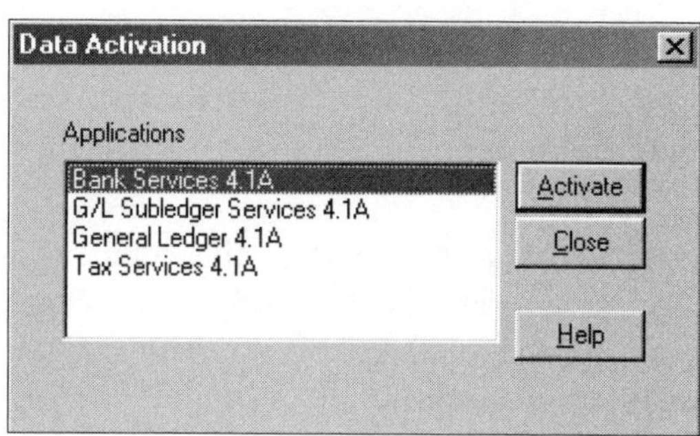

ACTIVATING THE GENERAL LEDGER

You will now activate the General Ledger. You can activate other ACCPAC for Windows applications in a similar fashion.

❑ Select: **General Ledger 4.1A**

❑ Click: **Activate** [Activate]

The GL Subledger Posting Activation dialog box will appear, as shown in Figure 7-6.

FIGURE 7-6
General Ledger Activation Dialog Box

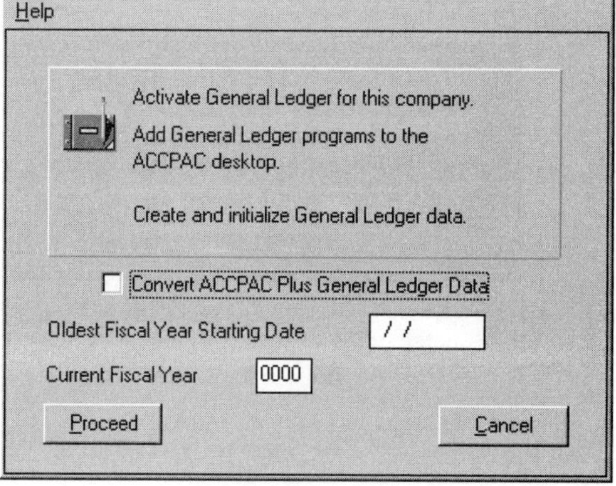

WARNING

If you are converting data from an earlier version of the application, consult the Getting Started manual that came with the new version of the application.

To create the General Ledger for Devine Designs Inc., enter the starting date for the fiscal year, and the year that the current fiscal year ends in.

❑ Click: the **Oldest Fiscal Year Starting Date** text box

❑ Type: **050109**

❑ Press: **Tab** [Tab]

- ❑ Type: **2010** in the Current Fiscal Year text box
- ❑ Click: **Proceed** Proceed

Once the activation is complete, the Data Activation dialog box will reappear on the screen and the name of the newly activated application will no longer be displayed on the list.

- ❑ Select: **G/L Subledger Services 4.1A**
- ❑ Click: **Activate** Activate

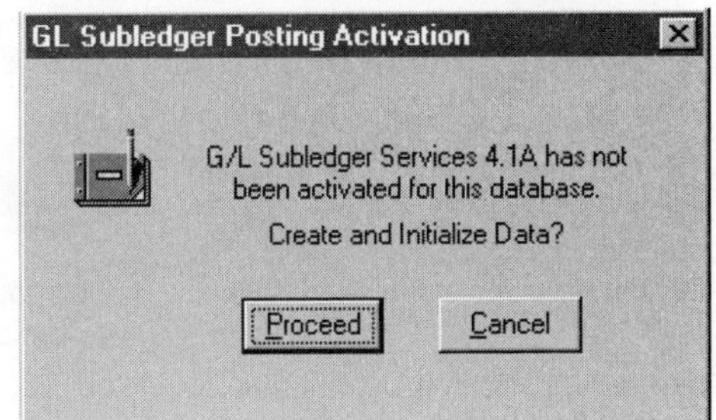

FIGURE 7-7 GL Subledger Posting Activation

- ❑ Click: **Close** Close to close the Data Activation window

The General Ledger icon should now appear on your desktop.

- ❑ Open: the **General Ledger** window, shown in Figure 7-8

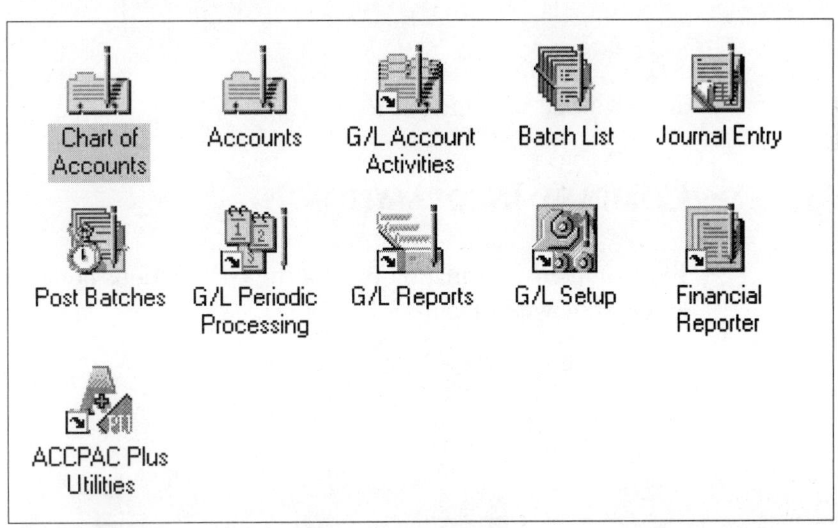

FIGURE 7-8 General Ledger Icons

The system administrator can use all of the eleven icons displayed in this window. As you work through the General Ledger for Devine Designs Inc., you will use all but the ACCPAC Plus Utilities icon. The use of each icon will be explained as you work through the General Ledger chapters.

SETUP

TIP
Whenever you need additional information, press **F1**.

Your first task is to use the General Ledger Options notebook to select the options Devine Designs Inc. wants to use. The options you choose will determine how the General Ledger system will operate and the types of data that will be stored and displayed.

❑ DClick: the **Setup** icon 

The G/L Setup Icons, Figure 7-9, will appear.

FIGURE 7-9
G/L Setup Icons

You will use each of the five icons displayed in the G/L Setup window as you set up the General Ledger for Devine Designs Inc.

OPTIONS

❑ DClick: the **Options** icon

COMPANY INFORMATION

The Company Information page of the G/L Options notebook will appear on your screen as shown in Figure 7-10.

FIGURE 7-10
Company Information Address Page

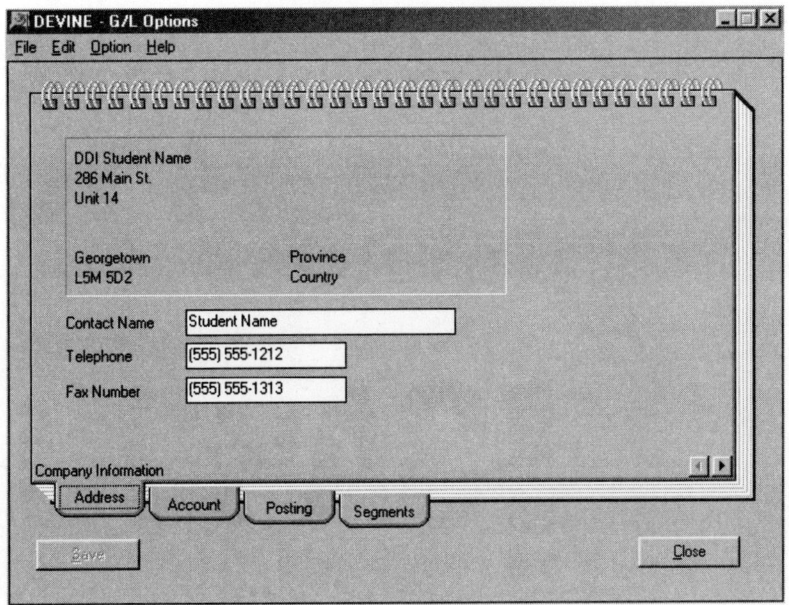

Information from the company database for Devine Designs Inc. has been transferred to the Company Information Address page. To change the company name and address, you would edit the Devine Designs Inc. company database. Because contact names and telephone numbers may be different for each ACCPAC accounting application or may change frequently, ACCPAC allows you to change this information on the Company Information Address page.

In the Contact Name text box, enter a name to identify a contact person or position in the company responsible for the General Ledger.

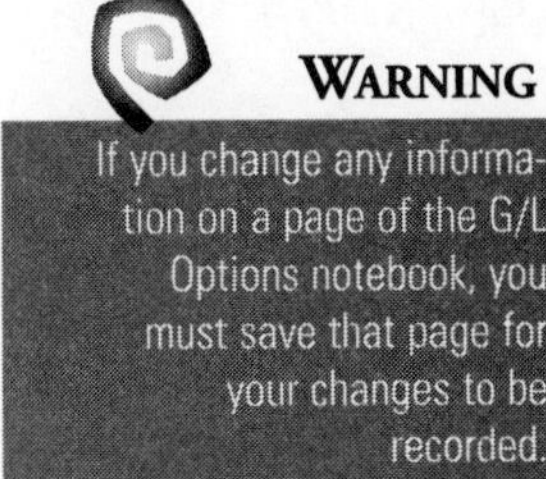

WARNING

If you change any information on a page of the G/L Options notebook, you must save that page for your changes to be recorded.

- ❑ Highlight: the text in the Contact Name text box
- ❑ Type: Hans Smith
- ❑ Press: **Tab** [Tab] to move to the Telephone Number field

The format used for telephone numbers depends on whether the Format Phone Numbers option is selected in the Company Profile window in Common Services. If these numbers have been changed since you created the company database, enter the new numbers.

Note that the save button has become active.

- ❑ Click: **Save** [Save]

ACCOUNT OPTIONS

❑ Click: the **Account** tab at the bottom of the notebook page, shown in Figure 7-11

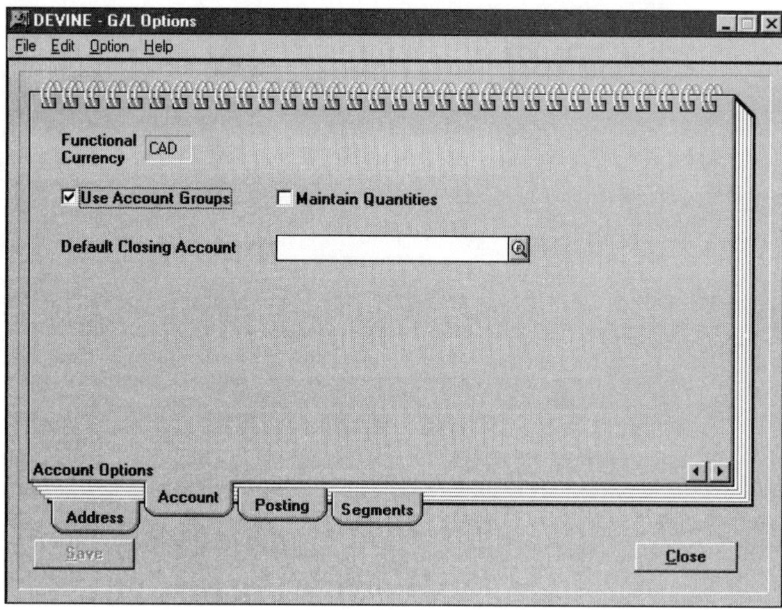

FIGURE 7-11
Account Options Page

Functional Currency

The functional currency code CAD has been transferred from the Devine Designs Inc. company database. You cannot change the functional currency. ACCPAC for Windows Small Business Series assigns a functional currency to enable upgrading to an ACCPAC multicurrency system.

Use Account Groups

The Financial Reporter uses account groups to create standard financial statements from your chart of accounts. If you decide to use Account Groups, assign each General Ledger account to one of the standard account groups, such as current assets, current liabilities, revenue, etc. If you choose not to activate the Account Groups option, you cannot use the balance sheet or income statement reports that come with ACCPAC.

Devine Designs Inc. will use the statements that come with ACCPAC. The Use Account Groups check box should already be active (as indicated by a check mark). If there is no check mark, click the check box to activate the Use Account Groups option.

Maintain Quantities

The Maintain Quantities option allows you to enter quantity information, such as the number of units sold, when you enter transactions for General Ledger accounts. Devine Designs Inc. will not record quantity information. If the Maintain Quantities option is active, click the check box to deactivate it.

Default Closing Account

At year-end, all corporations transfer the revenue and expense account balances to a Retained Earnings account. The procedure is much the same for a sole proprietorship. Enter the General Ledger code for the Retained Earnings account to which you want to close these temporary accounts. The Retained Earnings account for Devine Designs Inc. is 3200. Since the chart of accounts has not yet been created, you cannot add the account code. You will return to this page later to add the Retained Earnings account.

POSTING OPTIONS

❑ Click: the **Posting** tab at the bottom of the notebook page

The Posting Options page will appear as shown in Figure 7-12.

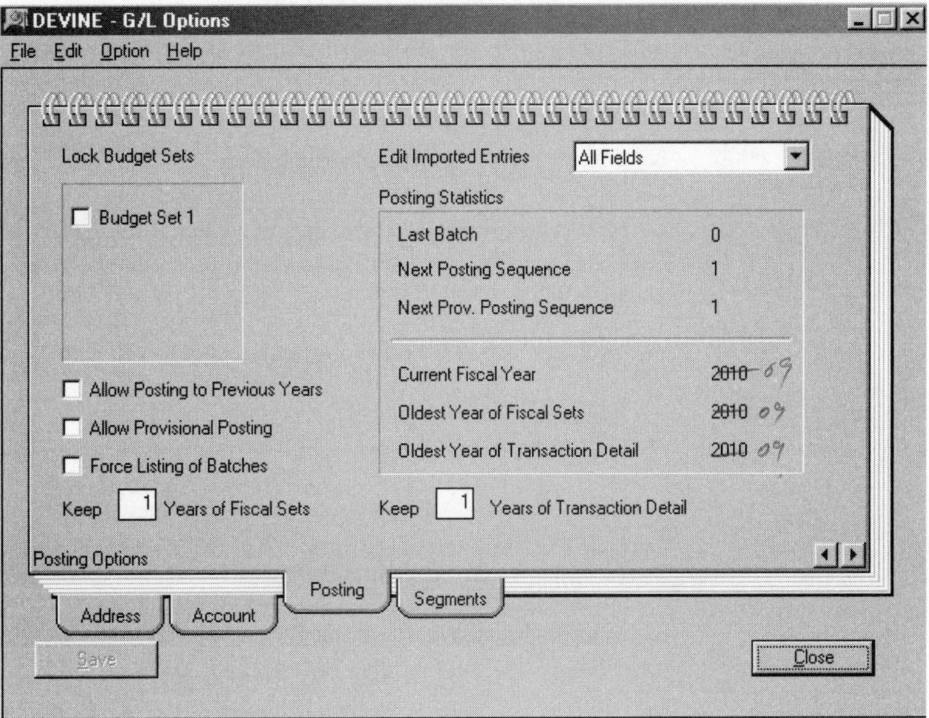

FIGURE 7-12
Posting Options Page

Lock Budget Sets

Once a budget is locked, it cannot be changed. Devine Designs Inc. will not create budgets at this time, so no changes to this option are necessary.

Allow Posting to Previous Years

You can set up the General Ledger to allow or prevent posting of batches to periods in the prior year. You can turn on this option as required for setup and end-of-year adjustments, and then turn it off to protect the integrity of "closed" years. In the future, Devine Designs Inc. may want to post to previous years.

❑ Click: the **Allow Posting to Previous Years** check box

Allow Provisional Posting

This feature allows you to post batches on a provisional basis to test the effects of transactions on the General Ledger and the financial statements before you permanently post the data. Provisional posting is particularly useful for estimating period-end or year-end adjustments. When the final adjustments are known, the provisional batch can be modified and permanently posted to the General Ledger. Devine Designs Inc. will select this option.

❑ Click: the **Allow Provisional Posting** check box

Force Listing of Batches

The Force Listing of Batches option requires you to print a listing for each batch and to correct any errors reported on the listing before you can post the batch. If this option is chosen, you must reprint the batch listing each time you make changes to that batch. Using this option helps you maintain a clear audit trail by ensuring that you post only error-free batches, so that all transactions entered in a batch are posted together. Devine Designs Inc. will select this option.

❑ Click: the **Force Listing of Batches** check box

Keep [ ] Years of Fiscal Sets

You can specify how many past years of financial and budget summary information you want to keep. You can keep up to 99 years of fiscal sets; however, two or three years will usually provide sufficient information.

❑ Highlight: the **default number** displayed in the text box
❑ Type: **2** in the text box
❑ Press: **Tab** [Tab]

Edit Imported Entries

The Edit Imported Entries function allows you to specify the types of changes or corrections you can make in batches transferred to the General Ledger from other ACCPAC programs. The choices are to edit all fields; to limit the editing to Fiscal Period, Year, and Transaction Date; or to prevent any editing of the batches.

Leave the default of All Fields unchanged.

Posting Statistics

ACCPAC will display posting statistics for information purposes only. The information will be updated each time you create or post a General Ledger batch of transactions.

As Devine Designs Inc. has just started operations, all three fiscal-year indicators should display 2010.

Keep [ ] Years of Transactions Detail Field

ACCPAC allows you to specify how many past years of posted transactions you want to keep. ACCPAC can keep up to 99 years of transaction details; however, two or three years will usually provide sufficient information. The number of Years of Transactions Detail you want to retain must equal the number of years of fiscal sets you want to save.

- ❑ Highlight: the **default number** displayed in the text box
- ❑ Type: **2** in the text box
- ❑ Click: **Save** [Save]

SEGMENT DEFINITION

- ❑ Click: the **Segments** tab at the bottom of the notebook page

The Segment Definition page of the G/L Options notebook will appear as shown in Figure 7-13.

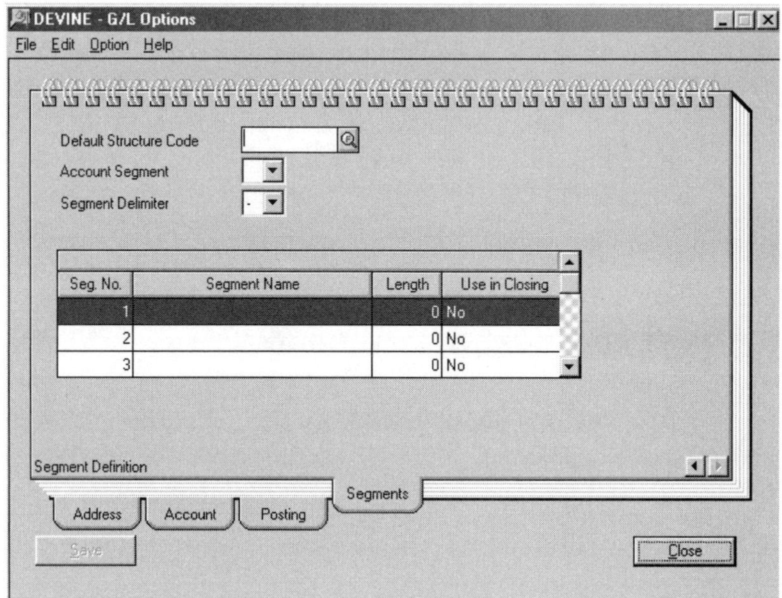

FIGURE 7-13
Segment Definition Page

This page allows you to define segments and to specify which segments can be used to close income summary accounts at the year-end. The segments are defined during setup. However, you can make changes in the segments definitions as follows:

- You can add new segments at any time, up to a maximum of ten.
- You can change the length of a segment at any time, provided it is not used in an account structure definition.
- You can change a segment description at any time.
- You can change the choice of using or not using the segment in closing at any time.

Default Structure Code

The Default Structure Code is automatically used for all General Ledger accounts added in the Accounts window. If you define more than one account structure, you can change the default for individual accounts as they are added.

Devine Designs Inc. has decided to use an account structure that will enable it to identify sales revenue from different sources. The Default Segmentation Code will be defined later in the G/L Account Structures window.

Eric has decided to use one segment that consists of a four-digit account number. A second two-digit segment identifies the different revenue sources.

Account Segment

If you have multiple segments for your account numbers, identify one of the segments as the account segment by selecting the account segment number (1 to 10). Devine

Designs Inc. uses the first segment to identify the account code.

- ❑ Click: the **Account Segment** list box
- ❑ Click: **1**

Segment Delimiter

The segment delimiter is the character that separates the segments of the account number to make the numbers easier to read.

- ❑ Click: the **Segment Delimiter** list box
- ❑ Click: **/**

Segment Information

make Backup

- ❑ Click: the **Segment Name** cell for segment number 1
- ❑ Type: **Account**
- ❑ Press: **Tab** [Tab] to move to the Length cell

Devine Designs Inc. uses four digits for the Account segment.

WARNING

Carefully review the information displayed. After saving, you cannot remove a segment, but you can change its name, length, and if it is used in closing.

- ❑ Type: **4**
- ❑ Press: **Tab** [Tab]
- ❑ Press: **Tab** [Tab] to leave the default **No** unchanged in the **Use in Closing** field

Devine Designs Inc. uses the second segment for revenue accounts to identify the type of activity that generates the sales revenue. The revenue account numbers that you will create have the following structure: Account/Activity. The account number is four digits long, followed by the two-digit activity identification.

TIP

Remember to save each page of the G/L Options notebook after making changes.

- ❑ Click: the **Segment Name** cell for segment number 2
- ❑ Type: **Activity**
- ❑ Press: **Tab** [Tab]
- ❑ Type: **2** in the Length cell
- ❑ Click: **Save** [Save]

PRINTING THE G/L OPTIONS REPORT

- ❑ Click: **File** on the G/L Options window menu bar
- ❑ Click: **Print** on the File menu
- ❑ Click: **Print** [Print] on the G/L Options Report window
- ❑ Click: **OK** [OK] on the Print window

Once you have reviewed your G/L Options Report,

- ❑ Click: **Close** [Close] on the G/L Options Report window

Compare your printout to that shown in Figure 7-14. If necessary, make corrections on the relevant pages of the Options notebook. Remember to save each page. Once you are satisfied it is correct, print the G/L Options Report again.

FIGURE 7-14
G/L Options Report

Date: Wednesday, July 05, 2000 11:22AM **DDI Student Name** Page 1
G/L Options (GLOPT01)

Company

DDI Student Name
286 Main St.
Unit 14

Georgetown Ontario
L7G 4Z1 Canada
ID: DEVINE Contact: Hans Smith Phone: (555) 555-1212 Fax: (555) 555-1313

Accounts

Functional Currency:	CAD	Use Account Groups:	Yes
Use Multicurrency:	No	Default Rate Type:	SP
Maintain Quantities:	No	Decimals in Quantities:	0
Keep Fiscal Sets for:	2 years	Default Closing Account.:	
Keep Transaction Details for:	2 years		

Posting Options

Allow Posting of Previous Year:	Yes		
Allow Provisional Posting:	Yes		
Force Listing Of Batches:	Yes	Edit Imported Entries:	All Fields
		Last Batch No:	0
Lock Budget Set 1:	No	Next Posting Sequence:	1
		Next Prov. Posting Sequence:	1
		Current Fiscal Year:	2010
		Oldest Year of Fiscal Sets:	2010
		Oldest Year of Transaction Detail:	2010

Account Segments

Default Structure Code: BASIC Segment Delimiter: / Account Segment: 1

Segment	Description	Length	Used in Closing
1	Account	4	No
2	Activity	2	No

❑ Close: the **G/L Options** window

SEGMENT CODES

Since you have defined two segments on the Segment Definition page of the Options notebook for Devine Designs Inc., you must use the Segment Codes window to enter the codes for the second segment. Enter a description for each code and assign a closing account to any of the segments that you indicated can be used in closing on the Segments page of the Options notebook.

Leslie, Eric, and John have decided to record sales using five categories. These categories must be entered as segment codes for the Activity segment before General Ledger account codes can be entered. Additional categories can be added as necessary. The five segment codes are:

- 10 Web Page Design
- 20 Web Page Maintenance

- 30 Web Site Hosting
- 40 Web Retail Sales
- 99 Misc. Sales

ACCPAC uses this information to verify segmented account numbers in the chart of accounts.

ENTERING SEGMENT CODES

❑ DClick: the **Segment Codes** icon 

If the segment name Activity is not displayed in the Segment Name text box as shown in Figure 7-15, click the list tool and select it from the options displayed.

FIGURE 7-15
G/L Segment Codes Window

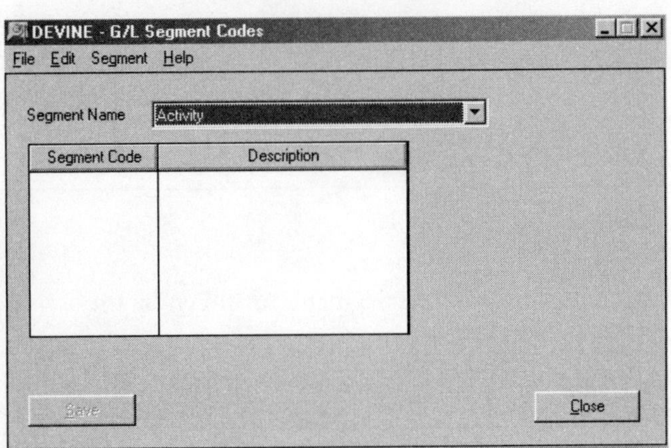

❑ Click: the **Segment Code** column to activate it
❑ Type: **10**
❑ Press: **Tab** [Tab] to move to the Description column
❑ Type: **Web Page Design**
❑ Press: **Enter** [Enter]

The program will add another highlighted line to the table, and the Save button will become active.

YOUR TURN

❑ Add the following four activity codes:
Segment Code 20 Web Page Maintenance
Segment Code 30 Web Site Hosting
Segment Code 40 Web Retail Sales
Segment Code 99 Misc. Sales

Once you have added the above codes, review them carefully and make any necessary corrections.

❑ Click: **Save** [Save]

PRINTING THE G/L SEGMENT CODE REPORT

The G/L Segment Code Report window is shown in Figure 7-16.

❑ Click: **File** on the G/L Segment Codes window menu bar
❑ Click: **Print** on the File Menu

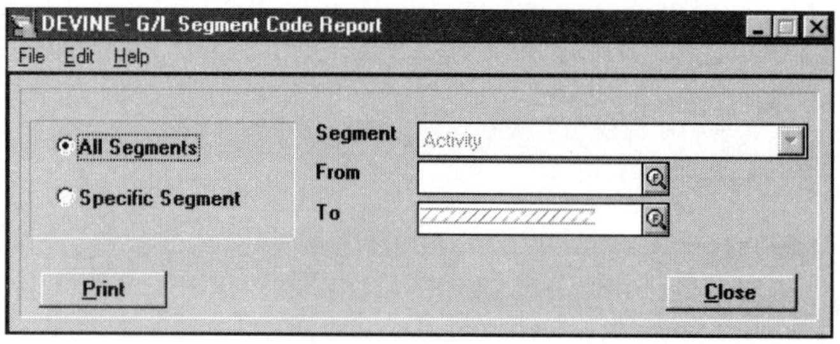

FIGURE 7-16
G/L Segment Code Report Window

TIP
If you have entered segment codes for more than one segment and only want to print the codes for one, click the Specific Segment button and use the list tool to identify the segment you want to print.

The default is to print All Segments as shown by the activated Option button.

❑ Click: **Print** [Print]
❑ Click: **OK** [OK] on the Print dialog box
❑ Close: the **G/L Segment Code Report** window
❑ Close: the **G/L Segment Codes** window

Use the printout to verify that you have recorded the Segment Codes correctly. If there is an error, return to the G/L Segment Codes window and correct it.

ACCOUNT STRUCTURES

The Account Structures window allows you to define multiple account structures for your company. An account structure defines the segments that an account number contains, and the order in which those segments appear.

You have to define an account structure for each combination of segments you will use in account numbers. You must define at least one account structure. Devine Designs Inc. is a small company and uses only two account structures—the default structure and the revenue account structure. When you add a new General Ledger account, the program compares the account number with the segments contained in the assigned structure.

ENTERING G/L ACCOUNT STRUCTURES

❑ DClick: the **Account Structures** icon [Account Structures] on the G/L Setup Window

The G/L Account Structures window should appear as shown in Figure 7-17.

FIGURE 7-17
G/L Account Structures Window

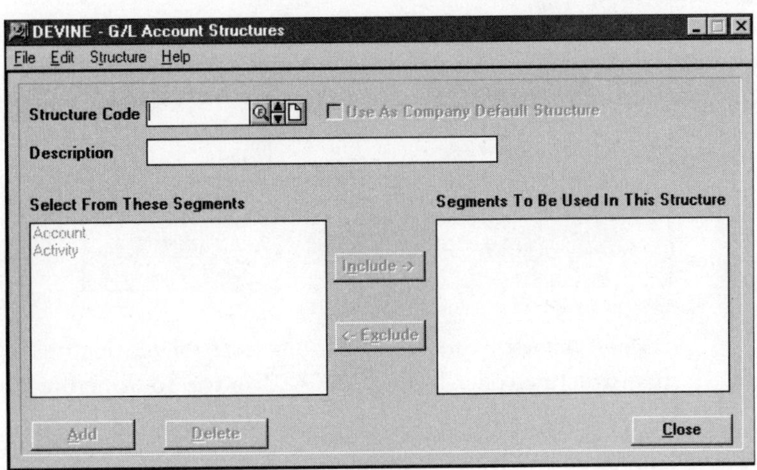

The insertion point should be displayed in the Structure Code text box. Structure codes can be up to seven characters long.

❑ Type: **BASIC** in the Structure Code text box
❑ Press: **Tab** [Tab] to move to the Description field
❑ Type: **For all acct's except revenue**
❑ Press: **Tab** [Tab] to move to the Select From These Segments field

The first item, Account, should be highlighted.

❑ Click: **Include** [Include ->] to move Account over to the Segments To Be Used In This Structure field

All of the accounts in the General Ledger, except the revenue accounts, will have the same structure, so you will select the BASIC structure code as the Company Default Structure.

❑ Click: the **Check box** for Use As Company Default Structure
❑ Click: **Add** [Add]

Add the REV account structure for revenue accounts.

❑ Click: the **New Document** icon for the Structure Code text box
❑ Type: **REV** in the Structure Code text box
❑ Press: **Tab** [Tab]
❑ Type: **Revenue accounts** in the Description text box
❑ Press: **Tab** [Tab]
❑ Include: both **Account** and **Activity** in the account structure
❑ Click: **Add** [Add]

Printing the G/L Account Structure Report

❑ Click: **File** on the G/L Account Structures window

❑ Click: **Print** [Print] on the File Menu

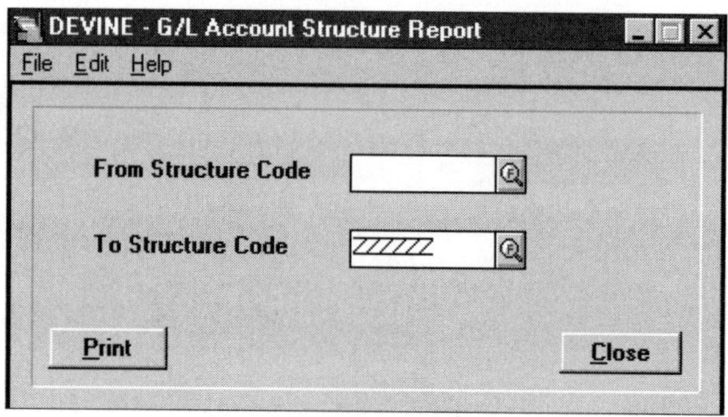

FIGURE 7-18
G/L Account Structure Report Window

If the From Structure Code text box is left blank (Figure 7-18), printing will start at the first structure code. Typing **ZZZZZZ** in the To Structure Code text box will ensure that all codes are printed.

❑ Click: **Print** [Print]

❑ Click: **OK** [OK] on the Print window

Review your printout to ensure that BASIC includes just the Account segment, and that REV includes both the Account and Activity segments. Make any corrections necessary and reprint the report.

❑ Close: the **G/L Account Structure Report** window

❑ Close: the **G/L Account Structures** window

Source Codes

A source code consists of two letters that identify the ACCPAC accounting module in which the transaction originates, followed by a dash and two letters that represent the type of transaction. All transactions entered in the General Ledger module must use a source code that begins with **GL**. ACCPAC automatically adds new source codes found in subledger transactions, such as accounts receivable or accounts payable, during posting. Source codes allow you to print source journals of posted transactions by transaction type for analysis and audit requirements.

Entering Source Codes

You must define at least one source code before you can record any transactions.

Devine Designs Inc. has decided to use the following two-letter groups to identify transaction types in the source codes:

GJ	General Journal
CR	Cash Receipts
CD	Cash Disbursements
PU	Purchases
SA	Sales

❑ DClick: the **Source Codes** icon on the G/L Setup window

FIGURE 7-19 G/L Source Codes Window

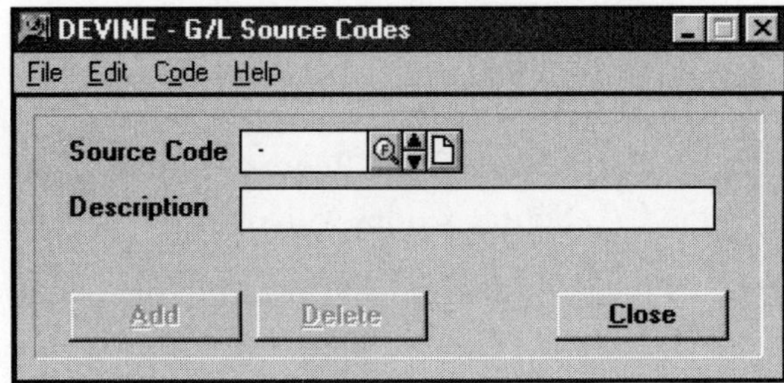

Ensure that the insertion point is displayed in the Source Code box (Figure 7-19).

❑ Type: **GLGJ**

You do not have to type the dash. All letters will be entered in upper case.

❑ Press: **Enter** to move the insertion point to the Description text box

❑ Type: **General Journal**

❑ Click: **Add**

YOUR TURN

❑ Click: the **New Document** icon to clear the text boxes

❑ Enter: the remaining source codes

Remember to click the Add button after entering each source code and to use the New Document icon to clear the text fields.

PRINTING THE SOURCE CODE REPORT

You will need the source codes when you enter transactions, so you should print a list of the source codes that you have entered.

❑ Click: **File** on the G/L Source Codes window menu bar

❑ Click: **Print** on the File Menu

FIGURE 7-20
G/L Source Code Report Window

The default settings, as shown in Figure 7-20—a blank From Source Code text box and **ZZ-ZZ** in the To Source Code text box—indicate that all source codes are to be printed.

- ❑ Click: **Print** [Print]
- ❑ Click: **OK** [OK] on the Print dialog box
- ❑ Close: the **G/L Source Code Report** window
- ❑ Close: the **G/L Source Codes** window

FIGURE 7-21
Source Code Report

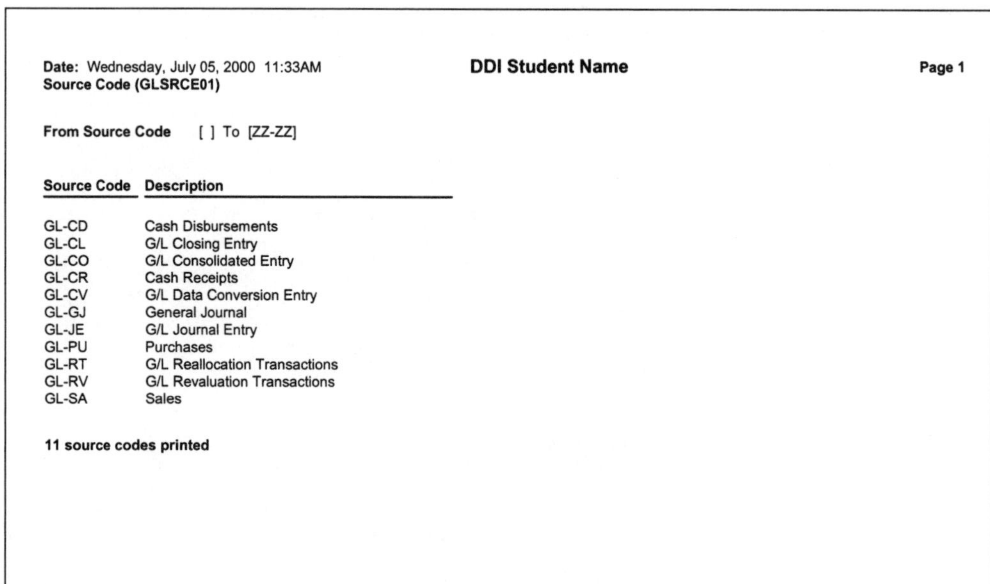

Date: Wednesday, July 05, 2000 11:33AM **DDI Student Name** **Page 1**
Source Code (GLSRCE01)

From Source Code [ ] To [ZZ-ZZ]

Source Code	Description
GL-CD	Cash Disbursements
GL-CL	G/L Closing Entry
GL-CO	G/L Consolidated Entry
GL-CR	Cash Receipts
GL-CV	G/L Data Conversion Entry
GL-GJ	General Journal
GL-JE	G/L Journal Entry
GL-PU	Purchases
GL-RT	G/L Reallocation Transactions
GL-RV	G/L Revaluation Transactions
GL-SA	Sales

11 source codes printed

SPECIAL SOURCE CODES

Compare your printout to that shown in Figure 7-21.

ACCPAC for Windows has created four source codes in addition to those you added.

- GL-CL is the G/L Closing Entry source code which is generated automatically for transactions created by the ACCPAC General Ledger at year-end.

- GL-CO, the G/L Consolidated Entry source code, is generated automatically for transactions consolidated by the ACCPAC General Ledger.
- GL-CV is the G/L Data Conversion Entry source code. This source code is generated by ACCPAC for Windows Small Business Series when data is converted from an earlier version of ACCPAC Plus.
- GL-JE is a generic G/L Journal Entry code that you can use in place of the General Journal source code you added earlier.

WARNING

Before you delete a source code, ensure that all batches in which it has been used have been posted. If necessary, change the source code in any unposted batches.

DELETING A SOURCE CODE

Since two source codes can be used for the same types of transactions, Devine Designs Inc. has decided to delete the GL-GJ source code.

❑ DClick: the **Source Codes** icon on the G/L Setup window

❑ Click: the **Finder** for the Source Code text box

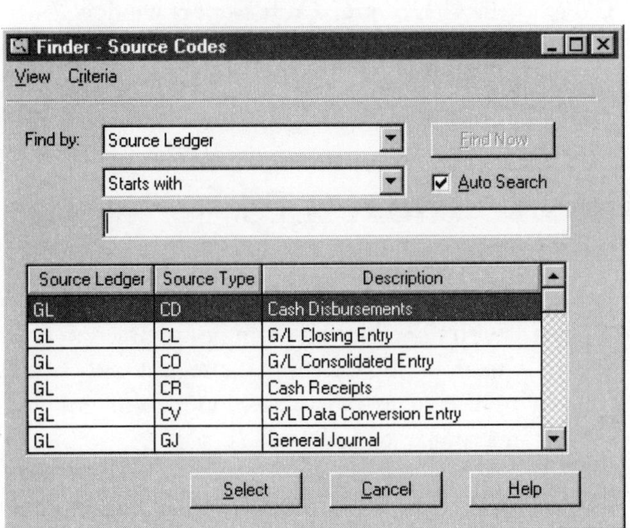

FIGURE 7-22
Finder - Source Codes

The Finder for Source Codes is shown in Figure 7-22. The Source Type Codes are arranged alphabetically.

❑ Click: the **GL GJ** row on the Finder table

❑ Click: **Select**

ACCPAC will transfer the information from the Finder to the G/L Source Codes window.

❑ Click: **Delete**

In most cases when data is to be removed, ACCPAC requires confirmation, as shown in Figure 7-23.

FIGURE 7-23
Warning Message

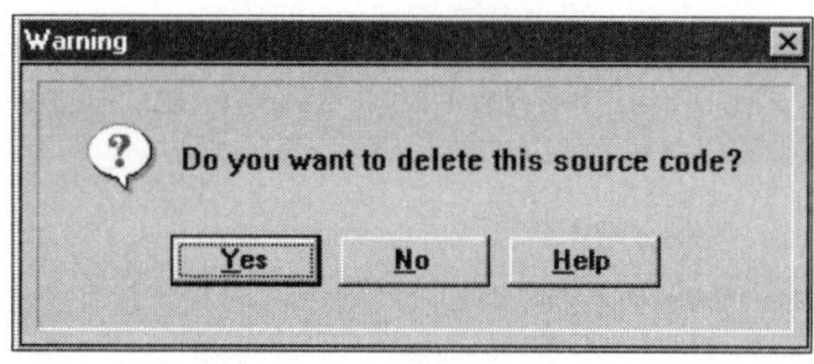

❑ Click: **Yes**

YOUR TURN

Devine Designs Inc. will not convert data from an earlier version of ACCPAC and will not need the GL-CV source code.

❑ Delete: the **GL-CV** source code
❑ Print: the **Source Code Report** again and file it for reference when entering transactions
❑ Close: the **G/L Source Code Report** window
❑ Close: the **G/L Source Codes** window

SOURCE JOURNAL PROFILES

The source codes you created in the previous section are used to organize and print source journals of transactions according to transaction type. You can use one source code for a source journal, or you can combine several types of transactions in one source journal. You may have as many journals as you require, but you must define the contents of each journal in a source journal profile.

Devine Designs Inc. has decided to print individual journals for Purchases, Sales, Cash Receipts, Cash Disbursements, and a General Journal.

ENTERING SOURCE JOURNAL PROFILES

❑ DClick: the **Source Journal Profiles** icon on the G/L Setup window

The insertion point should be in the Source Journal Name text box, as shown in Figure 7-24. If necessary, click in this text box to activate the insertion point.

❑ Type: **Cash Receipts Journal**
❑ Press: **Tab** three times

The General Ledger has a built-in source journal definition, GLSJ01F, which will be used by Devine Designs Inc.

FIGURE 7-24
G/L Source Journal Profiles Window

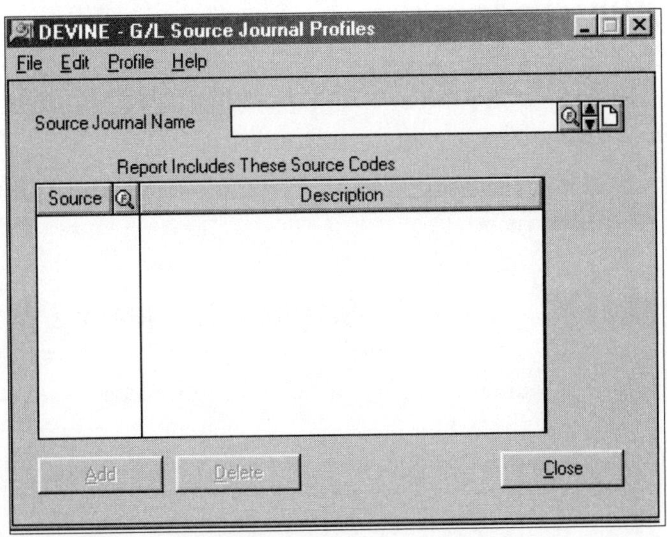

- ❑ Click: the **Finder** in the Source column
- ❑ Click: the **GL CR** row in the Finder table
- ❑ Click: **Select**

ACCPAC will transfer the source code and its description to the G/L Source Journal Profiles window.

- ❑ Click: **Add**

The next source journal profile that you will add will be for the General Journal. This source journal profile incorporates three of the four source codes created by ACCPAC.

- ❑ Click: the **New Document** icon
- ❑ Type: **General Journal**
- ❑ Press: **Tab** three times
- ❑ Click: the **Finder** in the Source column
- ❑ Click: the **GL JE** row in the Finder table
- ❑ Click: **Select**
- ❑ Press: **Tab** to add another line for a source code
- ❑ Click: the **Finder** in the Source column
- ❑ Click: the **GL CL** row in the Finder table
- ❑ Click: **Select**
- ❑ Press: **Tab** to add another line for a source code
- ❑ Click: the **Finder** in the Source column
- ❑ Click: the **GL CO** row in the Finder table
- ❑ Click: **Select**
- ❑ Click: **Add**

YOUR TURN

Devine Designs Inc. needs additional individual source journals for Cash Disbursements, Purchases, and Sales.

❑ Add individual source journal profiles for the Cash Disbursements, Purchases, and Sales Journals.

PRINTING THE G/L SOURCE JOURNAL PROFILE REPORT

The Source Journal Profile report allows you to verify that you have defined the source journals properly.

❑ Click: **File** on the G/L Source Journal Profiles window menu bar
❑ Click: **Print** on the File Menu

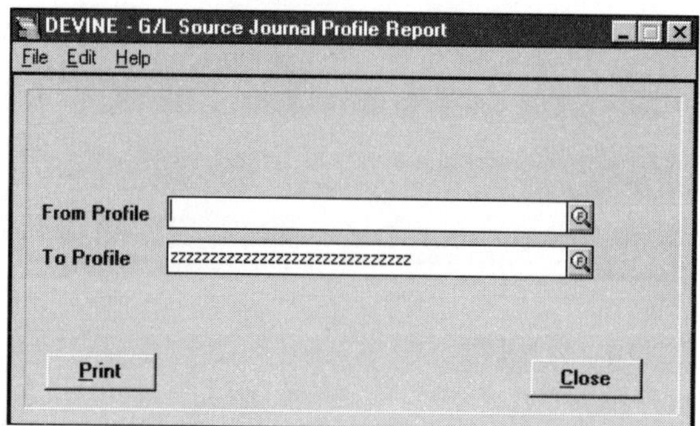

FIGURE 7-25
G/L Source Journal Profile Report Window

The defaults shown in Figure 7-25, a blank From Profile text box and multiple copies of the letter z in the To Profile text box, will print all source journal profiles in the report.

❑ Click: **Print** [Print]
❑ Click: **OK** [OK] on the Print dialog box

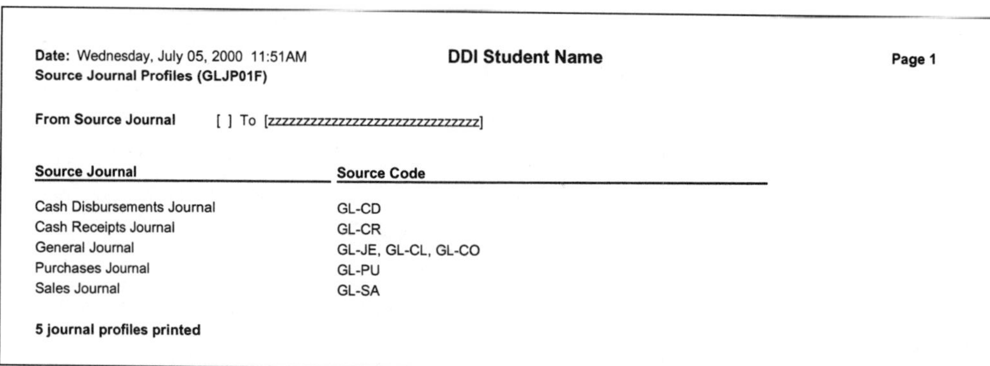

Date: Wednesday, July 05, 2000 11:51AM — DDI Student Name — Page 1
Source Journal Profiles (GLJP01F)

From Source Journal [ ] To [zzzzzzzzzzzzzzzzzzzzzzzzzzzzzz]

Source Journal	Source Code
Cash Disbursements Journal	GL-CD
Cash Receipts Journal	GL-CR
General Journal	GL-JE, GL-CL, GL-CO
Purchases Journal	GL-PU
Sales Journal	GL-SA

5 journal profiles printed

FIGURE 7-26
Source Journal Profile Report

Compare your printout to that shown in Figure 7-26. If necessary, make corrections and print the report again.

- ❑ Close: the **G/L Source Journal Profile Report** Window
- ❑ Close: the **G/L Source Journal Profiles** window
- ❑ Exit: **ACCPAC**

Review Questions

1. What is the purpose of the Options notebook?
2. When working on the Account page of the Options notebook, what would happen if you chose not to activate the Account Groups option?
3. Describe the purpose of provisional posting.
4. What is the purpose of the Force Listing of Batches option?
5. What is the purpose of the Edit Imported Entries function?
6. What is the purpose of the Account Structures window?
7. Describe the structure and purpose of the source codes used by ACCPAC Small Business Series for Windows.

Exercise

- ❑ Sign on to the your exercise company using 041210 as the Session Date.
- ❑ Set up the General Ledger using **05/01/09** as the Oldest Fiscal Year Starting Data and **2010** as the Current Fiscal Year.
- ❑ Enter your name in the Contact Name text box on the Address page.
- ❑ Make sure that the Use Account Groups check box is active on the Accounts page.
- ❑ Make sure that the Allow Posting to Previous Years check box is active on the Posting page.
- ❑ Make sure the Allow Provisional Posting check box is active.
- ❑ Make sure the Force Listing of Batches check box is active.
- ❑ Keep [2] Years of Fiscal Sets.
- ❑ Keep [2] Years of Transactions Detail.
- ❑ On the Segments page, select 1 as the account segment and the slash (/) as the delimiter.
- ❑ Name Seg. No. 1 Account and set the length to 4.
- ❑ Name Seg. No. 2 Activity and set the length to 2.

- ❑ Save the setup options and print the G/L Options Report.
- ❑ Create the following Segment Codes for the Activity segment:
  - 10 Web Page Design
  - 20 Web Page Maintenance
  - 30 Web Site Hosting
  - 40 Web Retail Sales
  - 99 Misc. Sales
- ❑ Print the G/L Segment Code report.
- ❑ Create the G/L Account Structure BASIC including the Account segment. This structure should be used as the Company Default Structure.
- ❑ Create the G/L Account Structure REV, including both the Account and Activity segments.
- ❑ Print the G/L Account Structure report.
- ❑ Create Source Codes for Cash Receipts, Cash Disbursements, Purchases, and Sales.
- ❑ Print the Source Code report.
- ❑ Create the appropriate Source Journal Profiles.
- ❑ Print the G/L Source Journal Profile report.
- ❑ Exit: **ACCPAC**

CHAPTER 8

CHART OF ACCOUNTS

All organizations use a systematic method of assigning identification numbers to their General Ledger accounts. A list of these accounts is called a Chart of Accounts. In this chapter, you will create the Chart of Accounts for Devine Designs Inc.

Computerized accounting systems may impose constraints on an organization's chart of accounts. To use the pre-programmed financial statements supplied with ACCPAC, each account must be assigned to one of 16 predetermined account groups. Each account will be given an identification code that is within the range for one of these account groups. Devine Designs Inc. will use the financial statements supplied with ACCPAC.

GETTING READY

- ❑ Start: **Windows 95/98**
- ❑ DClick: the **ACCPAC** shortcut icon on the Windows desktop
- ❑ Enter: **ADMIN** in the User ID text box
- ❑ Enter: **ADMIN** in the Password text box

- ❑ Select: **DDI** line in the Company list box
- ❑ Use: **04/12/10** as the Session Date
- ❑ Click: **OK**
- ❑ Open: the **General Ledger** window

ADDING BALANCE SHEET ACCOUINTS

- ❑ DClick: the **Accounts** icon on the General Ledger window

The Account Detail page of the G/L Accounts notebook will appear as shown in Figure 8-1.

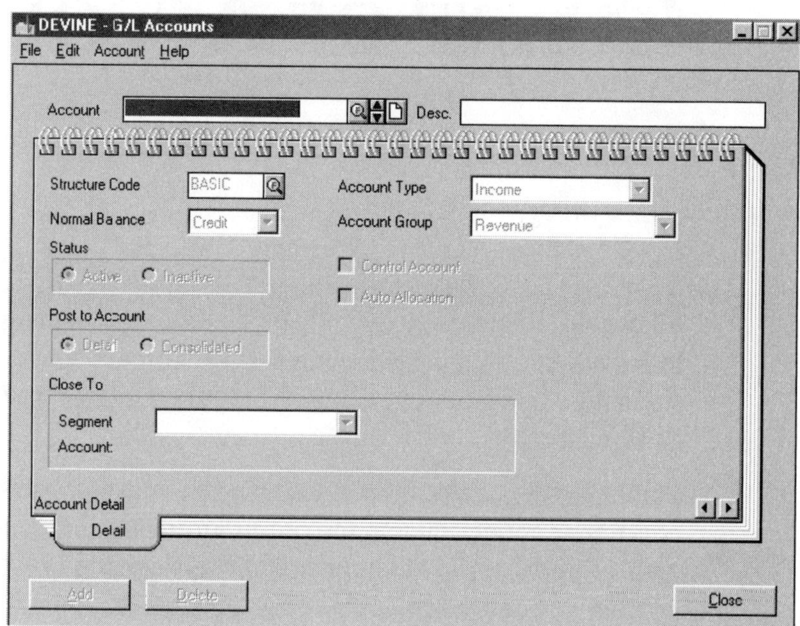

FIGURE 8-1
Account Detail Page

The G/L Accounts notebook can contain up to two pages of information about each General Ledger account. The Detail page contains the information that is required for every account. If you specify Auto Allocation for an account, an additional page will be created.

The Account and Description text boxes located above the notebook page are common to all pages.

ACCOUNT

ACCPAC will accept account numbers up to 45 characters long. Each account number may include as many as 10 segments. ACCPAC can accept a range of account number structures, from a very simple one for a small business to very complex ones for extremely large organizations.

Eric has decided to use a simple structure of two segments in the account numbers for Devine Designs Inc. The first four digits are the account segment. The second two digits identify the activity for revenue accounts. The two parts of the account number will be separated by a slash (/) as the delimiter.

Devine Designs Inc. uses numbers rather than letters or combinations of letters and numbers for the account code, since it is easier to define numeric ranges for account groups. Accounts are numbered in the order in which they appear, within their assigned account group, on reports or in financial statements.

The first account to be added is account number 1000 for the company bank account at First Bank Corp.

- ❑ Click: the **Account** text box
- ❑ Type: 1000
- ❑ Press: **Tab** [Tab] to move the insertion point to the Desc. text box

Description

In the Desc. text box, enter the name of the account exactly as you want the name to appear in reports or financial statements. This account description may be as many as 31 characters long.

- ❑ Type: **Bank - First Bank Corp.**

Account Detail Page

- ❑ Press: **Tab** [Tab] to activate the Detail tab at the bottom of the page

Note that all options on the Detail page and the Add button are now active, as indicated by the darker type. If you do not use the Auto Allocation option, you can record all the information for an account on the Account Detail page.

Some information is automatically entered in the Account Detail page to reduce the amount of data entry required. You can change this information for each individual account that you add.

Structure Code

The Structure Code text box on the Account Detail page is used to enter one of the structure codes that were recorded for the company when you set up the General Ledger. In Chapter 7 you created the segment codes, and used that information to create an account structure code—BASIC. You specified that BASIC would be the default structure code as most of the accounts would use this structure. BASIC should be displayed in the Structure Code text box as shown in Figure 8-1.

When you select a Structure Code, ACCPAC compares that Structure Code to the account number to verify that they are compatible.

❑ Click: the **Finder** for the Structure Codes text box

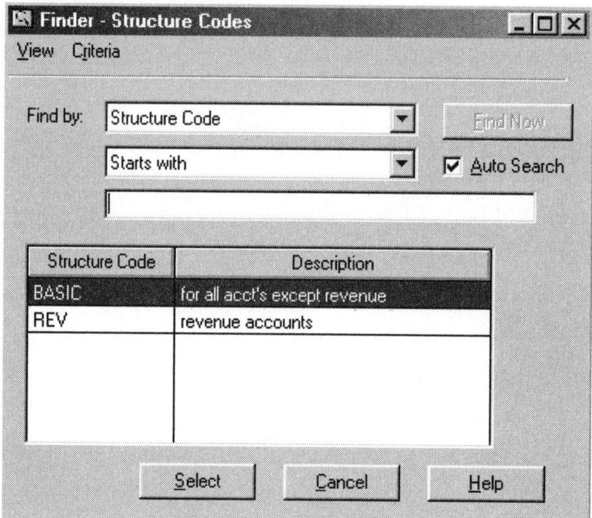

FIGURE 8-2
Finder - Structure Codes

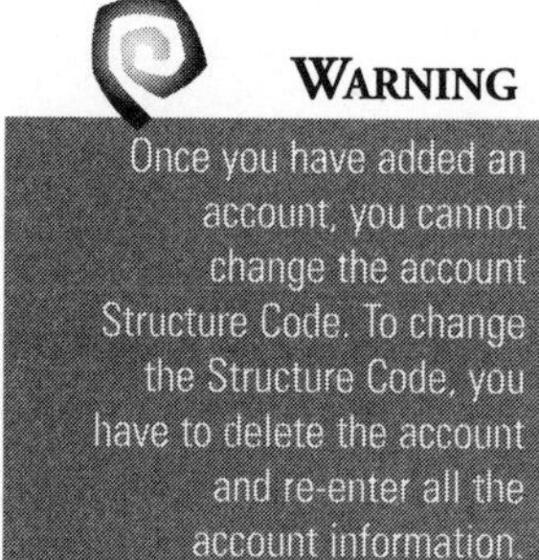

As shown in Figure 8-2, Devine Designs Inc. defined two Structure Codes. BASIC is the default Structure Code that will be used for most numbers. REV is the Structure Code that will be used for revenue accounts. To change the Structure Code, click on the new code and then click the Select button.

Account 1000 will use the BASIC Structure Code.

❑ Click: **Select** Select

ACCOUNT TYPE

The Account Type list box allows you to specify whether an account balance is a balance sheet, income statement, or retained earnings account. Balance sheet accounts do not close at the end of a fiscal year. Income statement accounts are temporary proprietorship accounts that are closed to a retained earnings account at the end of the fiscal year.

Bank accounts are current assets and are balance sheet accounts.

❑ Click: the **list tool** beside the Account Type list box

The list box will open and display the three choices: Income, Balance Sheet, and Retained Earnings.

❑ Click: **Balance Sheet**

Note that when you select Balance Sheet or Retained Earnings as the account type, the Close To portion of the screen disappears. Only Income Statement accounts use this option.

Normal Balance

The Normal Balance text box lets you specify whether the account balance is usually a debit or credit amount. Most asset and expense accounts have debit balances, while most liability, revenue, and shareholders' equity accounts have credit balances.

❑ Click: the **list tool** for the Normal Balance text box

The list box shows the two options available: Debit and Credit. Bank accounts are current assets and normally would have a debit balance.

❑ Click: **Debit**

Account Group

Account Groups are used by the ACCPAC Financial Reporter to create standard financial reports. If you do not use the Account Group option, you have to create your own financial statements. Since Devine Designs Inc. has decided to use ACCPAC's standard financial reports, each account must be assigned to one of the 16 account groupings used by ACCPAC for Windows.

The general structure of the chart of accounts for Devine Designs Inc. is shown below.

Account Group	Account Number Range
Current Assets	1000-1400
Fixed Assets	1500-1540
Other Assets	1600
Accumulated Depreciation	1700-1740
Current Liabilities	2000-2250
Long-Term Liabilities	Unused
Shareholders' Equity	3000-3300
Revenue	4000-4070
Cost of Sales	5000
Opening Inventory	Unused
Purchases	Unused
Closing Inventory	Unused
Costs and Expenses	6000-6200
Other Income and Expenses	6500
Provision for Income Taxes	Unused
Other	Unused

Note that the first two digits in the account numbers identify the balance sheet or income statement classification of the account. The last two digits identify specific accounts within each range. Devine Designs Inc. also uses the segment codes created in Chapter 7 to further classify sales by product or category.

To keep the Chart of Accounts as simple as possible, Devine Designs Inc. does not plan to use the ACCPAC account groups for other long-term liabilities, provision for income taxes, or other. As Devine Designs Inc. sells either services or copies of graphics and applet files, it will not be necessary to use the opening inventory, purchases, or closing inventory account groups. Account number ranges have been made available in case it becomes necessary to add accounts in these account groups.

❑ Click: the **list tool** for the Account Group list box

The list box displays the names of six of the sixteen possible account groups in the order listed previously. To change the account group displayed, click the scroll arrows to the right of the list box.

Bank accounts are a current asset.

❑ Scroll: until **Current assets** is displayed
❑ Click: **Current assets**

STATUS

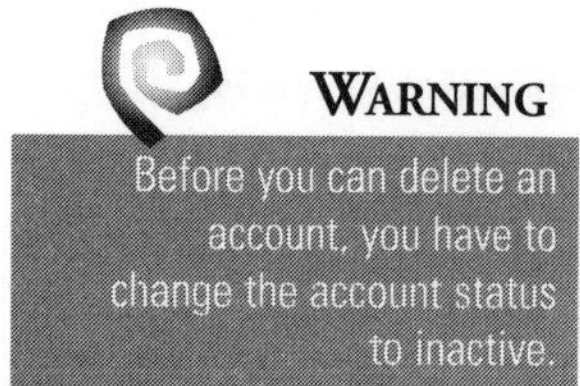

ACCPAC only allows transactions to be posted to active accounts. You can change the status of an account at any time. You would designate an account as inactive if you plan to delete it and do not want any transactions posted to that account. For Devine Designs Inc., all accounts will be active.

If the option button to the left of Active in the Status field is not enabled, as indicated by a dot in the middle of the button, click this button to make it active.

POST TO ACCOUNT

When an account is posted in detail, all debits and credits posted to it are retained, and can be listed individually on source journals and the G/L Listing. If an account is consolidated when posted, these separate details are combined during posting into single amounts for each fiscal period and source code. Eric has decided that all accounts should be posted in detail.

If the button in front of Detail for the Post to Account field is not active, as indicated by a dot in the button, click this button to activate it.

CONTROL ACCOUNT

ACCPAC allows you to specify if an account is a control account for a subledger, such as Accounts Receivable or Accounts Payable. When you select this option, you can only post subledger batches to the account. Transactions recorded in a general ledger transaction batch, with a source code starting with GL, cannot be posted to control accounts. A check mark in the check box indicates that the option has been activated for this account.

Account 1000 is not a subledger control account. If a check mark appears in this check box, click the check box to deactivate it.

AUTO ALLOCATION

The Auto Allocation option allows you to identify accounts whose balances will be periodically allocated to other accounts. This option is useful for allocating overhead expense account balances to different departments. When you select this option, the Auto Allocation page becomes available to record allocation details.

Devine Designs Inc. does not use the Auto Allocation option for any accounts. If a check mark appears in this check box, click the check box to deselect Auto Allocation. Note that if Auto Allocation is activated, a second page is added to the G/L Account notebook.

MAINTAIN QUANTITIES

If you had chosen to maintain quantities when you set up the General Ledger, a check box for Maintain Quantities would be displayed on your screen. When this option is selected for an account, you can record both monetary and quantity information in transactions for the account.

ADDING THE ACCOUNT

Before adding the account, you should compare your Account Detail page to that shown in Figure 8-3 and make any necessary corrections.

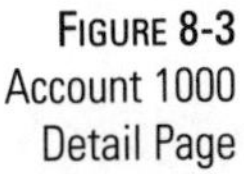
FIGURE 8-3 Account 1000 Detail Page

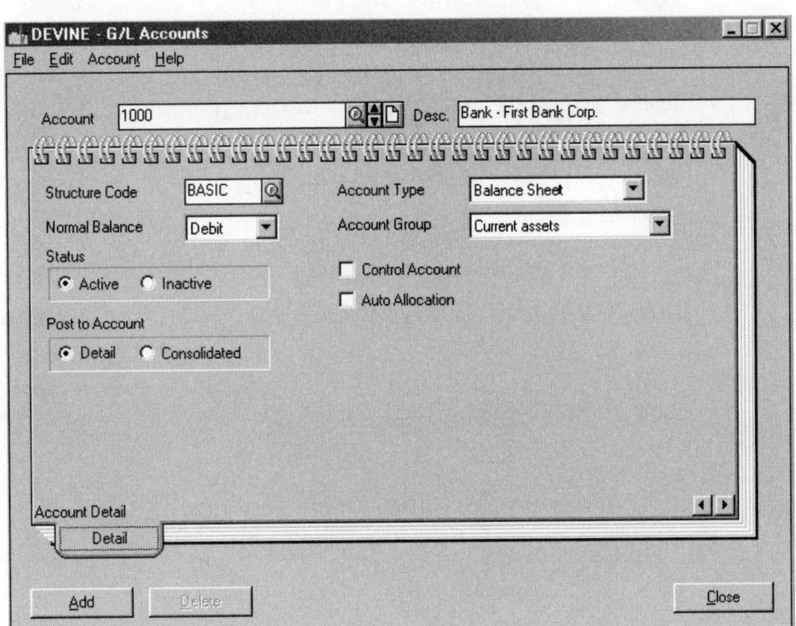

❑ Click: **Add** [Add]

Do not worry if there was an error in account 1000. Later in this chapter, you will be shown how to change account details.

YOUR TURN

TIP

If you are adding accounts with the same structure code, you do not have to click the New button to clear the Account Number, Description, Text Boxes, or to reset the Detail page to the defaults to your system. You can edit the Account and Description text boxes and make any other changes necessary to the Detail page. Then add the account and repeat the process as you add other accounts.

You will now add most of the remaining balance sheet accounts for Devine Design Inc. All of these accounts will use the Structure Code BASIC, the Account Type "Balance Sheet," the "Active" Status, and will Post to Account in "Detail." You will have to determine the Account Group for each account. Do not identify the accounts receivable and accounts payable as Subledger Control Accounts. These accounts will be edited after the Accounts Receivable and Accounts Payable have been activated.

Accounts to be added:

Account	Description	Normal Balance
1025	Bank - E-Bank.com	Debit
1040	Bank - Payroll Account	Debit
1100	Accounts Receivable	Debit
1120	Accounts Receivable, Control	Debit
1160	Allowance for Bad Debts	Credit
1200	Inventory	Debit
1300	Office Supplies	Debit
1400	Prepaid Expenses	Debit
1500	Machinery & Equipment	Debit
1520	Fixtures & Furniture	Debit
1540	Software	Debit
1600	Organization Costs	Debit
1700	Acc Dep-Machinery & Equipment	Credit
1720	Acc Dep-Fixtures & Furniture	Credit
1740	Acc Dep-Software	Credit
2010	Accounts Payable	Credit
2020	Accounts Payable, Control	Credit
2050	Bank Credit Line	Credit
2100	Retail Sales Tax Payable	Credit
2200	G.S.T. (V.A.T.) Payable	Credit
2205	G.S.T. (V.A.T.) Recoverable	Debit
2210	Prepayments Received	Credit
3000	Common Stock	Credit
3300	Dividends	Debit

Later in this chapter, you will print the Chart of Accounts and learn how to correct any accidental errors that you have made.

Retained Earnings Account

Before adding income statement accounts, you should add at least one retained earnings account. In a complex Chart of Accounts, ACCPAC can be configured to close accounts to different retained earnings accounts. This capacity can be used for divisional or regional reporting.

Devine Designs Inc. will add one retained earnings account and designate it as the default retained earnings account for the company.

Adding a Retained Earnings Account

- ❑ Click: the **New Document** icon to clear the account information
- ❑ Add: account 3200 Retained Earnings using the following information

Account Number	**3200**
Description	**Retained Earnings**
Structure Code	**Basic**
Normal Balance	**Credit**
Account Type	**Retained Earning**
Account Group	**Shareholders Equity**
Status	**Active**
Post to Account	**Detail**

Compare your Account Detail page with that shown in Figure 8-4 and make any necessary corrections.

FIGURE 8-4 Account 3200 Detail Page

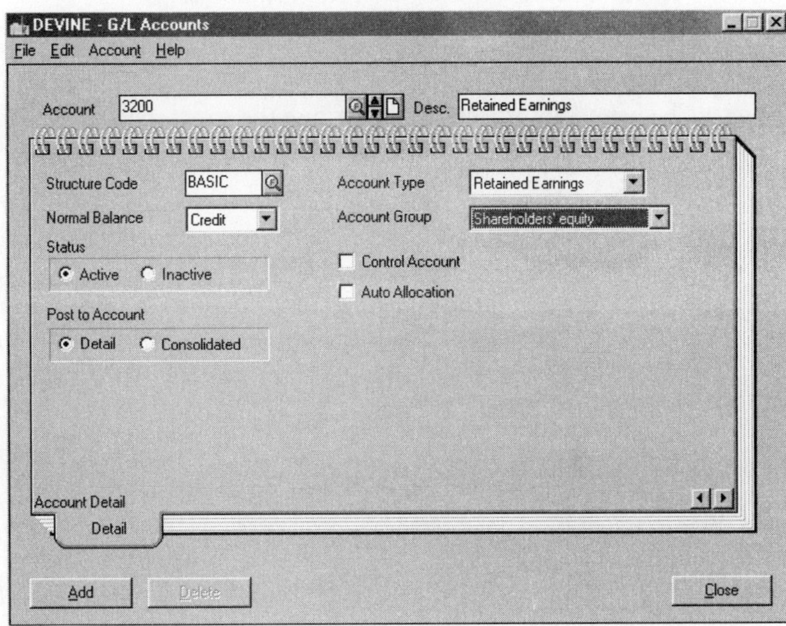

- ❑ Click: **Add**
- ❑ Close: the **G/L Accounts** window

Default Retained Earnings Account

Now that you have created a retained earnings account, return to the Options notebook in the G/L Setup window and specify the default Retained Earnings account.

- ❑ DClick: the **G/L Setup** icon on the General Ledger window
- ❑ DClick: the **Options** icon on the G/L Setup window
- ❑ Click: the **Account** tab at the bottom of the G/L Options notebook
- ❑ Click: the **Default Closing Account** text box
- ❑ Type: **3200**
- ❑ Press: **Enter** to complete the entry
- ❑ Click: **Save**
- ❑ Close: the **G/L Options** notebook

Income Statement Accounts

Adding Income Statement accounts is basically the same as adding Balance Sheet accounts, with two additional considerations.

The first consideration is that Devine Designs Inc. uses a different structure code for revenue accounts so that the type of activity producing the revenue can be identified. Therefore, for revenue accounts, use the structure code REV; for other Income Statement accounts, use BASIC as the structure code.

The second consideration is that at year-end all Income Statement accounts must be closed to a retained earnings account. You have just designated account 3200 as the default retained earnings account for Devine Designs Inc.

Adding an Income Statement Account

Adding account 4000/10 Sales - Web Page Design will illustrate the two additional considerations for Income Statement accounts.

- ❑ Open: the **G/L Accounts** window
- ❑ Type: **4000/10** in the Account text box
- ❑ Press: **Tab**

- ❑ Type: **Sales - Web Page Design** in the Desc. Text box
- ❑ Press: **Tab** [Tab]
- ❑ Select: **REV** in the Structure Code text box

ACCPAC compares the account number with the structure code selected. You cannot add the account if the account number does not match the structure code.

- ❑ Select: **Credit** in the Normal Balance text box
- ❑ Select: **Income** in the Account Type text box
- ❑ Select: **Revenue** in the Account Group text box

In complex Charts of Accounts with income accounts closing to different accounts, you have to enter this information for each income account individually. Devine Designs Inc. closes all income accounts to the same retained earnings account.

FIGURE 8-5
Account 4000/10
Detail Page

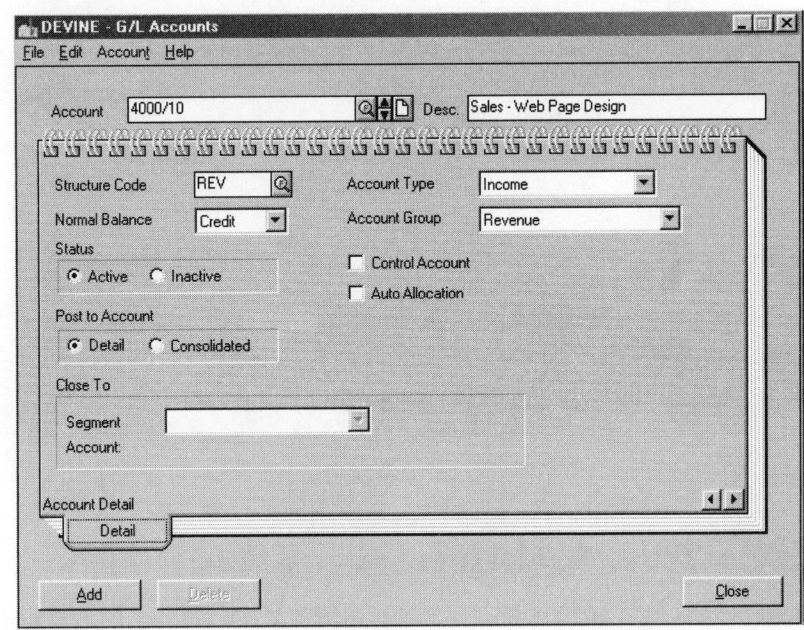

Compare your Account Detail page with that shown in Figure 8-5 and make any necessary corrections.

- ❑ Click: **Add** [Add]

YOUR TURN

You will now add the remaining Income Statement accounts for Devine Designs Inc. Remember to select the correct structure code—REV for revenue accounts and BASIC for all other accounts. All of the accounts will use the Account Type "Income," "Active" Status, and will Post to Account in "Detail." You will have to determine the Account Group for each account.

❑ Add the accounts in shown in Figure 8-6.

FIGURE 8-6 Accounts to Be Added

Account	Description	Normal Balance
4000/20	Sales - Web Page Maintenance	Credit
4000/30	Sales - Web Site Hosting	Credit
4000/40	Sales - Web Retail Sales	Credit
4000/99	Sales - Misc.	Credit
4010	Sales Discounts	Debit
5000	Cost of Sales	Debit
6000	Advertising Expense	Debit
6020	Bad Debt Expense	Debit
6040	Bank Service Charges	Debit
6050	Bank Clearing Errors	Debit
6060	Communication Expense	Debit
6080	Computer Rent	Debit
6100	Depreciation Expense	Debit
6120	Insurance Expense	Debit
6140	Internet Services Expense	Debit
6160	Office Rent Expense	Debit
6180	Salary Expense	Debit
6200	Supplies Expense	Debit
6500	Interest Income	Credit

❑ Close: the **G/L Accounts** window

VIEWING THE CHART OF ACCOUNTS

There are several ways to access the Chart of Accounts. You can display the Chart on screen or you can print it.

❑ DClick: the **Chart of Accounts** icon on the General Ledger window

Use the horizontal scroll bar to display additional information. The vertical scroll bar allows you to display additional accounts, as shown in Figure 8-7.

FIGURE 8-7
G/L Chart of Accounts Window

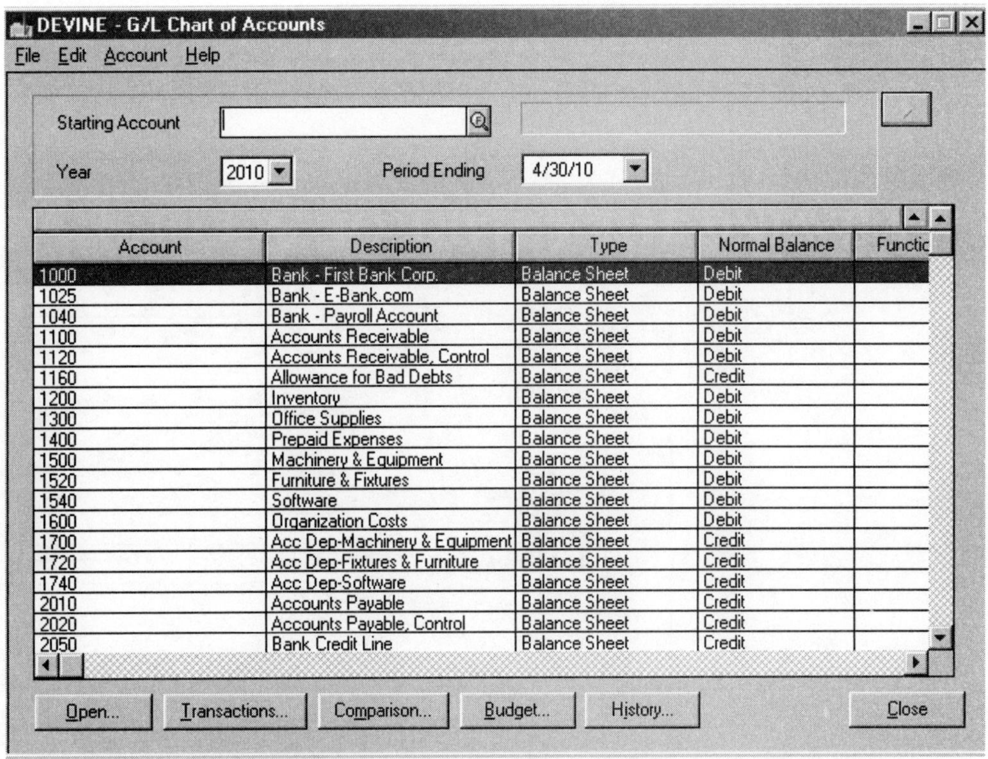

❑ Click: **Close**

PRINTING THE CHART OF ACCOUNTS

You will need a printout of the Chart of Accounts for reference when you enter transactions.

❑ DClick: the **G/L Reports** icon on the General Ledger window

FIGURE 8-8
G/L Reports Icons

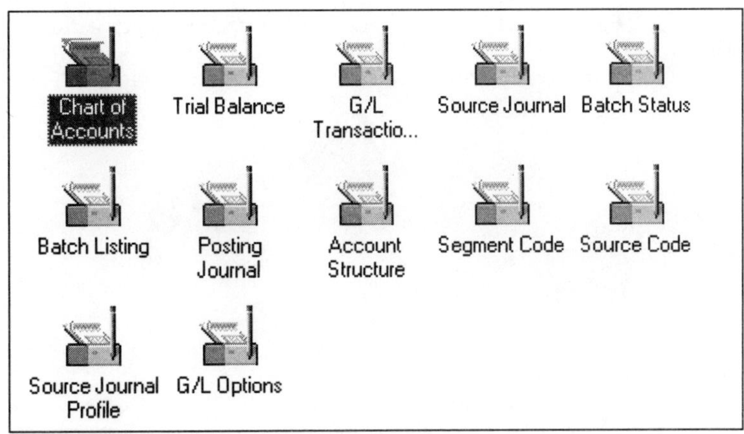

The twelve icons on this window (Figure 8-8) enable you to print a variety of reports, but not financial statements. Notice that there are icons for the reports that you printed in Chapter 7.

❑ DClick: the **Chart of Accounts** icon 

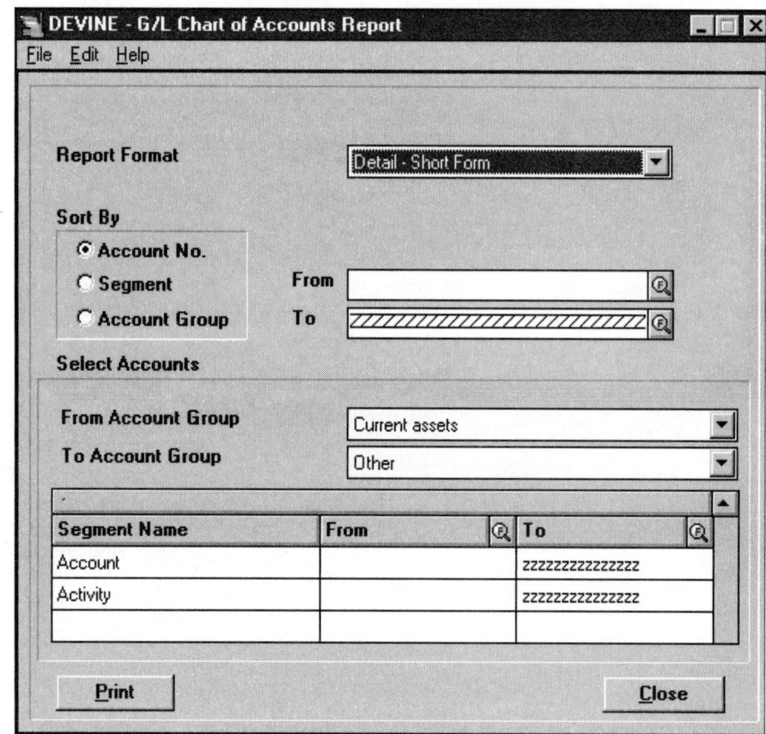

FIGURE 8-9
G/L Chart of Accounts Report Window

The default is to print all the accounts, sorted by Account No. in Detail - Short Form (Figure 8-9).

❑ Click: **Print** [Print]
❑ Click: **OK** [OK] on the Print window
❑ Close: the **G/L Chart of Accounts Report** window

Compare your printout with the one shown in Figure 8-10. Mark any errors for correction.

FIGURE 8-10
Chart of Accounts

Date: Sunday, May 28, 2000 12:09PM **DDI Student Name** **Page 1**
Chart Of Accounts - Short Form (GLCHTA01)

From Account No. [ ] To [ZZZZZZZZZZZZZZZZZZZZZZZZZZZZZZZZZZZZZZZZZZZZZZZ]
From Account Group [Current assets] To [Other]
Sort By [Account Number]

Account Number	Description	Status	Acct Config.	Post In	Structure Code	Qty.	Units	Auto Alloc.	Cntrl. Acct.
1000	Bank - First Bank Corp.	Active	B,DR,F	Detail	BASIC				
1025	Bank - E-Bank.com	Active	B,DR,F	Detail	BASIC				
1040	Bank - Payroll Account	Active	B,DR,F	Detail	BASIC				
1100	Accounts Receivable	Active	B,DR,F	Detail	BASIC				
1120	Accounts Receivable, Control	Active	B,DR,F	Detail	BASIC				
1160	Allowance for Bad Debts	Active	B,CR,F	Detail	BASIC				
1200	Inventory	Active	B,DR,F	Detail	BASIC				
1300	Office Supplies	Active	B,DR,F	Detail	BASIC				
1400	Prepaid Expenses	Active	B,DR,F	Detail	BASIC				
1500	Machinery & Equipment	Active	B,DR,F	Detail	BASIC				
1520	Furniture & Fixtures	Active	B,DR,F	Detail	BASIC				
1540	Software	Active	B,DR,F	Detail	BASIC				
1600	Organization Costs	Active	B,DR,F	Detail	BASIC				
1700	Acc Dep-Machinery & Equipment	Active	B,CR,F	Detail	BASIC				
1720	Acc Dep-Fixtures & Furniture	Active	B,CR,F	Detail	BASIC				
1740	Acc Dep-Software	Active	B,CR,F	Detail	BASIC				
2010	Accounts Payable	Active	B,CR,F	Detail	BASIC				
2020	Accounts Payable, Control	Active	B,CR,F	Detail	BASIC				
2050	Bank Credit Line	Active	B,CR,F	Detail	BASIC				
2100	Retail Sales Tax Payable	Active	B,CR,F	Detail	BASIC				
2200	G.S.T (V.A.T.) Payable	Active	B,CR,F	Detail	BASIC				
2205	G.S.T (V.A.T.) Recoverable	Active	B,DR,F	Detail	BASIC				
2210	Prepayments Received	Active	B,CR,F	Detail	BASIC				
3000	Common Stock	Active	B,CR,F	Detail	BASIC				
3200	Retained Earnings	Active	R,CR,F	Detail	BASIC				
3300	Dividends	Active	B,CR,F	Detail	BASIC				
4000/10	Sales - Web Page Design	Active	I,CR,F	Detail	REV				
4000/20	Sales - Web Page Maintenance	Active	I,CR,F	Detail	REV				
4000/30	Sales - Web Site Hosting	Active	I,CR,F	Detail	REV				
4000/40	Sales - Web Retail Sales	Active	I,CR,F	Detail	REV				
4000/99	Sales - Misc.	Active	I,CR,F	Detail	REV				
4010	Sales Discounts	Active	I,DR,F	Detail	BASIC				
5000	Cpst of Sales	Active	I,DR,F	Detail	BASIC				
6000	Advertising Expense	Active	I,DR,F	Detail	BASIC				
6020	Bad Debt Expense	Active	I,DR,F	Detail	BASIC				
6040	Bank Service Charges	Active	I,DR,F	Detail	BASIC				
6050	Bank Clearing Errors	Active	I,DR,F	Detail	BASIC				
6060	Communication Expense	Active	I,DR,F	Detail	BASIC				
6080	Computer Rent	Active	I,DR,F	Detail	BASIC				
6100	Depreciation Expense	Active	I,DR,F	Detail	BASIC				
6120	Insurance Expense	Active	I,DR,F	Detail	BASIC				
6140	Internet Services Expense	Active	I,DR,F	Detail	BASIC				
6160	Office Rent Expense	Active	I,DR,F	Detail	BASIC				
6180	Salary Expense	Active	I,DR,F	Detail	BASIC				
6200	Supplies Expense	Active	I,DR,F	Detail	BASIC				
6500	Interest Income	Active	I,CR,F	Detail	BASIC				

46 accounts printed

CHANGING ACCOUNT INFORMATION

You can use the G/L Accounts notebook to change any account information except for the account number and structure code. If you want to change either of these, delete the account and then add a new account.

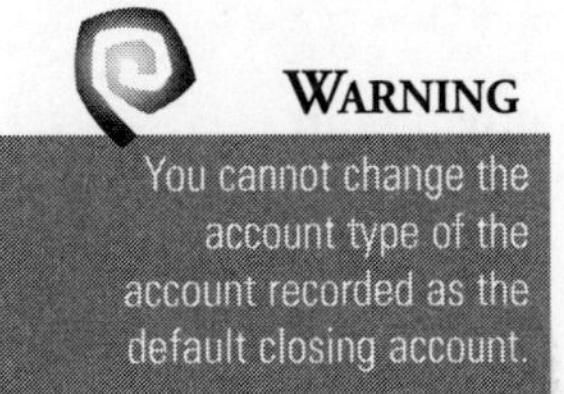

WARNING

You cannot change the account type of the account recorded as the default closing account.

Changing an Income Statement-type account to a Balance Sheet account can cause problems in the General Ledger if you post batches to a prior year. Changing the account type can also have an effect on your account groups. Before you change any account type, ensure that the account group is still correct.

Leslie noticed that account 1500 was called Machinery & Equipment, rather than Computers & Equipment.

- ❑ DClick: the **Accounts** icon on the General Ledger window
- ❑ Click: the **Finder** for the Account field
- ❑ Select: **1500 - Machinery & Equipment**

If necessary, Click and Drag the insertion point over the name in the Description field.

- ❑ Type: **Computers & Equipment**
- ❑ Press: **Tab** [Tab]

If other changes are required for this account, make them now.

- ❑ Click: **Save** [Save]

YOUR TURN

The description of the accumulated depreciation account, account 1700, should also be changed to match the new name for account 1500.

- ❑ Change: the **Description** for account 1700

Reviewing the Chart of Accounts, Erik decided to add an account, Prompt Payments Disc. Earned. Use account number 6400, account group Other Income and Expenses, and normal balance credit to add this income statement account.

- ❑ Add: account 6400

Remember to save the changes.

- ❑ Make any other necessary corrections.
- ❑ Close: the **G/L Accounts** window

DELETING ACCOUNTS

Occasionally, you may wish to delete an inactive account from the General Ledger. When you execute the period-end maintenance, the system can delete inactive accounts that contain zero balances for current and historical periods. If, however, you want to delete individual accounts during the year, you may do so through the G/L Accounts notebook.

ACCPAC for Windows will allow you to delete accounts only if:

- the current year opening and current balances for the account are both zero;
- the status of the account is inactive;
- no transactions have been posted to the account during the current year;
- there are no balances in the account for the number of years set up to keep fiscal sets in the G/L Options notebook;
- the account is not defined as the default closing account.

As Devine Designs Inc. is a small company, it doesn't need a separate bank account to control the payroll, so it has decided to delete account 1040, Bank - Payroll.

- ❑ DClick: the **Accounts** icon on the **General Ledger** window
- ❑ Click: the **Finder** for the Account text box
- ❑ Select: **1040 Bank - Payroll**

Before attempting to delete the account, change the Status to Inactive.

- ❑ Click: the **Inactive** option button for Status
- ❑ Click: **Save**

Now that the Status is Inactive, you can delete account 1040.

- ❑ Click: **Delete**

The warning message shown in Figure 8-11 will appear.

FIGURE 8-11
Warning Message

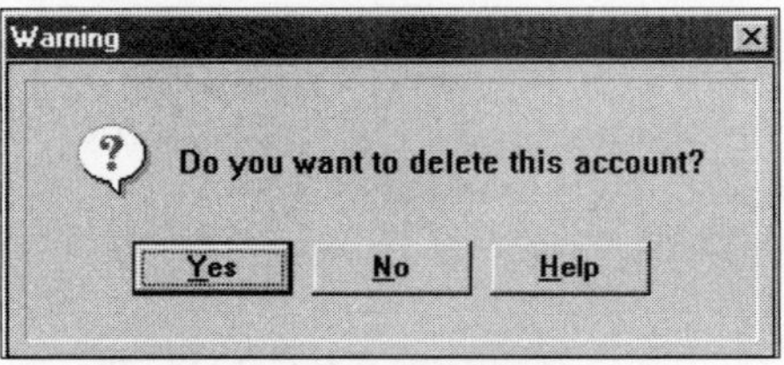

- ❑ Click: **Yes**

The account will not vanish from the screen automatically. This is another safeguard in case you have deleted the wrong account.

- ❑ Click: **Close**
- ❑ Exit: **ACCPAC**

REVIEW QUESTIONS

1. What is the purpose of a Chart of Accounts?
2. What is the purpose of the Structure Code text box?
3. What is the purpose of the Account Group?
4. Explain the difference between posting an account in detail and in consolidated formats.
5. What is the Auto Allocation option?
6. The number of accounts that can be identified as Default Retained Earnings is restricted. Why?

7. You must identify the account type for each account. Name and describe the three types of General Ledger accounts.
8. Why will the Delete Accounts option work only if the account that you wish to delete has a zero balance for both the current and previous year, the status of the account is inactive, no transactions have been posted to the account during the current year, there are no balances in the account for the number of years set up to keep fiscal sets in the G/L Options notebook, and the account is not defined as the Default Closing Account?
9. Why should you leave unallocated account codes between the ledger accounts you create? Explain.

EXERCISE

In this exercise, you will export the Chart of Accounts information from Devine Designs Inc. to a file. This information will then be imported from the file to your company. This will save adding each account individually.

EXPORTING THE CHART OF ACCOUNTS

❑ Sign on to Devine Designs Inc. as the system administrator using 04/12/10 as the Session Date.
❑ Open: the **General Ledger** window
❑ DClick: the **Accounts** icon
❑ Click: **File** on the Menu bar of the G/L Accounts window
❑ Click: **Export** on the File Menu

The File Import/Export Selection window will appear on your screen.

❑ Select: **Basic Account Profile**
❑ Click: **OK** OK

The Export Accounts window will appear, as shown in Figure 8-12. You want to include all of the options.

❑ Click: **All** to move all the accounts to the "Export These Fields" area

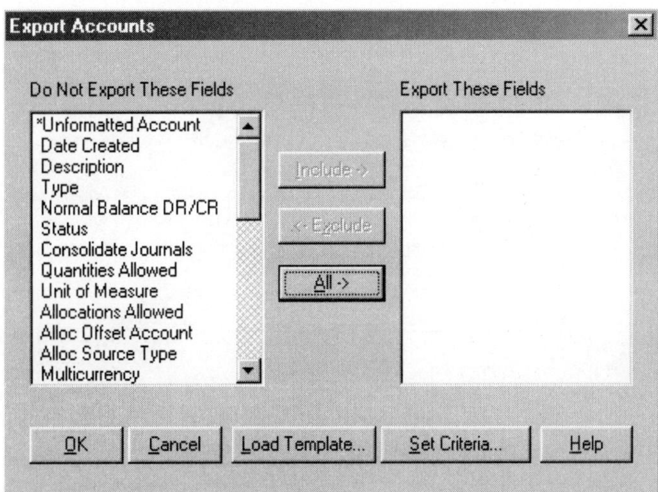

FIGURE 8-12
Export Accounts Master Window

- ❑ Click: **OK**

The Export Accounts window will appear. Note that the file you are about to create will be stored in C:\ACCPAC\Runtime.

- ❑ Type: **glmastex.exe** in the File Name text box
- ❑ Click: **OK**

Once the General Ledger Master Export file has been created and the information placed in it, the Export Account window will appear, telling you the number of records that have been exported.

- ❑ Click: **OK**
- ❑ Close: the **GL Accounts** window
- ❑ Exit: **ACCPAC** (Devine Designs Inc.)

IMPORTING THE CHART OF ACCOUNTS

- ❑ Sign on to your company using 04/12/10 as the Session Date.
- ❑ Open: the **General Ledger** window
- ❑ DClick: the **Accounts** icon
- ❑ Click: **File** on the Menu bar of the G/L Accounts window
- ❑ Click: **Import** on the File Menu
- ❑ Select: **Basic Account Profile**
- ❑ Click: **OK**

The Import Accounts window will appear (Figure 8-13). You want to include all of the options you exported from Devine Designs Inc.

FIGURE 8-13
Import Accounts
Master Window

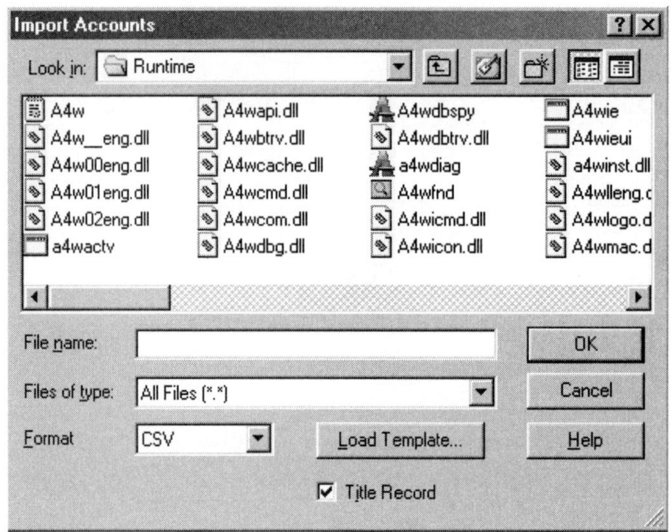

- ❑ Type: **glmastex.exe** in the File Name text box
- ❑ Click: **OK** [OK]
- ❑ Select: **Insert and Update** in the Option field on the Import Accounts master window
- ❑ Click: **OK** [OK]
- ❑ Print: the Chart of Accounts
- ❑ Compare your printout to Figure 8-10.

There should be 45 accounts listed. Account 1040 (Bank - Payroll) has been deleted since you printed the Chart of Accounts shown in Figure 8-10.

- ❑ Go back to G/L Options and record Account 3200 as the default retained earnings account.
- ❑ Exit: **ACCPAC**

CHAPTER 9

ENTERING TRANSACTIONS

In this chapter, you will enter a representative series of transactions in the first transaction batch. You will then edit the transaction batch to correct sample errors. Next, you will enter transactions for a second batch to practise your new skills.

SALES TAX MODELS USED IN THIS SIMULATION

Governments are relying more and more on taxes on the sale of goods and services to generate revenue. Retail or end-user sales taxes (RST) are levied by most provinces in Canada and by most states in the United States. Value Added Tax (VAT) is levied by the government of Canada and the governments of most European countries. In Canada, this tax is called the Goods and Services Tax (GST). As a result, you may have to record one or more types of sales tax data for several different governments. Each government has its own rules and regulations governing these types of taxes.

In this simulation you will work with a basic, non-cumulative retail sales tax and a value added tax model.

No retail sales taxes are collected on the purchase of goods for resale. A retail sales tax of 8% must be collected and rebated to the government on all merchandise and service sales to non-resellers of the goods, except for those outside of Canada. Devine Designs Inc. must collect sales tax on all merchandise sales unless the purchaser has documents to prove that he or she is exempt from retail sales tax. Retail sales tax must also be collected on the amount charged for services provided to end-users.

GST, or VAT, of 7% must be paid on all purchases of goods and services. All purchases made by Devine Designs Inc. are subject to the 7% GST. The GST paid on all purchases is deductible from the GST payable to the government.

As a provider of services, Devine Designs Inc. must pay RST of 8% and GST of 7% on all purchases.

GETTING READY

In this section, you will sign on to ACCPAC as the system administrator.

- ❑ DClick: the **ACCPAC** icon on the Windows desktop
- ❑ Enter: **ADMIN** in the User ID text box
- ❑ Enter: **ADMIN** in the Password text box
- ❑ Select: **DDI** in the Company list box
- ❑ Enter: **04/30/10** as the Session Date
- ❑ Press: **Tab** [Tab] to record the session date
- ❑ Click: **OK** [OK]

ENTERING THE FIRST TRANSACTION

The first transaction that you will enter records the contribution of $500.00 each by Leslie, Eric, and John for the initial capital of the company. The transaction took place on May 1, 2009, and the funds were deposited into the account at First Bank Corp.

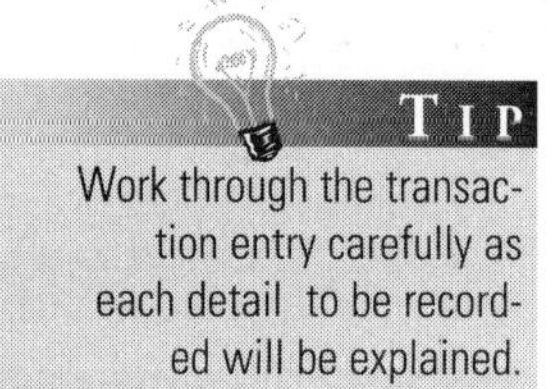

Work through the transaction entry carefully as each detail to be recorded will be explained.

- ❑ DClick: the **Journal Entry** icon on the General Ledger window

The G/L Journal Entry window (Figure 9-1) will appear.

The G/L Journal Entry window is divided into three sections for entering data and two areas that display information on the data entered.

The first data entry area, the Batch line, allows you to enter the number for an existing batch, or to create a new batch and enter a short description for it. The second data entry area allows you to enter information about an entry that records general information about a transaction.

The third data entry area is a table that enables you to enter detailed information about the transaction. Each line in this table is similar to a line in a manual journal entry, except that the information is recorded by a computer rather than manually. You will use this table to enter the first transaction. A form is also available for entering transaction

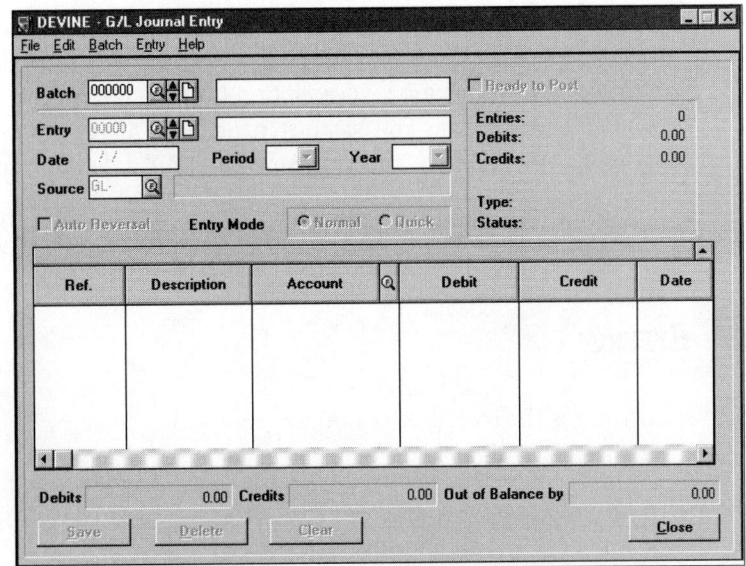

FIGURE 9-1 Sign-on Dialog Box

details. This form will be used to enter the second transaction in the simulation for Devine Designs Inc.

The data display area at the right above the detail entry table displays information about the batch of transactions, including all complete entries. The data displayed below the detail entry table displays information for the current entry or transaction only.

BATCH

ACCPAC for Windows Small Business Series is a batch-oriented accounting system. Before you can post transactions to the general ledger, you must first enter the transactions in a batch. Batching allows you to print, verify, and correct transaction information before you post. This gives you greater control over the system to ensure that the information is reliable, detailed, and complete. ACCPAC also has a provisional posting capability that allows you to review the effect of your batches before they are posted permanently to the accounts.

Batch Number

To maintain a clear audit trail, ACCPAC assigns a new number to each new batch. The batch number is used to recall an existing batch for editing, deleting, or posting. Once a batch has been deleted, you cannot reuse its number. Batch numbers are posted with each journal entry detail so you can trace the posted detail back to the original entry. Batch numbers are listed on the Posting Journals, the G/L Listing, and the Source Journal printouts. The batch number is reset to 1 when you check that option in the Period End maintenance window for the year- or period-end processing.

❑ Click: the **New Document** icon for the Batch text box

Note that both the Batch number and Entry number now display the number 1, which is the next number in sequence.

Batch Description

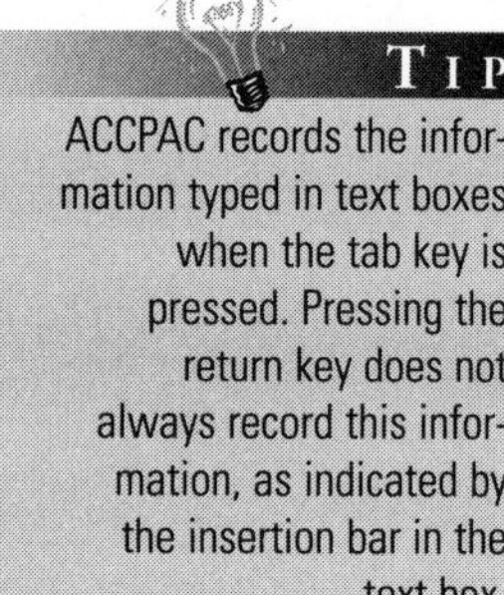

ACCPAC records the information typed in text boxes when the tab key is pressed. Pressing the return key does not always record this information, as indicated by the insertion bar in the text box.

You may enter a 30-character description for each transaction batch. This description will be printed on batch lists and batch status reports. If you import a batch from one of the other ACCPAC modules, the program will create a description for you.

- ❑ Type: **Company Organization**
- ❑ Press: **Tab** [Tab] to complete entering the Batch description

ENTRY

Each entry is the record of a complete transaction.

Entry Number

Each entry will be assigned a unique, sequential number. You can use the entry number to recall an entry for editing or deleting, and to track the entry after posting. Entry numbers are listed on batch listings and posting journals. If the details are not consolidated, the entry numbers also appear on the G/L Listing and source journals.

When you delete an entry, you can reuse that number for your next entry. If you do not add a new entry to replace the deleted entry and you post the batch, the posting journal will include an error report that lists the entry number as deleted. The error report becomes your audit trail of the deleted entry number.

Entry Description

You may enter a description of up to 30 characters for each transaction entry. This description will be displayed in the Finder table for entries, but will not be printed on the batch listing.

- ❑ Click: the **Description** text box
- ❑ Type: **Initial Investment**
- ❑ Press: **Tab** [Tab]

Date

The default date displayed is the session date you entered when you signed on to ACCPAC. The data displayed in the Period and Year list boxes are determined by this date and the fiscal calendar information entered in the company database.

The default date assumes that you are entering the transaction on the current date. Adopt a consistent policy of using the date the transaction took place. This gives you a handy auditing tool if you also have dated source documents to which you can trace transactions.

- ❑ Type: **050109** in the Date text box
- ❑ Press: **Tab** [Tab]

ACCPAC compares the date entered with the session date and the fiscal period number displayed. As the date entered is not in the current fiscal period, ACCPAC displays the warning message shown in Figure 9-2. This is a safeguard against errors in date entry. You must confirm that the date is correct.

FIGURE 9-2
Warning Message

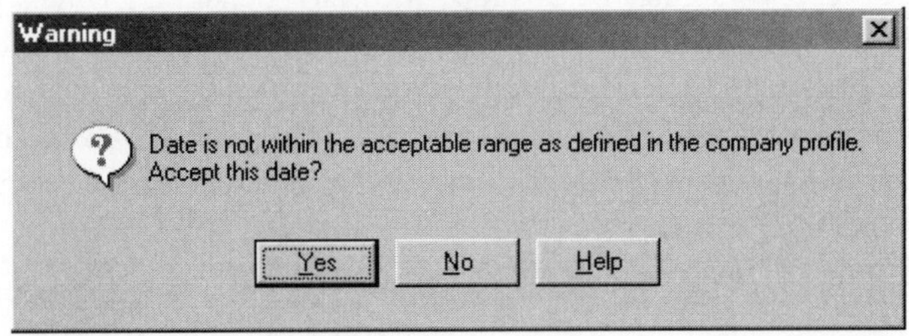

- ❑ Click: **Yes** [Yes]

Note that the Period and Year list boxes are automatically adjusted to reflect the changed date.

Period

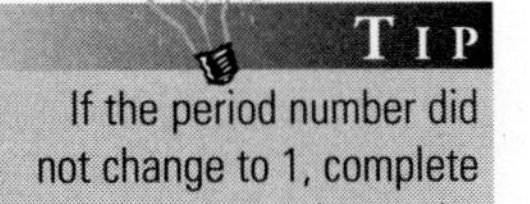

TIP

If the period number did not change to 1, complete the entries and save the batch. Modify the fiscal calendar using the System Manager and then edit the batch to display the correct period.

You must include a fiscal period number with each entry. The default period number displayed corresponds with the date you entered when signing on. If the session date entered is outside the fiscal year, the program enters a default period number in the fiscal period field. If you start with a session date that precedes the current year, 1 is displayed as the fiscal period number. If the session date is after the current year, the number assigned is 12 if you have a 12-period ledger, or 13 if you use 13 periods.

You can enter only one fiscal period for each entry. However, a batch can contain entries with different fiscal periods.

When you changed the Date to 05/01/09, ACCPAC should have adjusted the period number to 1 based on the dates recorded in the fiscal calendar.

- ❑ Press: **Tab** [Tab]

Year

You must identify the posting year for each entry. The default posting year for the data entry session is the same as the Session Date in the Sign-on window. You can change the year if necessary. If you need to post to a prior year, select the Allow Posting to Previous Years option on the Posting page of the G/L Options notebook. The previous fiscal year must be active, and the fiscal periods you are posting to in the previous year must be unlocked.

When you changed the Date to 05/01/09, ACCPAC should not have adjusted the year based on the dates recorded in the fiscal calendar. May 1, 2009 is the first day in fiscal year 2010.

❑ Press: **Tab** [Tab] to accept Year 2010

Source

A source code must be included with each detail on a batch entry to identify the type of transaction, such as a cash payment or cash receipt, and to identify the accounting application used to record the transaction. The first two characters of the code identify the accounting application used to record the transaction. All transactions recorded in the General Ledger module will start with the letters GL. You can enter or change the remaining two characters using the codes you defined earlier.

The source code for this transaction is GL-CR, the source code for G/L Cash Receipts.

❑ Click: the **Finder** for the Source text box

FIGURE 9-3
Finder - Source Codes

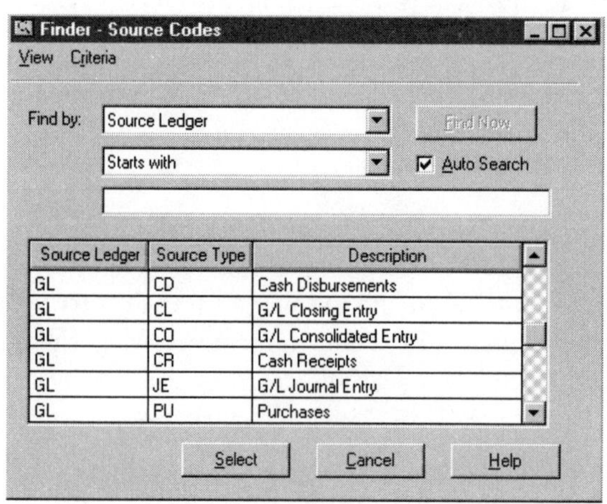

The General Ledger source codes are displayed in the Finder - Source Codes window, Figure 9-3.

❑ Click: **GL CR Cash Receipts** on the Finder table

❑ Click: **Select** [Select]

ACCPAC verifies that GL-CR has been entered as a source code, and displays the source code name Cash Receipts Journal to the right of the Source list box.

Auto Reversal

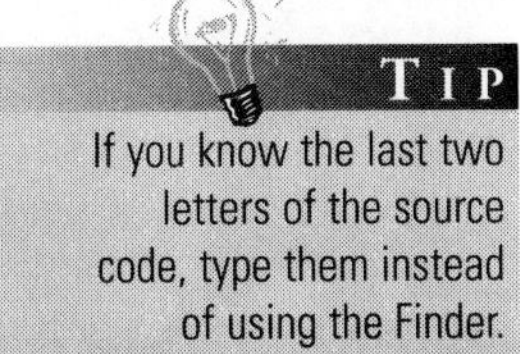

If you know the last two letters of the source code, type them instead of using the Finder. Remember to press the **Tab** key to complete the entry.

If this option is selected, the journal entry is reversed in the following fiscal period. This option is useful when making estimated accrual entries at period end for expense items, depreciation, or inventory levels. When exact amounts are known, another batch of transaction entries can be created and posted to the prior period.

This transaction records the actual receipt of funds in period 1 and is not an estimated accrual entry to be reversed next period. If there is a check mark in the check box for Auto Reversal, click to remove it.

Entry Mode

Entry Mode controls the fields at which the cursor stops as you enter transactions. Quick Entry saves keystrokes by entering the same reference and description for each detail line.

When you use Normal Entry, the cursor continues to visit each field for every detail line. Use this mode if you want to assign different source codes, dates, references, or descriptions to individual detail lines for one entry.

The selection you make applies only to the time you are working with the batch. If you recall an existing batch for editing, select the entry mode again and use the Normal Entry mode to add comments or change information you entered earlier in the Quick Entry mode.

The transaction you are entering will record the receipt of $500.00 each from Leslie, Eric, and John as their original investment in Devine Designs Inc. The source code, date, reference, and description will be the same for each detail line.

- ❑ Click: the **Quick** option button
- ❑ Press: **Tab** [Tab]

FIRST TRANSACTION DETAIL

When you use the Quick Entry mode, you can enter only one reference and one description for all the detail lines in each entry. If the account is not consolidated, the reference and description are printed with all the detail lines on the batch listing and posting journal for the batch and on the G/L Listing. For consolidated accounts, the G/L Listing displays a description of "Consolidated posting" for accounts which were consolidated by the Consolidate Posted Transactions function.

You can display more information by using the scroll bars or changing column widths on the detail table.

TIP

You can change the width of table columns by moving the pointer to the line between column headings. When the pointer changes shape, drag it to make the column wider or narrower.

Reference

Each reference can be up to 22 characters long. Wherever possible, use a reference that leads you back to the source document. Invoice numbers, purchase order numbers, check numbers, bank deposit slip numbers, and expense report numbers are all good references. For unusual items, it is sometimes not possible to use a source document number as the reference.

Because you can print source journals by reference, it is important to enter the same reference for associated details, such as multiple expense allocations for one check. In the quick entry mode, ACCPAC automatically copies the reference from the first line to all other lines in the entry.

- ❑ Type: **Common Stock** in the Ref. cell
- ❑ Press: **Tab** [Tab]

Description

The description can be 30 characters long. Try to keep descriptions as concise, but informative, as possible. You can add more detail later in the Comments cell. In the quick entry mode, ACCPAC automatically copies the description from the first line to all other lines in the entry.

Enter a description for each transaction. This description will be printed on the Batch Listing.

- ❑ Type: **Initial Share Purchase** in the Description cell
- ❑ Press: **Tab** [Tab]

Account

For each detail line, enter the account to which the debit or credit will be posted. For this transaction, the funds were deposited into what would become the new company account at First Bank Corp.

You can enter an account number by typing it or by using the Finder. If you type an account code that has not been entered into the Chart of Accounts, the computer displays an error message, as shown in Figure 9-4.

- ❑ Type: **1111**
- ❑ Press: **Tab** [Tab]

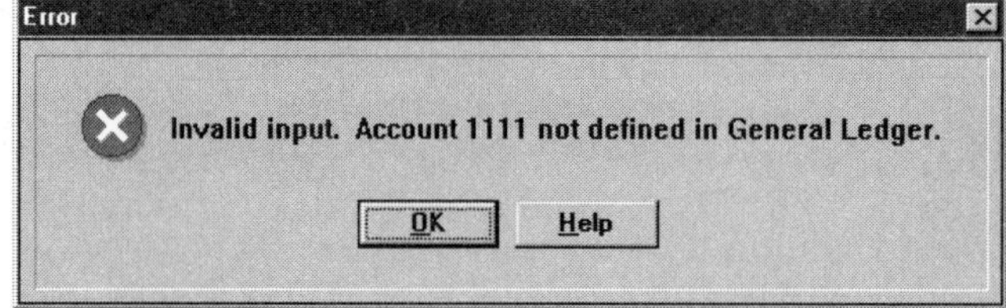

FIGURE 9-4
Error Message

As ACCPAC could not find Account 1111 in the Chart of Accounts for Devine Designs Inc., the error message is displayed.

❑ Click: **OK**
❑ Click: the **Finder** for the Account column

ACCPAC will display the Finder - Account Master, similar to that shown in Figure 9-5.

FIGURE 9-5
Finder - Account Master

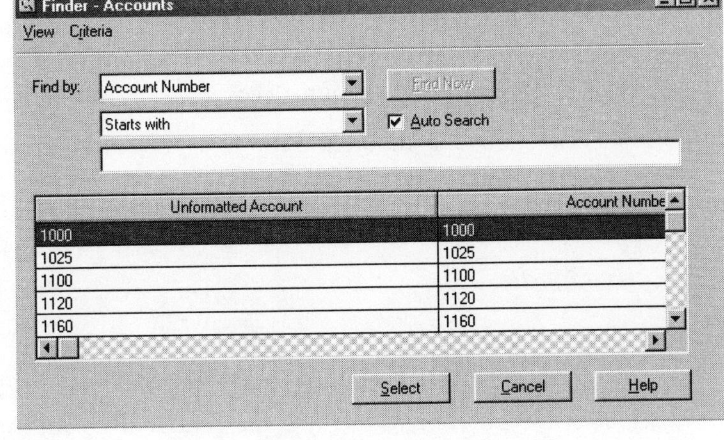

TIP
You can change the width of table columns by moving the pointer to the line between column headings. When the pointer changes shape, drag it to make the column wider or narrower. You can also use the scroll bars to view additional information.

Your Finder chart may not show information as compactly as in Figure 9-5.

❑ Select: **1000 Bank - First Bank Corp.**

Amount

The amount is entered in either the debit or credit cell for each entry line. The receipt of funds is a debit.

❑ Click: the **Debit** cell

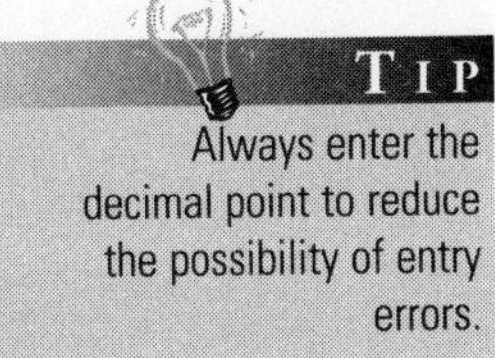

TIP
Always enter the decimal point to reduce the possibility of entry errors.

Do not type the currency signs or commas, but you can insert the decimal point. If you do not type a decimal point, the program will insert one, allowing for the number of decimal places in the functional currency recorded in the System Manager. If you enter a minus sign with either a debit or credit detail, ACCPAC will record the amount as the opposite type of entry.

Each debit or credit amount you enter is added to the total for the entry displayed at the bottom of the screen, along with the amount by which the entry is out of balance. You can add an entry that does not balance, but you cannot post it until it does balance.

Each detail line you enter updates the displayed totals for the entry. The debit and credit totals for the batch, displayed in the upper right corner of the screen, are updated when you save the entry.

❑ Type: **1500.00** in the Debit field

Date

The date is copied from the date entered for the entry. In most cases, you will not change the date on the detail line.

Source Ledger

The ACCPAC accounting module used to create the entry automatically enters its two-letter code in the Source Ledger cell. All transactions recorded using the General Ledger application will be given the Source Ledger "GL." You cannot change this entry.

Batches of transactions imported from other ACCPAC accounting applications will also be given their appropriate two-letter code.

Source Code

The source code is copied from the one selected in the entry information section. You can change the source code for each detail line by typing the new source code or by using the Finder. Devine Designs Inc. uses the same source code for all detail lines in an entry.

Comments

❑ Press: **Tab** [Tab] until the Comments cell is highlighted

TIP
Press the Tab key to record the comment without creating a new detail line.

If you cannot fit all of the comments text for a detail line in the Reference and Description fields, use the Comment field to add further information. Each Comment can contain up to 255 characters.

❑ Type: **Initial stock purchase funds deposited to First Bank Corp. account**
❑ Press: **Enter** [Enter] to record the entry and create another detail line

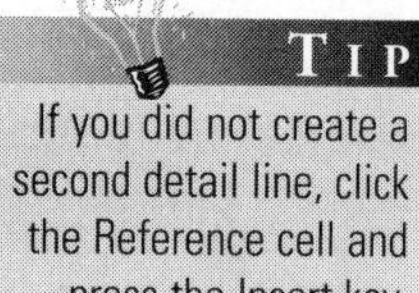

TIP
If you did not create a second detail line, click the Reference cell and press the Insert key.

SECOND TRANSACTION DETAIL

ACCPAC should have copied the reference, description, date, and source code information to the second line. The insertion point will appear in the Reference cell as seen by the dotted line surrounding the cell. Note that the first transaction is intentionally out of balance.

❑ Press: **Tab** [Tab] to accept the reference displayed
❑ Press: **Tab** [Tab] to accept the description displayed
❑ Click: the **Finder** for the Account field
❑ Select: **3000 Common Stock**
❑ Click: the **Credit** cell
❑ Type: **1400.00**

WARNING
This detail entry will be out of balance by $100. The error will be corrected later in this chapter.

- ❑ Press: **Tab** [Tab] to move to the Comments cell
- ❑ Type: **$500 each from Leslie, Eric & John**
- ❑ Press: **Enter** to complete the entry

Once you have entered these balances, the Debits total should equal 1500.00 and the Credits total should equal 1400.00. The amount shown in the Out of Balance field should be 100.00. ACCPAC for Windows will allow you to save a batch that is incomplete or out of balance but will not allow that batch to be posted.

- ❑ Click: **Add**

ENTERING THE SECOND TRANSACTION

In working through the second entry, you will enter the data to record the issuance of cheque number 0001 to Bruce's Business Services, in the amount of $725, dated May 1, 2009, for the fees to incorporate Devine Designs.

- ❑ Click: the **New Document** icon for the **Entry** text box

The batch number should remain unchanged, but the entry number updates to number 2, allowing you to create a new journal entry.

- ❑ Click: the **Entry description** text box
- ❑ Type: **Incorporation Fees**
- ❑ Press: **Tab** [Tab]
- ❑ Type: the date **050109**
- ❑ Press: **Tab** [Tab]

The date error message will appear again.

- ❑ Click: **Yes** to accept the date

Note that the period and year fields have both adjusted to reflect the date of the transaction.

- ❑ Press: **Tab** [Tab] twice to move to the Source list box
- ❑ Select: **CD Cash Disbursements** using the Finder
- ❑ Press: **Tab** [Tab] to move to the Entry Mode field
- ❑ Select: **Quick**
- ❑ Click: the **Ref.** Column on the detail table

Using the Journal Entry Form

To enter transaction details, you will now use the form rather than the table.

- ❑ Press: **F9**

The detail entry form has been layered over the table form as shown in Figure 9-6. You can still see the batch number and description above the form. The entry amounts totals are also shown below the form.

In this example the check number will be used as the reference.

FIGURE 9-6
Detail Entry Form

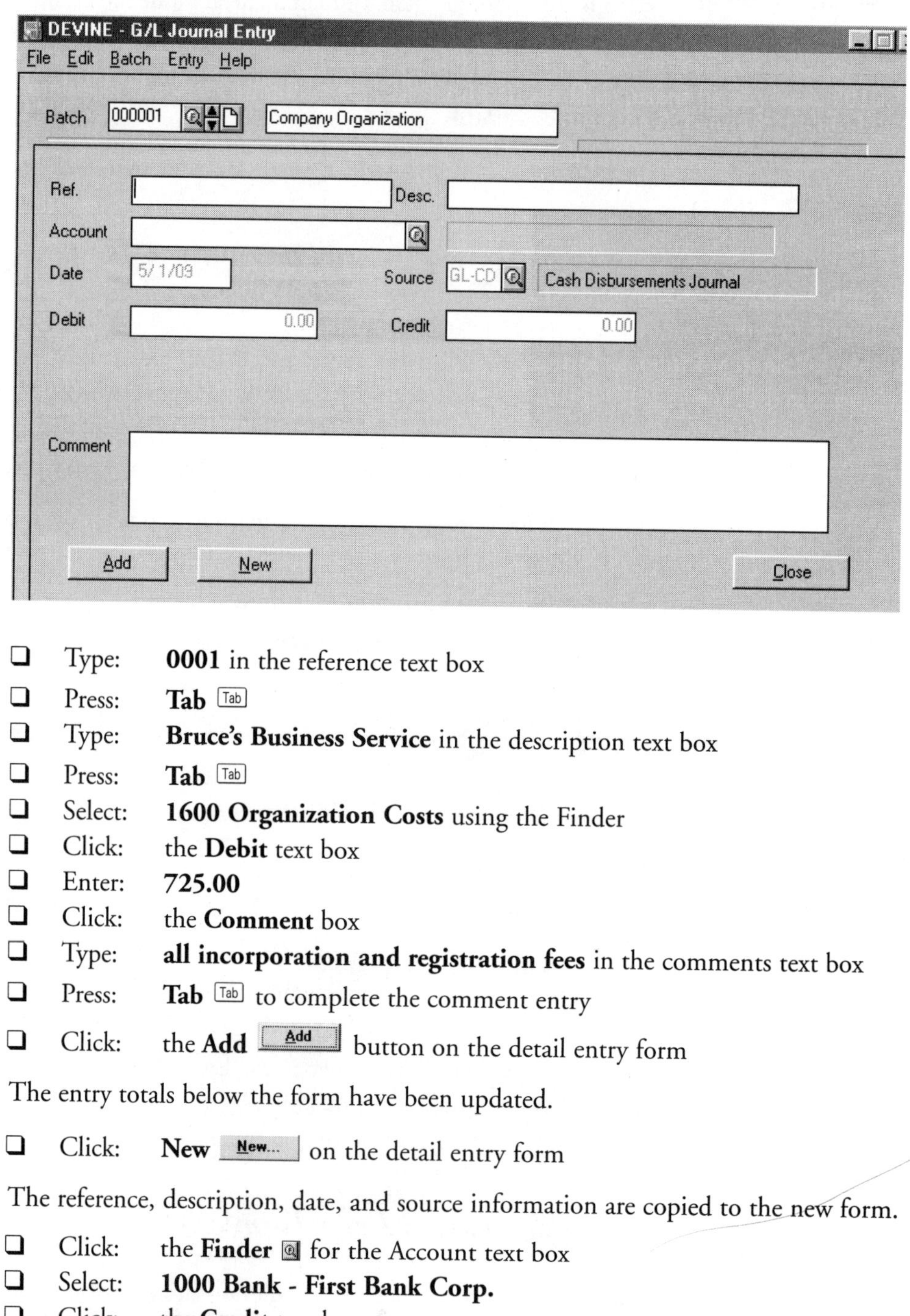

- ❑ Type: **0001** in the reference text box
- ❑ Press: **Tab** [Tab]
- ❑ Type: **Bruce's Business Service** in the description text box
- ❑ Press: **Tab** [Tab]
- ❑ Select: **1600 Organization Costs** using the Finder
- ❑ Click: the **Debit** text box
- ❑ Enter: **725.00**
- ❑ Click: the **Comment** box
- ❑ Type: **all incorporation and registration fees** in the comments text box
- ❑ Press: **Tab** [Tab] to complete the comment entry
- ❑ Click: the **Add** [Add] button on the detail entry form

The entry totals below the form have been updated.

- ❑ Click: **New** [New...] on the detail entry form

The reference, description, date, and source information are copied to the new form.

- ❑ Click: the **Finder** for the Account text box
- ❑ Select: **1000 Bank - First Bank Corp.**
- ❑ Click: the **Credit** text box
- ❑ Type: **725.00**

❑ Press: **Tab** [Tab]

You do not have to repeat the comment.

❑ Click: **Add** [Add] on the detail entry form

❑ Click: **Close** [Close] on the detail entry form

ACCPAC will return the display to the table entry.

❑ Click: the **Add** button [Add] to add entry 2 to the batch

❑ Click: **Close** [Close] to close the G/L Journal Entry window

PRINTING THE BATCH LISTING

The Transaction Batch List shows all the transactions in the batch. You should print this list so you can verify the entries. You should keep it as a permanent printed copy of the transactions, since ACCPAC denies access to a batch once you have posted it to the General Ledger.

❑ DClick: the **G/L Reports** icon [G/L Reports] on the General Ledger window

❑ DClick: the **Batch Listing** icon [Batch Listing]

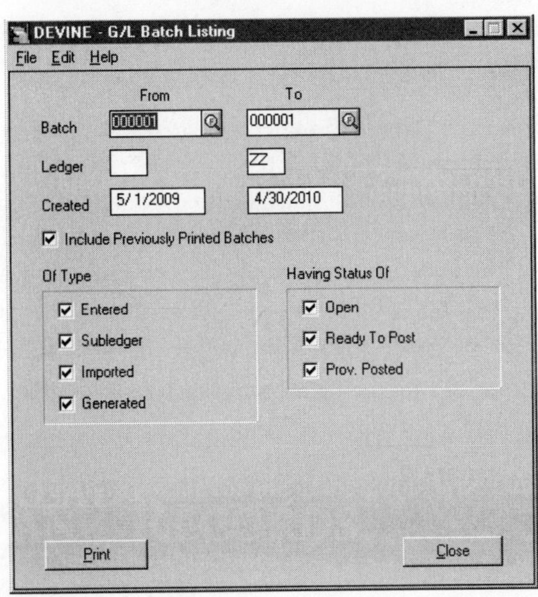

FIGURE 9-7
G/L Batch Listing Window

The default selections displayed in the G/L Batch Listing window (Figure 9-7) will print all the transaction batches that you have entered. You could select a group of batches by batch number, date, type, or status. As only one batch has been entered, you do not have to change any of the settings on this window.

❑ Click: **Print** [Print]

❑ Click: **OK** [OK] on the Print window

Once the batch has printed, the program will return to the G/L Batch Listing window.

❑ Click: **Close** [Close]

FIGURE 9-8 Batch Listing Printout

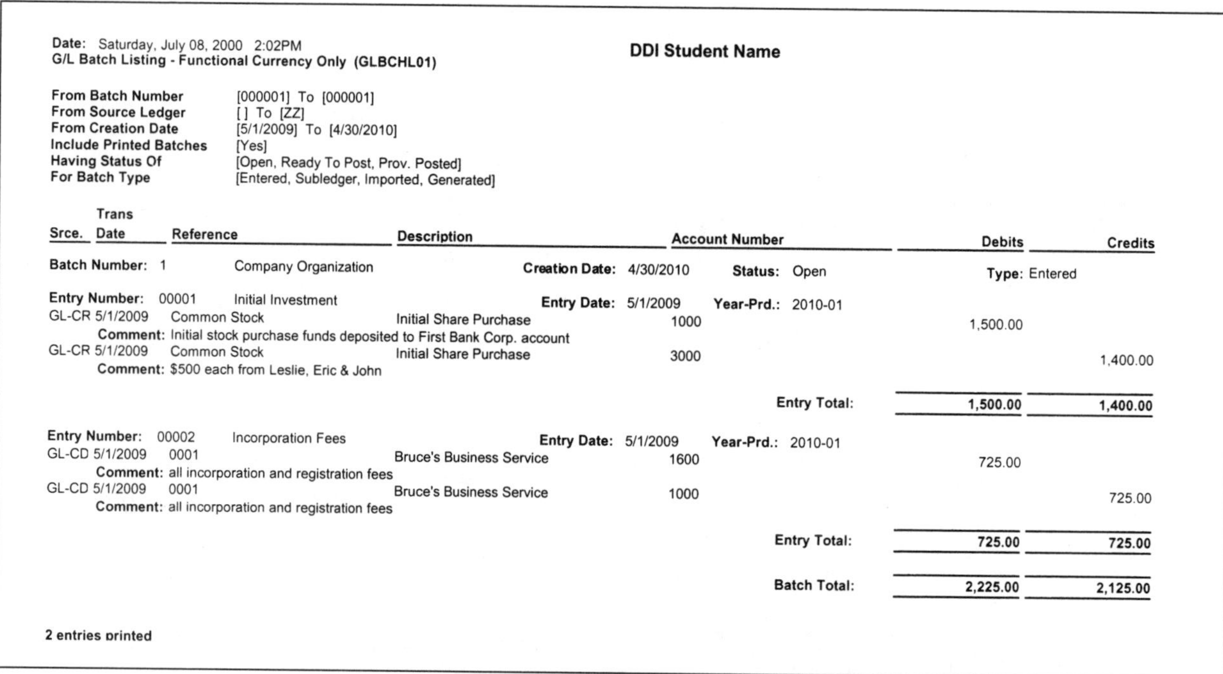

Date: Saturday, July 08, 2000 2:02PM
G/L Batch Listing - Functional Currency Only (GLBCHL01)

DDI Student Name

From Batch Number [000001] To [000001]
From Source Ledger [] To [ZZ]
From Creation Date [5/1/2009] To [4/30/2010]
Include Printed Batches [Yes]
Having Status Of [Open, Ready To Post, Prov. Posted]
For Batch Type [Entered, Subledger, Imported, Generated]

Srce.	Trans Date	Reference	Description	Account Number	Debits	Credits
Batch Number: 1		Company Organization	Creation Date: 4/30/2010	Status: Open	Type: Entered	
Entry Number: 00001		Initial Investment	Entry Date: 5/1/2009	Year-Prd.: 2010-01		
GL-CR	5/1/2009	Common Stock	Initial Share Purchase	1000	1,500.00	
		Comment: Initial stock purchase funds deposited to First Bank Corp. account				
GL-CR	5/1/2009	Common Stock	Initial Share Purchase	3000		1,400.00
		Comment: $500 each from Leslie, Eric & John				
				Entry Total:	1,500.00	1,400.00
Entry Number: 00002		Incorporation Fees	Entry Date: 5/1/2009	Year-Prd.: 2010-01		
GL-CD	5/1/2009	0001	Bruce's Business Service	1600	725.00	
		Comment: all incorporation and registration fees				
GL-CD	5/1/2009	0001	Bruce's Business Service	1000		725.00
		Comment: all incorporation and registration fees				
				Entry Total:	725.00	725.00
				Batch Total:	2,225.00	2,125.00

2 entries printed

Figure 9-8 shows the printed Transaction Batch Listing. The date and time that the batch was printed appears in the upper left corner of the printout. The name of the company appears at the top of each page, centred between the date and the page number. The name of the printout, G/L Batch Listing, appears below the date and time. The next five lines show the specifications you chose. The line below the column headings lists the batch number and description, the date the batch was created, and the batch status and type. After that, the columns show the transaction data that you entered for each entry.

In Figure 9-8, notice that the batch is out of balance because of an error in account 3000. The amount was entered as $1400 credit; it should have been entered as $1500 credit.

If your debits and credits are different from those shown above, you have made additional incorrect entries. Don't panic! Once you have corrected the error in account 3000, you can use the same technique to correct data entry errors in any other line of the batch.

If you have accidentally created additional empty batches, don't worry; you can enter transactions in these batches later.

❑ Mark any other errors on your printout for correction later.

EDITING A BATCH

You can edit or change a batch at any time before the batch is posted. Remember to print the batch before trying to post it.

If there is an error in a batch that you have posted to the General Ledger, you should create a new batch, reverse the original error, enter the correct transaction details, and post the new batch to the General Ledger.

You will now correct the intentional error that we made in entry 1 of batch 1.

❑ DClick: the **Journal Entry** icon [Journal Entry] on the General Ledger window

Specify the batch to be edited by typing its number in the Batch text box or by selecting the batch from the Finder.

❑ Select: Batch Number **000001 Company Organization** from the Finder - Batch Control

ACCPAC will retrieve the batch data. The display shows the batch data and the data for the first entry, as in Figure 9-9.

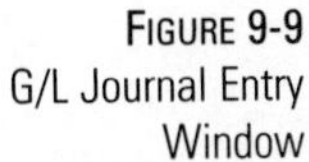

FIGURE 9-9
G/L Journal Entry Window

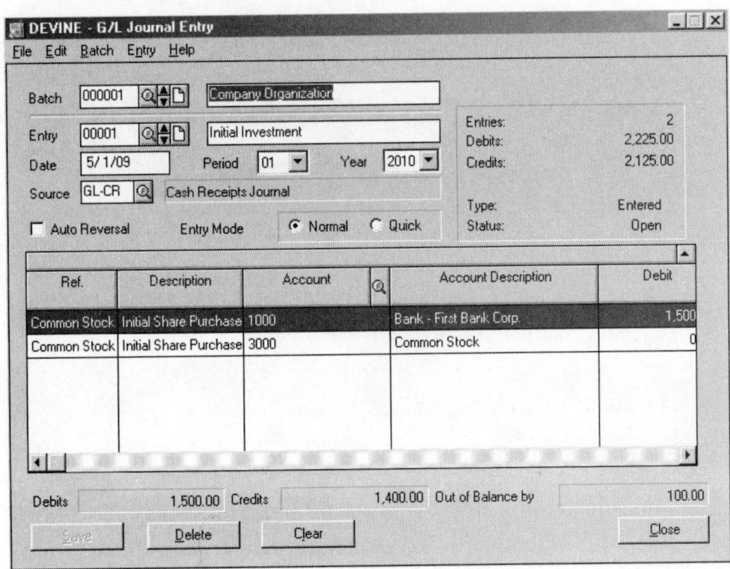

ACCPAC requires confirmation if you attempt to do something that will damage or delete data that you have entered.

As shown in Figure 9-9, there are three buttons active at the bottom of the G/L Journal Entry window. Clicking the Close button will close the window without damaging or destroying data. Clicking either the Delete or Clear button can destroy data.

❑ Click: **Delete** [Delete] on the G/L Journal Entry window for batch 000001

ACCPAC assumes that you wish to delete the entry displayed on the screen and requires confirmation that you wish to do so, as shown in Figure 9-10.

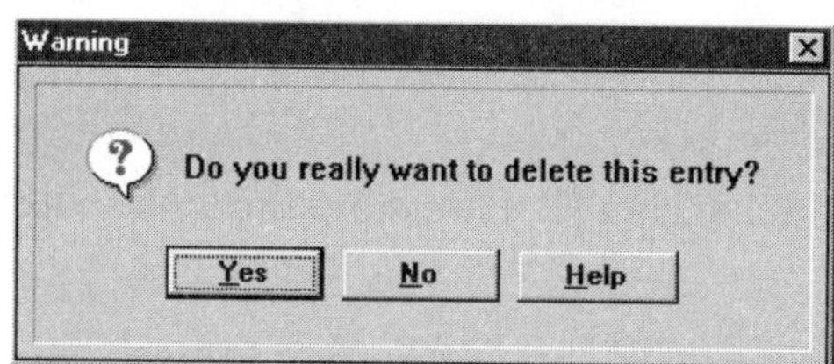

FIGURE 9-10
Warning Message

If you click Yes, the data for the entry displayed on the screen will be destroyed. Remember that you can use this entry number to record another entry.

Devine Designs Inc. wants this entry corrected, not deleted.

❑ Click: **No** [No]

The other button that could be clicked accidentally is the Clear button.

❑ Click: **Clear** [Clear]

ACCPAC assumes that you want to erase the details for the current entry and displays a slightly different warning, as shown in Figure 9-11.

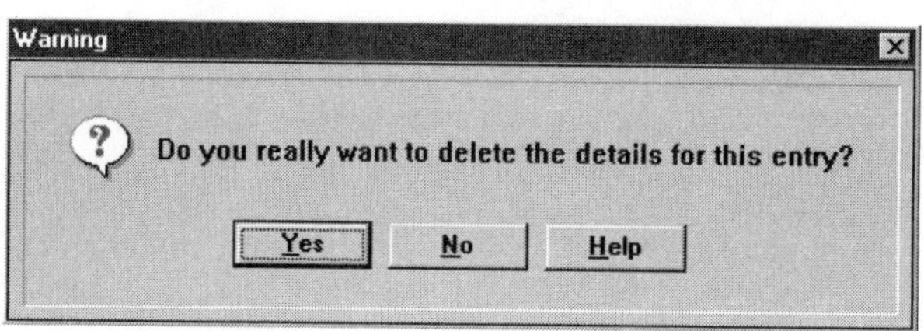

FIGURE 9-11
Warning Message

If you click the Yes button, you will destroy the data for the entry displayed. Remember that Devine Designs Inc. wants to change the data to correct an error, not to destroy the data.

❑ Click: **No** [No]

Now you will correct the error in entry 1.

The information displayed on the screen indicated that entry 1 is out of balance by 100.00. The entry recorded the contribution of $500.00 each from Leslie, Eric, and John to the initial capital of the company. The 1,500.00 debit to account 1000 is correct. The 1,400.00 credit to account 3000 must be corrected.

To edit an entry in the table entry format, double click the cell that you want to change and enter the new information.

❑ DClick: the **Credit** cell in the line for account 3000

Note that the whole cell is no longer coloured; only the entry is coloured and the insertion point at the right of the entry.

- ❑ Type: **1500.00**
- ❑ Press: **Tab** [Tab] to complete the credit entry

The Save button will now be activated, as you have changed the entry.

- ❑ Click: **Save** [Save] to save the changed entry

Note that, unless there are other errors, both the entry and the batch should now be balanced. You can correct any other errors using the same techniques, but remember to change the entry number if the errors are not in entry 1.

> **TIP**
> Use the Reports icon on the General Ledger window to print the batch listing.

- ❑ Correct any other errors and save your changes.
- ❑ Close: the **G/L Journal Entry** window
- ❑ Print the revised batch listing.

FIGURE 9-12 Batch Listing Printout

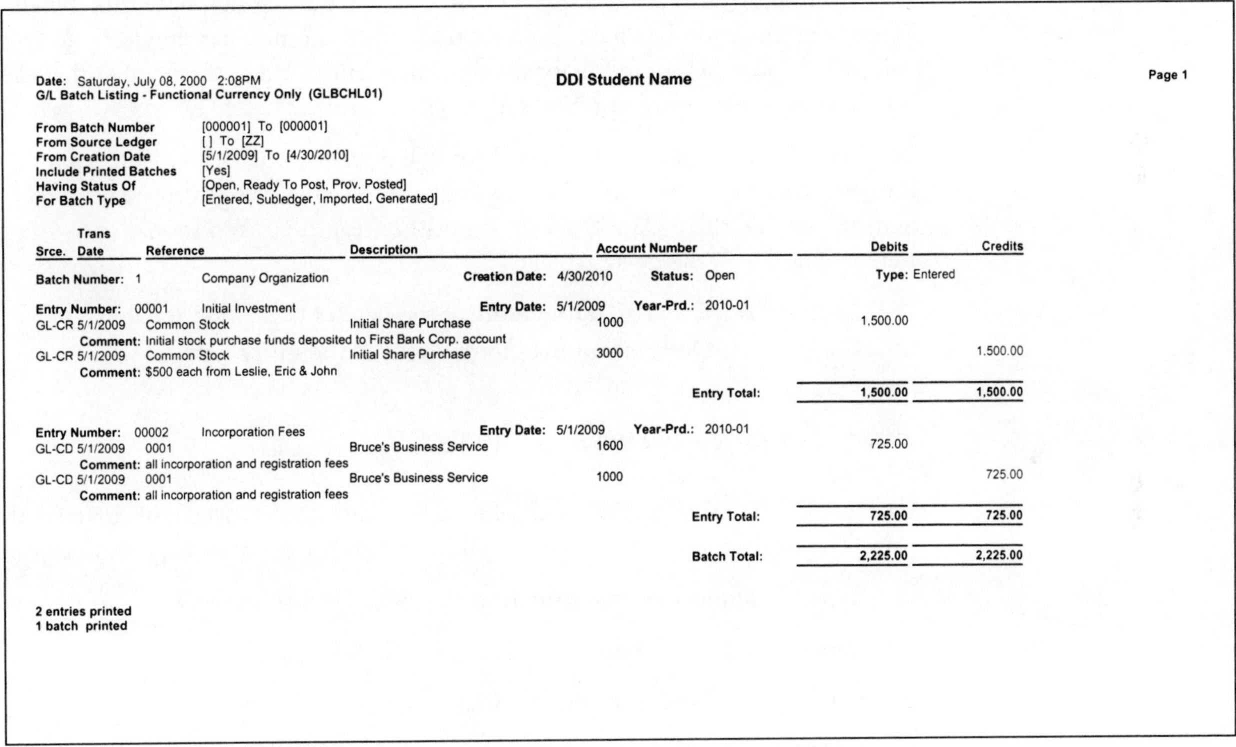

Date: Saturday, July 08, 2000 2:08PM
G/L Batch Listing - Functional Currency Only (GLBCHL01)

DDI Student Name

Page 1

From Batch Number	[000001] To [000001]
From Source Ledger	[] To [ZZ]
From Creation Date	[5/1/2009] To [4/30/2010]
Include Printed Batches	[Yes]
Having Status Of	[Open, Ready To Post, Prov. Posted]
For Batch Type	[Entered, Subledger, Imported, Generated]

Srce.	Trans Date	Reference	Description	Account Number	Debits	Credits
Batch Number: 1		Company Organization	**Creation Date:** 4/30/2010	**Status:** Open	**Type:** Entered	
Entry Number: 00001		Initial Investment	**Entry Date:** 5/1/2009	**Year-Prd.:** 2010-01		
GL-CR	5/1/2009	Common Stock	Initial Share Purchase	1000	1,500.00	
	Comment: Initial stock purchase funds deposited to First Bank Corp. account					
GL-CR	5/1/2009	Common Stock	Initial Share Purchase	3000		1,500.00
	Comment: $500 each from Leslie, Eric & John					
				Entry Total:	**1,500.00**	**1,500.00**
Entry Number: 00002		Incorporation Fees	**Entry Date:** 5/1/2009	**Year-Prd.:** 2010-01		
GL-CD	5/1/2009	0001	Bruce's Business Service	1600	725.00	
	Comment: all incorporation and registration fees					
GL-CD	5/1/2009	0001	Bruce's Business Service	1000		725.00
	Comment: all incorporation and registration fees					
				Entry Total:	**725.00**	**725.00**
				Batch Total:	**2,225.00**	**2,225.00**

2 entries printed
1 batch printed

Compare your printout with that shown in Figure 9-12. Both the entry and batch totals should now be balanced.

This is a good time for you to take a break.

- ❑ Close: the **G/L Batch Listing** window
- ❑ Close: the **G/L Reports** window
- ❑ Exit: **ACCPAC**

YOUR TURN

You will now record a set of representative transactions for April 2010. Using the Source Code list, Chart of Accounts, and the description of each transaction, prepare your entries on paper. This allows you to concentrate on accounting to prepare the data to be entered.

- ❑ Sign on to Devine Designs Inc. with User ID, ADMIN, and Session Date, 04/30/10.
- ❑ Open: the **G/L Journal Entry** window

You must first create a new batch for the April 2010 transactions. This batch will be entered on April 30, 2010.

- ❑ Click: the **New Document** icon

ACCPAC for Windows will display the next available batch number in the Batch field. Since one transaction batch has been entered, this batch number should be 2. The Entry field will display the number 1 for the first entry in this batch. Remember that each entry should completely record one, and only one, transaction.

The Date, Period Number, and Year fields will display the relevant information based on the Session Date you entered when signing on to Devine Designs Inc. The entry information should display Date 4/30/10, Period 12, Year 2010. You should enter the actual transaction date in the detail table.

- ❑ Type: **April 2010 Transactions** in the Batch Description text box
- ❑ Click: the **Description** field to the right of the Entry field

Entry 1- Stock Purchase

On April 1, 2010, Leslie, Eric, and John each bought $9,500 worth of shares in the company. The total of $28,500 was deposited in the bank account at First Bank Corp.

- ❑ Type: **additional investment** in the entry description field

The source code for this transaction is CR for Cash Receipts.

- ❑ Click: the **Finder** for the Source field
- ❑ Select: **GL CR**
- ❑ Select: **Quick Entry Mode**

In most cases, it is best to use the Quick Entry Mode when first entering transaction information. The Normal Entry Mode is best used when modifying or editing a batch, or when different references or descriptions are required for each detail line.

- ❑ Click: the **Ref.** column to create the first detail line

You can use either the table or form method for entering details.

- ❑ Enter: **common stock** as the reference
- ❑ Enter: **additional share purchase** as the description

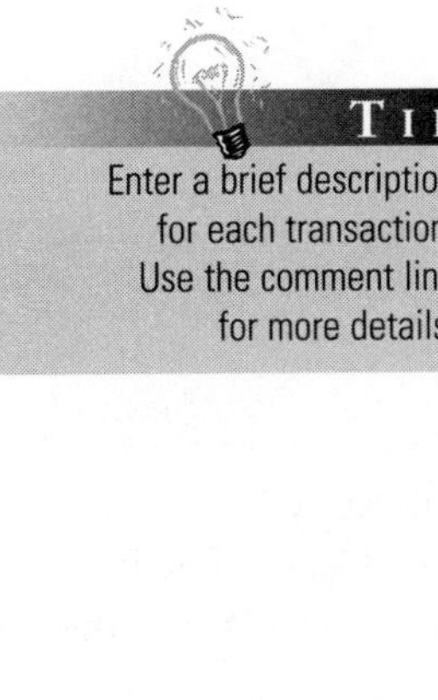

TIP Enter a brief description for each transaction. Use the comment line for more details.

- ❑ Select: account **1000 First Bank Corp.** using the Finder
- ❑ Enter: **28500.00** in the Debit cell

This transaction occurred on April 1, 2010, and should be recorded as of that date.

- ❑ Enter: **04/01/10** in the Date cell
- ❑ Enter: **Leslie, Eric & John each bought a further $9,500 worth of stock** as the comment
- ❑ Press: **Tab** [Tab] to create a second line
- ❑ Select: account **3000 Common Stock** using the Finder
- ❑ Enter: a credit of **28500.00**
- ❑ Enter: **04/01/10** in the Date cell
- ❑ Click: the **Add** [Add] to add the entry to the batch

TIP Remember to use the New Document icon to create each new entry.

You have to enter the remaining transactions because the information will be used later to demonstrate the budgeting functions and to prepare financial statements. Detailed descriptions for each entry are not given. If you have difficulties, use the step-by-step instructions described on the prior pages to work through these entries. Note that the RST is incorporated into Expense/Asset. Accept the GST calculations as accurate.

Entry 2 - Office Rent

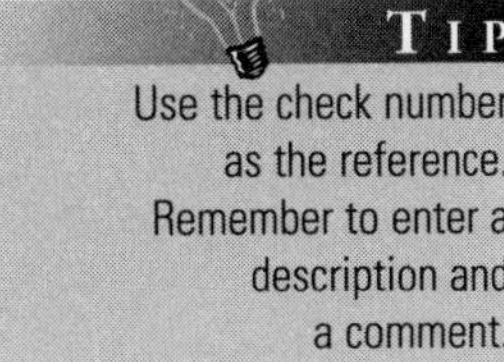

TIP Use the check number as the reference. Remember to enter a description and a comment.

Devine Designs Inc. leased office space from Prestige Properties Ltd. The monthly rent of $2,500 includes heating, air conditioning, electricity, and property taxes. The first month's rent was paid on April 1 with check number 0002.

6160	Office Rent	2500.00	
1000	Bank		2500.00

TIP Remember to add the entry and create a new entry.

Entry 3 - Furniture Purchase

On April 1, Devine Designs Inc. purchased used office furniture for the rented office from Hayen Business Interiors Ltd. The materials were delivered on Hayen's invoice number HBI78654 at a cost of $3,350, plus RST of $268 and GST of $234.50. The invoice was paid upon delivery using check number 0003.

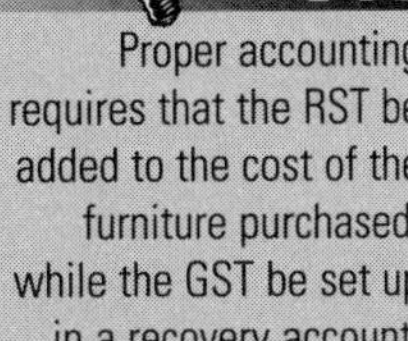

TIP Proper accounting requires that the RST be added to the cost of the furniture purchased, while the GST be set up in a recovery account.

1520	Fixtures & Furniture	3618.00	
2205	GST (VAT) Recoverable	234.50	
1000	Bank		3852.50

Entry 4 - Telephone Installation

On April 2, the local telephone company installed telephones that had been ordered earlier. The installation charge was paid by check number 0004 immediately upon completion of the installation. The telephone company's work order was PCI 3421. The invoiced cost for the work was $314, plus RST and GST.

TIP

Remember to enter the actual transaction date in all detail lines.

6060	Communications Expense	339.12	
2205	GST (VAT) Recoverable	21.98	
1000	Bank		361.10

Entry 5 - Printing Costs

On April 2, Eric ordered business cards and stationery from Kevin's Kopy Service, a print shop in the office building. The print shop insisted on payment in advance. The invoice amount was for $475, plus RST and GST. The invoice number was KK3425 and the full amount of $546.25 was paid with check number 0005.

1300	Office Supplies	513.00	
2205	GST(VAT) Recoverable	33.25	
1000	Bank		546.25

Entry 6 - Office Supplies

On April 2, John purchased office supplies from Prestonia Office Products. The invoice amount was for $532, plus RST and GST. The invoice number was POP9807 and the full amount of $611.80 was paid with check number 0006.

1300	Office Supplies	574.56	
2205	GST(VAT) Recoverable	37.24	
1000	Bank		611.80

Entry 7 - Computer Lease

On April 5, Devine Designs Inc. negotiated a two-year lease with Summit Peak Computers for three servers and a high resolution colour printer. The initial payment on the lease was $7,000, plus taxes, paid with check number 0007. The lease contract number was SP 9801. The lease called for a payment of $1,540, plus taxes, on the first of each month. The lease runs for two years, and allows the lessee to purchase the computers at the end for $3,300. The three partners have no intention of purchasing the computers since they expect the equipment to be outdated within that time period. The lease will be treated as an operating lease.

6080	Computer Rent	7560.00	
2205	GST(VAT) Recoverable	490.00	
1000	Bank		8050.00

Entry 8 - Office Furnishings

On April 5, Devine Designs Inc. purchased a small refrigerator, microwave, and coffee maker for the office. The purchase was made from Stoodley's Appliances on credit, invoice number 5556. The invoice was for $650, plus RST and GST. Payment is due on April 20.

1520	Fixtures & Furniture	702.00	
2205	GST(VAT) Recoverable	45.50	
2010	Accounts Payable		747.50

Entry 9 - Internet Connection

On April 6, a contract was signed with AS-Tech Computers for Internet connection services including an ATM line to their office in the same building. There will be a monthly charge of $125, plus taxes. The first month's service fees were paid with check number 0008.

6140	Internet Services Expense	135.00	
2205	GST(VAT) Recoverable	8.75	
1000	Bank		143.75

Entry 10 - Production Software

On April 6, production software was purchased from MicroWare Ltd. at a cost of $2,500, plus taxes, on invoice MW 345632. Terms were 2/10, n/30.

1540	Software	2,700.00	
2205	GST(VAT) Recoverable	175.00	
2010	Accounts Payable		2,875.00

Entry 11 - Accounting Software

On April 6, John ordered accounting software from Software Depot. The total cost was $1,500, plus taxes. Invoice SD334488, terms 2/10, n/30, accompanied the software.

1540	Software	1,620.00	
2205	GST(VAT) Recoverable	105.00	
2010	Accounts Payable		1,725.00

Entry 12 - Image Multimedia Ltd.

On April 12, Devine Designs Inc. received a phone call from the production manager at Image Multimedia Ltd. about a contract for the design of a company Web site. The estimate was that this would require 100 hours of work and would have to be completed by Friday, April 30. Leslie negotiated a fee of $50 per hour with an immediate payment of $2,000, plus taxes. Upon completion of the project the balance of $3,000, plus taxes, was due. An invoice was prepared, 10-0001, on April 12, for $2,000, plus taxes, with the remainder to be billed and paid on April 30. Image Multimedia delivered their check for $2,300 that afternoon.

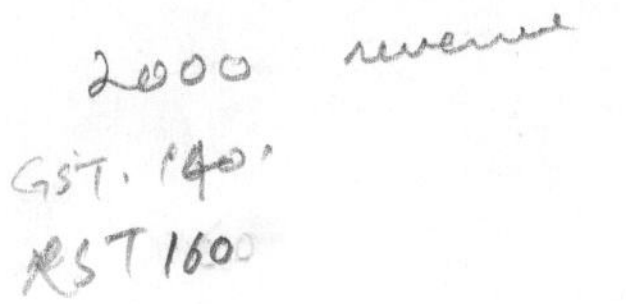

1000	Bank	2,300.00	
4000/10	Sales - Web Page Design		2,000.00
2100	Retail Sales Tax Payable		160.00
2200	GST Payable		140.00

Entry 13 - Invoicing Image Multimedia Ltd.

Image Multimedia Ltd. invoice 10-0002, due April 30 after completion of Web page installation.

1100	Accounts Receivable	3,450.00	
4000/10	Web Page Installations		3,000.00
2100	Retail Sales Tax Payable		240.00
2200	GST Payable		210.00

Entry 14

Leslie, Eric, and John agreed to draw montly salaries of $1500.00 each for the first six months. These salaries would be paid at the middle and end of each month. On April 15, 2010, Devine Designs Inc. issued their first pay checks (check numbers 0009, 0010, and 0011) for $750.00 each.

6180	Salary Expense		2250.00
1000	Bank		2250.00

Entry 15

On April 19, 2010, check number 0012 was issued to Stoodley's Appliances to pay invoice 5556 that was recorded as an account payable on April 5.

2010	Accounts Payable	747.50	
1000	Bank		747.50

Entry 16

On April 23, 2010, John arranged for banner advertising and links to Devine Designs Inc.'s home page for the months of May, June, and July 2010 on the WebMaster Guild Web site. John got a special rate of $2,000, plus taxes, by agreeing to pay immediately. Check number 0013 was issed to WebMaster Guild.

6000	Advertising Expense	2,160.00	
2205	GST (VAT) Recoverable	140.00	
1000	Bank		2,300.00

Devine Designs invoice number was 10-0002.

Entry 17

On April 30, 2010, John and Leslie delivered and installed the Web page for Image Multimedia. On the way back to the office, they deposited Image Multimedia's check number IM04532 to Devine Designs' account at First Bank Corp.

1000	Bank	3,450.00	
1100	Accounts Receivable		3,450.00

Entry 18

On April 30, 2010, Devine Design issued salary checks (numbers 0014, 0015, and 0016) for $750.00 to Leslie, Eric, and John.

6180	Salary Expense	2,250.00	
1000	Bank		2,250.00

Entry 19

Eric had started to prepare for setting up the accounts receivable and accounts payable accounting modules. He decided to pay the outstanding payables in April as this would make setting up the accounts payable module much easier.

On April 30, 2010, check number 0017 for $2,875.00 was issued to MicroWare Ltd. in payment of invoice MW 34532.

2010	Accounts Payable	2,875.00	
1000	Bank		2,875.00

Entry 20

On April 30, 2010, check number 0018 for $1,725 was issued to Software Depot in payment of invoice SD334488.

2010	Accounts Payable	1,725.00	
1000	Bank		1,725.00

Check Figure

When you have finshed the batch, you should have 20 entries in batch 2 for a balanced total of $71,260.40. You should print the Batch Listings and review them for errors.

❑ Print: the **Batch Listings**

Review the second batch listing carefully and compare it to that shown in Figure 9-13. Each entry should be balanced and the batch totals should be $71,260.40. Verify that there are no errors. If necessary, make corrections using the Normal Entry mode and reprint the batch listings.

FIGURE 9-13 Batch Listing Printout

Date: Saturday, July 08, 2000 3:30PM **DDI Student Name** Page 1
G/L Batch Listing - Functional Currency Only (GLBCHL01)

From Batch Number	[000002] To [000002]
From Source Ledger	[ ] To [ZZ]
From Creation Date	[5/1/2009] To [4/30/2010]
Include Printed Batches	[Yes]
Having Status Of	[Open, Ready To Post, Prov. Posted]
For Batch Type	[Entered, Subledger, Imported, Generated]

Srce.	Trans Date	Reference	Description	Account Number	Debits	Credits
Batch Number: 2		April 2010 transactions	**Creation Date:** 4/30/2010	**Status:** Open	**Type:** Entered	
Entry Number: 00001		additional investment	**Entry Date:** 4/30/2010	**Year-Prd.:** 2010-12		
GL-CR	4/1/2010	common stock	additional share purchase	1000	28,500.00	
		Comment: Leslie, Eric & John each bought a further $9,500 worth of stock				
GL-CR	4/1/2010	common stock	additional share purchase	3000		28,500.00
		Comment: Leslie, Eric & John each bought a further $9,500 worth of stock				
				Entry Total:	**28,500.00**	**28,500.00**
Entry Number: 00002		April Rent Prestige Properties	**Entry Date:** 4/1/2010	**Year-Prd.:** 2010-12		
GL-CD	4/1/2010	CK 0002		6160	2,500.00	
GL-CD	4/1/2010	CK 0002		1000		2,500.00
				Entry Total:	**2,500.00**	**2,500.00**
Entry Number: 00003		Furniture Purchase	**Entry Date:** 4/1/2010	**Year-Prd.:** 2010-12		
GL-CD	4/1/2010	CK 003	Hayen Business Interiors HBI78	1520	3,618.00	
GL-CD	4/1/2010	CK 003	Hayen Business Interiors HBI78	2205	234.50	
GL-CD	4/1/2010	CK 003	Hayen Business Interiors HBI78	1000		3,852.50
				Entry Total:	**3,852.50**	**3,852.50**
Entry Number: 00004		Telephone Installation	**Entry Date:** 4/2/2010	**Year-Prd.:** 2010-12		
GL-CD	4/2/2010	CK 0004	Telephone Company PCI 3421	6060	339.12	
GL-CD	4/2/2010	CK 0004	Telephone Company PCI 3421	2205	21.98	
GL-CD	4/2/2010	CK 0004	Telephone Company PCI 3421	1000		361.10
				Entry Total:	**361.10**	**361.10**
Entry Number: 00005		Business cards & stationary	**Entry Date:** 4/2/2010	**Year-Prd.:** 2010-12		
GL-CD	4/2/2010	CK 0005	Kevin's Kopy Service KK3425	1300	513.00	
GL-CD	4/2/2010	CK 0005	Kevin's Kopy Service KK3425	2205	33.25	
GL-CD	4/2/2010	CK 0005	Kevin's Kopy Service KK3425	1000		546.25
				Entry Total:	**546.25**	**546.25**
Entry Number: 00006		Office Supplies	**Entry Date:** 4/2/2010	**Year-Prd.:** 2010-12		
GL-CD	4/2/2010	CK 0006	Prestonia Office Products POP9	1300	574.56	
GL-CD	4/2/2010	CK 0006	Prestonia Office Products POP9	2205	37.24	

Date: Saturday, July 08, 2000 3:30PM

G/L Batch Listing - Functional Currency Only (GLBCHL01)

DDI Student Name

Page 2

Srce.	Trans Date	Reference	Description	Account Number		Debits	Credits
GL-CD	4/2/2010	CK 0006	Prestonia Office Products POP9	1000			611.80
					Entry Total:	**611.80**	**611.80**
Entry Number: 00007		Computer Lease	**Entry Date:** 4/5/2010	**Year-Prd.:** 2010-12			
GL-CD	4/5/2010	CK 0007	Summit Peak Comuters SP9801	6080		7,560.00	
GL-CD	4/5/2010	CK 0007	Summit Peak Comuters SP9801	2205		490.00	
GL-CD	4/5/2010	CK 0007	Summit Peak Comuters SP9801	1000			8,050.00
					Entry Total:	**8,050.00**	**8,050.00**
Entry Number: 00008		Office Furnishings	**Entry Date:** 4/5/2010	**Year-Prd.:** 2010-12			
GL-PU	4/5/2010	5556	Stoodley's Appliances	1520		702.00	
GL-PU	4/5/2010	5556	Stoodley's Appliances	2205		45.50	
GL-PU	4/5/2010	5556	Stoodley's Appliances	2010			747.50
					Entry Total:	**747.50**	**747.50**
Entry Number: 00009		Internet Connection	**Entry Date:** 4/6/2010	**Year-Prd.:** 2010-12			
GL-CD	4/6/2010	CK 0008	AS-Tech Computers	6140		135.00	
GL-CD	4/6/2010	CK 0008	AS-Tech Computers	2205		8.75	
GL-CD	4/6/2010	CK 0008	AS-Tech Computers	1000			143.75
					Entry Total:	**143.75**	**143.75**
Entry Number: 00010		Production Software	**Entry Date:** 4/6/2010	**Year-Prd.:** 2010-12			
GL-PU	4/6/2010	MW 345632	MicroWare Ltd	1540		2,700.00	
GL-PU	4/6/2010	MW 345632	MicroWare Ltd	2205		175.00	
GL-PU	4/6/2010	MW 345632	MicroWare Ltd	2010			2,875.00
					Entry Total:	**2,875.00**	**2,875.00**
Entry Number: 00011		Accounting Software	**Entry Date:** 4/6/2010	**Year-Prd.:** 2010-12			
GL-PU	4/6/2010	SD334488	Software Depot	1540		1,620.00	
GL-PU	4/6/2010	SD334488	Software Depot	2205		105.00	
GL-PU	4/6/2010	SD334488	Software Depot	2010			1,725.00
					Entry Total:	**1,725.00**	**1,725.00**
Entry Number: 00012		Image Multimedia Ltd.	**Entry Date:** 4/12/2010	**Year-Prd.:** 2010-12			
GL-CR	4/12/2010	Inv 10-0001	Image Multimedia	1000		2,300.00	
GL-CR	4/12/2010	Inv 10-0001	Image Multimedia	4000/10			2,000.00
GL-CR	4/12/2010	Inv 10-0001	Image Multimedia	2100			160.00
GL-CR	4/12/2010	Inv 10-0001	Image Multimedia	2200			140.00
					Entry Total:	**2,300.00**	**2,300.00**

Figure 9-13 Batch Listing Printout (continued)

Date: Saturday, July 08, 2000 3:30PM
G/L Batch Listing - Functional Currency Only (GLBCHL01)

DDI Student Name — Page 3

Trans Srce.	Date	Reference	Description	Account Number	Debits	Credits
Entry Number: 00013		Image Multimedia Ltd.	**Entry Date:** 4/30/2010	**Year-Prd.:** 2010-12		
GL-SA	4/30/2010	Inv 10-0002	Image Multimedia	1100	3,450.00	
GL-SA	4/30/2010	Inv 10-0002	Image Multimedia	4000/10		3,000.00
GL-SA	4/30/2010	Inv 10-0002	Image Multimedia	2100		240.00
GL-SA	4/30/2010	Inv 10-0002	Image Multimedia	2200		210.00
				Entry Total:	**3,450.00**	**3,450.00**
Entry Number: 00014		Salaries	**Entry Date:** 4/15/2010	**Year-Prd.:** 2010-12		
GL-CD	4/15/2010	CK 0009/10/11	April mid month salaries	6180	2,250.00	
GL-CD	4/15/2010	CK 0009/10/11	April mid month salaries	1000		2,250.00
				Entry Total:	**2,250.00**	**2,250.00**
Entry Number: 00015		Invoice Payment	**Entry Date:** 4/19/2010	**Year-Prd.:** 2010-12		
GL-CD	4/19/2010	CK 0012	Stoodley's Appliances 5556	2010	747.50	
GL-CD	4/19/2010	CK 0012	Stoodley's Appliances 5556	1000		747.50
				Entry Total:	**747.50**	**747.50**
Entry Number: 00016		banner advertising	**Entry Date:** 4/23/2010	**Year-Prd.:** 2010-12		
GL-CD	4/23/2010	CK 0013	WebMaster Guild	6000	2,160.00	
GL-CD	4/23/2010	CK 0013	WebMaster Guild	2205	140.00	
GL-CD	4/23/2010	CK 0013	WebMaster Guild	1000		2,300.00
				Entry Total:	**2,300.00**	**2,300.00**
Entry Number: 00017		Image Multimedia payment	**Entry Date:** 4/30/2010	**Year-Prd.:** 2010-12		
GL-CR	4/30/2010	inv 10-0002	Image Multimedia IM04532	1000	3,450.00	
GL-CR	4/30/2010	inv 10-0002	Image Multimedia IM04532	1100		3,450.00
				Entry Total:	**3,450.00**	**3,450.00**
Entry Number: 00018		Salaries	**Entry Date:** 4/30/2010	**Year-Prd.:** 2010-12		
GL-CD	4/30/2010	CK 0014/15/16	End of month salaries	6180	2,250.00	
GL-CD	4/30/2010	CK 0014/15/16	End of month salaries	1000		2,250.00
				Entry Total:	**2,250.00**	**2,250.00**
Entry Number: 00019		MicroWare Ltd	**Entry Date:** 4/30/2010	**Year-Prd.:** 2010-12		
GL-CD	4/30/2010	CK 0017	Microware inv MW34532	2010	2,875.00	
GL-CD	4/30/2010	CK 0017	Microware inv MW34532	1000		2,875.00
				Entry Total:	**2,875.00**	**2,875.00**

Date: Saturday, July 08, 2000 3:30PM
G/L Batch Listing - Functional Currency Only (GLBCHL01)

DDI Student Name — Page 4

Trans Srce.	Date	Reference	Description	Account Number	Debits	Credits
Entry Number: 00020		Software Depot	**Entry Date:** 4/30/2010	**Year-Prd.:** 2010-12		
GL-CD	4/30/2010	CK 0018	Software Depot SD334488	2010	1,725.00	
GL-CD	4/30/2010	CK 0018	Software Depot SD334488	1000		1,725.00
				Entry Total:	**1,725.00**	**1,725.00**
				Batch Total:	**71,260.40**	**71,260.40**

20 entries printed
1 batch printed

- ❑ Close: the **G/L Batch Listing**
- ❑ Close: **G/L Journal Entry**
- ❑ Exit: **ACCPAC**

REVIEW QUESTIONS

1. Why is it good practice to prepare a list of the transactions to be entered?
2. What is a transaction batch?
3. What is the purpose of the Reference field? Why is this information important?
4. What will happen if you type an account number that is not included in the Chart of Accounts?
5. How do you know if an entry you just made is not in balance?
6. Why should you print a Transaction Batch List before posting that batch to the General Ledger?
7. Describe the differences between the Quick entry and Normal entry modes. Under what conditions would you use each of these options?
8. How would you make corrections to a batch entry already posted to the General Ledger?

EXERCISE

- ❑ Sign on to your company as the system administrator using 04/30/10 as the Session Date.

APRIL 2010 TRANSACTIONS

- ❑ Enter the following transactions using a new batch dated April 30, 2010. It would be useful if you prepared a data entry sheet for the following transactions. Terms for all are n/30. Retail sales tax (RST) of 8% and goods and services tax (GST) of 7% are applied on all sales.

April 1, 2010

Sold Web Page Design services on credit to VanVoort Ltd. The invoice was for $2,000 plus sales taxes. Invoice #001.

April 1, 2010

Paid $600 to Joe Neimi Enterprises for April furnished office rent, check #001. Use Account 1000 for the disbursement.

April 2, 2010

Invoice #002 to Renrak & Co. $1,700 for Web Page Design services rendered during March plus RST and GST.

April 5, 2010

Invoice #003 to Renrak & Co. $1,000 plus RST and GST for Web Page Maintenance on its Web site.

April 7, 2010

Issued 10,000 shares of common stock to yourself for $10,000 cash.

April 10, 2010

Sold Web Site Hosting services on credit to B. Eady & Co. for $1,500 plus RST and GST. Invoice #004.

April 12, 2010

Cash sale of Java applets for $759 plus RST and GST to Beaudoin Ltd. The sale was recorded on invoice #005. Allocate the sale to Misc.

April 15, 2010

Purchased laptop computer on purchase order PO002 from Currys Inc. for $6,325. This amount includes the original cost of $5,500 plus GST and RST. The invoice (number JK4550) was dated April 15, with terms of Net 30.

April 15, 2010

Invoice #006 to MacMillan & Johnson $1,700 for Web Page Design services rendered during April plus RST and GST.

April 19, 2010

Invoice #007 to MacMillan & Johnson $1,200 plus RST and GST for Web Page Maintenance on its existing site.

April 23, 2010

Received a check in full payment from VanVoort Ltd. Invoice #001.

April 25, 2010

Received a check in full payment from Renrak & Co. for invoices #002 and 003.

April 26, 2010

Paid invoice #JK4550 to Currys Inc. in full, check number 002.

April 28, 2010

Received a check in full payment from B. Eady & Co. for invoice #004.

April 30, 2010

Received a check in full payment from MacMillan & Johnson for invoices #006 and 007.

- ❑ Print the Transaction Batch Lists.
- ❑ Compare your Batch Lists with Figure 9-14, as shown on pages 148–149.

Figure 9-14 April 2010 Transaction

Date: Saturday, July 15, 2000 11:33AM
G/L Batch Listing - Functional Currency Only (GLBCHL01)

John & Erik

Page 1

From Batch Number	[000001] To [000001]
From Source Ledger	[ ] To [ZZ]
From Creation Date	[5/1/2009] To [4/30/2010]
Include Printed Batches	[Yes]
Having Status Of	[Open, Ready To Post, Prov. Posted]
For Batch Type	[Entered, Subledger, Imported, Generated]

Srce.	Trans Date	Reference	Description	Account Number	Debits	Credits
Batch Number: 1		April 2010 Transactions	**Creation Date:** 4/30/2010	**Status:** Open	**Type:** Entered	
Entry Number: 00001		Van Voort Ltd	**Entry Date:** 4/1/2010	**Year-Prd.:** 2010-12		
GL-SA	4/1/2010	inv 001	web page design	1100	2,300.00	
GL-SA	4/1/2010	inv 001	web page design	2100		160.00
GL-SA	4/1/2010	inv 001	web page design	2200		140.00
GL-SA	4/1/2010	inv 001	web page design	4000/10		2,000.00
				Entry Total:	**2,300.00**	**2,300.00**
Entry Number: 00002		JoeNeimi Enterprises	**Entry Date:** 4/1/2010	**Year-Prd.:** 2010-12		
GL-CD	4/1/2010	ck 001	April rent	6160	600.00	
GL-CD	4/1/2010	ck 001	April rent	1000		600.00
				Entry Total:	**600.00**	**600.00**
Entry Number: 00003		Renrak & Co.	**Entry Date:** 4/2/2010	**Year-Prd.:** 2010-12		
GL-SA	4/2/2010	inv 002	design services	1100	1,955.00	
GL-SA	4/2/2010	inv 002	design services	2100		136.00
GL-SA	4/2/2010	inv 002	design services	2200		119.00
GL-SA	4/2/2010	inv 002	design services	4000/10		1,700.00
				Entry Total:	**1,955.00**	**1,955.00**
Entry Number: 00004		Renrak & Co.	**Entry Date:** 4/5/2010	**Year-Prd.:** 2010-12		
GL-SA	4/5/2010	inv 003	page maintenance	1100	1,150.00	
GL-SA	4/5/2010	inv 003	page maintenance	2100		80.00
GL-SA	4/5/2010	inv 003	page maintenance	2200		70.00
GL-SA	4/5/2010	inv 003	page maintenance	4000/20		1,000.00
				Entry Total:	**1,150.00**	**1,150.00**
Entry Number: 00005		common stock issued	**Entry Date:** 4/7/2010	**Year-Prd.:** 2010-12		
GL-JE	4/7/2010	stock	stock issued to your name	1000	10,000.00	
GL-JE	4/7/2010	stock	stock issued to your name	3000		10,000.00
				Entry Total:	**10,000.00**	**10,000.00**
Entry Number: 00006		B. Eady & Co.	**Entry Date:** 4/7/2010	**Year-Prd.:** 2010-12		
GL-SA	4/7/2010	inv 004	site hosting	1100	1,725.00	

Date: Saturday, July 15, 2000 11:33AM
G/L Batch Listing - Functional Currency Only (GLBCHL01)

John & Erik

Page 2

Srce.	Trans Date	Reference	Description	Account Number	Debits	Credits
GL-SA	4/7/2010	inv 004	site hosting	2100		120.00
GL-SA	4/7/2010	inv 004	site hosting	2200		105.00
GL-SA	4/7/2010	inv 004	site hosting	4000/30		1,500.00
				Entry Total:	1,725.00	1,725.00
Entry Number: 00007		Beaudoin Ltd.		Entry Date: 4/10/2010 Year-Prd.: 2010-12		
GL-SA	4/10/2010	inv 005	Java aplets	1000	872.85	
GL-SA	4/10/2010	inv 005	Java aplets	2100		60.72
GL-SA	4/10/2010	inv 005	Java aplets	2200		53.13
GL-SA	4/10/2010	inv 005	Java aplets	4000/99		759.00
				Entry Total:	872.85	872.85
Entry Number: 00008		Currys Inc.		Entry Date: 4/15/2010 Year-Prd.: 2010-12		
GL-PU	4/15/2010	po 002	laptop inv JK4550	1500	5,885.00	
GL-PU	4/15/2010	po 002	laptop inv JK4550	2205	440.00	
GL-PU	4/15/2010	po 002	laptop inv JK4550	2010		6,325.00
				Entry Total:	6,325.00	6,325.00
Entry Number: 00009		MacMillan & Johnson		Entry Date: 4/15/2010 Year-Prd.: 2010-12		
GL-SA	4/15/2010	inv 006	design services	1100	1,955.00	
GL-SA	4/15/2010	inv 006	design services	2100		136.00
GL-SA	4/15/2010	inv 006	design services	2200		119.00
GL-SA	4/15/2010	inv 006	design services	4000/10		1,700.00
				Entry Total:	1,955.00	1,955.00
Entry Number: 00010		MacMillan & Johnson		Entry Date: 4/19/2010 Year-Prd.: 2010-12		
GL-SA	4/19/2010	inv 007	maintenance	1100	1,380.00	
GL-SA	4/19/2010	inv 007	maintenance	2100		96.00
GL-SA	4/19/2010	inv 007	maintenance	2200		84.00
GL-SA	4/19/2010	inv 007	maintenance	4000/20		1,200.00
				Entry Total:	1,380.00	1,380.00
Entry Number: 00011		Van Voort Ltd.		Entry Date: 4/25/2010 Year-Prd.: 2010-12		
GL-CR	4/25/2010	inv 001	payment	1000	2,300.00	
GL-CR	4/25/2010	inv 001	payment	1100		2,300.00
				Entry Total:	2,300.00	2,300.00
Entry Number: 00012		Renrak & Co.		Entry Date: 4/25/2010 Year-Prd.: 2010-12		
GL-CR	4/25/2010	inv002/3	payment	1000	3,105.00	

Date: Saturday, July 15, 2000 11:33AM
G/L Batch Listing - Functional Currency Only (GLBCHL01)

John & Erik

Page 3

Srce.	Trans Date	Reference	Description	Account Number	Debits	Credits
GL-CR	4/25/2010	inv002/3	payment	1100		3,105.00
				Entry Total:	3,105.00	3,105.00
Entry Number: 00013		Currys Inc.		Entry Date: 4/26/2010 Year-Prd.: 2010-12		
GL-CD	4/26/2010	ck 002	inv JK4550	2010	6,325.00	
GL-CD	4/26/2010	ck 002	inv JK4550	1000		6,325.00
				Entry Total:	6,325.00	6,325.00
Entry Number: 00014		B. Eady & Co.		Entry Date: 4/28/2010 Year-Prd.: 2010-12		
GL-CR	4/28/2010	inv 004	payment	1000	1,725.00	
GL-CR	4/28/2010	inv 004	payment	1100		1,725.00
				Entry Total:	1,725.00	1,725.00
Entry Number: 00015		MacMillan &Johnson		Entry Date: 4/30/2010 Year-Prd.: 2010-12		
GL-CR	4/30/2010	inv 006/7	payment	1000	3,335.00	
GL-CR	4/30/2010	inv 006/7	payment	1100		3,335.00
				Entry Total:	3,335.00	3,335.00
				Batch Total:	45,052.85	45,052.85

15 entries printed
1 batch printed

- ❑ Make any corrections necessary and print the Batch Lists again.
- ❑ Exit: **ACCPAC**

CHAPTER 10

POSTING

In this chapter, you will post the transaction batches that you created in Chapter 9 to the General Ledger.

GETTING READY

In Chapter 4, when you activated Common Services, ACCPAC created a fiscal calendar with two fiscal years. Year 2009, starting on May 1, 2008 and ending on April 30, 2009, was created for recording historic information. Year 2010 is the current fiscal year.

- ❑ Sign on to Devine Designs Inc. as the system administrator. Use April 30, 2010 as the Session Date.
- ❑ DClick: the **Periodic Processing** icon on the **General Ledger** window

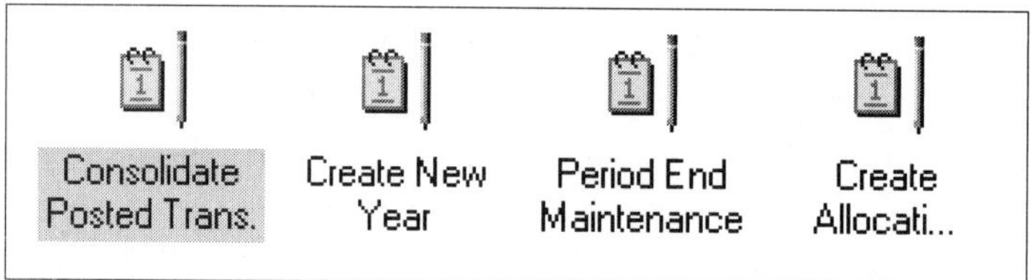

FIGURE 10-1
G/L Periodic Processing Icons

Four icons are displayed on the G/L Periodic Processing window (Figure 10-1). The Consolidate Posted Transactions and Period End Maintenance icons are used to reduce the amount of storage used by the company files. The Create Allocation Batch icon is used to create batches for accounts using the Auto Allocation option. The Create New Year icon is used to prepare the General Ledger for processing in the next fiscal year.

BATCH STATUS REPORT

Before you post batches to the General Ledger, verify the status of each batch. The Batch Status report tells you what activity has taken place in all the unposted batches and in batches that have been posted or deleted since the last time the data for the report were cleared. The report includes the number of errors in the unposted batches. It can be used as an audit trail of batch numbers and dates of activity in the batches.

You can print the Batch Status report at any time. The only time you must print and clear this report is before running the Change Fiscal Year function, which is described in Chapter 12.

- ❑ DClick: **Reports** [G/L Reports] on the General Ledger window
- ❑ DCick: **Batch Status** [Batch Status] on the G/L Reports window

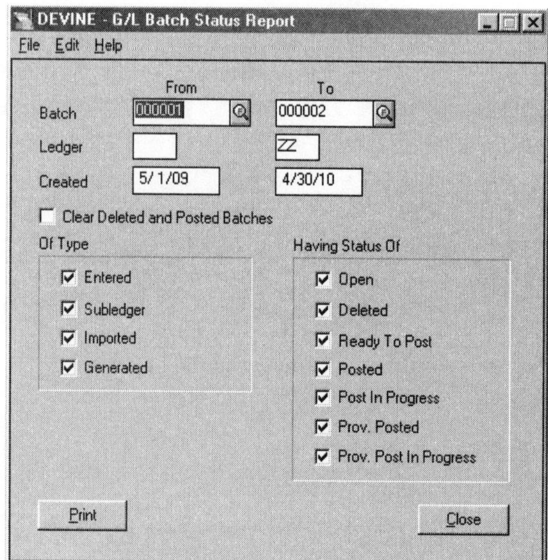

FIGURE 10-2
G/L Batch Status Report Window

The G/L Batch Status Report window (Figure 10-2) is divided into three sections.

In the upper section, you can use the Batch list boxes to specify a particular batch number or range of batch numbers. Text boxes also allow you to specify the Ledgers and the Dates for which you want the Batch Status report printed. The check box for Clear All Deleted and Posted Batches enables you to eliminate redundant information from the Batch Status report.

The check boxes in the Of Type section in the lower left of the window allow you to select the type of batch to be reported. The type of batch refers to how the batch was created. An Entered batch has been created with the ACCPAC General Ledger module. Subledger batches are created with other ACCPAC modules, such as Accounts Receivable and Accounts Payable. Imported batches are data files that are brought, or imported, into ACCPAC from other programs. Generated batches are created by ACCPAC; an example of a generated batch is the transactions generated by ACCPAC at year-end when the temporary equity accounts are closed. The default displays a check mark in each check box to print the status of every type of batch.

The "Having Status of" section refers to the processing of the batch. The two batches that you have entered are Open and Printed; that is, transactions have been entered and the batch lists printed, but the batches have not been processed further.

The default will print a Batch Status report for all batches that have not been cleared from the data files. If you want to change the report options for batch Of Type and Having Status Of, click on the check boxes for those items that you do not want to appear on the report.

- ❑ Click: **Print** [Print] on the G/L Batch Status Report window
- ❑ Click: **OK** [OK] on the Print dialog box

FIGURE 10-3 Batch Status Report

Date: Sunday, May 28, 2000 9:29PM **DDI Student Name** **Page 1**
Batch Status (GLBTCH01)

From Batch Number	[000001] To [000002]
From Ledger	[ ] To [ZZ]
From Creation Date	[5/1/09] To [4/30/10]
Of Type	[Entered, Subledger, Imported, Generated]
Having Status Of	[Open, Deleted, Posted, Prov. Posted, Post In Progress, Ready To Post, Prov. Post In Progress]

Batch Number	Description	Srce	No. of Entries	Date Created	Date Last Edited	Status	Printed	Type	Post Seq.	Errors	Debits	Credits
000001	Company Organization	GL	2	04/30/2010	05/28/2000	Open	Yes	Entered	0	0	2,225.00	2,225.00
000002	April 2010 Transactions	GL	20	04/30/2010	05/28/2000	Open	Yes	Entered	0	0	71,260.40	71,260.40

2 batches printed

Summary

Type	No. Of Entries	No. Of Batches	Total Debits	Total Credits	Status	No. Of Entries	No. Of Batches	Total Debits	Total Credits
Entered	22	2	73,485.40	73,485.40	Open	22	2	73,485.40	73,485.40
Subledger	0	0	0.00	0.00	Deleted	0	0	0.00	0.00
Imported	0	0	0.00	0.00	Posted	0	0	0.00	0.00
Generated	0	0	0.00	0.00	Prov. Posted	0	0	0.00	0.00
					Ready To Post	0	0	0.00	0.00
					Post In Progress	0	0	0.00	0.00
					Prov. Post In Prog.	0	0	0.00	0.00

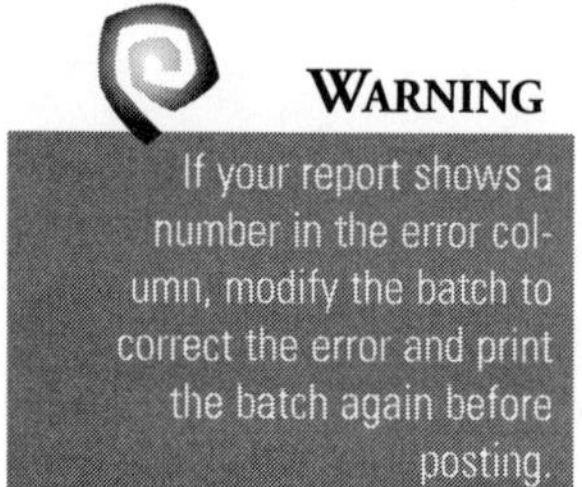

As shown in Figure 10-3, the first area on the Batch Status report identifies the date and time that the report was printed. It also indicates the selections entered on the G/L Batch Status Report window.

The second area lists each batch by batch number and describes each batch.

The table on the lower left of the report summarizes the transactions by the batch type, while the table on the lower right summarizes transactions by the status of the batches to which they have been entered.

If necessary,

- ❑ Print: the **batches**, then
- ❑ Print: the **Batch Status Report** again
- ❑ Close: the **G/L Batch Status Report** window

Posting to the General Ledger

Before you can post a batch, it has to be set to Ready to Post.

- ❑ DClick: the **Batch List Icon** on the General Ledger window

The G/L Batch List window will appear as displayed by Figure 10-4.

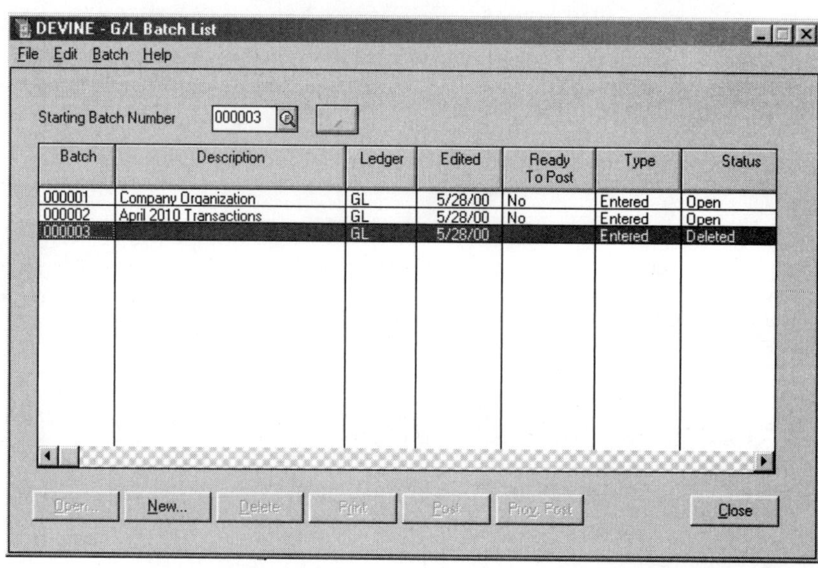

FIGURE 10-4
Batch List Window

The fifth column from the left is called Ready to Post. To change the status to Yes, you have to double click the contents of the cell for each batch you want to post.

- ❑ DClick: the **Ready to Post Cell** for batches 1 and 2
- ❑ Close: the **G/L Batch List** window

On the Posting page of the G/L Options notebook, Devine Designs Inc. selected the Force Listing of Batches option. When this option is selected, all printed batches are ready for posting. If this option is not selected, each batch has to be set ready to post, using the G/L Journal Entry window, before posting it to the General Ledger.

❑ DClick: the **Post Batches** icon [Post Batches] on the General Ledger window

The G/L Post Batches window will appear as shown in Figure 10-5.

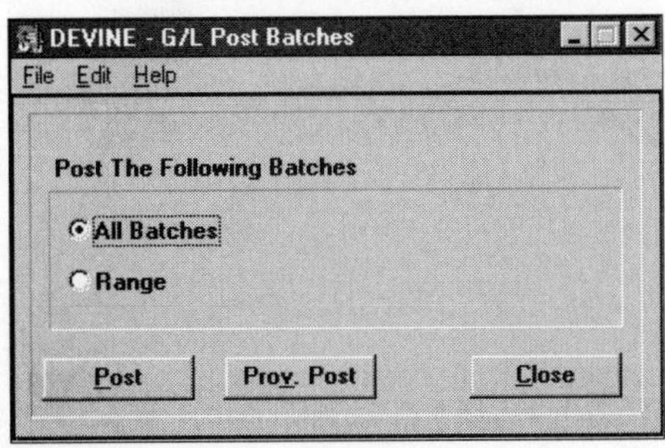

FIGURE 10-5
G/L Post Batches Window

TIP
You can also use the G/L Batch List window to post individual batches.

You can choose to post all the printed batches or you can specify a range of batches to post. When you select the range option, two list boxes are displayed that enable you to select the first and last batches in the range to be posted.

❑ Select: the **All Batches** option

❑ Click: **Post** [Post]

❑ Click: **OK** when you see the Posting Sequence 1 Completed message

❑ Click: **OK** [OK]

❑ Close: the **G/L Post Batches** window

Batch Errors

If you try to post a batch that contains errors identifiable by ACCPAC, those entries that are correct will be posted, and the entries containing errors will be placed in a new batch, which uses the next available number. The program cannot detect certain errors, such as duplicate document numbers, until you post the batch, and those errors will not be reported on the batch listing. If you use the Force Listing of Batches option, all the batches must be error free, and you must have printed listings for them before trying to post.

If errors were found by the program and placed in a new batch during posting, print a batch list for the error batch, correct the errors, and then print and post the error batch.

Provisional Posting

Provisional Posting copies actual fiscal set amounts to a Provisional fiscal set, and updates the Provisional fiscal set so you can see the combined effect. Batches are not deleted when you post them provisionally; you can, if necessary, make changes to them before permanent posting. On the Batch Status report, they are marked as Provisionally Posted, and the date and the posting sequence number are included. You can include provisional transactions on the Batch Status and Trial Balance reports.

You can use the Posting Journal window to print an audit trail report of posted transactions. To report provisional transactions, select the Provisional Posting Journal. When ready, you can post the provisional batches permanently.

DUPLICATE POSTING

If you are not certain that you posted a batch to the General Ledger, try to make a duplicate posting by returning to the G/L Post Batches and try to post the batches again. Provided no error batches were created during the previous posting, ACCPAC will display the message "There are no batches that are ready to post." ACCPAC will not allow you to post a batch twice.

PRINTING THE POSTING JOURNAL

The Posting Journal provides an audit trail of all details posted to the General Ledger.

❑ DClick: the **G/L Reports** icon on the General Ledger window

❑ DClick: the **Posting Journal** icon

The G/L Posting Journals window will appear as shown in Figure 10-6.

FIGURE 10-6
G/L Posting Journals Window

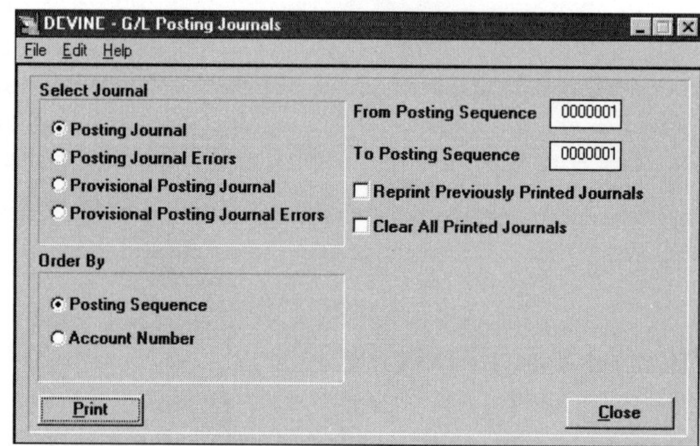

Select Journal

The Select Journal area allows you to select the journal to be printed. You print either the Posting Journal, the Provisional Posting Journal, or you can print the errors from either report. A posting error report is always printed after the journal if entries could not be posted.

❑ Ensure that the Posting Journal option button is active.

Posting Sequence Range

❑ Press: **Tab** [Tab] to move to the From Posting Sequence text box

Specify the range of posting sequences you want to print. The default is to print all unprinted journals.

❑ Press: **Tab** [Tab] twice to accept the full default range of batches

Reprint Previously Printed Journals

Activate the Reprint Previously Printed Journals box if you want to reprint posting journals. Devine Designs Inc. has not printed any posting journals yet, so this check box should be left empty.

❑ Press: **Tab** [Tab] to leave this check box empty

Clear All Printed Journals

Devine Designs Inc. has decided not to clear printed journals at this time. The journal information will be retained in case it is necessary to reprint the journals.

You must clear the posting journals before you can run the Change Fiscal Year function as described in Chapter 12. When you clear the posting journals, the detail information in the source journals and the General Ledger is unaffected.

❑ Press: **Tab** [Tab] to leave this check box empty

Order By

You can print the G/L Posting Journals sorted in order by posting sequence, or sorted in order by account codes. Devine Designs Inc. prints in order of posting sequence.

❑ Ensure that the Posting Sequence option has been selected.

❑ Click: **Print** [Print]

❑ Click: **OK** [OK]

FIGURE 10-7
G/L Posting Journal Report

Date: Saturday, July 08, 2000 3:44PM **DDI Student Name** **Page 1**
G/L Posting Journal - Functional Currency Only (GLPJ01)

From Posting Sequence [0000001] To [0000001]
Sorted By [Posting Sequence]

Posting Sequence Number: 1

Batch-Entry/ Trans. Date	Period/ Source Code	Year/ Reference	Entry Date/ Description	Account Number	Debits	Credits
1-1	01	2010	5/1/2009			
5/1/2009	GL-CR	Common Stock	Initial Share Purchase	1000	1,500.00	
	Comment:	Initial stock purchase funds deposited to First Bank Corp. account				
5/1/2009	GL-CR	Common Stock	Initial Share Purchase	3000		1,500.00
	Comment:	$500 each from Leslie, Eric & John				
				Entry Total:	**1,500.00**	**1,500.00**
1-2	01	2010	5/1/2009			
5/1/2009	GL-CD	0001	Bruce's Business Service	1600	725.00	
	Comment:	all incorporation and registration fees				
5/1/2009	GL-CD	0001	Bruce's Business Service	1000		725.00
	Comment:	all incorporation and registration fees				
				Entry Total:	**725.00**	**725.00**
2-1	12	2010	4/30/2010			
4/1/2010	GL-CR	common stock	additional share purchase	1000	28,500.00	
	Comment:	Leslie, Eric & John each bought a further $9,500 worth of stock				
4/1/2010	GL-CR	common stock	additional share purchase	3000		28,500.00
	Comment:	Leslie, Eric & John each bought a further $9,500 worth of stock				
				Entry Total:	**28,500.00**	**28,500.00**
2-2	12	2010	4/1/2010			
4/1/2010	GL-CD	CK 0002		6160	2,500.00	
4/1/2010	GL-CD	CK 0002		1000		2,500.00
				Entry Total:	**2,500.00**	**2,500.00**
2-3	12	2010	4/1/2010			
4/1/2010	GL-CD	CK 003	Hayen Business Interiors HBI78	1520	3,618.00	
4/1/2010	GL-CD	CK 003	Hayen Business Interiors HBI78	2205	234.50	
4/1/2010	GL-CD	CK 003	Hayen Business Interiors HBI78	1000		3,852.50
				Entry Total:	**3,852.50**	**3,852.50**
2-4	12	2010	4/2/2010			
4/2/2010	GL-CD	CK 0004	Telephone Company PCI 3421	6060	339.12	
4/2/2010	GL-CD	CK 0004	Telephone Company PCI 3421	2205	21.98	
4/2/2010	GL-CD	CK 0004	Telephone Company PCI 3421	1000		361.10
				Entry Total:	**361.10**	**361.10**
2-5	12	2010	4/2/2010			

Date: Saturday, July 08, 2000 3:44PM **DDI Student Name** **Page 2**
G/L Posting Journal - Functional Currency Only (GLPJ01)

Batch-Entry/ Trans. Date	Period/ Source Code	Year/ Reference	Entry Date/ Description	Account Number	Debits	Credits
4/2/2010	GL-CD	CK 0005	Kevin's Kopy Service KK3425	1300	513.00	
4/2/2010	GL-CD	CK 0005	Kevin's Kopy Service KK3425	2205	33.25	
4/2/2010	GL-CD	CK 0005	Kevin's Kopy Service KK3425	1000		546.25
				Entry Total:	**546.25**	**546.25**
2-6	12	2010	4/2/2010			
4/2/2010	GL-CD	CK 0006	Prestonia Office Products POP9	1300	574.56	
4/2/2010	GL-CD	CK 0006	Prestonia Office Products POP9	2205	37.24	
4/2/2010	GL-CD	CK 0006	Prestonia Office Products POP9	1000		611.80
				Entry Total:	**611.80**	**611.80**
2-7	12	2010	4/5/2010			
4/5/2010	GL-CD	CK 0007	Summit Peak Comuters SP9801	6080	7,560.00	
4/5/2010	GL-CD	CK 0007	Summit Peak Comuters SP9801	2205	490.00	
4/5/2010	GL-CD	CK 0007	Summit Peak Comuters SP9801	1000		8,050.00
				Entry Total:	**8,050.00**	**8,050.00**
2-8	12	2010	4/5/2010			
4/5/2010	GL-PU	5556	Stoodley's Appliances	1520	702.00	
4/5/2010	GL-PU	5556	Stoodley's Appliances	2205	45.50	
4/5/2010	GL-PU	5556	Stoodley's Appliances	2010		747.50
				Entry Total:	**747.50**	**747.50**
2-9	12	2010	4/6/2010			
4/6/2010	GL-CD	CK 0008	AS-Tech Computers	6140	135.00	
4/6/2010	GL-CD	CK 0008	AS-Tech Computers	2205	8.75	
4/6/2010	GL-CD	CK 0008	AS-Tech Computers	1000		143.75
				Entry Total:	**143.75**	**143.75**
2-10	12	2010	4/6/2010			
4/6/2010	GL-PU	MW 345632	MicroWare Ltd	1540	2,700.00	
4/6/2010	GL-PU	MW 345632	MicroWare Ltd	2205	175.00	
4/6/2010	GL-PU	MW 345632	MicroWare Ltd	2010		2,875.00
				Entry Total:	**2,875.00**	**2,875.00**
2-11	12	2010	4/6/2010			
4/6/2010	GL-PU	SD334488	Software Depot	1540	1,620.00	
4/6/2010	GL-PU	SD334488	Software Depot	2205	105.00	
4/6/2010	GL-PU	SD334488	Software Depot	2010		1,725.00
				Entry Total:	**1,725.00**	**1,725.00**
2-12	12	2010	4/12/2010			
4/12/2010	GL-CR	Inv 10-0001	Image Multimedia	1000	2,300.00	
4/12/2010	GL-CR	Inv 10-0001	Image Multimedia	4000/10		2,000.00

Date: Saturday, July 08, 2000 3:44PM
G/L Posting Journal - Functional Currency Only (GLPJ01)

DDI Student Name

Page 3

Batch-Entry/ Trans. Date	Period/ Source Code	Year/ Reference	Entry Date/ Description	Account Number	Debits	Credits
4/12/2010	GL-CR	Inv 10-0001	Image Multimedia	2100		160.00
4/12/2010	GL-CR	Inv 10-0001	Image Multimedia	2200		140.00
				Entry Total:	2,300.00	2,300.00
2-13	12	2010	4/30/2010			
4/30/2010	GL-SA	Inv 10-0002	Image Multimedia	1100	3,450.00	
4/30/2010	GL-SA	Inv 10-0002	Image Multimedia	4000/10		3,000.00
4/30/2010	GL-SA	Inv 10-0002	Image Multimedia	2100		240.00
4/30/2010	GL-SA	Inv 10-0002	Image Multimedia	2200		210.00
				Entry Total:	3,450.00	3,450.00
2-14	12	2010	4/15/2010			
4/15/2010	GL-CD	CK 0009/10/11	April mid month salaries	6180	2,250.00	
4/15/2010	GL-CD	CK 0009/10/11	April mid month salaries	1000		2,250.00
				Entry Total:	2,250.00	2,250.00
2-15	12	2010	4/19/2010			
4/19/2010	GL-CD	CK 0012	Stoodley's Appliances 5556	2010	747.50	
4/19/2010	GL-CD	CK 0012	Stoodley's Appliances 5556	1000		747.50
				Entry Total:	747.50	747.50
2-16	12	2010	4/23/2010			
4/23/2010	GL-CD	CK 0013	WebMaster Guild	6000	2,160.00	
4/23/2010	GL-CD	CK 0013	WebMaster Guild	2205	140.00	
4/23/2010	GL-CD	CK 0013	WebMaster Guild	1000		2,300.00
				Entry Total:	2,300.00	2,300.00
2-17	12	2010	4/30/2010			
4/30/2010	GL-CR	inv 10-0002	Image Multimedia IM04532	1000	3,450.00	
4/30/2010	GL-CR	inv 10-0002	Image Multimedia IM04532	1100		3,450.00
				Entry Total:	3,450.00	3,450.00
2-18	12	2010	4/30/2010			
4/30/2010	GL-CD	CK 0014/15/16	End of month salaries	6180	2,250.00	
4/30/2010	GL-CD	CK 0014/15/16	End of month salaries	1000		2,250.00
				Entry Total:	2,250.00	2,250.00
2-19	12	2010	4/30/2010			
4/30/2010	GL-CD	CK 0017	Microware inv MW34532	2010	2,875.00	
4/30/2010	GL-CD	CK 0017	Microware inv MW34532	1000		2,875.00
				Entry Total:	2,875.00	2,875.00
2-20	12	2010	4/30/2010			

Date: Saturday, July 08, 2000 3:44PM
G/L Posting Journal - Functional Currency Only (GLPJ01)

DDI Student Name

Page 4

Batch-Entry/ Trans. Date	Period/ Source Code	Year/ Reference	Entry Date/ Description	Account Number	Debits	Credits
4/30/2010	GL-CD	CK 0018	Software Depot SD334488	2010	1,725.00	
4/30/2010	GL-CD	CK 0018	Software Depot SD334488	1000		1,725.00
				Entry Total:	1,725.00	1,725.00
				Posted Total:	73,485.40	73,485.40

22 entries printed
1 posting sequence printed

Figure 10-7 shows you the printed G/L Posting Journal. The date and time that the batch was printed appears in the upper-left corner of the page. The name of the company appears at the top of each page, centred between the date and page number. The name of the report, G/L Posting Journal, appears below the date and time. The next two lines display the posting sequence and the sorting sequence you chose.

The G/L Posting Journal arranges the transactions by date. It shows the Period and Source Code, Year and Reference, Entry Data Description, Account Numbers to which the entries are posted, and the Debit and Credits. The end of the G/L Posting Journal also gives the hash totals for the debit and credit columns.

You can reprint journals as often as necessary, until you clear the file. Once printing is finished, ensure that you have a clear copy of the report, then file it with other audit trail reports.

- ❑ Click: **Close** Close to return to the G/ L Reports window

PRINTING A SOURCE JOURNAL

Source journals list the details of posted transactions for the source codes that you included in the source journal definition.

❑ DClick: the **Source Journal** icon on the G/L Reports window

JOURNAL SELECTION PAGE

The Journal Selection page of the G/L Source Journal Report notebook will appear as shown in Figure 10-8.

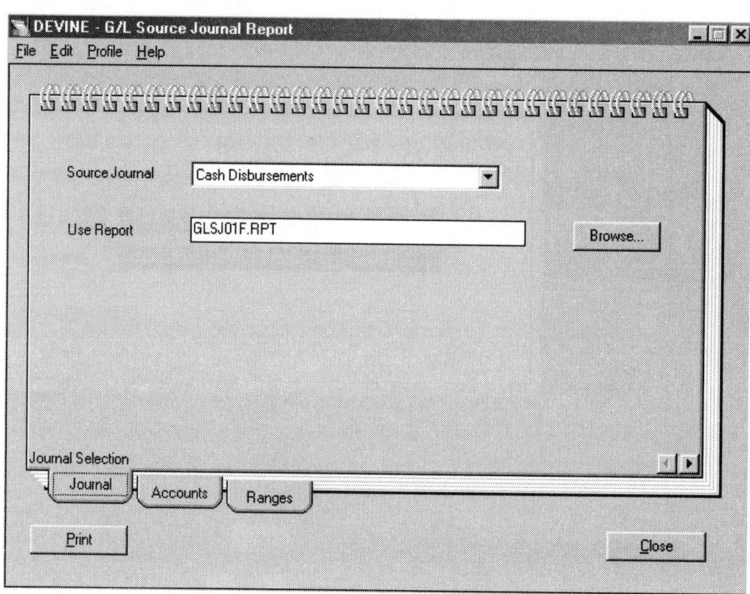

FIGURE 10-8
Journal Selection Page

The G/L Source Journal notebook contains three pages. The Journal Selection page is used to select the journal to be printed.

❑ Click: the **list tool** for Source Journal

The list box will display the names of the Source Journals that have been defined for Devine Designs Inc.

❑ Select: **Cash Receipts Journal**

ACCOUNT SELECTION PAGE

❑ Click: the **Accounts** tab at the bottom of the notebook page

The Account Selection page will appear as shown in Figure 10-9.

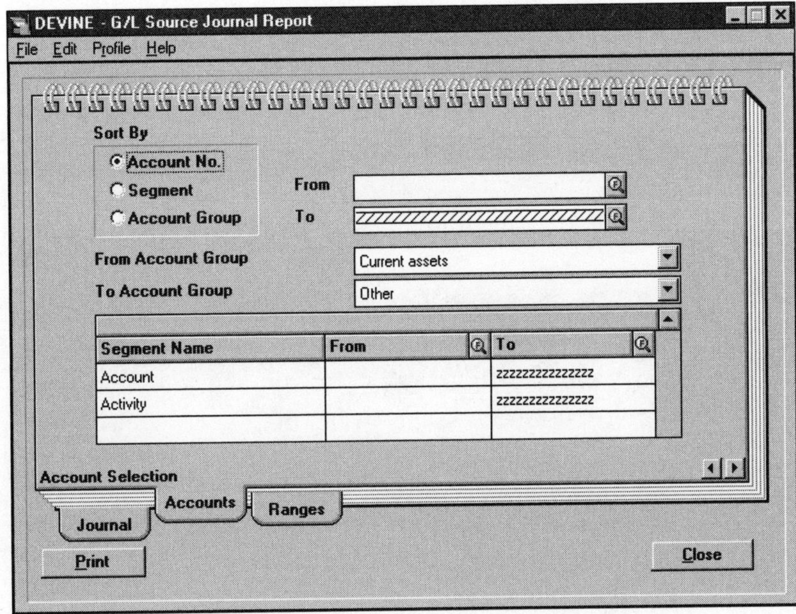

FIGURE 10-9
Account Selection Page

The defaults displayed on the Account Selection page will print all accounts in all account groups sorted by account number.

Sort By

You can print the report in order of account number, segment, or account group. Devine Designs Inc. prints in account number order.

- ❑ Ensure that the Account No. Option is active.

Account Range

The From and To text boxes identify the range of General Ledger account numbers you want included in the report. A blank From text box and a To text box full of multiple copies of the letter Z include all the ledger accounts in the report.

Account Group Range

The From Account Group and To Account Group list boxes are used when Account Group has been selected as the Sort By option. Use these list boxes to identify the range of General Ledger account groupings you want to include in the report. The default is to print all account groups.

Segment Name Table

This table is used when Segment has been selected as the Sort By option.

Select Ranges Page

- ❑ Click: the **Ranges** tab at the bottom of the notebook page

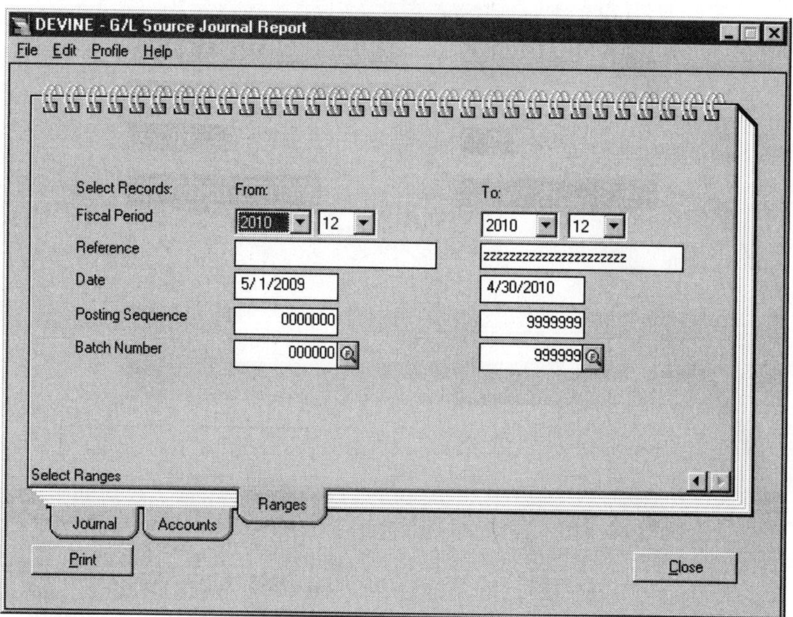

FIGURE 10-10 G/L Source Journal Report Window

The Select Ranges page (Figure 10-10) is used to specify the ranges of fiscal periods, references, dates, posting sequences, batch numbers, and, if you have a multicurrency ledger, source currencies.

The defaults displayed print the full range for each category for the current period of the current fiscal year. Devine Designs Inc. has posted transactions in both period 1 and period 12.

- ❑ Click: the **list tool** for period in the From column
- ❑ Select: **1**
- ❑ Print: the **Source Journal Report** for the General Journal

Once the report is printed, ACCPAC for Windows Small Business Series returns to the G/L Source Journal report.

TIP
Use the Source Journal list box on the Journal Selection page.

YOUR TURN

- ❑ Print the four other Source Journal Reports.
- ❑ Close: the **G/L Source Journal Report** notebook

PRINTING THE GENERAL LEDGER

❑ DClick: the **G/L Transactions Listing** icon [G/L Transactio...] on the G/L Reports window

The G/L Transactions Listing window will appear as shown in Figure 10-11.

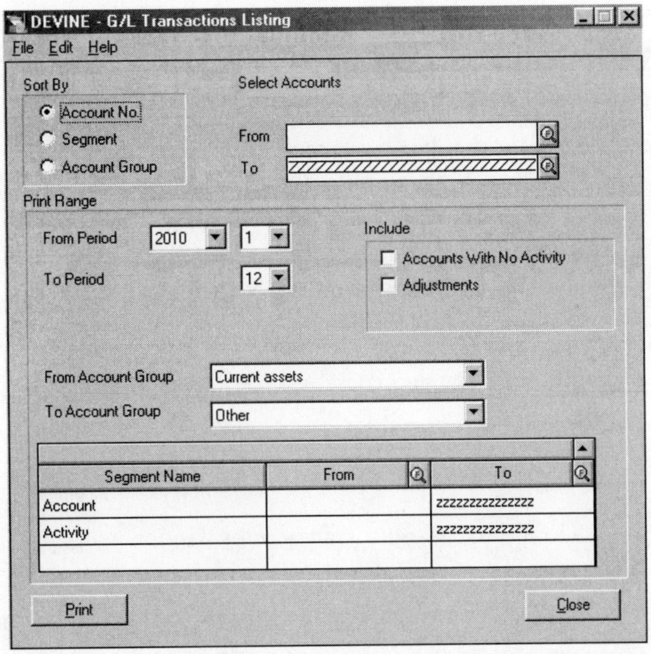

FIGURE 10-11
G/L Transactions Listing Window

The upper area of the G/L Transactions Listing window allows you to set the range of accounts to be printed and the order in which they print. The default is to print the full range of account numbers. You can change the Sort By field to specify sorting by segment or account group.

In the lower area, you can set options that further control the information to be printed. If you want to include all accounts, even if no transactions were posted to them in the reporting period, select Include Accounts With No Activity. Devine Designs Inc. has decided not to print inactive accounts.

❑ Ensure that the **Include Accounts With No Activity** check box is unselected.

Devine Designs Inc. has not posted adjustments to the adjustment period.

❑ Ensure that the **Adjustments** check box is unselected.

The three Period list boxes allow you to select the year and range of fiscal periods for the report. The default should be for year 2010 and periods 1 to 12.

❑ Ensure that year **2010** and periods **1** to **12** have been selected.

❑ Click: **Print** [Print]

❑ Click: **OK** [OK]

Comments do not appear in this report. Information about each detail includes the batch entry number, posting entry number, source code, descriptive and reference text, and the debit or credit amount. This report allows you to trace transactions to the batch listings and posting journals for audit purposes.

❑ Close: the **G/L Transactions Listing** window

CONSOLIDATE POSTED TRANSACTIONS

> **TIP**
> Always back up your data files before consolidating the posted entries.

You do not want the detailed entry information to accumulate in the General Ledger accounts indefinitely since this wastes storage space on your disk, slows down processing, and wastes paper by making reports longer. You can combine many transaction details into a single line using the Consolidate Posted Transactions function. Consolidate the posted transactions after printing the Source Journals.

❑ DClick: the **G/L Periodic Processing** icon [G/L Periodic Processing] in the General Ledger window

❑ DClick: the **Consolidate Posted Trans.** icon [Consolidate Posted Trans.]

The G/L Consolidate Posted Transactions window will appear as shown in Figure 10-12.

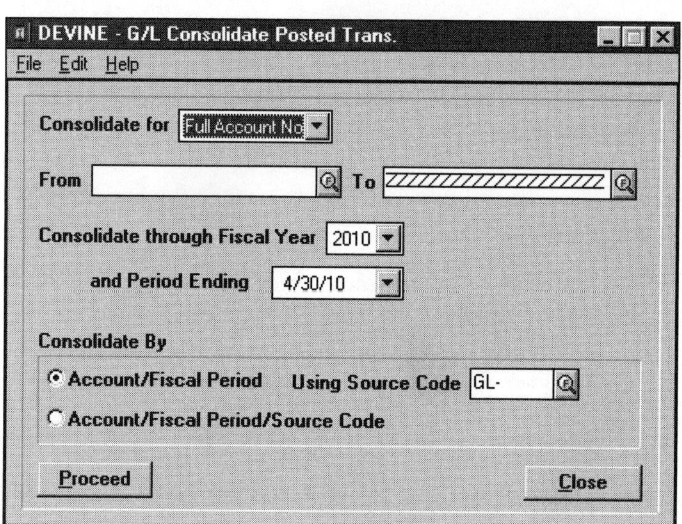

FIGURE 10-12
G/L Consolidate Posted Transactions Window

The defaults shown on the G/L Consolidate Posted Transactions window combine the transactions for all accounts up to and including the current fiscal period. For each account, the transactions are combined by Account and Fiscal period, using the Source Code you identify.

When you consolidate a group of transactions, the individual details are combined into a single number and cannot be listed on source journals or on the G/L Transactions Listing. The posting entry numbers and batch entry numbers associated with details are removed, the batch and entry numbers are identified as CNSLD, and the description and reference fields are set to Consolidated.

You can consolidate when posting by using the Post to Account in Consolidated option on the Detail page of the G/L Chart of Accounts notebook to identify the accounts you want to consolidate when you post batches. This could lead to difficulty in tracing transactions, however, so it is not suggested.

- ❑ Click: the **Finder** for the Using Source Code text box
- ❑ Select: **GL CO G/L Consolidated Entry**
- ❑ Click: **Proceed** Proceed

ACCPAC will display an information message, "Consolidation Completed."

- ❑ Click: **OK** OK
- ❑ Close: the **G/L Consolidate Posted Trans.** window
- ❑ Print the G/L Transactions Listing again.

Compare the new General Ledger Listing with that printed earlier. Note the consolidated postings and the reduced number of transactions printed. For the few transactions that have been posted for Devine Designs Inc., the benefits of consolidation are not significant. For companies recording hundreds of transactions each period, however, the benefits of consolidating the posted transactions are great.

- ❑ Exit: **ACCPAC**
- ❑ Back up your data files.

REVIEW QUESTIONS

1. What is the purpose of the Batch Status report?
2. Is it possible to post a transaction batch twice? What will happen if you try?
3. What types of error is an accounting program unable to prevent? Give several examples.
4. What is the purpose of provisional posting?
5. Describe a good control system that would allow you to review transactions before posting them to the General Ledger.
6. How does ACCPAC Small Business Series for Windows handle errors when they are identified?
7. What is the purpose of the Consolidate Posted Transactions function?

Exercise

- ❑ Sign on to your company as the system administrator using 04/30/10 as the Session Date.
- ❑ Set the batch status to **Ready to Post**
- ❑ Print: the **Batch Status Report**
- ❑ Post: the **General Ledger batches**
- ❑ Print: the **Posting Journal**
- ❑ Print: the **Source Journals**
- ❑ Print: the **General Ledger Transactions Listing**
- ❑ Exit: **ACCPAC**

CHAPTER 11

FINANCIAL REPORTS

In this chapter, you will use the data that you posted to the General Ledger in Chapter 10 to produce financial statements.

ACCPAC for Windows allows you to create financial statements for your company based on predefined specifications, or you can design your own financial reports. You can use the Statement Designer to modify existing reports and create new ones. Devine Designs Inc. will use the defined specifications that are supplied with ACCPAC.

FINANCIAL REPORTER

The Financial Reporter comes with two sets of six standard financial statements. Each statement is printed using an Excel spreadsheet. Devine Designs Inc. will use the "Quik" statements rather than the European design statements.

These six financial statements and their filenames are:

- Quikbal1 - Single Column Balance Sheet
- Quikbal2 - Comparative Balance Sheet (Current Year/Previous Year)

These statements depend on the proper assignment of account groups. If you did not assign account groups to the General Ledger accounts, you cannot use these statements.

- Quikbal3 - Comparative Balance Sheet (Current Period/Previous Period)
- Quikinc1 - Single Column Income Statement
- Quikinc2 - Comparative Income Statement (Current YTD/Last YTD)
- Quikinc3 - Comparative Income Statement (Current YTD/Budget YTD)

The standard financial specifications are located in the ENG subdirectory of the General Ledger program directory.

❑ Sign on to Devine Designs Inc. as the system administrator, using April 30, 2010 as the Session Date.

❑ DClick: the **Financial Reporter** icon [Financial Reporter] on the General Ledger window

The Financial Reporter icons will appear as shown in Figure 11-1.

FIGURE 11-1 Financial Reporter Icons

The Statement Designer icon is used to start Excel with the Financial Reporter add-in. You would use this icon to modify an existing specification or to create a new specification, but not to print financial reports using specifications that have already been created.

❑ DClick: the **Print Financial Statements** icon 

FIGURE 11-2
Financial Statements Window

DEVINE - Financial Statements

File Edit Help

Statement Name [ ] Browse...

Fiscal Option: Year 2010; Period 12
Report Type: Actual; Provisional
Report As: Separate; Consolidated
Include: Report Options; Audit Information; Formulas

Sort by: Account No.; Segment; Account Group
Account
From
To ZZZZ

Select Accounts
From Account Group: Current assets
To Account Group: Other

Segment Name	From	To	Report As
Activity		ZZ	Consolidated

Print Close

The Financial Statements window (Figure 11-2) allows you to select the report you want and to set printing criteria. As you print the Income Statement for Devine Designs Inc., each option will be reviewed.

INCOME STATEMENTS

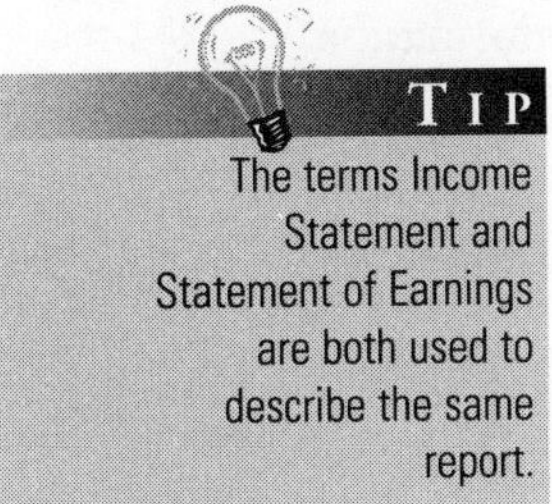

TIP
The terms Income Statement and Statement of Earnings are both used to describe the same report.

An Income Statement summarizes the results of a company's activity over a period of time. Income Statements are typically reported for a number of periods ending at a specific date.

PRINTING THE INCOME STATEMENT

Devine Designs Inc. will print a single column Income Statement.

Statement Name

In the Statement Name text box, enter the path to the statement specification file that you wish to use. Rather than trying to memorize the pathname, use the browse button.

- ❑ Click: **Browse** Browse...

ACCPAC will open a dialog box that allows you to select the financial statement file that you wish to use.

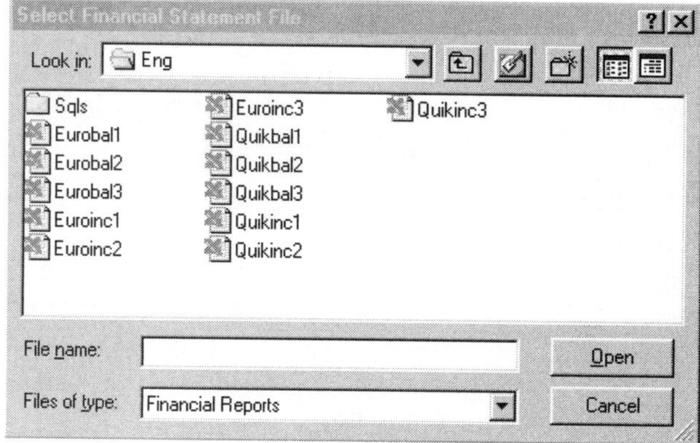

FIGURE 11-3
Select Financial Statement File Dialog Box

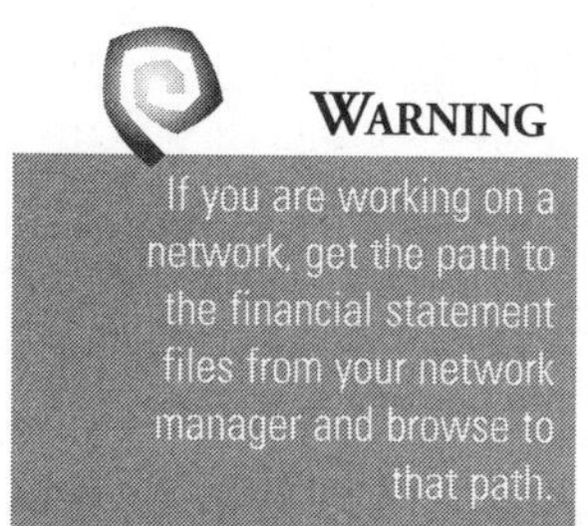

WARNING

If you are working on a network, get the path to the financial statement files from your network manager and browse to that path.

The default path to the financial statement files is C:\program Files\Accpac\G141a\Eng. If necessary, ensure that the Eng folder is open.

The Select Financial Statement File box should list the financial statement files as shown in Figure 11-3.

The filename for the single column Income Statement is Quikinc1.xls

- ❑ DClick: **Quikinc1.xls** on the file name scroll box

TIP

If you do not want to see the Excel file names, select SCW Reports in the List files of type list box.

Fiscal Option

The Fiscal Option area of this window allows you to select the fiscal year and period for your statement. The defaults displayed are for the current year and period as entered as the Session Date.

Devine Designs Inc. wants to print the Income Statement for the 12 periods of fiscal year 2010. If necessary, use the list tools and select the proper information.

Report Type

You can print two types of reports. The Actual Report Type includes data permanently posted to the General Ledger, but not data that have been provisionally posted. The Provisional Report Type includes provisionally posted data.

Devine Designs Inc. wants to print an Actual Income Statement. If necessary, click the radio button for Actual to activate it.

Report As

The Report As area has only one active option, Consolidated. The Separate option becomes available if you select Segment in the Sort By area and then select a segment other than the account segment. You could then activate Separate in the Report As area. This option is used, for example, to print divisional reports for a company that has structured its chart of accounts with a division segment.

Devine Designs Inc. wants to print a Consolidated Income Statement.

Include

Only one of the three check boxes in this area should be active. The Audit Information and Formulas options depend on special codes entered in the financial statement specifications. The standard specifications do not use these codes.

If you select Report Options, the first page printed is a report of the options that you select on this window. This report becomes part of your audit trail.

❑ Click: the **Report Options** check box

Sort By

The selections that you make in the Sort By area determine the order in which data is printed in your report.

If you added accounts in the Chart of Accounts in order of the default account group order, select Account No. to print your report. The Segment and Account Group options allow you to print a report based on one segment (i.e., a division) or part of a report based on a range of account groups.

Devine Designs Inc. entered account numbers in a numerical sequence that agrees with the order of account groups used by ACCPAC.

❑ Ensure that the radio button for **Account No.** is active.

Select Accounts

Use this area only if you wish to print partial statements based on accounts assigned to account groups. The default settings should select Current Assets as the From Account Group and Other as the To Account Group.

❑ Click: **Print** [Print] on the Financial Statements window

❑ Click: **OK** [OK] on the Print dialog box

When you use an Excel Worksheet containing macros, Excel may display a warning (Figure 11-4) that the macros may contain viruses.

FIGURE 11-4
Microsoft Excel Macro Warning

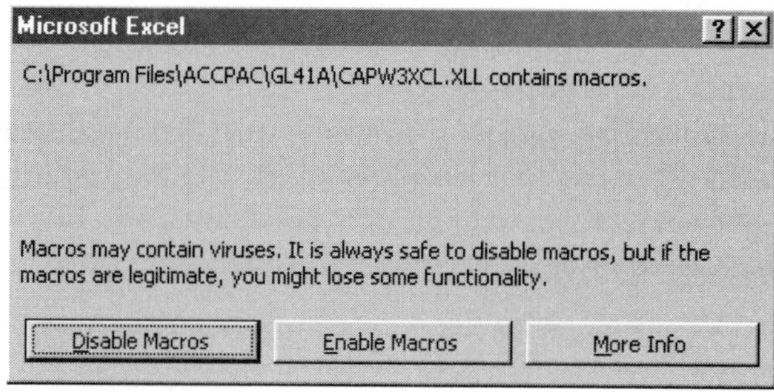

If your screen displays a message similar to that shown in Figure 11-4, you should click the **Enable Macros** button.

As ACCPAC prepares your report for printing, you can see the spreadsheet in the background. The first printed page reports the options selected on the Financial Statements window. The second page is the single column Income Statement for Devine Designs Inc. for the period ending April 30, 2010.

FIGURE 11-5
Statement of Earnings

Sheet1

DDI Student Name
Statement of Earnings
For The Year Ending April 30, 2010

Unaudited

	Current YTD
Revenue:	
Sales	5,000.00
	5,000.00
Cost of sales:	
	0.00
Gross profit	5,000.00
Costs and expenses:	
Advertising Expense	2,160.00
Communication Expense	339.12
Computer Rent	7,560.00
Internet Services Expense	135.00
Office Rent Expense	2,500.00
Salary Expense	4,500.00
	17,194.12
Earnings (loss) from operations	(12,194.12)
Other income and expenses:	
	0.00
Earnings (loss) before income taxes	(12,194.12)
Provision for income taxes:	
	0.00
Net earnings (loss) for period	(12,194.12)

Statement of Earnings Analysis

On the printed Statement of Earnings (Figure 11-5), note that the names of all income-related account groups are printed, but within each account group, only those accounts with a non-zero balance are printed. As a result, the detail lines for Cost of sales, Other income and expenses, and Provision for income taxes are blank, but the subtotals show 0.00.

For Revenue and Costs and expenses, you can see the accounts with non-zero balances. As no supplies expenses or depreciation expenses have been posted to the General Ledger, these accounts do not appear in the Income Statement.

Preparing an Income Statement, or a Statement of Earnings, calculates the Earnings (loss) before income taxes on the report. This amount less the provision for income taxes is temporarily transferred to the Profit (loss) for period line in the shareholder's equity section of the Balance Sheet.

While reviewing the Statement of Earnings, Eric notices several problems that should be corrected before closing the books and starting a new fiscal year. The first problem is that the advertising expense of $2,160.00 should be recorded as a prepaid expense because the advertising will not occur until the new fiscal year. The second problem is that there are no expense items for depreciation. Both of these problems will be cleared up in Chapter 12, before Devine Designs Inc. starts a new fiscal year.

YOUR TURN

TIP
To save paper and printing time, turn off the Reports Options in the Include area of the Financial Statements window.

Eric wants to see what the other two Statements of Earnings look like.

- ❑ Print: **Quikinc2.xls**, the Comparative Income Statement (Current Year/Last Year)
- ❑ Print: **Quikinc3.xls**, the Comparative Income Statement (Current YTD/Budget YTD)

While reviewing these printed statements, Eric realizes that in the new fiscal year, a year-to-year comparison will not be meaningful because Devine Designs Inc. was not active for the first 11 periods of fiscal 2010.

John suggested that the comparison with budgets offered by Quikinc3 would be a useful management tool in the new fiscal year. Eric and Leslie agreed and decided to enter budget information in the new fiscal year. Budget information for the new fiscal year will be entered in Chapter 13.

Balance Sheet

A Balance Sheet is like a freeze-frame picture of a company. The Balance Sheet reports the company's assets and liabilities at a particular instant in time.

PRINTING A BALANCE SHEET

Select the same options for printing a Balance Sheet as you selected for printing the matching Income Statement. Devine Designs Inc. wants to print a single column Balance Sheet as of the end of period 12 for fiscal year 2010.

❑ Click: **Browse** [Browse...] on the Financial Statements window

The Select Financial Statements File dialog box will appear as shown in Figure 11-3.

❑ DClick: **Quikbal1.xls**

The information displayed should print a Balance Sheet as of the end of period 12, 2010. The printed statement will be an actual report in a consolidated format sorted by account number. If necessary, change the options selected on the Financial Statements window to specify this report.

❑ Click: **Print** [Print]

❑ Click **OK** on the Print dialog box

❑ Click **Enable Macros** [Enable Macros]

While ACCPAC prepares the report for printing, the actual spreadsheet will appear in the background.

BALANCE SHEET ANALYSIS

The Balance Sheet is printed in two sections, each starting on a new page. These two sections are combined (see Figure 11-6).

FIGURE 11-6
Single Column Balance Sheet

Sheet1

DDI Student Name

Balance Sheet
As At April 30, 2010

Unaudited

ASSETS

Current assets:	
Bank First Bank Corp.	6,812.10
Office Supplies	1,087.56
Total current assets	7,899.66
Fixed assets:	
Fixtures & Furniture	4,320.00
Software	4,320.00
	8,640.00
Other assets:	
Organization Costs	725.00
	725.00
	17,264.66

Sheet1

LIABILITY AND SHAREHOLDER'S EQUITY

Current liabilities:	
Retail Sales Tax Payable	400.00
G.S.T V.A.T. Payable	350.00
G.S.T V.A.T. Recoverable	(1,291.22)
Total current liabilities	(541.22)
Long term liabilities:	
	0.00
Shareholder's equity:	
Common Stock	30,000.00
Profit (loss) for period	(12,194.12)
Total shareholder's equity	17,805.88
	17,264.66

In the ASSETS portion of the Balance Sheet, only account groups and accounts with a non-zero balance are printed.

In the LIABILITY AND SHAREHOLDER'S EQUITY portion, there are two things to note. The "Long-term liabilities" heading is printed but no amount is shown, as Devine Designs Inc. does not have any long-term liabilities. The second thing to note is that the "Profit (loss) for period" has been transferred to the Balance Sheet calculations.

YOUR TURN

Eric wants to see the format of the other Income Statements to see if they would be useful in the next fiscal year.

- ❑ Print: statement **Quikbal2** comparing the current year to the prior year's balances
- ❑ Print: statement **Quikbal3** comparing the current year to the budget
- ❑ Close: the **Financial Statements** window
- ❑ Exit: **ACCPAC**

REVIEW QUESTION

1. Describe the types of Income Statements and Balance Sheets available from the Financial Reporter icon.

EXERCISE

- ❑ Sign on to your company as the system administrator using 04/30/10 as the Session Date.
- ❑ Print all six versions of the financial statements.
- ❑ Exit: **ACCPAC**

CHAPTER 12

YEAR END

In this chapter, you will work through a typical year-end closing of the General Ledger. Before closing the accounts, you will print a Trial Balance. After closing the accounts, you will prepare a Post Closing Trial Balance, an opening Income Statement, and a Balance Sheet showing the starting position for the new fiscal year. In the new fiscal year, you will post the finalized adjustments to the previous fiscal year.

Make permanent copies of your data files before closing the accounts at year-end. In addition to using these files to print provisional financial statements, post the auditor's finalized adjustments to these files and then print the financial statements. A business would normally keep several identical copies of these files in different locations as a safety precaution.

BATCH STATUS REPORT

You must print a Batch Status Report and clear all posted and deleted batches before completing the year-end closing procedures. The Batch Status Report also allows you to verify that all batches have been posted to the General Ledger.

- ❑ Sign on to Devine Designs Inc. as the system administrator using April 30, 2010 as the Session Date.
- ❑ DClick: the **G/L Reports** icon [G/L Reports] on the General Ledger desktop
- ❑ DClick: the **Batch Status** icon [Batch Status]

The G/L Batch Status Report window will appear as shown in Figure 12-1.

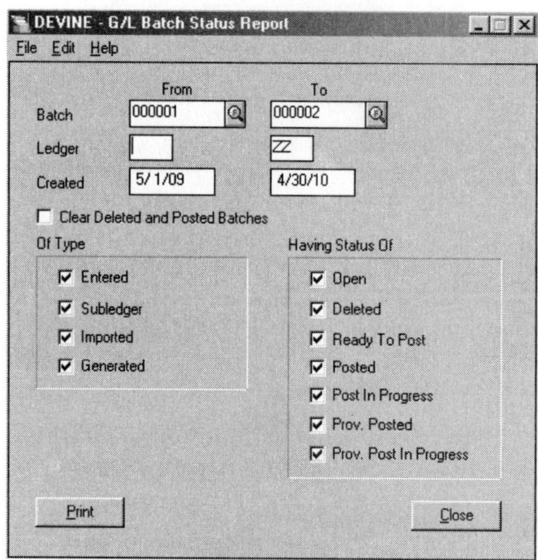

FIGURE 12-1
G/L Batch Status Report Window

TIP
If empty batches have not been posted, delete them using the Batch List icon on the General Ledger window.

The options available in this window were explained in Chapter 10.

- ❑ Click: the Finder for the To field to verify that all batches are included in your report

Before closing the fiscal year, clear all deleted and posted batches.

- ❑ Click: the **Clear Deleted and Posted Batches** check box to activate it
- ❑ Print: the **G/L Batch Status Report**

Verify that all batches have either been Posted or Deleted. The total Debits and Credits columns should balance at 73,485.40. Your totals may be larger if you corrected posted transaction recording errors by reversing the error and entering the correct transaction information. If there are Open or Printed batches, either post or delete these batches. If necessary, print and clear the new posting journals, then print the Batch Status report again.

You will see a message on your screen detailing the number of batches that have been removed.

- ❑ Click: **OK** [OK]
- ❑ Close: the **G/L Batch Status Report** window

CLEARING THE POSTING JOURNALS

Before closing the accounts, verify that all posting journals have been printed and cleared.

❑ DClick: the **Posting Journal** icon  on the G/L Reports window

FIGURE 12-2
G/L Posting Journals Window

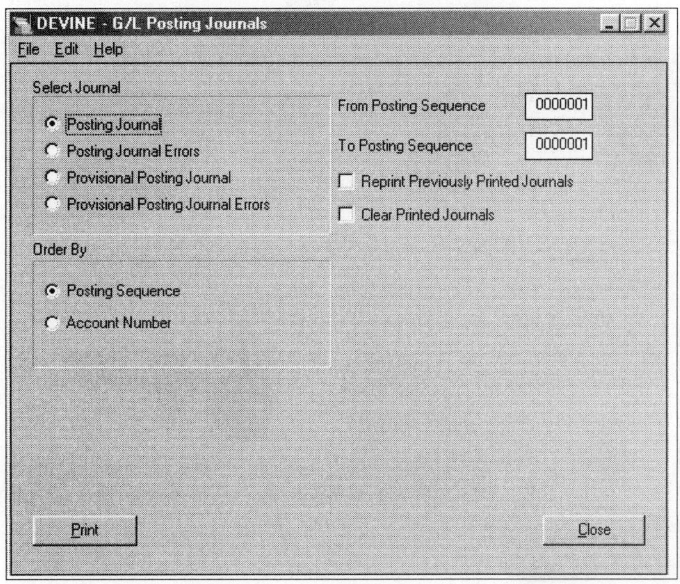

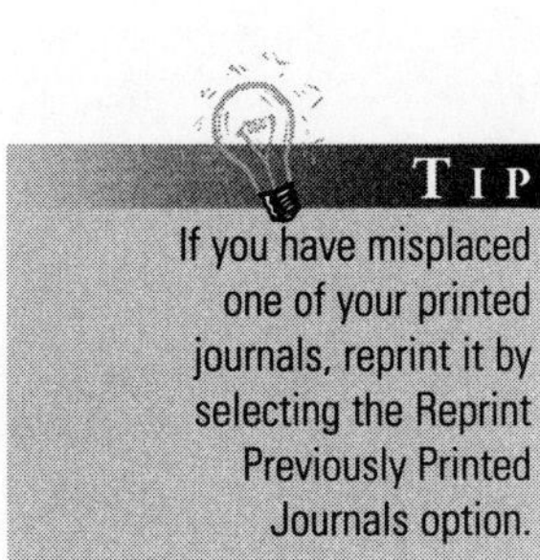

TIP
If you have misplaced one of your printed journals, reprint it by selecting the Reprint Previously Printed Journals option.

The components of the G/L Posting Journals window (Figure 12-2) were discussed in Chapter 10.

❑ Click: the **Clear Printed Journals** check box to activate it

❑ Click: **Print** [Print]

❑ Click: **OK** [OK]

If there are any unprinted journals, ACCPAC will print them and then clear all the printed journals. If all journals had been printed previously, ACCPAC will print a blank page and then clear the printed journals.

❑ Close: the **G/L Posting Journals** window

TRIAL BALANCE

Print the General Ledger Trial Balance worksheet before closing the books, since you will transfer the balances from the temporary equity accounts to retained earnings upon closing. ACCPAC allows you to print the Closing General Ledger Trial Balance in a worksheet format with columns for the auditor's adjusting entries, or in a report format. Normally, an auditor's adjustments would be returned a few months after the year-end, so you would enter these transactions through the Journal Entry window, making certain that the correct date and period are used so that the entries appear in the correct year. An identical batch containing the auditor's adjustments must also be posted to your backup copies of the previous year's archive files.

❑ DClick: the **Trial Balance** icon on the G/L Reports window

The G/L Trial Balance Report window will appear, as shown in Figure 12-3.

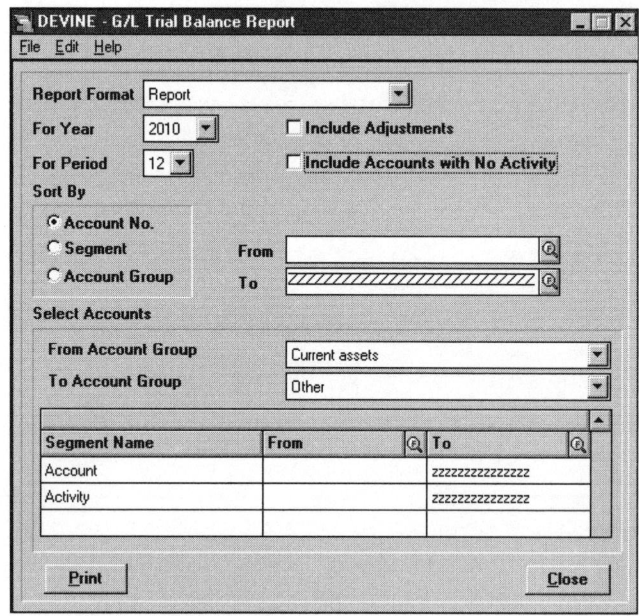

FIGURE 12-3
G/L Trial Balance Report Window

The default options print all of the accounts sequentially and include the balances at the end of the current period. Devine Designs Inc. prints both the report and worksheet formats, including accounts with zero balances.

❑ Click: the **list tool** for Report Format

In the Report Format, the balances of the accounts print out in a traditional trial balance format with all the balances listed as either a debit or a credit and column headings repeated at the top of each page. In a worksheet format, the report prints with debits and credits columns for Trial Balance, Adjustments, Income Statement, and Balance Sheet. Three additional options are available if batches have been provisionally posted.

❑ Select: **Report** as the Report Format
❑ Click: the **Include Accounts with No Activity** check box
❑ Print: the **Trial Balance**

Once the Trial Balance has finished printing, the screen will return to the G/L Trial Balance Report window.

❑ Print: the **Trial Balance** in worksheet format
❑ Close: the **G/L Trial Balance Report** window

Creating a New Fiscal Calendar

Before you create a new fiscal year, you have to create a fiscal calendar for the next year using the Common Services Fiscal Calendar window.

❑ DClick: the **Fiscal Calendar** icon on the Common Services window

The Fiscal Calendar window will appear as shown in Figure 12-4, displaying information for the current year.

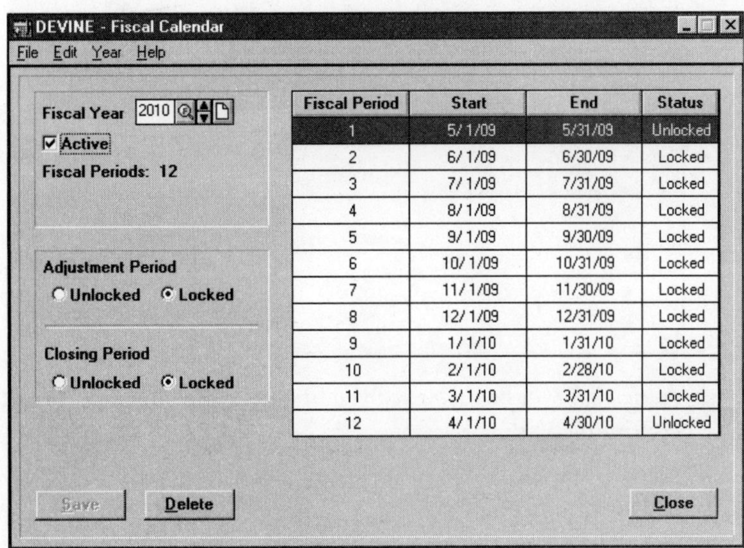

FIGURE 12-4
Fiscal Calendar Window

❑ Click: the **New Document** icon for the Fiscal Year text box

ACCPAC automatically increases the year by one for each fiscal period but the status for each period is unchanged.

❑ Click: **Add**

Notice that the Adjustment and Closing Periods are locked. Both must be unlocked to continue with closing the fiscal year.

❑ Click: the **back** button for Fiscal Year to display 2010
❑ Click: the **Unlocked** option button for Adjustment Period
❑ Click: the **Unlocked** option button for Closing Period
❑ Click: **Save**
❑ Close: the **Fiscal Calendar** window
❑ Exit: **ACCPAC**
❑ Back up your data files using the instructions in Chapter 6.

CREATING THE NEW YEAR

- ❑ Sign on to Devine Designs Inc. as the system administrator using April 30, 2010 as the Session Date.
- ❑ Open: the **Periodic Processing** window
- ❑ DClick: **G/L Periodic Processing** from the General Ledger window
- ❑ DClick: the **Create New Year** icon

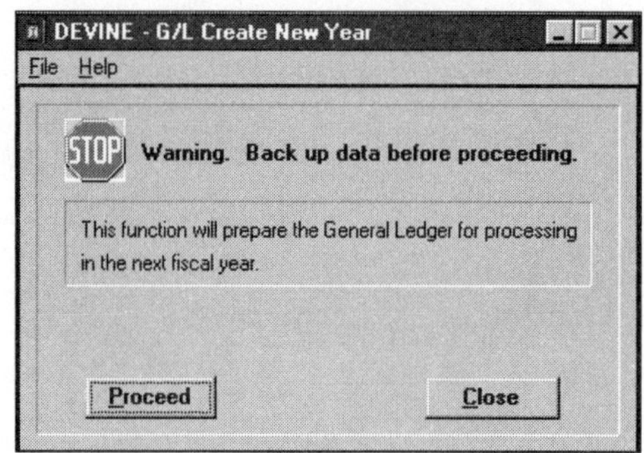

FIGURE 12-5
G/L Create New Year Warning Message

A message will be displayed (Figure 12-5) warning you to back up the data files before continuing with the Create New Year function. Whenever a program suggests that you make a backup before proceeding, it is wise to do so since failure to comply could result in the loss of important data. If you did not make a backup at the end of the previous section of this chapter, do so now.

The Create New Year window creates and posts a batch of transactions to close the temporary proprietorship accounts and enter the opening account balances for the new fiscal year. The opening balances for the Balance Sheet accounts will remain the same as the prior year's closing balances, but the income and expense accounts will have the opening balances reduced to zero. The fiscal year will be changed to the next year.

You may continue to post transactions to the year you have just closed. Whenever you do so, the General Ledger will create all appropriate closing entries to update the retained earnings.

- ❑ Click: **Proceed**

The process takes only a few seconds. Once it is complete, the message "Posting Sequence 2 completed" appears. Note that this is message 1 of 2.

- ❑ Click: **Next**

The second message informs you that "New year 2011 has been created."

- ❑ Click: **OK**
- ❑ Close: the **G/L Create New Year** window

Printing and Clearing the Closing Posting Journal

The Create New Year function creates and posts entries closing the Income Statement accounts to the retained earnings account. Print and clear the posting journal before proceeding.

- ❑ Open: the **G/L Reports** window
- ❑ DClick: the **Posting Journal** icon
- ❑ Click: the **Clear Printed Journals** check box
- ❑ Print: the **Posting Journal**

Review the printed Posting Journal. All entries should be in period 15, a special closing period created by ACCPAC. The source code for each entry should be GL-CL and the posted total should be 22,194.12.

- ❑ Close: the **G/L Posting Journals** window

Period End Maintenance

The final task in creating the new fiscal year for Devine Designs Inc. is to reset the batch and posting sequence number to 1.

- ❑ Open: the **G/L Periodic Processing** window on the General Ledger window
- ❑ DClick: the **Period End Maintenance** icon on the G/L Periodic Processing window

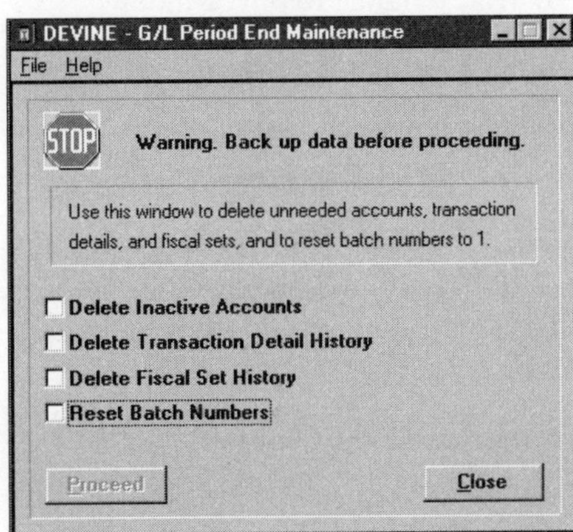

FIGURE 12-6
G/L Period End Maintenance Window

When he sees the G/L Period End Maintenance window (Figure 12-6), Eric realizes that there are inactive accounts in the Devine Designs Inc. Chart of Accounts. He does not delete them, however, as he expects to use most of them in the new fiscal year.

As this is only the start of the second fiscal year, it is not necessary to delete transaction detail or fiscal set history.

Eric has decided to reset the batch and posting sequence numbers to 1.

- ❑ Click: the **Reset Batch Numbers** check box
- ❑ Click: **Proceed** Proceed
- ❑ Close: the **G/L Period End Maintenance** window
- ❑ Exit: **ACCPAC**

Preparing Opening Financial Statements

After you have closed the General Ledger for the year, confirm that the opening Income Statement figures are all zeros and that the new opening Balance Sheet exactly reflects the General Ledger.

❑ Sign on to Devine Designs Inc. as the system administrator using May 1, 2010 as the Session Date.

- ❑ DClick: the **G/L Reports** icon G/L Reports on the General Ledger window
- ❑ DClick: the **Trial Balance** icon Trial Balance
- ❑ Print: the **G/L Trial Balance Report** for year 2011, period 1 in report format, and include all accounts

The Income Statement account opening balances should be zero. Make a note on the printout that the printout is an opening Trial Balance as of May 1, 2010.

- ❑ Close: the **G/L Trial Balance Report** window

Print the opening Income Statements and Balance Sheets.

- ❑ Open: the **Financial Reporter** window
- ❑ Open: the **Print Financial Statements** window
- ❑ Print: the **Balance Sheet Quickbal1**

The figures on the Balance Sheet should be the same as on the Balance Sheet you printed in Chapter 11. Make a note on the printed report that the report is an Opening Balance Sheet as of May 1, 2010.

- ❑ Print: the **Income Statement Quikinc1**

All figures on the Income Statement should be zeros, proving the clearing of the accounts for the beginning of the year. Make a note on the printout to this effect and date it May 1, 2010.

- ❑ Close: the **Financial Statements** window

Prior Year Adjustments

Eric has decided to process adjusting entries to properly record the advertising expense for May, June, and July as a prepaid expense, and to depreciate the office furniture and fixtures and the computer software.

- ❑ Open: the **Journal Entry** window found on the General Ledger window
- ❑ Create: a new **Batch**

ACCPAC should assign the batch the number 000001, with a default date of 5/1/10, period 1, year 2011.

- ❑ Enter: **year 2010, period 12 adjustmts** in the batch description text box

The first adjustment will be for the May, June, and July advertising that was recorded as a $2,160.00 debit to account 6000 Advertising Expense. The debit should have been recorded to account 1400 Prepaid Expenses. The reference should be ADJ-01.

- ❑ Enter: **error s/b dr to Prepaid Exps.** in the entry description text box
- ❑ Click: the **Period** list tool
- ❑ Scroll: to the bottom of the list box

Note that there are two additional periods available. CLS is period 15 and is used by ACCPAC for closing entries when creating a new fiscal year. ADJ is period 14 and is used for recording the auditors' final adjustments that cannot reasonably be charged to specific periods. The adjustment that you are entering can be charged directly to period 12.

- ❑ Select: **12**

This entry will be posted to the previous year, year 2010.

- ❑ Click: the **Year** list tool
- ❑ Select: **2010**
- ❑ Select: **GL-JE** as the Source

TIP
Use the last date in the period as the transaction date for adjusting entries.

1400	Prepaid Expenses	2,160.00	
6000	Advertising Expense		2,160.00

- ❑ Using the detail description and the comment line for documentation, add the adjusting entry.

Devine Designs Inc. estimates that the office furniture and fixtures will have a useful life of five years. Straight line depreciation over a 60-month period will be used. Make sure Period 12, 2010 is selected as the year.

6100	Depreciation Expense	72.00	
1720	Acc Dep - Fixtures & Furniture		72.00

- ❑ Add: the appropriate entry

Devine Designs Inc. estimates that software has an average useful life of 24 months and will use straight line depreciation. Make sure Period 12, 2010 is selected as the year.

6100	Depreciation Expense	180.00	
1740	Acc Dep - Software		180.00

- ❑ Add: the appropriate entry
- ❑ Print: the **Batch Listing**
- ❑ Post: the **Batch**
- ❑ Print & Clear: the **Posting Journal**
- ❑ Print: the single column **Income Statement** for the 12 periods ending April 30, 2010

Compare your printout to that printed in Chapter 11. Note that the Advertising Expense of $2,160.00 has been removed, while a Depreciation Expense of $252.00 has been added. The net loss for the period has been reduced to $10,286.12.

- ❑ Print: the single column **Balance Sheet** as at April 30, 2010

Compare your printout to that printed in Chapter 11. The $2,160.00 has been added as a prepaid expense, a current asset. The fixed assets now reflect the $252.00 charged to depreciation expense.

- ❑ Close: the **Financial Statements** window
- ❑ Exit: **ACCPAC**
- ❑ Back up your data files.

Review Questions

1. What is the purpose of closing a General Ledger at year-end?
2. Why is it important to make a permanent file copy of the General Ledger before closing the year's accounts?
3. What is the purpose of the G/L Posting Journal that is printed after you have finished closing the General Ledger?
4. What does the Create New Year function do?
5. What period number is allocated to the entries posted after the year-end that will be posted to the preceding year?
6. What is Period 15 used for?

EXERCISE

- ❑ Sign on to your company as the system administrator using 04/30/10 as the Session Date.
- ❑ Print: the **Batch Status Report**

If you have any error batches, or unposted batches, make the necessary adjustments and post them now.

- ❑ Clear: the **Deleted and Posted batches**
- ❑ Print the **Batch Status Report**
- ❑ Reprint
  & Clear: the **Posting Journal** (You should get a blank sheet.)
- ❑ Print: the **Trial Balance** in worksheet format
- ❑ Create: the **Fiscal Calendar** for 2011
- ❑ Create: the **new fiscal year**
- ❑ Print
  & Clear: the **Closing Posting Journal**
- ❑ Reset: the Batch Numbers.
- ❑ Print: an opening **Income Statement for period 1, year 2011**. Use the comparison to last YTD formats.
- ❑ Exit: **ACCPAC**

CHAPTER 13

ACCOUNT ACTIVITIES

The Account Activities window allows you to perform the normal housekeeping tasks associated with maintaining a General Ledger. It allows you to access the Account History Inquiry, Budget Maintenance, Transaction History, and Fiscal Set Comparison windows.

GETTING READY

- ❑ Sign on to Devine Designs Inc. as the system administrator using May 1, 2010 as the Session Date.
- ❑ DClick: the **G/L Account Activities** icon 

The G/L Account Activities window should contain the four icons shown in Figure 13-1.

FIGURE 13-1
G/L Account Activities Icons

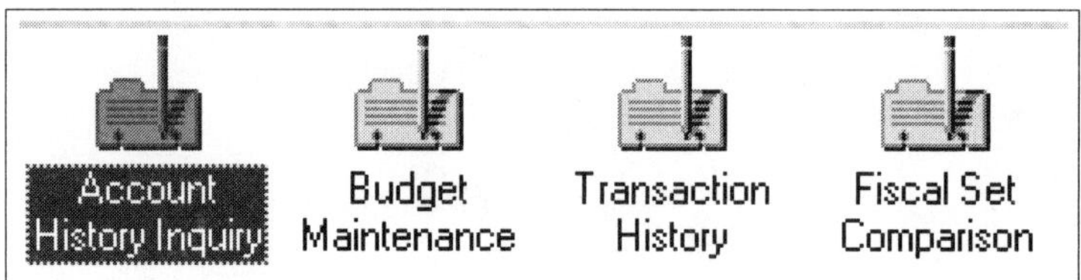

ACCOUNT HISTORY INQUIRY

The Account History Inquiry option allows you to look at a summary of a year's activity in an account. ACCPAC will maintain the account history for the number of years you specified when you set the Keep Years of Fiscal Sets field in the G/L Options window.

❑ DClick: the **Account History Inquiry** icon 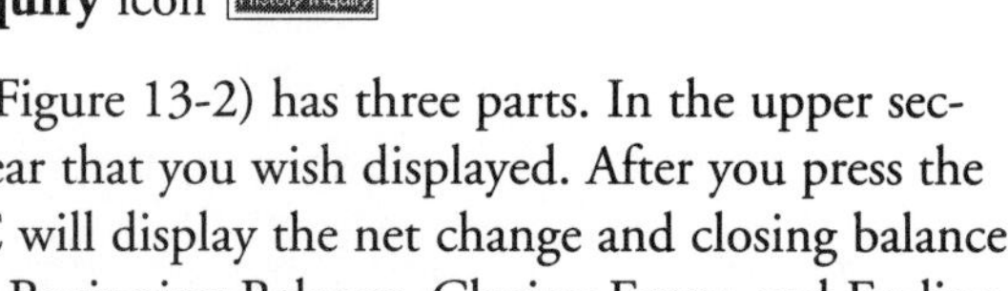

The Account History Inquiry window (Figure 13-2) has three parts. In the upper section, you select the account and fiscal year that you wish displayed. After you press the GO button (a green triangle), ACCPAC will display the net change and closing balance for each period in the central table. The Beginning Balance, Closing Entry, and Ending Balance for the year are displayed along the bottom of the window.

FIGURE 13-2
G/L Account History Inquiry Window

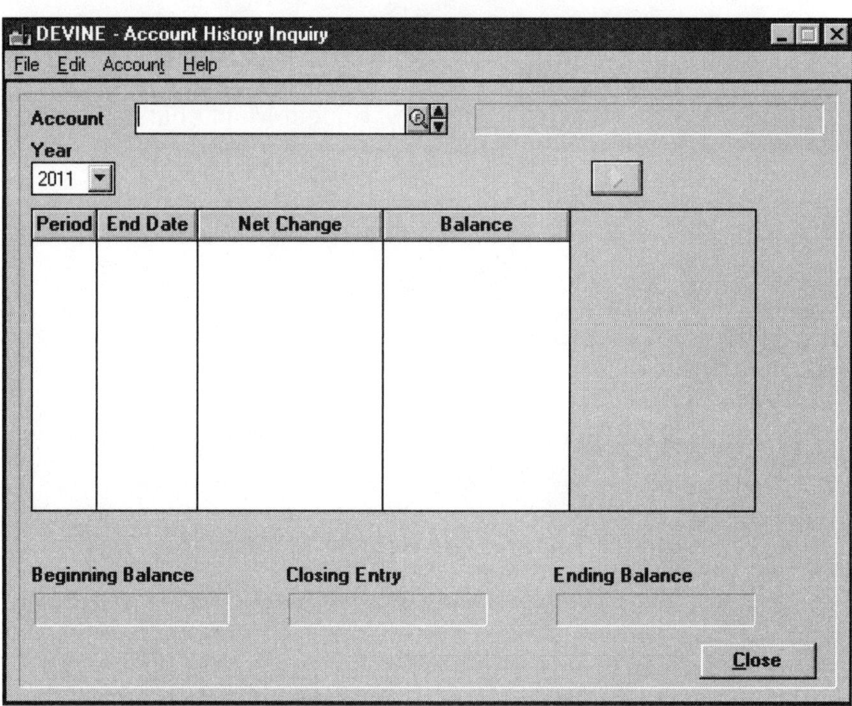

You can select the account by the Finder to the right of the Account text line, or you can type the account number in the Account text box. Leslie has decided to view the information for Depreciation Expense.

- ❑ Click: the **Finder** for the Account field
- ❑ Select: **6100 Depreciation Expense**

The Year list box should display 2011, the current fiscal year based on the Session Date (05/01/10) entered during sign-on. Leslie wants to review the Depreciation Expense for the 2010 fiscal year.

- ❑ Click: the **list tool** for the Year list box
- ❑ Select: **2010**
- ❑ Click: **GO**

The account history for Depreciation Expense will be displayed as shown in Figure 13-3. Note that activity has occurred in only two periods—period 12 and period 14, the special closing period. As Depreciation Expense is an Income Statement account, it was closed at the end of the fiscal year as noted by the closing entry in period 14.

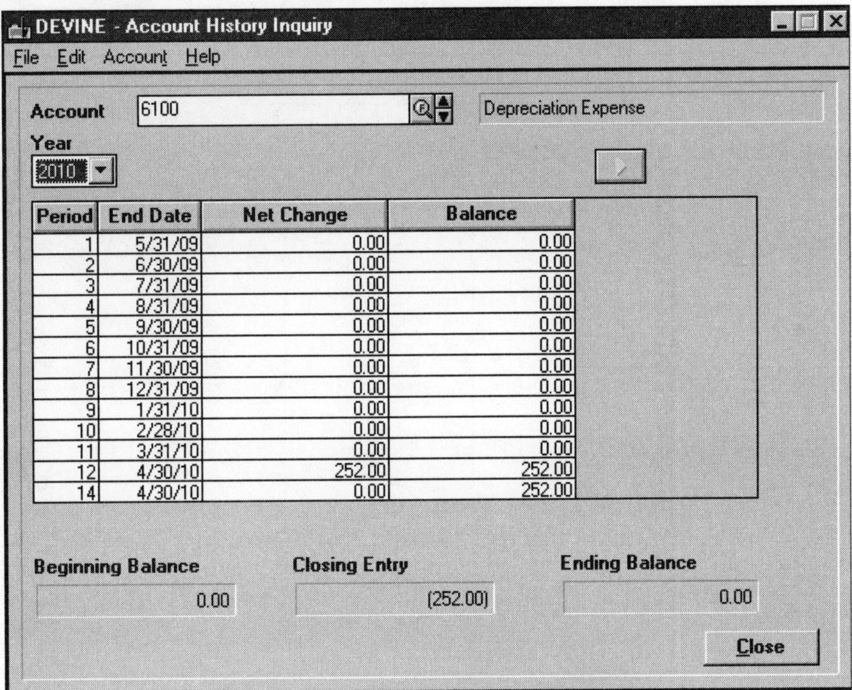

Period	End Date	Net Change	Balance
1	5/31/09	0.00	0.00
2	6/30/09	0.00	0.00
3	7/31/09	0.00	0.00
4	8/31/09	0.00	0.00
5	9/30/09	0.00	0.00
6	10/31/09	0.00	0.00
7	11/30/09	0.00	0.00
8	12/31/09	0.00	0.00
9	1/31/10	0.00	0.00
10	2/28/10	0.00	0.00
11	3/31/10	0.00	0.00
12	4/30/10	252.00	252.00
14	4/30/10	0.00	252.00

FIGURE 13-3
G/L Account History Inquiry Window

To see the transactions that comprise a period's balance, double click on the line for which you want details. ACCPAC will then open the Transaction History window showing the transactions for the account through the period you have selected.

- ❑ DClick: period **12**

Note the details for the two adjusting entries that were recorded in period 12. If necessary, you can adjust the column widths to display more information. To do this, move the mouse pointer to the line between the column headings and, when the pointer changes shape, drag the column to the width that you want.

- ❑ Close: the **G/L Transaction History** window
- ❑ Close: the **G/L Account History Inquiry** window

BUDGET MAINTENANCE

You cannot add, change, or delete information contained in a locked budget set. To see if Budget Set has been set to Locked, look on the Posting page of the G/L Options notebook. Devine Designs Inc. did not lock the Budget Set on the Posting page of the G/L Options notebook.

- ❑ DClick: the **Budget Maintenance** icon

FIGURE 13-4
G/L Budget Maintenance Window

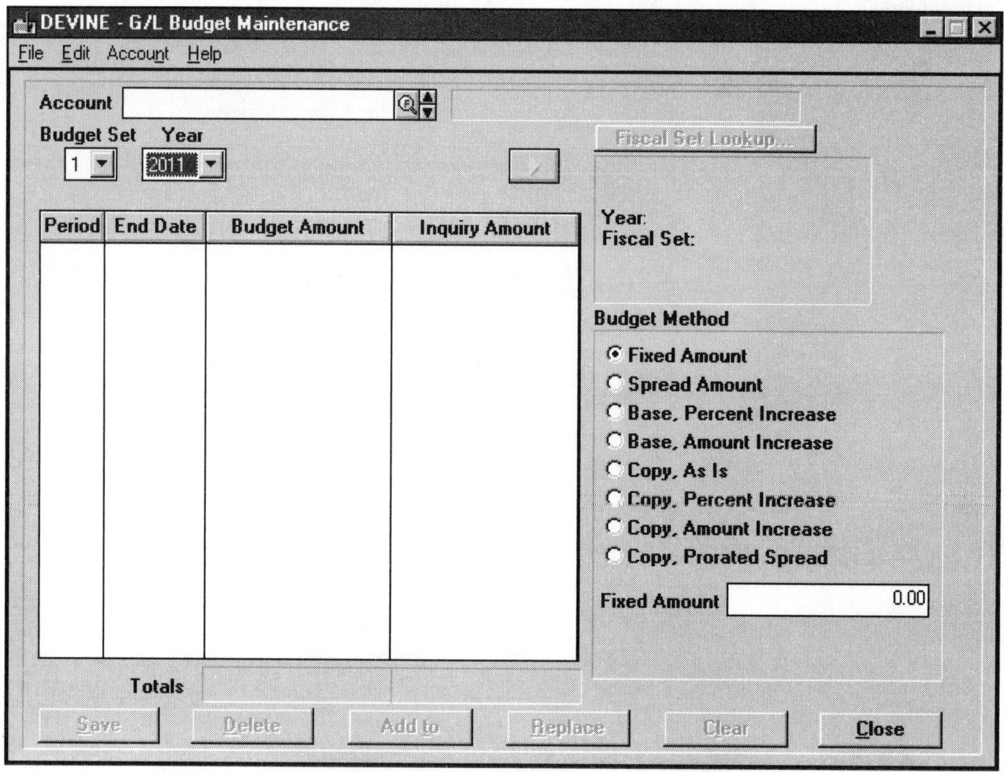

The G/L Budget Maintenance window (Figure 13-4) has five components. The upper portion of the window is used to select the Account, Budget Set, and Year. Budget and Inquiry Amounts are displayed in the table at the left. The buttons at the bottom of the window are used to save or delete the budget set, to move information from the inquiry column to the budget column, to clear the inquiry column, and to close the window.

WARNING

Budget amounts must reflect the normal balance for the account. Credit balance amounts must be entered with a minus sign. Comparative Income Statements will not be meaningful if normal account balances are not used.

The Budget Method area at the right allows you to select one of eight budgeting methods and then enter the budget information. You can also type budget amounts directly into cells on the table. As you work through this chapter, you will use the first four methods. The other four methods, the ones that start with the word Copy, are used to calculate budget amounts based on amounts in the inquiry column.

DIRECT ENTRY

The direct entry method is best suited for amounts that do not change in a regular pattern from one period to the next. Devine Designs Inc. has a budget for increasing its work force and increasing salaries. The anticipated costs will be $5,000 per month for the first three months, then $6,500 for each month in the second quarter, $8,000 for each month in the third quarter, and $10,000 per month for the last quarter.

- ❑ Select: Account **6180**
- ❑ Select: Year **2011**
- ❑ Click: **GO**

ACCPAC will display the account name, activate the Add and Fiscal Set Lookup buttons, and fill the table display area. You can clear any previously budgeted amounts from an account before changing a budget. In this case, there is nothing existing in the budget, but to ensure that everything has been cleared:

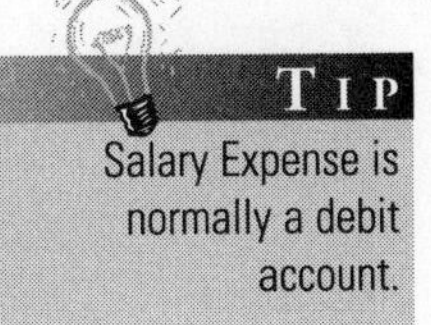

TIP

Salary Expense is normally a debit account.

- ❑ Click: **Clear** Clear
- ❑ Click: **Yes** Yes to confirm that you want to reduce all budget amounts to zero
- ❑ Click: the **Fixed Amount** option button
- ❑ Click: the **Budget Amount** cell for period **1**
- ❑ Enter: **5,000.00** in the Budget Amount cell for period 1

When entering budget amounts, do not enter the decimal point or decimals.

- ❑ Press: Enter ENTER

FIGURE 13-5
Salary Expense Budget

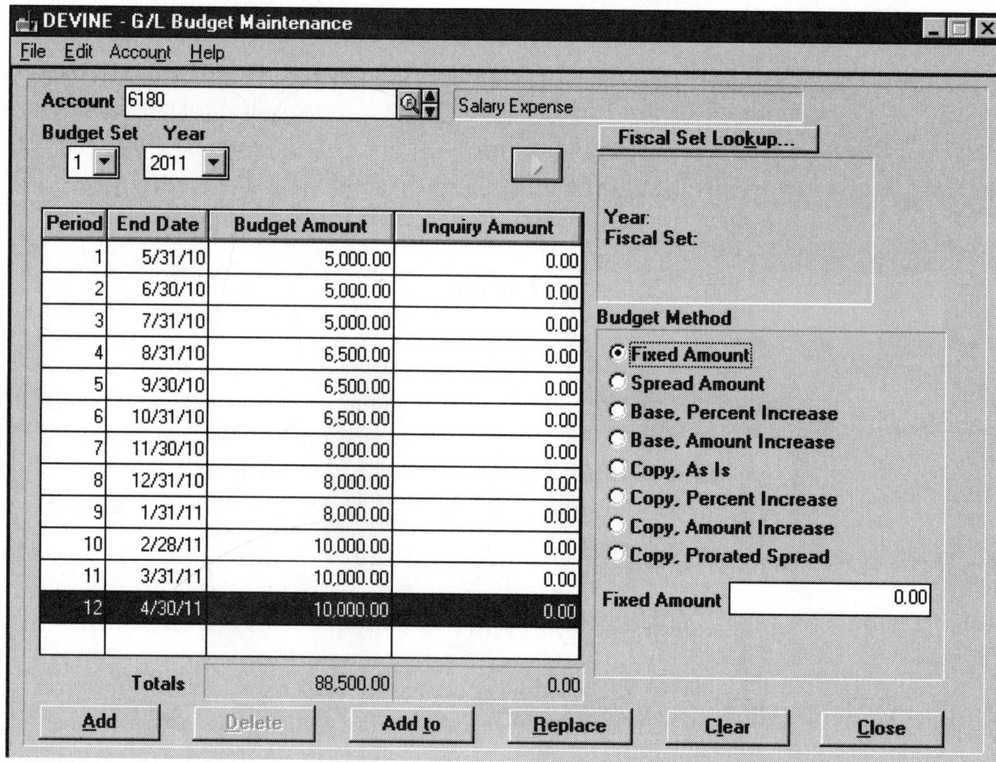

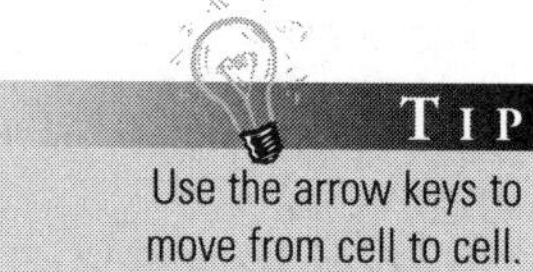

TIP
Use the arrow keys to move from cell to cell.

WARNING
You must click Add each time to save your final budget amounts.

- ❑ Complete the budget as shown in Figure 13-5.
- ❑ Click: Add [Add]

FIXED AMOUNT

TIP
Expense accounts are normally debit balance accounts.

The Fixed Amount option allows you to enter an amount once and transfer it to the budget amounts for each period. Devine Designs Inc. will budget $1,540 each period for the computer lease from Summit Peak Computers.

- ❑ Select: Account **6080**
- ❑ Select: Year **2011**
- ❑ Click: **GO**
- ❑ Click: the **Fixed Amount** option button
- ❑ Enter: **1,540.00** in the Fixed Amount text box
- ❑ Click: **Replace** [Replace]

FIGURE 13-6
Computer
Lease Budget

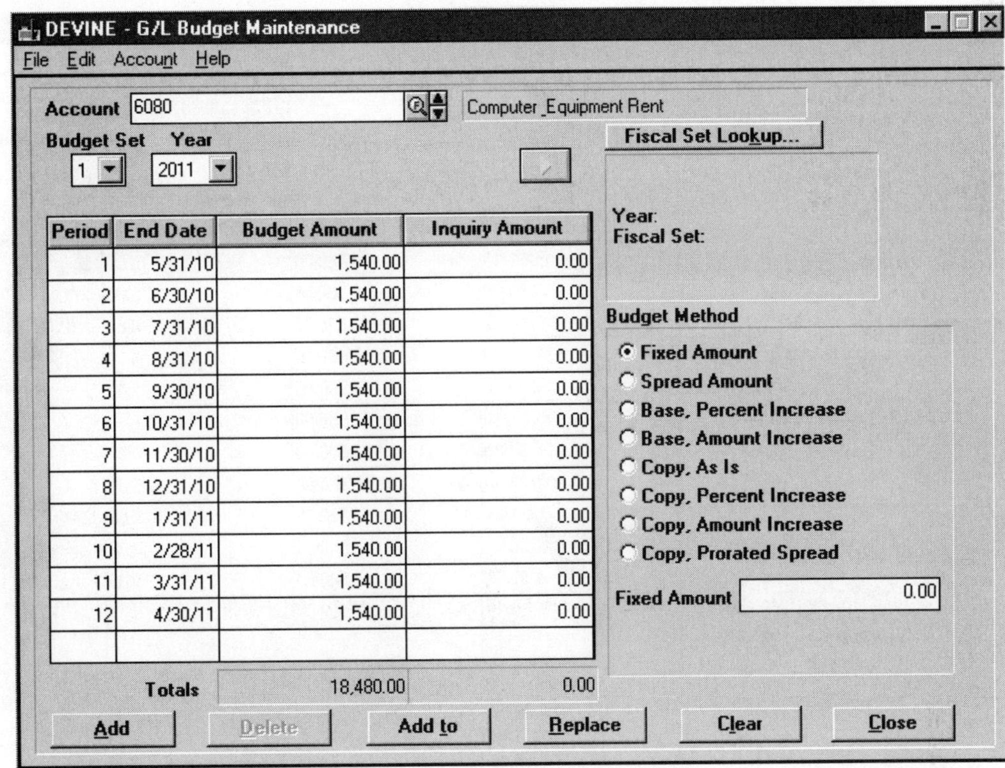

Compare the budget shown on your screen to Figure 13-6. If necessary, clear the amounts and enter the budget amounts again.

- ❑ Click: Add

SPREAD AMOUNT

Use this option to enter an amount that will be evenly divided across the budget amounts for each period. Devine Designs Inc. rents office space from Prestige Properties for $30,000 per year.

Expense accounts are normally debit balance accounts.

- ❑ Select: Account **6160**
- ❑ Select: Year **2011**
- ❑ Click: **GO**
- ❑ Click: the **Spread Amount** option button
- ❑ Enter: **30,000.00** in the Spread Amount text box
- ❑ Click: **Replace**

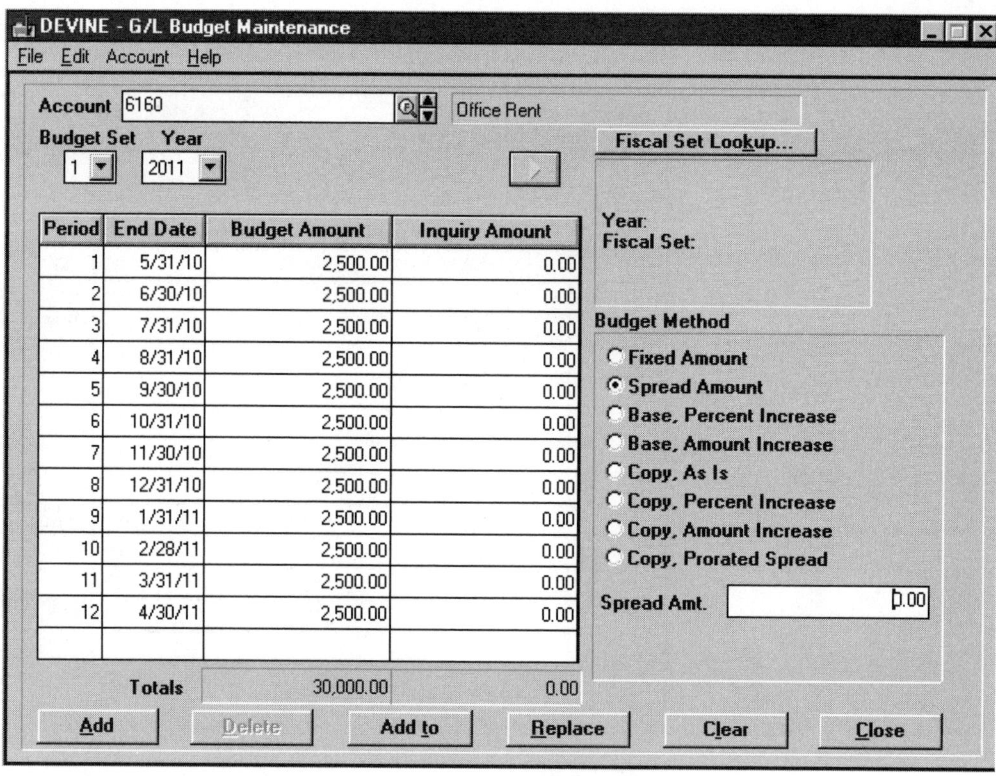

FIGURE 13-7
Office Rent Budget

Compare your budget amounts with those shown in Figure 13-7. $2,500 should appear in each period's Budget Amount field, with the total, $30,000, at the bottom. Make any necessary corrections.

❑ Click: Add [Add]

BASE, PERCENT INCREASE

Use this option when you want to start with a base amount for Period 1 and then increase each of the following periods by a percentage. Devine Designs Inc. expects Web Page Design sales to be $6,000 in May and then to increase at the rate of 5% per month.

TIP
Revenue accounts are normally credit balance accounts.

❑ Select: Account **4000/10**
❑ Select: Year **2011**
❑ Click: **GO** [GO]
❑ Click: the **Base, Percent Increase** option button
❑ Enter: **-6,000.00** in the Base Amount text box
❑ Enter: **5.000** in the % Increase text box
❑ Click: **Replace** [Replace]

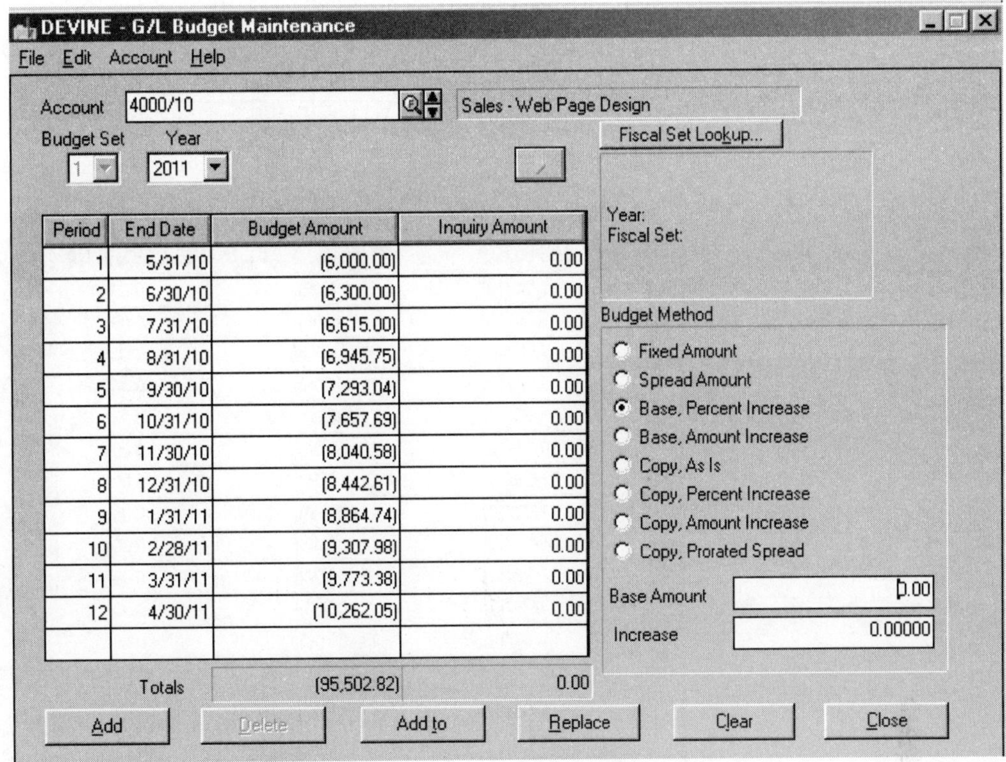

FIGURE 13-8 Web Page Design Budget

The new budget for Sales - Web Page Design will appear (Figure 13-8), increasing at the compounded rate of 5% per month.

- ☐ Click: **Add**

BASE, AMOUNT INCREASE

Use this option when you want to start with a base amount for Period 1 and then increase each of the following periods by a fixed amount. Devine Designs Inc. expects Web Page Maintenance sales to be $500 in May and then to increase $300 each month.

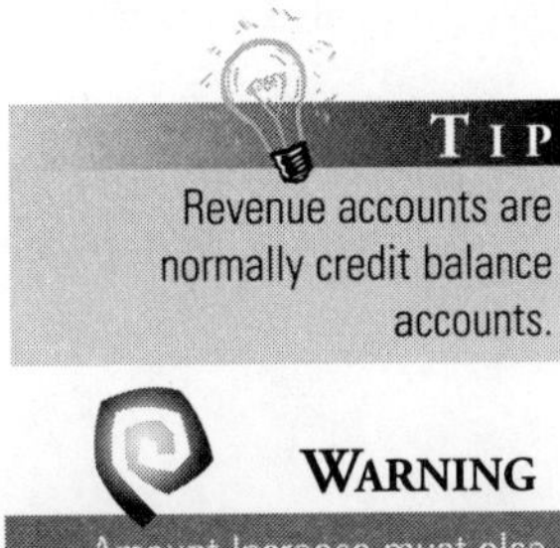

TIP

Revenue accounts are normally credit balance accounts.

WARNING

Amount Increase must also reflect the normal account balance.

- ☐ Select: Account **4000/20**
- ☐ Select: Year **2011**
- ☐ Click: **GO**
- ☐ Click: the **Base, Amount Increase** option button
- ☐ Enter: **-500.00** in the Base Amount text box
- ☐ Enter: **-300.00** in the Amt. Increase text box
- ☐ Click: **Replace**

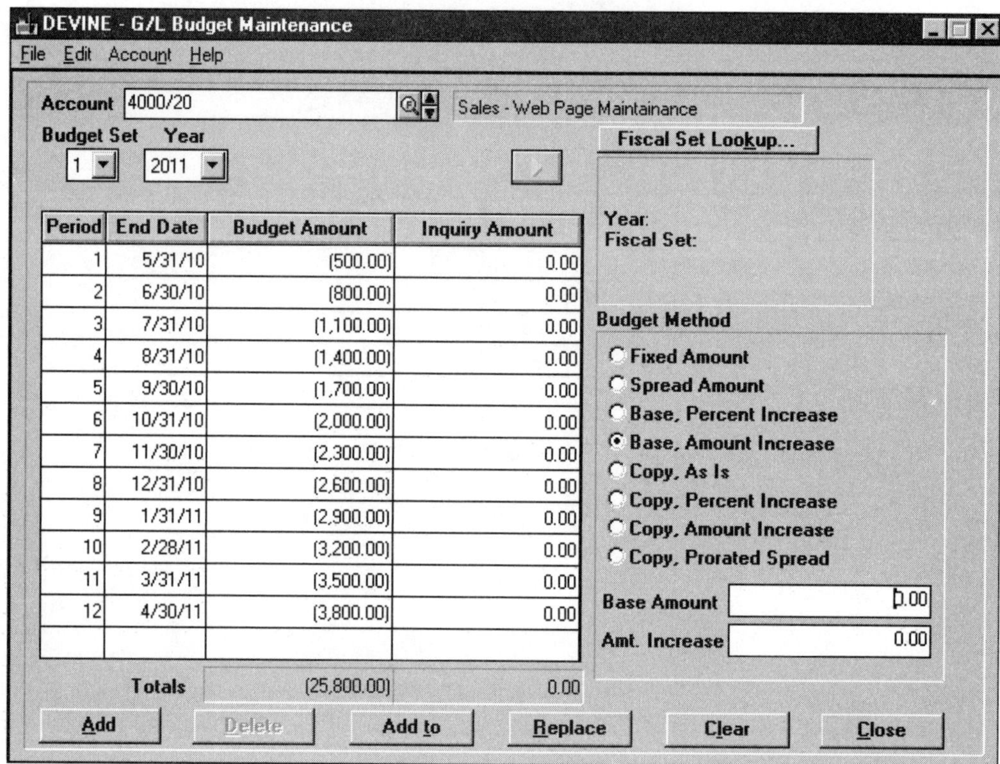

FIGURE 13-9 Web Page Maintenance Budget

The new budget for Sales -Web Page Maintenance will appear (Figure 13-9), increasing at the rate of $300 per month.

❑ Click: **Add** [Add]

COPY AS IS

This option is used to copy the exact amounts in the Inquiry Amount cells into the matching periods of the Budget Amount cells. Devine Designs Inc. estimates that Web Site Hosting sales will equal sales for Web Site Maintenance.

The first step is to copy the budget amounts for Web Site Maintenance to the Inquiry Amount cells.

❑ Click: **Fiscal Set Lookup** [Fiscal Set Lookup...]

The Fiscal Set Lookup will appear as shown in Figure 13-10.

FIGURE 13-10
Fiscal Set Lookup
Dialog Box

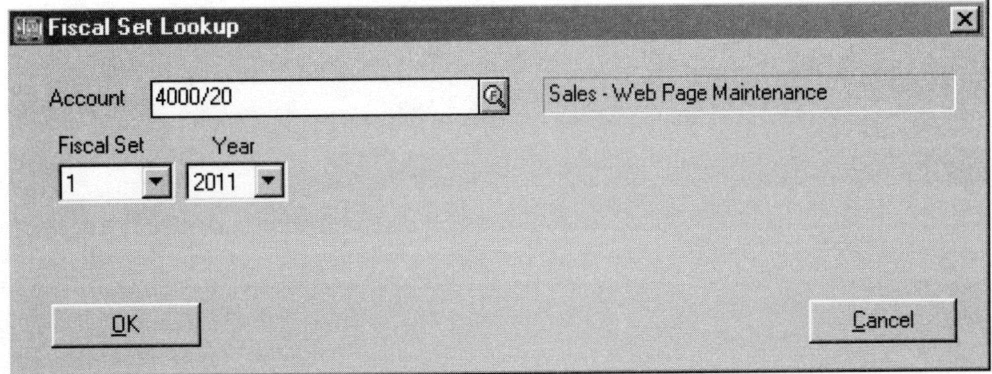

- ❑ Select: Account **4000/20**
- ❑ Select: Year **2011**
- ❑ Click: **OK**

The amounts you entered in the Budgeted Amount column now also appear in the Inquiry Amount column. The amounts in this column will remain when you call up another account.

- ❑ Select: Account **4000/30**
- ❑ Select: Year **2011**
- ❑ Click: **GO**

The amounts in the Inquiry Amount column should remain on your screen.

- ❑ Click: the **Copy, As Is** option button
- ❑ Click: **Replace**

FIGURE 13-11
Web Site Hosting
Budget

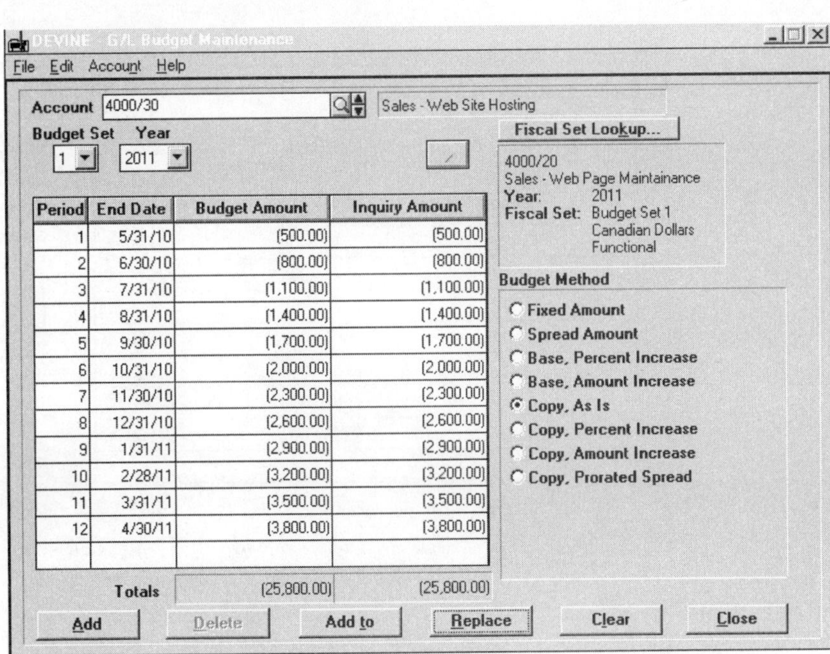

The Inquiry amounts now appear in the Budget Amount column as shown in Figure 13-11.

❑ Click: **Add**

Copy, Percent Increase

Use this option to copy the amounts from the Inquiry Amount column, with a fixed percentage increase, into the Budget Amount column. Devine Designs Inc. wants to see a budget for Web Site Hosting that is 5% higher than the budget for Web Site Maintenance.

❑ Click: **Clear**

❑ Click: **Yes** to reset the Budget Amounts to zero

❑ Click: the **Copy, Percent Increase** option button

❑ Enter: **5.000** in the Increase text box

❑ Click: **Replace**

Each number in the Budgeted column is now increased by 5% as shown in Figure 13-12. As you have already added a budget set for this account, the Add button is replaced by a Save button.

FIGURE 13-12
Revised Web Site Hosting Budget

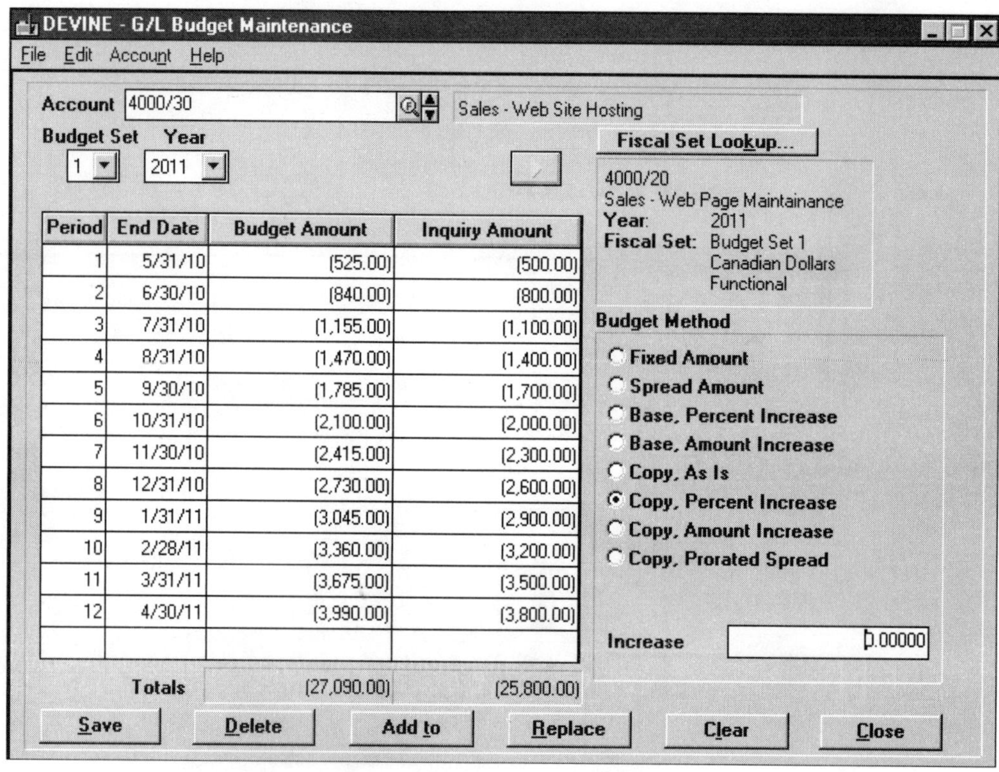

Period	End Date	Budget Amount	Inquiry Amount
1	5/31/10	(525.00)	(500.00)
2	6/30/10	(840.00)	(800.00)
3	7/31/10	(1,155.00)	(1,100.00)
4	8/31/10	(1,470.00)	(1,400.00)
5	9/30/10	(1,785.00)	(1,700.00)
6	10/31/10	(2,100.00)	(2,000.00)
7	11/30/10	(2,415.00)	(2,300.00)
8	12/31/10	(2,730.00)	(2,600.00)
9	1/31/11	(3,045.00)	(2,900.00)
10	2/28/11	(3,360.00)	(3,200.00)
11	3/31/11	(3,675.00)	(3,500.00)
12	4/30/11	(3,990.00)	(3,800.00)
	Totals	(27,090.00)	(25,800.00)

❑ Click: **Save** to save the revised budget

Copy, Amount Increase

This option is used to copy amounts from the Inquiry Amount column to the Budget Amount column while adding an increase of a fixed amount for each period. Devine Designs Inc. will sell images and Java applets over the Web. Leslie estimates that these sales should be $1,000 per period higher than the sales for Web Page Maintenance.

- ❑ Select: Account **4000/40**
- ❑ Select: Year **2011**
- ❑ Click: **GO**
- ❑ Click: **Fiscal Set Lookup**
- ❑ Select: Account **4000/20**
- ❑ Select: Year **2011**
- ❑ Click: **OK**
- ❑ Click: the **Copy, Amount Increase** option button
- ❑ Enter: **-1000.00** in the Amt. Increase text box
- ❑ Click: **Replace**

Figure 13-13
Retail Sales Budget

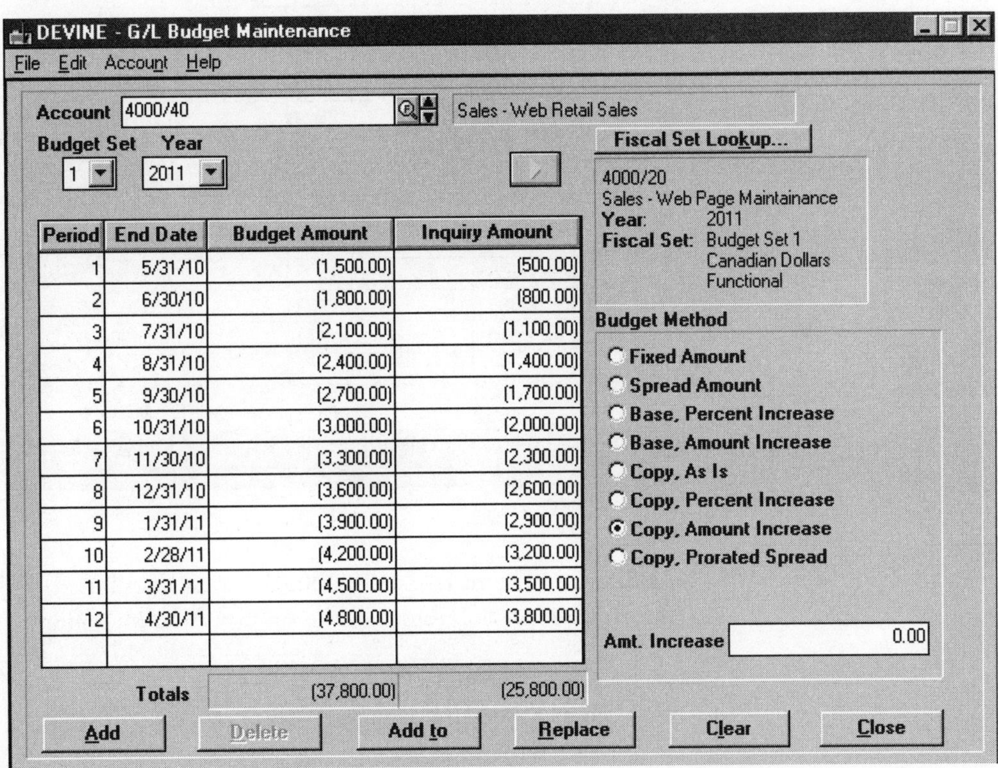

Each number in the Budget Amount Column is now increased by $1,000, as shown in Figure 13-13.

- ❑ Click: **Add**

Copy, Prorated Spread

Revenue accounts are normally credit balance accounts.

This method allows you to allocate a total amount to the 12 periods on the same percentage basis as the amounts in the Inquiry Amount column. Devine Designs Inc. wants to see the period budget amounts for $30,000 of Web Retail Sales allocated in the same proportions as the Web Page Maintenance Sales.

- ❑ Click: the **Copy, Prorated Spread** option button
- ❑ Enter: **-30,000.00** in the Spread Amt. text box
- ❑ Click: **Replace** [Replace]

Figure 13-14
Revised Retail Sales Budget

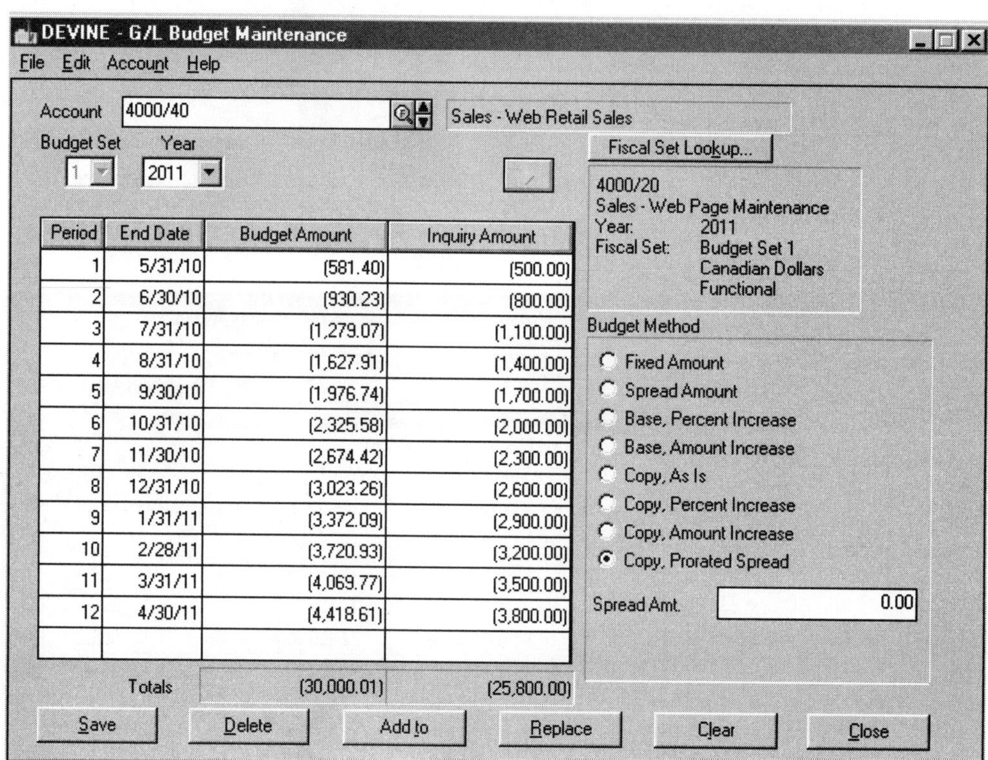

As shown in Figure 13-14, 30,000.01 is now distributed to the Budget Amount cells in the same proportion found in the Inquiry Amount column.

- ❑ Click: **Save** [Save]
- ❑ Close: the **G/L Budget Maintenance** window

Comparative Income Statement

ACCPAC allows you to compare actual to budgeted amounts by printing a comparative Income Statement.

❑ Open: the **Financial Reporter** window
❑ Open: the **Print Financial Statements** window
❑ Select: **Quikinc3** as the Statement Name
❑ Select: **2011** as the Fiscal Year
❑ Select: period **1**
❑ Select: **Actual** as the Report Type
❑ Select: **Account No** as the Sort By method
❑ Click: **Print** [Print]
❑ Click: **OK** [OK] on the Print window

TIP
If the Revenue amount is negative, you did not enter the amounts as credits when setting the budgets.

Review your printout. The Current YTD column should contain zeros as Devine Designs Inc. has not recorded any transactions in the new fiscal year. The amounts in the Budget YTD column reflect the budget information you have just entered. Devine Designs Inc. has budgeted to lose $1,433.60 in the first period of fiscal 2011.

❑ Print the same comparative Income Statement for the first quarter of fiscal 2011.

Note the decrease in the loss from operations.

❑ Close: the **Financial Statements** window

TRANSACTION HISTORY

The Transaction History icon enables you to show transaction details that have been posted to an account in the same format as accessed earlier from the G/L Account History window.

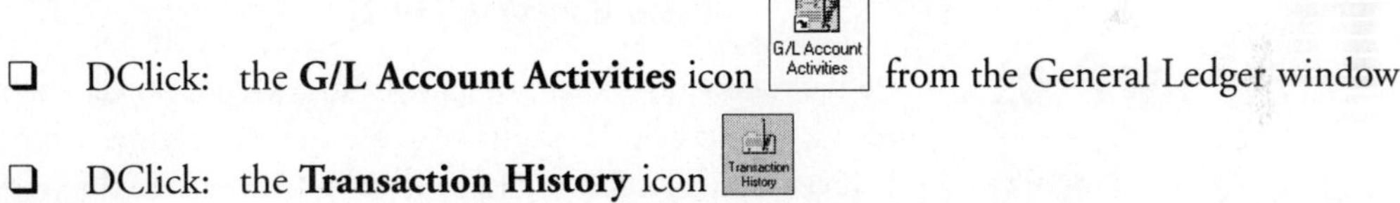

❑ DClick: the **G/L Account Activities** icon from the General Ledger window

❑ DClick: the **Transaction History** icon

FIGURE 13-15
G/L Transaction History Window

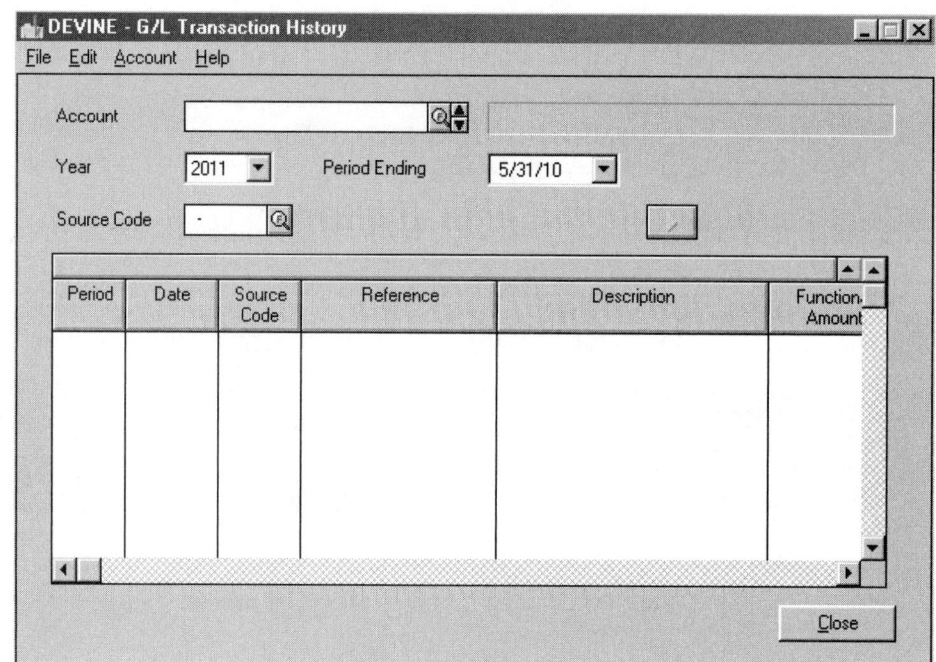

Use the upper portion of the window in Figure 13-15 to specify the information you want displayed in the table on the lower portion of the window.

❑ Select: Account **1000**

The Year and Period Ending text boxes show defaults based on the Session Date entered when signing on.

❑ Select: Year **2010**

❑ Select: Period Ending **04/30/10**

TIP
You can clear the Source Code text box by selecting its contents with the mouse and pressing the delete key.

To see the transactions that originate from a single source, enter the source code in the Source Code text box. If you want to see the transactions from all sources, leave the Source Code text box blank. Devine Designs Inc. wants to see the transactions for all source codes.

❑ Click: **GO**

As you can see, the transaction history for Bank - First Bank Corp. shows activity in periods 1 and 12.

❑ Close: the **G/L Transaction History** window

FISCAL SET COMPARSION

The Fiscal Set Comparison window allows you to compare the balances and the net and percentage change between two fiscal sets. Devine Designs Inc. has not accumulated enough data to make comparison realistic, but will compare the actual results for Web Page Design sales for fiscal 2010 to the budget for fiscal 2011 to show how this function works.

❑ DClick: the **Fiscal Set Comparison** icon 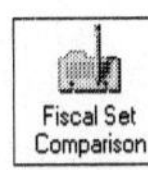

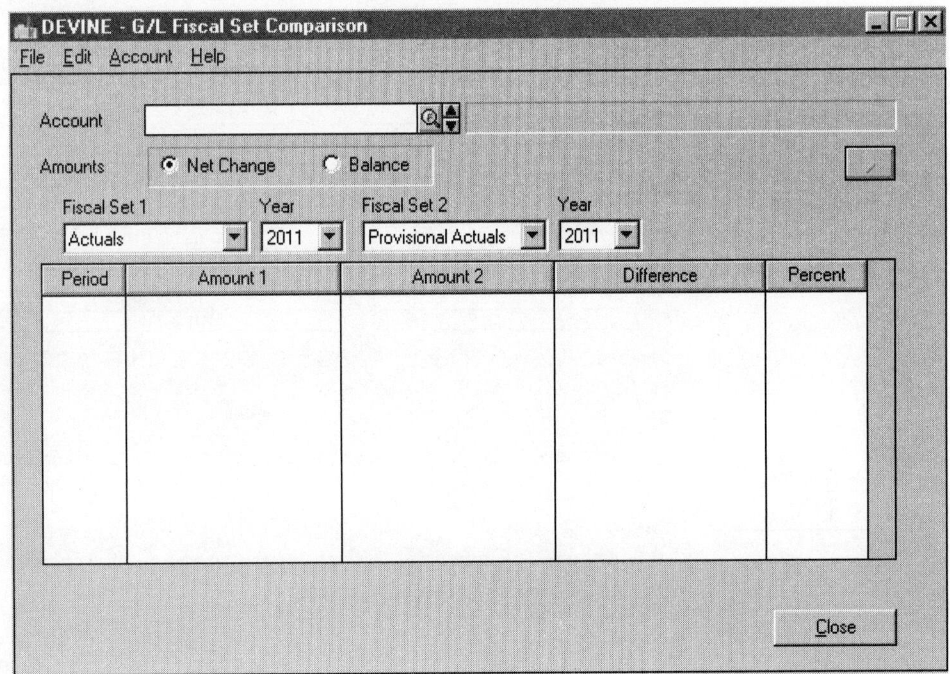

FIGURE 13-16
G/L Fiscal Set Comparison Window

The upper portion of the window in Figure 13-16 allows you to specify the comparison that will be displayed in the table in the lower portion of the window.

❑ Select: Account **4000/10**

The Amounts option allows you to select whether you want to view the Net Change or the Balance of the account for each period.

❑ Click: the **Net Change** option button

Devine Designs Inc. will compare the actual results for fiscal 2010 with the budget for fiscal 2011.

❑ Select: **Actuals** for Fiscal Set 1
❑ Select: **2010** for Fiscal Set 1
❑ Select: **Budget 1** for Fiscal Set 2
❑ Select: **2011** for Fiscal Set 2
❑ Click: **GO**

The G/L Fiscal Set Comparison will appear as shown in Figure 13-17.

FIGURE 13-17
Fiscal Set Comparison

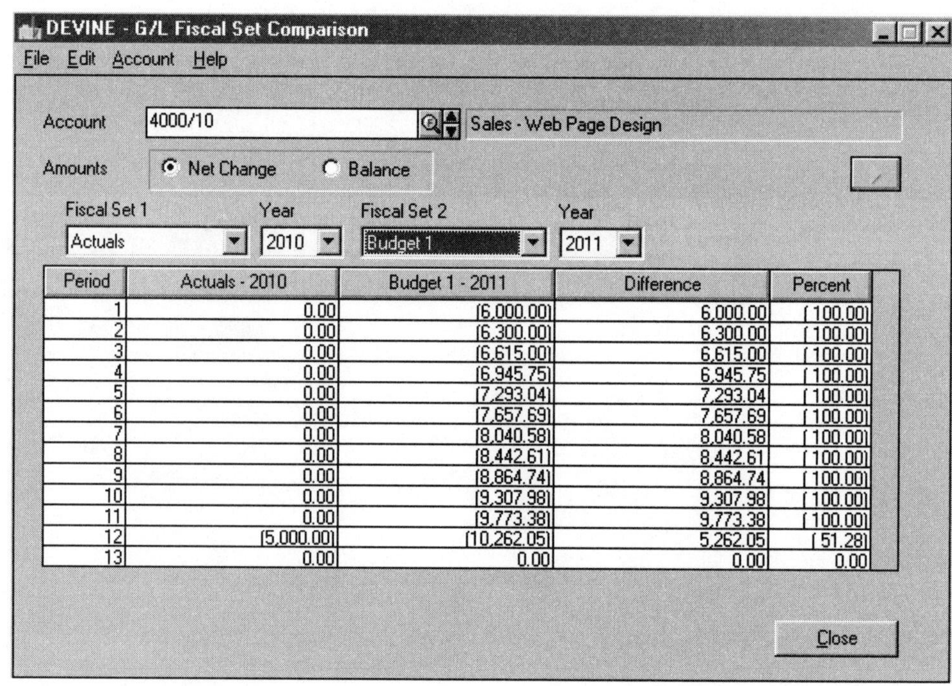

Period	Actuals - 2010	Budget 1 - 2011	Difference	Percent
1	0.00	(6,000.00)	6,000.00	(100.00)
2	0.00	(6,300.00)	6,300.00	(100.00)
3	0.00	(6,615.00)	6,615.00	(100.00)
4	0.00	(6,945.75)	6,945.75	(100.00)
5	0.00	(7,293.04)	7,293.04	(100.00)
6	0.00	(7,657.69)	7,657.69	(100.00)
7	0.00	(8,040.58)	8,040.58	(100.00)
8	0.00	(8,442.61)	8,442.61	(100.00)
9	0.00	(8,864.74)	8,864.74	(100.00)
10	0.00	(9,307.98)	9,307.98	(100.00)
11	0.00	(9,773.38)	9,773.38	(100.00)
12	(5,000.00)	(10,262.05)	5,262.05	(51.28)
13	0.00	0.00	0.00	0.00

- ❑ Click: **Close** [Close] to return to the G/L Account Activities window
- ❑ Exit: **ACCPAC**

REVIEW QUESTIONS

1. What is the purpose of the Account History Inquiry option?
2. What is the purpose of the Transaction History Inquiry option?
3. What is the purpose of the Fiscal Set Comparison option?
4. What is the purpose of the Budget Maintenance option?
5. List and describe the budgeting options available through the Budget Maintenance window.
6. How do you identify a number as a credit when adding it to the G/L Budget Maintenance window?

EXERCISE

- ❑ Sign on to your company using May 1, 2010 as the Session Date.
- ❑ Create a budget for account 6120, Insurance Expense, of $200 per month.
- ❑ Create a budget for account 6100, Depreciation Expense, of $1,800 per year.
- ❑ Create a budget for account 1100, Accounts receivable, of $5,000 in the first period with each subsequent period increasing by $150.
- ❑ Create a budget for account 6060, Communication Expense, with a monthly increment of 5% on a base of $250.
- ❑ Exit: **ACCPAC** and back up your data files

CASE 1

MURPHBALLS & CO. GENERAL LEDGER CASE

Murphballs & Co. was created on July 1, 2010, by two laid-back and over-relaxed hounds known as Calhoun Jazz and Sassy Lips. The company supplies the latest hound fad, a service in which family pets can hire another dog to chase balls thrown by their master, keeping the owner exercised and happy, while allowing the family mutt to relax and enjoy his walk. Ruff Tuff McDuff, a Scottish terrier that manages the company, has hired you to set up and maintain the company books. Murphballs & Co.'s fiscal year begins on July 1, 2010, and ends June 30, 2011. In the world of hounds, there is an 8% retail sales tax and a 7% goods and services tax.

After completing this case, organize and submit Murphballs & Co.'s printouts. Each printout must contain your initials followed by the company name. Save the data files for your instructor to evaluate and for you to use in the other cases.

CREATE A NEW SYSTEM DATABASE

- ❑ Create a new System Database with the following specifications:

Database ID:	**MURBLS**
Database Category:	**System**
Description:	**Professional Retrievals**

Create a New Company Database

- ❑ Create a new company database using the following information:

Database ID:	**MURPH**
Database Category:	**Company**
System Database ID:	**MURBLS**
Description:	**XX Murphballs & Co.**

- ❑ Enter your initials in place of "XX" before the company name in the description.
- ❑ Verify that the database is error free before you start to enter information.

Activate Services

- ❑ Sign on to Murphballs & Co. using the administrator User ID and **July 31, 2010** as the Session Date.
- ❑ Activate Administrative Services.
- ❑ Activate Common Services using **07/01/10** as the Fiscal Year Starting Date.

Create the Company Profile

- ❑ Create the Company Profile using the following information:

Name:	**XX Murphballs & Co.** (where XX are your initials)
Address:	**706 Hound Dog Way**
	Muttsville Junction
	BOW WOW
Contact:	**Ruff Tuff McDuff**
Telephone:	**555-555-9999**
Fax:	**555-555-9998**
Fiscal Periods:	**12**
Location Code:	**Doggone**
Country Code:	**DOG**
Branch:	**1**
Warning Date Range:	**30 days**
Functional Currency:	**Select the currency that you normally use.**

Activate the General Ledger

- ❑ Activate the General Ledger using the following information:

  The Oldest Fiscal Year Starting Date is **July 1, 2010.**
  The Current Fiscal Year is **2011.**

- ❑ Activate the G/L Subledger Services.
- ☑ Print the Company Profile.

Add a User

- ❑ Add the following user:

User ID:	**RUFF**
Name:	**Ruff Tuff McDuff**
Language:	**English**
Password:	**Ruff**

- ❑ Print the Users report.

Add a Security Group

- ❑ Add the following Security Group:

Group ID:	**TOPDOGS**
Description:	**The Leaders of the Pack**

Allow the "TOPDOGS" to use all the functions in Administrative Services, Common Services, and General Ledger.

- ❑ Print the Security Groups report.

User Authorization

- ❑ Authorize Ruff Tuff McDuff as one of the "TOPDOGS" for Administrative Services, Common Services, General Ledger, and G/L Subledger Services.
- ❑ Print the User Authorizations report.

Edit the Fiscal Calendar

- ❑ Edit the Fiscal Calendar using the following information:

Fiscal Year:	**2011**
Fiscal Period Status:	**unlocked (All Periods)**

- ❑ Print the Fiscal Calendar.

Create the General Ledger

Create the General Ledger using the following information:

Contact Name: **Put your own name as the contact person**
Posting: **Do not allow posting to previous years.**
Provisional Posting: **Allow provisional posting**
Force Listing of Batches
Keep [**2**] Years of Fiscal Sets
Keep [**2**] Years of Transactions Detail
Segment Definition

Account Segment:	**1**
Segment Delimiter:	**/**
Segment Name:	**Account**
Length:	**4**
Account Segment 2:	**Activity**
Length:	**2**

❑ Print the G/L Options report.

Add a Segment Code

❑ Add the following segment code for the Activity segment:

Segment Code	**10**
Description	**Retail Sales**

❑ Print the G/L Segment Code Report.

Add Account Structures

❑ Create two account structures with the following specifications:

Structure Code:	**BASIC**
Description:	**for all accounts except rev.**
Segments To Be Used In This Structure:	**Account**
Use As Company Default Structure:	**Activate**
Structure Code:	**REV**
Description:	**Revenue Accounts**
Segments To Be Used in This Structure:	**Account and Activity**

❑ Print the G/L Structure Report.

Add Source Codes

❑ Add the following Source Codes:

GL CR	**Cash Receipts**
GL CD	**Cash Disbursements**

GL PU	**Purchases**
GL SA	**Sales**

- ☐ Print the Source Code Report.

Create Source Journal Profiles

- ☐ Create the following Source Journal Profiles:

Cash Receipts	**GL CR**
General	**GL JE / GL CL / GL CO**
Cash Disbursements Journal	**GL CD**
Purchases Journal	**GL PU**
Sales Journal	**GL SA**

- ☐ Print the Source Journal profile report.

Create a Chart of Accounts

- ☐ Add the accounts listed below to the General Ledger.

Be careful to identify each account by the proper Account Type (Income Statement, Balance Sheet, or Retained Earnings) and Group. All accounts will have a Normal Balance. All accounts are to be posted in "Detail form" with an "Active" status. There are no automatic reallocations. The Structure Code for all accounts except the revenue accounts is "BASIC." The Revenue accounts use the "REV" Structure Code.

Note: Do not set up the Accounts Receivable or Accounts Payable as Control Accounts at this point.

Account	Name of Account
1101	Cash Working Funds
1201	Accounts Receivable
1205	Allowance for Doubtful Accounts
1301	Office Supplies Inventory
1401	Prepaid Expenses
1450	Inventory
1501	Office Equipment
1601	Accum. Amort., Office Equip.
2101	Accounts Payable
2105	RST Payable
2110	GST Payable
2111	GST Recoverable
2115	Prepayment Liability

2120	Bank Loan Payable
3101	Common Stock
3200	Retained Earnings
4101/10	Sales, Ball Chasing Services
4110/10	Sales, Other
4115	Sales Allowances and Discounts
5000	Cost of Goods Sold
6000	Advertising Expense
6005	Amortization Expense
6010	Bad Debts Expense
6020	Bank Interest and S/C Expense
6030	Entertainment Expense
6040	Insurance Expense
6050	Office Supplies Expense
6060	Payroll Expense
6070	Property Rent Expense
6150	Supplies Expense
6500	Interest Income

- ❑ Return to the Options notebook in the G/L Setup window to specify account 3200 as the default Closing account.
- ❑ Print the Chart of Accounts.
- ❑ Ensure that the General Ledger is set to the year 2011, not 2010.

Recording Initial Balances

- ❑ Create a transaction batch to record the initial account balances in the General Ledger as of July 1, 2010.

Account Name	Debit	Credit
Cash, Working Funds	2310.00	
Office Supplies Inventory	40.00	
Office Equipment	2650.00	
Common Stock		5000.00

- ❑ Print the Batch Listing.

Recording July Transactions

- ❑ Create another transaction batch as of July 31, 2010, to record the following transactions.

Assume that all sales are subject to 8% retail sales tax and 7% goods and services tax. Purchases of goods for resale are exempt from retail sales tax. No discounts are allowed for prompt payment.

Advertising

On credit, Murphballs purchased advertising in the Dogs' World News to announce the service to all well-read canines. The ad cost $800 plus GST and RST. Murphballs' purchase order was number M200. Dogs' World News issued invoice DW7499 on July 10, 2010.

Cash Sales

The July cash sales for ball-chasing services amounted to $750 plus GST and RST

Credit Sale

Sale of ball-chasing services on credit to Murphballs' first client, Bobbytomlack. The invoice was for $100 plus GST and RST. The invoice was number 001, dated July 13, 2010.

Credit Sale

Sale of ball-chasing services on credit to Hezaplasher dated July 23, invoice number 002, for $150.00 plus GST and RST.

Office Supplies

The purchase of office supplies for $350 plus GST and RST from Dog Chow Supplies Ltd. was made on credit. Murphballs' purchase order number was M201. Dog Chow's invoice number was DC010, dated July 31, 2010.

Insurance

Murphballs purchased a one-year insurance policy from Dog Catchers Insurance for $120 on July 1, using check number 101. Only Retail Sales Tax (no GST) applies to this purchase. The insurance guarded against wrongful imprisonment.

Salary

On July 31, 2010, payment of $70 was made to Sweetums Poodle, the office employee, from the working funds account. The check number was 102. No sales taxes apply to this transaction.

Office Rent

Rent of the office for July was $50, paid by check number 103 issued on July 29, 2010, to Stargazer Realty Inc. No sales taxes apply to this transaction.

Entertainment

Entertainment expenses for a howling good time amounted to $5 plus GST and RST This was paid with check number 104 on July 29. The check was payable to Backdoor Luigi's Restaurant.

Payment of Invoice

On July 30, 2010, paid for the advertising expense owing to Dogs' World News, using check number 105.

Payment of Invoice

On July 31, paid Dog Chow Supplies Ltd. the full amount owed. Payment was made using check number 106.

Payment Received

Received payment in full from Bobbytomlack for invoice number 001 on July 30, 2010.

Payment Received

Received payment in full from Hezaplasher for invoice number 002 on July 30, 2010.

- ☐ Print the Batch Listing.

Recording Adjusting Entries

❑ Prepare a third transaction batch to record the necessary adjustments based on the following information.

Supplies

At the end of July, you found that the office supplies inventory (account 1301) was reduced by $75.

Amortization

Estimated monthly amortization on the office equipment was $80.

Insurance

By July 31, the first month's Dog Catcher's Insurance had expired $10.80.

❑ Print the Batch Listing.

Make sure the batches have been set Ready to Post.

Post Transactions

❑ Post the transaction batches to the General Ledger.

❑ Print and clear the printing journals.

❑ Print the General Ledger Transactions listing.

Print Financial Statements

❑ Print a single-column Income Statement for July.

❑ Print a single-column Balance Sheet at the end of the first month of operation.

❑ Exit ACCPAC.

❑ Back up your data files.

UNIT 4

BANK AND TAX SERVICES

CHAPTER 14

BANK SERVICES

Bank Services are part of the Common Services for all the integrated ACCPAC applications for a company. Bank Services are not required if the company is using only the General Ledger, but are required for integrating Accounts Receivable and Accounts Payable with the General Ledger.

Bank Services centralizes payments and receipts for all the ACCPAC for Windows Small Business Series accounting programs. It is used to maintain banking information, track payments, record transfers of funds, reverse cheques, return NSF customer cheques, perform reconciliations with bank statements, and create General Ledger batches from bank reconciliations and miscellaneous monthly transactions. Bank Services must be activated before you activate Accounts Receivable, Accounts Payable, or Payroll.

BANK SERVICES ACTIVATION

- ❑ Sign on to Devine Designs Inc. as the system administrator using 05/01/10 as the Session Date.

Bank Services must be activated using Administrative Services.

❑ Open: the **Administrative Services** window

❑ DClick: the **Data Activation** icon

ACCPAC will display the Backup Warning message shown in Figure 14-1. If you did not back up your data at the end of the last chapter, you should do so now.

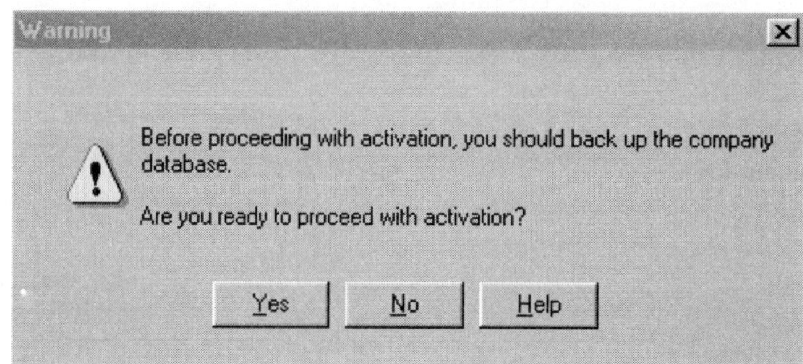

FIGURE 14-1
Warning Message

❑ Click: **Yes**

The Data Activation window on your screen may include additional applications to those shown in Figure 14-2.

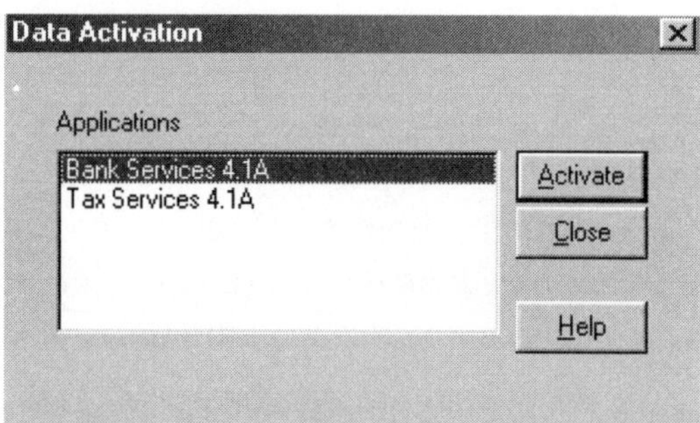

FIGURE 14-2
Data Activation Window

❑ Select: **Bank Services 4.1A**

❑ Click: **Activate**

ACCPAC will ask for confirmation as shown in Figure 14-3.

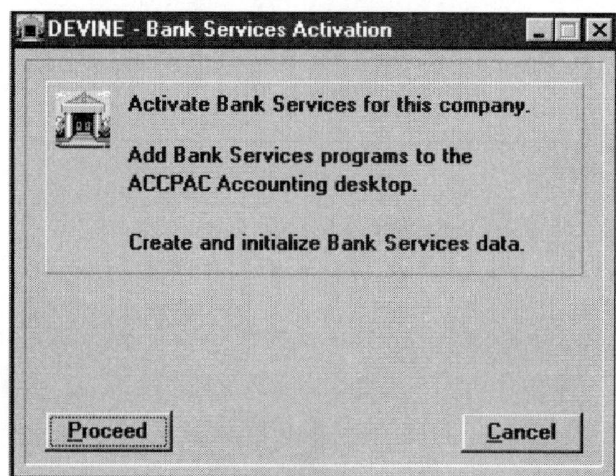

FIGURE 14-3
Bank Services Activation Window

- ❑ Click **Proceed** Proceed

As activation proceeds, ACCPAC will display an information window that shows the progress. Once complete, the Data Activation window will become active. Note that Bank Services has been removed from the applications list.

- ❑ Close: the **Data Activation** window
- ❑ Open: the **Common Services** window

FIGURE 14-4
Common Services Icon

ACCPAC has now added the Bank Services icon to the Common Services window.

BANK SERVICES

- ❑ DClick: the **Bank Services** icon 

The Bank Services window contains four icons, as shown in Figure 14-5.

FIGURE 14-5
Bank Services Icons

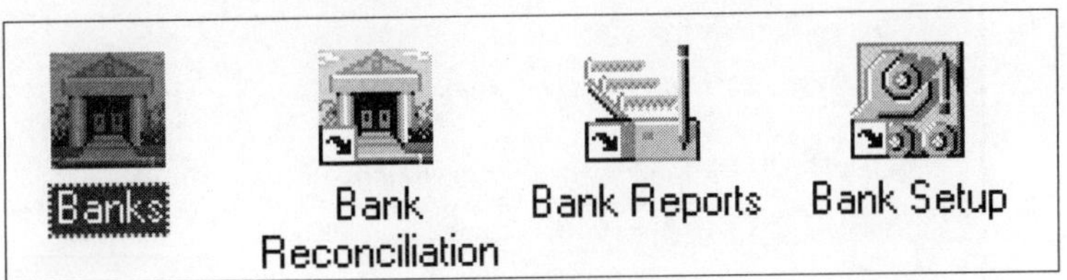

When working with actual company files, organize the following information before you begin:

- A list of the bank accounts used in your General Ledger, including addresses, phone numbers, contact persons, bank account numbers, and transit numbers.
- A list of the types of transactions that are processed through each of your bank accounts. Transaction types could include bank service charges, transfers of funds between accounts, and interest income.
- Records of your most recent bank reconciliation for each bank account, with each General Ledger bank account reconciled up to the end of its most recent bank statement.
- A list of outstanding transactions for each bank account.
- The check stubs and deposit slips used for each bank account, or a list of the next check numbers and deposit slip numbers to be used for the accounts.

You will be provided with this information for Devine Designs Inc. as you need it.

Setup

❑ DClick: the **Setup** icon [Bank Setup] on the Bank Services window

The Bank Setup window, shown in Figure 14-6, contains two icons.

FIGURE 14-6
Bank Setup Icons

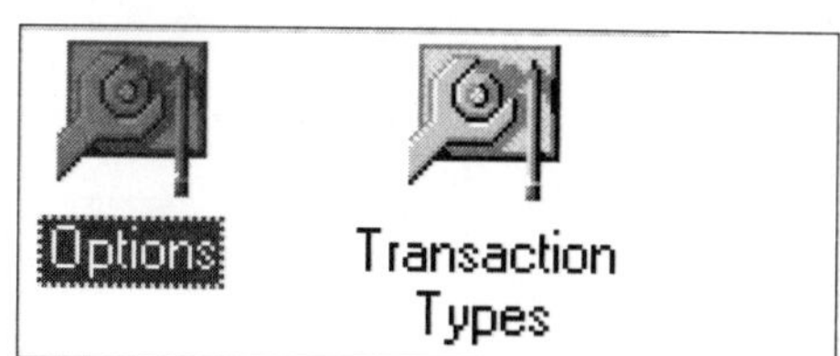

Setting Bank Options

❑ DClick: the **Options** icon [Options]

The Bank Options window will appear as shown in Figure 14-7.

FIGURE 14-7
Bank Options Window

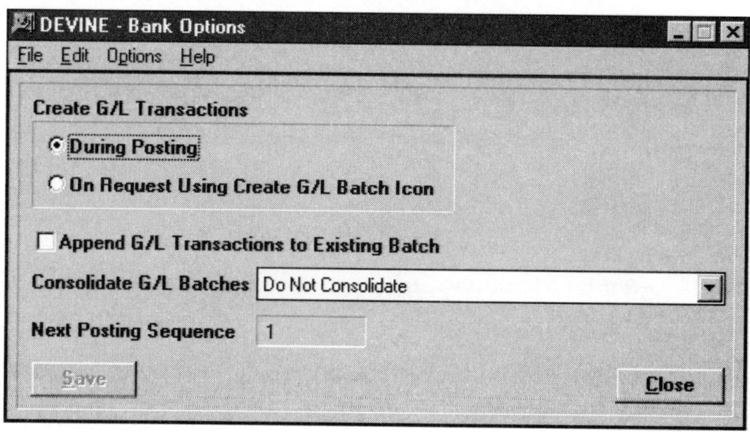

Creating G/L Transactions

You can create General Ledger transactions either During Posting or On Request Using Create G/L Batch Icon. If you want to create General Ledger transactions automatically when you post reconciliations, select the During Posting option. If you select During Posting, you cannot print the Bank G/L Transactions report in Bank Services. You have to print a record of the transactions by opening the General Ledger and printing the Batch Listing report.

If you want to use the Create G/L Batch window to create General Ledger transactions, select the On Request Using Create G/L Batch Icon. If you want to print the Bank G/L

Transactions report, you must select this option. The recommended option is On Request Using Create G/L Batch Icon. You can change this option later if you want to.

- ❑ Click: the **On Request Using Create G/L Batch Icon** option button

Append Option

The Append G/L Transactions to Existing Batch option allows you to add new General Ledger transactions to existing G/L batches. Do not select this option if you want to create a new General Ledger batch every time you produce General Ledger transactions. Devine Designs Inc. will create a new batch every time General Ledger transactions are produced by Bank Services.

Do not select the Append option. If there is a check mark in the check box, de-select it.

Consolidate G/L Batches

You use this option to specify whether to combine transaction details for the same General Ledger account into single lines, or to send the unconsolidated transaction details to the General Ledger. The options are:

- Do Not Consolidate—The General Ledger transaction batch includes separate details for each bank transaction.
- Consolidate by Account and Fiscal Period—The Bank Services program will combine all information with the same General Ledger account number into one detail.
- Consolidate by Account, Fiscal Period, and Source—The Bank Services program will combine all information with the same General Ledger account number, fiscal period, and source code into one detail.

Devine Designs Inc. wants as much detail as possible transferred to the General Ledger.

- ❑ Click: the **List Tool** for Consolidate G/L Batches
- ❑ Select: **Do Not Consolidate**

Source Codes

TIP
If you install General Ledger after activating Bank Services, you will have to enter the source codes manually in the General Ledger.

The Bank Services program uses the following source codes:

BK-CK	Bank Checks
BK-CO	Bank Consolidated Entry
BK-DP	Bank Deposits
BK-EN	Bank Entries
BK-CR	Bank Reconciliation Discrepancies

Since you have already created the ACCPAC General Ledger, these codes were automatically created when Bank Services was activated.

Next Posting Sequence

The Next Posting Sequence is displayed for information only; you cannot change it. If you completed the Year-End proceedure in Chapter 12 properly, the Next Posting Sequence should be 1.

Review your entries.

- ❑ Click: **Save** [Save]
- ❑ Close: the **Bank Options** window

ADD TRANSACTION TYPES

The Transaction Types option identifies the General Ledger account you will debit or credit to offset the amount posted to the Bank Control account. Devine Designs Inc. has decided to use its account at E-Bank.com as the control account for Bank Services. A Transaction Type should be added for transfers of funds between the E-Bank.com and First Bank Corp. accounts.

- ❑ DClick: the **Transaction Types** icon [Transaction Types] on the Bank Setup window

The Transaction Types window will appear as shown in Figure 14-8.

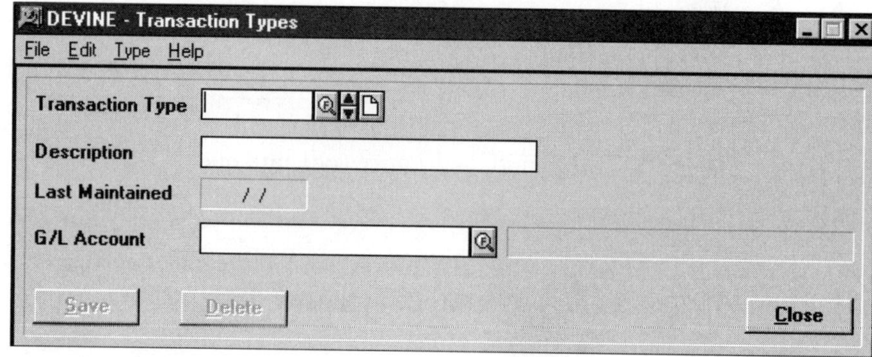

FIGURE 14-8 Transaction Types Window

Transaction Type

Each type of transaction must be identified by a name or code. Transaction Type codes can be six characters long. You can add or delete Transaction Type codes as needed.

Devine Designs Inc. will create a Transaction Type called XFER-1 that will be used to transfer funds betweent account 1000, Bank - First Bank Corp., and account 1025, Bank - E-Bank.com, the bank control account, in Bank Services.

- ❑ Click: the **New Document** icon
- ❑ Enter: **XFER1** in the Transaction Type text box
- ❑ Press: **Tab** [Tab]

Description

The description of the Transaction Type may be 30 characters long.

- ❑ Enter: **Xfer-1st Bank Corp/E-Bank.com** in the Description text box
- ❑ Press: **Tab** [Tab]

Last Maintained

The Last Maintained area displays information only. ACCPAC will update this field with the Windows system date when you add a new transaction type or make a change to an existing record. This area should be blank.

G/L Account

The G/L Account field is used to identify the General Ledger account to which offsetting entries for this transaction type are made. This first transaction type is used to transfer funds between the First Bank Corp. account and the E-Bank.com account.

- ❑ Click: the **Finder** for the G/L Account text box
- ❑ Select: **1000 Bank - First Bank Corp.**
- ❑ Click: **Add** [Add]

YOUR TURN

- ❑ Add a transaction type for Bank Service Charges using the following information:

Transaction Type	**SVCE**
Description	**Bank Service Charges**
G/L Account	**6040**

- ❑ Add a Transaction Type for Bank Services set up as follows:

Transaction Type	**SETUP**
Description	**Bank Services Setup**
G/L Account	**1000**

- ❑ Close: the **Transaction Types** window

ADDING BANK RECORDS

A Bank Record contains the General Ledger account and currency information that defines the characteristics of the bank account. It determines what kinds of transactions you can record. You have to add a record for each bank account in your chart of accounts.

Profile Information Page

- ❑ DClick: the **Banks** icon on the Bank Services window

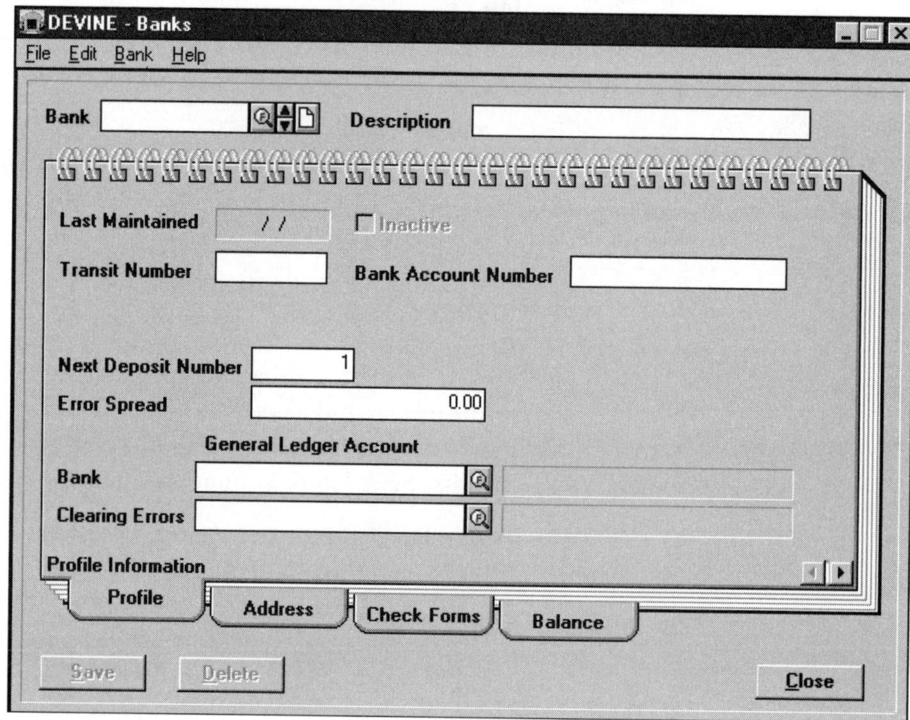

FIGURE 14-9
Profile Information Page

The Profile Information page, Figure 14-9, contains the General Ledger and system information you have to enter for each bank.

Bank

The Bank code is a unique code of up to eight alphanumeric characters. The first Bank code you will enter is for the E-Bank.com account.

- ❑ Click: the **New Document** icon
- ❑ Type: **EBANK**
- ❑ Press: **Tab** [Tab] to move to the Description text box

The Description may be up to 30 characters.

- ❑ Type: **E-Bank.com Working Funds**
- ❑ Press: **Tab** [Tab] to complete the entry

Last Maintained

ACCPAC updates this display with the Windows system date after you add a new bank account or make changes to an existing account. The field is currently blank because no maintenance on E-Bank has been performed.

Inactive

When an account is made inactive, a date appears to the right, to show when it was made inactive. An account can be made inactive at any time. You would set an account to inactive if the bank account has been closed, or you could temporarily make the account inactive to prevent additional checks from being issued if it is low on funds.

Transit Number

Each bank branch has a transit number that identifies it. This information is optional but should be recorded.

- ❑ Click: the **Transit Number** text box
- ❑ Type: **35421**
- ❑ Press: **Tab** [Tab] to move to the Bank Account Number text box

You can enter the bank account number assigned by your bank. This information is also optional but recommended.

- ❑ Type: **01-5555**
- ❑ Press: **Tab** [Tab]

Next Deposit Number

You can enter the number that you want Bank Services to assign to the next deposit batch for this account. When you create a deposit batch in Accounts Receivable, the Bank Services program will assign a number to the batch.

- ❑ Press: **Tab** [Tab] to accept the default number 1

Error Spread

This Error Spread is the maximum amount of error that you will accept without investigating the cause of the error. If the bank clears a check or deposit with an amount that differs from your records, and the difference is less than or equal to the error spread, the Bank Services program will post the difference to the General Ledger Clearing Errors account. If the difference is greater than the error spread, you have the choice of clearing the difference to the Clearing Errors account or marking it Cleared with Bank Error, which flags the difference as pending further action, such as phoning the bank to request a correction of the error, or making an adjustment entry if the error is due to a data entry error.

- ❑ Press: **Tab** [Tab] to leave the Error Spread at 0.00

General Ledger Accounts

This text box records the General Ledger account number for the bank you are setting up.

- ❑ Click: the **Finder** for the Bank text box
- ❑ Select: **1025 Bank - E-Bank.com**

Select the General Ledger account to which you will post the small differences between the bank statement and the General Ledger.

- ❑ Click: the **Finder** for the Clearing Errors text box
- ❑ Select: **6050 Bank Clearing Errors**

Review your entries to ensure that they are correct.

- ❑ Click: **Add** [Add]

Address Information Page

This page contains the address and telephone information of your bank account. Each line of the address can contain as many as 30 characters.

- ❑ Click: the **Address** tab at the bottom of the notebook

The Address Information page will appear as shown in Figure 14-10.

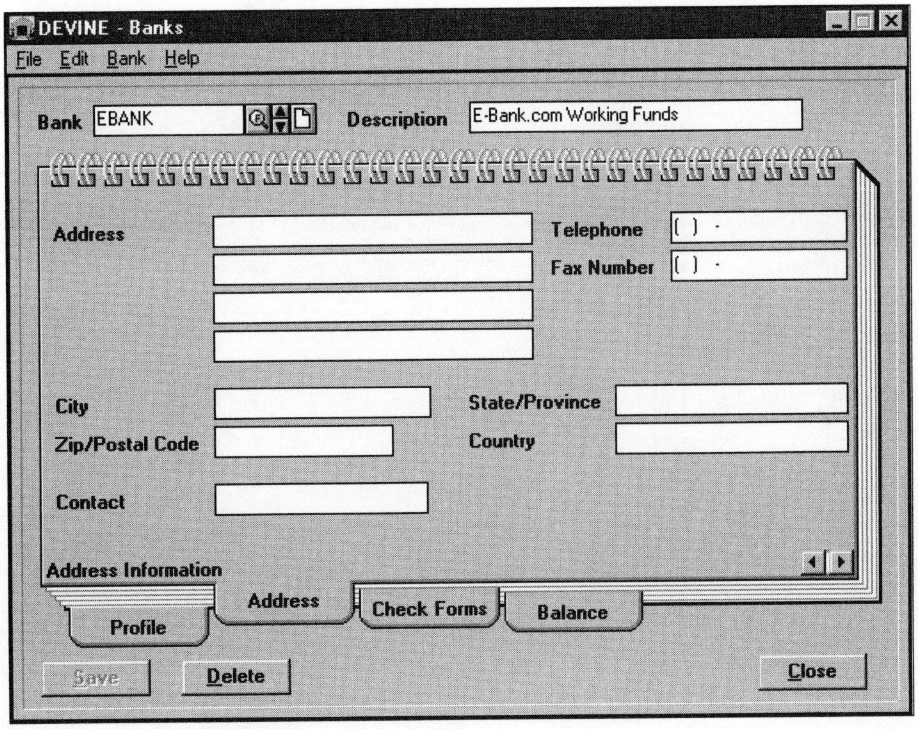

FIGURE 14-10
Address Information Page

- ☐ Enter the following address:

  1732 Upper Greenback Way
  Georgetown
  Your Province or State
  K8H 4S2
  Your Country

Your personal banker is Rosemary Satco.

- ☐ Enter: **Rosemary Satco** in the Contact text box
- ☐ Enter: **905 555 1732** in the Telephone text box
- ☐ Enter: **905 555 1854** in the Fax Number text box
- ☐ Click: **Save** Save

CHECK FORMS PAGE

- ☐ Click: the **Check Forms** tab at the bottom of the notebook

Some of the information necessary to complete this page (Figure 14-11) will not be available until the Accounts Payable module is installed. Devine Designs Inc. will complete this page later.

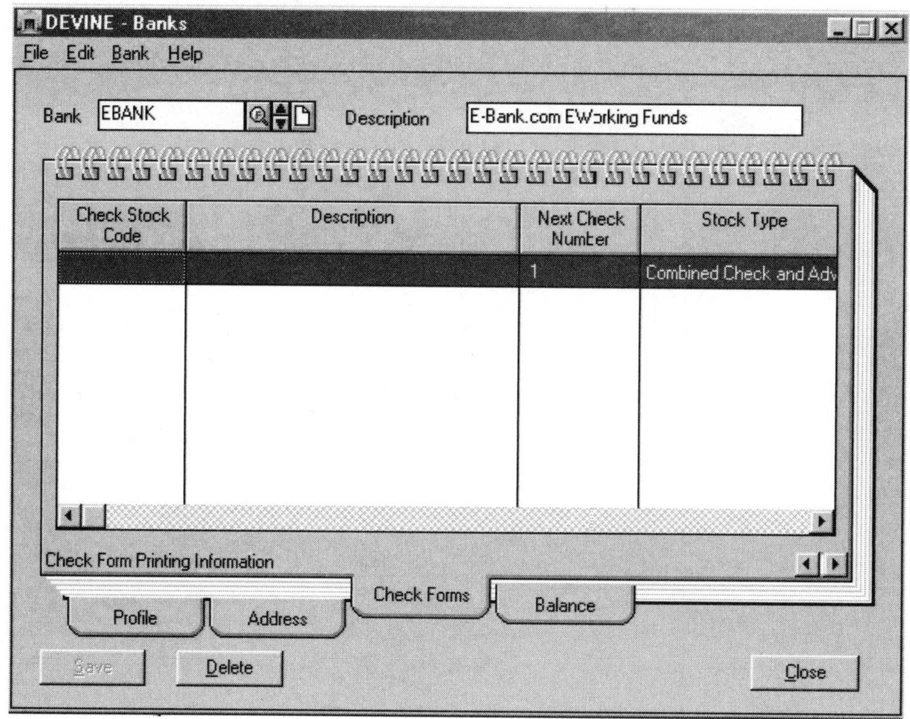

FIGURE 14-11
Check Forms Page

BALANCE PAGE

❑ Click: the **Balance** tab at the bottom of the notebook

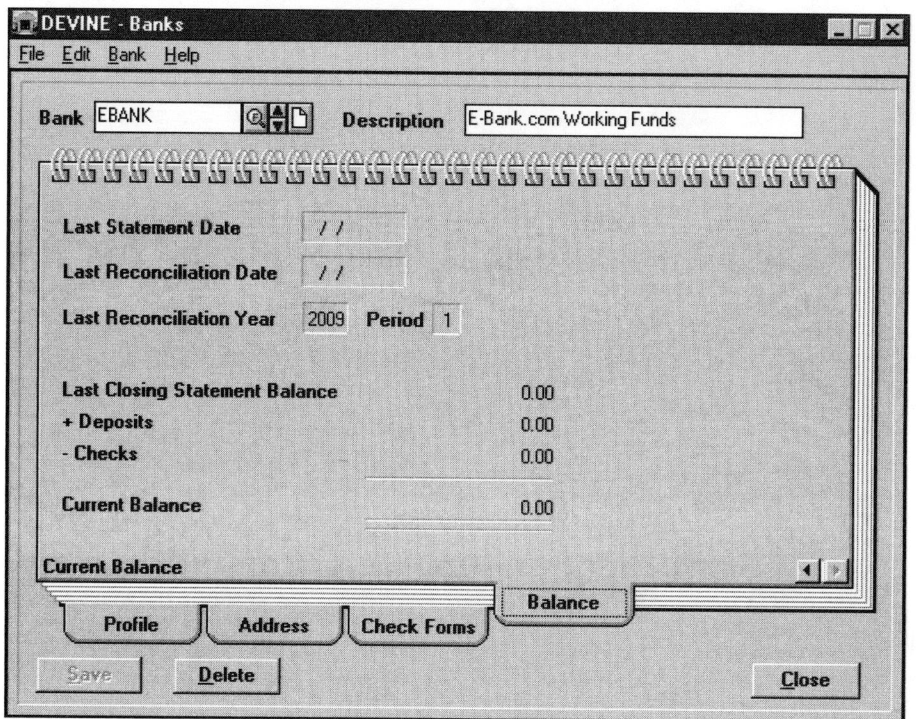

FIGURE 14-12
Current Balance Window

The Balance page shown in Figure 14-12 displays current information for the bank account. The amounts displayed are zeros, but will change after Devine Designs Inc. enters the balance later in this chapter.

YOUR TURN

You will now add the First Bank Corp.

- ❑ Click: the **New Document** icon for Bank
- ❑ Enter: **1STBK** in the Bank text box
- ❑ Enter: **First Bank Corp** in the Description text box
- ❑ Enter the following information on the Profile Information page:

Transit Number	**39821**
Bank Account Number	**09-5753**
Next Deposit Number	**1**
Error Spread	**0.00**
Bank General Ledger Account	**1000**
Clearing Errors	**6050**

- ❑ Click: **Add** Add
- ❑ Click: the **Address** tab
- ❑ Enter the following address:

  17 Melrose Place
  Georgetown
  Your Province or State
  K8H 4S8
  Your Country

Your personal banker is Harry Shore.

- ❑ Enter: **Harry Shore** in the Contact text box
- ❑ Enter: the telephone number **905 555 1717**
- ❑ Enter: the fax number **905 555 1818**

Review your input. Once you are satisfied it is correct,

- ❑ Click: **Save** Save

The Check Forms page will be completed as you work through the Accounts Payable.

- ❑ Close: the **Banks** notebook

ESTABLISHING BANK BALANCES

For each General Ledger bank account that has a balance, you must set up a matching balance in Bank Services by performing a setup reconciliation. The best time to do this reconciliation is at the end of a fiscal period. Devine Designs Inc. will reconcile the account for First Bank Corp. on May 1, 2011, the start of the new fiscal year. There are no outstanding checks or deposits and the balance on the bank statement, sent electronically from First Bank Corp. that morning, matches that in the General Ledger account.

- ❑ DClick: the **Bank Reconciliation** icon [Bank Reconciliation] on the Bank Services window
- ❑ DClick: the **Reconcile Statements** icon [Reconcile Statements] on the Bank Reconciliation window
- ❑ Select: Bank **1STBK** using the Finder

SUMMARY PAGE

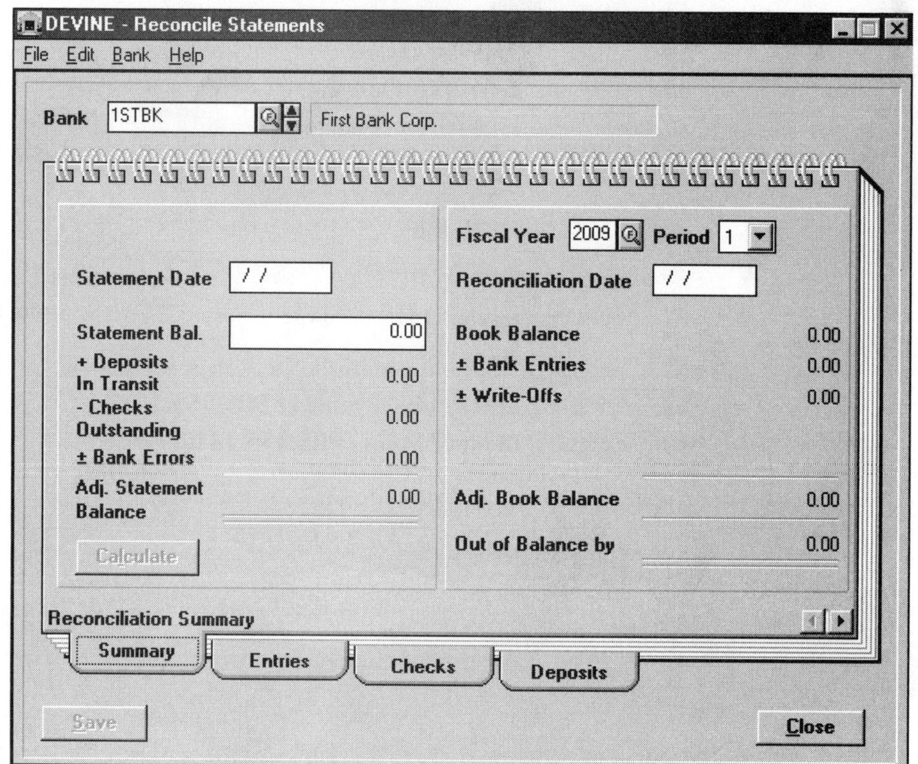

FIGURE 14-13
Summary Page

The summary page is shown in Figure 14-13.

Statement Date

The statement from First Bank Corp. is dated April 30, 2010.

- ❑ Click: the **Statement Date** text box
- ❑ Type: **04302010** in the **Statement Date** text box
- ❑ Press: **Tab** [Tab]

Statement Balance

The balance on the statement is $6,812.10.

- ❑ Type: **6812.10** in the Statement Bal. text box
- ❑ Press: **Tab** [Tab]

Fiscal Year

TIP You could also use the Finder to select the Fiscal Year.

Select the fiscal year in which the reconciliation occurs. Devine Designs Inc.'s fiscal year ended on April 30, 2010.

- ❑ Type: **2010** in the Fiscal Year text box
- ❑ Press: **Tab** [Tab]

Period

April is period 12 in Devine Designs Inc.'s Fiscal Calendar.

- ❑ Select: Period **12** using the List Tool
- ❑ Press: **Tab** [Tab]

Reconciliation Date

In this text box, enter the date that ended the most recent fiscal period. In this case, the statement date is also the last day in fiscal period 12.

- ❑ Type: **043010**
- ❑ Press: **Tab** [Tab]

Calculate

Changing the Fiscal Year or Period causes the summary amounts to be out of date as indicated by the active Calculate button. Clicking the Calculate button updates the summary amounts.

- ❑ Click: **Calculate** [Calculate]

Note that the Summary page is out of balance by $6,812.10.

ENTRIES PAGE

❑ Click: the **Entries** tab at the bottom of the Reconcile Statements notebook

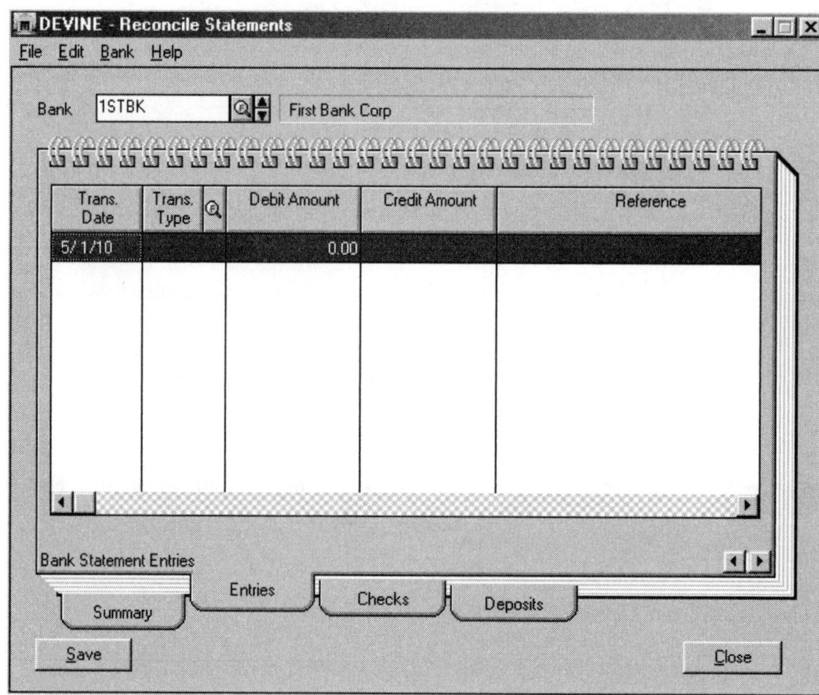

FIGURE 14-14
Entries Page

TIP
To display the data entry form, press **F9**.

Use the Entries page (Figure 14-14) to enter the bank statement ending balance as the starting point for establishing the General Ledger bank account balance. You can enter the information directly into the table cells or you can use a data entry form. Devine Designs Inc. will enter the information directly into the table.

Transaction Date

This cell is used to record the last date of the most recent fiscal period. The default displayed is the Session Date entered when signing on.

❑ Click: the **Transaction Date** cell
❑ Type: **043010**

Transaction Type

❑ Select: **SETUP** using the Finder

Debit Amount

If the account balance on the bank statement is positive, enter that balance in this cell. Devine Designs Inc.'s account at First Bank Corp. has a positive balance of $6,812.10.

- ❑ Click: the **Debit Amount** cell
- ❑ Type: **6812.10**

Credit Amount

If the bank statement shows a negative balance, add that amount in this cell.

Reference

A reference is optional but recommended. Devine Designs Inc. will use Bank Statement as the reference.

- ❑ Click: the **Reference** cell
- ❑ Type: **April 30, 2010, Bank Statement**

Description

A description is also optional but recommended.

- ❑ Click: the **Description** cell
- ❑ Type: **Setup Reconciliation**
- ❑ Click: **Save** Save

Verification

You now want to verify that the General Ledger bank account and the balance in Bank Services match.

- ❑ Click: the **Summary** tab at the bottom of the Reconcile Statements notebook

The Book Entries on the left of the window should display 6,812.10 and there should be a zero amount in the Out of Balance by display. If there are errors, make the necessary corrections and save the information again.

CHECKS PAGE /withdrawals.

- ❑ Click: the **Checks** tab at the bottom of the notebook

Use this page to enter outstanding checks for this account. Devine Designs does not have any outstanding checks.

DEPOSITS PAGE

- ❑ Click: the **Deposits** tab at the bottom of the notebook

This page is used to enter deposits that are outstanding as of the reconciliation date. Devine Designs Inc. does not have any outstanding deposits.

RETURNS PAGE

The Returns page is not visible until Accounts Receivable has been activated.

- ❑ Close: the **Reconcile Statements** window

POSTING THE RECONCILIATION

- ❑ DClick: the **Post Reconciliations** icon [Post Reconciliati...] on the Bank Reconciliation window

FIGURE 14-15
Post Reconciliation
Dialog Box

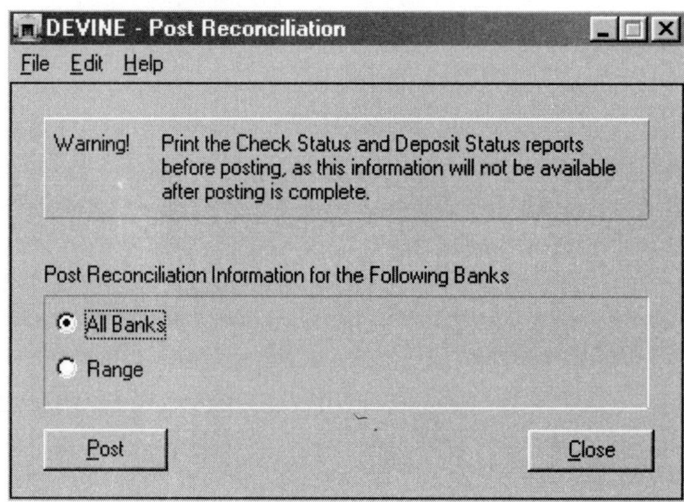

Devine Designs Inc. will not print the Check Status and Deposit Status reports referred to in the dialog box of Figure 14-15, as no information has been entered for these reports. Devine Designs Inc. will only post reconciliation information to the First Bank Corp. Records.

- ❑ Click: the **Range** option button
- ❑ Select: **1STBK** in the From text box
- ❑ Select: **1STBK** in the To text box
- ❑ Click: **Post** [Post]

After posting is completed, an information message indicating successful posting will be displayed.

- ❑ Click: **OK** [OK]

PRINTING REPORTS

❑ DClick: the **Bank Reports** icon on the Bank Services window

FIGURE 14-16
Banks Reports Icons

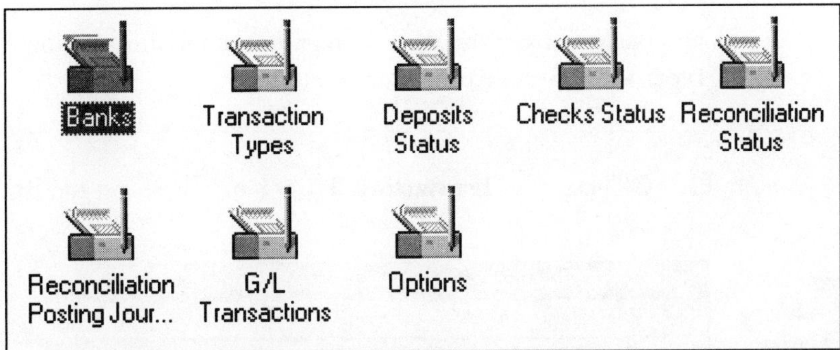

The Bank Reports window, Figure 14-16, contains eight icons. You will now use four to print reports. The other four icons will be used in Accounts Receivable and Accounts Payable.

PRINTING THE BANK OPTIONS REPORT

The Bank Options Report prints the information that you entered using the Options icon on the Bank Setup window.

❑ DClick: the **Options** icon on the Bank Reports window
❑ Click: **Print** on the Bank Options Report window
❑ Click: **OK** on the Print dialog box

FIGURE 14-17
Bank Options Report

Date: Monday, May 29, 2000 2:53PM **DDI Student Name** **Page 1**
Bank Options (BK1480)

Create G/L Transactions:	On Request Using Create G/L Batch Icon
Append G/L Transactions To Existing Batch:	No
Consolidate G/L Transactions:	Do Not Consolidate
Next Posting Sequence:	2

Compare your report to that shown in Figure 14-17. If there are errors, correct them using the Options icon on the Bank Setup window and print the report again.

❑ Close: the **Bank Options Report** window

PRINTING THE BANK TRANSACTION TYPES REPORT

The Bank Transaction Types Report prints the information entered using the Transaction Types icon on the Bank Setup window.

❑ DClick: the **Transaction Types** icon  on the Bank Reports window

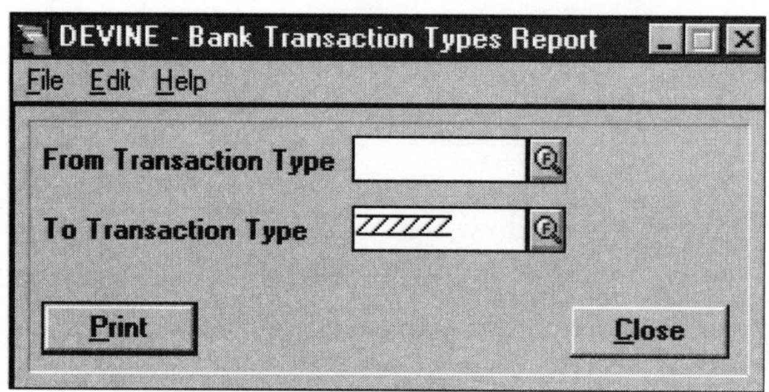

FIGURE 14-18
Bank Transaction Types Report Dialog Box

The default settings shown in Figure 14-18 print all Transaction Types. You could use the Finder to print an alphabetical range or a single Transaction Type.

❑ Click: **Print** Print

❑ Click: **OK** OK on the Print dialog box

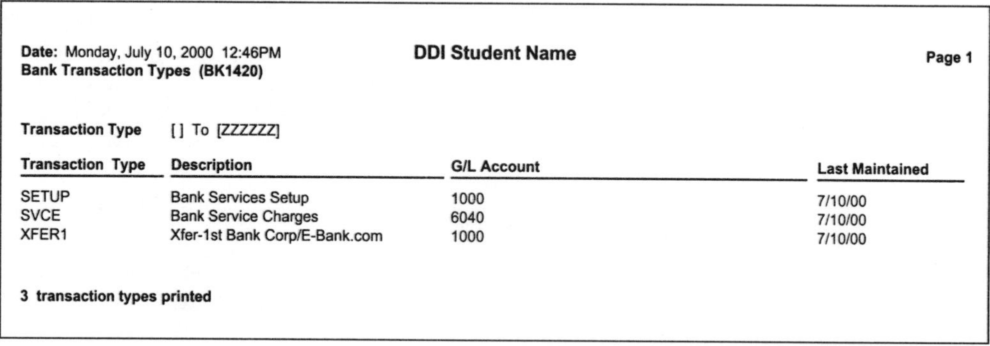

Date: Monday, July 10, 2000 12:46PM — **DDI Student Name** — **Page 1**

Bank Transaction Types (BK1420)

Transaction Type [] To [ZZZZZZ]

Transaction Type	Description	G/L Account	Last Maintained
SETUP	Bank Services Setup	1000	7/10/00
SVCE	Bank Service Charges	6040	7/10/00
XFER1	Xfer-1st Bank Corp/E-Bank.com	1000	7/10/00

3 transaction types printed

FIGURE 14-19
Bank Transaction Types Report

Compare your report with that shown in Figure 14-19. The Last Maintained date should be different as this date is the Windows system date for when the Transaction Types were added or modified. If there are errors, make the appropriate corrections and reprint the report.

❑ Close: the **Bank Transaction Types Report** dialog box

PRINTING THE BANKS REPORT

The Banks Report prints the information entered in the Banks notebook.

❑ DClick: the **Banks** [Banks] icon on the Banks Report window

The default settings, as shown in Figure 14-20, will print information for all banks in alphabetical order by bank code. You could use the Finder to select a range or a single bank for printing.

FIGURE 14-20
Banks Report Dialog Box

❑ Click: **Print** [Print]

❑ Click: **OK** [OK]

Compare your report to that shown in Figure 14-21. Note that the Last Maintained dates will not be the same on the two reports. If there are any other errors, make the necessary corrections and reprint the report.

FIGURE 14-21
Banks Report

Date: Monday, May 29, 2000 2:56PM **DDI Student Name** **Page 1**
Banks (BK1410)

From Bank Code [ ] To [ZZZZZZZZ]

Bank Code	Name/Address	Telephone / Fax / Transit Number Bank Account	Contact	Status	Date Inactive
1STBK	Firct Bank Corp 17 Melrose Place Georgetown, Province K8H 4S8 Canada	**Telephone:** (905)555-1717 **Fax:** (905)555-1818 **Transit No.:** 39821 **Bank Acct.:** 09-5753	Harry Shore	Active	

Next Deposit No.	Last Reconciliation Date	Last Maintained	Bank G/L Account	Clearing Errors G/L Account	Error Spread
1	4/30/10	5/29/00	1000	6050	0.00

Bank Code	Name/Address	Telephone / Fax / Transit Number Bank Account	Contact	Status	Date Inactive
EBANK	E-Bank.com Working Funds 1732 Upper Greenback Way Georgetown, Province K8H 4S2 Canada	**Telephone:** (905)555-1732 **Fax:** (905)555-1854 **Transit No.:** 35421 **Bank Acct.:** 01-5555	Rosemary Satco	Active	

Next Deposit No.	Last Reconciliation Date	Last Maintained	Bank G/L Account	Clearing Errors G/L Account	Error Spread
1		5/29/00	1025	6050	0.00

2 banks printed

❑ Close: the **Banks Report** dialog box

PRINTING THE RECONCILIATION POSTING JOURNAL

The Reconciliation Posting Journal is an essential part of the audit trail.

❑ DClick: the **Reconciliation Posting Journal** icon 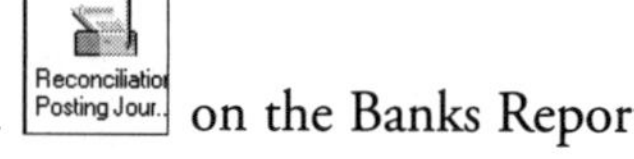 on the Banks Report window

The default settings, as shown in Figure 14-22, are to print all Reconciliation Posting Journals that have not been printed before and to retain the current reconciliation information.

FIGURE 14-22
Bank Reconciliation Posting Journal Dialog Box

DEVINE - Bank Reconciliation Posting Journal

File Edit Help

From Posting Sequence 1

To Posting Sequence 1

☐ Reprint Previously Printed Journals

☐ Clear All Printed Journals

Print Close

❑ Click: **Print** Print

❑ Click: **OK** OK

Compare your printouts to those shown in Figure 14-23. Page 2 prints a classical bank reconciliation showing that your opening balances are correct.

❑ Close: the **Bank Reconciliation Posting Journal** dialog box

FIGURE 14-23
Bank Reconciliation Posting Journal

Date: Monday, May 29, 2000 2:58PM **DDI Student Name** **Page 1**

Bank Reconciliation Posting Journal (BK1470)

From Posting Sequence [1] To [1]

Deposit / Check No.	Srce. Appl.	Deposit / Check Date	Reconciliation Status	Document Amount	Reconciliation Amt. Cleared	Clearing Difference
Posting Sequence: 1						
Bank: 1STBK - Firct Bank Corp			**Statement Currency** CAD			
Entries:						
		4/30/10	Bank Services Setup	6,812.10	6,812.10	0.00
				6,812.10	6,812.10	0.00
			Bank Total:	6,812.10		

FIGURE 14-23
Bank Reconciliation Posting Journal, continued

Date: Monday, May 29, 2000 2:58PM | DDI Student Name | Page 2

Bank Reconciliation Posting Journal (BK1470)

Deposit / Check No.	Srce. Appl.	Deposit / Check Date	Reconciliation Status	Document Amount	Reconciliation Amt. Cleared	Clearing Difference

Reconciliation Summary for 1STBK - Firct Bank Corp

		Fiscal Year	2010
		Fiscal Period	12
Statement Date	4/30/10	Reconciliation Date	4/30/10
Statement Balance	6,812.10	Book Balance	0.00
+ Deposits in Transit	0.00	+/- Bank Entries	6,812.10
- Checks Outstanding	0.00	+/- Write-offs	0.00
+/- Bank Errors	0.00	Exchange Gain	0.00
		Exchange Loss	0.00
Adjusted Statement Balance	6,812.10	Adjusted Book Balance	6,812.10
		Out of Balance	0.00

CREATING THE G/L BATCH

Now that the reconciliation has been documented, you complete establishing the bank balances by creating a General Ledger batch and then deleting that batch in the General Ledger. This prevents the posting of the setup information to the bank account in the General Ledger.

- ❑ DClick: the **Bank Reconciliation** icon on the Bank Services window
- ❑ DClick: the **Create G/L Batch** icon

The default setting, as shown in Figure 14-24, will create a General Ledger transaction batch containing all the information entered in Bank Services. The detailed information will then be removed from Bank Services so that it cannot be included in other General Ledger batches.

- ❑ Click: **Process**

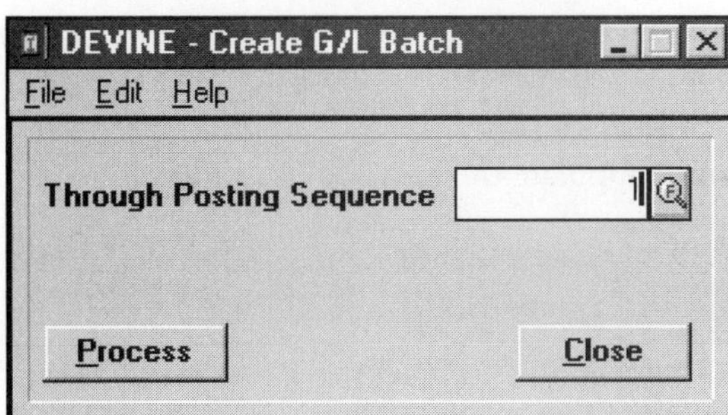

FIGURE 14-24
Create G/L Batch Dialog Box

ACCPAC will display an information message that the General Ledger batch has been successfully created.

- ❑ Click: **OK**
- ❑ Open: the **General Ledger** window
- ❑ DClick: the **Batch List** icon
- ❑ DClick: the **BK#1-#1** line on the G/L Batch List table
- ❑ Click: **Delete**

ACCPAC requires you to confirm that you want the batch deleted.

- ❑ Click: **Yes**

After the batch has been deleted, its status is changed to Deleted in the Batch List table.

- ❑ Close: the **G/L Journal Entry** window
- ❑ Close: the **G/L Batch List** window

Bank Services are now set up for use with Accounts Receivable. In Accounts Payable, you will have to add additional information on the Check Forms page of the Banks notebook.

- ❑ Exit: **ACCPAC**

REVIEW QUESTIONS

1. Do you need Bank Services if you are using only the General Ledger? When must you add the Bank Services?
2. Describe the purpose of Bank Services.
3. When setting up the bank options, you can choose to create General Ledger batches either During Posting or On Request Using Create G/L Batch Icon. Explain the differences between these two choices.
4. What does the Append G/L Transactions to Existing Batch option allow you to do?
5. List the source codes added by the Bank Services program.
6. What is the purpose of the Transaction Types?
7. How do you manipulate the Last Maintained field in the Transaction Types window?

EXERCISE

- ❑ Sign on to your company, using May 1, 2010 as the session date.

Activate the Bank Services using the same procedures and options chosen for Devine Designs Inc.

Set the Bank Options using the same procedures and options chosen for Devine Designs Inc.

Add the Transaction Types using the Setup Transaction Types created for Devine Designs Inc.

On the Profile Information page for 1STBK, create the same General Ledger and system information setup as Devine Designs Inc. Leave the Error Spread at 0.00. You can go to the bank that is closest to you and use their address, telephone, and transit number. Talk to a personal banker in the branch and use that preson's name in the Contact box.

Establishing Bank Balances:

- ❑ Select: **1STBK**
- ❑ Type: **04302010** in the Statement Date box
- ❑ Balance: **$14,412.85**

Ensure that you make the appropriate entries on the Entries page, following the example from Devine Designs Inc.

- ❑ Post the **Reconciliation**
- ❑ Print: the **Bank Options** report
- ❑ Print: the **Bank Transaction Types** report
- ❑ Print: the **Banks** report
- ❑ Print: the **Reconciliation Posting Journal**
- ❑ Create: the **G/L batch** from the Bank Reconciliation window, then delete it
- ❑ Exit: **ACCPAC**

CHAPTER 15

TAX SERVICES

In this chapter, you will set up Tax Services to be used with the Accounts Receivable and Accounts Payable accounting applications. Tax Services is used to create records for the tax authorities and the tax classes that you assign to item records, to customer accounts in Accounts Receivable, and to vendor records in Accounts Payable.

When you record invoices for items in Accounts Receivable, ACCPAC calculates all taxes, using the sales tax rates entered in Tax Services. When you enter transactions for vendors in Accounts Payable, ACCPAC calculates all taxes, using the purchases tax rates entered in Tax Services. When you post invoice batches, Accounts Receivable and Accounts Payable create General Ledger transactions for the tax accounts defined for the tax authorities and list the information on the posting journals.

TAX SERVICES ACTIVATION

- ❑ Sign on to Devine Designs Inc. as the system administrator using 05/01/10 as the Session Date.

You use Administrative Services to activate Tax Services.

❑ Open: the **Administrative Services** window

❑ DClick: the **Data Activation** icon

ACCPAC will display a warning message. If you did not back up your data at the end of the last chapter, you should do so now.

❑ Click: **Yes**

The Data Activation window on your screen may include additional applications to those shown in Figure 15-1.

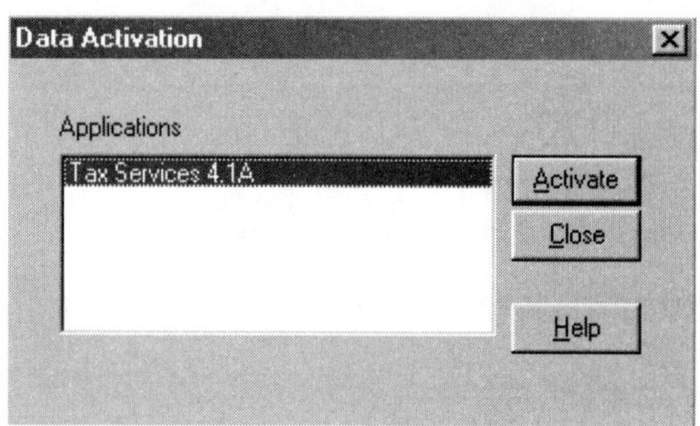

FIGURE 15-1
Data Activation Window

❑ Select: **Tax Services 4.1A**

❑ Click: **Activate**

ACCPAC will ask for confirmation as shown in Figure 15-2.

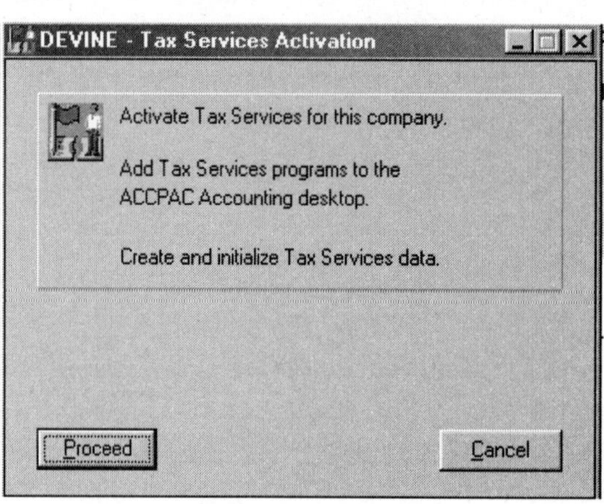

FIGURE 15-2
Tax Services Activation Window

❑ Click **Proceed**

As activation proceeds, ACCPAC will display a Tax Services Activation window that shows the progress. Once complete, the Data Activation window will become active. Note that Tax Services has been removed from the application list.

❑ Close: the **Data Activation** window

❑ Open: the **Common Services** window

ACCPAC has now added the Tax Services icon to the Common Services window.

Tax Services

❑ DClick: the **Tax Services** icon 

The Tax Services window, Figure 15-3, contains five icons.

FIGURE 15-3
Tax Services Icons

Adding Tax Authorities

You have to add a record for each tax authority or jurisdiction to which the company remits taxes. Devine Designs Inc. remits taxes to two levels of government: GST or Value Added Tax to the federal government, and RST to the provincial or state government. This tax model is simplified for learning purposes; in reality, a company may have many more tax remitting requirements.

❑ DClick: the **Tax Authorities** icon 

The Tax Authorities Window is a two-page notebook. The Tax Authority and Description text boxes are displayed for each page of the notebook.

Tax Authority

The Tax Authority text box can accept up to six alphanumeric characters. You should devise a meaningful, unique code for each jurisdiction to which you remit taxes.

Devine Designs Inc. uses three letters to describe the tax (RST or GST) and the international two-letter code to represent the province, state, or country. The first Tax Authority that Devine Designs Inc. adds is for Retail Sales Tax (RST) in the province of Ontario (ON).

❑ Enter: **RSTON** in the Tax Authority text box

❑ Press: **Tab** [Tab]

Description

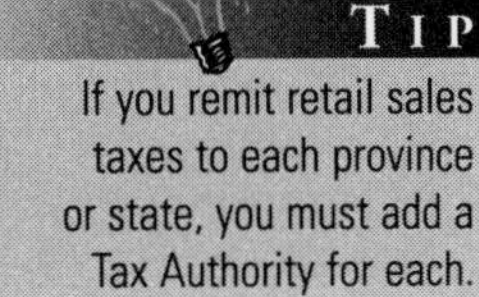

TIP

If you remit retail sales taxes to each province or state, you must add a Tax Authority for each.

You can enter up to 30 characters in the Description text box.

❑ Enter: **Retail Sales Tax - Ontario** in the Description text box

❑ Press: **Tab** [Tab]

Profile Page

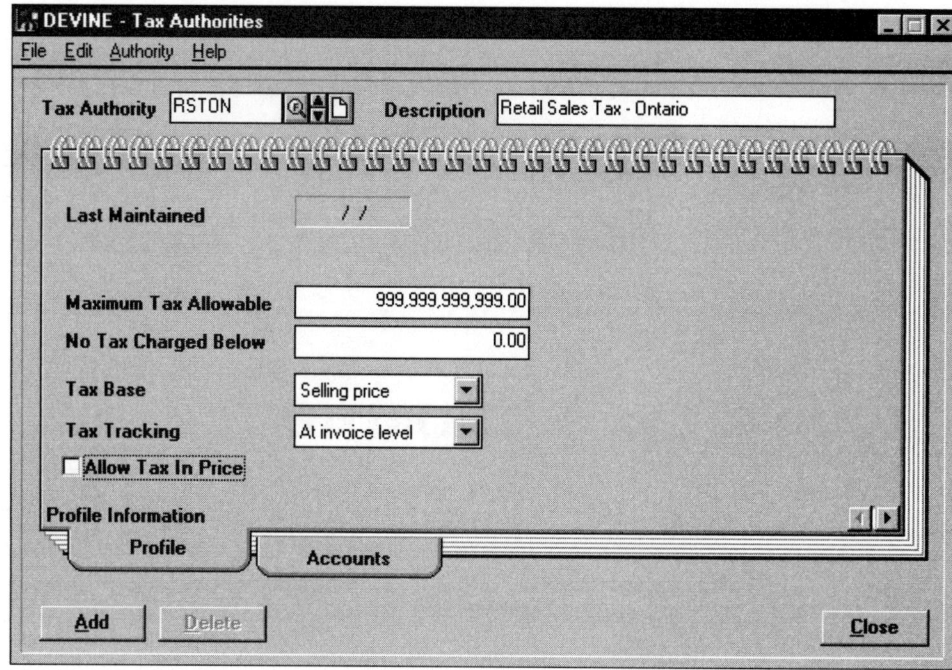

Figure 15-4
Profile Page

The Tax Authorities profile page is shown in Figure 15-4.

Last Maintained

ACCPAC updates this display with the Windows system date after you add a new tax authority or make a change to an existing one. The field is blank because no maintenance has been performed yet.

Maximum Tax Allowable

The default for the Maximum Tax Allowable is $999,999,999,999.00, assuming that there is no upper limit on the amount of tax an authority is willing to accept. Devine Designs Inc. must collect and remit the full amount of RST on all eligible sales.

Do not change the default amount.

No Tax Charged Below

The default in the No Tax Below field is 0.00, assuming that there is no minimum amount of tax charged. Devine Designs Inc. must collect and remit tax on all eligible sales.

Do not change the default amount of 0.00.

Tax Base

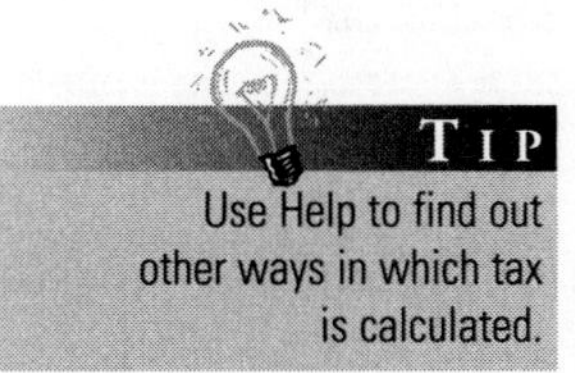

You use this list box to identify the base on which the tax is calculated. The list box offers five options. Most tax authorities collect sales tax based on Selling Price, so the base for calculating tax on an invoice or credit note is the number of units in the transaction multiplied by the price per unit.

Devine Designs Inc. must collect and remit RST based on the selling price of its services or retail sales items.

❑ Select: **Selling price**

Tax Tracking

Different tax authorities require different levels of documentation for auditing a firm's collections and remittances. Devine Designs Inc. is required to keep tax audit information for this authority At Invoice Level, printing tax information for each invoice level on the Tax Tracking report. The tax information can be cleared after printing the Tax Tracking Report.

❑ Select: **At invoice level**

If you select the No Reporting option, tax audit information is not kept and the Tax Tracking Report will be blank. It is recommended that tax audit information be retained by all companies.

Allow Tax in Price

You select this option if taxes charged by the authority can be included in the selling price. You should not include this option if you have customers who are tax exempt. Devine Designs Inc. will have tax exempt customers and so will not include RST in its selling prices.

The Allow Tax in Price check box should be empty.

ACCOUNTS PAGE

❑ Click: the **Accounts** tab on the bottom of the Tax Authorities notebook

The Account Information page will appear as shown in Figure 15-5.

Tax Liability Account

Use the Tax Liability Account text box to record the General Ledger account number to which sales taxes for this authority are posted. The amount your company will remit is the total sales tax calculated for the authority in all the tax groups. Any subledger that calculates sales tax will use this account.

FIGURE 15-5
Accounts Page

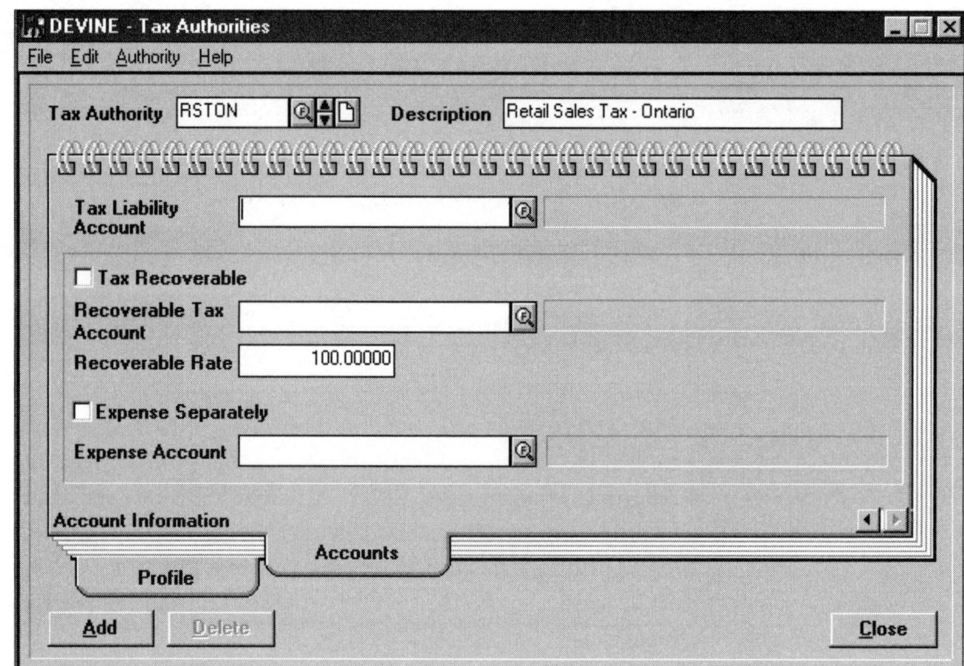

Devine Designs Inc. uses account 2100 to record RST payable.

❑ Select: Account **2100** using the Finder

Tax Recoverable

In general, retail sales taxes are not recoverable, but Value Added Tax is recoverable. The RST that Devine Designs Inc. collects for Ontario is not recoverable. If the Tax Recoverable check box is active, click it.

Expense Separately

You select this option if you record the sales tax as an expense. As a rule, retail sales taxes are not expensed separately.

❑ Click: **Add**

YOUR TURN

You will now add the Tax Authority for the federal government, which collects a value added tax. For Devine Designs Inc., the tax authority is the federal government, which collects a 7% GST on all sales. Companies are allowed to recover the GST paid on their purchases.

- ❑ Click: the **Profile** tab at the bottom of the notebook
- ❑ Click: the **New Document** icon for the Tax Authority text box
- ❑ Enter: **GSTFED** in the Tax Authority text box
- ❑ Enter: **Federal Goods & Services Tax** in the Description text box

The federal government requires that the actual amount of GST be collected on all purchases based on the Selling Price At Invoice Level.

- ❑ Select the appropriate options on the Profile page.
- ❑ Click: the **Accounts** tab at the bottom of the notebook

Devine Design Inc. uses account 2200 to record GST payable.

- ❑ Select: Tax Liability Account **2200**

The federal government allows companies to recover 100% of the GST paid on purchases. Devine Designs Inc. uses account 2205 to record GST recoverable.

- ❑ Click: the **Tax Recoverable** check box
- ❑ Select: **2205** in the Recoverable Tax Account text box
- ❑ Enter: **100** in the Recoverable Rate text box
- ❑ Click: **Add** [Add]
- ❑ Close: the **Tax Authorities** window

PRINTING THE TAX AUTHORITIES REPORT

- ❑ DClick: the **Tax Reports** icon [Tax Reports] on the Tax Services window

You will then see the Tax Reports window, shown in Figure 15-6.

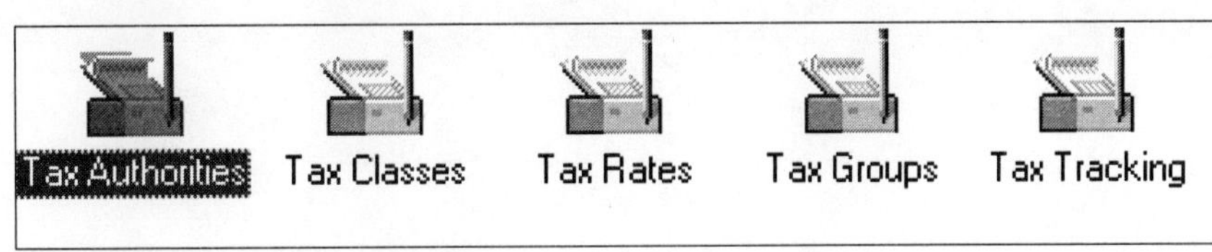

FIGURE 15-6
Tax Reports Icons

You will use the first four icons as you complete this chapter. Tax Tracking Reports will be printed in Accounts Receivable and Accounts Payable.

- ❑ DClick: the **Tax Authorities** icon [Tax Authorities]

FIGURE 15-7
Tax Authorities Report Dialog Box

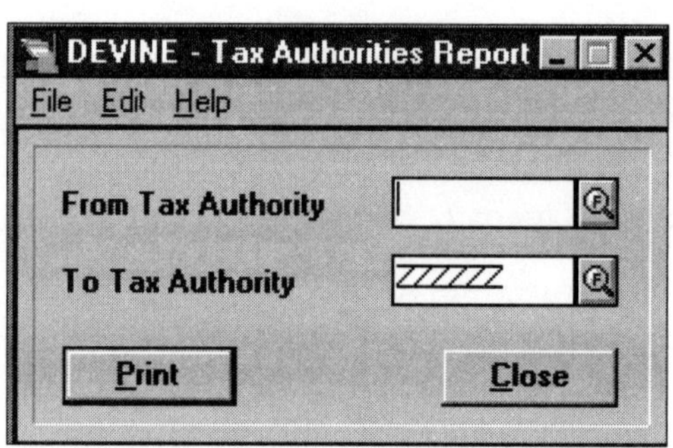

The default settings, shown in Figure 15-7, print all Tax Authorities in alphabetical order. Devine Designs will print all Tax Authorities.

- ❑ Click: **Print** [Print]
- ❑ Click: **OK** [OK] on the Print dialog box
- ❑ Close: the **Tax Authorities Report** dialog box

FIGURE 15-8
Tax Authorities Report

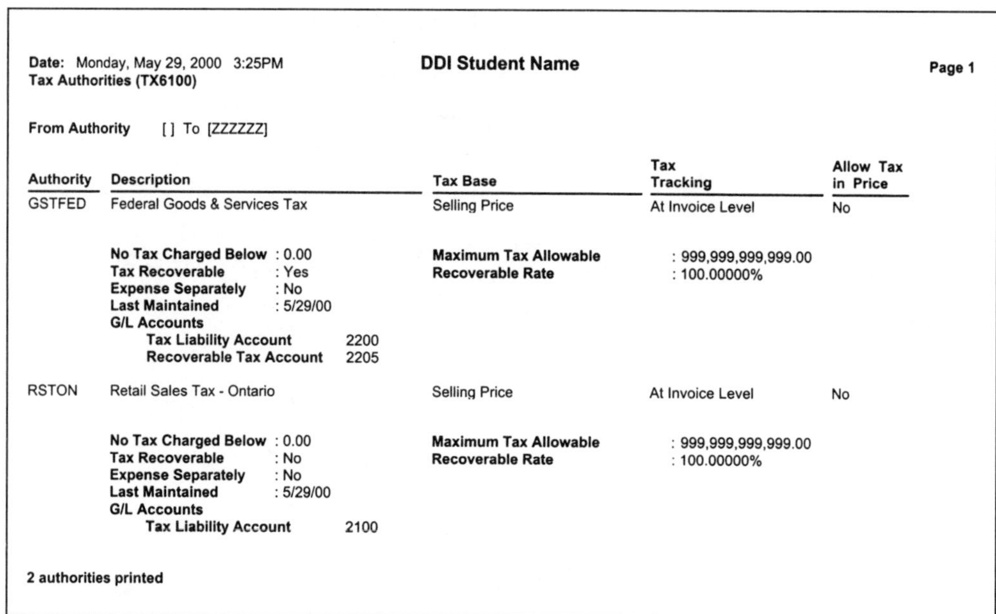

Date: Monday, May 29, 2000 3:25PM **DDI Student Name** **Page 1**
Tax Authorities (TX6100)

From Authority [ ] To [ZZZZZZ]

Authority	Description	Tax Base	Tax Tracking	Allow Tax in Price
GSTFED	Federal Goods & Services Tax	Selling Price	At Invoice Level	No

No Tax Charged Below : 0.00 — **Maximum Tax Allowable** : 999,999,999,999.00
Tax Recoverable : Yes — **Recoverable Rate** : 100.00000%
Expense Separately : No
Last Maintained : 5/29/00
G/L Accounts
Tax Liability Account 2200
Recoverable Tax Account 2205

Authority	Description	Tax Base	Tax Tracking	Allow Tax in Price
RSTON	Retail Sales Tax - Ontario	Selling Price	At Invoice Level	No

No Tax Charged Below : 0.00 — **Maximum Tax Allowable** : 999,999,999,999.00
Tax Recoverable : No — **Recoverable Rate** : 100.00000%
Expense Separately : No
Last Maintained : 5/29/00
G/L Accounts
Tax Liability Account 2100

2 authorities printed

Compare your printout to that shown in Figure 15-8. Make any necessary corrections and print the report again.

ADDING TAX CLASSES

For each tax authority you have added, you have to define Tax Classes. Tax Classes are required for both sales and purchases. Sales classes consist of customers and items, whereas purchase classes consist of vendors and items. Tax Classes for Vendors and Items will be added at the beginning of the Accounts Payable module.

❑ DClick: the **Tax Classes** icon [Tax Classes] on the Tax Services window

The Tax Classes window will appear as shown in Figure 15-9.

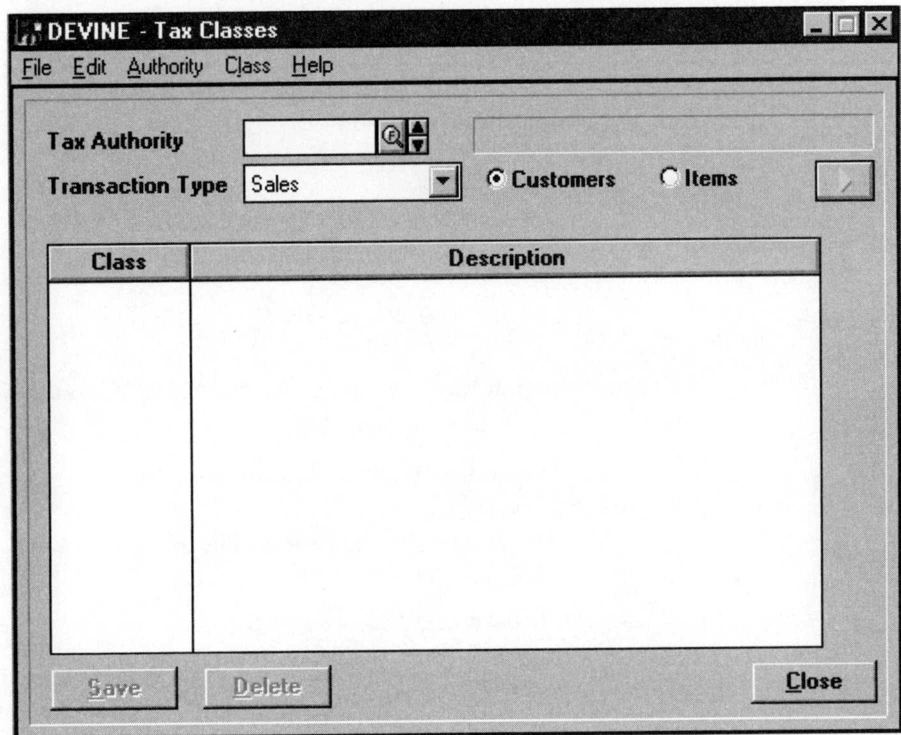

FIGURE 15-9
Tax Classes Window

The first Tax Class that Devine Designs Inc. will enter is for RST on sales.

Tax Authority

❑ Click: the **Finder** for Tax Authority

❑ Select: **RSTON**

Transaction Type

There are two choices of Transaction Types: Sales and Purchases.

❑ Select: **Sales**

ACCPAC requires that you enter at least one customer/vendor class and one item class in order to be able to enter tax rates.

❑ Ensure that the **Customers** option button is active.
❑ Click: **GO**

Class 1 will appear.

❑ Press: **Tab** [Tab] to move to the Description cell
❑ Type: **Taxable**

In this simulation, all of Devine Designs Inc.'s domestic customers will be taxable.

❑ Press: **Tab** [Tab]

The screen will create a second line. Class 2 is for sales to customers who are tax exempt.

❑ Click: the **Description** cell
❑ Type: **Exempt**
❑ Press: **Enter** [ENTER]

You can add up to ten classes for each Tax Authority and Transaction type combination. Taxable and Exempt Classes are sufficient for the Devine Designs Inc. simulation.

❑ Click: **Save** [Save]

You must enter at least one Items class for ACCPAC to use when it creates a Tax Rate table.

❑ Click: the **Items** option button
❑ Click: **GO**
❑ Enter: **All items** in the Description cell for Class 1
❑ Press: **Enter** [ENTER]
❑ Click: **Save** [Save]

Devine Designs Inc. must also create Tax Classes for the federal GST for both sales and purchases.

❑ Select: **GSTFED** in the Tax Authority text box
❑ Select: **Sales** in the Transaction Type list box
❑ Select: the **Customers** option button
❑ Click: **GO**
❑ Add: Class 1 **Taxable**
❑ Add: Class 2 **Exempt**
❑ Click: **Save** [Save]
❑ Select: the **Items** option button
❑ Click: **GO**
❑ Add: Class 1 **All Sales**
❑ Click: **Save** [Save]
❑ Select: **GSTFED** in the Tax Authority text box
❑ Select: **Purchases** in the Transaction Type list box
❑ Select: the **Vendors** option button

- ❑ Click: **GO**
- ❑ Add: Class 1 **Taxable**
- ❑ Add: Class 2 **Exempt**
- ❑ Click: **Save** Save
- ❑ Enter the corresponding Items classes
- ❑ Select: **GSTFED** in the Tax Authority text box
- ❑ Select: **Purchases** in the Transaction Type list box
- ❑ Select: the **Items** option button
- ❑ Click: **GO**
- ❑ Add: Class 1 **All Purchases**
- ❑ Click: **Save** Save

PRINTING THE TAX CLASSES REPORT

- ❑ Click: **File** on the Tax Classes window menu bar
- ❑ Click: **Print** on the File menu

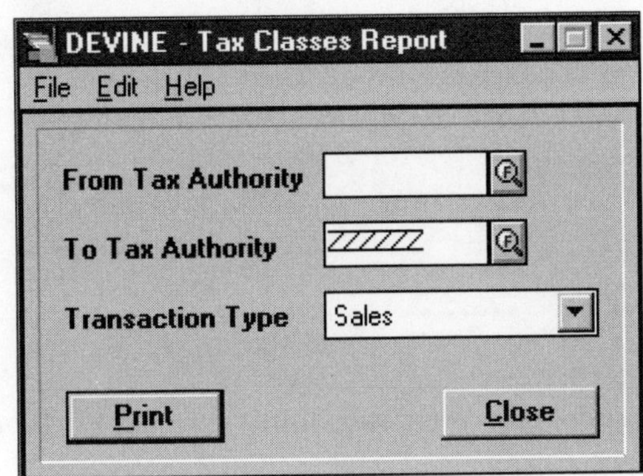

FIGURE 15-10
Tax Classes Report Dialog Box

The Tax Classes Report dialog box is shown in Figure 15-10. The default settings will print a report in alphabetical order for all Tax Authorities for the transaction type you select.

- ❑ Select: **Sales** in the Transaction Type list box
- ❑ Click: **Print** Print
- ❑ Click: **OK** OK on the Print dialog box
- ❑ Print the same report for **Purchases**.

FIGURE 15-11
Tax Classes Report

Date: Monday, July 10, 2000 10:17AM
Sales Tax Classes (TX6200)

DDI Student Name

Page 1

From Authority [ ] To [ZZZZZZ]

Authority	Description	Class Type	Class	Description
GSTFED	Federal Goods & Services Tax			
		Customer		
			1	Taxable
			2	Exempt
		Item		
			1	All Sales
RSTON	Retail Sales Tax - Ontario			
		Customer		
			1	Taxable
			2	Exempt
		Item		
			1	All items

2 authorities printed

Date: Monday, July 10, 2000 10:17AM
Purchases Tax Classes (TX6200)

DDI Student Name

Page 1

From Authority [ ] To [ZZZZZZ]

Authority	Description	Class Type	Class	Description
GSTFED	Federal Goods & Services Tax			
		Vendor		
			1	Taxable
			2	Exempt
		Item		
			1	All Purchases

1 authority printed

Compare your printouts to those shown in Figure 15-11. If necessary, make corrections and print the reports again.

❑ Close: the **Tax Classes Report** dialog box
❑ Close: the **Tax Classes** window

ENTERING TAX RATES

Tax Services creates sales and purchases tax tables, using the tax classes you have created. A sales tax table consists of customer classes and item classes, while a purchase tax table consists of vendor classes and item classes. The tax rates that you enter in these tables are used by the Accounts Receivable program to determine the tax charges to customers, and the Accounts Payable to determine the tax charges from vendors.

❑ DClick: the **Tax Rates** icon on the Tax Services window
❑ Select: **RSTON** in the Tax Authority text box
❑ Select: **Sales** in the Transaction Type list box
❑ Click: **GO**

FIGURE 15-12
Tax Rates Window

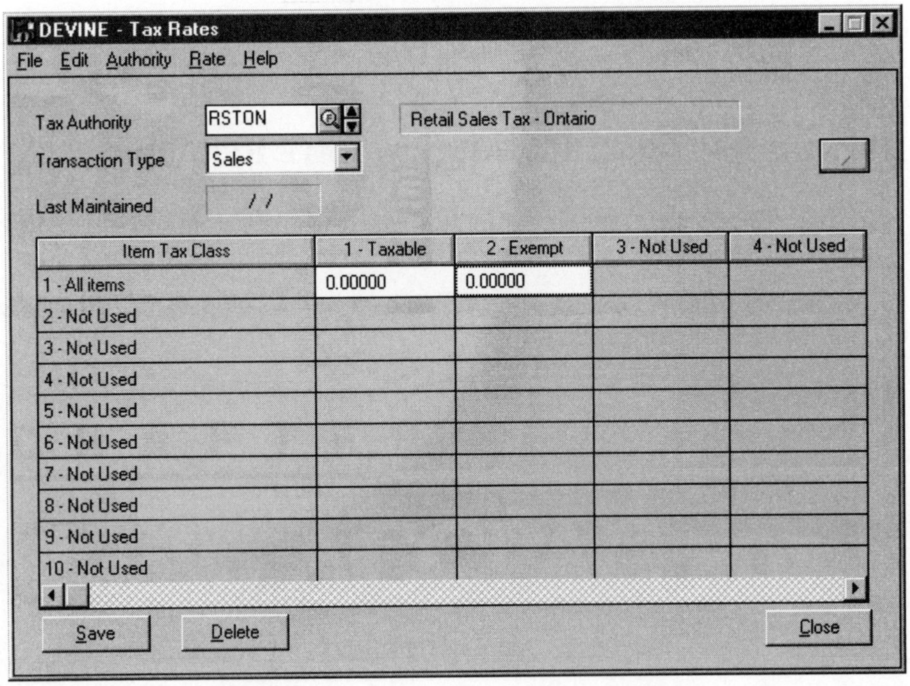

The Tax Rates window will appear as shown in Figure 15-12. Note that the Customer classes you added appear as the column headings, and the Items classes appear as the row headings. There are two active cells in which you can enter tax rates.

- ❑ DClick: the **Taxable** cell in row 1 - All Sales
- ❑ Type: **8**
- ❑ Press: **Enter**
- ❑ Click: **Save**

Devine Designs Inc. must also enter rates for both sales and purchases for the federal GST.

- ❑ Select: **GSTFED**
- ❑ Select: **Sales**
- ❑ Click: **GO**
- ❑ DClick: the **Taxable** cell
- ❑ Type: 7
- ❑ Press: **Enter**
- ❑ Click: **Save**
- ❑ Enter the rate for the Transaction Type Purchases.
- ❑ Select: **GSTFED**
- ❑ Select: **Purchases**
- ❑ Click: **GO**
- ❑ Click: the **Taxable** cell
- ❑ Type: 7
- ❑ Press: **Enter**

- ❑ Click: **Save** [Save]
- ❑ Close: the **Tax Rates** window

PRINTING THE TAX RATE REPORT

- ❑ Open: the **Tax Reports** window
- ❑ DClick: the **Tax Rates** icon [Tax Rates] on the Tax Reports window

The Tax Rates Report dialog box is shown in Figure 15-13.

FIGURE 15-13
Tax Rates Report Dialog Box

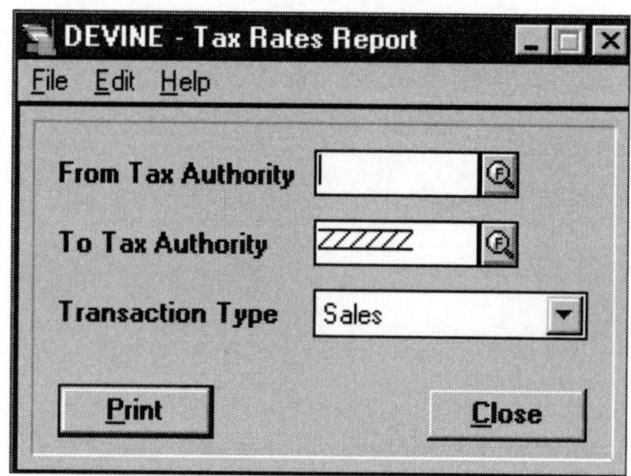

- ❑ Select: **Sales** in the Transaction Type list box
- ❑ Click: **Print** [Print]
- ❑ Click: **OK** [OK] on the Print dialog box
- ❑ Print: the **Tax Rate Report** for **Purchases**
- ❑ Close: the **Tax Rates Report** dialog box

Compare your printouts to those shown in Figure 15-14. Make any necessary corrections and print the reports again.

FIGURE 15-14
Tax Rates Report

Date: Monday, July 10, 2000 10:21AM
Sales Tax Rates (TX6400)

DDI Student Name

Page 1

From Authority [] To [ZZZZZZ]

Authority	Customer Tax Class	Item Tax Class	Tax Rate
GSTFED	1-Taxable	1-All Sales	7.00000%
	2-Exempt	1-All Sales	0.00000%
RSTON	1-Taxable	1-All items	8.00000%
	2-Exempt	1-All items	0.00000%

2 authorities printed

Date: Monday, July 10, 2000 10:22AM
Purchases Tax Rates (TX6400)

DDI Student Name

Page 1

From Authority [] To [ZZZZZZ]

Authority	Vendor Tax Class	Item Tax Class	Tax Rate
GSTFED	1-Taxable	1-All Purchases	7.00000%
	2-Exempt	1-All Purchases	0.00000%

1 authority printed

ADDING TAX GROUPS

A Tax Group consists of all Tax Authorities that charge sales tax in a particular area. In this simulation, Devine Designs Inc. is subject to RST and GST on domestic sales and purchases. Foreign sales or purchases are not subject to sales tax. Devine Designs Inc. will require two Tax Groups for the domestic market.

❑ DClick: the **Tax Groups** icon on the Tax Services window

The Tax Groups window will appear as shown in Figure 15-15

❑ Type: **DOMSAL** in the Tax Group text box
❑ Press: **Tab** Tab
❑ Select: **Sales** as the Transaction Type
❑ Click: **GO**

FIGURE 15-15
Tax Groups Window

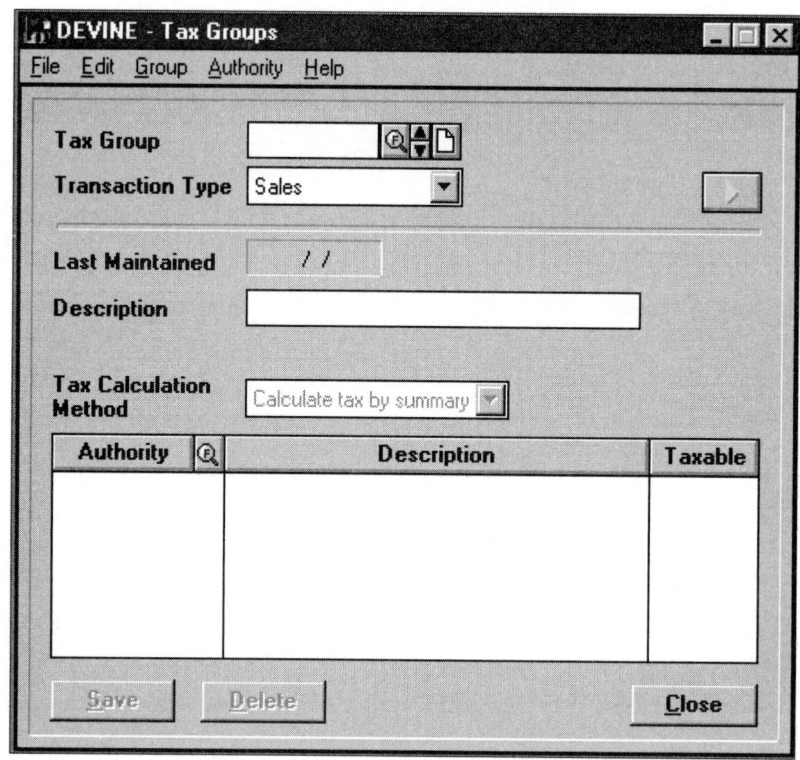

An inquiry message may appear requiring confirmation that you want to add Tax Group DOMSAL. If the message appears,

- ❑ Click: **Yes** [Yes]
- ❑ Type: **Domestic Sales** in the Description text box
- ❑ Press: **Tab** [Tab]

Tax Calculation Method

You have two choices for the Tax Calculation method. If you select Calculate tax by detail, the program will calculate tax on each invoice by multiplying the tax base by the tax rate. The total tax for the invoice is the sum of the tax calculated for each detail line. The second method is Calculate tax by summary. In this option, the program calculates tax on the invoice total by multiplying the document amount by the tax rate.

The results of one method may differ from the other due to rounding. It is usually better to use the Calculate tax by detail method if any authority in the group allows tax to be included in the price.

- ❑ Select: **Calculate tax by summary**
- ❑ Press: **Tab** [Tab] to move to the Authority cell
- ❑ Select: **GSTFED**

Taxable

If you have to pay taxes on the taxes you charge on your invoices, you would change the Taxable field to Yes by typing Yes or double-clicking the No to effect the change. Generally speaking, the sales taxes charged on invoices represent a liability to the company, not a revenue, and are therefore not taxable.

- ❑ Press: **Tab** [Tab] to create a second line
- ❑ Select: **RSTON** for the second authority
- ❑ Click: **Add** [Add]

- ❑ Add the following Tax Group:

Tax Group:	**DOMPUR**
Transaction Type:	**Purchases**
Description:	**Domestic Purchases**
Tax Calculation Method:	**Calculate tax by summary**
Tax Authorities:	**GSTFED and RSTON**
Taxable:	**No**

TIP
Remember to add this Tax Group.

After adding these tax groups:

- ❑ Close: the **Tax Groups** window

PRINTING THE TAX GROUPS

- ❑ Open: the **Tax Reports** window
- ❑ DClick: the **Tax Groups** icon

FIGURE 15-16
Tax Groups Report Dialog Box

The defaults shown in Figure 15-16 will print all Tax Groups for the transaction type Sales in alphabetical order.

- ❑ Click: **Print** [Print]
- ❑ Click **OK**

Once printing has finished,

❑ Print: the **Tax Group Report** for Transaction Type **Purchases**

Compare your reports to those shown in Figure 15-17. Make any necessary corrections and print the reports again.

❑ Close: the **Tax Groups Report** dialog box

FIGURE 15-17
Tax Groups Reports

Date: Monday, July 10, 2000 10:27AM
Sales Tax Groups (TX6300)

DDI Student Name **Page 1**

From Group [ ] To [ZZZZZZ]

Tax Group	Description	Tax Calculation Method	Tax Authority	Description	Taxable	Currency
DOMSAL	Domestic Sales	Calculate tax by summary	1-GSTFED	Federal Goods & Services Tax	No	
			2-RSTON	Retail Sales Tax - Ontario	No	

1 group printed

Date: Monday, July 10, 2000 10:27AM
Purchases Tax Groups (TX6300)

DDI Student Name **Page 1**

From Group [ ] To [ZZZZZZ]

Tax Group	Description	Tax Calculation Method	Tax Authority	Description	Taxable	Currency
DOMPUR	Domestic Purchases	Calculate tax by summary	1-GSTFED	Federal Goods & Services Tax	No	

1 group printed

MAINTAINING TAX SERVICES RECORDS

Tax rates and authorities change from time to time. You can edit tax authority records, tax classes and rates, and tax groups as needed. If you edit a tax rate, the new rate will apply only to invoices entered after you save the tax rate changes. If you need to edit the tax already calculated on invoices in unposted batches, you have to use the Invoice Distribution window in Accounts Receivable.

❑ Exit: **ACCPAC**

Review Questions

1. What are Tax Services?
2. Define "Tax Authority."
3. Define "Tax Group."
4. What are the Tax Authorities within your own region?
5. Name and describe the two methods in the Tax Groups window used to calculate taxes.
6. If you edit a tax rate and change it, what effect will that have on invoices prepared before the change?
7. Can you delete a Tax Authority?

Exercise

- ❑ Sign on to your company.
- ❑ The date sequence for this exercise will be the same as that used in the chapter.
- ❑ Enter 050110 in the Session Date box.
- ❑ Your company resides in the same province (or state) and country as Devine Designs Inc. and, as such, is responsible for the same taxes and rates as Devine Designs. Your exercise for this chapter is to reenter the information you have just finished putting into Devine Designs Inc., but this time into your own company. The best way to accomplish this project would be to start your company, then repeat the chapter.
- ❑ Print the same reports that were required as you worked through the chapter.

CASE 2

Murphballs & Co. Bank and Tax Services

This case continues from the General Ledger case presented earlier in the text. After Murphballs & Co.'s first month of operations, Ruff Tuff McDuff decided to add the ACCPAC for Windows Small Business Series Accounts Receivable module to the computerized accounting system. The Accounts Payable module will be added later. Bank Services must be activated before you integrate the Accounts Receivable or Accounts Payable with the General Ledger. Tax Services is used to create records for the tax authorities and tax classes you assign. Your assignment in this case is to set up the Bank Services and then the Tax Services.

After completing this case, organize and submit Murphballs & Co.'s printouts. Each printout *must* contain your initials followed by the company name. If you are given no instructions regarding a field, leave the defaults unchanged.

Sign on to Murphballs & Co. as the system administrator using July 31, 2010 as the Session Date.

Follow the steps and procedures in the Bank Services and Tax Services chapters to complete the required tasks.

ACTIVATE BANK SERVICES

❑ Activate: **Bank Services 4.1A**

From the Banks Setup window, set up the following Bank Options:

Create G/L Transactions:	**During Posting**
Append G/L Transactions to Existing Batch:	**Leave inactive**
Consolidate G/L Batches:	**Do Not Consolidate**

From the Transaction Types window create the following:

The first Transaction Type is for Bank Service Charges:

Transaction Type:	**SVCE**
Description:	**Bank Service Charges**
G/L Account:	**6020**

Create a Transaction Type for the Bank Services set up.

Transaction Type:	**SETUP**
Description:	**Bank Services Setup**
G/L Account:	**1101**

Create a Bank Profile

Create the Bank Profile using the Banks icon.

Bank:	**BBB**
Description:	**Buried Bone Bank**
Transit Number:	**98765**
Bank Account Number:	**000001**
Next Deposit:	**1**
Error Spread:	**0.00**

G/L Accounts:

Bank:	**1101**
Clearing Errors:	**6020**

Address Information:

	77 Tailchase Ave.
	Muttsville Junction
Zip/Postal:	**BOW WOW**
Contact:	**Halfconchess**
Telephone:	**555-555-1122**
Fax:	**555-555-1123**

Establishing the Bank Balance

Add the following information to the Reconciliation Summary page:

Bank:	**BBB**
Statement Date:	**07/31/2010**
Bank Statement Balance:	**$1,882.15**
Fiscal Year:	**2011**
Period:	**1**
Reconciliation Date:	**07/31/2010**

Entries Page:

Transaction Date:	**07/31/10**
Transaction Type:	**SETUP**
Debit Amount:	**$1,882.15**
Reference:	**Bank Statement**
Description:	**Setup Reconciliation**

There are no outstanding checks or deposits.

- ❑ Post: the Reconciliation
- ❑ Print: the Bank Options report
- ❑ Print: the Bank Transaction Types report
- ❑ Print: the Banks report
- ❑ Print and clear the Bank Reconciliation Posting journal.

TAX SERVICES

Using Administrative Services, activate Tax Services 4.1A.

Add the following Tax Authorities:

RSTON:	**Retail Sales Tax**
Tax Base:	**Selling Price**
Tax Tracking:	**At invoice level**
Tax Liability Account:	**2105**
GSTFED:	**Federal Goods & Services Tax**
Tax Base:	**Selling Price**
Tax Tracking:	**At invoice level**
Tax Liability Account:	**2110**
Activate:	**the Tax Recoverable check box**
Recoverable Tax Account:	**2111**
Recoverable Tax Rate:	**100**

- ❑ Print: the Tax Authorities Report

TAX CLASSES

For every Tax Authority, both Transaction Types (Sales and Purchases), and for customers, vendors, and items, create Class 1, Taxable and Class 2, Exempt.

❑ Print: the Tax Classes report

Tax Rates

Add the following Tax Rates.

RSTON	**Sales Taxable:**	**8**
RSTON	**Purchases Taxable:**	**8**
GSTFED	**Sales Taxable:**	7
GSTFED	**Purchases Taxable:**	7

❑ Print: the Tax Rate report for both Sales and Purchases

Tax Groups

Create the following Tax Group.

Tax Group:	**BALLCH**
Transaction Type:	**Sales**
Description:	**Ball Chasing Services**
Tax Calculation Method:	**Calculate tax by detail**
First Authority:	**GSTFED**
Second Authority	**RSTON**

Ensure that both authorities show "**No**" in the Taxable column.

Add the following second Tax Group.

Tax Group:	**PURCH**
Transaction Type:	**Purchases**
Description:	**Purchases**
Tax Calculation Method:	**Calculate tax by detail**
First Authority:	**GSTFED**
Second Authority	**RSTON**

Ensure that both authorities show "Yes" in the Taxable column.

❑ Print: the Sales Tax Groups report for both groups.

❑ Exit: ACCPAC

UNIT 5

ACCOUNTS RECEIVABLE

CHAPTER 16

SETTING UP ACCOUNTS RECEIVABLE

In Part 5, you will add the Accounts Receivable module for Devine Designs Inc. Devine Designs Inc. is already using the ACCPAC System Manager and General Ledger modules and has decided to add the Accounts Receivable. Each chapter will guide you through one step in setting up and operating the ACCPAC Accounts Receivable module.

If you have not completed Part 2: System Manager, Part 3: General Ledger, and Part 4: Bank and Tax Services, do so now.

INSTALLING ACCOUNTS RECEIVABLE

WARNING

You must have an Activation Code to complete installation of the System Manager. If you do not have one, complete the form at www.accpac.com/ products/ activfm.htm.

In this section, you will install the ACCPAC Accounts Receivable. The procedure is very similar to that used in Chapter 2 to install the System Manager and General Ledger.

❑ Display the Windows Desktop on your screen.

❑ DClick: the **My Computer** icon

❑ DClick: the **Control Panel** icon in the My Computer window

❑ DClick: the **Add/Remove Programs** icon in the Control Panel window

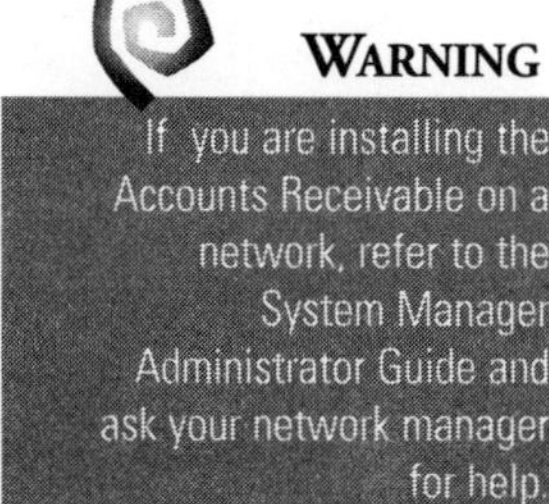

WARNING

If you are installing the Accounts Receivable on a network, refer to the System Manager Administrator Guide and ask your network manager for help.

The upper portion of the Install/Uninstall page is used to install programs. As a program is installed, Windows will monitor the installation and save the information necessary for removing the program. The lower portion of the page is used to uninstall or remove programs.

❑ Click: **Install**

The Install Program window reminds you to insert the first installation floppy disk or CD-ROM.

❑ Insert the ACCPAC for Windows Small Business Series Accounts Receivable CD-ROM.

Windows will scan the CD you just inserted and the screen will display the Accounts Receivable Installation information shown in Figure 16-1.

FIGURE 16-1
Accounts Receivable Installation

❑ Click: **Install ACCPAC (32-bit)**

ACCPAC will load the installation software and then display a series of dialog boxes that enable you to enter the information required for the installation of Accounts Receivable. The Welcome window will remind you to close all other Windows programs before running the Accounts Receivable Setup program. If necessary, click Cancel, exit any other Windows programs, and then start the installation over again.

❑ Click: **Next**

The next window displayed contains a copy of the licensing agreement for installing and using ACCPAC. Use the scroll bar to view the whole agreement.

- ❑ Click: **Yes** [Yes] to accept the terms of the license agreement
- ❑ Select: the radio button for **I have an activation code**
- ❑ Click: **Next** [Next >] to display the second Activation window

You must fill in the text boxes with the exact information supplied by ACCPAC International in response to your activation code request. The name and company text boxes will display the information that you entered as you installed the System Manager.

TIP

Staple a copy of the activation information received from ACCPAC International onto the first page of each of the Accounts Receivable manuals.

- ❑ Type: the **name of the software vendor** in the Dealer text box
- ❑ Press: **Tab** [Tab]
- ❑ Type: the **name of the qualified installer** in the QI text box
- ❑ Press: **Tab** [Tab]
- ❑ Type: the **Product ID number** in the Product ID/Serial # text box
- ❑ Press: **Tab** [Tab]
- ❑ Type: the **Activation Code** in the Activation Code text box

As you enter the Activation Code, the Next button will become active. Check that you have entered the information exactly as on the form you received from ACCPAC International.

- ❑ Click: **Next** [Next >]

The Select Components window identifies the different options you can install and shows the default directory C:\Program Files\ACCPAC. If you install the General Ledger to a different drive or directory, click the browse button and select the appropriate location for the files. The Select Components window is shown in Figure 16-2.

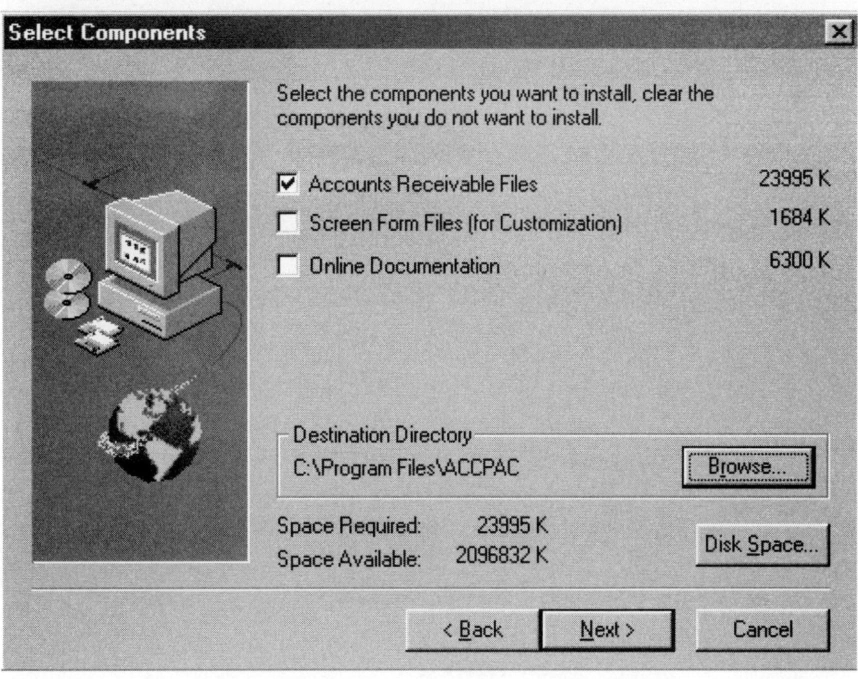

FIGURE 16-2 Select Components

- ❑ Click: **Next** [Next >]

WARNING

If you are installing the Accounts Receivable in a networked environment, ask the network manager for the proper location for installing the Accounts Receivable.

The Select Program Folder dialog box is used to add program icons to a folder in the Windows 95/98 Start menu. The Program Folder text box displays ACCPAC 32-bit as the default. The scroll box lists the existing folders. If necessary, change the default in the Program Folders text box.

❑ Click: **Next** [Next >] to accept the default ACCPAC folder

Before copying files to your hard drive, ACCPAC displays the Start Copying Files dialog box, shown in Figure 16-3.

FIGURE 16-3
Start Copying Files Window

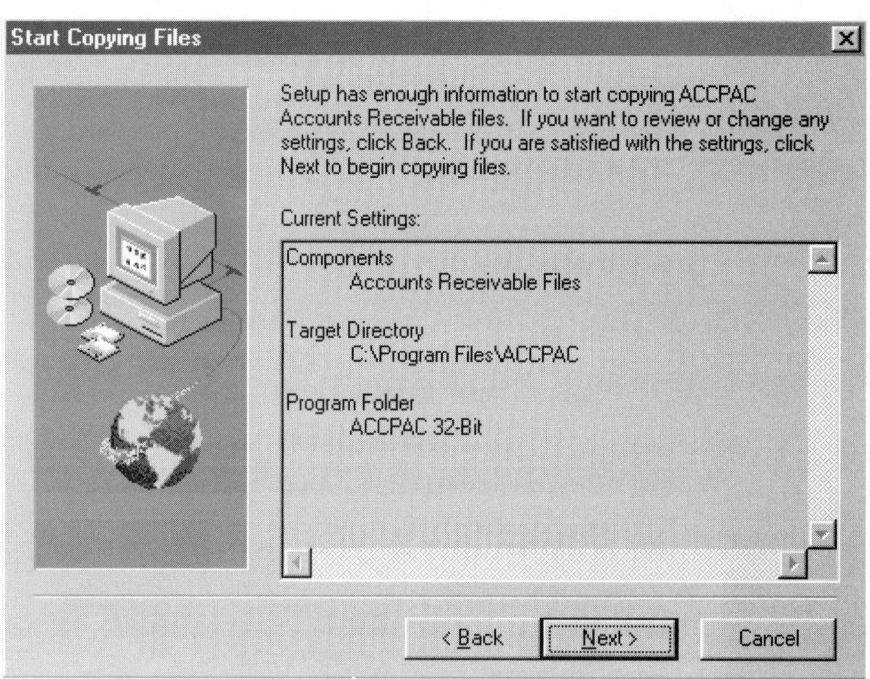

Carefully review the components to be installed and the directories to be used. The target directory should be C:\Program Files\ACCPAC and the folder should be ACCPAC 32-bit.

WARNING

If you are installing on a network, confirm these settings with your network manager.

❑ Click: **Next** [Next >]

After all the Accounts Receivable files have been copied, ACCPAC will inquire if you want to view the Accounts Receivable README file. To inform users of changes that have not yet been added to their printed manuals, most software manufacturers include README files on disk. Whenever you install a new or upgraded software package, print and read the README file and follow any additional installation steps described. Then make the necessary changes in the manual.

TIP

Print the README file and tape a copy of it into your manual. Cut up a second copy of the printout and tape it to the related pages in your manuals.

❑ Click: **Finish** [Finish] to view the README file in WordPad

To print the information,

❑ Click: the **Print** icon [Print]
❑ Close: the **WordPad** window

If you are asked if you wish to save changes to the README file, click **No.**

- ❑ Close: the **ACCPAC 32-bit** window
- ❑ Exit: the **Accounts Receivable Installation** window
- ❑ Close: the **Install Program** window
- ❑ Close: the **Install** window
- ❑ Close: the **Control Panel** window
- ❑ Remove: the ACCPAC CD from the computer and store it in a safe place.

ACCPAC International creates modified versions of program modules that are not full upgrades or product replacements. These program temporary fixes (PTF) or Service Packs should be installed by an ACCPAC authorized Qualified Installer. You should contact your ACCPAC Qualified Installer and have the most recent Accounts Receivable Service Pack installed.

ACTIVATING ACCOUNTS RECEIVABLE

- ❑ Start: **ACCPAC**
- ❑ Sign on to Devine Designs Inc. as the system administrator using 05/01/10 as the Session Date.
- ❑ Open: the **Administrative Services** window

TIP
Close all other program windows for the company before activating the data.

Only the system administrator is allowed to activate data files.

- ❑ DClick: the **Data Activation** icon

A warning message will appear cautioning you to make a backup of your data files before continuing.

- ❑ Click: **Yes** to continue activation

The Data Activation window will appear as shown in Figure 16-4.

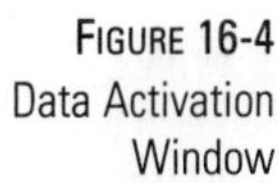

FIGURE 16-4
Data Activation Window

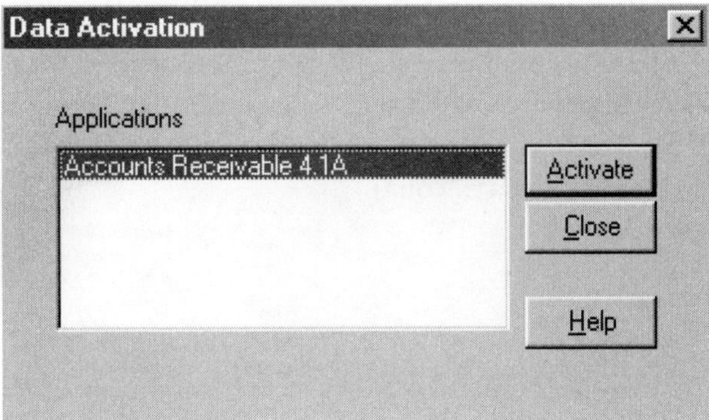

❑ Select: **Accounts Receivable 4.1A**

❑ Click: **Activate** Activate

You may see a message informing you that Accounts Receivable 4.1A requires a System Manager 4.1A with a PTF dated 20000115 or later. The PTF is a temporary fix created by ACCPAC International to solve difficulties with the software. You require a user ID and password to access the ACCPAC website to obtain these service packs. Contact your qualified installer to update your system manager.

A warning screen will appear requiring confirmation that you want to activate Accounts Receivable for this company and to Add Accounts Receivable Programs to the ACCPAC for Windows desktop.

❑ Click: **Proceed** Proceed

Once activation is complete,

❑ Click: **Close** Close to return to the Administrative Services window

❑ Click: **Accounts Receivable**

The Accounts Receivable icon is now displayed on the Company Desktop, indicating that the Accounts Receivable has been activated.

FIGURE 16-5
Accounts Receivable Icons

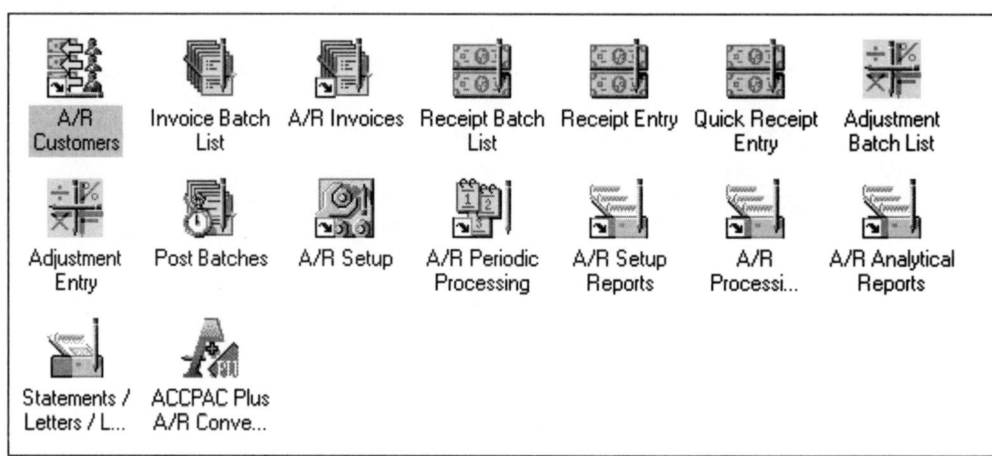

You will use fifteen of the sixteen icons in the window shown in Figure 16-5 as you work through the Accounts Receivable part of this book. The last icon, ACCPAC Plus A/R Conversion, would be used if you were converting Accounts Receivable data files from a DOS version of ACCPAC. As you work through the rest of this chapter, you will use the Setup and Setup Reports icons.

SETUP

❑ DClick: the **A/R Setup** icon on the Accounts Receivable window

FIGURE 16-6
A/R Setup Icons

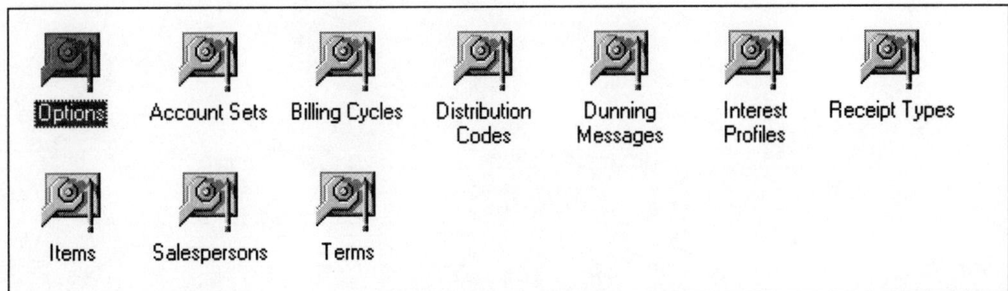

There are ten icons on the A/R Setup window shown in Figure 16-6. It looks complicated, but each icon represents information that ACCPAC needs to properly operate the Accounts Receivable for a company. Using the Devine Designs Inc. simulation, you will see how to enter this seemingly complex information. You will use each icon as you set up the Accounts Receivable for Devine Designs Inc.

OPTIONS

The first step is to use the Options notebook to choose the options that tell Accounts Receivable how to operate, how information is transferred to the General Ledger, and the type of data it will accept and display.

❑ DClick: the **Options** icon on the A/R Setup window

FIGURE 16-7
Company Options Page

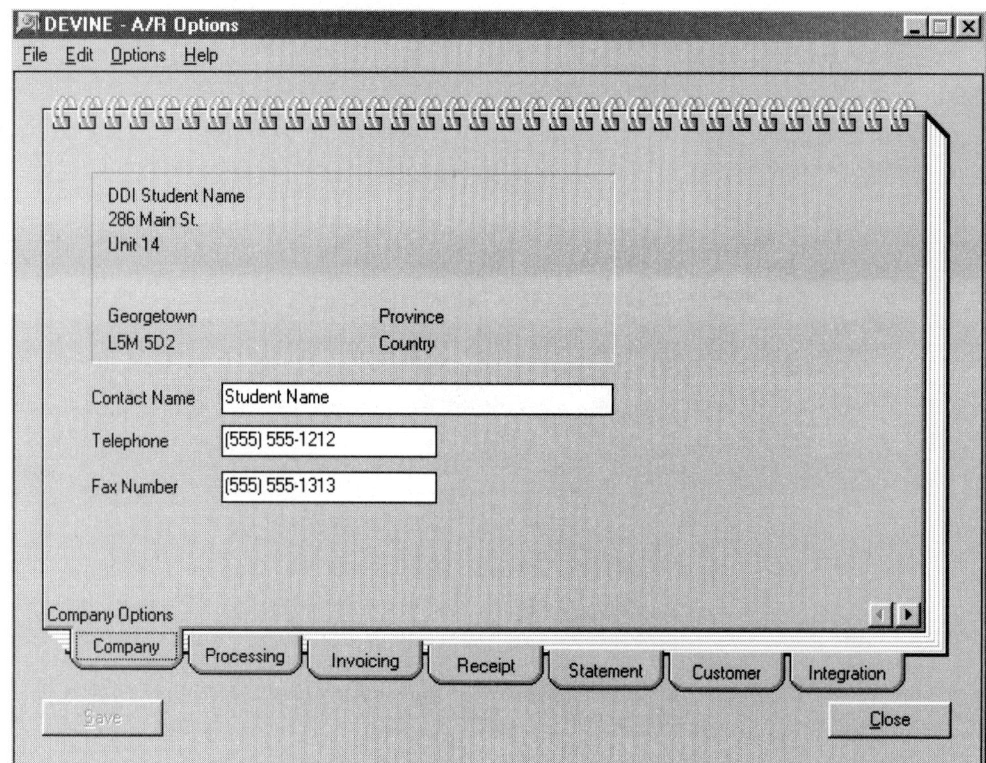

The Setup Options notebook consists of seven pages, as indicated by the tabs at the bottom of the notebook (see Figure 16-7).

COMPANY OPTIONS

The Company Options page of the A/R Options notebook, shown in Figure 16-7, displays information from the Company Profile window in Common Services. The information in the upper area can only be changed through Common Services. You can enter a separate contact name, telephone number, and fax number on this page for your Accounts Receivable database. For Devine Designs Inc., no changes are necessary.

PROCESSING OPTIONS

❑ Click: the **Processing** tab at the bottom of the A/R Options notebook

The Processing Options page, shown in Figure 16-8, has five different sections.

Figure 16-8
Processing Options Page

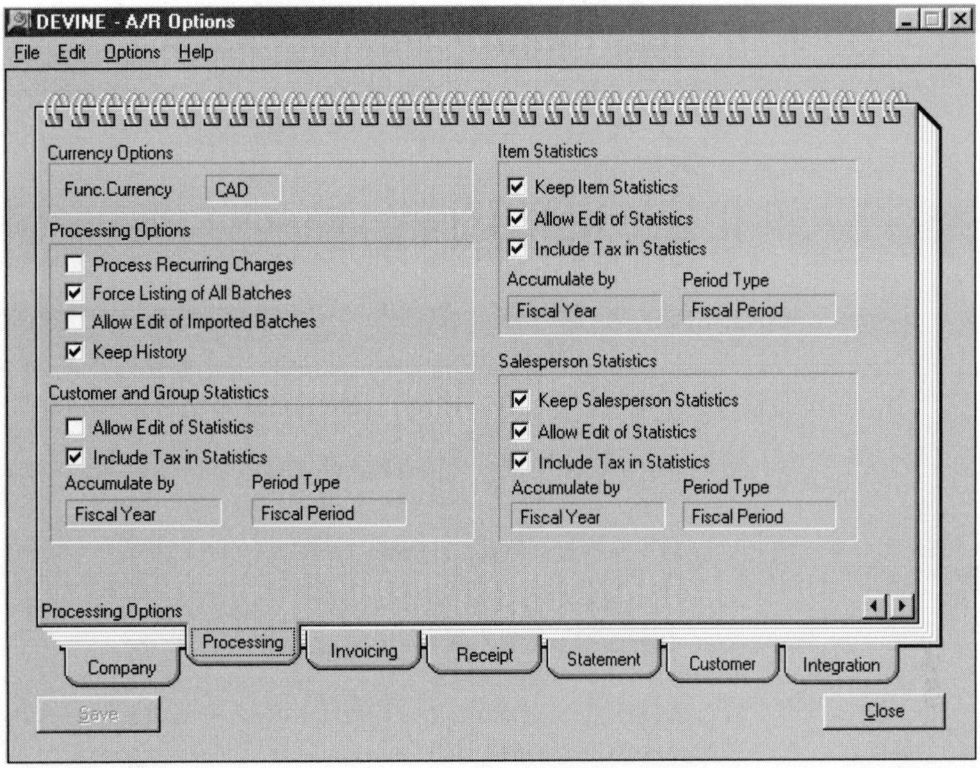

Currency Options

The Currency Options section of the Processing Options page displays the functional currency selected when the system database was created. The functional currency cannot be changed in Accounts Receivable.

Processing Options

The Processing Options section enables you to select four options for processing the Accounts Receivable.

The Process Recurring Charges option allows you to preset recurring charges that are to be applied to a customer's account. Select this option to automatically create invoices for customers to whom you bill standard amounts on a regular basis. Devine Designs Inc. will use this option to create recurring-charge records and assign them to customers for Web Site Maintenance and Web Site Hosting.

❑ Select: **Process Recurring Charges**

Selecting the Force Listing of All Batches option requires you to print a listing for each batch and correct any errors reported on the listing before you post the batch. When this option is activated, you must reprint the batch listing each time you make changes to it. Devine Designs Inc. will select this option as the printed batches will be part of its audit trail.

❑ Select: **Force Listing of All Batches**

Selecting the Allow Edit of Imported Batches option lets you edit batches retrieved from other ACCPAC accounting applications or imported from another program. Devine Designs Inc. will not use an invoicing or order entry program.

❑ De-select: the **Allow Edit of Imported Batches option**

Selecting the History Option lets you store all the details of posted invoices, receipts and adjustments until you clear the history. If selected, transaction details are available to allow you to re-open batches and reprint posted invoices and deposit slips. Furthermore, if you keep history, you can drill down to these accounts receivable transactions from the General Ledger.

❑ Select: **Keep History**

Customer and Group Statistics

ACCPAC Accounts Receivable accumulates statistics from the transactions you post to customer accounts.

The Allow Edit of Statistics option allows you to edit the year-to-date and last-year invoice sales, payments, discounts taken, interest charges, and credit notes, as well as total days to pay and total paid invoices, for a customer account. As Devine Designs Inc. is just starting its second fiscal year, this option will not be selected.

❑ De-select: the **Allow Edit of Statistics** check box

Selecting the Include Tax in Statistics option allows you to include tax amounts in invoice totals that are kept with the year-to-date and the last-year statistics for each customer. Devine Designs Inc. wants to keep statistics that do not reflect changes in government tax policy, so this option will not be selected.

❑ De-select: the **Include Tax in Statistics** check box

A warning message will appear, advising that changing this option can cause incorrect reporting of statistcs.

You would normally change this option only at year-end. In this case, nothing has been recorded in the accounts receivable so you do not have to worry about corrupting your statistics.

❑ Click: **OK** [OK]

Accumulate By

The program uses the Accumulate by list box to indicate whether you choose to report statistics by calendar or fiscal year. If you choose to accumulate by Calendar Year, the starting date for statistics will be January 1. If you choose to accumulate by fiscal year, the starting date will be the first day of your fiscal year as specified in the fiscal calendar in Common Services. Devine Designs Inc. reports statistics by fiscal year.

The Period Type list box indicates the period for which statistics will be reported. Normally, you would change this option only at the beginning of a fiscal year. Devine Designs Inc. reports statistics by Fiscal Period for consistency with other reports.

Item Statistics

You use this section to save statistics about the inventory items you sell. If you select Keep Item Statistics, you would use the other options in this section to specify how the item statistics are processed. These options are identical in function to those in the Customer section. Devine Designs Inc. will not keep statistics on items.

❑ De-select: the **Keep Item Statistics** check box

The options for controlling how item statistics are kept should disappear from the screen.

Salesperson Statistics

This option allows a company to gather statistics by sales representative. A company might select this option if it had many salespersons and paid them commission on sales. Devine Designs Inc. will not use this option.

❑ De-select: the **Keep Salesperson Statistics** check box

❑ Click: **Save** Save

INVOICING OPTIONS

❑ Click: the **Invoicing** tab at the bottom of the A/R Options notebook

The Invoicing Options page (Figure 16-9) has four input sections and displays next number for both invoice batch and invoice posting sequence.

FIGURE 16-9
Invoicing Options Page

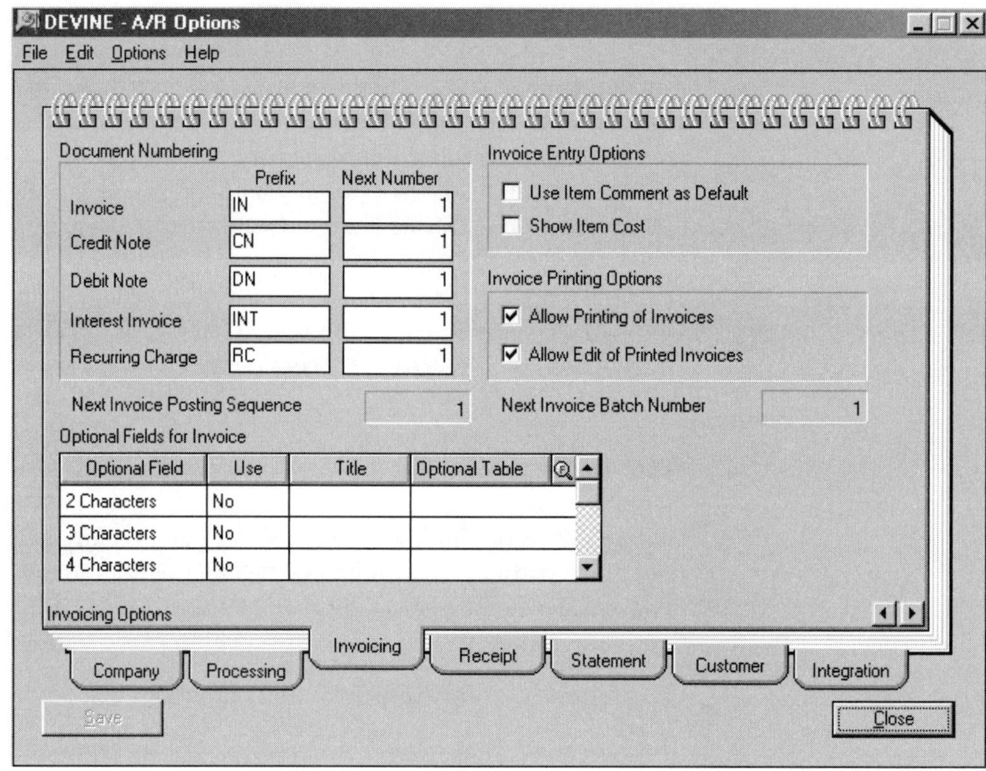

Document Numbering

Accounts Receivable assigns a number to each document you add to an invoice batch. To differentiate between different types of documents, a prefix identifies each type. You can select the default prefix as shown on the screen or create your own. Devine Designs Inc. has decided to use the default prefixes and document numbers. ACCPAC will sequentially assign the next number to identify each specific transaction.

Do not change the defaults displayed in this section.

Invoice Entry Options

You use this section to display any comments or costs from item records when you enter invoice details. Devine Designs Inc. does not use item records.

❑ De-select: the **Use Item Comment as Default** check box
❑ De-select: the **Show Item Cost** check box

Invoice Printing Options

ACCPAC allows you to print invoices from the Accounts Receivable without requiring the Invoicing module. Select this option if you want to use the Accounts Receivable to print invoices directly onto a company's preprinted forms. Devine Designs Inc. will use Accounts Receivable to print customer invoices.

❑ Select: the **Allow Printing of Invoices** check box

You can select the Allow Edit of Printed Invoices option only if you have chosen the Allow Printing of Invoices option. This option allows you to make changes in invoice batches after the invoices have been printed.

❑ Select: the **Allow Edit of Printed Invoices** check box

Next Invoice Posting Sequence

This field displays the posting sequence number that will be assigned the next time you post invoice batches. The Accounts Receivable module updates the number each time you post invoice batches.

Next Invoice Batch Number

This field displays the number that will be assigned to the next invoice batch created. These invoice batches may also include credit and debit notes. The Accounts Receivable module updates the number each time you create a new batch.

Optional Fields for Invoice

You use this section to add fields containing specific information that your company may require on customer invoices. You can add up to eight fields from the list. For example, you can add a text field to contain a warranty number, then add a date field to contain the date when the warranty expires. Devine Designs Inc. will not use optional fields on customer invoices.

❑ Do not change any of the entries in the Use column from No to Yes.

RECEIPT PROCESSING OPTIONS

❑ Click: the **Receipt** tab at the bottom of the A/R Options notebook

The Receipt Processing Options page appears as shown in Figure 16-10.

Default Receipt Type

This field identifies the type of receipt that you get most often. The choices are Cash and Check. When you enter receipts, you will have to identify the receipt type only if it is different from the default you set here.

FIGURE 16-10
Receipt Processing Options Page

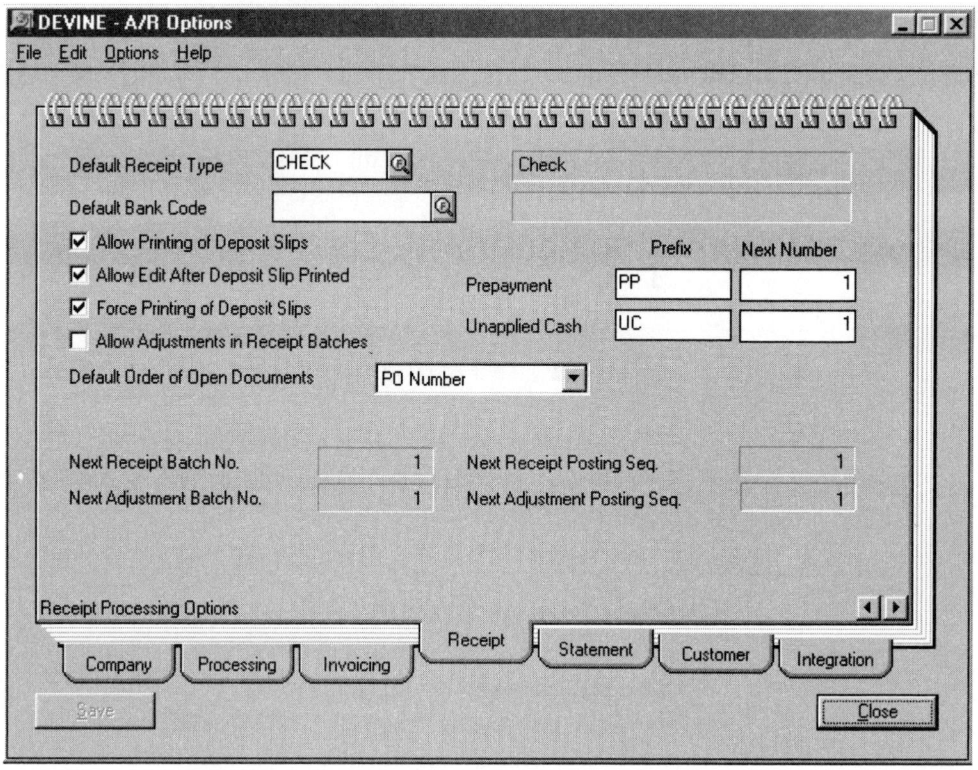

Click:	the **Finder** for the Default Receipt Type text box
Select:	**CHECK**

If you want to create another type of receipt (for example, electronic deposit or credit card), you must first add it using the Receipt Types window, as described later in this chapter.

Default Bank Code

This field is used to select the code for the bank account that you use normally to deposit receipts. You must use one of the bank codes defined in the Bank Services window in Common Services.

Click:	the **Finder** for the Default Bank Code text box
Select:	**1STBK**

Allow Printing of Deposit Slips

When this option is activated, you can print deposit slips for the deposits you enter in the Receipt Entry window. You can print the slips both before and after posting the batches. Devine Designs Inc. will use Accounts Receivable to print deposit slips.

Select:	the **Allow Printing of Deposit Slips** check box

Allow Edit After Deposit Slip Printed

This option only appears when the Allow Printing of Deposit Slips option has been selected. Selecting this option allows you to edit or delete receipt batches after printing the related deposit slips. Devine Designs Inc. has decided not to select this option.

❑ Deselect: **Allow Edit After Deposit Slip Printed**

Force Printing of Deposit Slips

This option appears only if you select the Allow Printing of Deposit Slips option. Devine Designs Inc. will select this option to ensure that deposit slips are printed before receipt batches are posted.

❑ Select: the **Force Printing of Deposit Slips** check box

Allow Adjustments to Receipt Batches

It is not uncommon to receive checks for an amount slightly less than the invoice amount due to a dispute over a minor invoice item that is not worth pursuing. This option would be selected if you want to be able to enter adjustments or to write off small amounts in the accounts as you enter receipts, rather than having to enter the transactions separately.

❑ Select: the **Allow Adjustments in Receipt Batches** check box

Default Order of Open Documents

You may choose the order in which you list documents when you apply cash, checks, or other receipts to customer accounts in the Receipt Entry. You can choose to list open documents by:

- Document Number, beginning with the lowest document number for each transaction type.
- PO Number, listing documents by customer purchase order number.
- Due Date, beginning with the earliest due date.
- Sales Order Number, listing documents by their sales order number.
- Document Date, listing documents by the date entered with the document.
- Balance Due, listing documents by their outstanding balances.

Devine Designs Inc. has decided to list documents by the document number.

❑ Select: **Document Number** using the list tool ▾

Assigning Numbers to Prepayments and Unapplied Cash Transactions

It is fairly common in some industries to receive payments in advance for goods or services to be provided at a later date. For example, a hotel might require a deposit for a function room for an office party in six months, or a customer may need an item that you would not normally carry, so you require payment before ordering the goods.

You must specify the numbers that will be assigned to prepayments and unapplied cash transactions during the entry of receipts and adjustments. Devine Designs Inc. has decided to leave the default Prefix and the next document number unchanged.

Sometimes you receive checks that cannot be traced in Accounts Receivable. This might occur if the Account Receivable is recorded under the name of a business, but in fact is a franchise operated by a company with another name. If the payer doesn't supply the name of the company, or the invoice number, you may not be able to identify what is being paid. Devine Designs Inc. has decided to leave the default Unapplied Cash Prefix and the next document number unchanged.

Next Number Displays

These four fields display the numbers that will be assigned to the next batches created and the posting sequence numbers that will be assigned the next time you post receipt, adjustment, and revaluation batches. The program updates the numbers each time you create or post a batch.

❑ Click: **Save** Save

STATEMENT PROCESSING OPTIONS

❑ Click: the **Statement** tab at the bottom of the A/R Options notebook

The Statement Processing Options page (Figure 16-11) allows you to specify the Aging Periods for the Accounts Receivable, to print a dunning or reminder message on customer statements based on the status of the account, and to print statements for zero balance accounts.

Aging Periods

Devine Designs Inc. will use the default aging periods of 30, 60, 90, and over 90 days.

Dunning Messages

Dunning messages are usually short messages asking customers to keep their accounts up to date. You may use up to 45 characters for each message. The messages you enter on this page become the default set of dunning messages that are printed on customer statements.

FIGURE 16-11
Statement Processing Options Page

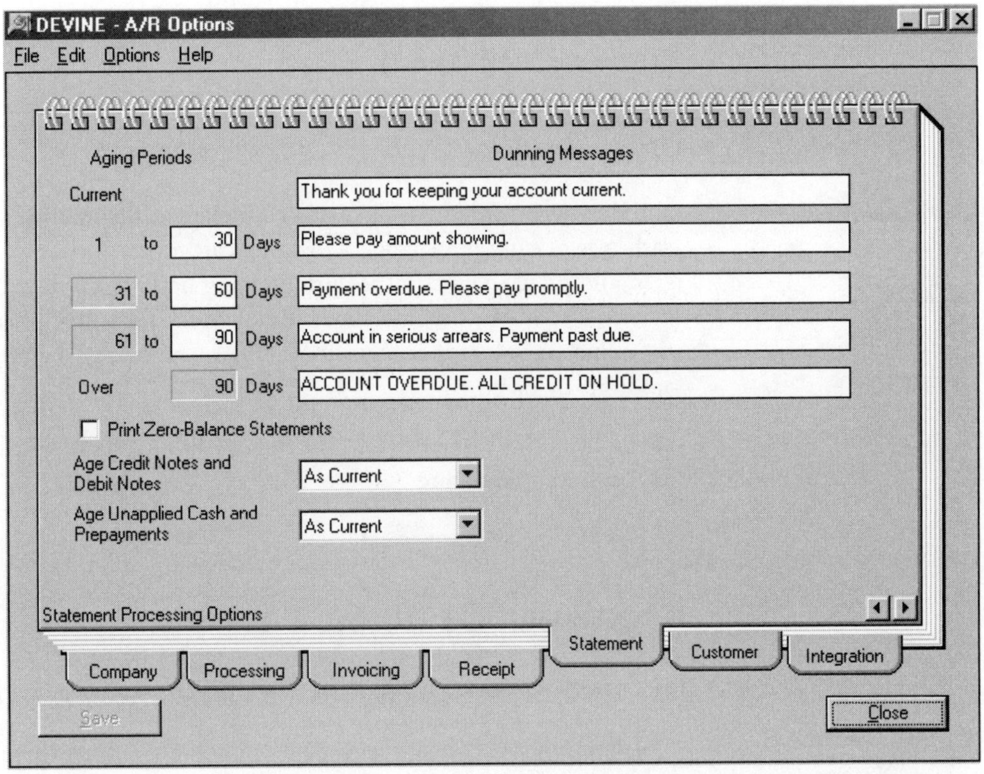

Aging Periods				Dunning Messages
Current				Thank you for keeping your account current.
1	to	30	Days	Please pay amount showing.
31	to	60	Days	Payment overdue. Please pay promptly.
61	to	90	Days	Account in serious arrears. Payment past due.
Over		90	Days	ACCOUNT OVERDUE. ALL CREDIT ON HOLD.

☐ Print Zero-Balance Statements

Age Credit Notes and Debit Notes: As Current

Age Unapplied Cash and Prepayments: As Current

Print Zero-Balance Statements

The Print Zero-Balance Statements option allows you to choose to print statements for customers with no outstanding balances in addition to printing statements for customers with outstanding balances. Devine Designs Inc. has decided to print statements for zero-balance accounts.

❑ Select: the **Print Zero-Balance Statements** check box

Age Credit and Debit Notes

You must select a method to use in aging unapplied credit and debit notes. If you want to assign the credit and debit notes to the current aging period, select As Current. When you select this option, Accounts Receivable will not use the notes in calculating the balances on which you charge interest. You cannot select credit notes and debit notes as transaction types to write off in the Create Write-Off Batch window if you have selected As Current.

The second method you may select is By Date. This method includes each unapplied credit and debit note in the aging period containing its document date. Devine Designs will age debt and credit notes By Date.

- ❑ Click: the **list tool** for Age Credit Notes and Debit Notes
- ❑ Select: **By Date**

Age Unapplied Cash and Prepayments

You may select either As Current or By Date as the method you want to use to assign cash receipts and prepayments to aging categories. As Current includes any unapplied cash and prepayments in the current aging period; it will not include these amounts when calculating interest charges. By Date includes unapplied cash and prepayments in the aging periods that contain their document dates. Devine Designs Inc. will age these amounts by date.

- ❑ Click: the **list tool** for Age Unapplied Cash and Prepayments
- ❑ Select: **By Date**
- ❑ Click: **Save** Save

CUSTOMER OPTIONAL FIELDS

- ❑ Click: the **Customer** tab at the bottom of the A/R Options notebook

The Customer Optional Fields page (Figure 16-12) has three input areas.

Days to Keep Comments

The Default Number of Days to Keep Comments field allows you to control the number of days that any comments you enter in the customer records will be retained. The default is 30 days. Devine Designs Inc. has decided that this is a reasonable period and will leave it unchanged.

Optional Fields for Customer and Group

You can add optional fields for extra information that you want to have appear for customers, and customer groups. The information that can be added ranges from service contract numbers to expiration date, deductible amounts, or lease types. You can give these fields any name you want, and you can assign them to optional tables, if optional tables were defined in Common Services, to validate entries.

Devine Designs Inc. has decided to add a 30-character field for comments.

- ❑ Scroll: to display the **30 characters** Optional Field for Customer and Group
- ❑ DClick: the **No** in the Use cell to change it to Yes
- ❑ Press: **Tab** Tab
- ❑ Type: **Comment** in the Title cell
- ❑ Press: **Tab** Tab

FIGURE 16-12
Customer Optional Fields Page

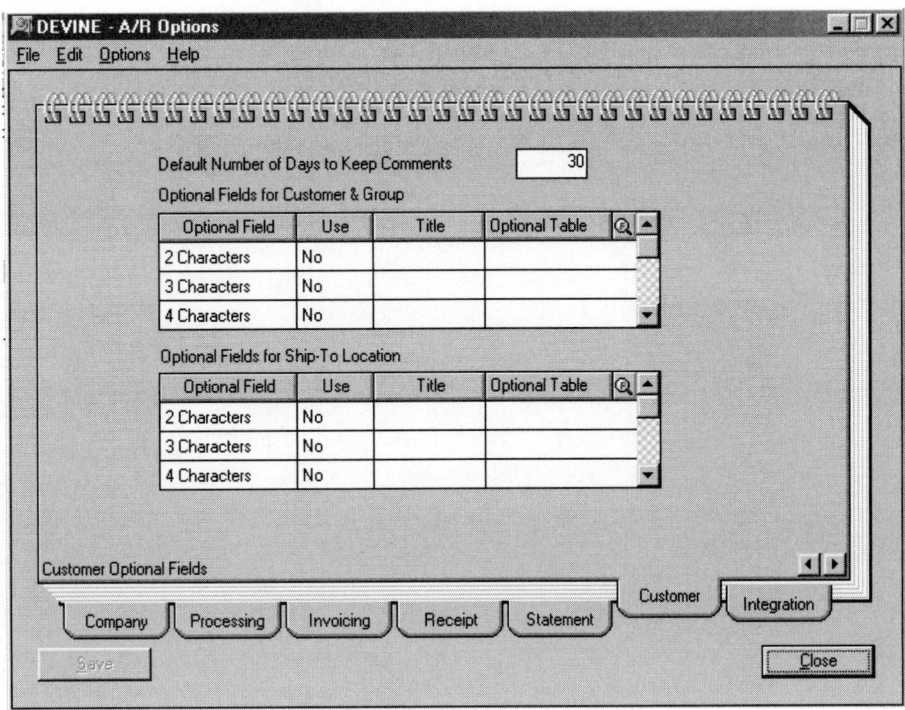

As Devine Designs Inc. did not define Optional Tables in Common Services, this cell must be left empty.

Optional Fields for Ship-To Location

Devine Designs Inc. has decided to include a 30-character field in the Ship-To Location area as well.

- ❑ Scroll: to display the **30 characters** Optional Field for Ship-To locations
- ❑ DClick: the **No** in the Use cell to change it to Yes
- ❑ Press: **Tab** [Tab]
- ❑ Type: **Comment** in the Title cell
- ❑ Press: **Tab** [Tab]

As Devine Designs Inc. did not define Optional Tables in Common Services, the Optional Tables cell must be left empty.

- ❑ Click: **Save** [Save]

INTEGRATION OPTIONS

- ❑ Click: the **Integration** tab at the bottom of the A/R Options notebook

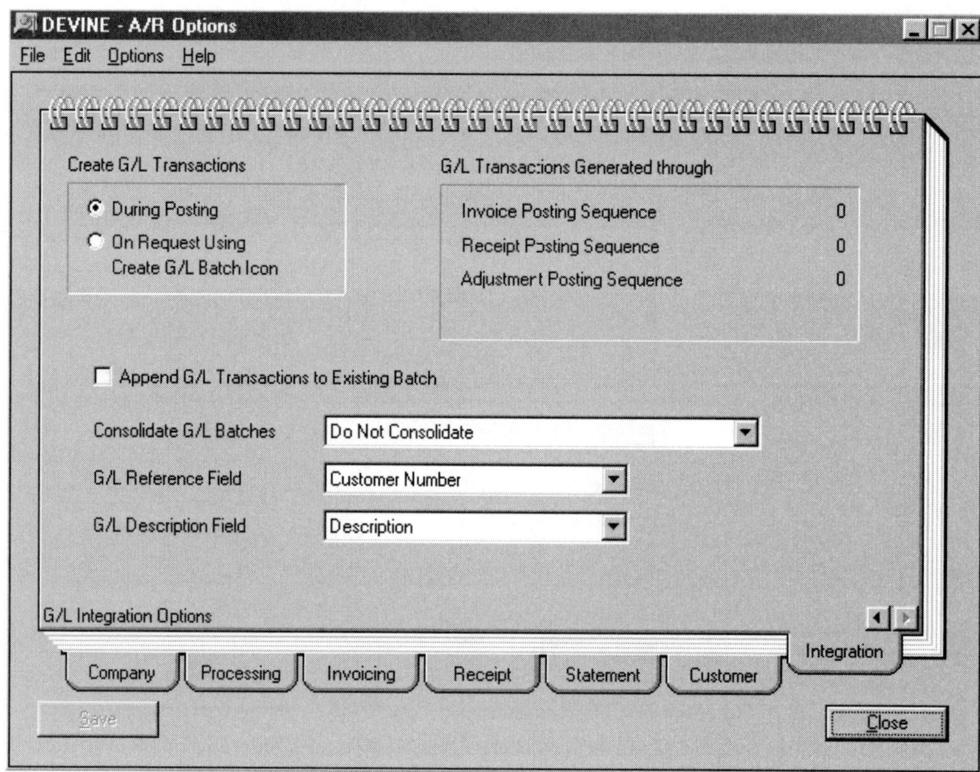

FIGURE 16-13
Integration Options Page

The G/L Integration Options page (Figure 16-13) has five option areas and one data display.

Create G/L Transactions

If you select During Posting, ACCPAC will automatically create General Ledger transactions when transaction batches are posted to Accounts Receivable. If you select On Request Using Create G/L Batch Icon, the General Ledger Transaction batch will be created when you use the Create G/L Batch window.

Devine Designs Inc. has decided to select the During Posting option.

❑ Select: the **During Posting** option button

G/L Transactions Generated Through

This data display is located in the upper right corner of the page. The three fields (Invoice Posting Sequence, Receipt Posting Sequence, and Adjustment Posting Sequence) display the number of the last posting sequences used. As Devine Designs Inc. has not posted batches to Accounts Receivable, these numbers should be zeros.

Append G/L Transactions to Existing Batch

ACCPAC Accounts Receivable automatically creates separate General Ledger batches for invoices, receipts, and adjustments. Selecting this option allows new General Ledger transactions to be added to existing batches. You would not select this option if you want to create a new General Ledger batch each time you produce General Ledger transactions. Devine Designs Inc. will select this option.

❑ Activate: the **Append G/L Transactions to Existing Batch** check box

Consolidate G/L Batches

You can choose to combine transaction details for the same General Ledger account into single lines for posting, or to send unconsolidated Accounts Receivable transactions to the General Ledger.

If Do Not Consolidate is selected, the General Ledger transaction batch includes separate details for each invoice, credit note, debit note, receipt, or adjustment posted to the Accounts Receivable. When initially setting up Accounts Receivable, it is recommended that you select this option so that the G/L Transactions report provides complete details of all the transactions you enter. You can then check the posting report against the source documents to ensure that you have entered all transactions accurately. You can change this option later as you become more confident of entering transactions correctly.

The Consolidation option combines all details with the same account number and fiscal period into one detail or combines all details with the same account number, fiscal period, and source code into one detail.

Devine Designs Inc. will not consolidate transaction information at this time.

❑ Select: **Do Not Consolidate** using the list tool ▾

G/L Reference Field

When unconsolidated Accounts Receivable transactions are retrieved by the General Ledger, cash payment, interest invoice, and recurring charge invoice information is transferred to the G/L Reference field. This allows you to select the information that you want to appear in the reference field for other transactions when they are retrieved by the General Ledger.

Devine Designs Inc. will track these other transactions by customer number.

❑ Select: **Customer Number** using the list tool ▾

G/L Description Field

The first part of the description field for unconsolidated transactions retrieved by the General Ledger consists of a posting sequence number, a batch number, and an entry number, all of which are assigned by ACCPAC. This option allows you to control the information that appears in the Description field for transactions when they are retrieved by the General Ledger.

Devine Designs Inc. will select the document number.

- ❑ Select: **Document Number** using the list tool
- ❑ Click: **Save** [Save]

PRINTING THE A/R OPTIONS REPORT

You should always print a listing of the options chosen to document the setup of the Accounts Receivable.

- ❑ Click: **File** on the A/R Options notebook's menu bar
- ❑ Click: **Print** [Print] on the File Menu
- ❑ Click: **Print** [Print] on the A/R Options Report dialog box
- ❑ Click: **OK** [OK] on the Print dialog box
- ❑ Click: **Close** [Close] to close the A/R Options Report dialog box

Compare your printed report to that shown in Figure 16-14. Make any corrections necessary. Save the corrections and print the report again.

FIGURE 16-14
A/R Options Report

Date: Tuesday, June 20, 2000 2:00PM
A/R Options (AROPT01)

DDI Student Name

Page 1

Company

Company Name	DDI Student Name
Address	286 Main St.
	Unit 14
	Georgetown, Province L5M 5D2
	Country

Contact: Student Name **Phone:** (555) 555-1212 **Fax:** (555) 555-1313

Processing Options

Currency Options:	
Functional Currency	CAD
Multicurrency	NO
Processing Options:	
Process Recurring Charges	Yes
Force Listing of All Batches	Yes
Allow Edit of Imported Batches	No
Keep History	Yes
Customer and Group Statistics:	
Allow Edit of Customer Statistics	No
Include Tax in Statistics	No
Accumulate Statistics By	Fiscal Year
Period Type	Fiscal Period

Item Statistics:	
Keep Item Statistics	No
Salesperson Statistics:	
Keep Salesperson Statistics	No

Invoicing Options

Document Numbering:

Invoice Prefix	IN	**Next Number**	1
Credit Note Prefix	CN	**Next Number**	1
Debit Note Prefix	DN	**Next Number**	1
Interest Invoice Prefix	INT	**Next Number**	1
Recurring Charge Prefix	RC	**Next Number**	1
Next Invoice Number	IN00000001	**Next Inv. Batch No.**	1
Next Invoice Posting Seq.	1		

Invoice Entry Options:	
Use Item Comment as Default	No
Show Item Cost	No
Invoice Printing Options:	
Allow Printing of Invoices	Yes
Allow Edit of Printed Invoices	Yes

Optional Field:	**Active**	**Field Title**	**Optional Table**
1 - 2 Characters	No		
2 - 3 Characters	No		
3 - 4 Characters	No		
4 - 12 Characters	No		
5 - 15 Characters	No		
6 - 30 Characters	No		
7 - Date Field	No		
8 - Amount Field	No		

Date: Tuesday, June 20, 2000 2:00PM
A/R Options (AROPT01)

DDI Student Name

Page 2

Receipt and Adjustment Options

Default Receipt Type	CHECK
Default Bank Code	1STBK
Allow Printing of Deposit Slips	Yes
Allow Edit After Deposit Slip Printed	No
Force Printing of Deposit Slips	Yes
Allow Adjustments in Receipt Batches	Yes
Default Order of Open Documents	Document No.
Prepayment Prefix	PP
Unapplied Cash Prefix	UC
Next Prepayment Number	1
Next Unapplied Cash Number	1
Next Receipt Batch Number	1
Next Receipt Posting Sequence	1
Next Adjustment Batch Number	1
Next Adjustment Posting Sequence	1

Statement Options

Aging Periods			**Dunning Messages**
Current			Thank you for keeping your account current.
1	to	30 days	Please pay amount showing.
31	to	60 days	Payment overdue. Please pay promptly.
61	to	90 days	Account in serious arrears. Payment past due.
Over		90 days	ACCOUNT OVERDUE. ALL CREDIT ON HOLD.

Print Zero-Balance Statements	Yes
Age Credit Notes/Debit Notes	By Date
Age Unapplied Cash/Prepayments	By Date

Customer and Ship-To Location Options

Default Number of Days to Keep Comments 30

Optional Fields for Customer and Group:

	Active	**Field Title**	**Optional Table**
1 - 2 Characters	No		
2 - 3 Characters	No		
3 - 4 Characters	No		
4 - 12 Characters	No		
5 - 15 Characters	No		
6 - 30 Characters	Yes	Comment	
7 - Date Field	No		
8 - Amount Field	No		

Optional Fields for Ship-To Location:

	Active	**Field Title**	**Optional Table**
1 - 2 Characters	No		
2 - 3 Characters	No		
3 - 4 Characters	No		
4 - 12 Characters	No		
5 - 15 Characters	No		
6 - 30 Characters	Yes	Comment	
7 - Date Field	No		
8 - Amount Field	No		

Date: Tuesday, June 20, 2000 2:00PM A/R Options (AROPT01)	DDI Student Name	Page 3
Integration Options		
Create G/L Processing Transactions	During Posting	
G/L Transactions Generated Through:		
Invoice Posting Sequence	0	
Receipt Posting Sequence	0	
Adjustment Posting Sequence	0	
Append G/L Transactions to Existing Batch	Yes	
Consolidate G/L Batches	Do not Consolidate	
G/L Reference Field	Customer Number	
G/L Description Field	Document Number	

- ❑ Click: **Close** [Close] to close the A/R Options Report notebook
- ❑ Click: **Close** [Close] to return to the A/R Setup window
- ❑ Exit: **ACCPAC**
- ❑ Back up your data files.

Review Questions

1. What is the purpose of README files?
2. Which window is used to access the Data Activation function?
3. When you access the Company Page of the A/R Options notebook, information about the company is already displayed. Where does this information come from?
4. What is the purpose of the Process Recurring Charges option?
5. Why is it advisable to select the Force Listing of Batches option?
6. What are the prefixes for the different types of documents found on the Invoicing page of the Options notebook?
7. Define the term: "Dunning Message"
8. What does "Consolidation" do?

EXERCISE

If you have not completed the General Ledger exercises, you will not be able to use the Finder or post the Accounts Receivable transactions to the General Ledger.

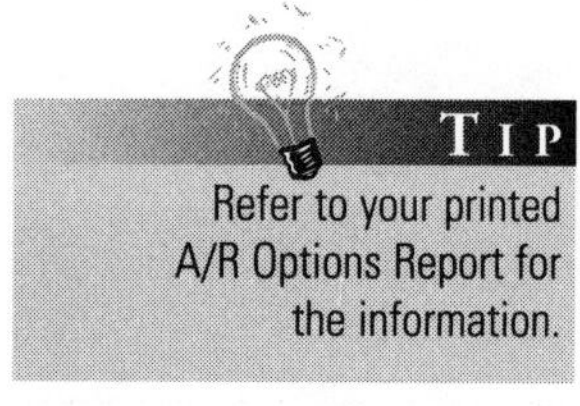

- ❑ Sign on to your company (EXERCO) as the system administrator using 05/01/10 as the Session Date.
- ❑ Activate Accounts Receivable for your company.
- ❑ Select the same setup options for your company as you selected for Devine Designs Inc.
- ❑ Print: the **A/R Options Report** for your company using the Setup Reports window
- ❑ Review the report, make any necessary corrections, and print the report again.
- ❑ Close: any open windows
- ❑ Exit: **ACCPAC**
- ❑ Back up your data files.

CHAPTER 17

ADDING SETUP RECORDS

This chapter will guide you through the process of adding the records and codes that you assign when adding customer accounts or entering transactions in Accounts Receivable. The information that you will enter in this chapter reduces the time required for recording transactions in Accounts Receivable.

GETTING READY

- ❑ Sign on to Devine Designs Inc. as the system administrator using 05/01/10 as the Session Date.
- ❑ Open: the **Accounts Receivable** window
- ❑ Open: the **A/R Setup** Window

Each of the icons on the A/R Setup window (Figure 17-1) enables you to add, modify, or delete information that is used when you record customer or transaction information.

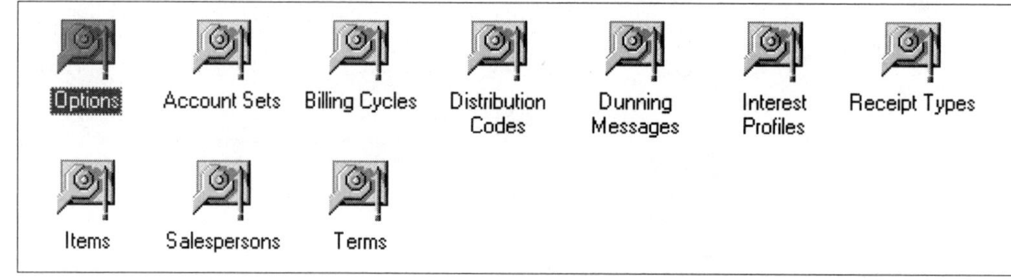

FIGURE 17-1
A/R Setup Window

MODIFYING SETUP RECORDS

You can modify and delete the records you set up in this chapter as needed. To modify a record, select the code that identifies it (for example, the Account Set Code), make your changes, and then save them. You can change everything in most records, except for the identifying code or number. To change a code or number, first add a record with the code or number you want to use, then delete the record you do not want.

You can delete dunning messages, receipt types, and items at any time. However, you can only delete account sets, billing cycles, distribution codes, and interest profiles when they are not assigned to customer records. If you want to delete a record that is assigned to a customer record, you must first assign a different code to the customer, or delete those records also.

ADDING ACCOUNT SETS

Account Sets allow you to specify the General Ledger accounts to be used when Accounts Receivable transaction information is posted to the General Ledger. You must define at least one Account Set before adding customers. Each Account Set consists of an Accounts Receivable control account, a bank account, a payment discounts account, and an interest income account.

Devine Designs Inc. has a simple set of books and will create only one Account Set.

❑ DClick: the **Account Sets** icon [Account Sets] on the Setup window to get the display shown in Figure 17-2

FIGURE 17-2
Account Sets Window

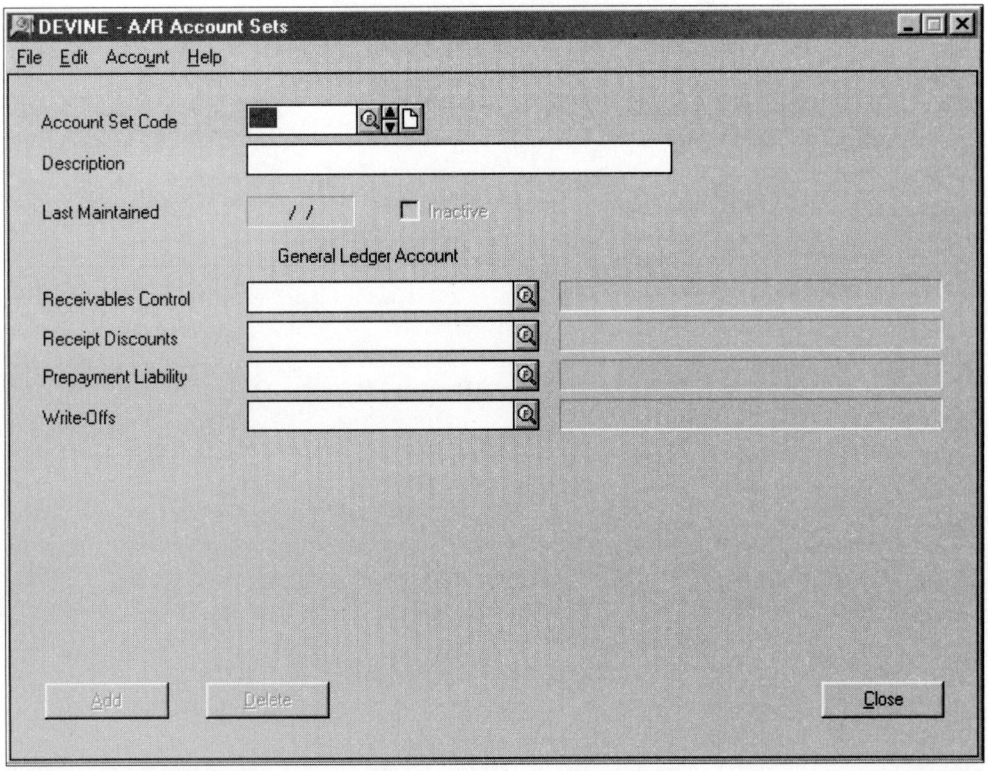

DEVINE - A/R Account Sets

File Edit Account Help

Account Set Code

Description

Last Maintained / / Inactive

General Ledger Account

Receivables Control

Receipt Discounts

Prepayment Liability

Write-Offs

Add Delete Close

Account Set Code

Enter a unique name or number, up to six characters long, to identify each Account Set.

- ❑ Type: **1**
- ❑ Press: **Tab** [Tab]

Description

WARNING

If there is an X in the Inactive check box, click the check box to remove the X and make the account code active.

- ❑ Type: **Accounts Receivable - General** in the Description text box
- ❑ Press: **Tab** [Tab]

Inactive

You do not want to designate this code as inactive.

- ❑ Press: **Tab** [Tab]

Receivables Control

Enter the Accounts Receivable Control account code from the General Ledger so that the information will be posted to the proper account.

Using the printed Chart of Accounts and typing the account numbers is faster than using the Finder.

- ❑ Click: the **Finder**
- ❑ Select: **1120** Accounts Receivable Control

The account description, Accounts Receivable Control, will be displayed to the right of the text box.

Receipt Discounts

- ❑ Enter: **4010** in the Receipts Discounts text box

Prepayment Liability

- ❑ Enter: **2210** in the Prepayment Liability text box

Write-Offs

TIP
Use Print on the File menu.

- ❑ Enter: **6020** in the Write-Offs text box
- ❑ Click: **Add** [Add]
- ❑ Print: the **A/R Account Sets Report**

FIGURE 17-3
Account Sets Report

Date: Tuesday, June 20, 2000 2:11PM **DDI Student Name** **Page 1**
A/R Account Sets (ARACCT1Z)

From Account Set [ ] To [ZZZZZZ]

Account Set	Description	Account Number	Last Maintained/ Account Desc.	Inactive On
1	Accounts Receivable - General		6/20/00	
	Receivables Control:	1120	Accounts Receivable, Control	
	Receipt Discounts:	4010	Sales Discounts	
	Prepayment Liability:	2210	Prepayments Received	
	Write-Offs:	6020	Bad Debt Expense	

Compare your printout to that shown in Figure 17-3 and verify that it is correct and complete.

- ❑ Close: the **A/R Account Sets Report** dialog box
- ❑ Close: the **A/R Account Sets** window

ADDING BILLING CYCLES

Billing Cycles are time intervals into which you group customers for billing. You can charge interest, print statements, invoice recurring charges, print the Customer Transactions and Aged Trial Balance reports, and create write-off transactions by Billing Cycle. If you charge interest by Billing Cycle on overdue balances, the Billing Cycle is frequently used in the calculation of interest charges.

When you process records by Billing Cycle, ACCPAC keeps track of the dates when you last printed statements and created invoices for interest charges and recurring charges for each billing cycle. At least one Billing Cycle must be added before you add any customer accounts.

Devine Designs Inc. will use a single Billing Cycle—the end of each month. You will clear transaction details by period-end rather than by Billing Cycle. The date that transactions are cleared is updated for all Billing Cycles when you clear transaction details after running the Period End function. If you were to choose to clear transaction details by Billing Cycle, the date would be updated when you print statements for that Billing Cycle.

❑ DClick: the **Billing Cycles** icon 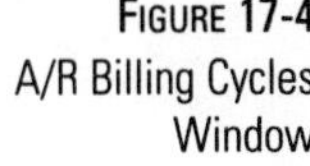 on the A/R Setup window

The A/R Billing Cycles window will appear as shown in Figure 17-4.

FIGURE 17-4
A/R Billing Cycles Window

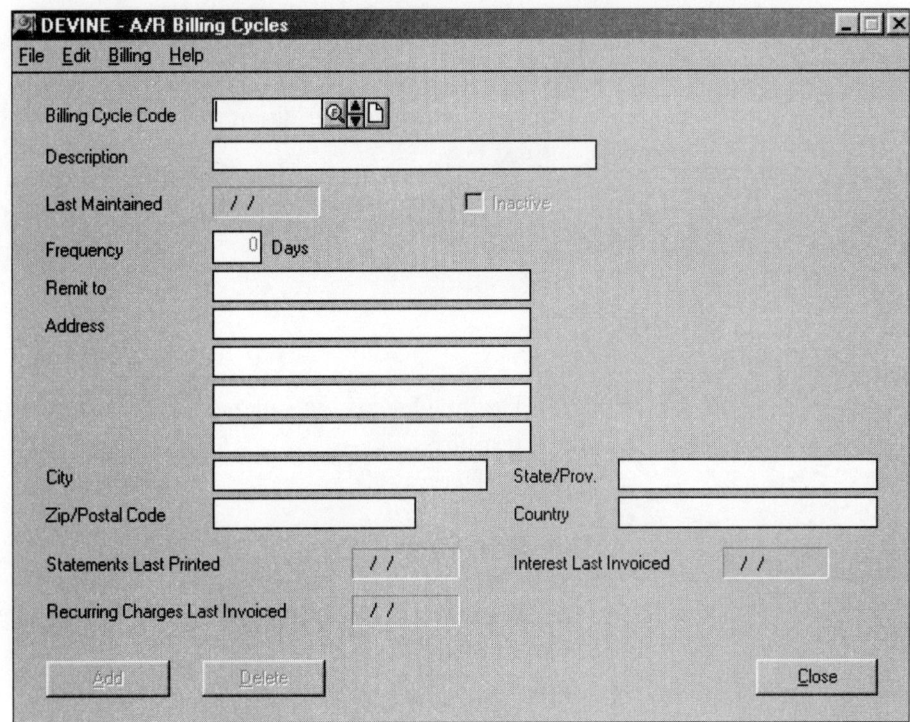

Billing Cycle Code

- ❑ Type: **MONTH** in the Billing Cycle Code text box
- ❑ Press: **Tab** [Tab]

Note that the Billing Cycle Code always appears in upper case.

Description

- ❑ Type: **Monthly Billing** in the Description field
- ❑ Press: **Tab** [Tab]

Inactive Check Box

Ensure that the Inactive check box is not selected.

- ❑ Press: **Tab** [Tab]

Frequency

- ❑ Type: **30** in the Frequency text box
- ❑ Press: **Tab** [Tab]

Remit To

Enter the name of the person or position to which you want customers to send their payments in this text box.

- ❑ Type: **Attn: Accounts Receivable**
- ❑ Press: **Tab** [Tab]

Address

- ❑ Enter: Devine Designs Inc.'s name and address information in the appropriate text boxes.

Use the following address:

286 Main Street
Unit 14
Georgetown
Your Province/State
Your Postal/Zip Code
Your Country

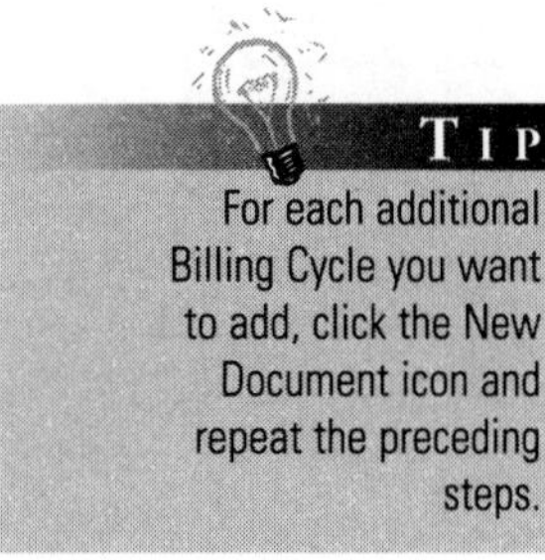

For each additional Billing Cycle you want to add, click the New Document icon and repeat the preceding steps.

- ❑ Click: **Add** [Add]

FIGURE 17-5
Billing Cycles Report

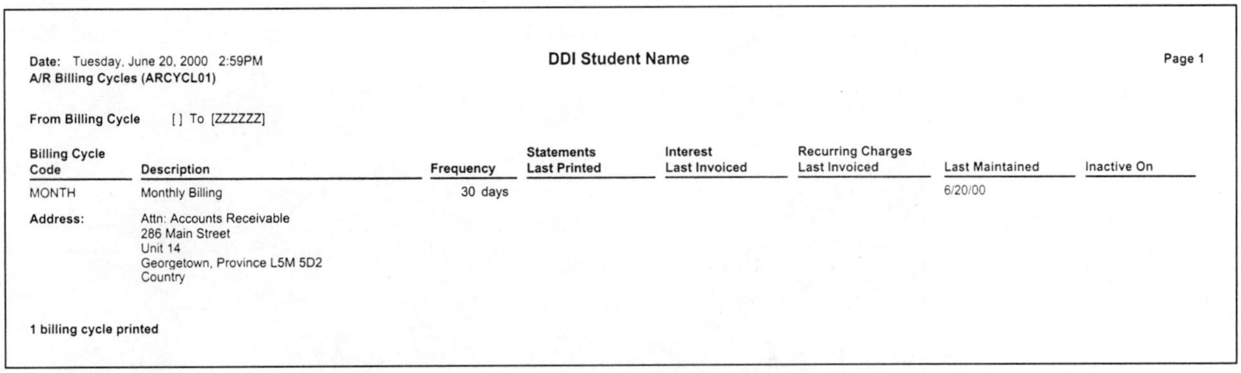

Date: Tuesday, June 20, 2000 2:59PM
A/R Billing Cycles (ARCYCL01)

DDI Student Name

Page 1

From Billing Cycle [] To [ZZZZZZ]

Billing Cycle Code	Description	Frequency	Statements Last Printed	Interest Last Invoiced	Recurring Charges Last Invoiced	Last Maintained	Inactive On
MONTH	Monthly Billing	30 days				6/20/00	
Address:	Attn: Accounts Receivable 286 Main Street Unit 14 Georgetown, Province L5M 5D2 Country						

1 billing cycle printed

- ❑ Print: the **A/R Billing Cycles Report**, as shown in Figure 17-5
- ❑ Close: the **A/R Billing Cycles Report** dialog box
- ❑ Close: the **A/R Billing Cycles** window

ADDING DISTRIBUTIONS

Distribution Codes identify the General Ledger accounts to which you post data from sales transactions. You must add at least one Distribution Code before you can add customer records. This function allows you to enter and maintain General Ledger distribution codes to speed up the entry of invoices, payments, and adjustments.

- ❑ DClick: the **Distribution Codes** icon [Distribution Codes] on the A/R Setup window

The A/R Distribution Codes window will appear as shown in Figure 17-6.

Distribution Code

The cursor should be displayed in the Distribution Code text box. When creating a distribution code, use a name or short form that is easy to remember. The distribution code can be up to six characters long.

- ❑ Type: **DESIGN**
- ❑ Press: **Tab** [Tab]

Description

- ❑ Type: **Sales - Web Page Design** in the Description text box

FIGURE 17-6
A/R Distribution Codes Window

DEVINE - A/R Distribution Codes
File Edit Code Help
Distribution Code
Description
Last Maintained / /
Inactive
General Ledger Account
Revenue
Inventory
Cost of Goods Sold
Add Delete Close

❑ Press: **Tab** [Tab]

Inactive

Do *not* select the Inactive box.

❑ Press: **Tab** [Tab]

TIP
Use your printed Chart of Accounts and type the account numbers in the text boxes.

General Ledger Accounts

ACCPAC requires that you add an account in the Revenue text box. You do not have to add accounts for Inventory or Cost of Goods Sold, but ACCPAC will prompt you with an error message if you leave these text boxes blank. Devine Designs Inc. will add account numbers in the Inventory and Cost of Goods Sold text boxes, but will not use them for most transactions.

❑ Click: the **Finder** for the Revenue text box
❑ Select: **4000/10** Sales - Web Page Design
❑ Type: **1200** in the Inventory text box
❑ Press: **Tab** [Tab]
❑ Type: **5000** in the Cost of Goods Sold text box
❑ Press: **Tab** [Tab]
❑ Click: **Add** [Add]

YOUR TURN

Devine Designs Inc. has decided to create Distribution codes for all five Segment Codes used to identify types of revenue. These Segment Codes were added in Chapter 7: Setting Up the General Ledger.

❑ Click: the **New Document** icon for the Distribution Code text box
❑ Add: the Distribution Code **UPDATE** for Sales - Web Page Maintenance

Use **4000/20** as the Revenue account, **1200** as the Inventory Account, and **5000** as the Cost of Goods Sold account.

❑ Click: **Add** [Add]
❑ Add: the Distribution Code **HOST** for Sales - Web Site Hosting

Use **4000/30** as the Revenue account, **1200** as the Inventory Account, and **5000** as the Cost of Goods Sold account.

❑ Click: **Add** [Add]
❑ Add: the Distribution Code **RETAIL** for Sales - Web Retail Sales

Use **4000/40** as the Revenue account, **1200** as the Inventory Account, and **5000** as the Cost of Goods Sold account.

❑ Click: **Add** [Add]
❑ Add: the Distribution Code **MISC** for Sales - Misc. Sales

Use **4000/99** as the Revenue account, **1200** as the Inventory Account, and **5000** as the Cost of Goods Sold account.

❑ Click: **Add** [Add]
❑ Print: the **A/R Distribution Codes Report** shown in Figure 17-7

FIGURE 17-7
Distribution Codes Report

Date: Tuesday, June 20, 2000 3:09PM **DDI Student Name** Page 1
A/R Distribution Codes (ARDIST1Z)

From Distribution Code [] To [ZZZZZZ]

Distribution Code	Description		Account Number	Account Description	Last Maintained	Inactive On
DESIGN	Sales - Web Page Design					6/20/00
		Revenue Account:	4000/10	Sales - Web Page Design		
		Inventory Account:	1200	Inventory		
		Cost of Goods Sold:	5000	Cost of Sales		
HOST	Sales - Web Page Hosting					6/20/00
		Revenue Account:	4000/30	Sales - Web Site Hosting		
		Inventory Account:	1200	Inventory		
		Cost of Goods Sold:	5000	Cost of Sales		
MISC	Sales - Misc. Sales					6/20/00
		Revenue Account:	4000/99	Sales - Misc.		
		Inventory Account:	1200	Inventory		
		Cost of Goods Sold:	5000	Cost of Sales		
RETAIL	Sales - Web Retail Sales					6/20/00
		Revenue Account:	4000/40	Sales - Web Retail Sales		
		Inventory Account:	1200	Inventory		
		Cost of Goods Sold:	5000	Cost of Sales		
UPDATE	Sales - Web Page maintenance					6/20/00
		Revenue Account:	4000/20	Sales - Web Page Maintenance		
		Inventory Account:	1200	Inventory		
		Cost of Goods Sold:	5000	Cost of Sales		

5 distribution codes printed

❑ Close: the **A/R Distribution Codes** window

ADDING INTEREST PROFILES

An Interest Profile must be added to each customer account, specifying the rate and methods to be used when charging interest on the customer's overdue invoices or account balances. You must add at least one Interest Profile before you can add customer records.

- ❑ DClick: the **Interest Profiles** icon  on the A/R Setup window

FIGURE 17-8
A/R Interest Profiles Window

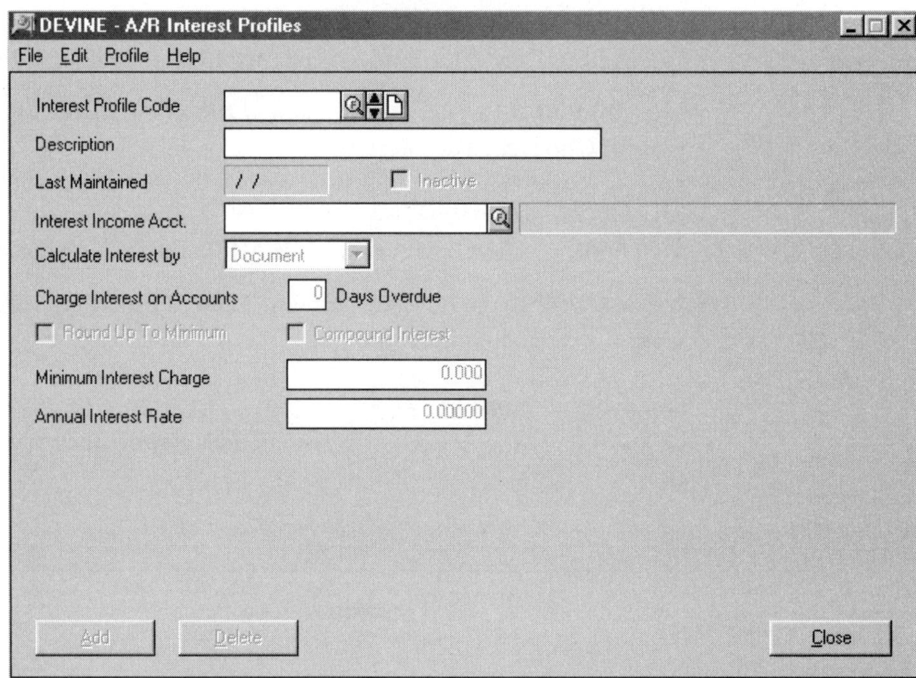

Devine Designs Inc. has decided to add two Interest Profile Codes; the first will charge a rate of 8% for most customers, and the second will charge a zero rate of interest for those customers who have negotiated special arrangements. Refer to the A/R Interest Profiles window shown in Figure 17-8.

Interest Profile Code

- ❑ Type: **NORMAL** in the Interest Profile Code text box
- ❑ Press: **Tab** [Tab]

Description

- ❑ Type: **8% for normal accounts** in the Description text box
- ❑ Press: **Tab** [Tab]

Inactive

- ❑ Ensure that the **Inactive** box has not been selected.
- ❑ Press: **Tab** [Tab]

Interest Income Account

- ❑ Select: **6500 Interest Income** using the Finder

Calculate Interest By

The Calculate Interest By field is used to indicate whether you will charge interest on each overdue invoice or on the overdue account balance. Devine Designs Inc. will charge interest on each overdue invoice.

- ❑ Select: **Document** using the list tool
- ❑ Press: **Tab** [Tab]

Days Overdue

The Charge Interest on Accounts { } Days Overdue field is used to identify the number of days an account must be overdue before interest is charged. Devine Designs Inc. has decided to allow customers a three-day grace period.

- ❑ Type: **3** in the Calculate Interest on Accounts text box
- ❑ Press: **Tab** [Tab]

Round Up To Minimum

Select this option if you round up interest charges to a minimum amount. If you do not have a minimum interest charge, or if you charge interest as calculated, do not select this option. Devine Designs Inc. has decided to charge interest only when the interest is $1.00 or more.

- ❑ De-select: the **Round Up To Minimum** option box
- ❑ Press: **Tab** [Tab]

Compound Interest

Select this option to include previous interest charges on the overdue total when calculating interest. Devine Designs Inc. will not use compound interest.

- ❑ De-select: the **Compound Interest** option box
- ❑ Press: **Tab** [Tab]

Minimum Interest Charge

In this text box, enter the minimum amount you charge as interest. If you charge interest as calculated, regardless of the amount, enter 0 (zero). Devine Designs Inc. has decided to charge a minimum of $1.00 interest.

- ❑ Type: **1.00** in the Minimum Interest Charge field
- ❑ Press: **Tab** [Tab]

Annual Interest Rate

Type the annual interest rate at which you charge interest. An annual rate of 8%, as charged by Devine Designs Inc., would be entered as .08.

- ❑ Type: **.08** in the Annual Interest Rate field
- ❑ Press: **Tab** [Tab]
- ❑ Click: **Add** [Add]

YOUR TURN

- ❑ Click: the **New Document** icon
- ❑ Add: the Interest Profile **CTRACT**
- ❑ Enter information so there are no interest charges for the CTRACT Interest Profile.
- ❑ Print: the **Interest Profiles Report** as shown in Figure 17-9

FIGURE 17-9
Interest Profiles Report

Date: Tuesday, June 20, 2000 3:15PM **DDI Student Name** **Page 1**
A/R Interest Profiles (ARINT01)

From Interest Profile [ ] To [ZZZZZZ]

Interest Profile	Interest Income Account	Charge Interest On	Charge Interest on Accounts	Compound Interest	Round Up To Min.	Minimum Interest	Annual Int. Rate
CTRACT	Contract - no interest charges		Last Maintained:		6/20/00		
	6500	Overdue Invoice	0 days overdue	No	No	0.00	0.00000
NORMAL	8% for normal accounts		Last Maintained:		6/20/00		
	6500	Overdue Invoice	3 days overdue	No	No	1.00	0.08000

2 interest profiles printed

- ❑ Close: the **A/R Interest Profiles** window

Adding Receipt Types

The Receipt Types window (Figure 17-10) identifies how customers pay you. Receipt Types include cash, checks, credit cards, or other methods, such as gift certificates. For each type of receipt your company accepts, enter a unique code of up to six characters, a description (such as the name of the credit card), and the type of receipt: cash, check, credit card, or other. You must add at least one receipt type before you can add customer records.

❑ DClick: the **Receipt Types** icon  Receipt Types on the A/R Setup window

Figure 17-10
A/R Receipt Types Window

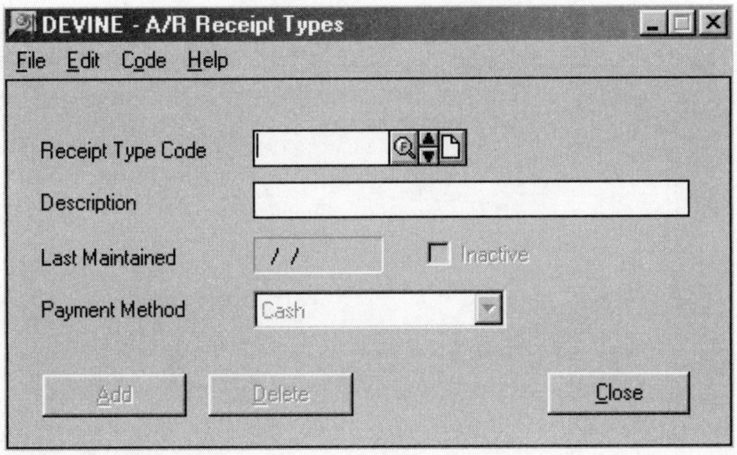

DEVINE - A/R Receipt Types

File Edit Code Help

Receipt Type Code

Description

Last Maintained / / Inactive

Payment Method Cash

Add Delete Close

In Chapter 16: Setting Up Accounts Receivable, you added receipt types for Checks and Cash. Devine Designs Inc. will also receive payment through e-cash, which includes credit card payments.

Receipt Type Code

The code may be as long as six characters to identify the Receipt Type.

❑ Type: **ECASH**

❑ Press: **Tab** Tab

Description

❑ Type: **e-cash - including credit card** in the Description text box

❑ Press: **Tab** Tab twice to move to the Payment Method field

Payment Method

You can choose Cash, Check, Credit Card, or Other to identify the payment method. Devine Designs Inc. will use Other to define payments received by e-cash.

- ❑ Select: **Other** using the list tool
- ❑ Click: **Add** [Add]
- ❑ Print: the **Receipt Types Report**

FIGURE 17-11
Receipt Types Report

Date: Tuesday, June 20, 2000 3:18PM — **DDI Student Name** — **Page 1**
A/R Receipt Types (ARPYTP01)

Receipt Type Code	Description	Receipt Type	Last Maintained	Inactive On
CASH	Cash	Cash		
CHECK	Check	Check		
ECASH	e-cash - including credit card	Other	6/20/00	

3 receipt codes printed

- ❑ Close: the **A/R Receipt Types Report** window, shown in Figure 17-11
- ❑ Close: the **A/R Receipt Types** window

ADDING TERMS

ACCPAC Accounts Receivable records the payment terms that your company uses to determine invoice due dates, to set the rates and eligibility periods of discounts for early payment, and to calculate discount bases in Terms Codes. You must record at least one Terms Code before you can enter accounts receivable transactions. The A/R Terms window is shown in Figure 17-12.

- ❑ DClick: the **Terms** icon [Terms] on the A/R Setup window

FIGURE 17-12
A/R Terms Window

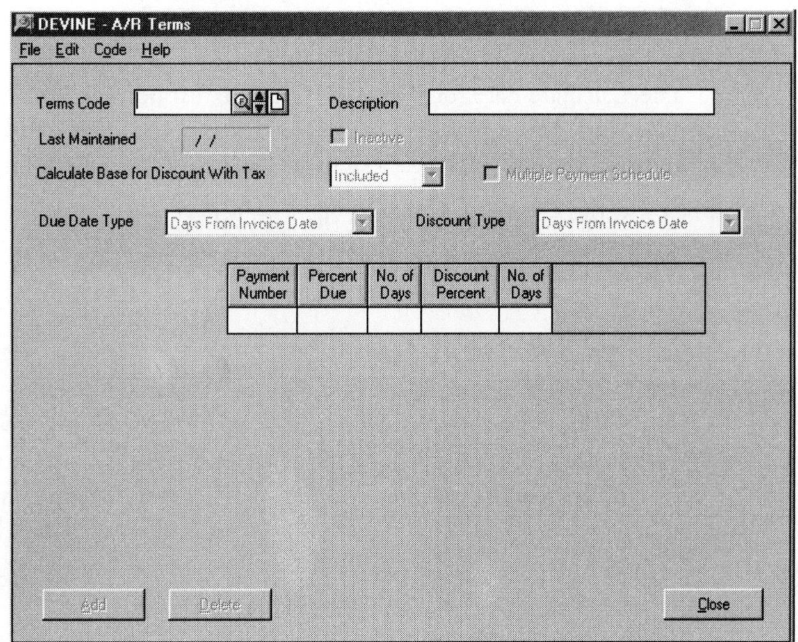

The first term that Devine Designs Inc. will add will allow clients a 2% discount if they pay invoiced amounts within 10 days of the invoice date. Otherwise, the full amount of the invoice is due within 30 days of the invoice date.

Terms Code

Each Terms Code is identified by a unique alpha-numeric name in the Terms Code text box.

- ❑ Type: **DISC** in the blank Terms Code text box
- ❑ Press: **Tab** [Tab]

Description

The description that you enter should describe the terms offered to the client.

- ❑ Type: **2/10, n/30** in the Description text box
- ❑ Press: **Tab** [Tab]

Inactive

This Terms Code should be active. If there is a tick in the Inactive check box, click it to make the Terms Code active.

- ❑ Press: **Tab** [Tab]

Calculate Base for Discount With Tax

The Calculate Base for Discount With Tax list box is used to specify how tax amounts are calculated. Select Included to allow a discount on taxes, and Excluded if discounts are not allowed on taxes. Devine Designs Inc. will not allow discounts on taxes.

❑ Select: **Excluded** using the list tool

❑ Press: **Tab** [Tab]

Multiple Payment Schedule

The Multiple Payment Schedule check box is selected if you allow customers to pay by installments. This field will be left inactive for this Terms Code. If there is a tick in this check box, click it to make the Multiple Payment Schedule inactive.

❑ Press: **Tab** [Tab]

Due Date Type

The Due Date Type list box allows you to select one of five different methods by which you determine invoice due dates.

- Days from Invoice Date is selected when invoices come due in a specific number of days after the invoice date.
- End of Next Month is used if the invoices are due on the last day of the next month.
- Day of Next Month is used if invoices are due on a specific day in the next month.
- Days from Day of Next Month is selected if invoices are due a standard number of days after a specific day in the next month.
- Due Date Table is selected if you use standard due dates for invoices entered within specific ranges of days.

Terms of 2/10, n/30 means that the full amount of the Invoice is due 30 days from the invoice date.

❑ Select: **Days from Invoice Date** using the list tool

❑ Press: **Tab** [Tab]

Discount Type

The Discount Type list box allows you to select the method used to calculate the last day on which customers are eligible for a discount. The options are the same as those for Due Date type.

❑ Select: **Days from Invoice Date** using the list tool

❑ Press: **Tab** [Tab]

Data Table

The data table should now be active. ACCPAC enters 1 in the Payment Number cell and 100 in the Percent Due cell because the Multiple Payment Schedule option was not selected. You must enter the data for the other three cells.

❑ Click: the first **No. of Days** cell

In this cell, enter the number of days from the invoice date that the full payment of the invoice is due.

❑ Type: **30**
❑ Press: **Tab** [Tab]

In the Discount Percentage cell, enter the amount of the discount that is granted for early payment of invoices.

❑ Type: **2.0** in the Discount Percentage cell
❑ Press: **Tab** [Tab]

In the second No. of Days cell, enter the number of days from the invoice date that the discount is offered.

❑ Type: **10** in the second No. of Days cell
❑ Press: **Tab** [Tab]
❑ Click: **Add** [Add]

YOUR TURN

Add the following terms records. In all cases, the Calculate Base for Discount With Tax field should be Excluded.

❑ Add: the term **CASH** for Cash Sales
❑ Add: the term **NODISC** for credit sales due in 30 days but with no discount

ADDING A MULTIPLE PAYMENT SCHEDULE

Devine Designs Inc. needs a Terms Code with a Multiple Payment Schedule. This Terms Code will be used for projects that take a month to complete. The client will be asked to pay 40% of the fee at the start of the contract, 30% when the project is delivered 30 days later, and the final 30% 30 days later. Devine Designs Inc. will issue the invoice at the start of the contract.

❑ Click: the **New Document** icon in the Terms Code field
❑ Type: **PROJ** in the Terms Code text box
❑ Press: **Tab** [Tab]
❑ Type: **30 day projects** in the Description text box
❑ Press: **Tab** [Tab]

- ❑ Select: Calculate Base for Discount With **Tax Excluded**
- ❑ Press: **Tab** [Tab]
- ❑ Click: the **Multiple Payment Schedule** check box
- ❑ Press: **Tab** [Tab]

ACCPAC opens an expanded Number of Payments section in the lower portion of the screen.

- ❑ Select: **Days from Invoice Date** in the Due Date Type list box
- ❑ Press: **Tab** [Tab]
- ❑ Select: **Days from Invoice Date** in the Discount Type list box
- ❑ Press: **Tab** [Tab]
- ❑ Click: the **Payment Number** column
- ❑ Press: **Tab** [Tab]
- ❑ Type: **40.0** on the Percent Due field
- ❑ Press: **Tab** [Tab] to move to the No. of Days cell
- ❑ Type: **0**

No discounts will be offered when a payment schedule has been arranged.

- ❑ Press: **Tab** [Tab] three times to create a new line
- ❑ Enter: **30** in the Percent Due cell
- ❑ Press: **Tab** [Tab]
- ❑ Enter: **30** in the No. of Days cell
- ❑ Press: **Tab** [Tab] until the row for payment three appears
- ❑ Enter: **30** in the Percent Due cell
- ❑ Press: **Tab** [Tab]
- ❑ Enter: **60** in the No. of Days cell
- ❑ Press: **Tab** [Tab]
- ❑ Click: **Add** [Add]

Printing the Terms Report

- ❑ Print: the **A/R Terms Code** report including Multiple Payment Schedules

FIGURE 17-13
Terms Report

Date: Tuesday, June 20, 2000 3:28PM
A/R Terms Codes (ARTERMS1)

DDI Student Name

From Terms Code [] To [ZZZZZZ]
Report Format [Profile and Multiple Payment Schedules]

Terms Code **Description**

CASH Cash Sales — Last Maintained: 6/20/00

Due Date
Type: Days From Invoice Date
Number of Days: 0

Discount Date
Type: Days From Invoice Date
Number of Days: 0
Calculate Base For Discount With Tax: Included
Discount %: 0.00000 %

DISC 2/10,n/30 — Last Maintained: 6/20/00

Due Date
Type: Days From Invoice Date
Number of Days: 30

Discount Date
Type: Days From Invoice Date
Number of Days: 10
Calculate Base For Discount With Tax: Excluded
Discount %: 2.00000 %

NODISC n/30 — Last Maintained: 6/20/00

Due Date
Type: Days From Invoice Date
Number of Days: 30

Discount Date
Type: Days From Invoice Date
Number of Days: 0
Calculate Base For Discount With Tax: Included
Discount %: 0.00000 %

PROJ 30 day projects — Last Maintained: 6/20/00 Use Multiple Payments: Yes

Due Date
Type: Days From Invoice Date

Discount Date
Type: Days From Invoice Date
Calculate Base For Discount With Tax: Excluded

	Payment			Discount		
Payment Number	**Percent Due**	**No. of Days**	**Day of Month**	**Percent**	**No. of Days**	**Day of Month**
1	40.00000 %	0	0	0.00000 %	0	0
2	30.00000 %	30	0	0.00000 %	0	0
3	30.00000 %	60	0	0.00000 %	0	0

4 terms codes printed

Review the printout, Figure 17-13, to verify that the Terms are correct and complete. Make any necessary corrections and print the report again.

- ❑ Close: the **A/R Terms Report** dialog box
- ❑ Close: the **A/R Terms** window
- ❑ Exit: **ACCPAC**

REVIEW QUESTIONS

1. When working with Setup records, you can modify or delete records whenever necessary, except for one item. What is that item, and how must you proceed to make changes?
2. What is the purpose of the Account Sets option?
3. What is the purpose of the Billing Cycles option?
4. What is the purpose of the Distribution Codes option?
5. What is the purpose of the Interest Profiles option?
6. What is the purpose of the Receipt Type option?
7. What is the purpose of the Terms option?
8. When would you use a Multiple Payment schedule?

EXERCISE

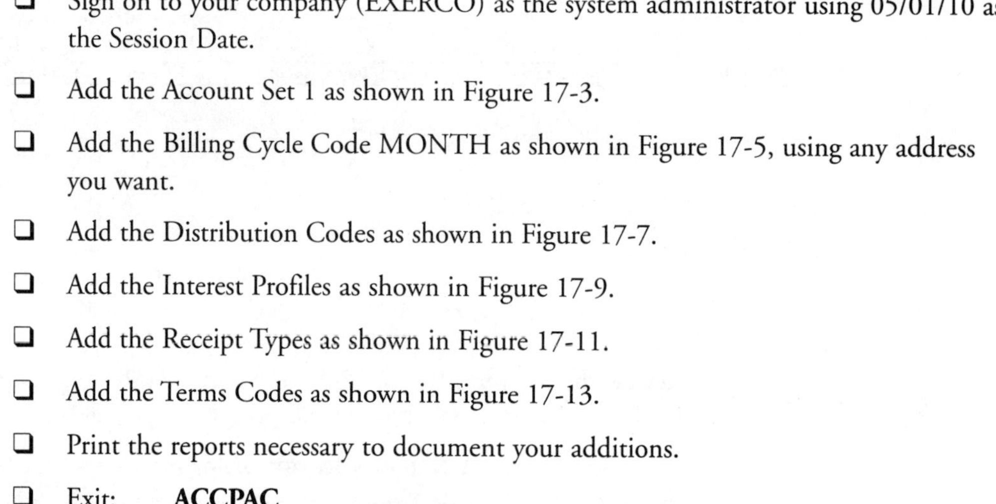

- ❑ Sign on to your company (EXERCO) as the system administrator using 05/01/10 as the Session Date.
- ❑ Add the Account Set 1 as shown in Figure 17-3.
- ❑ Add the Billing Cycle Code MONTH as shown in Figure 17-5, using any address you want.
- ❑ Add the Distribution Codes as shown in Figure 17-7.
- ❑ Add the Interest Profiles as shown in Figure 17-9.
- ❑ Add the Receipt Types as shown in Figure 17-11.
- ❑ Add the Terms Codes as shown in Figure 17-13.
- ❑ Print the reports necessary to document your additions.
- ❑ Exit: **ACCPAC**

TIP

Use the Setup Reports icon on the Accounts Receivable window.

CHAPTER 18

CUSTOMER RECORDS

ACCPAC Accounts Receivable allows you to keep very detailed records about your customers, and provides several options with which you can customize the records for your business requirements. This chapter takes you through the process of adding customer records to ACCPAC Accounts Receivable and choosing the options that will let you process customer information and transactions to suit your company's requirements.

GETTING READY

- ❑ Sign on to Devine Designs Inc. as the system administrator using 05/01/10 as the Session Date.
- ❑ Open: the **Accounts Receivable** window
- ❑ DClick: the **A/R Customers** icon 

FIGURE 18-1
A/R Customers Window

Customers

Ship-To
Locations

Ship-To
Locati...

Customer
Activity

Each of the icons on the Customers window (Figure 18-1) enables you to add, modify, or delete customer information.

ADDING A CUSTOMER GROUP

Use Customer Groups to classify the customer records into groups that share similar characteristics; for example, regional locations or industry types. Some of the information that you enter in the Customer Group will become the default information for customer accounts within the group. This transfer of information reduces the amount of data that must be entered when individual customer accounts are added.

You must add at least one customer group before you can add individual customer records. Additional customer groups can be added when necessary.

Devine Designs Inc. has decided to use one customer group for all sales.

- ❑ DClick: the **Customer Groups** icon  on the A/R Customers window

The Customer Groups notebook (Figure 18-2) consists of three pages with two identifying text boxes displayed above each notebook page.

Group Code

WARNING

Group Codes cannot be changed. Be sure to create your Group Code carefully.

The Group Code may be up to three characters long. Devine Designs Inc. has decided to assign the Group Code, DOM (domestic), to the initial account group.

- ❑ Type: **DOM** in the Group Code text box
- ❑ Press: **Tab** [Tab]

If you must change a Group Code, first create the new customer group and then reassign all the customers from the old group to the new group. Then delete the old customer group.

FIGURE 18-2
Customer Groups Notebook

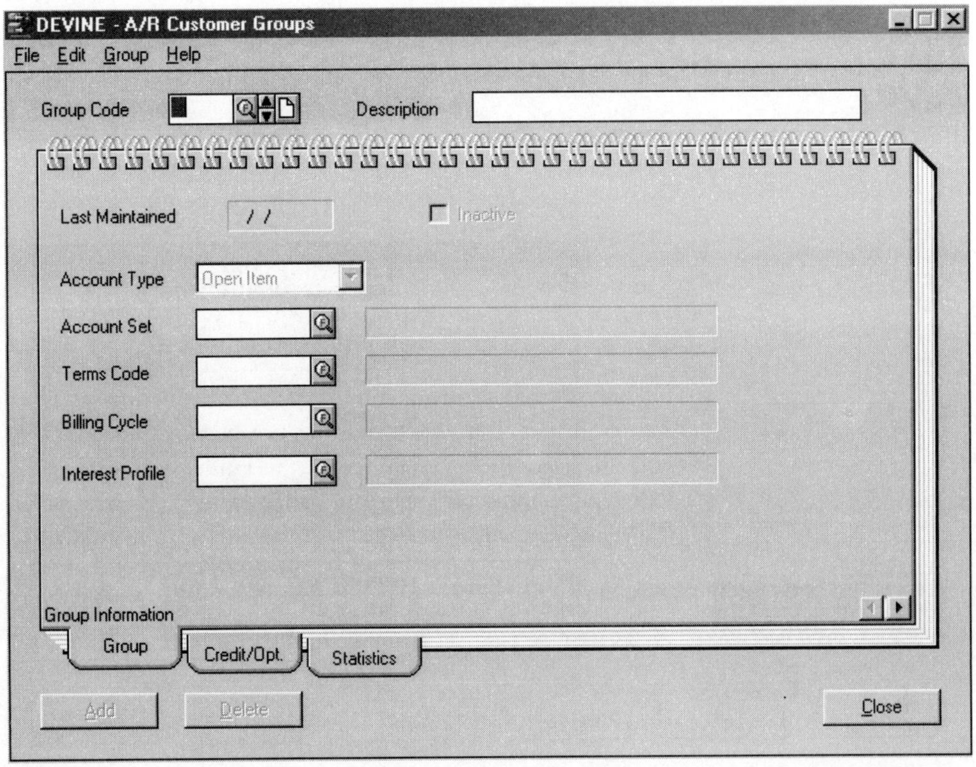

Description

- ❑ Type: **Domestic Sales** in the Description field
- ❑ Press: **Tab** [Tab]

GROUP INFORMATION PAGE

Inactive

Select Inactive only if you are preparing to delete a customer group and want to ensure that no further transactions are posted to customers assigned to the group. Devine Designs Inc. will not select this option when setting up the initial customer group.

Account Type

ACCPAC maintains customer accounts as either Open Item or Balance Forward accounts. You can change the default for any specific customer as required.

Choose the Open Item option when you want to track each transaction for the customer. Payments, credit notes, and debit notes are applied to specific invoices and are shown as such on the customer's statement. The Open Item option provides more detailed information on unpaid invoices and, therefore, better control of Accounts Receivable.

Choose the Balance Forward option if it is not necessary to keep itemized transactions from previous periods. When this option is selected, ACCPAC applies the amounts of payments, credit notes, or debit notes to the oldest customer transactions. Customer statements show a balance brought forward plus the current transactions.

Most of Devine Designs Inc.'s customers will have Open Item accounts.

❑ Select: **Open Item** using the list tool

For the rest of this page, you can enter information by typing or by selecting from the Finder. If you type a code that has not been added, ACCPAC will display the Finder and you can select the proper code. If the Finder does not display the proper code, save the Customer Group, add the appropriate code, and then edit the Customer Group to enter the remaining information.

TIP
If you type the information, press **Tab** to complete the entry.

Account Set

❑ Select: Account Set **1** using the list tool

Terms Code

Select the Terms Code that you will assign to most of the customers in the group. When you add customers, you can change this default Terms Code for individual customers. You can also change the default Terms Code for individuals' invoices. Devine Designs Inc. will offer most customers 2/10, n/30 terms.

❑ Select: **DISC** using the Finder

Billing Cycle

A company could use several different Billing Cycles for different kinds of customers. Devine Designs Inc. has decided to use a monthly Billing Cycle for all customers.

❑ Select: **MONTH** using the Finder

Interest Profile

Select the Interest Profile that you will assign to most of the customers in the group. When you add customers, you can change this default Interest Profile for individual customers. You can also change the default Interest Profile for individuals' invoices. Devine Designs Inc. will select the Interest Profile, NORMAL, to charge customers 8% interest on invoices that are three days overdue.

❑ Select: **NORMAL** using the Finder

Credit Information Page

❑ Click: the **Credit/Opt.** tab at the bottom of the A/R Customer Groups Notebook

The Credit Information page will appear as shown in Figure 18-3.

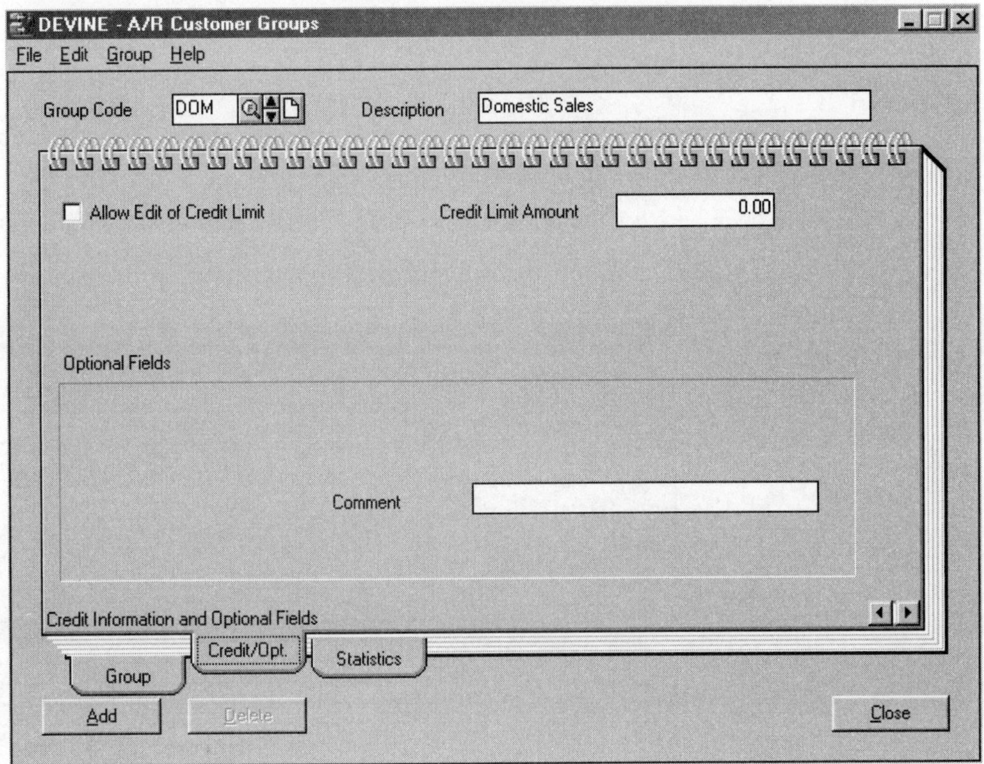

FIGURE 18-3
Credit Information Page

Allow Edit of Credit Limit

This option allows you to change the default credit limit for individual customer accounts. Devine Designs Inc. has decided to set a default credit limit of $2,000 for all domestic customers, but will change the credit limit where necessary.

❑ Click: the **Allow Edit of Credit Limit** check box

❑ Press: **Tab** [Tab]

Credit Limit Amount

The amount entered in the Credit Limit Amount text box will appear as the default credit limit for new customers you add to the group. When invoices are posted that cause a customer's balance to exceed his or her credit limit, ACCPAC will produce a warning message.

- ❑ Type: **2000.00**
- ❑ Press: **Tab** [Tab]

Devine Designs Inc. will not add a comment at this time.

- ❑ Click: **Add** [Add]

Group Statistics Page

If the Allow Edit of Customer Statistics option in the Options notebook has not been selected, this page will not be available.

- ❑ Click: the **Statistics** tab at the bottom of the A/R Customer Groups notebook

The Group Statistics page will appear as shown in Figure 18-4.

Figure 18-4
Group Statistics Page

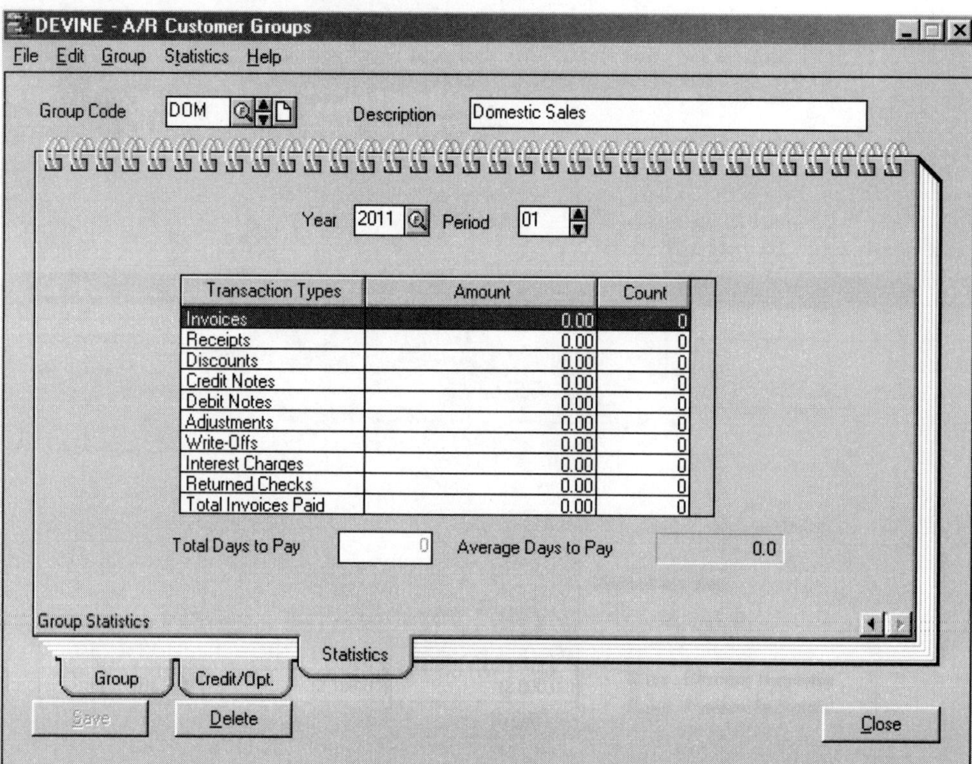

ACCPAC keeps track of the year-to-date amounts and the dates of the highest balance and largest invoice in the current and previous years. It also keeps track of the last invoice, receipt, credit note, debit note, adjustment, write-off, interest invoice, and returned check posted to the customer's account. The total invoices paid, total days to pay, and average days to pay for the customer group are also calculated.

Devine Designs Inc. has decided not to add information about the previous fiscal year. ACCPAC will accumulate statistics on the current fiscal year that has just begun.

PRINTING THE A/R CUSTOMER GROUPS FILE MENU

❑ Select: **Print** from the A/R Customer Groups File menu

FIGURE 18-5
A/R Customer Groups Report Window

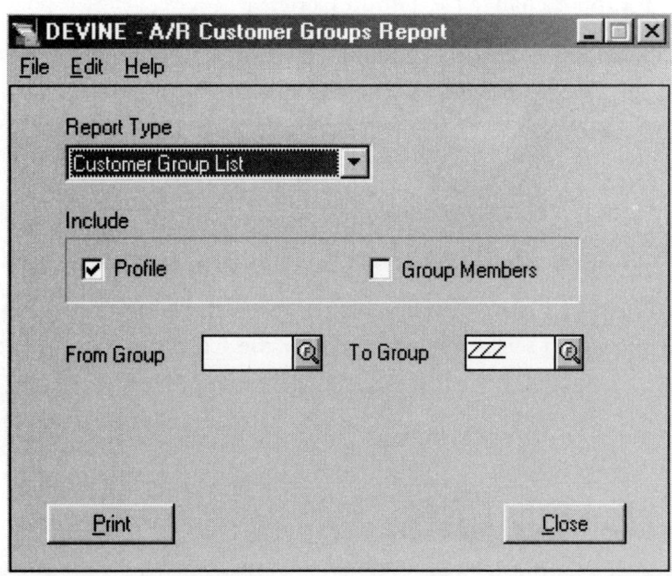

The default settings shown in Figure 18-5 will print a report listing the profiles of all Customer Groups. This window can also be used to list all customers within a group or to print group statistics. Enter any necessary changes to display the information shown in Figure 18-5.

❑ Press: **Print** [Print] on the A/R Customer Groups Report window

❑ Click: **OK** [OK] on the Print dialog box

FIGURE 18-6
A/R Customer Group Report

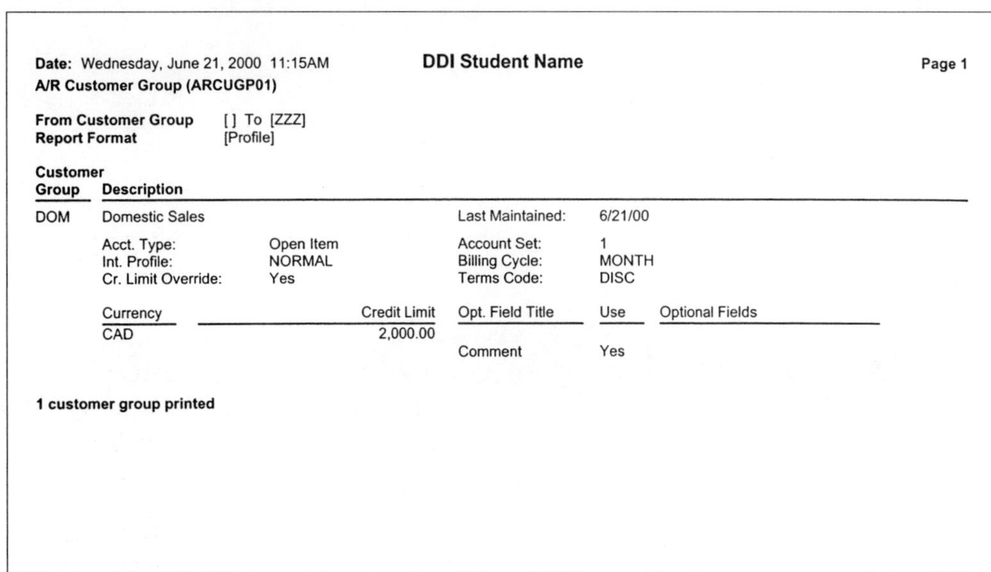

Date: Wednesday, June 21, 2000 11:15AM **DDI Student Name** **Page 1**
A/R Customer Group (ARCUGP01)

From Customer Group [ ] To [ZZZ]
Report Format [Profile]

Customer Group	Description			
DOM	Domestic Sales		Last Maintained:	6/21/00
	Acct. Type:	Open Item	Account Set:	1
	Int. Profile:	NORMAL	Billing Cycle:	MONTH
	Cr. Limit Override:	Yes	Terms Code:	DISC

Currency	Credit Limit	Opt. Field Title	Use	Optional Fields
CAD	2,000.00			
		Comment	Yes	

1 customer group printed

Compare your printout to that shown in Figure 18-6. Make any necessary changes and print the report again. You can edit the information in a Customer Group by selecting the notebook for that Customer Group, entering the changes that you want to make, then saving the Customer Group.

You cannot change the Group Code.

❑ Close: the **A/R Customer Groups Report** dialog box
❑ Close: the **A/R Customer Groups** window

Deleting a Customer Group

You cannot delete a Customer Group that is assigned to an individual customer account.

To delete a Customer Group, first assign the customer accounts to another Customer Group, then select the notebook for the Customer Group and click Delete.

Adding Customers

Individual customer records must be added before you can enter and process transactions in Accounts Receivable. The first customer that Devine Designs Inc. adds is Image Multimedia Ltd.

❑ DClick: the **Customers** icon [Customers] on the A/R Customers window

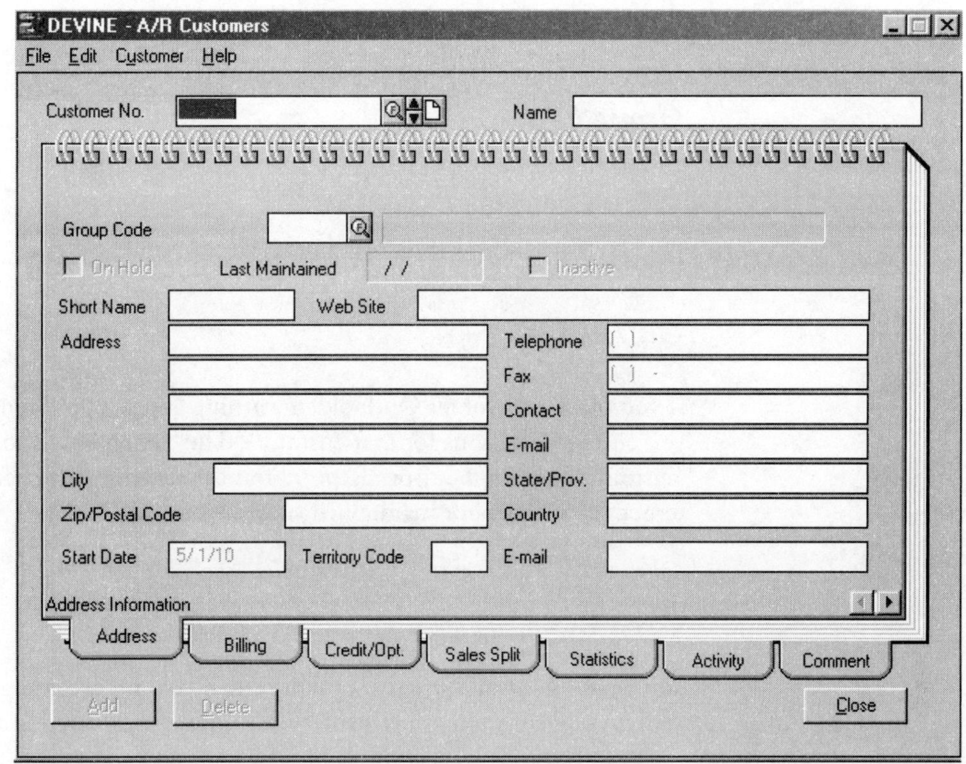

FIGURE 18-7
A/R Customers Notebook

The Customer's notebook (Figure 18-7) contains seven pages with two common fields displayed above the pages.

Customer Number

ACCPAC will accept any combination of up to twelve characters or digits as a customer number. Use at least four characters to allow for an increase in the number of customers. You cannot change a customer's number after you have created the customer account record.

Devine Designs Inc. will use a simple sequential numbering method using four numbers.

- ❑ Type: **1001** in the Customer No. text box
- ❑ Press: **Tab** [Tab]

Name

The Customer Name may have up to 28 letters and/or digits. Enter it exactly as you want it to appear on statements and reports.

- ❑ Type: **Image Multimedia Ltd.** in the Name text box
- ❑ Press: **Tab** [Tab]

Address Information Page

Group Code

Image Multimedia Ltd. is a domestic account.

- ❑ Select: **DOM** using the Finder

On Hold

If you place a customer On Hold, a warning appears on the invoice entry screen when you enter transactions for that customer. The customer is also flagged as On Hold on the Customer List and Statistics Report. You can activate this check box later if the customer's account is not maintained satisfactorily.

Inactive

You would select the Inactive option only if you are preparing to delete a customer record and want to ensure that no further transactions are posted to the account.

Short Name

This field is used to create a nickname for the customer. The name may be composed of as many as ten letters. Companies commonly enter the first ten letters of the name. For several reports, you can sort the customer accounts according to this short name. If you wish to change it, type the new name over the current one and press the Tab key. Alternatively, you can leave this field blank.

Devine Designs Inc. will create short names for each customer.

- ❑ Enter: **Image MM** in the Short Name text box
- ❑ Press: **Tab** Tab

Web Site

If this customer has a Web site, you can record the Web site address in this field.

- ❑ Type: **imagemultimedia.com**
- ❑ Press: **Tab** Tab

Be careful! Invoices and statements print the address information entered here.

Address Information

- ❑ Enter: **Suite 5210**
  First Place Tower
  1 King St.
  Toronto, Ontario
  L4Y 4M4
  Canada

Telephone

- ❑ Type: **416 1IMAGE1**
- ❑ Press: **Tab** Tab

Fax

Devine Designs Inc. will not use faxes; documents will be sent by e-mail.

- ❑ Press: **Tab** Tab

Contact

Bud Jaccin is the Supervisor, Accounts Payable, at Image Multimedia Ltd.

- ❑ Type: **Bud Jaccin** in the Contact text box
- ❑ Press: **Tab** Tab

Contact E-mail

If your contact has an e-mail address, you can record it in the E-mail field below the contact field.

- ❑ Type: **bud.jaccin@sympatico.com**
- ❑ Press: **Tab** Tab

Start Date

This text box allows you to enter the date on which this customer started doing business with you. The default displayed is the Session Date. Image Multimedia Ltd. signed the contract with Devine Designs Inc. on April 12, 2010.

- ❑ Type: **04/12/10** in the Start Date text box
- ❑ Press: **Tab** Tab

Territory Code

You can create a code of two characters to assign the customer to a territory within the customer group that is used in your company. Devine Designs Inc. has decided to use province or state designations as the territory code.

❑ Type: **ON** in the Territory Code text box

❑ Press: **Tab** Tab

Company E-mail

Enter the company's e-mail address in the E-mail field beside the Territory Code-field.

❑ Type: **imagemm@sympatico.com**

❑ Press: **Tab** Tab

BILLING INFORMATION PAGE

❑ Click: the **Billing** tab at the bottom of the A/R Customers notebook

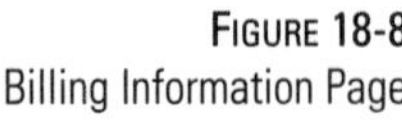

FIGURE 18-8
Billing Information Page

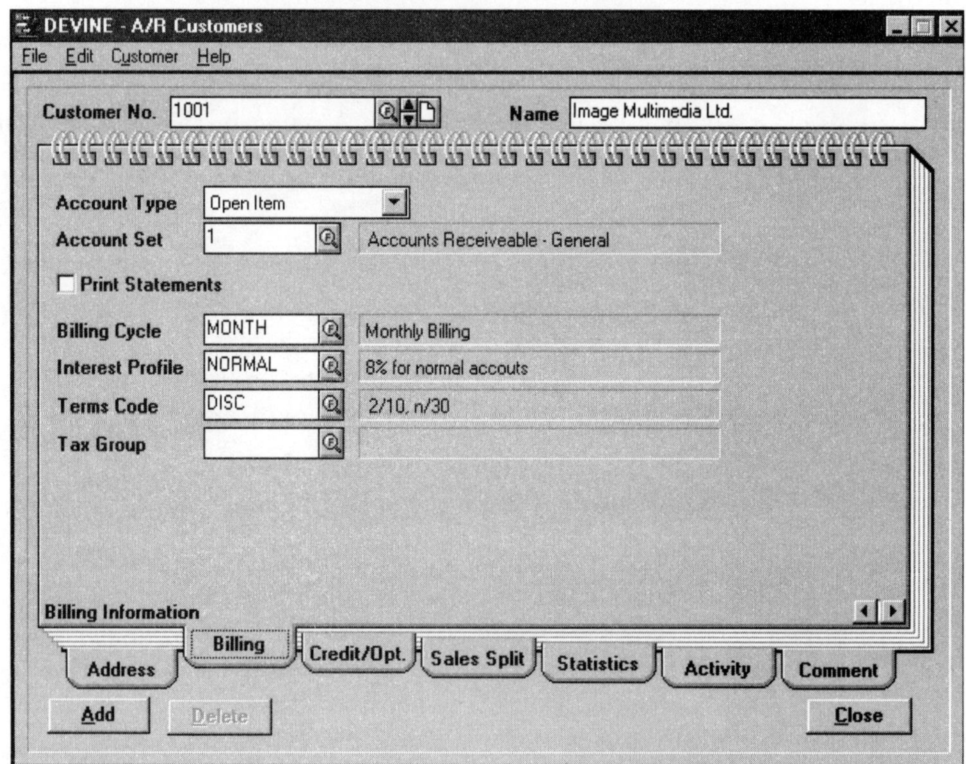

Most of the text boxes on the Billing Information page (Figure 18-8) display default information entered when customer groups were created. The defaults can be changed for individual customers.

Account Type

The default account type is Open Item. You can change the account type for individual customer accounts. Devine Designs Inc. will use the Open Item method for all customer accounts.

Account Set

The default displayed in the Account Set text box is 1, the code assigned to the customer group. As Devine Designs Inc. has only created one Account Set, no changes are necessary.

Print Statements

If you want to print statements for the customer, select this option. If you do not choose the option, you will not be able to print statements for this customer. Devine Designs Inc. will print statements for all customers.

- ❑ Activate: the **Print Statements** check box

Billing Cycle

The default Billing Cycle MONTH was assigned to the customer group DOM. You can change the code for individual customers which are not assigned to a national account. Devine Designs Inc. will use the MONTH Billing Cycle for all customers.

Interest Profile

The default Interest Profile, NORMAL, was assigned to the customer group DOM. Devine Designs Inc. will use the NORMAL Interest Profile as the default for all customers. If necessary, changes will be entered on individual transaction documents.

Terms Code

The default Terms Code DISC was assigned to the customer group DOM. You can change the Terms Code for any customer accounts. Devine Designs Inc. will use DISC for all customers. If necessary, changes will be entered on individual transaction documents.

Tax Group

Tax groups and other tax information were set up in Tax Services, which supplies this information to other ACCPAC applications.

❑ Click: the **Finder** for Tax Group

Select the code that represents the tax group to which the customer belongs. Devine Designs Inc. created one Tax Group in Tax Services.

❑ Select: **DOMSAL**

Tax Data Table

The scroll box that appears on the window allows you to select the Tax Class and enter the customer's registration number for each Tax Authority. Devine Designs Inc. created Taxable and Exempt Tax Classes for both the Federal and Provincial Tax Authorities. Image Multimedia Ltd. must pay both GST and RST.

The line displayed should be for the Federal Goods and Services Tax.

❑ Select: Class **1 Taxable** using the Finder

❑ Press: **Tab** Tab

The Registration No. cell allows you to record the customer's tax-exemption or tax-registration number.

❑ Type: **12345A** in the Registration No. cell

❑ Press: **Tab** Tab to display the line for Retail Sales Tax - Ontario

The Default Tax Class 1 is for taxable sales. Devine Designs Inc. will record Image Multimedia Ltd.'s provincial tax registration number.

❑ Enter: **987654-987ON** in the Registration No. Cell

❑ Press: **Tab** Tab

When the Address and Billing pages have been completed, ACCPAC will allow you to add the customer account.

❑ Click: **Add** Add

TIP
After completing another page, save the customer account information.

CREDIT INFORMATION AND OPTIONAL FIELDS PAGE

❑ Click: the **Credit/Opt.** tab at the bottom of the A/R Customers notebook to access the Credit Information and Optional Fields page, shown in Figure 18-9

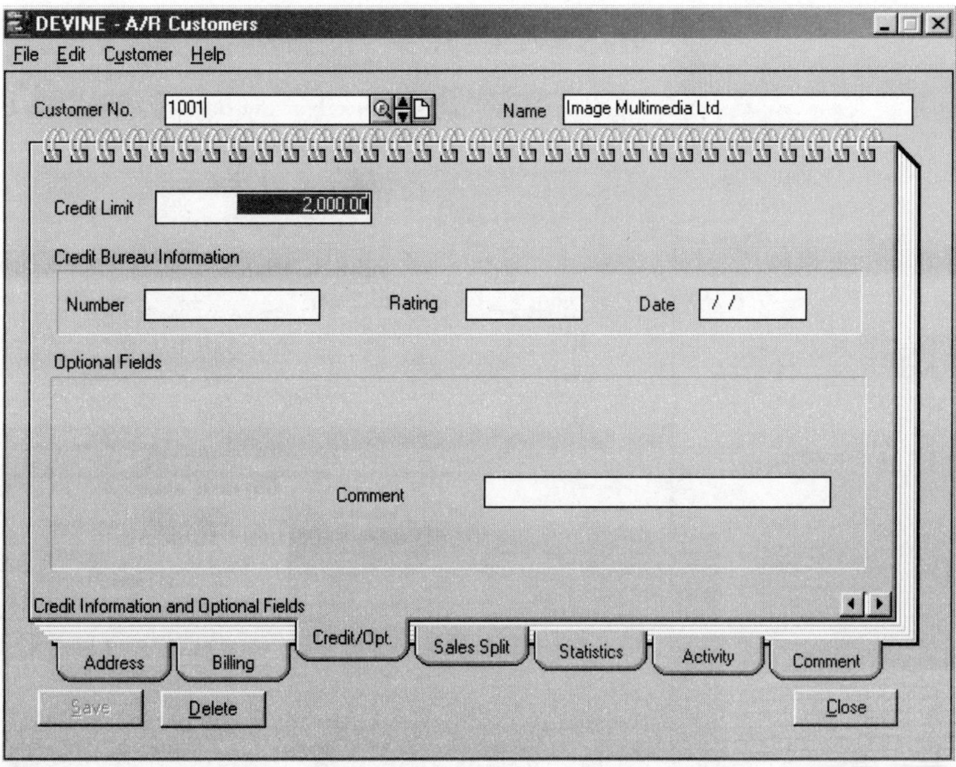

FIGURE 18-9
Credit Information and Optional Fields Page

Credit Limit

The Credit Limit text box should display the default credit limit (2,000.00) entered for the Customer Group DOM. Devine Designs Inc. has decided to set the initial credit limit for Image Multimedia Ltd. at $5,000.

- ❑ Type: **5000.00** in the Credit Limit text box
- ❑ Press: **Tab** [Tab]

Credit Bureau Information

If you use credit bureau information, you may enter the credit bureau number, the credit rating for the account, and the date of the credit rating in the three text boxes provided. Devine Designs Inc. has not decided on a credit reporting agency, so these text boxes will be left blank.

Optional Fields

Devine Designs Inc. will not enter a comment at this time.

- ❑ Click: **Save** [Save]

Salesperson Information Page

❑ Click: the **Sales Split** tab at the bottom of the A/R Customers notebook

FIGURE 18-10
Salesperson Information Page

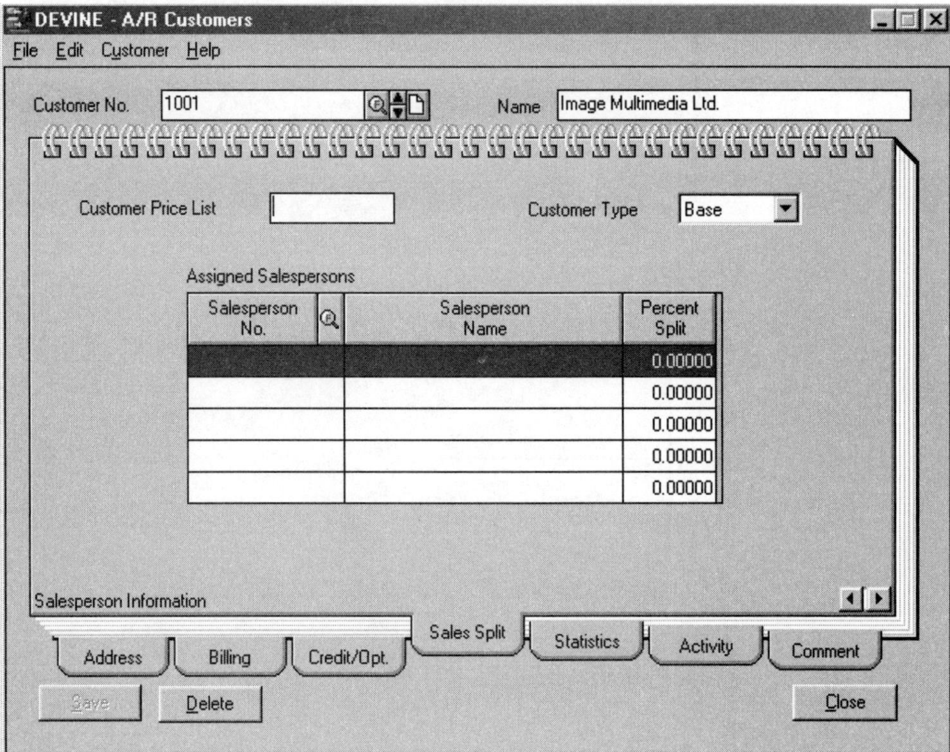

The Salesperson Information page (Figure 18-10) allows you to integrate ACCPAC Accounts Receivable with ACCPAC Order Entry and Inventory applications and to assign salespersons to an account. As Devine Designs Inc. will not use Order Entry, Inventory Control, or salespersons, no entries will be made on this page.

Period Statistics Page

❑ Click: the **Statistics** tab at the bottom of the A/R Customers notebook

FIGURE 18-11
Period Statistics Page

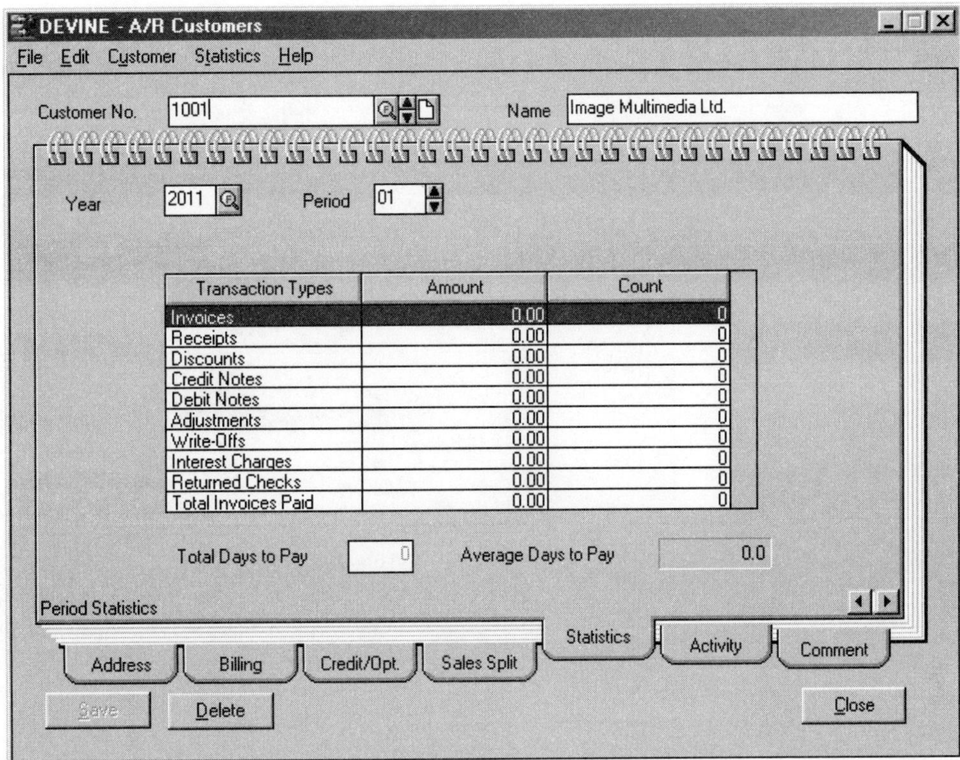

The Period Statistics page (Figure 18-11) displays statistics calculated by ACCPAC for each Period. As Devine Designs Inc. has not processed any transactions in Accounts Receivable, the amounts displayed for period 1, fiscal year 2011, should be zeros. As transactions are processed in Accounts Receivable, the statistics on the page will be updated.

ACTIVITY STATISTICS PAGE

❑ Click: the **Activity** tab at the bottom of the A/R Customers notebook

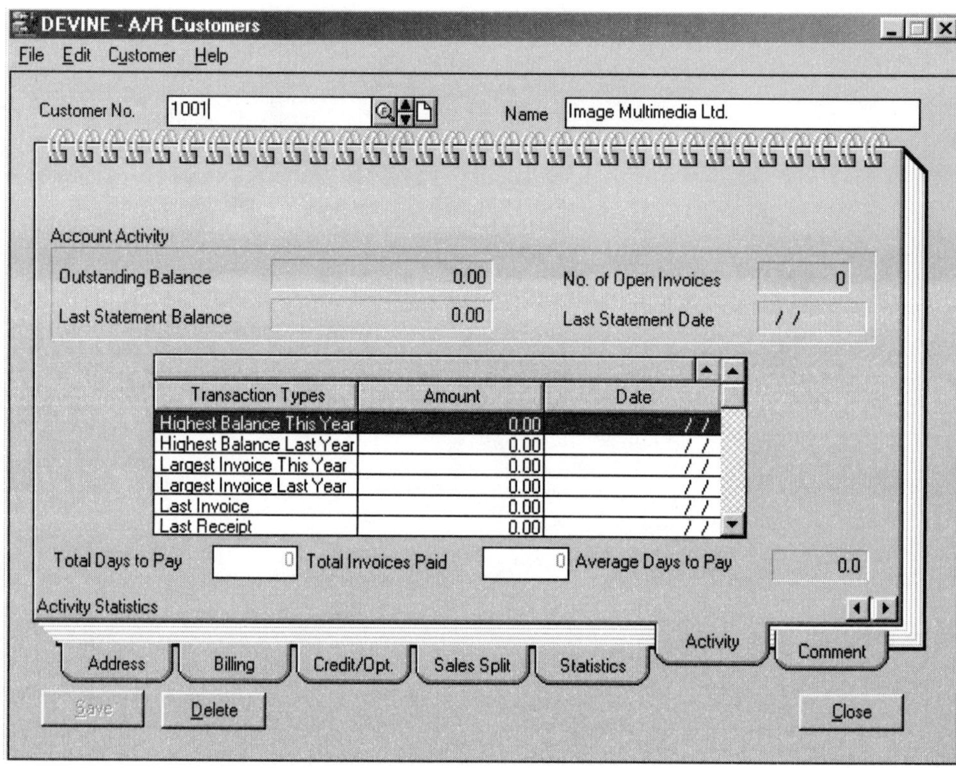

FIGURE 18-12
Activity Statistics Page

The Activity Statistics page (Figure 18-12) displays statistics calculated by ACCPAC for the current and last year. As Devine Designs Inc. has not processed any transactions in Accounts Receivable, the amounts displayed should be zeros. As transactions are processed in Accounts Receivable, the statistics on the page will be updated.

CUSTOMER COMMENTS PAGE

❑ Click: the **Comment** tab at the bottom of the A/R Customers notebook

The Comments page (Figure 18-13) allows comments to be recorded in a customer's account.

Date Entered

The Date Entered text box is used to record the date on which the comment was entered. The default displayed is the Session Date.

Follow-up Date

The Follow-up Date text box is used to record the date on which you want to follow up on your comment.

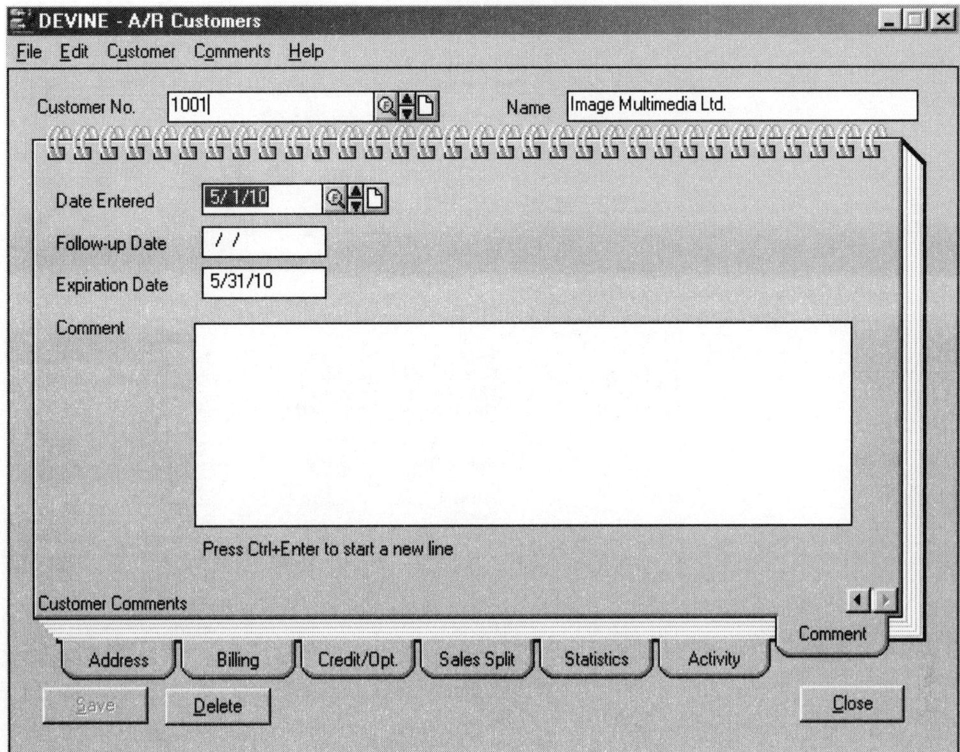

FIGURE 18-13 Customer Comments Page

Expiration Date

The Expiration Date text box is used to record the date on which you want to delete your comment. ACCPAC will display the date that is the same number of days later than the Date Entered date that you specified for the Default Number of Days To Keep Comments option in the Options notebook.

Comment

The comment text box holds up to 250 characters. You may type your comment in one single long line, or in several shorter lines. Press the Ctrl and Enter keys together whenever you want to start a new line.

Devine Designs Inc. will not enter any comments at this time.

YOUR TURN

You will now add six new customers for Devine Designs Inc.

- ❑ Click: the **Address Tab**
- ❑ Click: the **New Document** icon for Customer No.
- ❑ Add the six new customers using the information shown in Figure 18-14.

FIGURE 18-14
A/R Customer List

Date: Friday, August 11, 2000 1:35PM **DDI Student Name** **Page 1**
A/R Customer List (ARCULT01)

From Customer No. [ ] To [ZZZZZZZZZZZZ]
Account Type [All Customers]
Report Format [Profile, Address]

Customer Number | **Description**

1001
Image Multimedia Ltd.
Suite 5210
First Place Tower
1 King St.
Toronto, Ontario
L4Y 4M4
Ganada

Last Maintained: 8/11/2000
Phone: (416) 1IM-AGE1
Fax:

Short Name: Image MM **Contact:** Bud Jaccin
Contact E-mail: bud.jaccin@sympatico.com
Web Site: imagemultimedia.com
E-mail: imagemm@sympatico.com

Cust. Group: DOM
Start Date: 4/12/2010 **Territory:** ON

Account Type: Open Item **Account Set:** 1
Print Stmts.: Yes **Currency:** CAD **Rate Type:** SP
Billing Cycle: MONTH **Int. Profile:** NORMAL **Terms Code:** DISC
Price List: **Cust. Type:** Base
Credit Limit: 5,000.00 **Tax Group:** DOMSAL

Credit Bureau Information:	**Tax Authority**	**Tx. Class**	**Registration No.**
Number:	GSTFED	1	12345A
Rating :	RSTON	1	987654-987ON
Date:			

Salesperson	**Percent Split**	**Opt. Field Title**	**Use**	**Optional Field**
		Comment	Yes	

1005
Caledon Hotel, The
6 Caledon Mountain Rd.
Caledon, Ontario
J8K 9S2
Canada

Last Maintained: 8/11/2000
Phone: (905) 555-3211
Fax: (905) 555-3311

Short Name: Caledon Ho **Contact:** Marty Lysander
Contact E-mail:
Web Site: caledonhotel.on.ca
E-mail: caledon.hotel@aol.ca

Cust. Group: DOM
Start Date: 5/1/2010 **Territory:** ON

Account Type: Open Item **Account Set:** 1
Print Stmts.: Yes **Currency:** CAD **Rate Type:** SP
Billing Cycle: MONTH **Int. Profile:** NORMAL **Terms Code:** DISC
Price List: **Cust. Type:** Base
Credit Limit: 5,000.00 **Tax Group:** DOMSAL

Credit Bureau Information:	**Tax Authority**	**Tx. Class**	**Registration No.**
Number:	GSTFED	1	33445L
Rating :	RSTON	1	546654-789ON
Date:			

Salesperson	**Percent Split**	**Opt. Field Title**	**Use**	**Optional Field**
		Comment	Yes	

1010
Newell Productions
786 7th line
Milto, Ontario
L7Y 3E6
Canada

Last Maintained: 8/11/2000
Phone: (905) 555-1819
Fax: (905) 555-1920

Short Name: Newell **Contact:** Darren Newell
Contact E-mail: daren.newell@hotmail.com
Web Site: newellproductions.com
E-mail:

Date: Friday, August 11, 2000 1:35PM
A/R Customer List (ARCULT01)

DDI Student Name

Page 2

Customer Number **Description**

Cust. Group: DOM
Start Date: 5/1/2010 **Territory:** ON

Account Type: Open Item **Account Set:** 1
Print Stmts.: Yes **Currency:** CAD **Rate Type:** SP
Billing Cycle: MONTH **Int. Profile:** NORMAL **Terms Code:** DISC
Price List: **Cust. Type:** Base
Credit Limit: 4,000.00 **Tax Group:** DOMSAL

Credit Bureau Information:	**Tax Authority**	**Tx. Class**	**Registration No.**
Number:	GSTFED	1	456345G
Rating :	RSTON	1	123465-123ON
Date:			

Salesperson	**Percent Split**	**Opt. Field Title**	**Use**	**Optional Field**
		Comment	Yes	

1015 Bow River Outfitters **Last Maintained:** 8/11/2000
14 Hot Springs Rd. **Phone:** (615) 555-9631
Banff, Alberta **Fax:** (615) 555-6754
P8P 7Y7
Canada
Short Name: Bow River **Contact:** Mike Reid
Contact E-mail: mread@hotmail.com
Web Site: bowriver.com
E-mail: bowriver@sympatico.com

Cust. Group: DOM
Start Date: 5/1/2010 **Territory:** AL

Account Type: Open Item **Account Set:** 1
Print Stmts.: Yes **Currency:** CAD **Rate Type:** SP
Billing Cycle: MONTH **Int. Profile:** NORMAL **Terms Code:** DISC
Price List: **Cust. Type:** Base
Credit Limit: 5,000.00 **Tax Group:** DOMSAL

Credit Bureau Information:	**Tax Authority**	**Tx. Class**	**Registration No.**
Number:	GSTFED	1	
Rating :	RSTON	2	
Date:			

Salesperson	**Percent Split**	**Opt. Field Title**	**Use**	**Optional Field**
		Comment	Yes	

1020 Kawartha Comedy Club **Last Maintained:** 8/11/2000
360 Water Rd. **Phone:** (613) 555-1236
Peterborough, Ontario **Fax:** (613) 555-1228
C3R 5G4
Canada
Short Name: Kawartha C **Contact:** Derry Carry
Contact E-mail: derry.carry@total.net
Web Site:
E-mail:

Cust. Group: DOM
Start Date: 5/1/2010 **Territory:** ON

Account Type: Open Item **Account Set:** 1
Print Stmts.: Yes **Currency:** CAD **Rate Type:** SP
Billing Cycle: MONTH **Int. Profile:** NORMAL **Terms Code:** DISC
Price List: **Cust. Type:** Base
Credit Limit: 2,000.00 **Tax Group:** DOMSAL

Credit Bureau Information:	**Tax Authority**	**Tx. Class**	**Registration No.**
Number:	GSTFED	1	75321S
Rating :	RSTON	1	951753-852ON
Date:			

Salesperson	**Percent Split**	**Opt. Field Title**	**Use**	**Optional Field**

Date: Friday, August 11, 2000 1:35PM
A/R Customer List (ARCULT01)

DDI Student Name

Page 3

Customer Number	Description						
9990	Misc Sales - Ontario		Comment	Yes			
				Last Maintained:	8/11/2000		
				Phone:			
				Fax:			
	Short Name:	Misc Sales	**Contact:**				
	Contact E-mail:						
	Web Site:						
	E-mail:						
	Cust. Group:	DOM					
	Start Date:	5/1/2010	**Territory:**	ON			
	Account Type:	Open Item	**Account Set:**	1			
	Print Stmts.:	No	**Currency:**	CAD		**Rate Type:**	SP
	Billing Cycle:	MONTH	**Int. Profile:**	NORMAL		**Terms Code:**	DISC
	Price List:		**Cust. Type:**	Base			
	Credit Limit:	0.00	**Tax Group:**	DOMSAL			
	Credit Bureau Information:		**Tax Authority**	**Tx. Class**	**Registration No.**		
	Number:		GSTFED	1			
	Rating :		RSTON	1			
	Date:						
	Salesperson	**Percent Split**	**Opt. Field Title**	**Use**	**Optional Field**		
			Comment	Yes			
9991	Misc Sales - Other			**Last Maintained:**	8/11/2000		
				Phone:			
				Fax:			
	Short Name:	Misc Sales	**Contact:**				
	Contact E-mail:						
	Web Site:						
	E-mail:						
	Cust. Group:	DOM					
	Start Date:	5/1/2010	**Territory:**	XX			
	Account Type:	Open Item	**Account Set:**	1			
	Print Stmts.:	No	**Currency:**	CAD		**Rate Type:**	SP
	Billing Cycle:	MONTH	**Int. Profile:**	NORMAL		**Terms Code:**	DISC
	Price List:		**Cust. Type:**	Base			
	Credit Limit:	0.00	**Tax Group:**	DOMSAL			
	Credit Bureau Information:		**Tax Authority**	**Tx. Class**	**Registration No.**		
	Number:		GSTFED	1			
	Rating :		RSTON	2			
	Date:						
	Salesperson	**Percent Split**	**Opt. Field Title**	**Use**	**Optional Field**		
			Comment	Yes			

7 customers printed

Remember to add each new customer and then use the New Document icon to clear the window for a new customer.

PRINTING THE CUSTOMER LIST

❑ Click: **File** on the menu bar of the A/R Customers window

❑ Click: **Print** on the File Menu

FIGURE 18-15
A/R Customers Report Window

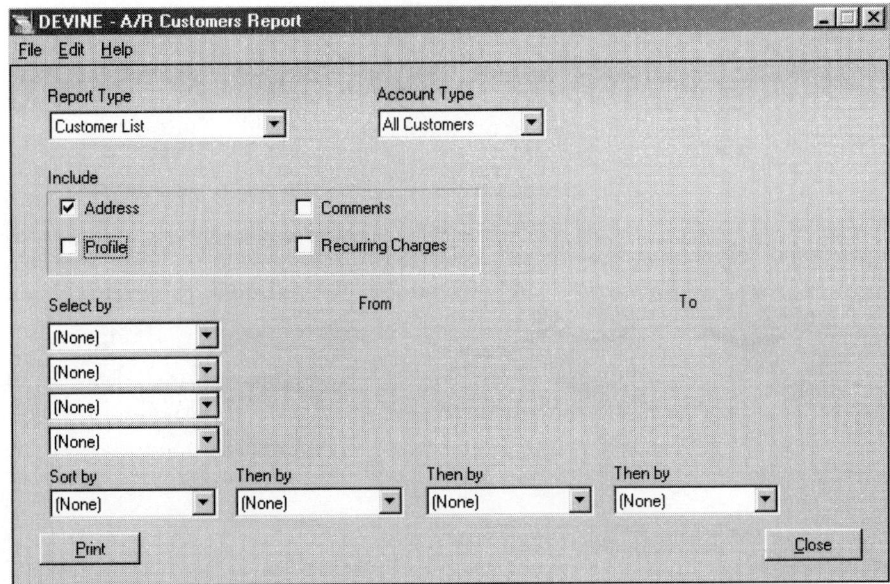

The Customers Report window (Figure 18-15) has five entry areas that allow you to control the format and content of the printed report.

Report Type

The Report Type list box allows you to print three types of reports: a Customer List, a Customer Activity Statistics report, or a Customer Period Statistics report. Devine Designs Inc. wants to print a Customer List.

❑ Select: **Customer List** using the list tool

Account Type

The Account Type list box allows you to select printing by account type (Open Item or Balance Forward), or to print All Customers (Open Item and Balance Forward). Devine Designs Inc. will include all customer accounts in the report.

❑ Select: **All Customers** using the list tool

Include

The Include area consists of four check boxes that allow you to select the information from the Customer Account record that will be included in the report. The default is to print only the customer address. Devine Designs Inc. will include the customer profile in this report. Devine Designs Inc. has not yet added Comments or Recurring Charges, so these options will not be activated.

❑ Activate: the **Profile** check box

Select By

The four Select by list boxes allow you to specify which customer accounts will be included in the report. Six selections are possible. The default, None, includes all customer accounts. If you use the list tool to select specific accounts, From and To text boxes with Finders will open beside the active list box. Devine Designs Inc. will print a report for all customers but will use the first list box to specify all customers.

❑ Select: **Customer No.** in the first list box using the list tool

From and To text boxes will open beside the active list box. The defaults of a blank From text box and ZZZZZ in the To text box will include all customers. If you want to print a specific group of customers, change the information in these text boxes. Devine Designs Inc. will print a report for all customers, so no changes are necessary.

Sort By

The four Sort by list boxes allow you to specify the order in which customer accounts will appear in the printed report. The default, None, will print the report in order of customer account number. As Devine Designs Inc. wants the report in order of customer account number, no changes are necessary.

❑ Click: **Print** Print

❑ Click: **OK** OK on the Print dialog box

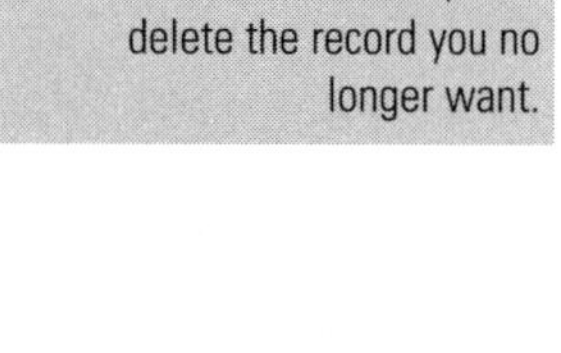

TIP

To change the customer number, set up a new customer record with a new number, then delete the record you no longer want.

Compare your printed report to that shown in Figure 18-14 and make any corrections necessary. If necessary, print the report again to document your changes.

❑ Print: the **Customer List** sorted by Customer Number

❑ Close: the **A/R Customers Report** window

❑ Close: the **A/R Customers** notebook for Devine Designs Inc.

SHIP-TO LOCATIONS

Ship-To Locations are different addresses to which a customer wants goods sent, with invoices and statements sent to the address entered on the customer record. ACCPAC allows you to enter many different Ship-To Locations for the same customer.

The Ship-To-Location Inquiry icon allows you to look up these different addresses for each customer.

Devine Designs Inc. has decided not to record this information in Accounts Receivable.

Customer Activity

The Customer Activity notebook consists of four pages (Activity, Aging, Transactions, and Receipts) that describe a customer's activity. ACCPAC updates this notebook for each customer as transactions are processed. Devine Designs Inc. will use this notebook later, after transactions have been processed.

- ❑ Close: the A/R **Customers** window
- ❑ Close: the **Accounts Receivable** window
- ❑ Exit: **ACCPAC**
- ❑ **Back up your data.**

Review Questions

1. What is the purpose of Customer Records?
2. What is the purpose of Customer Groups?
3. Describe the difference between "Open Item" and "Balance Forward" accounts.
4. Why is it necessary to set a realistic credit limit for a customer account?
5. Group Statistics keeps track of what information?
6. What constraints are there on the deletion of Customer Groups?
7. What will happen if you place a customer "On Hold" and then attempt to record an invoice?
8. Explain the purpose of "Ship-To" locations.

Exercise

- ❑ Sign on to your company (EXERCO) as the system administrator.
- ❑ The date sequence for this exercise will be the same as that used in the chapter.
- ❑ Enter 050110 in the Session Date box.

1. Create the same Customer Group as Devine Designs.
2. Print the A/R Customer Groups List.
3. Add the customers shown on the following list.
4. Print the Customer list as show in Figure 18-16.

FIGURE 18-16

Date: Thursday, August 17, 2000 12:36PM **John & Erik** **Page 1**
A/R Customer List (ARCULT01)

Account Type [All Customers]
Report Format [Profile, Address]

Customer Number	Description						
1050	B. Eady & Co.			**Last Maintained:**	8/17/2000		
	33 Tedwyn Dr.			**Phone:**	(905) 555-1598		
	Oakville, Ontario			**Fax:**			
	L8H G6H						
	Canada						
	Short Name:	B. Eady	**Contact:**	Bob Eady			
	Contact E-mail:						
	Web Site:						
	E-mail:						
	Cust. Group:	DOM					
	Start Date:	5/1/2010	**Territory:**	ON			
	Account Type:	Open Item	**Account Set:**	1			
	Print Stmts.:	Yes	**Currency:**	CAD		**Rate Type:**	SP
	Billing Cycle:	MONTH	**Int. Profile:**	NORMAL		**Terms Code:**	DISC
	Price List:		**Cust. Type:**	Base			
	Credit Limit:	2,000.00	**Tax Group:**	DOMSAL			
	Credit Bureau Information:		**Tax Authority**	**Tx. Class**	**Registration No.**		
	Number:		GSTFER	1	GST 1234		
	Rating :		RSTON	1	RST 9876		
	Date:						
	Salesperson	**Percent Split**	**Opt. Field Title**	**Use**	**Optional Field**		
			Comment	Yes			
1130	MacMillan & Johnson			**Last Maintained:**	8/17/2000		
	5268 Dundas St. West			**Phone:**	(905) 555-1478		
	Mississauga, Ontario			**Fax:**			
	L5L H9K						
	Canada						
	Short Name:	MacMillan	**Contact:**	Gary			
	Contact E-mail:						
	Web Site:						
	E-mail:						
	Cust. Group:	DOM					
	Start Date:	5/1/2010	**Territory:**	ON			
	Account Type:	Open Item	**Account Set:**	1			
	Print Stmts.:	Yes	**Currency:**	CAD		**Rate Type:**	SP
	Billing Cycle:	MONTH	**Int. Profile:**	NORMAL		**Terms Code:**	DISC
	Price List:		**Cust. Type:**	Base			
	Credit Limit:	5,000.00	**Tax Group:**	DOMSAL			
	Credit Bureau Information:		**Tax Authority**	**Tx. Class**	**Registration No.**		
	Number:		GSTFER	1	GST 9753		
	Rating :		RSTON	1	RST 1625		
	Date:						
	Salesperson	**Percent Split**	**Opt. Field Title**	**Use**	**Optional Field**		
			Comment	Yes			
1180	RenRak Ltd.			**Last Maintained:**	8/17/2000		
	220 Eglington Ave East			**Phone:**			
	Toronto, Ontario			**Fax:**			
	M4P 1K7						
	Canada						
	Short Name:	RenRak Ltd	**Contact:**				
	Contact E-mail:						
	Web Site:						
	E-mail:						
	Cust. Group:	DOM					
	Start Date:	5/1/2010	**Territory:**	ON			

Date: Thursday, August 17, 2000 12:36PM **John & Erik** **Page 2**
A/R Customer List (ARCULT01)

Customer Number	Description					
	Account Type: Open Item		**Account Set:** 1			
	Print Stmts.: Yes		**Currency:** CAD		**Rate Type:** SP	
	Billing Cycle: MONTH		**Int. Profile:** NORMAL		**Terms Code:** DISC	
	Price List:		**Cust. Type:** Base			
	Credit Limit: 2,500.00		**Tax Group:** DOMSAL			
	Credit Bureau Information:		**Tax Authority**	**Tx. Class**	**Registration No.**	
	Number:		GSTFER	1	GST 8076	
	Rating :		RSTON	1	RST 9146	
	Date:					
	Salesperson	**Percent Split**	**Opt. Field Title**	**Use**	**Optional Field**	
			Comment	Yes		
1220	VanVoort Ltd			**Last Maintained:**	8/17/2000	
	1725 Apple Orchard Street			**Phone:**	(905) 555-9514	
	Hamilton, Ontario			**Fax:**		
	J6H 4D6					
	Canada					
	Short Name: VanVoort L		**Contact:**	Richard Van		
	Contact E-mail:					
	Web Site:					
	E-mail:					
	Cust. Group: DOM					
	Start Date: 5/1/2010		**Territory:**	ON		
	Account Type: Open Item		**Account Set:** 1			
	Print Stmts.: Yes		**Currency:** CAD		**Rate Type:** SP	
	Billing Cycle: MONTH		**Int. Profile:** NORMAL		**Terms Code:** DISC	
	Price List:		**Cust. Type:** Base			
	Credit Limit: 5,000.00		**Tax Group:** DOMSAL			
	Credit Bureau Information:		**Tax Authority**	**Tx. Class**	**Registration No.**	
	Number:		GSTFER	1	GST 9757	
	Rating :		RSTON	1	RST 2939	
	Date:					
	Salesperson	**Percent Split**	**Opt. Field Title**	**Use**	**Optional Field**	
			Comment	Yes		
9990	Miscellaneous Sales - Ontario			**Last Maintained:**	8/17/2000	
				Phone:		
				Fax:		
	Short Name: Miscellane		**Contact:**			
	Contact E-mail:					
	Web Site:					
	E-mail:					
	Cust. Group: DOM					
	Start Date: 5/1/2010		**Territory:**	ON		
	Account Type: Open Item		**Account Set:** 1			
	Print Stmts.: No		**Currency:** CAD		**Rate Type:** SP	
	Billing Cycle: MONTH		**Int. Profile:** NORMAL		**Terms Code:** DISC	
	Price List:		**Cust. Type:** Base			
	Credit Limit: 0.00		**Tax Group:** DOMSAL			
	Credit Bureau Information:		**Tax Authority**	**Tx. Class**	**Registration No.**	
	Number:		GSTFER	1		
	Rating :		RSTON	1		
	Date:					
	Salesperson	**Percent Split**	**Opt. Field Title**	**Use**	**Optional Field**	
			Comment	Yes		
9991	Misc. Sales - Other			**Last Maintained:**	8/17/2000	
				Phone:		
				Fax:		

Date: Thursday, August 17, 2000 12:36PM

A/R Customer List (ARCULT01)

John & Erik

Page 3

Customer Number	**Description**					
	Short Name:	Misc. Sale	**Contact:**			
	Contact E-mail:					
	Web Site:					
	E-mail:					
	Cust. Group:	DOM				
	Start Date:	5/1/2010	**Territory:**			
	Account Type:	Open Item	**Account Set:**	1		
	Print Stmts.:	No	**Currency:**	CAD	**Rate Type:**	SP
	Billing Cycle:	MONTH	**Int. Profile:**	NORMAL	**Terms Code:**	DISC
	Price List:		**Cust. Type:**	Base		
	Credit Limit:	0.00	**Tax Group:**	DOMSAL		

Credit Bureau Information:	**Tax Authority**	**Tx. Class**	**Registration No.**
Number:	GSTFER	1	
Rating :	RSTON	2	
Date:			

Salesperson	**Percent Split**	**Opt. Field Title**	**Use**	**Optional Field**
		Comment	Yes	

6 customers printed

CHAPTER 19

INVOICE PROCESSING

In this chapter, you will create an Invoice Batch and record individual invoices for a typical set of transactions. You will also create recurring transactions for transactions that occur every month.

GETTING READY

- ❑ Sign on to Devine Designs Inc. as the system administrator using 05/14/10 as the Session Date.
- ❑ Open: the **Accounts Receivable** window
- ❑ DClick: the **A/R Invoices** icon 

The Invoices window (Figure 19-1) contains three icons that you will use in this chapter.

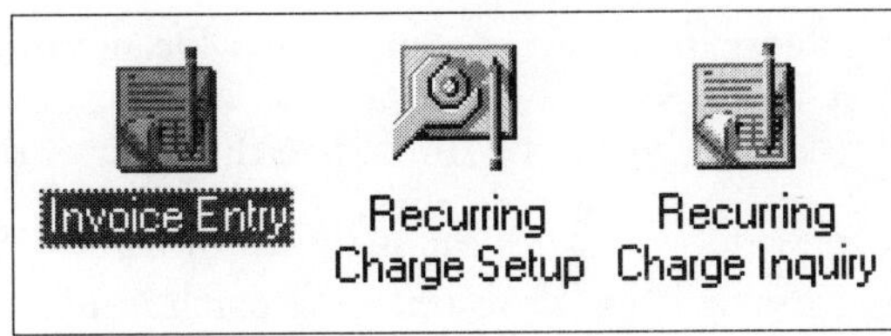

FIGURE 19-1
A/R Invoices Icons

Adding an Invoice

You use the Invoice Entry notebook (Figure 19-2) to enter and edit invoices, credit notes, debit notes, and prepayments.

❑ DClick: the **Invoice Entry** icon  on the A/R Invoices window

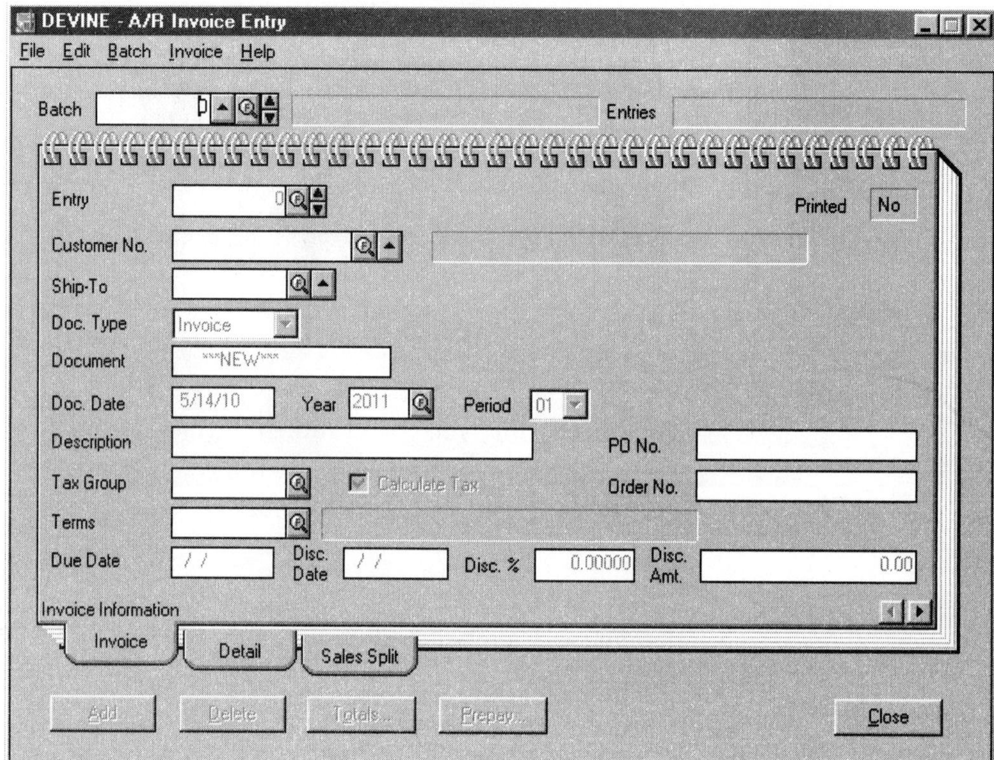

FIGURE 19-2
Invoice Entry Notebook

The Invoice Entry notebook contains four pages with a common batch identification area above the pages.

Batch Header

There is an expanded window for entering Batch Header information.

❑ Click: the **Zoom** button ▪ directly to the right of the Batch text box

The Batch Header window will appear as shown in Figure 19-3. The Batch text box is used to select an existing batch or to open the batch header in order to create a batch or modify header information. Devine Designs Inc. will create a new batch.

FIGURE 19-3
Batch Header Window

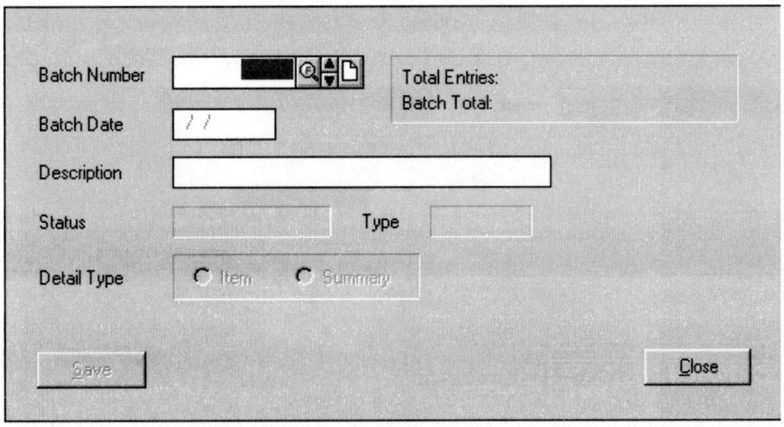

- ❑ Click: the **New Document** icon for the Batch Number text box

ACCPAC assigns the next available batch number to the new Invoice Batch. Number 1 should be displayed in the Batch Number box. The batch number is an important part of the audit trail, and cannot be assigned to another invoice batch. The batch number appears with each transaction on the posting journal.

ACCPAC automatically displays the current Session Date.

- ❑ Press: **Tab** [Tab] to move to the Description text box
- ❑ Type: **May 2010 Invoices**
- ❑ Press: **Tab** [Tab]

The Detail Type option button allows you to select Item or Summary detail. Summary details include the General Ledger revenue account, a description of the transaction, and the amount. Enter this detail type when you do not use an item list in Accounts Receivable, or when the invoice does not include item numbers.

Item details include an item number, distribution code, and description, as well as quantity and pricing information. Enter item details when you use an Accounts Receivable item list and want to update the Inventory and Cost of Goods Sold General Ledger accounts from the invoices you post in Accounts Receivable.

Devine Designs Inc. will select Summary detail.

- ❑ Select: the **Summary** option button
- ❑ Click: **Save** [Save]
- ❑ Click: **Close** [Close]

DOCUMENT HEADER INFORMATION PAGE

The Invoice Entry notebook is used to add or edit invoices, credit and debit notes, and individual interest invoices. You can add all four document types to a single batch, or you can use separate batches for each type.

The first invoice entered is to Image Multimedia Ltd. for Web page design work completed on May 13, 2010. The invoice amount is $1,800, plus taxes.

Entry

Since this transaction is the first to be entered, the Entry number will be 1. If you cancel or delete an entry, the entry number will not be available for use in that batch.

Customer Number

A customer number must be entered for each document. You can type the customer number in the text box or select it using the Finder.

- ❑ Click: the **Finder** for Customer No.
- ❑ Select: **1001 Image Multimedia Ltd.**

ACCPAC displays the customer's name at the right and fills in the text boxes using the default information recorded in the customer's account.

Ship-To

Ship-To is used when goods are shipped to one location and the invoice sent to another location. The ship-to locations are entered in the customer's account and can be selected using the Finder. You can also enter Ship-To locations by clicking on the zoom button to the right of the Finder.

Devine Designs Inc. delivered the new Web pages to Image Multimedia Ltd. by e-mail and will invoice the customer at its regular address.

- ❑ Press: **Tab** [Tab] to leave the Ship-To text box blank

Document Type

You can select Invoice, Credit Note, Debit Note or Interest as the document type using the list tool.

- ❑ Select: **Invoice** using the list tool
- ❑ Press: **Tab** [Tab]

Document

You can enter your own invoice numbers in the Document text box provided that each number is unique. You cannot use duplicate numbers for other types of Accounts Receivable documents, such as credit and debit notes. Transactions that duplicate a previously posted document number are placed in an error batch during posting.

If this text box is left showing ***NEW***, ACCPAC will assign the document number using the prefix specified in the Options notebook and the next available number. Devine Designs Inc. will use this automatic numbering feature whenever possible. In this case, ACCPAC will assign the invoice number IN1.

❑ Press: **Tab** [Tab] to move to the Doc. Date text box

Document Date

The default Document Date is the Session Date. This date is used for aging and statistical purposes. If necessary, you can type a new date in this text box.

Devine Designs Inc. completed the Web page and sent it Image Multimedia Ltd. on May 13, 2010, but will issue the invoice on May 14, 2010.

❑ Press: **Tab** [Tab] to accept the Session Date as the Document Date

Year and Period

ACCPAC displays the fiscal year and period based on the date entered in the Doc. Date text box and the information in the company's Fiscal Calendar. Only rarely will you change this information.

❑ Press: **Tab** [Tab] twice to move to the Description field

Description

This text box can be used to enter a brief description for the invoice. A brief description and longer comments can be entered for each detail added to the invoice. This invoice will cover work done on Image Multimedia Ltd.'s site map.

❑ Type: **site mapping** in the Description text box

❑ Press: **Tab** [Tab]

Purchase Order Number

The PO No. text box is used to record the customer's purchase order number. Image Multimedia Ltd.'s purchase order number was IMM 14335

❑ Type: **IMM 14335**

❑ Press: **Tab** [Tab]

Order Number

The Order No. text box is used when a company assigns sales order numbers to each purchase order received from customers. Many order entry and inventory control systems do this automatically. Devine Designs Inc. will not use sales order numbers.

❑ Press: **Tab** [Tab]

Tax Group

ACCPAC displays the default Tax Group entered in the customer's profile. For Image Multimedia Ltd., this is DOMSAL.

❑ Press: **Tab** [Tab]

Calculate Tax

A tax amount is calculated for invoices, credit notes, and debit notes if the customer is subject to tax. The document contains taxable item details, and tax rates have been entered for the tax authorities and classes in Tax Services.

❑ Press: **Tab** [Tab]

Terms

For each invoice, ACCPAC will display the default terms recorded in the customer's account. This information is used to calculate the information displayed in the Due Date, Discount Date, Discount %, and Discount Amount text boxes. Devine Designs Inc. will extend the default 2/10 n/30 to Image Multimedia Ltd.

DETAIL PAGE

At least one detail must be entered for each document before the document can be added to the batch.

❑ Click: the **Detail** tab at the bottom of the A/R Invoice Entry notebook

FIGURE 19-4
Detail Information Page

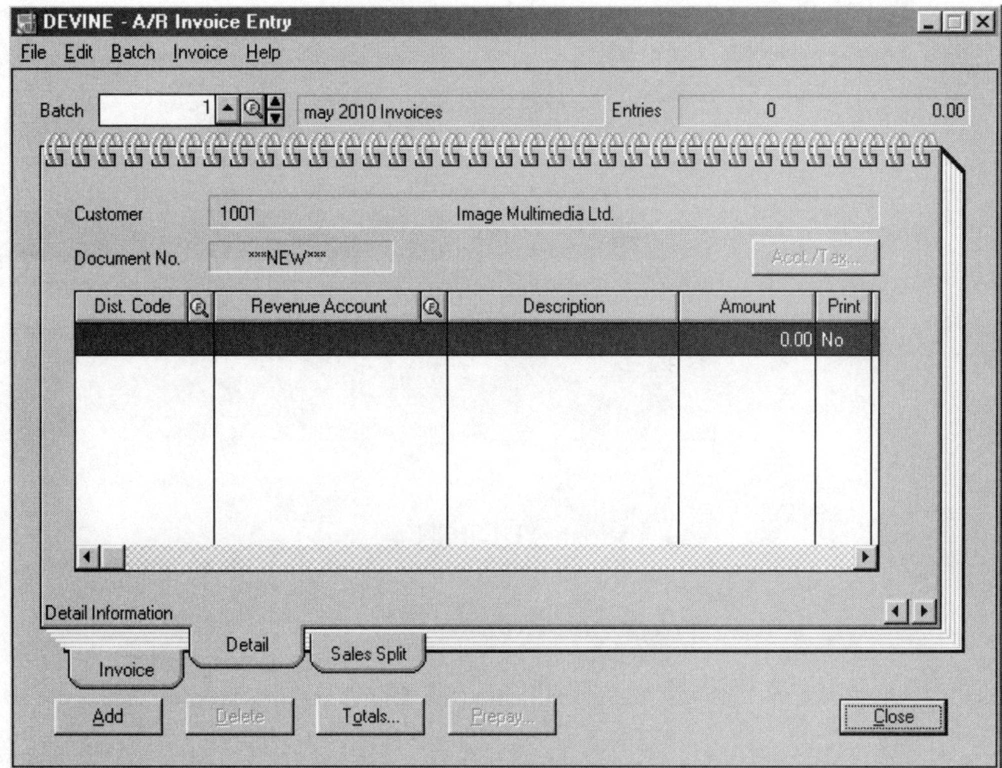

The Detail Information page (Figure 19-4) enables you to enter the information needed to generate an invoice. If the first two columns are Item No. and Units of Measure, you selected Item Detail on the Batch Header window and should change that selection to Summary Detail.

Distribution

You may enter either a distribution code or a General Ledger account number. Devine Designs Inc. created Distribution Codes for all types of sales revenue.

❑ Click: the **Finder** for the Dist. Code Column

The Finder should display the five Distribution codes shown in Figure 19-5.

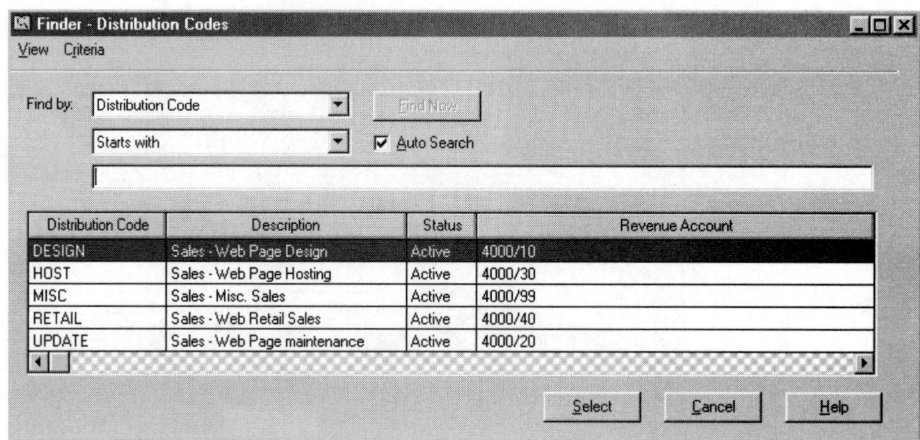

FIGURE 19-5
Finder - Distribution Codes

❑ Select: **DESIGN**

Revenue Account

ACCPAC will enter the default revenue account associated with the distribution code. If necessary, this can be changed by typing the new account number or by selecting the account using the Finder.

Description

The Description cell on each detail line is used to briefly describe the item or service for that detail.

❑ Click: the **Description** cell on the first row

❑ Type: **site mapping**

❑ Press: **Tab** [Tab]

Amount

❑ Type: **1800.00** in the Amount cell

❑ Press: **Tab** [Tab]

Print

The Print cell allows you to control printing of the Comment cell when the invoice is printed. Devine Designs Inc. will describe the services rendered more completely in the Comment cell and will print that information on the invoice.

❑ DClick: the **Print** cell to display Yes

Comment

The Comment cell is optional, but will be used by Devine Designs Inc. to more fully describe the services being invoiced.

- ❑ Click: the **Comment** cell
- ❑ Type: **mapping site and mounting site map pages**
- ❑ Press: **Tab** [Tab]
- ❑ Click: **Add** [Add] to record this invoice

If you need to change a line on the invoice, click the line with the mouse, then type the new information. If you want to delete a line, click on it, then press the Delete key.

TOTALS

- ❑ Click: the **Totals** button [Totals...] at the bottom of the page

The Document Totals window (Figure 19-6) is used to verify amounts and to print invoices. If necessary, the customer's tax classes can be changed using the Finder, but the tax base cannot be changed on this window.

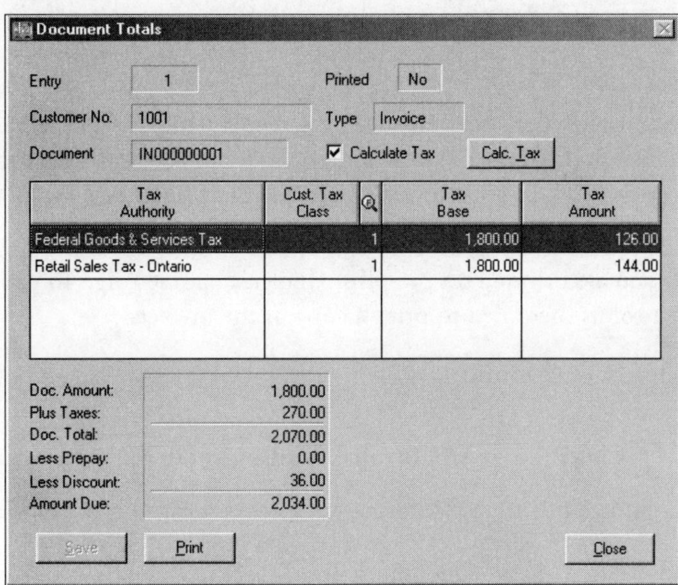

FIGURE 19-6 Document Totals Window

The Calc. Tax button is used to recalculate the amounts after you change the customer's tax classes. Tax amounts are also calculated when you add an invoice, even if you do not use the Calc. Tax button.

The summary area under the Tax working fields is used to check the invoice totals against those on the source document.

Printing an Invoice

After verifying the invoice information against the source documents, you can print the invoice. The Print button will be active only if the Allow Printing Of Invoices option was selected in the Options notebook.

Devine Designs Inc. will print the complete invoice on plain paper.

❑ Click: **Print** [Print]

An A/R Invoice Printing window will appear as displayed in Figure 19-7.

FIGURE 19-7
A/R Batch Printing Window

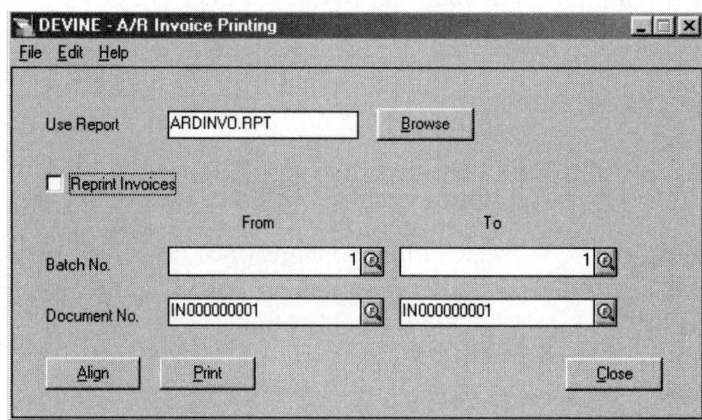

The Use Report field identifies the report template that will be used to print the invoice. The Batch Numbers From and To fields allow you to select the range of batches from which you will print invoices, and the Document No. From and To fields identify the documents you want to print.

If you are printing on pre-printed forms, choose Align to print a test copy. The Print button is then used to print a copy of the invoice.

❑ Click: **Print** [Print]

❑ Click: **OK** [OK] on the Print dialog box

❑ Close: the **A/R Invoice Printing** window

Compare the printed information to that shown on the Document Totals window.

❑ Close: the **Document Totals** [Totals...] window

❑ Close: the **A/R Invoice Entry** notebook

PAYMENTS

In many cases, businesses like Devine Designs Inc. negotiate a prepayment with a new customer when the service to be provided to that customer represents a significant commitment of time and resources by the business.

In this example, Bow River Outfitters wants to develop the concept of a Web-based retailer of high-quality camping, canoeing, and hiking equipment. Bow River Outfitters would also like to take reservations over the Internet for their white water rafting trips, wilderness horseback rides, and other escorted trips. Mike Reid, the owner of Bow River Outfitters, was referred to Devine Designs Inc. by Image Multimedia Ltd. On May 4, 2010, Devine Designs Inc. agreed to develop a preliminary design for Bow River Outfitters by May 29, for a fee of $3,000, with a prepayment of $1,000.

A prepayment can be entered through the Invoice Entry notebook or as a receipt. Devine Designs Inc. will record the prepayment using the Invoice Entry notebook.

- ❑ Open: the **Invoice Entry** notebook
- ❑ Select: **Batch 1** using the Finder

DOCUMENT HEADER

ACCPAC displays the information for the first entry in the batch on the Document Header page.

- ❑ Click: the **New Document** icon button for the Entry text box

ACCPAC will clear the displayed information for Entry 1 so that you can enter the new invoice information. The new entry will be Entry 2.

Customer Number

- ❑ Select: **1015** Bow River Outfitters using the Finder

ACCPAC will display default information in many of the text boxes based on the information entered in the customer account (Figure 19-8).

FIGURE 19-8
Invoice Entry Notebook

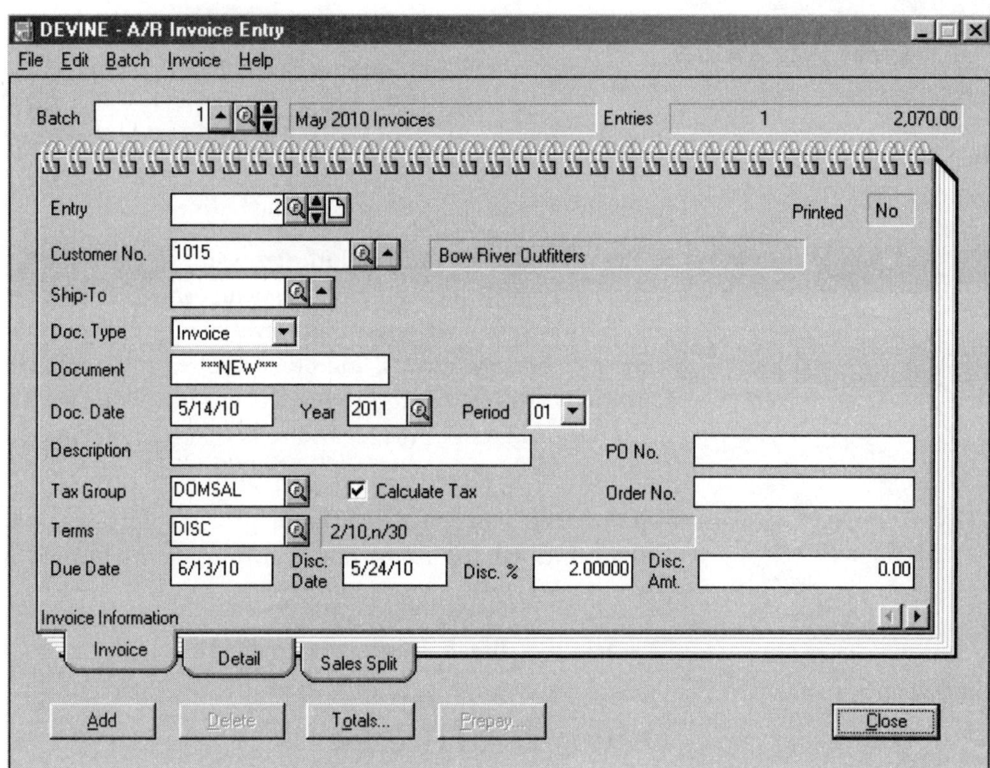

The default information in the Ship-To, Document Type, and Document text boxes should not be changed.

Document Date

Devine Designs Inc. will issue an invoice dated May 29, 2010, but will record the prepayment as of May 3, 2010.

- ❑ Select: the **date** in the Doc. Date text box
- ❑ Type: **052910**
- ❑ Press: **Tab** [Tab] to complete the entry

Description

- ❑ Type: **preliminary design** in the Description text box
- ❑ Press: **Tab** [Tab] to complete the entry

Purchase Order Number

Bow River Outfitters' purchase order number was 99507.

- ❑ Type: **99507** in the PO No. Text box
- ❑ Press: **Tab** [Tab] to complete the entry

DETAIL PAGE

- ❑ Click: the **Detail** tab at the bottom of the A/R Invoice Entry notebook
- ❑ Select: **DESIGN** as the Distribution Code
- ❑ Click: the **Amount** cell
- ❑ Type: **3000.00**
- ❑ Press: **Tab** [Tab] to complete the entry
- ❑ Press: the **spacebar** to change the Print cell to Yes
- ❑ Type: **preliminary design for web based retailing** in the Comment cell
- ❑ Press: **Tab** [Tab] to complete the entry
- ❑ Click: **Add** [Add]

The Prepayment button [Prepay...] should now be active.

PREPAYMENTS WINDOWS

- ❑ Click: the **Prepay...** button [Prepay...]

The Prepayments window (Figure 19-9) has two sections. The upper section displays the information that has been entered. The lower section consists of text boxes that allow you to record the prepayment.

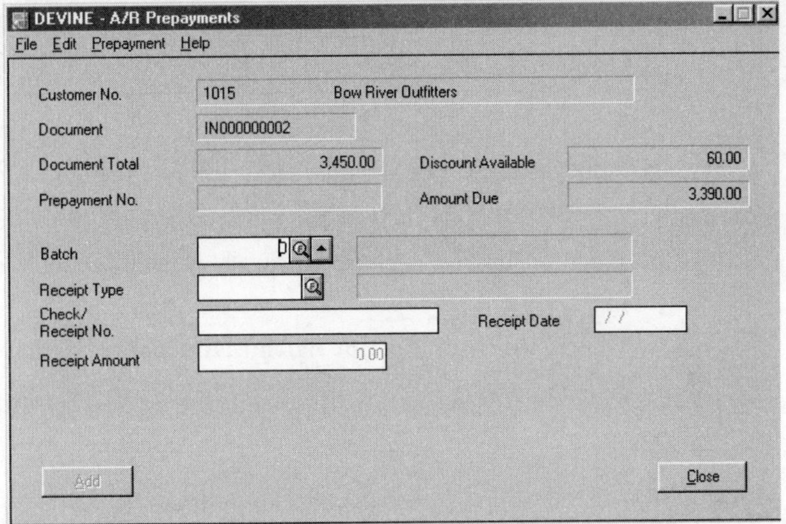

FIGURE 19-9
Prepayments Window

Receipt Batch

A prepayment may be added to an existing Receipt Batch, or a new batch may be created.

❑ Click: the **arrowhead** icon next to the Batch text box

The A/R Receipt Batch Maintenance window will appear as shown in Figure 19-10.

Devine Designs Inc. must create a new Receipt Batch to record the receipt of the $1,000.00 prepayment.

❑ Click: the **New Document** icon

ACCPAC will assign the next available number (1) to the Receipt Batch and display the Session Date in the Batch Date text box.

❑ Press: **Tab** [Tab] to accept 05/14/10
❑ Type: **May 14 Receipts** in the Description field
❑ Press: **Tab** [Tab]

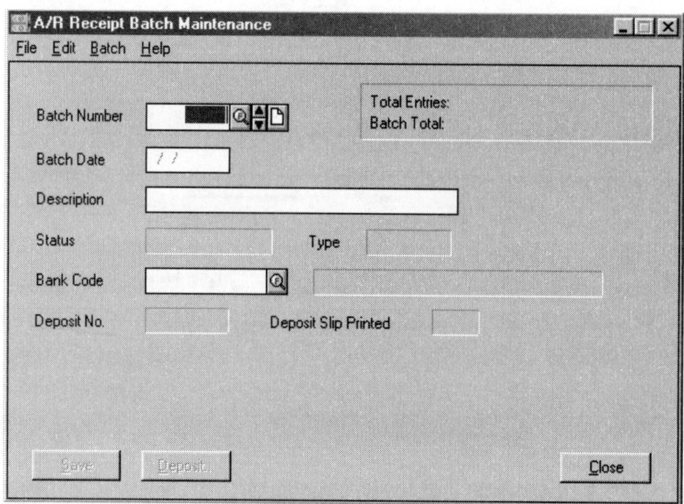

FIGURE 19-10 Receipt Batch Maintenance Window

The Bank Code text box should display 1STBK, the Bank Code that you entered in Banking Services.

❑ Press: **Tab** [Tab] again to accept the default Bank Code
❑ Click: **Save** [Save]
❑ Close: the **A/R Receipt Batch Maintenance** window

Batch number 1, May 14, 2010, Receipts should be displayed on the A/R Prepayments window.

Receipt Type

The default Receipt Type is CHECK. If necessary, you can select another Receipt Type using the Finder.

❑ Press: **Tab** [Tab] to accept CHECK

Check/Receipt Number

Bow River Outfitters' check number is 789-434.

- ❑ Type: **789-434** in the Check/Receipt Number text box
- ❑ Press: **Tab** [Tab]

Receipt Date

The default Receipt Date is the Session Date.

- ❑ Press: **Tab** [Tab] to accept 05/14/10

Receipt Amount

Bow River Outfitters prepaid $1,000.00.

- ❑ Type: **1000.00** in the Receipt Amount text box
- ❑ Press: **Tab** [Tab]
- ❑ Click: **Add** [Add]

ACCPAC adds the prepayment and assigns the prepayment number using the prefix and next number specified in the Options notebook for prepayment transactions. Once you process a prepayment and close the Prepayment window, you cannot open it again for that prepayment. If you need to change the prepayment information, use the Receipt Entry window.

- ❑ Close: The **A/R Prepayments** window

PRINTING THE INVOICE

- ❑ Click: **Totals** [Totals...] on the Invoice Entry notebook

Note that the discount calculated is based on the Document Amount ($3,000.00).

- ❑ Click: **Print** [Print]
- ❑ Click: **Print** on the A/R Invoice Printing window
- ❑ Click: **OK** [OK] on the Print dialog box
- ❑ Close: the **A/R Invoice Printing** window
- ❑ Close: the **Document Totals** window
- ❑ Click: the **Invoice** tab at the bottom of the notebook

ADDING AN INVOICE WITH A PAYMENT SCHEDULE

In the Web page design market, most large projects are completed within 30 days. The industry practice is for the customer to pay 40 percent of the fee when the contract is signed, 30 percent when the pages are delivered, and the last 30 percent 30 days after the initial delivery. The holdback of 30 percent for 30 days ensures that firms like Devine Designs Inc. will correct any deficiencies in the product that they deliver. Devine Designs Inc. has created the Terms Code PROJ for this type of project.

On May 10, 2010, Newell Productions issued a contract to Devine Designs Inc. to develop an interactive banner ad. This banner ad will be placed on various commercial Web pages that charge for this type of advertising. The ad enables people to purchase the product advertised by credit card by filling out a form on the Web, without going to the advertiser's home page. It also offers the customer security by encrypting all information on the form and then authorizing the customer's purchase by the credit card company. The design of these complex interactive banner ads is expensive and time consuming. Nowell Productions and Devine Designs Inc. agreed on a fee of $8,200 with a payment of 40 percent ($3,280.00) on May 14, 2010, when Devine Designs Inc. starts work on the project.

❑ If necessary, open the Invoice Entry notebook and select Invoice Batch 1.

A new entry must be created for each transaction.

Entry

❑ Click: the **New Document** icon for Entry

ACCPAC should display Entry 3, the next available entry number.

Customer

❑ Select: **1010 Newell Productions** using the Finder

Document Date

❑ Type: **051410** in the Document Date text box

Description

❑ Click: the **Description** text box
❑ Type: **Banner ad development**
❑ Press: **Tab** [Tab]

Terms

- ❑ Select: **PROJ** using the Finder

The PROJ Terms Code was created to divide an invoice total into three payments set 30 days apart, with 40 percent of the total due in the first payment and 30 percent due in the second and third. When you change the Terms Code, the Due Date and Discount fields disappear and the Schedule tab appears at the bottom of the page.

Detail Page

You must enter the details of the invoice before making entries on the Schedule page.

- ❑ Click: the **Detail** tab at the bottom of the A/R Invoice Entry notebook
- ❑ Click: the **Finder** for the Distribution Code column
- ❑ Select: **Design**

ACCPAC will display the default Revenue Account (4000/10) in the Revenue Account cell.

- ❑ Click: the **Amount** cell
- ❑ Type: **8200.00**
- ❑ Press: **Tab** [Tab]

The invoice must be added to the batch before payment schedule information is entered.

- ❑ Click: **Add** [Add]
- ❑ Click: **OK** [OK] on the credit limit message

Schedule Page

- ❑ Click: the **Schedule** tab at the bottom of the notebook

The Payment Schedule page is shown in Figure 19-11.

ACCPAC uses the As of Date to calculate the due dates in the payment schedule table. The default displayed is the Document Date. If necessary, change the As of Date by entering another date and clicking the green Go button to recalculate the schedule.

The amounts due are calculated using the information entered in the terms code. If necessary, they can be changed by clicking the appropriate cell and entering the new amounts.

You can only increase the number of payments in a schedule by changing the number in the Terms Record code. To reduce the number of payments in a schedule you enter with an invoice, allocate the total due to as many payments as you need, then enter zeros for the remaining payment lines.

FIGURE 19-11
Payment Schedule Page

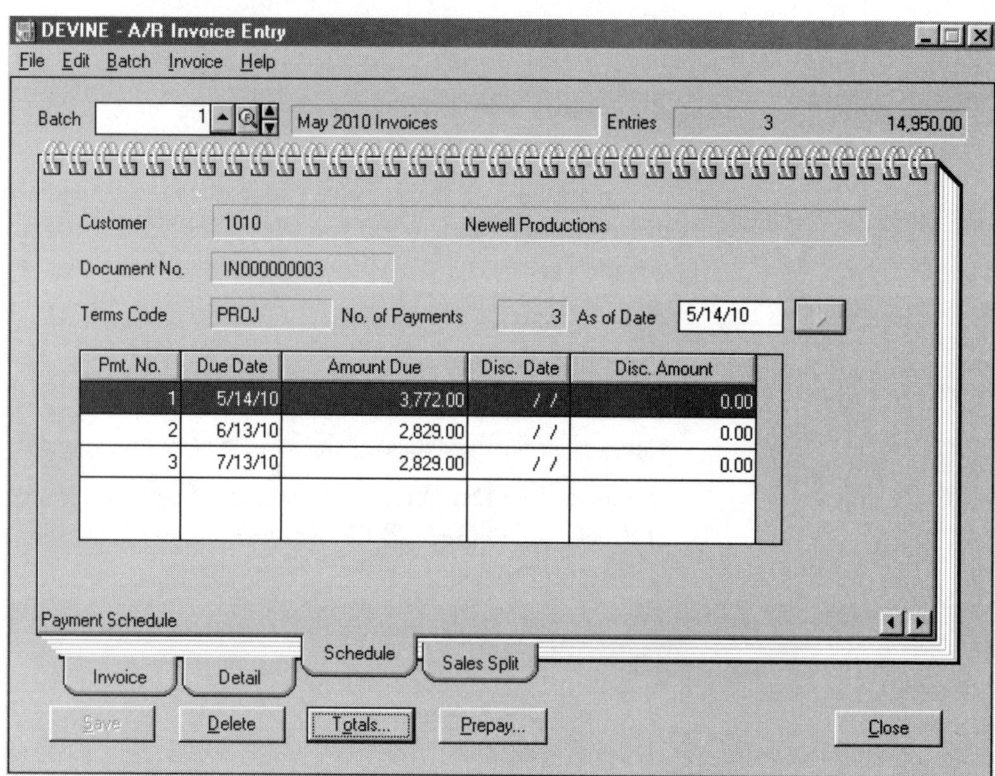

❑ Print the invoice using the Totals page.

The first payment from Newell Productions will be added later when you process receipts.

TIP
Remember to click the New Document icon to create each new invoice.

YOUR TURN

❑ Add the following invoices to the batch:

The Caledon Hotel

On May 3, 2010, Devine Designs Inc. completed the design of a simple Web page for the Caledon Hotel.

The amount of the invoice will be entered as $1,750, plus taxes, due to a typing error. This error will be corrected later with a credit note.

❑ Enter this invoice and print it.

Kawartha Comedy Club

On May 10, 2010, Devine Designs Inc. completed maintenance work on the Kawartha Comedy Club's home page. The invoice amount is $462. plus taxes.

❑ Enter and print this invoice.

Jimmy's Fish & Chips

TIP

Use customer number 9990 and prepayments for this invoice.

On May 12, 2010, Jimmy Scott brought in a disk with the files he tried to mount on a community Web site. The photos of his meals were discoloured. Devine Designs Inc. has photo-editing software and agreed to fix the colours. Later that afternoon, Jimmy picked up his corrected files and paid the fee of $85.00, plus taxes.

❑ Enter and print the invoice for Jimmy.

PRINTING AN INVOICE BATCH

Each batch should be printed and the printout compared to the source documents. If errors are found, they should be corrected and the batch printed again.

❑ Click: **File** on the A/R Invoice Entry menu bar

❑ Click: **Print** on the File menu

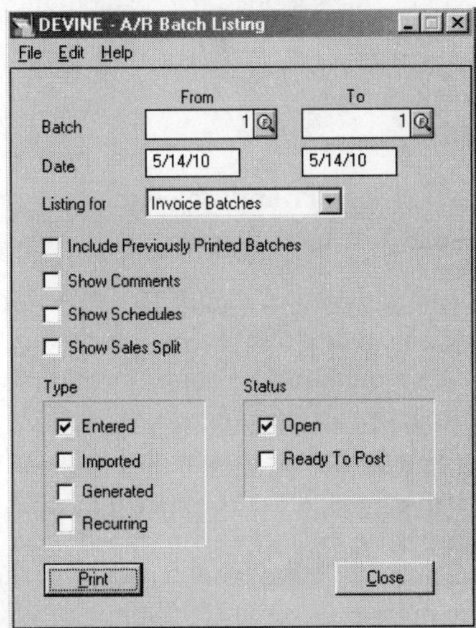

FIGURE 19-12 Batch Listing Dialog Box

The Batch Listing dialog box (Figure 19-12) has three sections. The defaults displayed in the upper section will print all invoice batches entered on the Session Date.

- ❑ Highlight: the **Date From** field
- ❑ Type: **050110**
- ❑ Press: **Tab** [Tab]

Show Schedules

The use of Show Schedules is optional. Devine Designs Inc. will show schedules on the batch listing printout.

- ❑ Click: the **Show Schedules** option box

Type

The Type options refer to the way in which the batch was created. Batch 1 was entered using the Invoice Entry notebook. Imported batches are batches created in other ACCPAC modules and imported into Accounts Receivable. Generated batches are batches created by Accounts Receivable, such as batches of interest invoices generated during periodic processing. Recurring batches are created by Accounts Receivable for items such as regular monthly charges to a customer.

- ❑ Click: the **Entered** option box

Status

Status refers to the processing done to the batch. An open batch has not yet been posted or printed. As Devine Designs Inc. specified that batches must be printed before posting, all printed batches are ready to post.

- ❑ Click: the **Open** option box
- ❑ Click: **Print** [Print]
- ❑ Click: **OK** [OK] on the Print dialog box
- ❑ Close: the **A/R Batch Listing** dialog box

Compare your printout to that shown in Figure 19-13. As long as you have not posted a batch, you can add, delete, or modify transaction information. If you want to change information, click the mouse pointer in the appropriate text box and enter the correct information. If you want to reopen a document, choose Previous or Next from the Entry menu (or click the previous [up] or next [down] arrow beside the Entry field).

- ❑ Make any necessary changes and print the batch listing again.

When Eric reviewed the batch listing, he found an error in the invoice to the Caledon Hotel. The amount of the invoice should be $750, not $1,750. This error could be corrected now, but will be corrected later with a credit note so that you see how to issue credit notes.

- ❑ Close: the **A/R Invoice Entry** notebook
- ❑ Close: **ACCPAC**

Figure 19-13
Batch Listing Printout

Date: Friday, August 11, 2000 3:42PM
A/R Batch Listing - Invoice (ARIBTCLZ)

DDI Student Name

Page 1

From Batch Number	[1] To [1]
From Creation Date	[5/1/2010] To [5/14/2010]
Listing For	[Invoice Batches]
Of Type	[Entered]
Having Status Of	[Open]
Show Comments	[N]
Show Schedules	[Y]
Show Sales Split	[N]

Batch No.: 1 **Description:** May 2010 Invoices **Total:** 17,351.55
Batch Date: 5/14/2010 **Type:** Entered **Status:** Open

Entry: 1 **Type:** IN **Document:** IN000000001 **Customer:** 1001 Image Multimedia Ltd. **Document Date:** 5/14/2010
PO No.: IMM 14335 **Order No.:** **Description:** site mapping **Period:** 01 **Year:** 2011
Terms: DISC **Due Date:** 6/13/2010 **Disc. Date:** 5/24/2010 **Discount Pct.:** 2.00000% **Discount Amt.:** 36.00

Dist. Code	Acct. Number/Acct. Description	Detail Description	Tax Authority	Tax Base	Amount
DESIGN	4000/10 Sales - Web Page Design	site mapping			1,800.00
			GSTFED	1,800.00	126.00
			RSTON	1,800.00	144.00
				Total Invoice:	2,070.00
				Total Taxes:	270.00

Payment	Due Date	Amount Due	Discount Date	Discount Amount
1	6/13/2010	2,070.00	5/24/2010	36.00

Entry: 2 **Type:** IN **Document:** IN000000002 **Customer:** 1015 Bow River Outfiters **Document Date:** 5/29/2010
PO No.: 99507 **Order No.:** **Description:** preliminary design **Period:** 01 **Year:** 2011
Terms: DISC **Due Date:** 6/28/2010 **Disc. Date:** 6/8/2010 **Discount Pct.:** 2.00000% **Discount Amt.:** 60.00
Payment: 1,000.00

Dist. Code	Acct. Number/Acct. Description	Detail Description	Tax Authority	Tax Base	Amount
DESIGN	4000/10 Sales - Web Page Design	Sales - Web Page Design			3,000.00
			GSTFED	3,000.00	210.00
			RSTON	3,000.00	
				Total Invoice:	3,210.00
				Total Taxes:	210.00

Payment	Due Date	Amount Due	Discount Date	Discount Amount
1	6/28/2010	3,210.00	6/8/2010	60.00

Entry: 3 **Type:** IN **Document:** IN000000003 **Customer:** 1010 Newell Productions **Document Date:** 5/14/2010
PO No.: **Order No.:** **Description:** Banner ad development **Period:** 01 **Year:** 2011
Terms: PROJ

Date: Friday, August 11, 2000 3:42PM
A/R Batch Listing - Invoice (ARIBTCLZ)

DDI Student Name

Page 2

Dist. Code	Acct. Number/Acct. Description	Detail Description	Tax Authority	Tax Base	Amount
DESIGN	4000/10 Sales - Web Page Design	Sales - Web Page Design			8,200.00 C
			GSTFED	8,200.00	574.00
			RSTON	8,200.00	656.00
				Total Invoice:	9,430.00
				Total Taxes:	1,230.00

Payment	Due Date	Amount Due	Discount Date	Discount Amount
1	5/14/2010	3,772.00		0.00
2	6/13/2010	2,829.00		0.00
3	7/13/2010	2,829.00		0.00
	Total:	9,430.00		0.00

Entry: 4 Type: IN Document: IN000000004 Customer: 1005 Caledon Hotel, The Document Date: 5/3/2010
PO No.: Order No.: Description: Design of a Web Page Period: 01 Year: 2011
Terms: DISC Due Date: 6/2/2010 Disc. Date: 5/13/2010 Discount Pct.: 2.00000% Discount Amt.: 35.00

Dist. Code	Acct. Number/Acct. Description	Detail Description	Tax Authority	Tax Base	Amount
DESIGN	4000/10 Sales - Web Page Design	Sales - Web Page Design			1,750.00
			GSTFED	1,750.00	122.50
			RSTON	1,750.00	140.00
				Total Invoice:	2,012.50
				Total Taxes:	262.50

Payment	Due Date	Amount Due	Discount Date	Discount Amount
1	6/2/2010	2,012.50	5/13/2010	35.00

Entry: 5 Type: IN Document: IN000000005 Customer: 1020 Kawartha Comedy Club Document Date: 5/10/2010
PO No.: Order No.: Description: Maintenance on Web Page Period: 01 Year: 2011
Terms: DISC Due Date: 6/9/2010 Disc. Date: 5/20/2010 Discount Pct.: 2.00000% Discount Amt.: 9.24

Dist. Code	Acct. Number/Acct. Description	Detail Description	Tax Authority	Tax Base	Amount
UPDATE	4000/20 Sales - Web Page Maintenance	Sales - Web Page Maintenance			462.00
			GSTFED	462.00	32.34
			RSTON	462.00	36.96
				Total Invoice:	531.30
				Total Taxes:	69.30

Payment	Due Date	Amount Due	Discount Date	Discount Amount
1	6/9/2010	531.30	5/20/2010	9.24

Entry: 6 Type: IN Document: IN000000006 Customer: 9990 Misc Sales - Ontario Document Date: 5/12/2010

Date: Friday, August 11, 2000 3:42PM
A/R Batch Listing - Invoice (ARIBTCLZ)

DDI Student Name

Page 3

PO No.: Order No.: Description: Jimmy's Fish & Chips Period: 01 Year: 2011
Terms: CASH Due Date: 5/12/2010

Dist. Code	Acct. Number/Acct. Description	Detail Description	Tax Authority	Tax Base	Amount
MISC	4000/99 Sales - Misc.	photo editing - colour balance			85.00 C
			GSTFED	85.00	5.95
			RSTON	85.00	6.80
				Total Invoice:	97.75
				Total Taxes:	12.75

Payment	Due Date	Amount Due	Discount Date	Discount Amount
1	5/12/2010	97.75		0.00

--- Summary ---

Total Invoices	17,351.55
Total Credit Notes	0.00
Total Debit Notes	0.00
Total Interest	0.00
Total For Batch 1	17,351.55

C: Indicates over credit limit

6 entries printed
1 batch printed

REVIEW QUESTIONS

1. When working with the Invoice Entry notebook, can you assign your own batch number?
2. Describe the difference between Item and Summary Detail Types.
3. What is the purpose of the Invoice Entry notebook?
4. What is the purpose of Ship-To Locations?
5. Can you use duplicate invoice numbers? What happens if you do?
6. When prepayments for goods or services are received, they can be recorded by two different means. What are they?

EXERCISE

- ❑ Sign on to your company (EXERCO), as the system administrator.
- ❑ Enter 051410 in the Session Date box.

1. Create a new batch to record the following invoices:
   a) May 1, B. Eady & Co., sale of Web Page Design services. P.O. EAD0897, Invoice number 001 for $1800 plus all sales taxes.
   b) May 1, Sold Web Page Design services on credit to VanVoort Ltd. The invoice was for $1350 plus all sales taxes. Invoice # 002.
   c) May 2, Invoice #003 to RenRak Ltd $800 plus all sales taxes for Web Page Design services.
   d) May 10, sold Web Page Maintenance services on credit to B. Eady & Co. for $1,500 plus all sales taxes. Invoice #004.
   e) May 12, cash sale of Java animations for $475 plus R.S.T. and G.S.T. to Sheldon Ltd. The sale was recorded on invoice #005. Hint—use Prepayments to record the receipt.
   f) May 14, Invoice #006 to MacMillan & Johnson $650 plus all sales taxes for Web Page Maintenance services.
   g) May 14, invoice #007 to MacMillan & Johnson. $1400 plus all sales taxes for Web Page Design services.
2. Print the invoices.

3. On May 14, you received an order to develop an interactive banner ad for MacMillan & Johnson. MacMillan & Johnson has agreed upon a fee of $8000 plus all sales taxes, with a payment of 40% ($3,680) on May 14, 2010. Check number 132 was received with the order. The remaining two payments will be for 30% each ($2,760). The first will be 30 days after the invoice date, and the remaining payment will be 60 days after. Create a payment schedule and record Invoice 008.

4. Print the MacMillan & Johnson invoice.

5. Batch 1 should have 8 entries totalling $18,371.25. If necessary, review each entry and make the required corrections.

6. Print the Invoice Batch Listing.

- ❑ Once you have finished, close the A/R Invoice Entry notebook and exit from ACCPAC Small Business Series for Windows.

CHAPTER 20

MORE INVOICE PROCESSING

In this chapter, you will post the invoice batch created in the last chapter to Accounts Receivable. You will then print reports to document the processing and to show the status of customer accounts.

Devine Designs Inc. will then correct the $1,000 error in the invoice to the Caledon Hotel. Because the invoice has already been faxed to the customer, a Credit Note will be issued.

Devine Designs Inc. invoices three customers each month for hosting their home pages on the Devine Designs Inc. Web server. Rather than creating individual invoices each month, Devine Designs Inc. will use the Recurring Charge feature to generate an invoice batch each month.

- ❑ Sign on to Devine Designs Inc. as the system administrator using 05/17/10 as the Session Date.
- ❑ Open: the **Accounts Receivable** window

POSTING AN INVOICE BATCH

The posting process enters the posted transactions into the customers' accounts, updates statistics in the customers' records, assigns a unique posting sequence number, produces a posting journal, and produces an error batch if there are incorrect entries that cannot be posted.

As Devine Designs Inc. selected the Setup option to create General Ledger transactions during posting, a General Ledger transaction batch will also be created each time transactions are posted to Accounts Receivable.

Devine Designs Inc. also chose the option of force printing batches before posting. This means that each batch must be printed after any changes before the batch can be posted.

Ready to Post and Posting

After a batch has been printed, it must be designated as Ready To Post before it can be posted.

You have to set a batch to Ready To Post using the Invoice Batch List window.

❑ DClick: the **Invoice Batch List** 

icon

The A/R Invoice Batch List window will appear as displayed in Figure 20-1.

FIGURE 20-1
Invoice Batch List Window

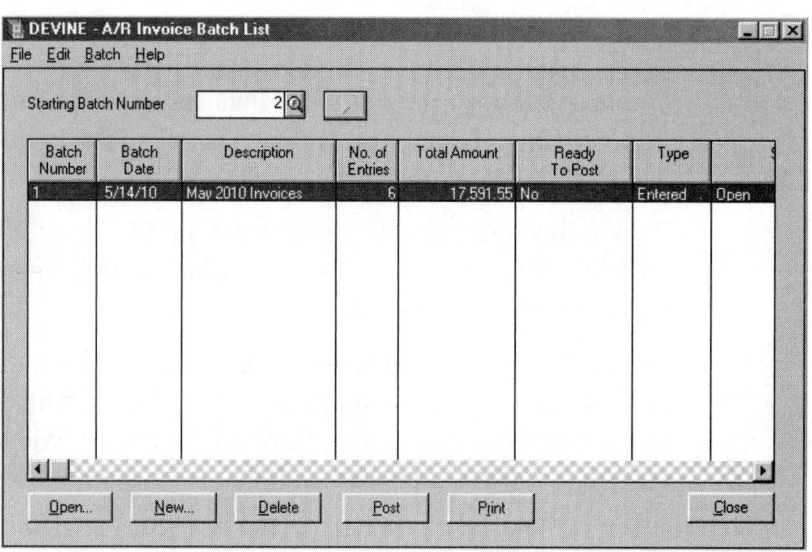

❑ Click: the first cell in the Ready to Post column.

❑ Press: the spacebar once to change "No" to "Yes"

❑ Click: **Post** [Post]

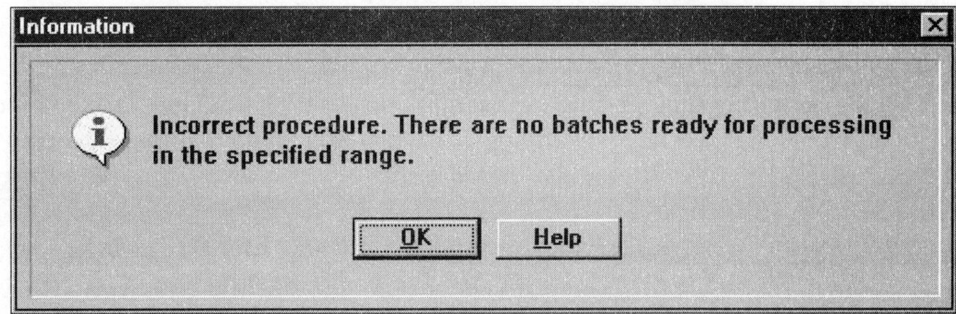

FIGURE 20-2
Information Message

If the batch is not ready to post, an incorrect procedure message (Figure 20-2) will be displayed. The most probable causes of this message are either that the batch list has not been printed since the last time the batch was accessed, or that the batch has not been designated as ready to post. In that case, click OK to close the message window and then print the batch again or designate the batch as ready to post.

As posting occurs, ACCPAC will display which transactions are being posted, first to Accounts Receivable and then to the General Ledger batch. ACCPAC assigns a posting sequence number to all batches posted together, and to each posted detail. If you have not activated the Consolidate Details During Posting option, you can use the number to track the details from the G/L transactions report back to the source documents. ACCPAC will then display two information windows. The first (Figure 20-3) confirms posting to the Accounts Receivable.

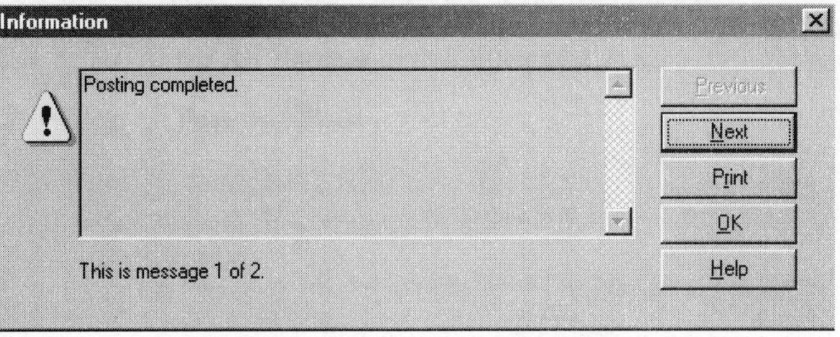

FIGURE 20-3
Information Window

❑ Click: **OK** [OK] to close the Information window

If there are errors in transactions which cannot be posted, ACCPAC will display an error message and create an error batch. This batch will use the next number available. Open the batch using the Invoice Entry notebook, make the necessary corrections, and process the batch.

❑ Close: the **A/R Invoice Batch List** window

PRINTING THE POSTING JOURNAL

The Posting Journal is a listing of the entries that have been posted. You should always print the Posting Journal immediately after posting batches to verify the report to the batch listing, then file it with other posting journals to form an audit trail.

❑ DClick: the **A/R Processing Reports** icon 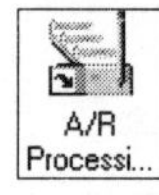 on the Accounts Receivable window

❑ DClick: the **Posting Journals** icon 

The A/R Posting Journals window (Figure 20-4) has two sets of option buttons and a range selection area.

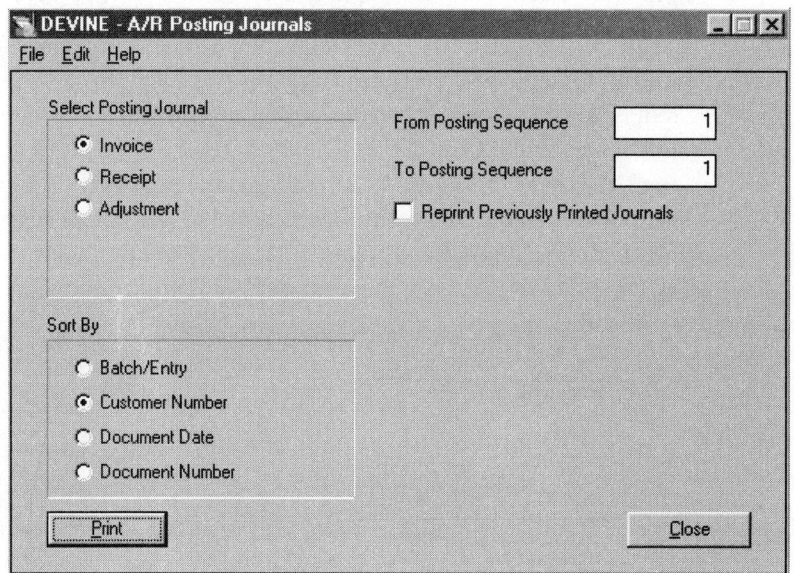

FIGURE 20-4
Posting Journals Window

Select Posting Journal

The three option buttons in this area allow you to select the Posting Journal by type. Devine Designs Inc. posted an invoice batch.

❑ Select: the **Invoice** option button

Sort By

The four options in this area control the order in which information is printed. Devine Designs Inc. wants to print the journal in the same order as the batch listing so that the two reports can be easily compared

❑ Select: the **Batch/Entry** option button

Range Selection

The defaults displayed on the right side of the dialog box print all posting journals that have not yet been printed. You can select specific posting journals by entering the posting sequence numbers in the From Posting Sequence and To Posting Sequence text boxes. The Reprint Previously Printed Journals check box allows you to print posting journals again.

- ❑ Click: **Print** [Print]
- ❑ Click: **OK** [OK] on the Print dialog box

Review the posting journal and compare it to the batch listing printed earlier. Ensure that all the transactions have been posted.

- ❑ Close the **A/R Posting Journals** window

Debit and Credit Notes

When a company accepts the return of goods that have been sold, it has to credit the customer's account and produce the General Ledger entries necessary to return the items to inventory. Similarly, if a customer is overcharged on an invoice, a credit note can be issued to credit the customer's account with the amount overcharged.

Debit notes are used when a customer has been undercharged on an invoice and the company does not wish to issue another invoice for the amount undercharged.

Adding a Credit Note

The processes for entering credit or debit notes are almost the same as the one used to enter an invoice. Devine Designs Inc. will issue a credit note to the Caledon Hotel for $1,000—the amount that the customer was overcharged.

- ❑ Open: the **A/R Invoices** window
- ❑ Open: the **Invoice Entry** notebook

Adding a New Batch

The Batch text box can be used to select an existing batch or to add a new batch header. Devine Designs Inc. will create a new batch for credit notes.

- ❑ Click: the **Zoom** button for Batch Number in the Batch Header window in Figure 20-5

FIGURE 20-5
Batch Header Window

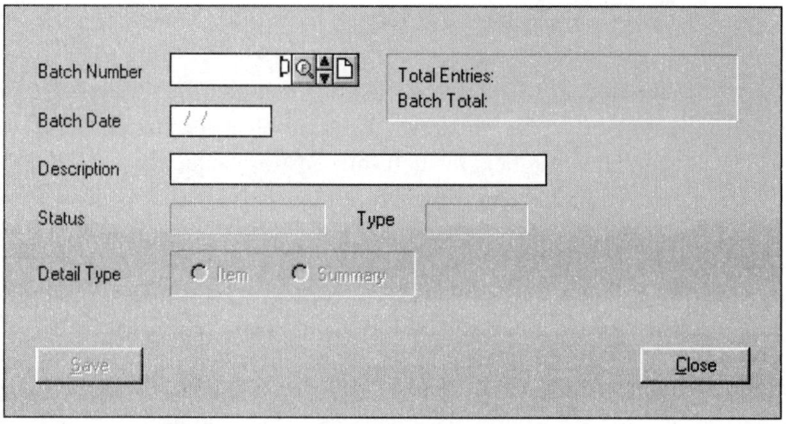

Batch Number		Total Entries:	
Batch Date	/ /	Batch Total:	
Description			
Status		Type	
Detail Type	○ Item ○ Summary		
Save			Close

Batch Number

❑ Click: the **New Document** icon for Batch Number

When you create a new batch, ACCPAC assigns the next available batch number to it. This number is part of the audit trail for the batch, and you cannot assign it to another invoice batch if you delete a batch you created. The batch number should be 2. Do not worry if you have created extra batches: they can be deleted later.

Batch Date

When you create a new batch, the Session Date is displayed in the Batch Date text box.

❑ Press: **Tab** [Tab] to accept the Session Date as the Batch Date

Batch Description

The Batch Description forms part of the information that is displayed for the batch in the Batch List window. You do not have to enter a description for every batch, but it is a valuable tool that helps you keep track of your batches.

❑ Type: **May 2010 Credit Notes** in the Description text box

❑ Press: **Tab** [Tab] to accept the Description

Status and Type

The Batch Status (Open) and Type (Entered) are automatically displayed by ACCPAC.

Detail Type

You can choose between two types of detail in Accounts Receivable. Summary details include the General Ledger revenue account, a description of the transaction, and the amount. Item details include an item number, distribution code, and description, as well as quantity and pricing information. Devine Designs Inc. uses the Summary Detail Type.

- ❑ Select: the **Summary** option button
- ❑ Click: **Save** [Save]
- ❑ Close: the **Batch Header** window

If you forget to save the header, a message appears inquiring whether you want to save the changes to the batch header. Make sure that your entries are correct, then select Yes.

The A/R Invoice Entry Form (Figure 20-6) displays the default settings.

FIGURE 20-6
A/R Invoice Entry Form

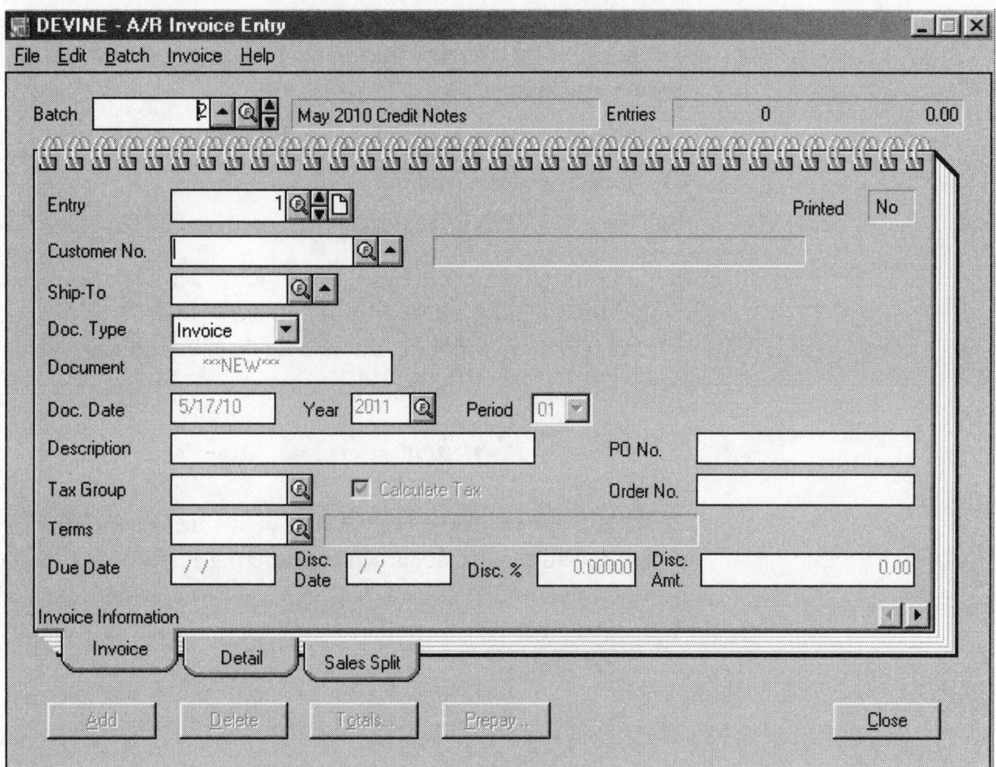

Entry

The Entry text box is used to create a new entry number or to select an entry number in a batch. As this is a new batch, Devine Designs Inc. will have to create a new entry for the credit note.

- ❑ Click: the **New Document** icon for Entry

The Entry number, 1, is assigned automatically by ACCPAC.

Customer Number

- ❑ Click: the **Finder** for Customer No.
- ❑ Select: **1005 Caledon Hotel, The**

When you select the customer, the fields on the Document Header Information page display the information that was entered for the customer in the customer's notebook.

Document Type

The Invoice Entry notebook allows you to enter invoices, credit notes, debit notes, or interest. Devine Designs Inc. wants to enter a credit note for $1,000 to correct the earlier typing mistake.

- ❑ Click: the **List Tool** for Doc. Type
- ❑ Select: **Credit Note**
- ❑ Press: **Tab** [Tab] to accept Credit Note as the Doc. Type

When you select Credit Note, the window will change to include only those items you would use to add a credit note. The Terms, Due Date, Discount Date, Discount Percentage, and Discount Amount fields all disappear.

Document Number

ACCPAC allows you to enter a unique document number in the Document text box or to use the automatic document numbering feature. Devine Designs Inc. will leave this text box showing NEW, so that ACCPAC will assign the document number. The prefix was specified for credit notes in the Options notebook and the number will be the next available number.

- ❑ Press: **Tab** [Tab] to accept automatic numbering

Apply To

The document number that the credit note is to be applied to can be entered in two ways. If the invoice has been posted, the document number can be selected using the Finder. If the invoice has not yet been posted, the invoice number can be typed in the text box.

When entering credit notes, you can leave this field blank if you do not know the document number. If you can determine the document number before you post the batch, you can edit the credit note and enter the document number. If you do not discover the number until after the batch has been posted, you can use the Receipt Entry window to apply the credit note to the account.

❑ Click: the **Finder** for the Apply To text box

The Finder will display all documents that have been posted to the customer's account. Use the scroll bar to review the information displayed. Devine Designs Inc. has only posted one document, IN000000004, to the Caledon Hotel's account.

❑ Select: **IN000000004** in the Apply To text box
❑ Press: **Tab** [Tab] to complete the entry

The document date, fiscal year, and period are determined by the Session Date and do not need to be changed.

Description

You may enter a brief description for the transaction in the Description text box.

❑ Click: the **Description** text box
❑ Type: **Invoiced wrong amount**
❑ Press: **Tab** [Tab] to complete the entry

DETAIL INFORMATION PAGE

❑ Click: the **Detail** tab at the bottom of the A/R Invoice Entry notebook

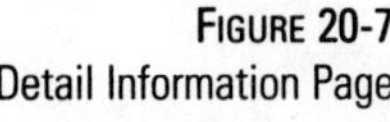

FIGURE 20-7
Detail Information Page

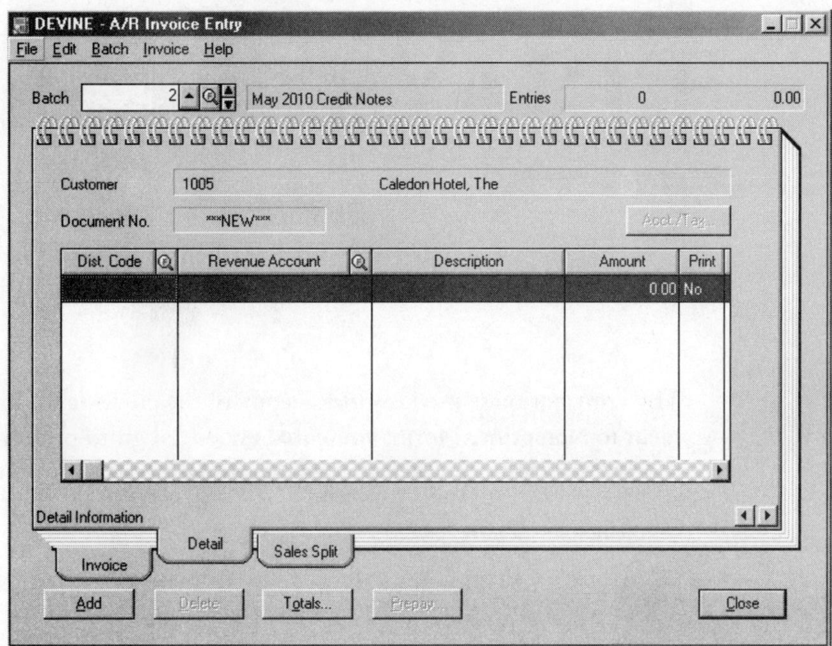

The Detail Information page (Figure 20-7) allows you to enter summary details to create an accounts receivable transaction for the customer's account.

- ❑ Click: the **Finder** for the Dist. Code column
- ❑ Select: **DESIGN**
- ❑ Click: the **Amount** cell
- ❑ Type: **1000.00**
- ❑ Press: **Tab** to complete the entry
- ❑ Click: **Add**

Printing the Credit Note

Debit and credit notes are printed in the same way as invoices.

- ❑ Click: the **Totals** button at the bottom of the notebook

Verify the amounts on the Document Totals window (Figure 20-8).

FIGURE 20-8 Document Totals Window

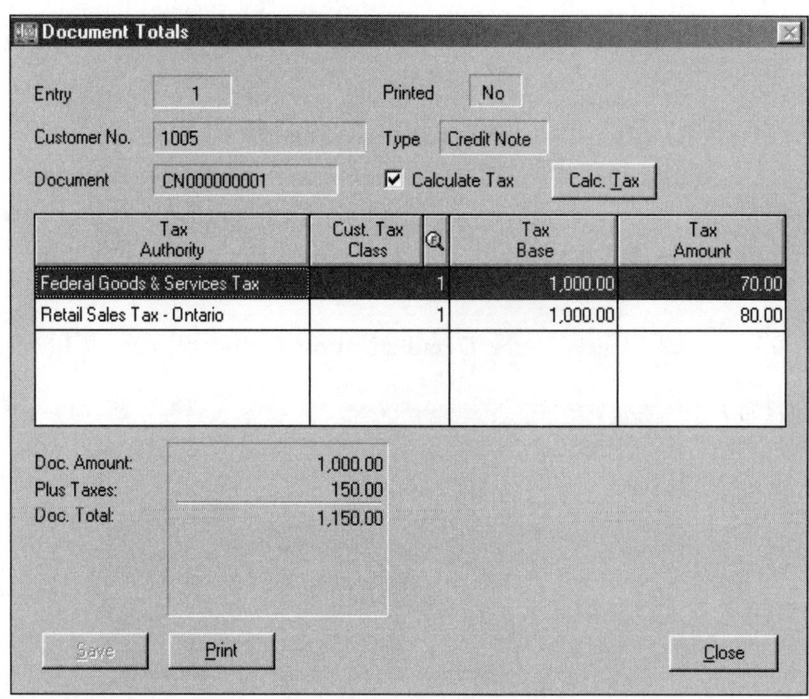

The Print button is used to print a copy of the credit note. If you are sending the document to a preprinted form, you could choose Align to print a test copy. Devine Designs Inc. will print the complete credit note using the form in ACCPAC.

- ❑ Click: **Print**
- ❑ Click: **Print** when the A/R Invoice Printing window appears

- ❑ Click: **OK** [OK]
- ❑ Close: the **A/R Invoice Printing** window
- ❑ Close: the **Document Totals** window

Processing the Credit Note

Devine Designs Inc. will print this batch with one credit note and then post it to Accounts Receivable.

Printing the Batch Listing

- ❑ Print: the **Invoice Batch Listing**

Ready to Post

- ❑ Open: the **Accounts Receivable** window
- ❑ Open: the **A/R Invoice Batch List** window
- ❑ Change: the status of the **Ready to Post** column to Yes

Posting the Batch

- ❑ Click: **Post** [Post]
- ❑ Close: the **Posting Information Dialog** box
- ❑ Close: the **A/R Invoice Batch List** window

Printing the Posting Journal

- ❑ Open: the **A/R Processing Reports** window
- ❑ Open: the **Posting Journals** window
- ❑ Select: the **Invoice** option button in the Select Posting Journal field
- ❑ Select: the **Customer Number** option button in the Sort By field
- ❑ Click: **Print** [Print]
- ❑ Click: **OK** [OK] on the Print dialog box
- ❑ Close: the **A/R Posting Journals** window

Adding Recurring Charges

Using the Recurring Charges option reduces the amount of data entry required for customers who are invoiced a standard fee each month, as you can make one entry for a customer that can be processed many times, rather than making many entries that are processed once.

Devine Designs Inc. has several customers who will be charged a standard fee each month for Web site hosting. Each customer will have a recurring charge set up that will then be processed periodically.

The first recurring charge will be set up for Web site hosting for the Caledon Hotel, with a regular monthly charge of $45.00, for a 12-month total of $540.00, plus taxes.

❑ DClick: the **A/R Invoices** icon A/R Invoices on the Accounts Receivable window

❑ DClick: the **Recurring Charge Setup** icon 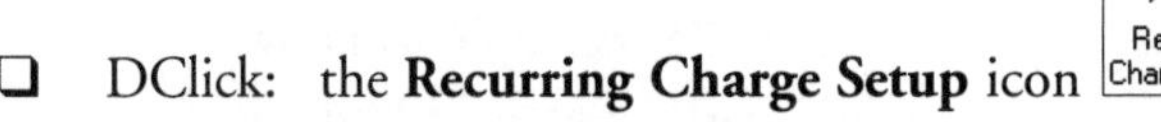

The Recurring Charge Setup notebook (Figure 20-9) consists of three notebook pages and a common header section.

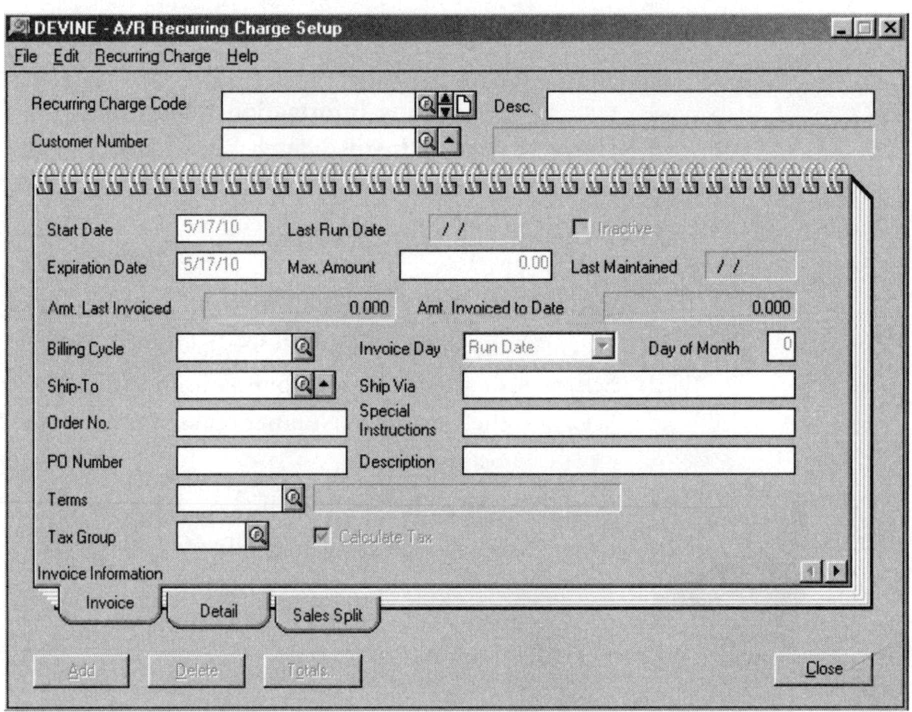

FIGURE 20-9
Recurring Charge Setup Notebook

Recurring Charge Code

The Recurring Charge Code text box holds up to 15 characters used to identify the recurring charge. Devine Designs Inc. will use the code PH followed by the customer number for the monthly Web page hosting fee charged to customers.

- ❑ Type: **PH1005** in the Recurring Charge Code text box
- ❑ Press: **Tab** [Tab] to complete the entry

Customer Number

The Customer Number field is used to record the customer number for which you are entering the recurring charge.

- ❑ Click: the **Finder** for Customer Number
- ❑ Select: **1005 The Caledon Hotel**

You can display the customer's name and billing address, as shown in Figure 20-10.

- ❑ Click: the **Zoom** button for Customer Number
- ❑ Close: the **Customer Information** display

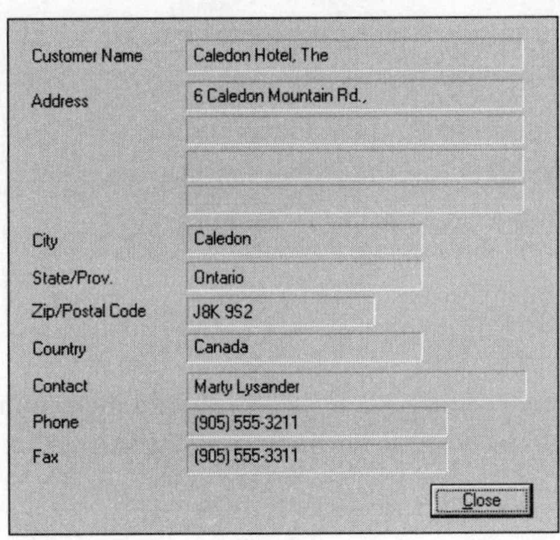

FIGURE 20-10
Customer Information

Description

- ❑ Type: **Monthly Web Page Hosting Fees** in the Description text box
- ❑ Press: **Tab** [Tab] to complete the entry

INVOICE INFORMATION PAGE

The Billing Cycle, Terms, and Tax Group information from the customer's records are transferred to the A/R Recurring Charge Setup notebook.

Start Date

The Start Date text box is used to enter the date on which the recurring charges take effect. The recurring charge goes into effect on May 1, 2010.

- ❑ Highlight: the contents of the Start Date field
- ❑ Type: **05/01/10** in the Start Date text box
- ❑ Press: **Tab** [Tab] to complete the entry

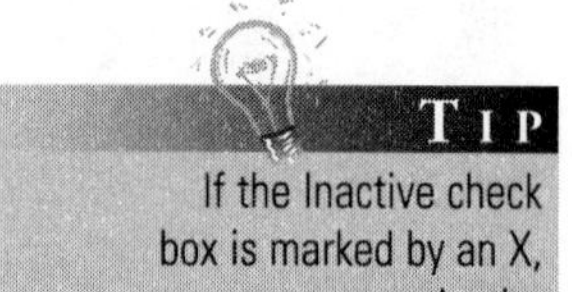

TIP
If the Inactive check box is marked by an X, you can make the recurring charge active by clicking on the Inactive check box to remove the X.

Last Run Date

The Last Run Date display tells you the last date on which the recurring charge was processed. This display should be empty when adding a new recurring charge.

Inactive

The Inactive check box allows you to prevent the processing of recurring charges.

Expiration Date

Use the Expiration Date text box to enter the date on which the recurring charge ceases. The recurring charge will expire in one year.

- ❑ Highlight: the contents of the Expiration Date field
- ❑ Type: **05/01/11** in the Expiration Date text box
- ❑ Press: **Tab** [Tab] to complete the entry

Maximum Amount

The Maximum Amount text box is used to enter the maximum amount that the customer has agreed to be charged for the period of the recurring charges.

- ❑ Type: **540.00** in the Maximum Amount text box
- ❑ Press: **Tab** [Tab] to complete the entry

The amount shown in the Maximum Amount field represents the maximum amount the customer will be invoiced during the period between the Start and Expiration dates. Once the maximum amount has been invoiced, no further invoices will be created for the recurring charge.

Last Maintained

The Last Maintained information field shows the last date on which changes were made for this recurring charge for this customer. When adding a new recurring charge, this field should be empty.

Amount Last Invoiced

The Amount Last Invoiced information field displays the amount invoiced to the customer the last time that recurring charges were processed.

Amount Invoiced to Date

This information field displays the amount of recurring charges that have been invoiced to the customer from the Start Date to the current date.

Billing Cycle

The billing cycle is the default Billing Cycle for the customer. If you want the recurring charge to be invoiced on a particular day of the month, enter it in the Day of Month field. This option is used if the invoice is to be dated on any day other than the last day of the month.

Invoice Day

You have three different options to choose from. You can select a day of the month, the last day of the month, or run date. Choose Select Day if you want to specify the day of the month that you want to invoice the recurring charge. If you select Last Day of Month, the invoice will be processed then. If you select Run Date, the charges will be process on the date you process recurring charges.

❑ Select: **Last Day of Month**

Purchase Order Number

The PO Number text box is used to record the customer's purchase order number.

❑ Type: **PO975** in the PO Number field

❑ Press: **Tab** [Tab] to complete the entry

Description

The Description text box is used to enter a description of the charge that will appear in the Invoice Entry notebook on invoices you create for the charge. You can change the description on individual invoices.

❑ Type: **Monthly Web Page Hosting Fee**

❑ Press: **Tab** [Tab] to complete the entry

Terms and Tax Group

The default Terms and Tax Group information from the customer account is displayed. No changes are necessary.

DETAIL INFORMATION

❑ Click: the **Detail** tab at the bottom of the notebook

The Detail Information page is shown in Figure 20-11.

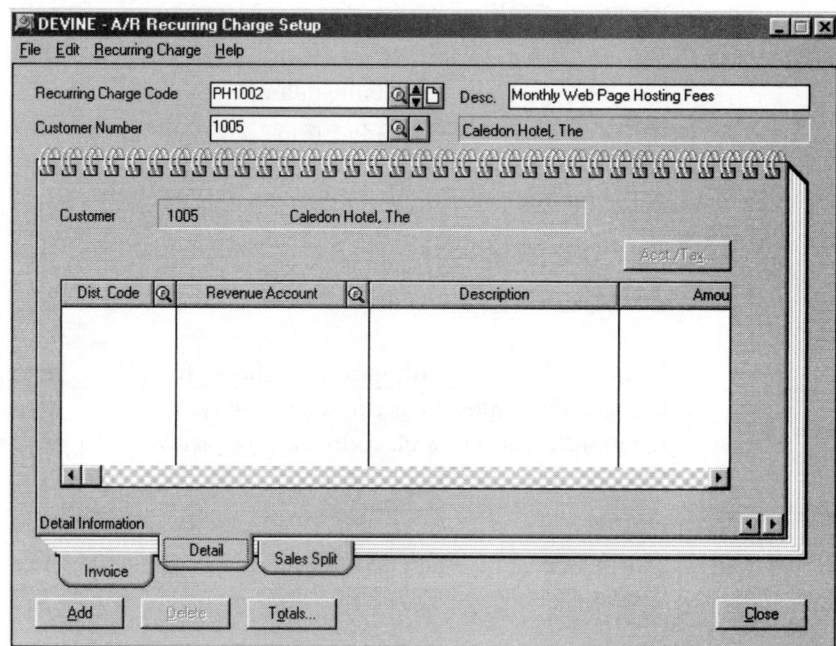

FIGURE 20-11 Detail Information Page

The Detail Information page displays the customer's account number and name, and a four-column table. The active cell in the table is indicated by a dotted outline around the cell. You can change the active cell by pressing the tab key or by clicking on the cell you wish to make active.

Distribution Code

Distribution codes allow you to identify the General Ledger revenue account to which you will post the recurring charge invoices.

❑ Click: the **Finder** for the Dist. Code cell
❑ Select: **HOST**

The General Ledger revenue account for this distribution will be displayed in the next cell.

TIP

If you need to include more than one line in the detail information table, press the Insert key to add another blank line. Then enter the information needed in each cell of the new line.

Description

The use of this Description cell is optional; it will be used by Devive Designs Inc. The general ledger account name appears in the description field.

Amount

- ❑ Click: the **Amount Field** to activate it
- ❑ Type: **45.00** in the Amount cell
- ❑ Press: **Tab** [Tab] to complete the entry
- ❑ Click: **Add** [Add]

Invoice Totals

You can use the Totals Page to verify the total of the recurring charge or to change the customer's tax class. Unlike the Totals page in the Invoice Entry notebook, this page cannot be used for printing invoices.

- ❑ Click: **Totals** [Totals...]

Verify that the Document Amount is $45.00.

- ❑ Close: the **Document Totals** page
- ❑ Close: the **A/R Recurring Charge Setup** notebook

YOUR TURN

Recurring charges for Web page hosting must also be added for Newell Productions and the Kawartha Comedy Club.

Newell Productions

- ❑ Add: the **Recurring Charge Code PH1010**
- ❑ Use the following information to create this recurring charge:

As of May 1, 2010, Devine Designs Inc. will host Newell Productions' home page on its Web server. The initial agreement is for one year, with a fee of $55.00 per month. Invoices will be issued on the last day of the month.

Kawartha Comedy Club

- ❑ Add: the **Recurring Charge Code PH1005**
- ❑ Use the following information to create this recurring charge:

As of May 1, 2010, Devine Designs Inc. will host Kawartha Comedy Club's home page on its Web server. The initial agreement is for one year, with a fee of $35.00 per month. Invoices will be issued on the last day of the month.

PRINTING THE RECURRING CHARGES

Devine Designs Inc. will document the recurring charges that have been entered by printing the Recurring Charges Report.

- ❑ DClick: the **A/R Setup Reports** icon 

 on the Accounts Receivable window
- ❑ DClick: the **Recurring Charges** icon 

 on the Setup Reports window

FIGURE 20-12 Recurring Charges Report Dialog Box

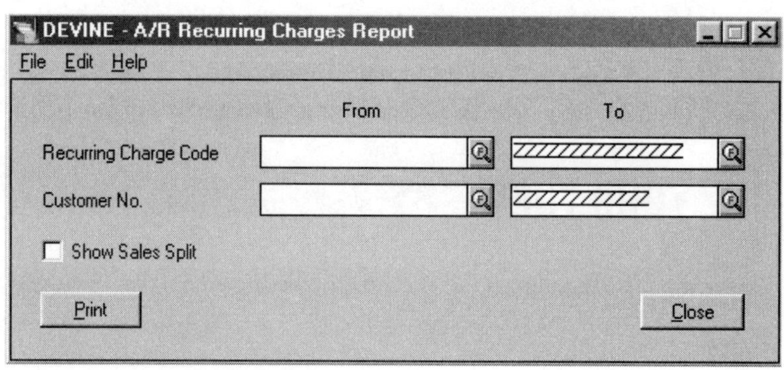

The defaults displayed on the Recurring Charges Reports dialog box (Figure 20-13) will print all recurring charges that have been entered for Devine Designs Inc.

- ❑ Click: **Print** [Print]
- ❑ Click: **OK** [OK] on the Print dialog box
- ❑ Close: the **A/R Recurring Charges Report** dialog box

Compare your printout to that in Figure 20-13. Make any necessary corrections and print the report again.

FIGURE 20-13

Date: Tuesday, August 15, 2000 1:12PM
A/R Recurring Charges (ARRCD01)

DDI Student Name

Page 1

From Recurring Charge Code [] To [ZZZZZZZZZZZZZZZ]
From Customer No. [] To [ZZZZZZZZZZZZ]

Recurring Charge Code: PH1005 Description: Monthly Web Page Hosting Fees

Customer Number: 1005 Customer Name: Caledon Hotel, The

Start Date: 5/1/2010
Last Run Date:
Expiration Date: 5/1/2011
Last Maintained: 8/15/2000
Terms: DISC
Tax Group: DOMSAL
Order Number:
PO Number: PO975

Max. Amount: 540.00
Amt. Last Invoiced: 0.00 Ship-To:
Amt. Invoiced to Date: 0.00 Ship Via:
Billing Cycle: MONTH
Invoice Day: Last Day of Month

Special Instructions:
Description: Monthly Web Page Hosting Fee

Dist. Code	Revenue Account	Description	Amount
HOST	4000/30	Sales - Web Site Hosting	45.00
		Customer Total:	45.00

Recurring Charge Code: PH1010 Description: Monthly Web Page Hosting Fees

Customer Number: 1010 Customer Name: Newell Productions

Start Date: 5/1/2010
Last Run Date:
Expiration Date: 5/1/2011
Last Maintained: 8/15/2000
Terms: DISC
Tax Group: DOMSAL
Order Number:
PO Number:

Max. Amount: 660.00
Amt. Last Invoiced: 0.00 Ship-To:
Amt. Invoiced to Date: 0.00 Ship Via:
Billing Cycle: MONTH
Invoice Day: Last Day of Month

Special Instructions:
Description:

Dist. Code	Revenue Account	Description	Amount
HOST	4000/30	Sales - Web Site Hosting	55.00
		Customer Total:	55.00

Recurring Charge Code: PH1020 Description: Monthly Web Page Hosting Fees

Customer Number: 1020 Customer Name: Kawartha Comedy Club

Start Date: 5/1/2010
Last Run Date:
Expiration Date: 5/1/2011
Last Maintained: 8/15/2000
Terms: DISC
Tax Group: DOMSAL
Order Number:
PO Number:

Max. Amount: 420.00
Amt. Last Invoiced: 0.00 Ship-To:
Amt. Invoiced to Date: 0.00 Ship Via:
Billing Cycle: MONTH
Invoice Day: Last Day of Month

Special Instructions:
Description:

Dist. Code	Revenue Account	Description	Amount
HOST	4000/30	Sales - Web Site Hosting	35.00
		Customer Total:	35.00

3 customers printed
3 recurring charges printed

Recurring charge invoices will be generated and printed in Chapter 22: Periodic Processing.

❑ Exit: **ACCPAC**

REVIEW QUESTIONS

1. What happens during the Posting process?
2. If a batch is not ready to post when you try to post an invoice batch, what happens? What are the most probable causes for the message?
3. What information does the Posting Journal contain? When should you print it?
4. Explain Debit and Credit Notes.
5. The Apply To option found on the Document Header Information page has two ways by which a credit note can be applied. Explain.
6. What is the purpose of having Recurring Charges?

EXERCISE

- ❑ Sign on to your company (EXERCO), as the system administrator.
- ❑ Enter 051710 in the Session Date box.

1. Set the invoice batch(es) you created in Chapter 19 to Ready to Post and post it (them).
2. Print the Posting Journal sorted by Customer Number
3. VanVoort Ltd.'s invoice was in the wrong amount. The agreed charge was $1,200, not $1,350 as invoiced. Issue a credit note dated May 1, 2010 for $150 plus taxes.
4. Print the credit note.
5. Print the batch listing for the credit note.
6. Set the new batch ready to post, post it, and print the posting journal.
7. RenRack Ltd. has requested Web Page Hosting services for the next twelve months. The agreed to fee is $150 per month plus all sales taxes. Create a Recurring Charge for RenRack Ltd. using the Recurring Charges option. The invoice number will be RC001. The charges are due on the last day of the month starting May 31, 2010. The P.O. number is RR3419.
8. Print the Recurring Charges report.

- ❑ Close: the A/R Recurring Charge Setup window
- ❑ Close: the A/R Invoices window
- ❑ Exit: from ACCPAC.

CHAPTER 21

PROCESSING RECEIPTS

In this chapter, you will record the payments received by Devine Designs Inc. in a Receipt Batch. These are representative payments; they are not intended to illustrate a complete month's work. After recording the receipts, you will print a deposit slip, print a batch listing, and post the receipts to Accounts Receivable.

Devine Designs Inc. also receives payments that do not affect a customer's account but should be recorded through Accounts Receivable. These transactions are recorded as miscellaneous receipts. As an example, you will process a receipt from Prestonia Office Products for the return of office supplies.

- ❑ Sign on to Devine Designs Inc. as the system administrator using 05/21/10 as the Session Date.

ENTERING A RECEIPT

- ❑ Open: the **Accounts Receivable** window
- ❑ DClick: the **Quick Receipt Entry** icon

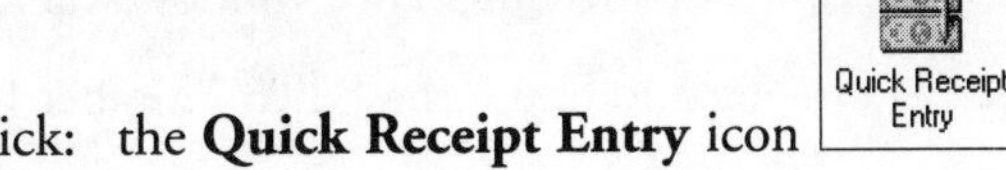

The Receipt Entry window (Figure 21-1) has a batch header section above a batch detail table.

FIGURE 21-1
Receipt Entry Window

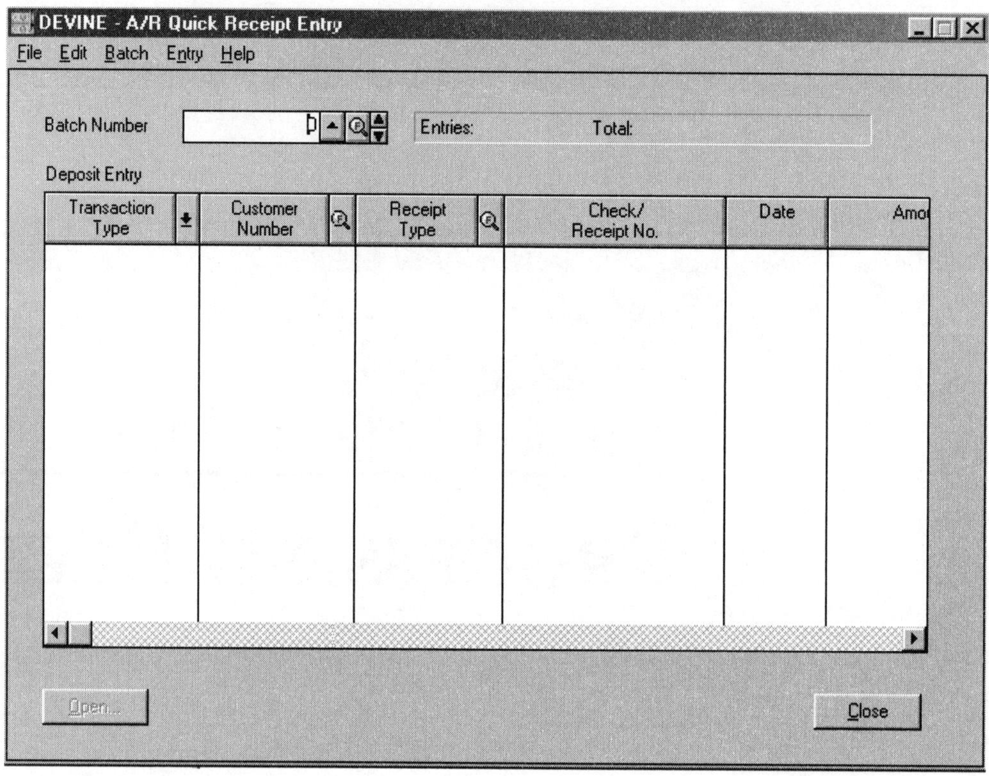

The Batch Number text box and the buttons beside it can be used in several ways to access existing batches or to create new batches.

Devine Designs Inc. has already recorded receipts in a batch when processing invoices with prepayments. This batch can be displayed using the Finder.

- ❑ Click: the **Finder** for Batch Number
- ❑ Select: **Batch Number 1**

The detail information for the batch will be displayed as shown in Figure 21-2.

Additional detail information can be displayed by scrolling the table to the left or right.

- ❑ Close: the **A/R Quick Receipt Entry** window

You can access existing batches or create new batches using the Zoom button.

- ❑ Open: the **Quick Receipt Entry** window
- ❑ Click: **Zoom** for the Batch Number text box

The A/R Receipt Batch Maintenance window will appear as shown in Figure 21-3.

To select an existing batch, use the Batch Number Finder.

To create a new batch, click the New Document icon for the Batch Number text box. Devine Designs Inc. will create another receipts batch for payments received on or before May 21, 2010.

FIGURE 21-2
Receipt Entry Window

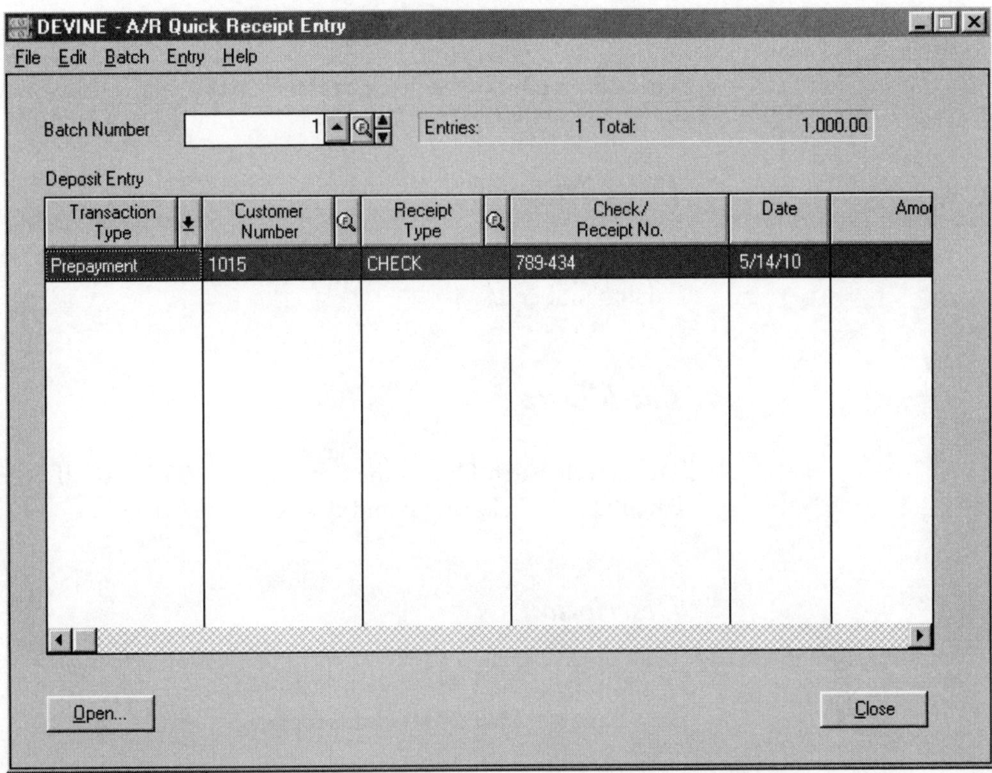

FIGURE 21-3
A/R Batch Maintenance Window

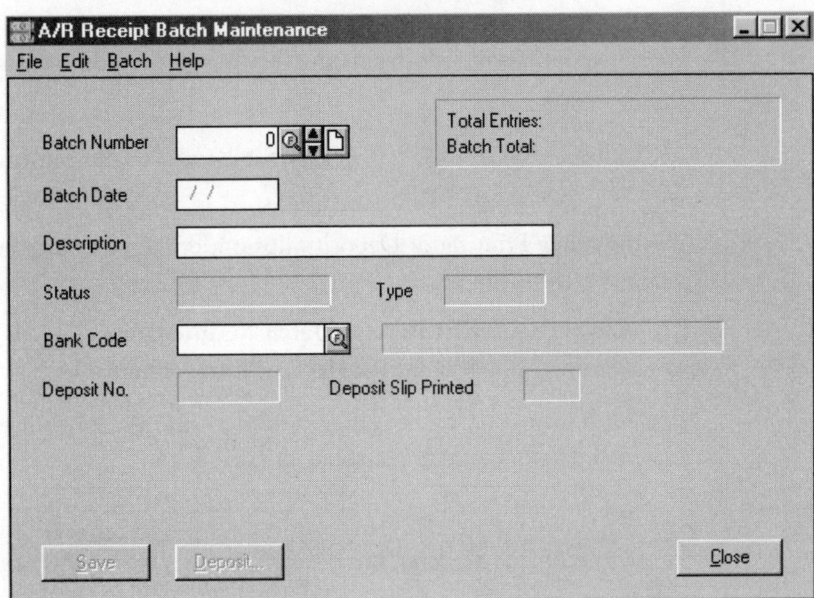

- ☐ Click: the **New Document** icon for Batch Number

The information in the Receipt Batch Maintenance window will be updated.

Batch Number

ACCPAC will automatically assign the next available Batch Number. This should be Batch Number 2.

Batch Date

The default Batch Date is the Session Date, 05/21/10. If necessary, you could change the Batch Date by selecting it and typing the new date.

Description

- ☐ Click: the **Description** text box
- ☐ Type: **May 2010 cash receipts**
- ☐ Press: **Tab** [Tab] to complete the entry

Bank Code

The insertion point will bypass the Status and Type displays and highlight the default Bank Code.

- ☐ Click: **Save** [Save] to save the Batch Header information

The Deposit Number is assigned by the system when you enter and save deposits. If you use the Allow Printing of Deposit Slips option, the Deposit Slip Printed field is updated when you print the deposit slip.

- ☐ Close: the **A/R Receipt Batch Maintenance** window
- ☐ Close: the **A/R Quick Receipt Entry** window

Receipt information can be entered directly into the table or using a data entry form. Devine Designs Inc. will use the data entry form.

- ☐ DClick: the **Receipt Entry** icon [Receipt Entry] on the Accounts Receivable window

The A/R Receipt Entry form (Figure 21-4) should be displayed.

Four types of transactions can be entered in this window. Receipts encompass payments received from customers for specific invoices paid on account. Prepayments, which you entered in Chapter 19, are receipts on an invoice that has not been prepared or posted yet. Unapplied Cash includes receipts from customers for invoices you cannot identify.

FIGURE 20-4
Receipt Entry Form

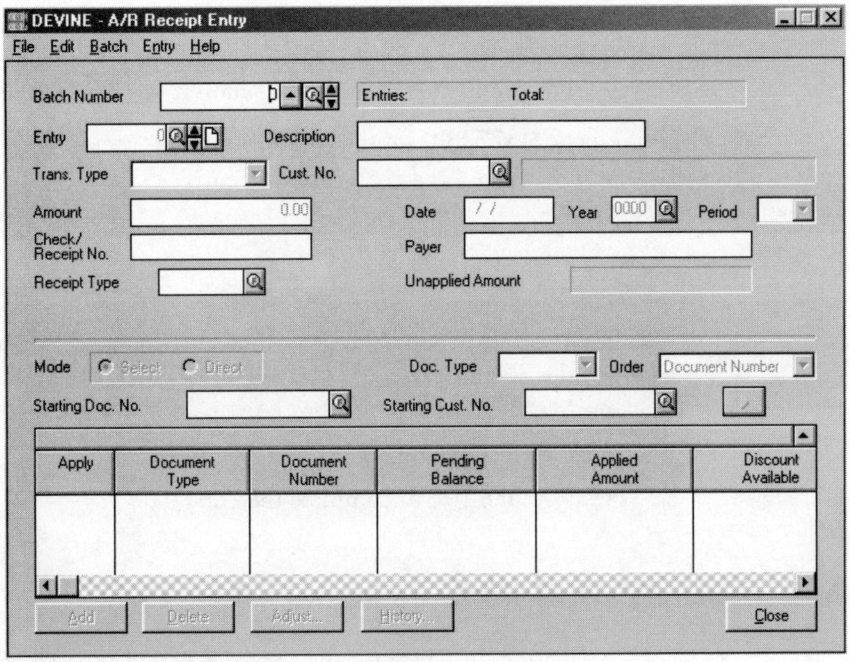

Miscellaneous Receipts are payments that do not affect customer accounts, such as a tax refund.

The upper portion of the form is used to enter information about the entry, and the lower portion is used to apply the transaction to the customer's account.

The first receipt that Devine Designs Inc. enters is for $3,772.00 ($3,280.00, plus taxes) from Newell Productions on May 14, 2010.

- ❑ Using: the **Finder,** select Batch Number 2

Entry Number

ACCPAC automatically assigns the next available Entry Number.

Entry Description

- ❑ Type: **Scheduled Payment** in the Entry Description text box
- ❑ Press: **Tab** [Tab] to complete the entry

Customer Number

- ❑ Click: the **Finder** for Customer Number
- ❑ Select: **1010 Newell Productions**

Amount

Newell Productions' check was in the amount of $3,772.00.

- ❑ Type: **3772.00** in the Amount text box
- ❑ Press: **Tab** [Tab] to complete the entry

Date

The Date text box is used to record the date a company actually receives a payment. The default is the Session Date, 05/21/10. Devine Designs Inc. received Newell Productions' check on May 14, 2010.

- ❑ Type: **051410** in the Date text box
- ❑ Press: **Tab** [Tab] to complete the entry

Year and Period

The information displayed for the Year and Period is based on the date entered in the Date text boxes. Only rarely would this information be changed.

- ❑ Press: **Tab** [Tab] twice

Check/Receipt Number

This text box is used to record the customer's check number or a receipt number for cash payments. Newell Productions' check was number 10-008877.

- ❑ Type: **10-008877** in the Check/Receipt No. Text box
- ❑ Press: **Tab** [Tab] to complete the entry

Payer

The Payer text box displays the customer name default. This information may be changed when a third party, such as a finance company, issues the check. In most cases, you will not change this information.

- ❑ Press: **Tab** [Tab] to accept Newell Productions

Receipt Type

Devine Designs Inc. created three receipt types in the Options notebook.

- ❑ Click: the **Finder** for Receipt Type
- ❑ Select: **CHECK**
- ❑ Click: **Add** [Add]

APPLYING A RECEIPT

Mode

The Direct Mode is used to apply receipts to the customer's total outstanding balance. Devine Designs Inc. will use the Select Mode to apply receipts to individual invoices.

❑ Select: **Select**

Document Type

The Doc. Type list box allows you to control the types of documents displayed in the table. You can display invoices, debit notes, credit notes, or all three.

❑ Select: **Invoice**

Order

The Order list box allows you to control the order in which documents are listed in the table.

❑ Select: **Document Number**

❑ Click: **GO** to display the table

The information for all invoices posted to Newell Productions' account will be displayed in the table in the lower portion of the form.

Apply

The Apply cell in each line allows you to apply the unapplied amount to that line in the document. If the unapplied amount is larger than the Pending Balance, the excess will remain unapplied and can be applied to other documents. Newell Productions' payment of $3,772.00 equals the Pending Balance.

❑ DClick: the **Apply** cell in the first row

The Apply cell should now display Yes and 3,772.00 should appear in the Applied Amount cell. Note that the Unapplied Amount in the upper portion of the form displays 0.00 and that the Save button is now active.

❑ Click: **Save** Save

YOUR TURN

You will now enter two more receipts for Devine Designs Inc. from The Caledon Hotel and Kawartha Comedy Club.

- ❑ Click: the **New Document** icon in the entry field

ACCPAC should display entry number 2.

- ❑ Enter the receipt from the Caledon Hotel using the following information:

On May 19, 2010, Devine Designs Inc. received check number 99-7788 from the Caledon Hotel. The check was in the amount of $763.50.

- ❑ Click: **Add** [Add] to add the receipt information
- ❑ Apply the payment against the outstanding invoice to the Caledon Hotel's account.

The amount of the payment is less than the Pending Balance. When the receipt is applied, the Caledon Hotel will have a net balance of $99.00, which will appear on its statement.

- ❑ Record the receipt of check 22-3456 from Kawartha Comedy Club on May 20, 2010. The check was for the amount of $522.06.
- ❑ Apply this receipt to the outstanding invoice for Kawartha Comedy Club.
- ❑ If necessary, enter the Discount Taken by typing 9.24 in the Discount Taken cell and pressing the Tab key.
- ❑ Click: **Add** [Add]
- ❑ Close: the **A/R Receipt Entry** form
- ❑ DClick: the **Quick Receipt Entry** [Quick Receipt Entry] icon
- ❑ Select: **Batch 2** using the finder

FIGURE 21-5
Receipt Entry Window

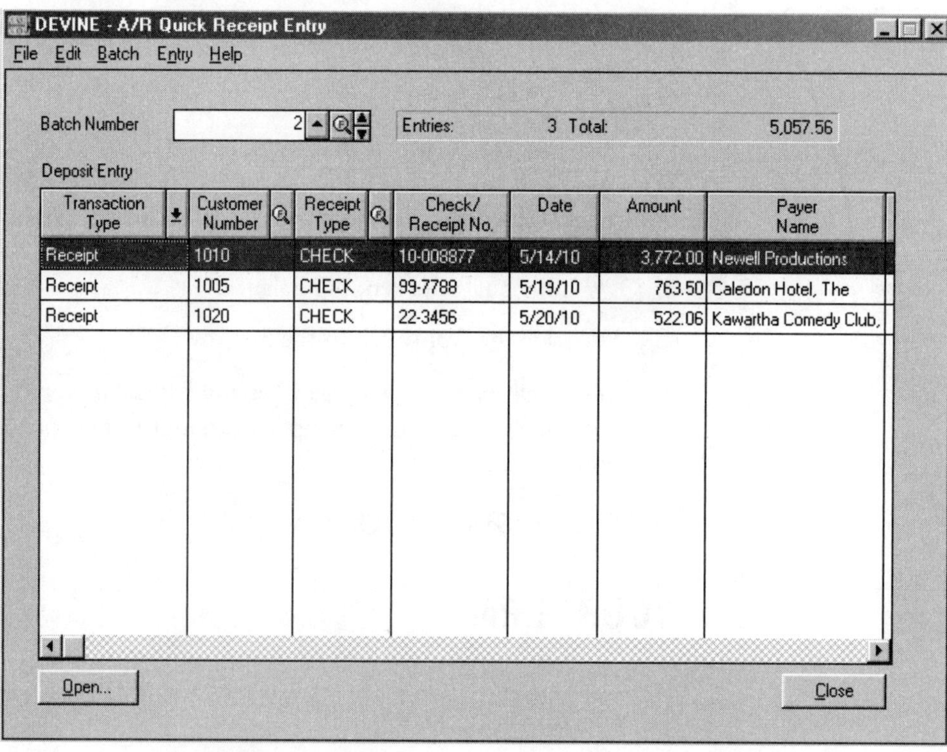

Transaction Type	Customer Number	Receipt Type	Check/ Receipt No.	Date	Amount	Payer Name
Receipt	1010	CHECK	10-008877	5/14/10	3,772.00	Newell Productions
Receipt	1005	CHECK	99-7788	5/19/10	763.50	Caledon Hotel, The
Receipt	1020	CHECK	22-3456	5/20/10	522.06	Kawartha Comedy Club,

The A/R Quick Receipt Entry window (Figure 21-5) should now display the three receipts that you have entered. You will have to use the scroll bar at the bottom to see the entire screen.

You can adjust the column width to show more information or you can use the scroll bars to see additional columns.

PRINTING THE RECEIPT BATCH

Devine Designs Inc. chose the Force Printing of Batches option.

- ❑ Click: **File** on the menu bar
- ❑ Click: **Print** on the File Menu

The Batch Listing dialog box is identical to that used to print invoice batches.

- ❑ Click: the **list tool** ▾ for Listing for
- ❑ Select: **Receipt Batches**
- ❑ Click: the **Entered** check box
- ❑ Click: the **Open** check box
- ❑ Click: **Print** [Print]
- ❑ Click: **OK** [OK] on the Print dialog box
- ❑ Close: the **Batch Listing** window

Compare your printout to the A/R Batch Listing - Receipt shown in Figure 21-6. Any errors in Batch 1, the batch containing the prepayments should be corrected by issuing a debit or credit note as these transactions cannot be edited. Correct any errors in Batch 2 by opening the batch and changing the information.

FIGURE 21-6
A/R Batch Listing—Receipt Printout

Date: Thursday, June 22, 2000 11:22AM
A/R Batch Listing - Receipt (ARCBTCLZ)

DDI Student Name

Page 1

From Batch Number	[2] To [2]
From Creation Date	[5/21/10] To [5/21/10]
Listing For	[Receipt Batches]
Of Type	[Entered]
Having Status Of	[Open]
Include Previously Printed Batches	[No]

Batch Number: 2 Description: May 2010 cash receipts Bank: 1STBK Total: 5,057.56
Batch Date: 5/21/10 Type: Entered Status: Open

Entry: 1 Customer: 1010 Newell Productions Check/Receipt No.: 10-008877 Check Amt: 3,772.00
Year: 2011 Period: 01 Account Set: 1 Check Date: 5/14/10 Receipt Type: CHECK
Description: Scheduled Payment

Type	Document No.-Schedule No.	Adj. No.	Adjustment Reference		Adjustment	Discount	Amount
PY	IN000000003-1				0.00	0.00	3,772.00
				Total :	0.00	0.00	3,772.00

Entry: 2 Customer: 1005 Caledon Hotel, The Check/Receipt No.: 99-7788 Check Amt: 763.50
Year: 2011 Period: 01 Account Set: 1 Check Date: 5/19/10 Receipt Type: CHECK
Description: Payment on account

Type	Document No.-Schedule No.	Adj. No.	Adjustment Reference		Adjustment	Discount	Amount
PY	IN000000004-1				0.00	0.00	763.50
				Total :	0.00	0.00	763.50

Entry: 3 Customer: 1020 Kawartha Comedy Club, The Check/Receipt No.: 22-3456 Check Amt: 522.06
Year: 2011 Period: 01 Account Set: 1 Check Date: 5/20/10 Receipt Type: CHECK
Description: Payment on account

Type	Document No.-Schedule No.	Adj. No.	Adjustment Reference		Adjustment	Discount	Amount
PY	IN000000005-1				0.00	9.24	522.06
				Total :	0.00	9.24	522.06

---Summary ---

	Adjustment	Discount	Amount
Total for Batch 2	0.00	9.24	5,057.56

3 entries printed
1 batch printed

PRINTING DEPOSIT SLIPS

Devine Designs Inc. must print deposit slips for a receipt batch before that batch can be designated as ready to post.

- ❑ Click: the **Zoom** button for Batch Number 2
- ❑ Click: **Deposit** [Deposit...] on the A/R Receipt Batch Maintenance window
- ❑ Click: **Print** [Print] on the A/R Deposit Slips window.
- ❑ Click: **OK** [OK] on the Print dialog box

The deposit slip number should match the receipt batch number. Deposit Slip 2 should total $5,057.56. Note that the Deposit button on the Receipt Batch Maintenance window is no longer active.

- ❑ Close: the **Receipt Batch Maintenance** window

ACCPAC will display a message (Figure 21-7) confirming that the deposit slip has been printed. No changes can be made to the entries in a batch after the deposit slip is printed.

FIGURE 21-7
Confirmation Message

- ❑ Click: **OK**
- ❑ Select: **Batch Number 1**
- ❑ Click: the **Zoom** button to display the Batch Maintenance window
- ❑ Print: the **Deposit Slip** for Receipt Batch 1
- ❑ Close: the Receipt Batch Maintenance window
- ❑ Click: **OK** on the Confirmation message
- ❑ Print: the **Batch Listing - Receipts** again

READY TO POST

After deposit slips have been printed, you cannot alter the entries in a batch, but you cannot post the batch until it has been designated Ready to Post.

- ❑ DClick: the **Receipt Batch List** icon

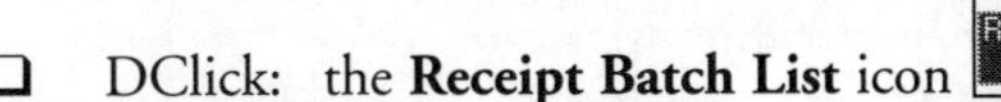

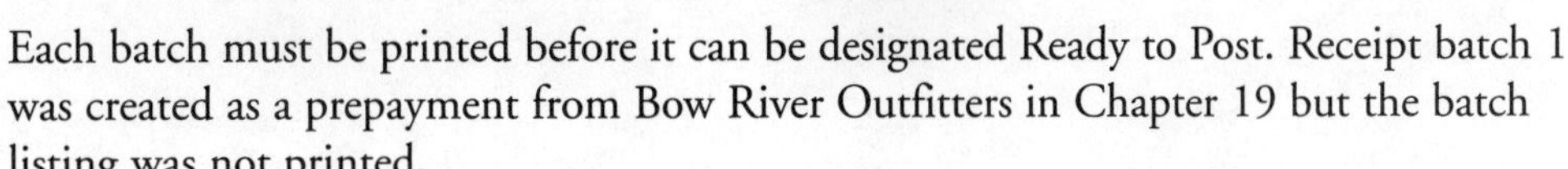

Each batch must be printed before it can be designated Ready to Post. Receipt batch 1 was created as a prepayment from Bow River Outfitters in Chapter 19 but the batch listing was not printed.

You set a Cash Receipt Batch as Ready to Post in the same way you set an Invoice Batch Ready to Post.

- ❑ DClick: the **Ready to Post Cell** for Batch 1
- ❑ Click: **Post**

After posting is completed, ACCPAC displays two Information messages. If there are errors in the batches, such as duplicate check numbers, ACCPAC creates an error batch and displays a message similar to that in Figure 21-8.

FIGURE 21-8
Information Message

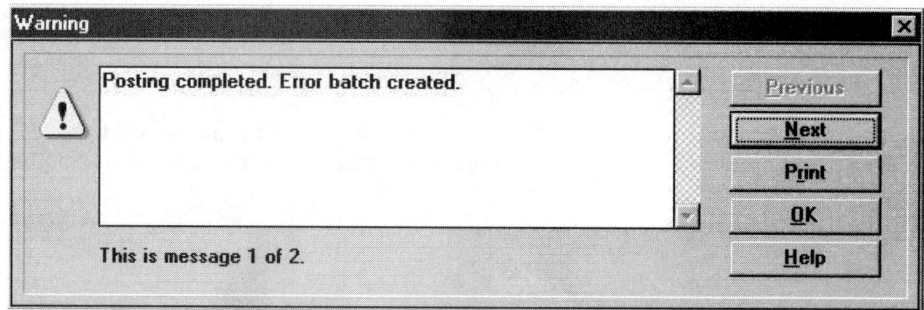

If you see this message, edit the error batch and process it so that you can post it.

- ❑ Click: **Next** [Next >]

The second Information message (Figure 21-9) confirms that the General Ledger transactions have been created.

FIGURE 21-9
Information Message

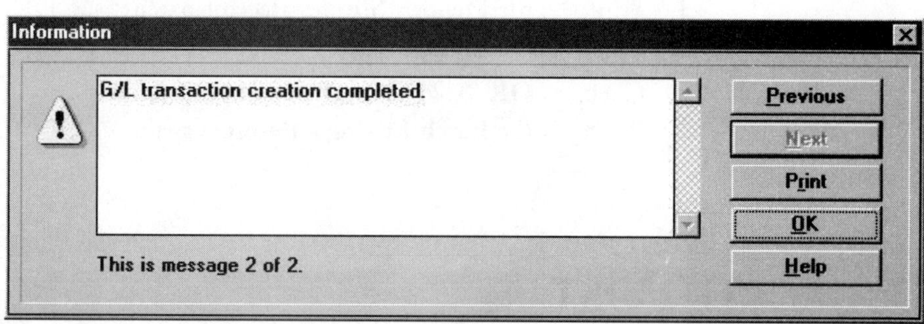

- ❑ Click: **OK** [OK] to clear the messages
- ❑ Select: **Batch Number 2**
- ❑ DClick: the **Ready to Post Cell** for Batch 2
- ❑ Click: **Post**
- ❑ Clear: the Information Messages
- ❑ Close: the **A/R Receipt Batch List** window

PRINTING POSTING JOURNAL

- ❑ Open: the **A/R Processing Reports** window
- ❑ Open: the **Posting Journals** dialog box

The Posting Journals dialog box (Figure 21-10) is identical to that used to print the Invoice Posting Journal.

- ❑ Select: the **Receipt** option button
- ❑ Select: the **Customer Number** option button
- ❑ Click: **Print** [Print]

FIGURE 21-10
Posting Journals
Dialog Box

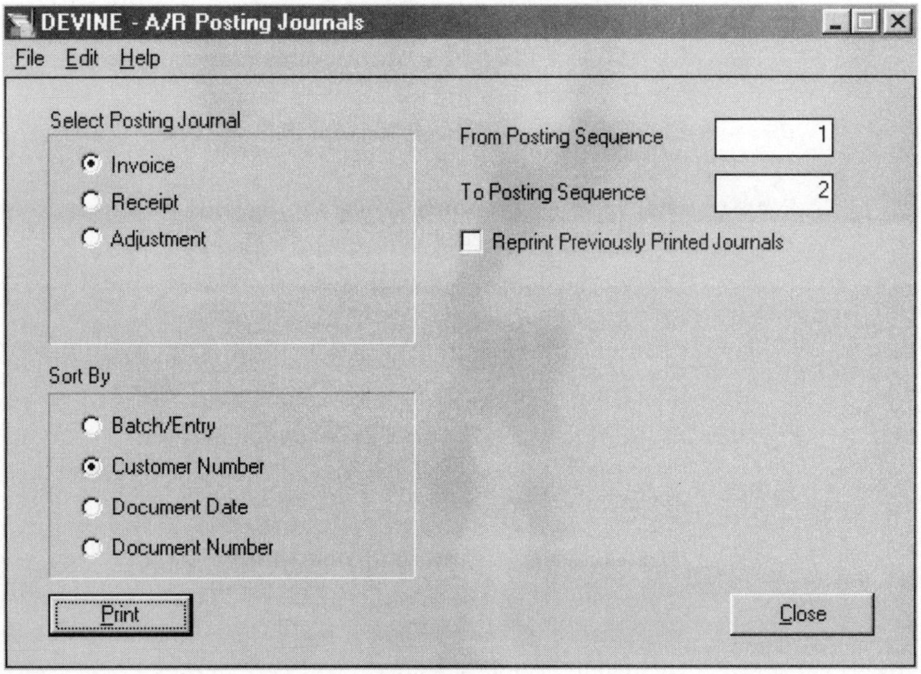

- ❑ Click: **OK** [OK] on the Print dialog box
- ❑ Close: the **A/R Posting Journals** dialog box

ENTERING A MISCELLANEOUS RECEIPT

Devine Designs Inc. received a check from Prestonia Office Products for office supplies that were returned. The check, number 44-8765 received on May 17, 2010, was for $163.30. As this transaction does not affect a customer's account, it will be entered as Miscellaneous Receipt Transaction in a new batch.

The receipt will be entered in the Deposit Entry window, and then the Miscellaneous Receipt Distribution window will be used to specify the General Ledger accounts to which the transaction will be posted.

- ❑ Open: the **Receipt Entry** window
- ❑ Click: the **Zoom** button for the Batch Number text box
- ❑ Click: the **New Document** icon for the Batch Number text box
- ❑ Enter: **051710** in the Batch Date text box
- ❑ Enter: **Miscellaneous Receipts** in the Description text box
- ❑ Select: **1STBK** in the Bank Code text box
- ❑ Click: **Save** [Save] to save the new batch information

- ❑ Click: **Close** [Close] to return to the Receipt Entry window
- ❑ Type: **163.30** in the **Amount** text box
- ❑ Press: **Tab** [Tab] to complete the entry
- ❑ Click: the **Check/Receipt No.** text box
- ❑ Type: **44-8765**
- ❑ Type: **Prestonia Office Products** in the **Payer** text box
- ❑ Press: **Tab** [Tab] to complete the entry
- ❑ Click: the **Finder** for the Receipt Type
- ❑ Select: **CHECK** as the Transaction Type
- ❑ Type: **Refund-returned supplies** in the **Description** text box
- ❑ Press: **Tab** [Tab] to complete the entry
- ❑ Click: the **list tool** for the Transaction Type column
- ❑ Select: **Misc. Receipt** for the Transaction Type
- ❑ Press: **Tab** [Tab]

The original transaction debited the Office Supplies account for the amount of the purchase, plus the Retail Sales Tax. The GST (VAT) Recoverable account was also debited for 7 percent of the purchase price of these supplies. Both of these accounts must be credited to record the refund.

- ❑ Click: the **Finder** for the Account column
- ❑ Select: **1300 Office Supplies**

The check stub shows that the refund is based on a purchase price of $142.00, plus PST (RST) of 8%, or $11.36. The total amount for the purchase price plus RST is $153.36.

- ❑ Click: the **Amount** cell
- ❑ Type: **153.36**
- ❑ Press: **Tab** [Tab] to complete the entry

You should save each distribution.

- ❑ Click: **Add** [Add]

The GST (VAT) on the purchase price of $142.00 would be $9.94.

- ❑ Press: the **Insert** key to add a new row to the table
- ❑ Click: the **Account cell**
- ❑ Click: the **Finder** for the Account text box
- ❑ Select: **2205 GST (VAT) Recoverable**
- ❑ Click: the **Amount cell**
- ❑ Type: **9.94**
- ❑ Press: **Tab** [Tab] to complete the entry
- ❑ Click: **Save** to save the distribution

Confirm that the Undistributed Amount is zero as you cannot post the receipt until it is fully distributed. If an amount remains undistributed, enter the correct amounts in the Amount column. Remember to save the corrections.

PRINTING THE DEPOSIT SLIP AND BATCH LISTING

The Batch Number field should still display the batch number used to record the miscellaneous receipt.

- ❑ Click: the **Zoom** button for the Batch Number text box
- ❑ Click: **Deposit** Deposit...
- ❑ Click: **Print** Print
- ❑ Click: **OK** OK on the Print dialog box
- ❑ Print: the **Receipt Batch Listing**
- ❑ Close: the **Receipt Batch Maintenance** window
- ❑ Close: the **A/R Receipt Entry** window

POSTING THE RECEIPT BATCH

- ❑ Open: the **A/R Receipt Batch List** window
- ❑ DClick: the **Ready to Post** cell for batch 3
- ❑ Close: the **A/R Receipt Batch List** window

Receipt Batches can be posted after the deposit slips have been printed and each batch designated as ready to post.

- ❑ Open: the **Post Batches** window
- ❑ Select: the **Receipt** option button
- ❑ Select: the **All Batches** option button
- ❑ Click: **Post** Post

After posting is completed, ACCPAC will display two Information messages. If there are errors in the batches, such as duplicate check numbers, ACCPAC creates an error batch and display a message.

- ❑ Click: **OK** OK to clear the messages
- ❑ Close: the **Post Batches** window
- ❑ Open: the **Processing Reports** window
- ❑ Open: the **Posting Journals** dialog box
- ❑ Select: the **Receipt** option button
- ❑ Select: the **Batch/Entry** option button
- ❑ Click: **Print** Print
- ❑ Click: **OK** OK on the Print dialog box
- ❑ Close: the **Posting Journals** dialog box
- ❑ Close: the **Processing Reports** window

Review Questions

1. What is the purpose of the A/R Receipt Entry window?
2. Can you create your own batch number for Cash receipts?
3. Four types of transactions can be entered on the Receipt Entry form. What are they?
4. What information do you enter in the Date field on the Receipt Entry window? What is normally displayed in the Date field?
5. What is the difference between the Direct mode of applying a payment and the Select mode?

Exercise

- ❑ Sign on to your company (EXERCO) as the system administrator.
- ❑ Enter 052110 in the Session Date box.

1. Three payments were received from the invoices issued early in May. Use A/R Receipt Entry batch 1 to record the following receipts.
   a) May 9, 2010, B. Eady & Co. Check # BE 0072, in payment of Invoice 001, $2,034.
   b) May 10, 2010, VanVoort Ltd. Check # VV00-132, in payment of Invoice 003, $1,353.
   c) May 15, 2010, RenRak Ltd. Check # 10-346, in payment of Invoice 003, $920.
2. Print the Deposit Slips.
3. Print the Receipt Batch.
4. Set the batch Ready to Post and post the receipt batch.
5. Print the A/R Posting Journal.

- ❑ Close the A/R Processing Reports window.
- ❑ Exit from ACCPAC.

CHAPTER 22

Periodic Processing

At the end of each period, a company typically processes recurring charges and interest charges on overdue accounts and prints customer statements.

In this chapter, Devine Designs Inc. will process recurring charges, using the recurring charges set up in Chapter 19, generating invoices and posting to the Accounts Receivable. Customer Statements and the Trial Balance will then be printed.

Interest Invoices will be created and posted to the Accounts Receivable on June 30, 2010.

The simulation will then move to the end of the fiscal year to illustrate Year-End Processing.

Periodic Processing

- ❑ Sign on to Devine Designs Inc. as the system administrator using May 31, 2010, as the Session Date.
- ❑ Open: the **Accounts Receivable** window
- ❑ DClick: the **A/R Periodic Processing** icon 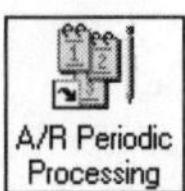

FIGURE 22-1
Periodic Processing Icons

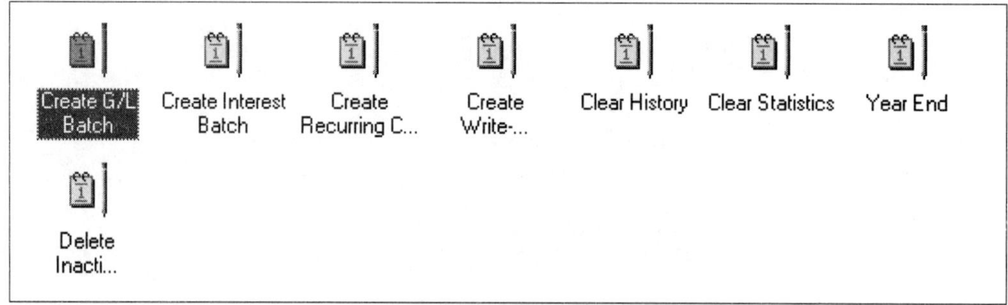

The Periodic Processing window contains eight icons (Figure 22-1). Devine Designs Inc. will not use the Create G/L Batch icon as it selected the option to have these batches created during posting. The Clear History, Clear Statistics and Delete Inactive Records icons will also not be used.

CREATING A RECURRING CHARGES BATCH

Recurring charges are used to reduce the amount of data entry necessary to produce invoices for goods or services that are issued to the same customers for the same amount on a regular basis. The recurring charge information is entered once for each customer and then used to generate the recurring charges as necessary. Devine Designs Inc. will use recurring charges to invoice customers at the end of each month for Web page hosting.

❑ DClick: the **Create Recurring Charge Batch** icon 

The A/R Create Recurring Charge Batch window will appear as shown in Figure 22-2.

FIGURE 22-2
Recurring Charge Dialog Box

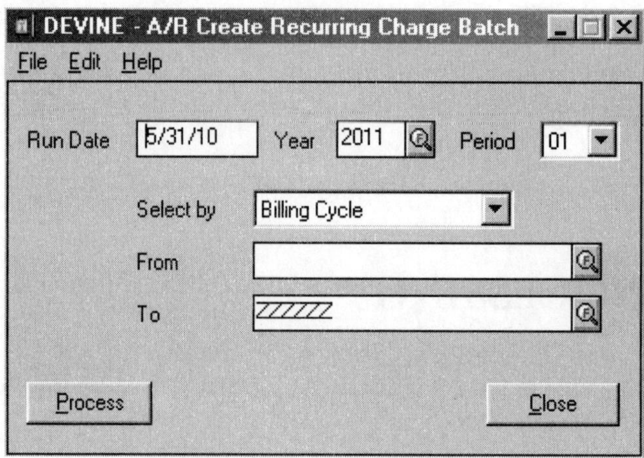

Run Date

The Run Date is recorded as the invoice date for each recurring charge generated. When the batch is posted, this date is entered in the Last Run Date for the recurring charge batch. The default Run Date is the Session Date.

- ❑ Press: **Tab** [Tab] to accept the default date

Year and Period

The information displayed in the Year and Period text boxes is based on the Run Date and the Fiscal Calendar for Devine Designs Inc. Only rarely would these be changed.

Select By

The Select by list box has four options:

The Recurring Charge Code option allows you to create invoices for a range of recurring charge codes. Other charges assigned to the customers are ignored if you do not include their recurring charge codes in the range of codes.

The Customer Number option is used to create invoices for all the recurring charges assigned to the customers in the range specified.

The Billing Cycle option creates invoices for all the recurring charges assigned to the customers who use the billing cycles specified.

The Customer Group and National Accounts options are used to create invoices for all the recurring charges assigned to customers who belong to the customer groups or national accounts specified.

Devine Designs Inc. will select the Recurring Charge Code option.

- ❑ Click: the **list tool** for Select by
- ❑ Select: **Recurring Charge Code**

From and To

You enter the range of records to select from in the From and To text boxes. If you want to specify a single record, enter its code in both text boxes. To select all records, leave the From text box blank and the To text box displaying multiple copies of the letter Z.

- ❑ Click: the **Finder** for the From text box

The Finder (Figure 22-3) should display the three Recurring Charge Codes that were set up in Chapter 19.

FIGURE 22-3
Finder-Recurring Charges

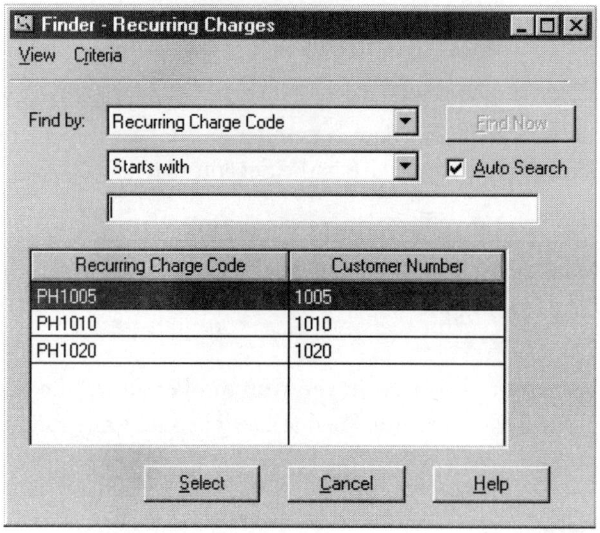

- ❑ Select: **PH1005**
- ❑ Click: the **Finder** for the To text box
- ❑ Select: **PH1020**
- ❑ Click: **Process** to create the batch

ACCPAC will automatically assign the next available batch number to the batch using the prefix selected in the Options notebook. No invoices will be created for recurring charges that have reached the limit allowed in the Maximum Amount field in the Recurring Charge record.

When processing is completed, ACCPAC displays an information message indicating that the processing is complete.

- ❑ Click: **OK**
- ❑ Close: the **A/R Create Recurring Charge Batch** window

PRINTING THE BATCH LISTING

The Batch Listing Dialog Box is shown in Figure 22-4.

- ❑ Open: the **A/R Processing Reports** menu
- ❑ DClick: the **Batch Listing** icon on the Processing Reports Window

Batch

The defaults displayed in the From and To text boxes will print all batch numbers corresponding to the other selections made on this dialog box.

Figure 22-4
Batch Listing Dialog Box

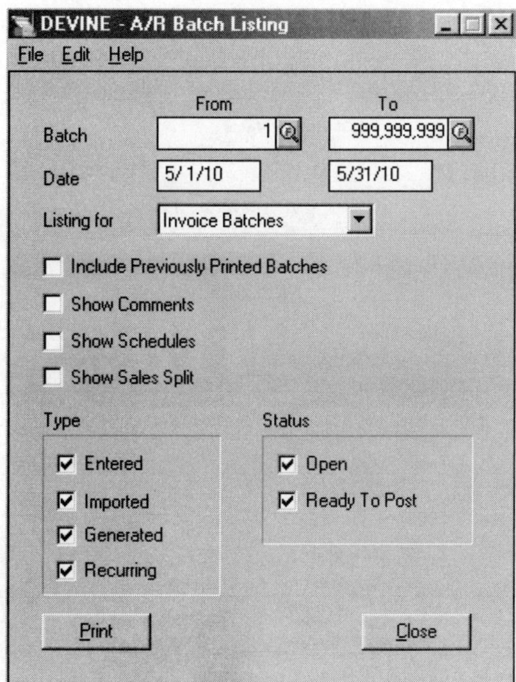

Date

The default dates displayed in the From and To text boxes will print all batches of the type selected that were created in the time period shown.

Listing For

Recurring Charges are invoices.

❑ Select: **Invoice Batches** using the list tool

Deselect

❑ Click: the **Entered, Imported,** and **Generated** check boxes to deselect them

Status

❑ Click: the **Ready to Post** check box to deselect it
❑ Click: **Print** [Print]
❑ Click: **OK** [OK] on the Print dialog box
❑ Close: the **A/R Batch Listing** window

FIGURE 22-5
Batch Listing - Invoices

Date: Tuesday, August 15, 2000 3:18PM **DDI Student Name** **Page 1**
A/R Batch Listing - Invoice (ARIBTCLZ)

From Batch Number [3] To [3]
From Creation Date [5/1/2010] To [5/31/2010]
Listing For [Invoice Batches]
Of Type [Recurring]
Having Status Of [Open]
Show Comments [N]
Show Schedules [N]
Show Sales Split [N]

Batch No.: 3 **Description:** Recurring Chgs 2010-05-31 RC **Total:** 155.25
Batch Date: 5/31/2010 **Type:** Recurring **Status:** Open

Entry: 1 **Type:** IN **Document:** RC000000001 **Customer:** 1005 Caledon Hotel, The **Document Date:** 5/31/2010
PO No.: PO975 **Order No.:** **Description:** Monthly Web Page Hosting Fee **Period:** 01 **Year:** 2011
Terms: DISC **Due Date:** 6/30/2010 **Disc. Date:** 6/10/2010 **Discount Pct.:** 2.00000% **Discount Amt.:** 0.90
Recurring Charge Code: PH1005

Dist. Code	Acct. Number/Acct. Description	Detail Description	Tax Authority	Tax Base	Amount
HOST	4000/30 Sales - Web Site Hosting	Sales - Web Site Hosting			45.00
			GSTFED	45.00	3.15
			RSTON	45.00	3.60
				Total Invoice:	51.75
				Total Taxes:	6.75

Entry: 2 **Type:** IN **Document:** RC000000002 **Customer:** 1010 Newell Productions **Document Date:** 5/31/2010
PO No.: **Order No.:** **Description:** **Period:** 01 **Year:** 2011
Terms: DISC **Due Date:** 6/30/2010 **Disc. Date:** 6/10/2010 **Discount Pct.:** 2.00000% **Discount Amt.:** 1.10
Recurring Charge Code: PH1010

Dist. Code	Acct. Number/Acct. Description	Detail Description	Tax Authority	Tax Base	Amount
HOST	4000/30 Sales - Web Site Hosting	Sales - Web Site Hosting			55.00 C
			GSTFED	55.00	3.85
			RSTON	55.00	4.40
				Total Invoice:	63.25
				Total Taxes:	8.25

Entry: 3 **Type:** IN **Document:** RC000000003 **Customer:** 1020 Kawartha Comedy Club **Document Date:** 5/31/2010
PO No.: **Order No.:** **Description:** **Period:** 01 **Year:** 2011
Terms: DISC **Due Date:** 6/30/2010 **Disc. Date:** 6/10/2010 **Discount Pct.:** 2.00000% **Discount Amt.:** 0.70
Recurring Charge Code: PH1020

Dist. Code	Acct. Number/Acct. Description	Detail Description	Tax Authority	Tax Base	Amount
HOST	4000/30 Sales - Web Site Hosting	Sales - Web Site Hosting			35.00
			GSTFED	35.00	2.45
			RSTON	35.00	2.80

Date: Tuesday, August 15, 2000 3:18PM **DDI Student Name** **Page 2**
A/R Batch Listing - Invoice (ARIBTCLZ)

Total Invoice: 40.25
Total Taxes: 5.25

--- Summary ---

Total Invoices	155.25
Total Credit Notes	0.00
Total Debit Notes	0.00
Total Interest	0.00
Total For Batch 3	155.25

C: Indicates over credit limit

3 entries printed
1 batch printed

Compare your printed output to Figure 22-5. Correct any errors using the Invoice Entry window and print the batch listing again.

PRINTING INVOICES

There are several ways to print invoices. In the chapters on invoices, invoices were printed individually from the Invoice Entry window. Invoices can also be printed using the Invoice Printing icon on the Processing Reports window.

❑ DClick: the **Invoice Printing** icon 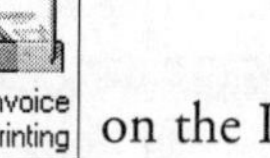 on the Processing Reports window

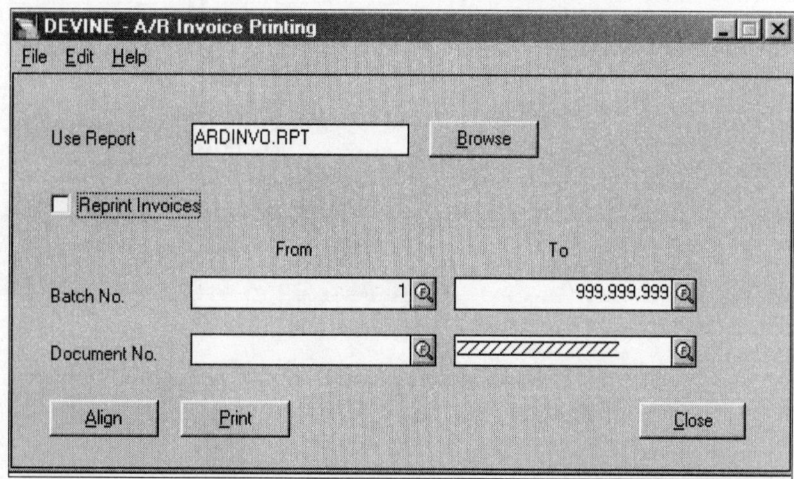

FIGURE 22-6
Invoice Printing Dialog Box

The defaults shown on the Invoice Printing dialog box (Figure 22-6) will print all unprinted invoices. You can reprint invoices using the Reprint Invoice check box. You can also select a batch or range of batches to print invoices from. Devine Designs Inc. will print all unprinted invoices using the Invoice From generated by ACCPAC.

❑ Click: **Print** [Print]
❑ Click: **OK** [OK] on the Print dialog box
❑ Close: the **A/R Invoice Printing** dialog box

POSTING THE INVOICE BATCHES

In the chapters on invoices, Devine Designs Inc. used the Post Batches window to post batches after they were designated Ready to Post. Invoices can also be printed using the Invoice Batch List icon.

❑ DClick: the **Invoice Batch List** icon  on the Accounts Receivable main window

FIGURE 22-7
Invoice Batch List Window

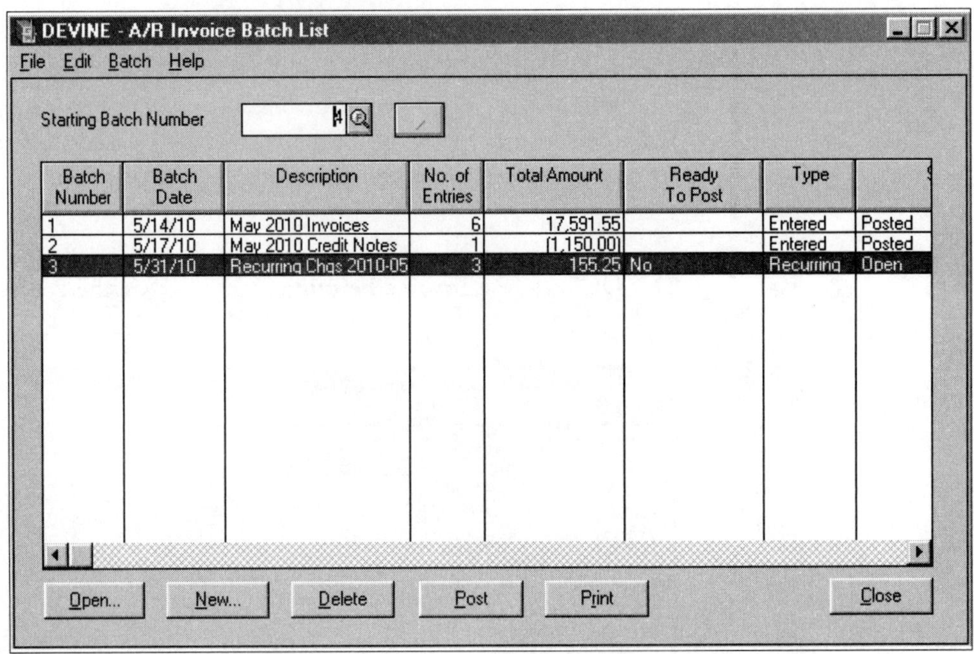

The line for the Recurring Batch should be highlighted when the table display is complete (Figure 22-7).

- ❑ DClick: the **Ready to Post** cell to display Yes
- ❑ Click: **Post** [Post]

When you post recurring charges, the amount of each invoice is entered in the Amount Last Entered field in the recurring charge record, and added to the total in the Amount Invoiced to Date field. Posting also updates the statistics for recurring charges that are kept in the customer records.

When posting is completed, ACCPAC displays the messages that posting and General Ledger transaction creation are completed.

- ❑ Click: **OK** [OK] to clear the messages

Note that the status of the recurring batch has been changed to posted.

- ❑ Close: the **A/R Invoice Batch List** window

PRINTING STATEMENTS

Devine Designs Inc. would normally create Interest Invoices before printing customer statements. As of May 31, 2010, no Interest Invoices would be created. Later you will create Interest Invoices using June 30, 2010, as the Session Date.

❑ DClick: the **Statements Letter/Labels** icon Statements / Letters / L... on the Accounts Receivable window to get the display shown in Figure 22-8

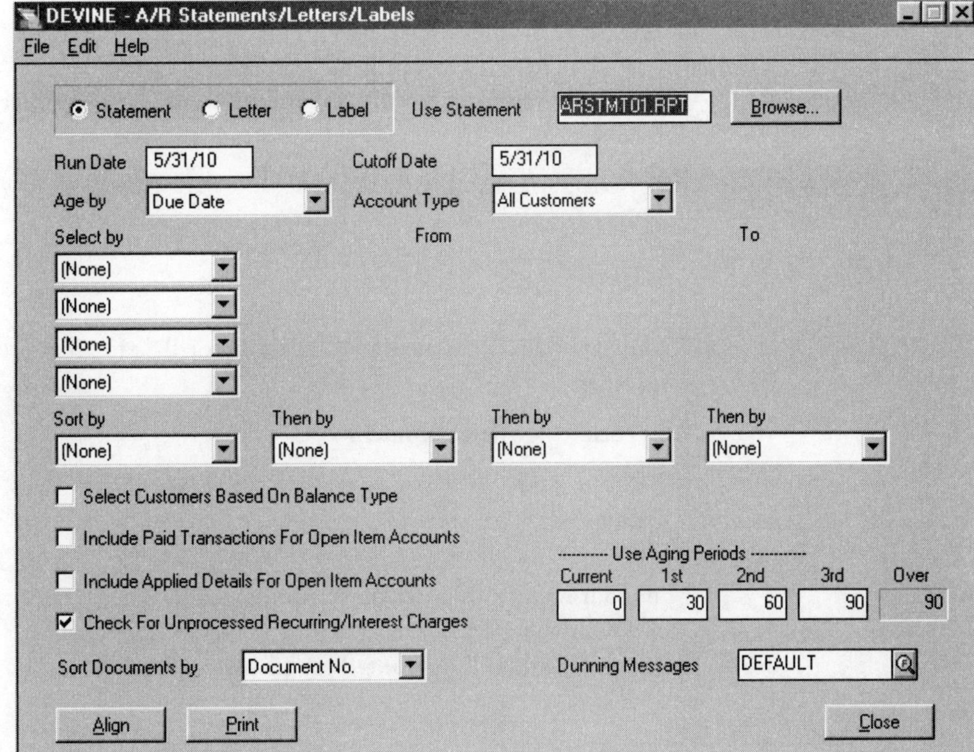

FIGURE 22-8
Statements Letters Labels Window

Document Type

This window can be used to print customer statements, customer letters that have been created, or envelope labels.

❑ Select: the **Statement** option button

Use Statement

Devine Designs Inc. uses the default printer generated statements that come with ACC-PAC. If you were printing on preprinted forms and had a statement specification file, you would use Browse to select that statement specification.

Run and Cutoff Dates

The defaults displayed should be the Session Date. You would use these text boxes if the dates on the statements and the last transactions reported were earlier or later than the session date; for example, when the end of the month is not a business day and customer statements are printed one or two days later. If necessary, change the Run Date and the Cutoff Date to 5/31/2010.

Age by

Transactions reported on the statement can be aged by either the Due Date or the Document Date. Devine Designs Inc. will age by Due Date.

- ❑ Select: **Due Date**

Account Type

Statements can be printed for Open Item or Balance Forward account types, or for all customers.

- ❑ Select: **All Customers**

Select by

The four rows in this area of the window allow you to restrict the selection of customers for whom you are printing statements. Devine Designs Inc. will use the default None so that statements will be printed for all customers.

Sort by

The Sort by list boxes allow you to control the order in which statements are printed. To facilitate bulk mailing, you could use this option to print statements in order of customers' postal codes. Devine Designs Inc. does not have enough customers to make this feature useful.

Select Customers Based on Balance Type

If this option is selected, you can choose not to print statements for customers with debit, credit, or zero balance accounts. Devine Designs Inc. will print statements for all customers.

Include Paid Transactions for Open Item Accounts

The default is not to include paid transactions on the statements for open item customers. Devine Designs Inc. wants to include these details on customer statements.

- ❑ Select: the **Include Paid Transactions for Open Item Accounts** check box

Include Applied Details for Open Item Accounts

Devine Designs Inc. wants to provide as much detail information to their customers as possible.

❑ Select: the **Include Applied Details for Open Item Accounts** check box

Use Aging Periods

The number of days displayed in these text boxes are the same as those Devine Designs Inc. entered in the Setup Options notebook. Only rarely would they be changed.

Dunning Messages

Dunning Messages are messages that are printed on customer statements to thank the customer for keeping the account current or to encourage payment of overdue invoices. Devine Designs Inc. entered a series of Dunning Messages in the Options notebook.

❑ Click: the **Finder** for Dunning Messages
❑ Select: **DEFAULT**
❑ Click: **Print** Print
❑ Click: **OK** OK on the Print dialog box

ACCPAC will display the warning message shown in Figure 22-9.

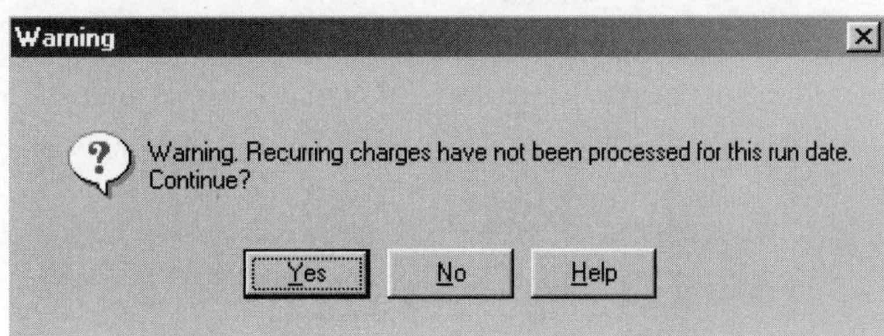

FIGURE 22-9
Warning Message

Recurring charges have been processed for the 05/31/10 Run Date. Devine Designs Inc. has decided not to process interest charges at this time.

❑ Click: **Yes** Yes to continue

After the statements are sent to the printer, ACCPAC displays another Warning message, shown in Figure 22-10.

FIGURE 22-10
Warning Message

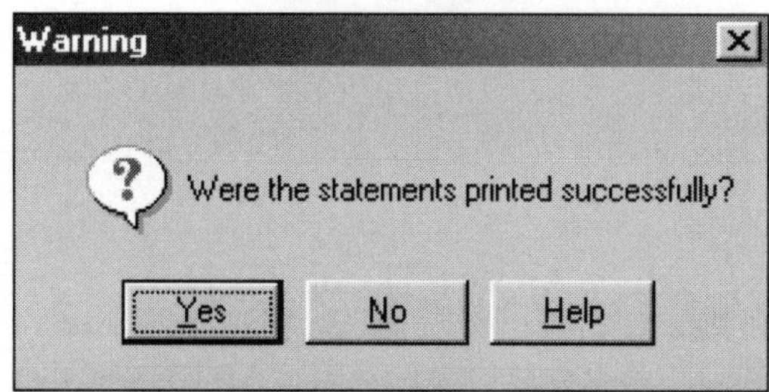

Get the statements from the printer before responding to this message. If the printouts are not satisfactory, click No, and print the statements again.

- ❑ Click: **Yes** [Yes] to clear the Warning message
- ❑ Click: **OK** [OK] to clear the Processing Completed information message
- ❑ Close: the **A/R Statements/Letters/Labels** window

ANALYTICAL REPORTS

ACCPAC allows you to print a series of Analytical Reports on posted transaction.

- ❑ DClick: the **A/R Analytical Reports** icon  on the Accounts Receivable window

The Analytical Reports window contains three icons (Figure 22-11). Devine Designs Inc. will not use the Item Sales History icon as it does not track inventory items or quantities.

FIGURE 22-11
Analytical Reports Icons

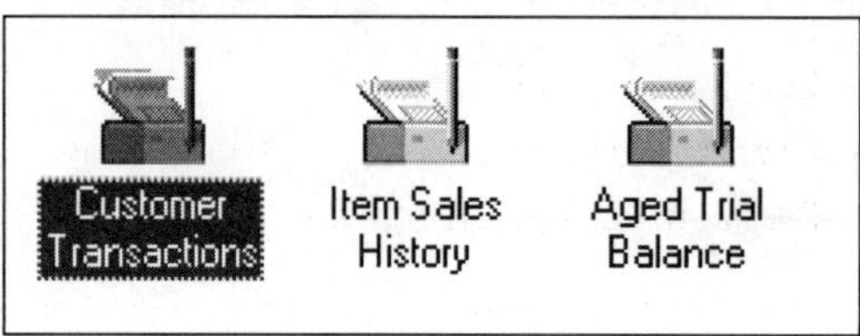

CUSTOMER TRANSACTIONS REPORT

- ❑ DClick: the **Customer Transactions** icon 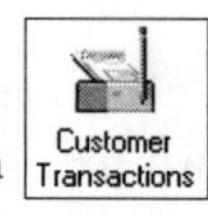

The A/R Customer Transactions Report window (Figure 22-12) has several areas that you have seen before and some new data entry areas.

FIGURE 22-12
Customer Transactions Report Window

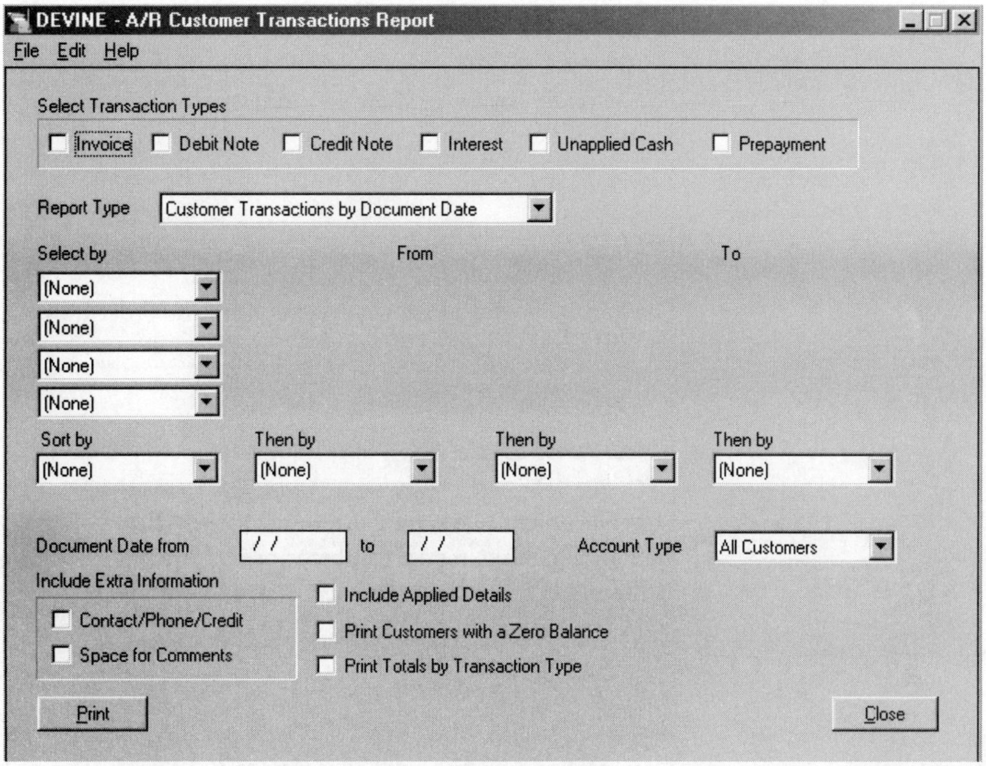

Select Transaction Types

The Select Transaction Type option buttons allow you to select specific types of transactions to be included in the report. To include all types of transactions, select all six option buttons. Devine Designs Inc. has only recorded Invoices, Credit Notes, and Prepayments.

- ❑ Select: the **Invoice** option button
- ❑ Select: the **Credit Note** option button
- ❑ Select: the **Prepayment** option button

If you have entered any other types of transactions, select the corresponding option buttons.

Report Type

You can print this report in order by document date, document number, or fiscal year and period. Devine Designs Inc. will print the report by document number.

- ❑ Select: **Customer Transactions by Document Number**

Select by

The Select by list boxes allow you to restrict the report to specific customers. The defaults of None exclude no customers, so the report includes all customers.

Sort by

The Sort by list boxes allow you to control the order in which customers are printed. The default is to print by customer number.

Document Date

The Document Date from and to text boxes allow you to specify a specific period of time for which the report will be printed. If these text boxes are left blank, ACCPAC will include all customer transactions in the current and history files.

Account Type

The Account Type list box allows you to print open item or balance forward customers, or all customers.

❑ Select: **All Customers**

Include Extra Information

The two check boxes in this area allow you to include the contact name, phone number, and credit limit from the customer account record and give space for additional comments. Devine Designs Inc. will include the contact name, phone number, and credit limit.

❑ Select: the **Contact/Phone/Credit** check box

Include Applied Details

Including applied details allows a more complete analysis of a customer's account.

❑ Select: the **Include Applied Details** check box

Print Customers with a Zero Balance

The default is not to print information on customers whose account is current. If you wish to include these customers, select the Include Customers with a Zero Balance check box.

Print Totals by Transaction Type

When this option is selected, an additional line for the total of each of the selected Transaction Types is added to the printout for each customer. Devine Designs Inc. will not use this analysis tool.

- ❑ Click: **Print** [Print]
- ❑ Click: **OK** [OK] on the Print dialog box
- ❑ Close: the **A/R Customer Transactions Report** window

Analyze your printout. You should be able to understand and explain each line. If necessary, look at your earlier printouts for help.

PRINTING THE AGED TRIAL BALANCE

The Aged Trial Balance shows the payment performance of customers and provides information on the status of the company's Accounts Receivable. It can be used to identify customers who are chronically slow payers and thus may be credit risks.

- ❑ Click: the **Aged Trial Balance** icon  on the Analytical Report window

FIGURE 22-13
Aged Trial Balance Report Window

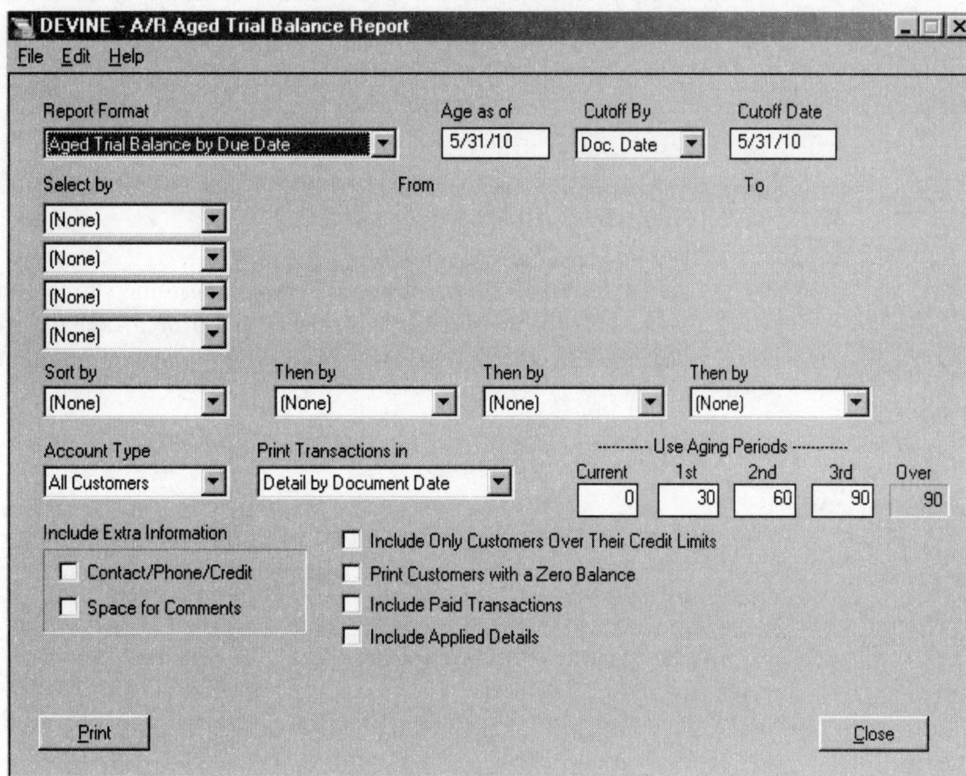

The Aged Trial Balance Report window (Figure 22-13) displays many features already familiar to you. It also has some unique features.

Report Format

The Report Format list box allows you to select printing the Aged Trial Balance or a report on Overdue Receivables. Each type of report can be printed by either Due Date or Document Number. Each of these four reports can be a useful analytical tool for helping the management of Accounts Receivable.

Devine Designs Inc. will print an Aged Trial Balance by Due Date.

❑ Select: **Aged Trial Balance by Due Date**

Age as of

The Age as of text box defaults to the Session Date and is used to calculate the age of receivables. In most cases, you would not change this date.

Cutoff By

The Cutoff By list box allows you to choose the method used to determine the date for including transactions in the report. If you select the default, Doc. Date (the document date), the Cutoff Date text box defaults to the Session Date, but you can change this Cutoff Date if necessary. If you choose Year/Period, the cutoff date becomes the last day of the current period based on the Session Date.

As the Session Date is May 31, 2010, which is also the last day of period 1 in the fiscal year 2011, Devine Designs Inc. does not have to make any changes.

Select by and Sort by

These list boxes allow you to select which customers to include in the Aged Trial Balance and to choose the order in which they are printed. The defaults displayed in Figure 22-13 will include all customers printed in order of customer number.

Account Type

The Account Type list box allows you to include Open item or Balance Forward customers in the report, or to include all customers. Devine Designs Inc. will include all customers.

❑ Select: **All Customers**

Print Transactions in

The Print Transactions in list box allows you to print either a summary or detailed report. The detailed report can be organized by document date or document number. Devine Designs Inc. will print a detailed report by document number.

❑ Select: **Detail by Document Date** using the list tool ▾

Use Aging Periods

The default Aging Periods were entered in the Options notebook by Devine Designs Inc.

Include Extra Information

The two check boxes in this area allow you to include information on the customer. Selecting Space for Comments gives you a blank space following each customer in which you can write notes. Devine Designs Inc. will include the contact name, phone number, and credit limit for each customer.

❑ Select: the **Contact/Phone/Credit** check box

Include Only Customers Over Their Credit Limits

Selecting this option reduces the number of customer accounts printed. You would choose this option if there were a large number of accounts and you wanted to review only those customers over their credit limit.

Print Customers with a Zero Balance

Devine Designs Inc. will choose this option as there are few customers and this will provide a more detailed report.

❑ Select: the **Print Customers with a Zero Balance** check box

Include Paid Transactions

Devine Designs Inc. will select this option to list documents that are fully paid, but not yet cleared from Accounts Receivable.

❑ Select: the **Include Paid Transactions** check box

Include Applied Details

Devine Designs Inc. will select this option as the printed report includes all documents, including receipts and credit notes, that were applied to each invoice reported.

- Select: the **Include Applied Details** check box
- Click: **Print** [Print]
- Click: **OK** [OK] on the Print dialog box

Review the printed Aged Trial Balance. Note that the recurring charges have been applied to customers 1005, 1010, and 1020. There should be a credit note applied to the regular invoice to the Caledon Hotel.

- Close: the **A/R Aged Trial Balance Report** window
- Exit: **ACCPAC**

INTEREST CHARGES

Devine Designs Inc. charges interest on overdue accounts at the end of each month.

For the purpose of creating an interest batch, we will assume that Devine Designs Inc. received no further payments in June 2010.

- Sign on to Devine Designs Inc. as the system manager using June 30, 2010 as the Session Date.
- Open: the **Accounts Receivable** main window
- Open: the **Periodic Processing** window

CREATING AN INTEREST BATCH

The Create Interest Batch window is used to create batches of interest invoices for customers whose accounts are overdue. ACCPAC assigns the next available interest invoice batch number to the interest batch, and selects Summary as the detail type.

- DClick: the **Create Interest Batch** icon 

The Create Interest Batch dialog box will appear as shown in Figure 22-14.

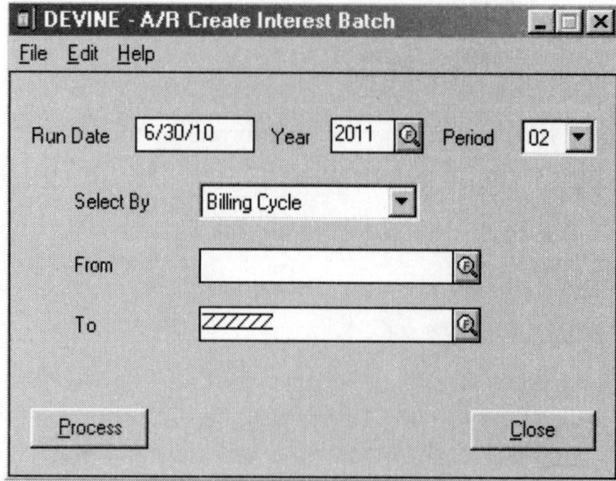

FIGURE 22-14
Create Interest Batch Dialog Box

Run Date

The Run Date is assigned as the document date for all interest invoices in the batch. Overdue interest is charged on all invoices and debit notes that were overdue by at least the number of days specified in the interest profile.

The default displayed in the Run Date text box is the Session Date. This also determines the default Year and Period.

Select By

The are four choices for the Select By list box. These are Customer Number, Customer Group, National Account, and Billing Cycle. Devine Designs Inc. will select all customers by Customer Number.

❑ Select: **Customer Number** using the list tool

The defaults displayed in the From and To text boxes include all customers.

❑ Click: **Process**

❑ Click: **OK** to clear the information message

❑ Close: the **A/R Create Interest Batch** dialog box

PROCESSING THE INTEREST INVOICES

The regular processing cycle should be followed for Interest Invoices.

Printing Interest Invoices

❑ Open: the **Invoice Printing** window 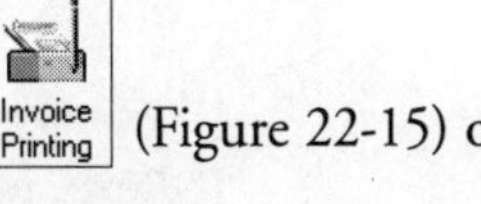

(Figure 22-15) on the A/R Processing Reports menu

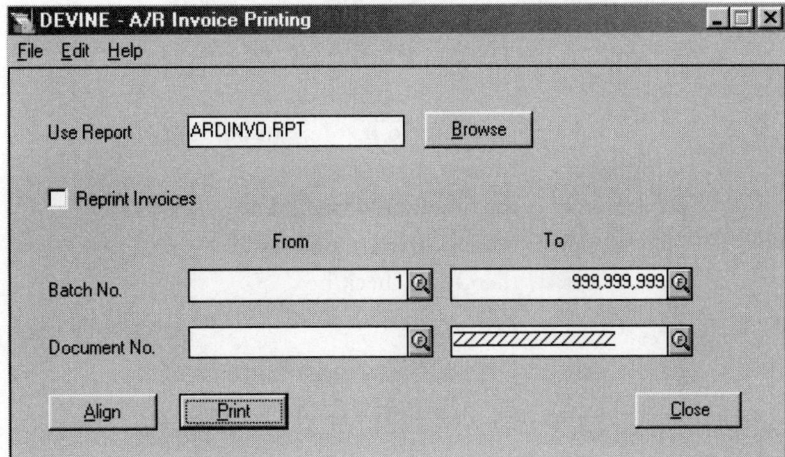

FIGURE 22-15 Invoice Printing Window

Devine Designs Inc. will print only the interest invoices. The Print Invoices Already Posted and Reprint Invoices check boxes should not be selected.

- ❑ Select: the **Interest Invoice batch** in both the From and To text boxes for Batch No.
- ❑ Click: **Print** [Print]
- ❑ Click: **OK** [OK] on the Print dialog box
- ❑ Close: the **A/R Invoice Printing** window

Printing the Batch List

- ❑ Open: the **A/R Processing Reports** window
- ❑ Open: the **Batch Listing** window (Figure 22-16)
- ❑ Use the finders to select the interest batch

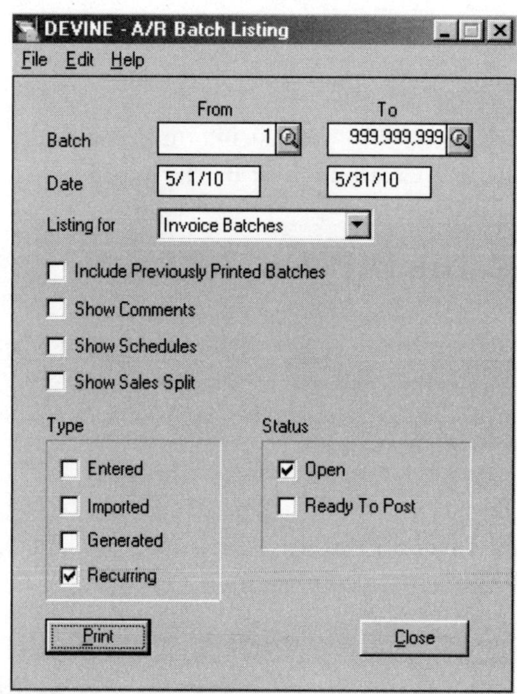

FIGURE 22-16
Batch Listing Report Window

- ❑ Change: the Date To text box to 06/30/2010
- ❑ Select: **Invoice Batches**
- ❑ Select: the **Generated** check box
- ❑ Deselect: the **Recurring** check box
- ❑ Select: the **Open** check box
- ❑ Click: **Print** [Print]
- ❑ Click: **OK** [OK] on the Print dialog box
- ❑ Close: the **A/R Batch Listing** window

Posting Interest Invoices

- ❑ DClick: the **Invoice Batch List** icon [Invoice Batch List] on the Accounts Receivable window
- ❑ Select: the **Interest Invoice** batch
- ❑ DClick: the **Ready to Post** cell to display Yes.
- ❑ Click: **Post** [Post]
- ❑ Click: **OK** [OK] to clear the information message

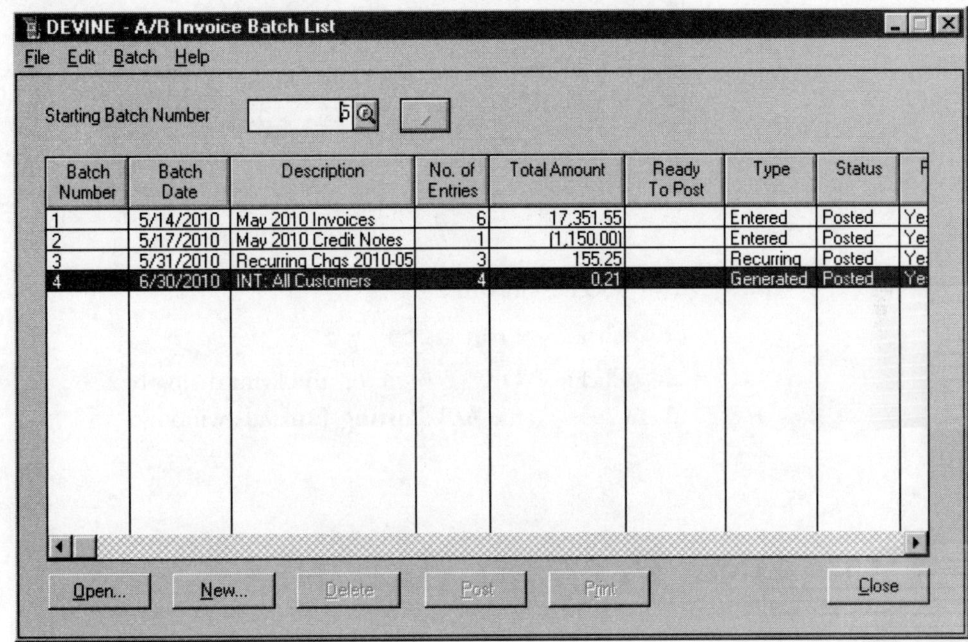

FIGURE 22-17 Invoice Batch List Window

- ❑ Close: the **A/R Invoice Batch List** window
- ❑ Open: the **A/R Processing Reports** window
- ❑ Open: the **Posting Journals** window

FIGURE 22-18
Posting Journal Window

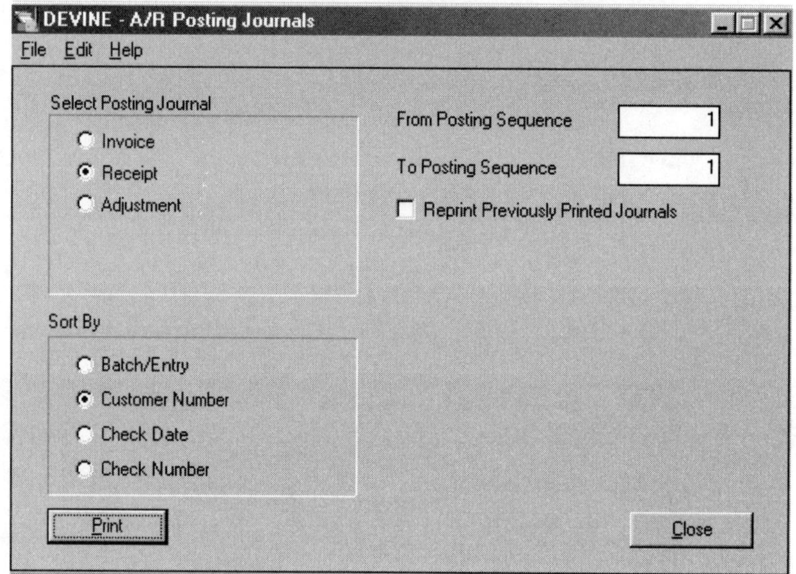

- ❑ Select: **Invoice**
- ❑ Click: **Print** [Print]
- ❑ Click: **OK** [OK] on the Print dialog box
- ❑ Close: the **A/R Posting Journals** window

CLEARING POSTED BATCHES

After batches have been posted and their posting journals printed, the information from these batches is in the customer records in Accounts Receivable. It is no longer necessary to keep the actual invoice batches as they are redundant.

- ❑ DClick: the **Batch Status** icon  on the Processing Reports window

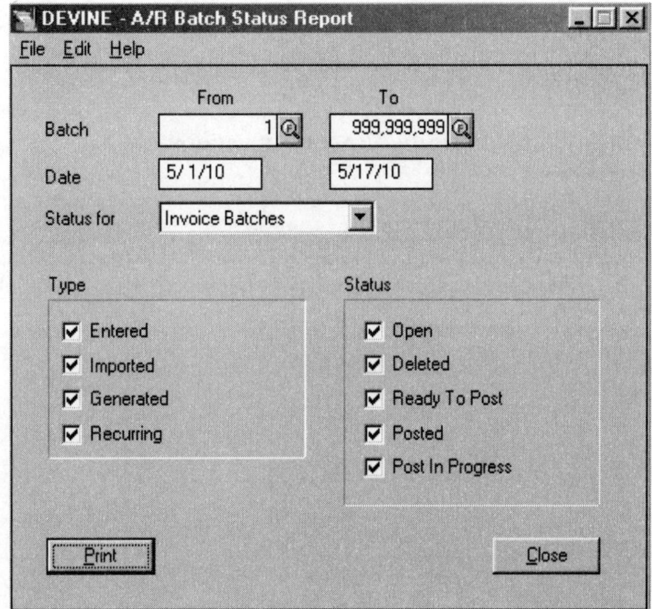

FIGURE 22-19
Batch Status Report Window

The Batch Status Report window (Figure 22-19) is used to print a Batch Status report and to clear deleted and posted batches.

- ❑ Type: 06/30/10 in the Batch To text box
- ❑ Select: **Invoice Batches**
- ❑ Select: the **Entered, Generated,** and **Recurring** check boxes for Type
- ❑ Select: All check boxes for Status
- ❑ Click: **Print** [Print]
- ❑ Click: **OK** [OK] on the Print dialog box
- ❑ Print: the **Batch Status Report** for Receipt Batches
- ❑ Close: the **A/R Batch Status Report** window

YEAR END PROCESSING

The purpose of this function is to reset batch numbers, so that the next batch of any group will start with the number 1. It will move customer account activity statistics for the current year into the previous year, and reduce to zero the statistical totals for the new year. The recurring Charge Amounts Invoiced to Date totals for the year will be set to zero, so that you can resume invoicing the charges in the new year. Lastly, it will reset to zero the number in the Total Days to Pay and Total Invoices Paid fields in customer and national account activity statistics.

Before you start the year-end processing, print and post all open batches, print posting journals and clear history, print customer statements and analytical reports, and then back up the data files.

❑ Open: the **Periodic Processing** window

❑ DClick: the **Year End** icon Year End

The Year End dialog box will appear as shown in Figure 22-20.

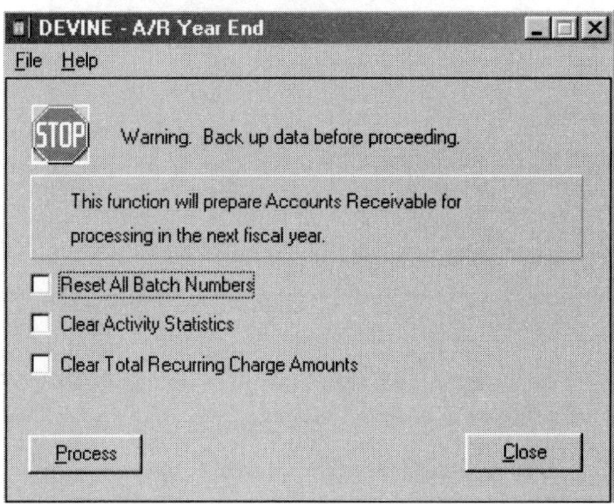

FIGURE 22-20
Year End Dialog Box

Reset All Batch Numbers

WARNING

This function is used only once each year. You must not run this function twice, or you will reset the customer statistics to zero for both the current year and the previous year.

The Reset All Batch Numbers option will reset the batch numbers for all types of batches to 1.

If you select this option, you will not be able to drill down to these batches from the General Ledger, view them from the Batch List windows, or reprint invoices or deposit slips for these batches, so you should ensure that you have a printed copy of all your documents properly filed so the information can be referenced at a later time.

Clear Activity Statistics

The Clear Activity Statistics option resets the current-year fields on the Activity Statistics pages in the Customers and National Accounts notebooks to zero, and transfers current-year statistical information to the corresponding fields for the prior year. When you select this option, the Clear Invoices Paid and Days to Pay Counter appears.

Clear Total Recurring Charge Amount

This option is used to set the amount in the Amount Invoices To Date field in all the recurring-charge records to zero. It should only be used if all recurring charge amounts are set up on a fiscal year basis.

Clear Invoices Paid and Days to Pay Counter

This option only appears if you have activated the Clear Activity Statistics check box. It is used if you want to enter zero in the Invoices Paid and Days to Pay fields on the Activity Statistics page in the Customers and National Accounts notebooks. Do not select this option if you want to include prior-year documents in the numbers you use to calculate the entry in the Average Days to Pay field for the account. You cannot clear these figures if you do not also clear the other activity statistics.

Devine Designs Inc. will not complete year-end processing at this time.

- ❑ Click: **Close** [Close]
- ❑ Exit: **ACCPAC**

REVIEW QUESTIONS

1. What is the purpose for creating recurring charges?
2. Can you create a recurring charge invoice for customers that have reached their maximum credit limit?
3. What two routes can be used to print invoices?
4. What is the purpose of the Accounts Receivable Aged Trial Balance?
5. What is the purpose of year-end processing?

EXERCISE

- ❑ Sign on to your company (EXERCO) as the system administrator.
- ❑ Enter 053110 in the Session Date box.

1. Create a Recurring Charges batch based on the recurring charge you set up in Chapter 20.
2. Print the Batch Listing.

3. Print the Recurring Charge invoice.
4. Set the Recurring Charge batch Ready to Post, post it, and print the posting journal.
5. Print the Customer statements.
6. Print the Customer Transactions report.
    a) Select invoice, credit note, and prepayment Transaction Types.
    b) Report Type; by document number.
    c) Include the Contact/Phone/Credit information.
    d) Include applied details.
7. Print the Aged Trial Balance.
   Tailor the Aged Trial Balance to meet your own needs.
8. Exit ACCPAC.

CASE 3

Murphballs & Co. Accounts Receivable

This case continues from the General Ledger, Bank, and Tax Services cases presented earlier in the text. After Murphballs & Co.'s first month of operations, Ruff Tuff McDuff decided to add the ACCPAC for Windows Small Business Series Accounts Receivable module to the computerized accounting system. The Accounts Payable module will be added later.

After completing this case, organize and submit Murphballs & Co.'s printouts. Each printout *must* contain your initials followed by the company name. If you are given no instructions regarding a field, leave the defaults unchanged.

Sign on to Murphballs & Co. as the system administrator using August 31, 2010 as the Session Date.

Follow the steps and procedures in the Accounts Receivable chapters to complete the required tasks.

ACTIVATE ACCOUNTS RECEIVABLE

- ❑ Activate: **Accounts Receivable 4.1A**

1. CREATE THE FOLLOWING A/R OPTIONS

SETUP OPTIONS

Contact Name:	Your own name
Process Recurring Charges:	Select
Force Listing of All Batches:	Select
Allow Edit of Imported Batches:	De-select
Keep History:	Select
Allow Edit of Statistics:	De-select
Include Tax in Statistics:	De-select
Keep Item Statistics:	De-select
Keep Salesperson Statistics:	De-select

INVOICING OPTIONS

Use Item Comment as Default:	De-select
Show Item Cost:	De-select
Allow Printing of Invoices:	Select
Allow Edit of Printed Invoices:	Select

RECEIPT OPTIONS

Default Receipt Type:	CHECK
Default Bank Code:	BBB – Buried Bone Bank
Allow Printing of Deposit Slips:	Select
Allow Edit After Deposit Slip Printed:	De-select
Force Printing of Deposit Slips:	De-select
Allow Adjustments in Receipt Batches:	Select
Default Order of Open Documents:	Document Number

Statement Processing Options

Accept the default aging periods of 1–30, 31–60, and 61–90.

Dunning Messages

The default dunning messages require no changes.

Print Zero-Balance Statements:	Select
Age Credit Notes and Debit Notes:	By Date
Age Unapplied Cash and Prepayments:	By Date

Customer Optional Fields

No changes are necessary on this page. Leave the defaults unchanged.

Integration Options

Create G/L Transactions:	During Posting
Append G/L Transactions to Existing Batch:	Select
Consolidate G/L Batches:	Do Not Consolidate
G/L Reference Field:	Customer Number
G/L Description Field:	Document Number

❑ Print: the A/R Options report

2. Add the Following Records

Add the Account Sets

Account Set Code:	1
Description:	Accounts Receivable - General
Receivables Control:	1201
Receipt Discounts:	4115
Prepayment Liability:	2115
Write-Offs:	6010

❑ Print: the A/R Account Sets report

Add Billing Cycle Codes

Billing Code Cycle:	MONTH
Description:	Monthly Billing
Frequency:	30 Days
Remit To:	Attn: Sweetums Poodle
Address:	Enter Murphballs & Co.'s name and address.

❑ Print: the A/R Billing Cycle Report

Add Distribution Codes

1.

Distribution Code:	SALES
Description:	Ball Reclamation Services
Revenue:	4101/10
Inventory:	1450
Cost of Goods Sold:	5000

2.

Distribution Code:	OTHER
Description:	Other Income
Revenue:	4110/10
Inventory:	1450
Cost of Goods Sold:	5000

❑ Print: the A/R Distribution Codes report

Add Interest Profiles

Interest Profile Code:	NORMAL
Description:	5% for overdue accounts
Interest Income Account:	6500
Calculate Interest By:	Document
Days Overdue:	30
Round up to Minimum:	De-select
Compound Interest:	De-select
Minimum Interest Charge:	Leave blank
Annual Interest Rate:	.05

❑ Print: the Interest Profiles report

Add Receipt Types

1.

Receipt Type Code:	CHECK
Description:	Payment by Check
Payment Method:	Check

2.

Receipt Type Code:	CASH
Description:	Cash Sales
Payment Method:	Cash

❑ Print: the Receipt Types report

Add Terms

There are two Terms codes.

1.

Terms Code:	DISC
Description:	2/10, n/30
Calculate Base for Discount With Tax field:	Excluded
Due Date Type:	Days From Invoice Date
Discount Type:	Days From Invoice Date

2.

Terms Code:	CASH
Description:	Cash Sales
Calculate Base for Discount With Tax field:	Excluded
Due Date Type:	Days From Invoice Date
Discount Type:	Days From Invoice Date

Cash sales are due within 1 day.

Murphballs & Co. will not have a multiple payment schedule.

❑ Print: the Terms report

Creating Customer Accounts

Murphballs has a total of five customers: the two found in the General Ledger case plus another three that have recently applied for credit. The full profiles for all five customers follow. All of the customers will be open accounts.

Adding Customer Groups

All of the customers belong to the same Customer Group. Add the following Customer Group.

Group Code:	DOD
Description:	Domesticated Dogs
Account Type:	Open Item
Account Set:	1
Terms Code:	DISC
Billing Cycle:	MONTH
Interest Profile:	NORMAL
Allow Edit of Credit Limit:	Select
Credit Limit Amount:	2000.00

❑ Print: the A/R Customer Groups report

Add Customer Accounts

Create the following customer accounts.

a)

Customer Number:	1010
Name:	Bobbytomlack
Group Code:	DOM
On Hold:	De-select
Inactive:	De-select
Short Name:	Bobbytom
Address:	1 Dog Days Street
	Muttsville Junction
	BOW WOW
Telephone:	555-555-4629
Fax:	555-555-4628
Contact:	Bobbytomlack
Start Date:	07/13/2010
Territory Code:	ON
Print Statements:	Activate
Billing Cycle:	MONTH
Interest Profile:	NORMAL
Terms Code:	DISC
Tax Group:	BALLCH
Tax Data Table:	1 – Taxable (create registration numbers)
Credit Limit:	2000

b) Customer Number: 1610
   Name: Hezaplasher
   Group Code: DOD
   On Hold: De-select
   Inactive: De-select
   Short Name: Hezaplash
   Address: 24 Doggy Gone Way
   Muttsville Junction
   BOW WOW
   Telephone: 555-555-9806
   Fax: 555-555-9804
   Contact: Hezaplasher
   Start Date: 07/23/2010
   Territory Code: ON
   Print Statements: Activate
   Billing Cycle: MONTH
   Interest Profile: NORMAL
   Terms Code: DISC
   Tax Group: BALLCH
   Tax Data Table: 1 – Taxable (create registration numbers)
   Credit Limit: 2500

c) Customer Number: 1650
   Name: Hipnscrappy
   Group Code: DOD
   On Hold: De-select
   Inactive: De-select
   Short Name: Hipnscra
   Address: 17 No Leash Way
   Muttsville Junction
   BOW WOW
   Telephone: 555-555-0264
   Fax: 555-555-8264
   Contact: Hipnscrappy
   Start Date: 07/31/2010
   Territory Code: ON
   Print Statements: Activate
   Billing Cycle: MONTH
   Interest Profile: NORMAL
   Terms Code: DISC
   Tax Group: BALLCH
   Tax Data Table: 1 – Taxable (create registration numbers)
   Credit Limit: 2000

d) Customer Number: 1810
Name: Rookapooka
Group Code: DOD
On Hold: De-select
Inactive: De-select
Short Name: Rookapoo
Address: Old Dog Pound
Muttsville Junction
BOW WOW
Telephone: 555-555-1362
Fax: 555-555-1361
Contact: Rookapooka
Start Date: 07/31/2010
Territory Code: ON
Print Statements: Activate
Billing Cycle: MONTH
Interest Profile: NORMAL
Terms Code: DISC
Tax Group: BALLCH
Tax Data Table: 1 – Taxable (create registration numbers) 67890D
Credit Limit: 2000

e) Customer Number: 1910
Name: Tarquinius
Group Code: DOD
On Hold: De-select
Inactive: De-select
Short Name: Tarquinius
Address: The Roots Under
The Big Maple Tree
Muttsville Junction
BOW WOW
Telephone: 555-555-0897
Fax: 555-555-0896
Contact: Tarquinius
Start Date: 07/31/2010
Territory Code: ON
Print Statements: Activate
Billing Cycle: MONTH
Interest Profile: NORMAL
Terms Code: DISC
Tax Group: BALLCH
Tax Data Table: 1 – Taxable (create registration numbers) 56789E
Credit Limit: 2000

❑ Print: the Customer List. Include both the address and profile.

3. Enter the Following August 2010 Invoice Transactions

Create a new batch for the following invoices. Give the document header an appropriate description. The Detail Type should be set to **Summary** in the document header. Enter the following invoices. Make sure that the RST is not calculated to include the GST as part of the invoice amount. Since you are now using the Accounts Receivable module, Ruff Tuff McDuff has decided to allow the program to assign the invoice numbers.

❑ Exit, and restart the company using August 31, 2010 as the session date.

1. August 5: Bobbytomlack purchased ball-chasing services on credit for $175 plus sales taxes, P.O. number BTL-1. You will charge 7% GST and 8% RST
2. August 7: Hezaplasher purchased ball-chasing services for $200 plus sales taxes, P.O. number Heza002.
3. August 14: Rookapooka purchased ball-chasing services for $225 plus sales taxes, P.O. number Rookapoo-98.
4. August 17: Hipnscrappy purchased ball-chasing services for $150 plus sales taxes, P.O. number Hipster 8.
5. August 27: Tarquinius purchased ball-chasing services for $200 plus sales taxes, P.O. number Tar 7.
6. August 30: Bobbytomlack purchased ball-chasing services for $160 plus sales taxes, P.O. number BTL-2.

❑ Print: the invoice batch

❑ Post: the invoice batch

❑ Print: the Invoice Posting Journal sorted by Document Number

❑ Print: the Aged Trial Balance by Document Date

4. Enter the Following August 2010 Credit Note Transaction

Hezaplasher's family has decided to go for an extended vacation to the south seas and has taken him along. Because Hezaplasher will not be able to use the ball-chasing services, and because he is fervently hoping that the family will leave him there he has applied for and been allowed a credit note for the balance of the unused services he purchased.

❑ Create: a new batch for the August 20 credit note to Hezaplasher in the amount of $75 plus GST and RST

- [x] Print: the new batch listing
- [x] Post: the batch
- [x] Print: the Posting Journal
- [x] Print: the Aged Trial Balance

5. Enter the Following August 2010 Cash Receipts

- [ ] Create: a new batch and enter the following cash receipts
  1. August 12: Check number 284 from Bobbytomlack in the amount of $197.75.
  2. August 25: Check number 1098 from Hipnscrappy in the amount of $169.50.
  3. August 30: Check number 472 from Hezaplasher in the amount of $140.87 for the invoice less the credit note.
- [x] Print: the Receipt Batch listing
- [x] Print: the Status Report for the Receipt batch
- [x] Print: the Deposit Slips
- [x] Post: the Receipt Batch
- [x] Print: the Posting Journal sorted by Customer Number

6. Periodic Processing

- [x] Print: the Customer Statements for August. Include the paid transactions.
- [x] Print: the Customer Transactions report
- [x] Print: the Accounts Receivable Aged Trial Balance. Include customers with a zero balance and include paid transactions.
- [x] Print: the Batch Status report for all invoice and receipt batches
- [ ] Post: the Accounts Receivable transactions to the General Ledger
- [ ] Print: the General Ledger G/L Transactions Listing sorted by Account Number

UNIT 6

Accounts Payable

CHAPTER 23

SETTING UP ACCOUNTS PAYABLE

In Unit 6, you will add the Accounts Payable module for Devine Designs Inc. Devine Designs Inc. is already using the ACCPAC System Manager, General Ledger and Accounts Receivable modules and has now decided to add the Accounts Payable. Each chapter will guide you through one step in setting up and operating the ACCPAC Accounts Payable module.

If you have not completed Unit 2 - System Manager, Unit 3 - General Ledger, and Unit 4 - Bank and Tax Services: do so now.

INSTALLING ACCOUNTS PAYABLE

WARNING

You must have an Activation Code to complete installation of the system manager. If you do not, complete the form at www.accpac.com/products/accpac.com/support/activation_codes

In this section, you will install the ACCPAC Accounts Payable. This procedure is very similar to that used in Chapter 2 to install the System Manager and General Ledger, and Chapter 16 to install the Accounts Receivable.

If you are installing the Accounts Payable on a network, refer to the System Manager Administrator Guide and ask your network manager for help.

❑ Display the Windows Desktop on your screen.

❑ DClick: the **My Computer** icon 

- ❑ DClick: the **Control Panel** icon [Control Panel] in the My Computer window
- ❑ DClick: the **Add/Remove Programs** icon in the Control Panel

The upper portion of the Install/Uninstall page is used to install programs. As a program is installed, Windows 95/98 will monitor the installation and save the information necessary for removing the program. The lower portion of the page is used to uninstall or remove programs.

- ❑ Click: **Install** [Install...]

The Install Program window reminds you to insert the first installation floppy disk or CD-ROM.

- ❑ Insert the ACCPAC for Windows Small Business Series Accounts Payable CD-ROM.
- ❑ Click: **Next** [Next >]

Windows 95/98 will scan the root directory of your disk drives for a setup program. It will not identify the setup.exe file in ACCPAC folder on your CD-ROM so you will have to enter the information manually.

ACCPAC will load the installation software and then display a series of dialogue boxes that enable you to enter the information required for the installation of the Accounts Payable. When the ACCPAC for Windows Installation window appears:

- ❑ Click: **Install ACCPAC (32-bit)**

The Welcome window will remind you to close all other Windows programs before running the Accounts Payable Setup program. If necessary click Cancel, exit any other Windows programs and then start installation over again.

- ❑ Click: **Next** [Next >]

The next window displayed contains a copy of the licensing agreement for installing and using ACCPAC. Use the scroll bar to view the whole agreement.

- ❑ Click: **Yes** [Yes] to accept the terms of the license agreement
- ❑ Select: the radio button for **I have an activation code**
- ❑ Click: **Next** [Next >] to display the second Activation window

You must fill in the text boxes with the exact information supplied by ACCPAC International in response to your activation code request. The name and company text boxes will display the information that you entered as you installed the System Manager.

TIP

Staple a copy of the activation information received from ACCPAC International on the first page of each of the Accounts Payable manuals.

- ❑ Type: the **name of the software vendor** in the Dealer text box
- ❑ Press: **Tab** [Tab]
- ❑ Type: the **name of the qualified installer** in the QI text box
- ❑ Press: **Tab** [Tab]
- ❑ Type: the **Product ID number** in the Product ID/Serial # text box
- ❑ Press: **Tab** [Tab]
- ❑ Type: the **Activation Code** in the Activation Code text box

As you enter the Activation Code, the Next button will become active. Check that you have entered the information exactly as on the form you received from ACCPAC International.

❑ Click: **Next** [Next >]

The Select Components window allows you to select the components of Accounts Payable to be installed. The selected components are indicated by a check mark in the box to the left of the component name. The hard drive storage space required for each component is shown at the right. The directory where the program files will be stored is shown at the bottom of the screen.

WARNING

If you are installing the Accounts Payable in a networked environment, ask the network manager for the proper location for installing the Accounts Payable.

❑ Select: **Accounts Payable Files**

❑ Click: **Next** [Next >]

The Select Program Folder window adds Program icons to the Program folder.

❑ Select: **ACCPAC 32-Bit**

❑ Click: **Next** [Next >]

Before copying files to your hard drive, ACCPAC displays the Start Copying Files dialog box, shown in Figure 23-1.

FIGURE 23-1 Start Copying Files Window

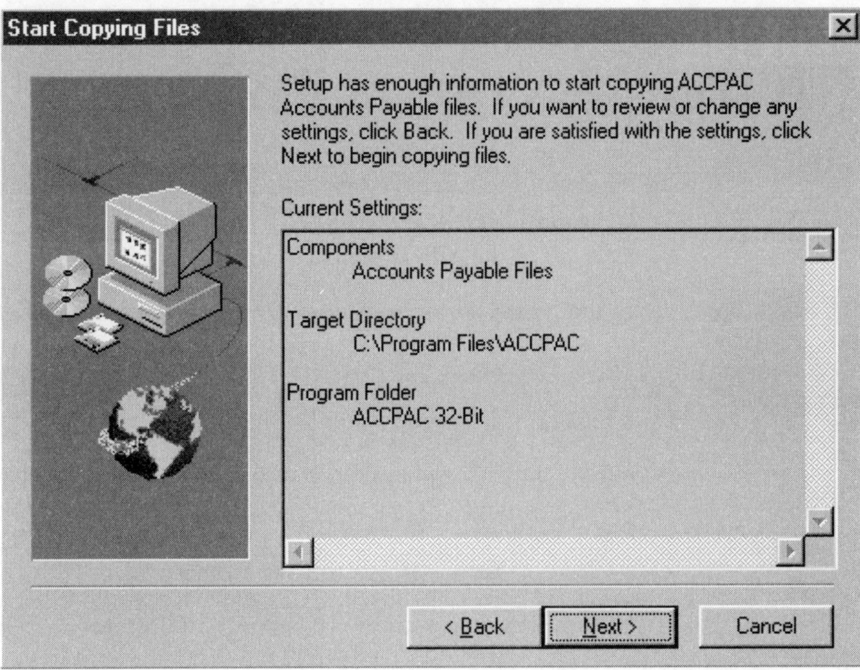

WARNING

If you are installing on a network, confirm these settings with your network manager.

Carefully review the components to be installed and the directories to be used. The target directory should be C:\Program Files\ACCPAC and the program folder should be ACCPAC 32-Bit.

❑ Click: **Next** [Next >]

Print the README file and tape a copy of it in your manual. A second copy of the printout can be cut up and taped to the related pages in your manuals.

After all the Accounts Payable files have been copied, ACCPAC will inquire if you want to view the Accounts Payable README file. To inform users of changes that have not yet been added to their printed manuals, most software manufactures include README files on disk. Whenever you install a new or upgraded software package, you should print and read the README file. You should then complete any additional installation steps as described. The README file contains information that is not included in the manual, or has information that has changed since the manual was printed. It is advisable to print the file, then make the necessary changes in the manual.

❑ Click: **Finish** [Finish] to view the Readme file in WordPad.

To print the information

❑ Click: the **Printer** icon
❑ Close: the **WordPad** window
❑ Close: the **ACCPAC 32-Bit** window
❑ Exit: the **ACCPAC for Windows Installation** window
❑ Close: the **Add/Remove Programs Properties** window
❑ Close: the **Control Panel** window
❑ Remove: the ACCPAC CD from the disk drive and store it in a safe place

ACTIVATING ACCOUNTS PAYABLE

❑ Sign-on to Devine Designs Inc. as the system administrator using 05/01/10 as the Session Date.
❑ Open: the **Administrative Services** window

Close all other program windows for the company before activating the data.

Only the system administrator is allowed to activate data files.

❑ DClick: the **Data Activation** icon [Data Activation]

A warning message will appear, cautioning you to make a back-up of your data files before continuing.

❑ Click: **Yes** [Yes] to continue activation

The Data Activation window will appear as displayed in Figure 23-2.

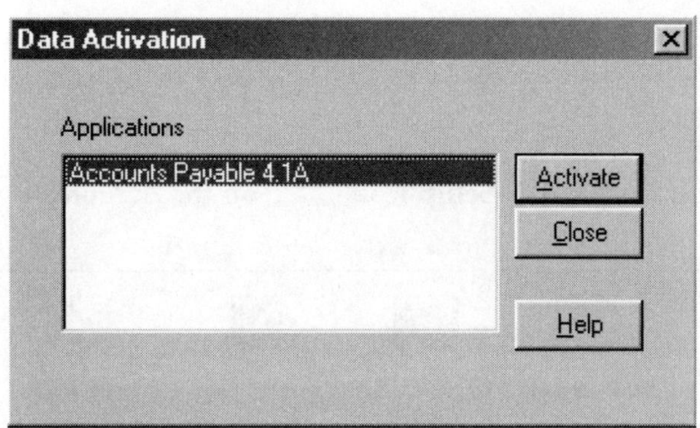

FIGURE 23-2
Data Activation Window

❑ Select: **Accounts Payable 4.1A**

❑ Click: **Activate** [Activate]

WARNING
Do not select Convert Accounts Payable Data.

A warning screen will appear, requiring you to confirm that you want to activate Accounts Payable for this company and to Add Accounts Payable Programs to the ACC-PAC for Windows desktop.

❑ Click: **Proceed** [Proceed]

Once the activation is complete

❑ Click: **Close** [Close] to return to the Administrative Services window

The Accounts Payable icon is now displayed as a reduced title bar on the left side of the Company Desktop, indicating that the Accounts Payable has been activated.

❑ Open: the **Accounts Payable** window

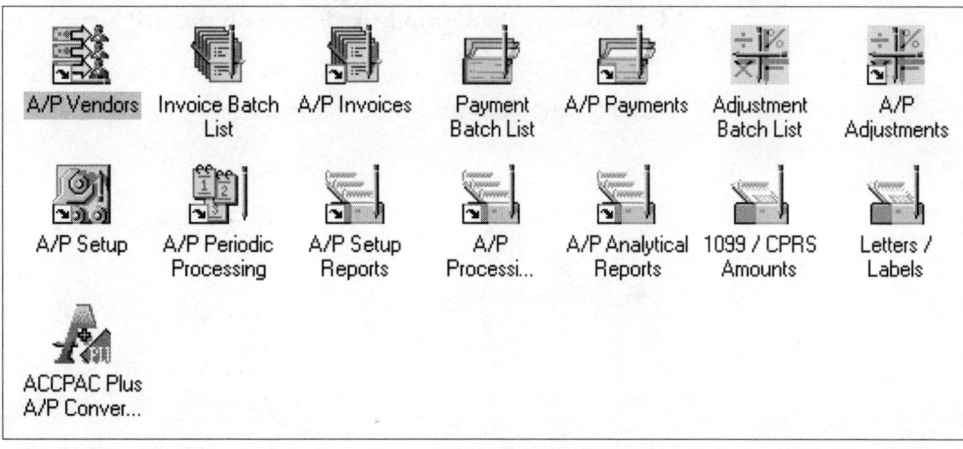

FIGURE 23-3
Accounts Payable Icons

You will use most of the icons in this window (Figure 23-3) as you work through Accounts Payable. The last icon, ACCPAC Plus A/P Conversion, would be used if you were converting Accounts Payable data files from a DOS version of ACCPAC. As you work through the rest of this chapter, you will use the Setup and Setup Reports icons.

SETUP

❑ DClick: the **A/P Setup** icon on the Accounts Payable window

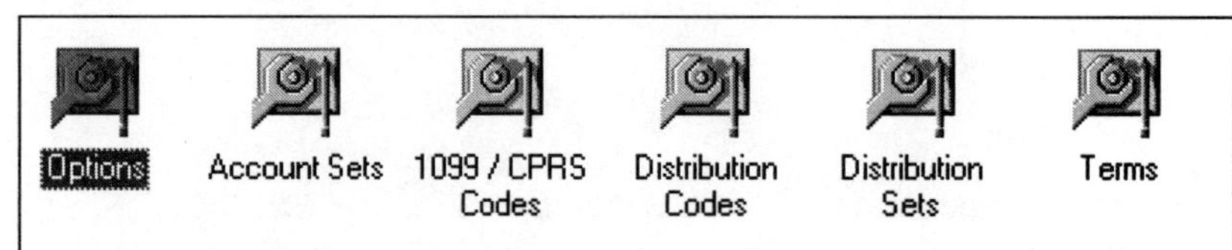

FIGURE 23-4
A/P Setup Icons

There are six icons on the A/P Setup window (Figure 23-4). It looks complicated, but each icon represents information that ACCPAC needs to properly operate the Accounts Payable for a company. Using the Devine Designs Inc. simulation, you will see how to enter this seemingly complex information. You will use each icon as you set up the Accounts Payable for Devine Designs Inc.

OPTIONS

The first step is to use the Options notebook to choose the options that tell ACCPAC Accounts Payable how to operate, how information is transferred to the General Ledger, and the type of data it accepts and displays.

❑ DClick: the **Options** icon on the A/P Setup window

The Setup Options notebook consists of six pages as indicated by the tabs at the bottom of the notebook as shown in Figure 23-5.

Figure 23-5
Company Options Page

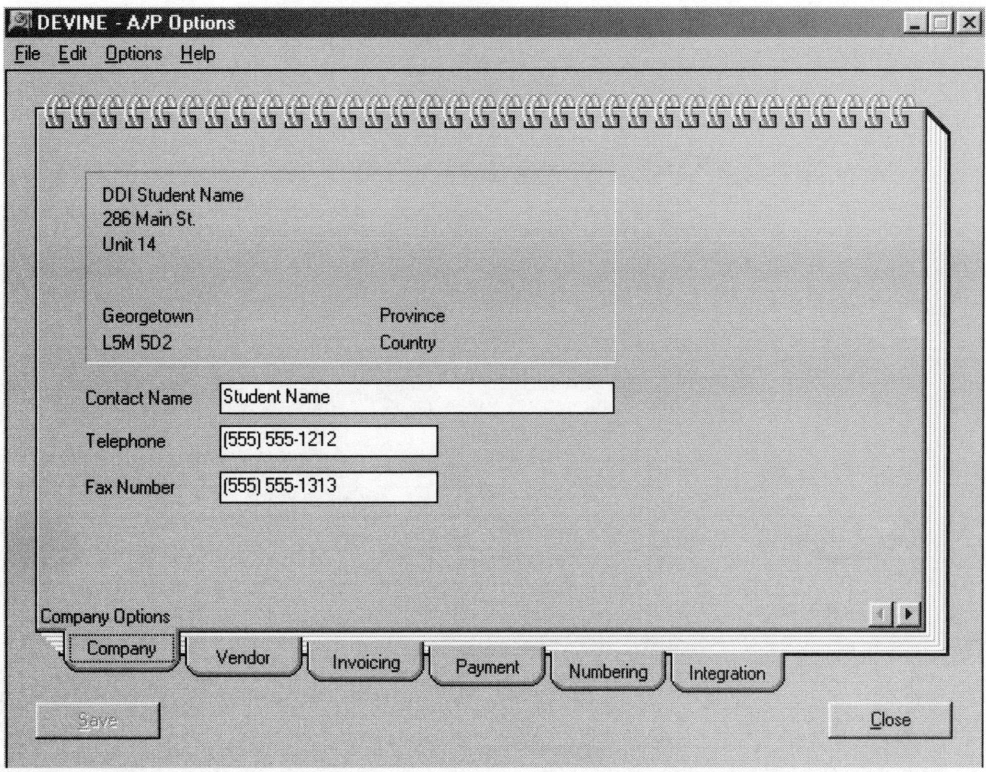

Company Options

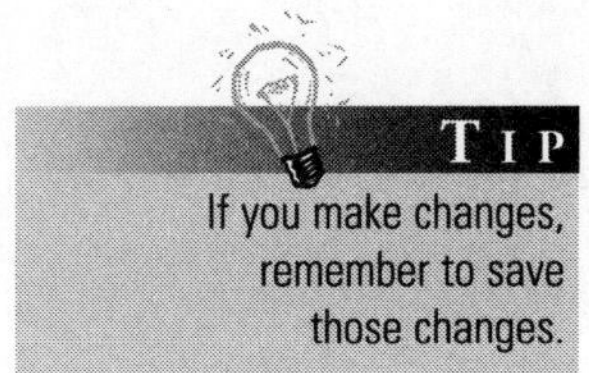

If you make changes, remember to save those changes.

The Company Options page of the A/P Options notebook, as displayed in Figure 23-5, displays information from the Company Profile window in Common Services. The information displayed in the upper area can only be changed through Common Services. You can enter a separate contact name, telephone number and fax number on this page for your Accounts Payable database. For Devine Designs Inc., no changes are necessary.

Vendor Options

❑ Click: the **Vendor** tab at the bottom of the A/P Options notebook

The Vendor Options Page shown in Figure 23-6 has five different sections.

FIGURE 23-6
Vendor Options Page

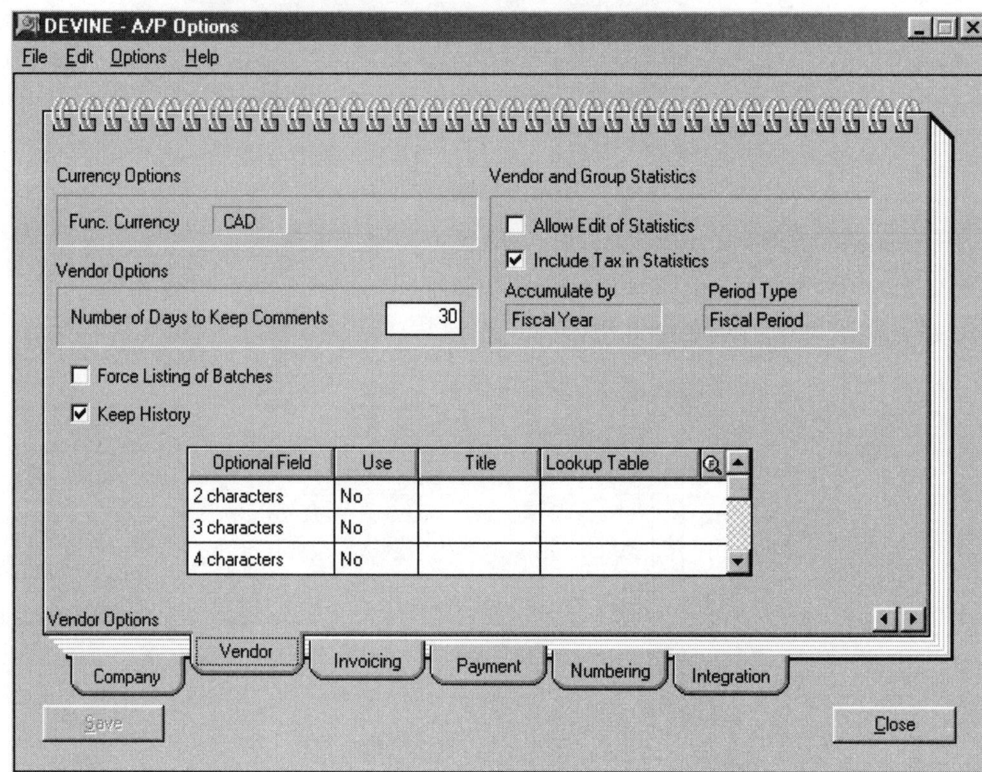

Currency Options

The Currency Options section of the Vendor Options page displays the functional currency selected when the system database was created. The functional currency cannot be changed in Accounts Payable.

Vendor Options

The Vendor Options section allows you to specify the default number of days for which you want to keep comments that have been entered in vendor records.

❑ Press: **Tab** to accept the 30-day default

Force Listing of Batches

Selecting the Force Listing of Batches option requires you to print a listing for each batch and correct any errors reported on the listing before you post the batch. When this option is activated, you must reprint the batch listing each time you make changes to a batch. Devine Designs Inc. will select this option as the printed batches will be part of its audit trail.

❑ Select: **Force Listing of Batches**

Keep History

When you activate this option, the program will store the details of all posted transactions in your company database. This option can be turned on or off at any time.

❑ Activate: **Keep History**

Vendor and Group Statistics

ACCPAC Accounts Payable accumulates statistics from the transactions you post to vendor accounts.

The **Allow Edit of Statistics** option allows you edit the year-to-date and last-year purchases, payments, discounts taken, interest charges, and debit notes, as well as total days to pay and total paid invoices for a vendor account. As Devine Designs Inc. is just starting its second fiscal year, the option will not be selected.

❑ De-select: the **Allow Edit of Statistics** check box

Selecting the **Include Tax in Statistics** option allows you to include tax amounts in purchase totals that are kept with the year-to-date and the last-year statistics for each vendor. Devine Designs Inc. wishes to keep statistics that do not reflect changes in government tax policy, so this option will not be selected.

❑ De-select: the **Include Tax in Statistics** check box

Accumulate By

The **Accumulate By** list box indicates whether you report statistics by calendar or fiscal year. If you chose to accumulate by Calendar Year, the starting date for statistics will be January 1. If you chose to accumulate by fiscal year, the starting date will be the first day of your fiscal year as specified in the fiscal calendar in Common Services. Devine Designs Inc. reports statistics by Fiscal Year.

The **Period Type** list box indicates the period for which statistics will be reported. Normally you would change this option only at the beginning of a fiscal year. Devine Designs Inc. reports statistics by Fiscal Period for consistency with other reports.

Optional Fields

You use this section to add up to eight fields containing specific information that your company may require on vendors. For example, you can add a text field to contain a service contract number, the name of your account representative, an expiration date, a deductible amount, or a lease type. Devine Designs Inc. will not use optional fields on customer invoices.

❑ Do not change any of the entries in the Use column from No to Yes.

❑ Click: **Save** Save

INVOICING OPTIONS

❑ Click: the **Invoicing** tab at the bottom of the A/P Options notebook

The Invoicing Options page (Figure 23-7) has three input sections.

FIGURE 23-7
Invoicing Options Page

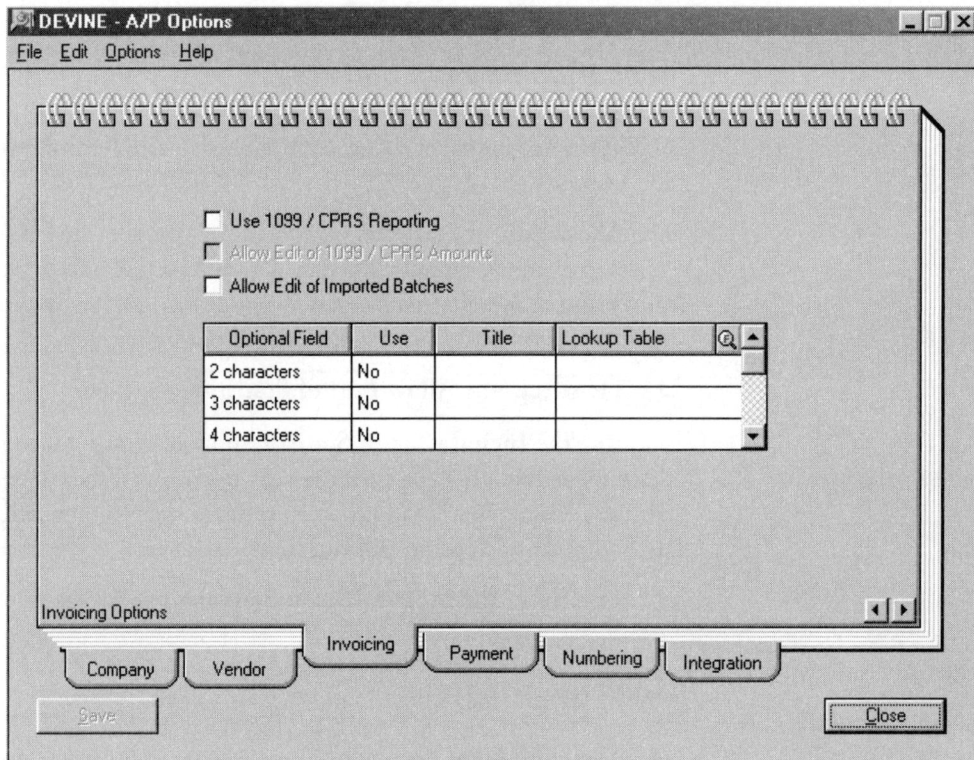

1099/CPRS Reporting

This option is used in the United States, where companies must report payments to vendors subject to 1099 reporting. Even if your company does not produce 1099 forms, you can use this option to accumulate payments to vendors during selected periods.

❑ Click: the **Use 1099/CPRS Reporting** check box to activate it

Allow Edit of Imported Batches

This option allows you to make changes to batches retrieved from other ACCPAC Small Business for Windows modules or imported from another program.

❑ De-select: **Allow Edit of Imported Batches**

Optional Fields

You can use as many as eight fields from the list. Ensure that you select fields with appropriate lengths for the data you want to record. You use the Vendor Options page in the Options notebook to define the Optional fields. Devine Designs Inc. will not use the optional fields.

- ❑ Do not change any of the entries in the Use column from No to Yes.
- ❑ Click: **Save** Save

PAYMENT PROCESSING OPTIONS

- ❑ Click: the **Payment** tab at the bottom of the A/P Options notebook

The Payment and Aging Options page appears as displayed in Figure 23-8.

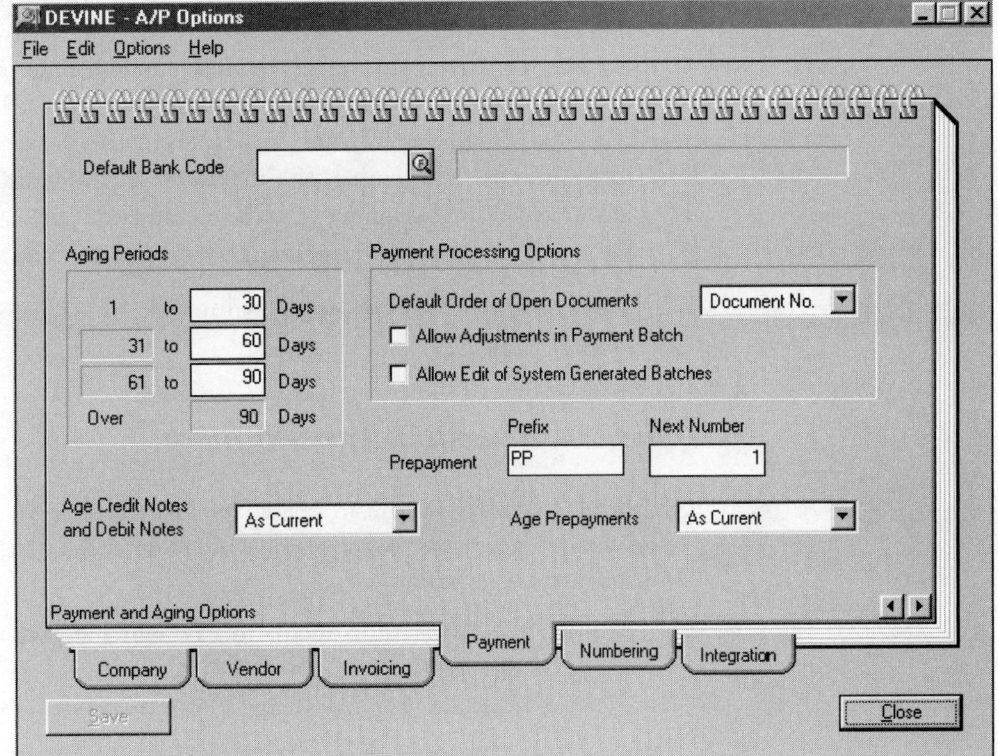

FIGURE 23-8 Payment and Aging Options Page

Default Bank Code

This field is used to select the code for the bank account that you normally use when you write checks. You must use one of the bank codes defined in the Bank Services window in Common Services.

❑ Click: the **Finder** for the Default Bank Code text box
❑ Select: **1STBK**

Default Aging Periods

ACCPAC Accounts Payable sorts outstanding items and balances for the Aged Trial Balance and Overdue Payables reports by the number of days entered in these fields. The default days are fairly standard, so Devine Designs Inc. has decided not to change them.

Default Order of Open Documents

You can select the order in which the documents (invoices, debit notes, and credit notes) are listed when you apply cash, checks, or other payments to vendor accounts. Open documents may be listed by:

- Document Number; beginning with the lowest document number for each transaction type.
- PO Number; listing documents by their purchase order numbers, beginning with the lowest purchase order number and earliest document.
- Due Date; beginning with the earliest due date.
- Sales Order No.; beginning with the lowest sales order number.
- Document Date; beginning with the oldest date.
- Balance Due; listing by outstanding balances, beginning with the smallest balance.

❑ Select: **Document No.** using the list tool
❑ Press: **Tab** Tab

Allow Adjustments in Payment Batch

Select this option if you want to be able to enter adjustments or write off small amounts when entering payments, rather than having to enter the transactions separately in the Adjustment Entry window.

❑ Activate: the **Allow Adjustments in Payment Batch** check box
❑ Press: **Tab** Tab

WARNING

If you edit check amounts, they will not match the pre-check register. The edit feature should be used only on an exception basis.

Allow Edit of System Generated Batches

Select this option if you want to be able to edit or delete payment batches after they have been generated. If this option is not selected, you cannot edit or delete checks, or delete a check batch.

❑ Press: **Tab** Tab to leave this option unselected

Assigning Numbers to Prepayments

It is fairly common in some industries to make payments in advance for goods or services to be provided at a later date. For example, a hotel might require a deposit for a function room for an office party in six months, or you might order an item from a vendor that would not normally be carried, so you require payment before ordering the goods.

ACCPAC Accounts Payable will automatically generate document numbers for prepayment transactions. Each of these numbers has a prefix of up to six characters to identify the transaction as a prepayment. The default prepayment prefix is PP.

You must specify the numbers that will be assigned to prepayments. Devine Designs Inc. has decided to leave the default Prefix and the next document number unchanged.

❑ Press: **Tab** [Tab] to leave the Prefix unchanged

Prepayment Next Number

The program will sequentially assign numbers to identify specific prepayment transactions. The number 1 is displayed as the default sequence number as the Accounts Payable module has yet to be used to generate prepayment transactions.

❑ Press: **Tab** [Tab] to leave the prepayment number unchanged

Age Credit Notes and Debit Notes

You may choose between two methods for aging credit and debit notes:

As Current: This includes unapplied credit notes and debit notes in the current aging period. The program will not use debit or credit notes in calculating the outstanding balances.

By Date: This includes each unapplied credit and debit note in the aging period.

❑ Select: **By Date** using the list tool

❑ Press: **Tab** [Tab]

Age Prepayments

Select the method you want to use to assign prepayments to aging categories:

As Current: This includes prepayment in the current aging period. The program will not include the transactions when calculating outstanding period balances.

By Date: This will include each unapplied cash payment and prepayments in the aging periods which contain their document dates.

❑ Select: **By Date** using the list tool

❑ Click: **Save** [Save]

Processing Sequence Number Page

❑ Click: the **Numbering** tab at the bottom of the A/P Options notebook

This screen displays the next batch numbers and posting sequence numbers. Since you have not entered any data into the system, all of the sequence number fields display "1".

Integration Options

❑ Click: the **Integration** tab at the bottom of the A/P Options notebook

The G/L Integration Options Page (Figure 23-9) has five option areas and one data display.

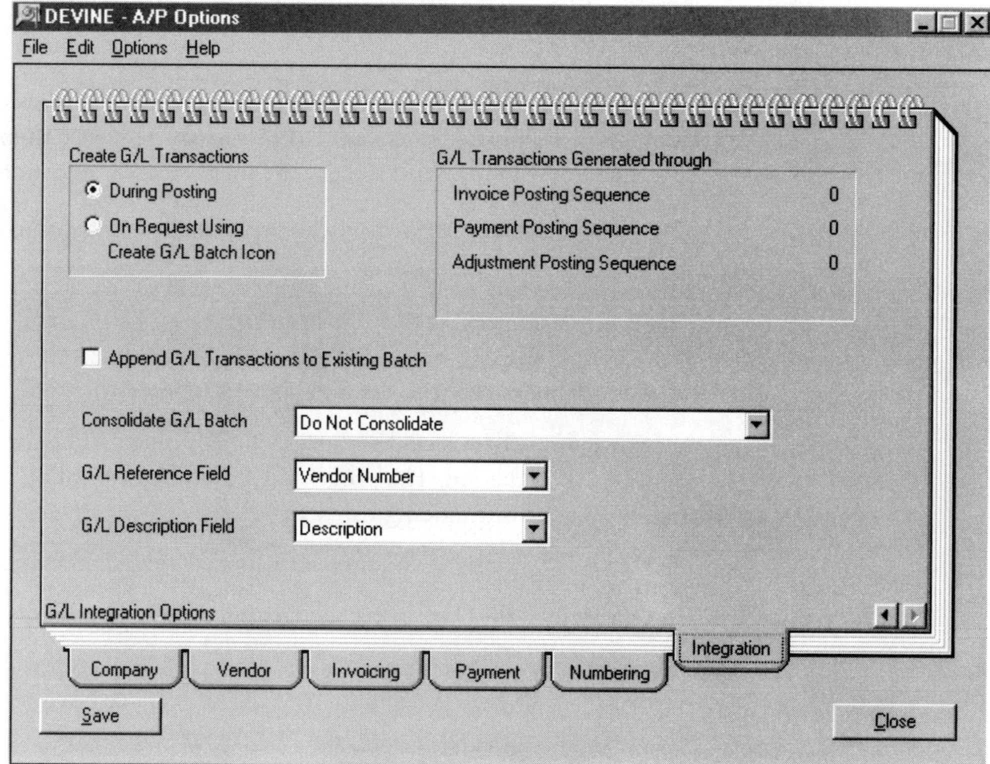

FIGURE 23-9 G/L Integration Options Page

G/L Transactions Generated Through

This data display is located in the upper right corner of the page. The three fields (Invoice Posting Sequence, Payment Posting Sequence, and Adjustment Posting Sequence) display the number of the last posting sequences used. As Devine Designs Inc. has not posted batches to Accounts Payable, these numbers display zeros.

Create G/L Transactions

If you select **During Posting**, ACCPAC will automatically create General Ledger transactions when transaction batches are posted to the Accounts Payable. If you select On Request Using Create G/L Batch Icon, the General Ledger transaction batch will be created when you use the Create G/L Batch window.

Devine Designs Inc. has decided to select the During Posting option.

❑ Select: the **During Posting** option button

Append G/L Transactions to Existing Batch

ACCPAC Accounts Payable automatically creates separate General Ledger batches for invoices, payments, and adjustments. Selecting this option allows new General Ledger transactions to be added to existing batches. You would not select this option if you want to create a new General Ledger batch each time you produce General Ledger transactions. Devine Designs Inc. will select this option.

❑ Select: the **Append G/L Transactions to Existing Batch** check box

Consolidate G/L Batches

You can choose to combine transaction details for the same General Ledger account into single lines for posting, or to send unconsolidated Accounts Payable transactions to the General Ledger.

If **Do Not Consolidate** is selected, the General Ledger transaction batch includes separate details for each invoice, credit note, debit note, payment, or adjustment posted to the Accounts Payable. When initially setting up Accounts Payable, it is recommended that you select this option, so that the G/L Transactions report provides complete details of all the transactions you enter. You can then check the posting report against the source documents to ensure that you have entered all transactions accurately. You can change this option later as you become more confident of entering transactions correctly.

The Consolidate G/L Batch option combines all details with the same account number and fiscal period into one detail, or combines all details with the same account number, fiscal period, and source code into one detail.

Devine Designs Inc. will not consolidate transaction information at this time.

❑ Select: **Do Not Consolidate** using the list tool

G/L Reference Field

When unconsolidated Accounts Payable transactions are retrieved by the General Ledger, transaction information is transferred to the G/L Reference field. The G/L Reference field allows you to select the information that you want to appear in the reference field for transactions when they are retrieved by the General Ledger.

Devine Designs Inc. will track these other transactions by Vendor Number.

❑ Select: **Vendor Number** using the list tool

G/L Description Field

The first part of the description field for unconsolidated transactions retrieved by the General Ledger consists of a posting sequence number, a batch number, and an entry number which are assigned by ACCPAC. This option allows you to control the information that appears in the Description field for transactions when they are retrieved by the General Ledger.

Devine Designs Inc. will select the document number.

❑ Select: **Document Number** using the list tool

❑ Click: **Save** Save

PRINTING THE A/P OPTIONS REPORT

Devine Designs Inc. will print a listing of the options chosen to document the setup of the Accounts Payable.

❑ Click: **File** on the A/P Options notebook's menu bar
❑ Click: **Print** on the File Menu
❑ Click: **Print** Print from the A/P Options Report
❑ Click: **OK** OK from the Print dialogue box
❑ Click: **Close** Close to close the A/P Options Report dialog box

Compare your printed report to that shown in Figure 23-10. Make any necessary corrections. Save the corrections and print the report again.

❑ Click: **Close** Close to close the A/P Options notebook
❑ Back up your data files.

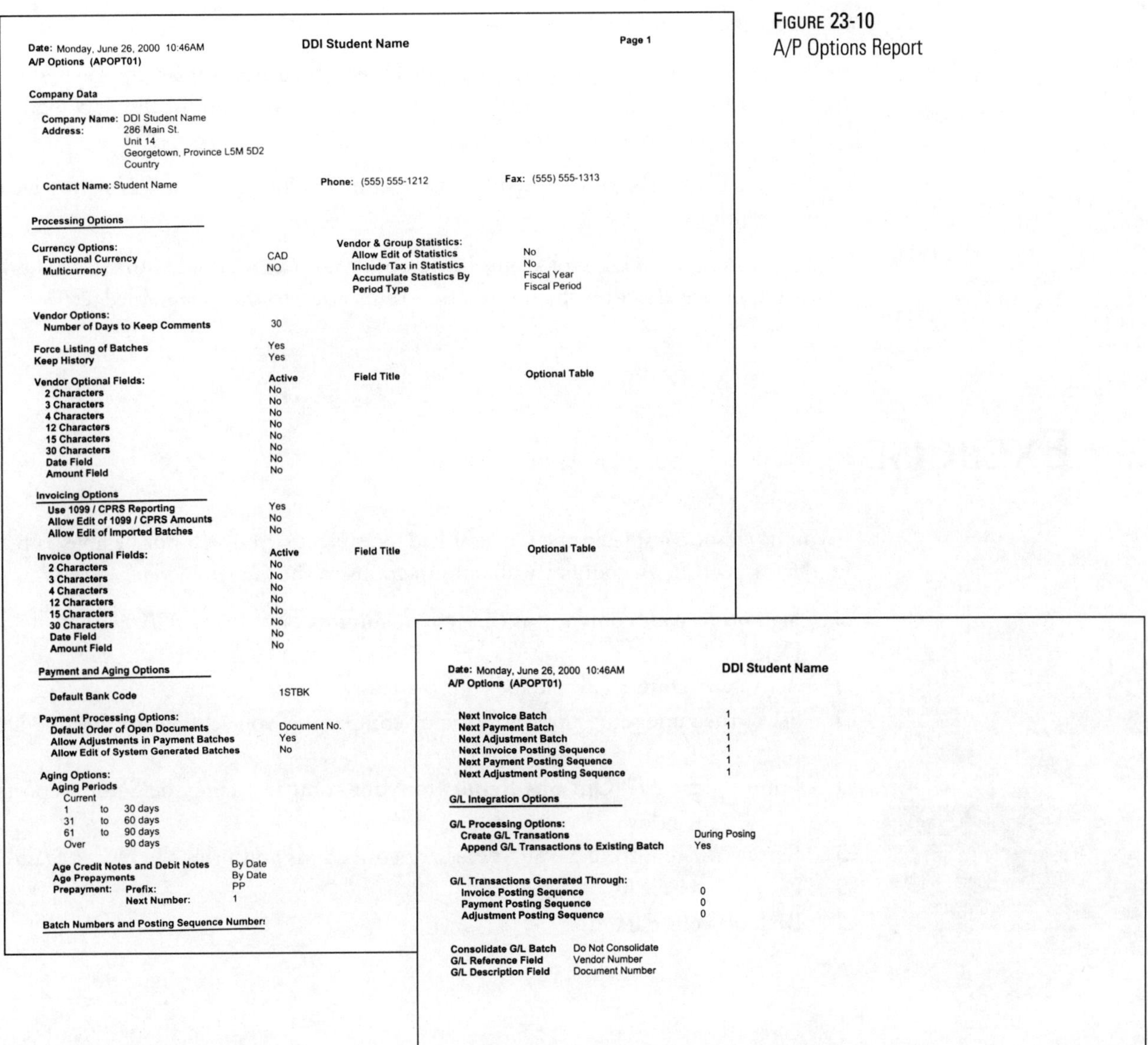

Date: Monday, June 26, 2000 10:46AM
A/P Options (APOPT01)

DDI Student Name

Page 1

Company Data

Company Name: DDI Student Name
Address: 286 Main St.
Unit 14
Georgetown, Province L5M 5D2
Country

Contact Name: Student Name
Phone: (555) 555-1212
Fax: (555) 555-1313

Processing Options

Currency Options:
Functional Currency CAD
Multicurrency NO

Vendor & Group Statistics:
Allow Edit of Statistics No
Include Tax in Statistics No
Accumulate Statistics By Fiscal Year
Period Type Fiscal Period

Vendor Options:
Number of Days to Keep Comments 30

Force Listing of Batches Yes
Keep History Yes

Vendor Optional Fields:	Active	Field Title	Optional Table
2 Characters	No		
3 Characters	No		
4 Characters	No		
12 Characters	No		
15 Characters	No		
30 Characters	No		
Date Field	No		
Amount Field	No		

Invoicing Options

Use 1099 / CPRS Reporting Yes
Allow Edit of 1099 / CPRS Amounts No
Allow Edit of Imported Batches No

Invoice Optional Fields:	Active	Field Title	Optional Table
2 Characters	No		
3 Characters	No		
4 Characters	No		
12 Characters	No		
15 Characters	No		
30 Characters	No		
Date Field	No		
Amount Field	No		

Payment and Aging Options

Default Bank Code 1STBK

Payment Processing Options:
Default Order of Open Documents Document No.
Allow Adjustments in Payment Batches Yes
Allow Edit of System Generated Batches No

Aging Options:
Aging Periods
Current
1 to 30 days
31 to 60 days
61 to 90 days
Over 90 days

Age Credit Notes and Debit Notes By Date
Age Prepayments By Date
Prepayment: Prefix: PP
Next Number: 1

Batch Numbers and Posting Sequence Numbers

Date: Monday, June 26, 2000 10:46AM
A/P Options (APOPT01)

DDI Student Name

Next Invoice Batch 1
Next Payment Batch 1
Next Adjustment Batch 1
Next Invoice Posting Sequence 1
Next Payment Posting Sequence 1
Next Adjustment Posting Sequence 1

G/L Integration Options

G/L Processing Options:
Create G/L Transations During Posing
Append G/L Transactions to Existing Batch Yes

G/L Transactions Generated Through:
Invoice Posting Sequence 0
Payment Posting Sequence 0
Adjustment Posting Sequence 0

Consolidate G/L Batch Do Not Consolidate
G/L Reference Field Vendor Number
G/L Description Field Document Number

FIGURE 23-10
A/P Options Report

REVIEW QUESTIONS

1. What is the purpose of the ACCPAC Plus A/P Conversion icon found on the Accounts Payable window?
2. Which window is used to access the Data Activation function?
3. When you access the Company Page of the A/P Options notebook, information about the company is already displayed. Where does this information come from?
4. What is the purpose of the **Allow Edit of Statistics** option that you would find on the Vendor Options page of the A/P Options notebook?

5. What is 1099/CPRS Reporting?
6. When you select the **Default Order of Open Documents** from the Payment and Aging Options page of the A/P Options notebook, you can list the documents by different choices. What are those choices?
7. What is the prefix for the prepayment documents found on the Payment page of the A/P Options notebook?
8. If you choose the Do Not Consolidate option to post your Accounts Payable, what would be the effect on the information transferred to the General ledger?

EXERCISE

If you have not completed the General Ledger exercises, you will not be able to use the Finder, or post the Accounts Payable transactions to the General ledger.

- ❑ Sign on to your company as the system administrator using 05/01/10 as the Session Date.
- ❑ Activate Accounts Payable for your company.
- ❑ Select the same setup options for your company as you selected for Devine Designs Inc.
- ❑ Print: the **A/P Options Report** for your company using the Setup Reports window
- ❑ Review the report, make any necessary corrections and print the report again.
- ❑ Exit: **ACCPAC**
- ❑ Back up your data files

Refer to your printed A/P Options Report for the information.

CHAPTER 24

COMPLETING ACCOUNTS PAYABLE SETUP

In Chapter 14, you set up the Bank Services for Accounts Receivable. You now have to modify the Bank Services for Accounts Payable. Then you will complete setting up the Accounts Payable.

❑ Sign on to Devine Designs Inc. as the system administrator using 05/01/10 as the Session Date.

You activated both the Bank and Tax Services earlier, so you do not have to activate them again.

BANK SERVICES

❑ Open: the **Common Services** window

❑ DClick: the **Bank Services** icon 

The Bank Services window contains four icons as shown in Figure 24-1.

FIGURE 24-1
Bank Services Icons

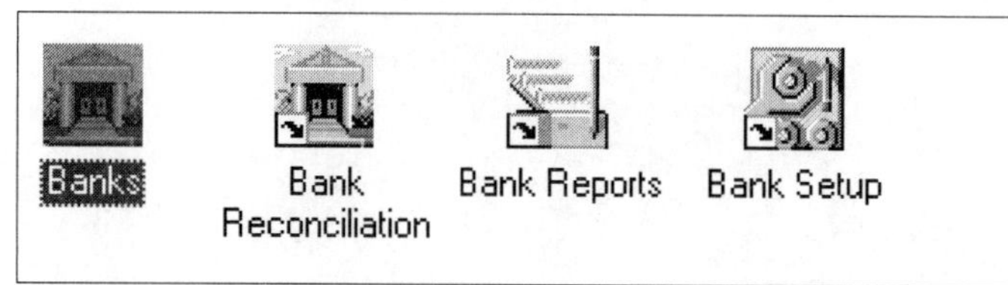

❑ DClick: the **Banks** icon [Banks] on the Bank Services window

The Banks window, shown in Figure 24-2, will appear.

FIGURE 24-2
Banks Window

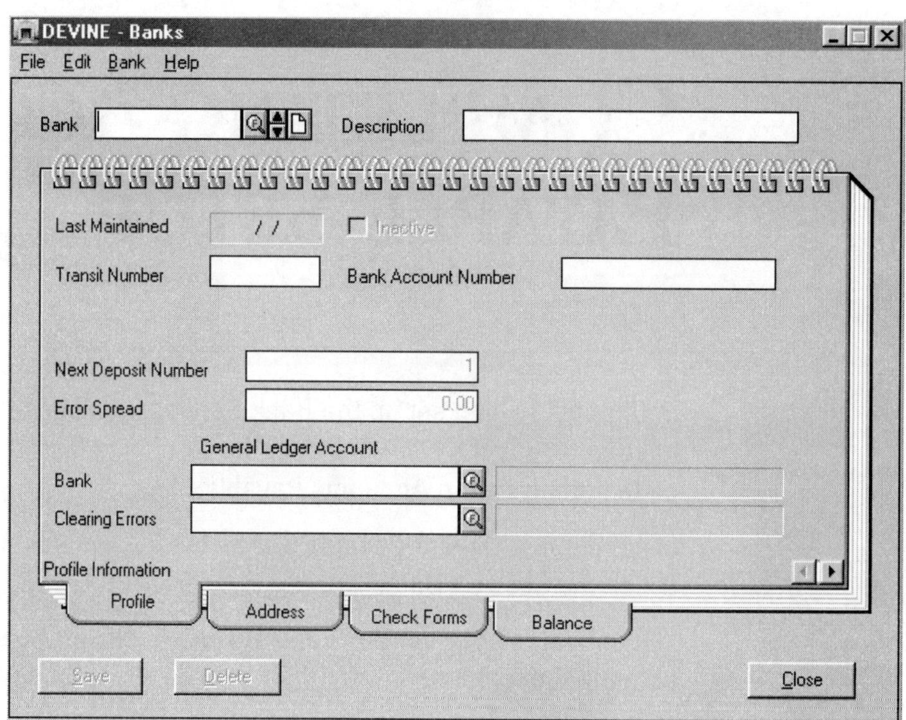

Banks Window

You have previously completed the Banking Profile, Address, and Balance pages, but you have not yet completed the Check Forms page.

❑ Click: the **Finder** for the Banks field at the top of the screen
❑ Select: **1STBK**
❑ Click: the **Check Forms** tab at the bottom of the Banks notebook

The **Check Form Printing Information** page of the Banks notebook, shown in Figure 24-3, will appear.

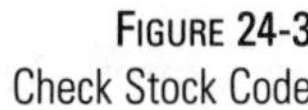
FIGURE 24-3
Check Stock Code

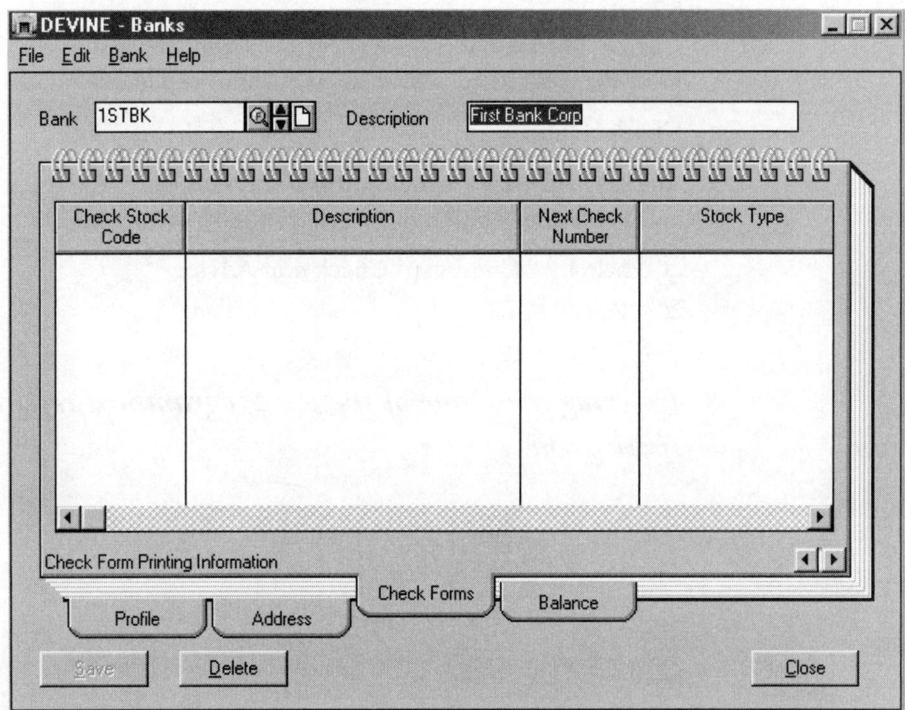

Check Stock Code

A Check Stock Code is made up of the physical check forms along with the report specifications contained in the software, plus the written language you will be using. You create the code yourself. It may contain up to six alphanumeric characters.

- ❑ Click: on the first line of the **Check Stock Code** field to activate it.
- ❑ Enter: **STD001**
- ❑ Press: **Tab** [Tab]

The Description may contain up to 30 characters to name the style of checks you use.

- ❑ Type: **Standard Forms**
- ❑ Press: **Tab** [Tab]

The Next Check Number field displays 1 as the default.

- ❑ Press: **Tab** [Tab]
- ❑ Click: the **list tool** ▾ for the Stock Type field

There are four forms available as follows:

Combined Check and Advice: The check form contains the advice portion on the same page as the check.

Checks Then Advices: The check form and advice slips are different forms. You have to print the checks first, then load and print the advice forms.

Checks Only: This option prints the checks only.

Advices Only: This option prints the advices only. You use this option if you write manual checks and want an individual printout for each check.

- ❑ Select: **Combined Check and Advice**
- ❑ Press: **Tab** [Tab]

Entering the name of the pre-programmed report specification for the check form.

- ❑ Click: **Browse** beside the **Check Form** button

The Select Report file window will appear as shown in Figure 24-4.

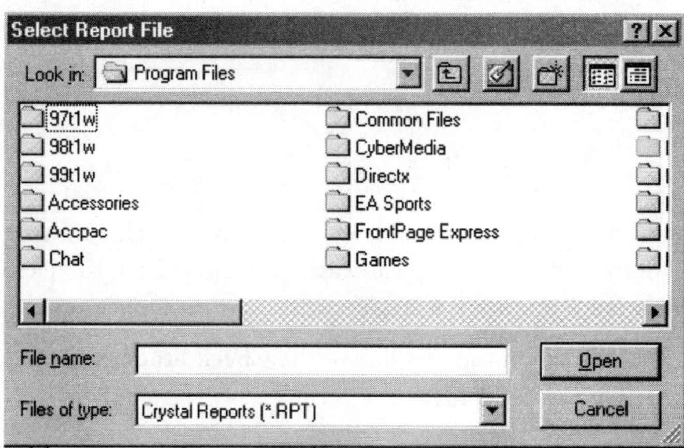

FIGURE 24-4 Select Report File Window

The files you need are found in the directory Program Files/ACCPAC/AP41a/ENG.

- ❑ DClick: **Program Files**
- ❑ DClick: **ACCPAC**
- ❑ DClick: **AP41a**
- ❑ DClick: **Eng**

Among the files available are the following:

APCHK01.RPT This produces a combined check and advice for laser printers.
APCHK02.RPT This produces a combined check and advice for dot matrix printers.

AP1099.RPT	This produces the 1099 form for laser printers.
APLETT01.RPT	This produces a sample letter.
APLBL01.RPT	This produces sample labels.

Review these forms carefully. The next instruction tells you to install the combined check and advice form for laser printers. If you are using a dot matrix printer, be sure to install the appropriate file.

❑ DClick: **APCHK01.RPT**

You cannot activate the Browse button for the Advice Form field since the check form you have selected includes both the check and advice. The two remaining fields, Advice Lines per Page and Language, have been filled in as the result of the check form you chose.

❑ Click: **Save** Save

❑ Close: the **Banks** window

This completes the installation of a file that will allow you to print combined checks and advices. If you require other check forms, repeat the process, and select the check form best suited to your needs.

Adding Tax Classes

For each tax authority you have added, you have to define Tax Classes. Tax Classes are required for both sales and purchases. You created the Tax Classes for sales and some purchases in Chapter 15; now you must create the Retail Sales Tax Classes for Purchases and Items.

❑ DClick: the **Tax Services** icon Tax Services from the Common Services Window

❑ DClick: the **Tax Classes** icon Tax Classes from the Tax Services Window

Tax Classes Window

The first Tax Class Devine Designs Inc. will enter is for Retail Sales Tax on purchases. Generally Retail Sales Tax is not accounted for in purchases because it is either exempt or not recoverable.

Tax Authority

❑ Click: the **Finder** for Tax Authority

❑ Select: **RSTON**

Transaction Type

There are two choices of Transaction Types: Sales and Purchases.

- ❑ Select: **Purchases**

ACCPAC requires that you enter at least one vendor class and one item class in order to be able to enter tax rates.

Ensure that the Vendors option button is active.

- ❑ Click: **GO**

Class 1 will appear.

- ❑ Press: **Tab** to move to the Description cell
- ❑ Type: **Taxable**
- ❑ Press: **Tab**

Class 2 will appear.

- ❑ Press: **Tab** to move to the Description cell
- ❑ Type: **Exempt**
- ❑ Press: **Tab**

You can add up to ten classes for each Tax Authority and Transaction type combination. Taxable and Exempt Classes are sufficient for the Devine Designs Inc. simulation.

- ❑ Click: **Save** Save

You must enter at least one item class for ACCPAC to use when it creates a Tax Rate table.

- ❑ Click: the **Items** option button
- ❑ Click: **GO**
- ❑ Enter: **All items** in the Description cell for Class 1
- ❑ Press: **Tab**
- ❑ Click: **Save** Save
- ❑ Close: the **Tax Classes** window

ENTERING TAX RATES

Tax Services creates sales and purchases tax tables, using the tax classes you have created. A sales tax table consists of customer classes and item classes, while a purchases tax table consists of vendor classes and item classes. The tax rates that you enter in these tables are used by the subledgers to determine the taxes charged to vendors and customers for those goods and services bought and sold. In Chapter 15, you added a number of Tax Rates. This chapter will complete the addition of required Tax Rates.

- ❑ DClick: the **Tax Rates** icon on the Tax Services window
- ❑ Select: **RSTON** from the Tax Authority text box using the Finder
- ❑ Select: **Purchases** in the Transaction Type list box
- ❑ Click: **GO**

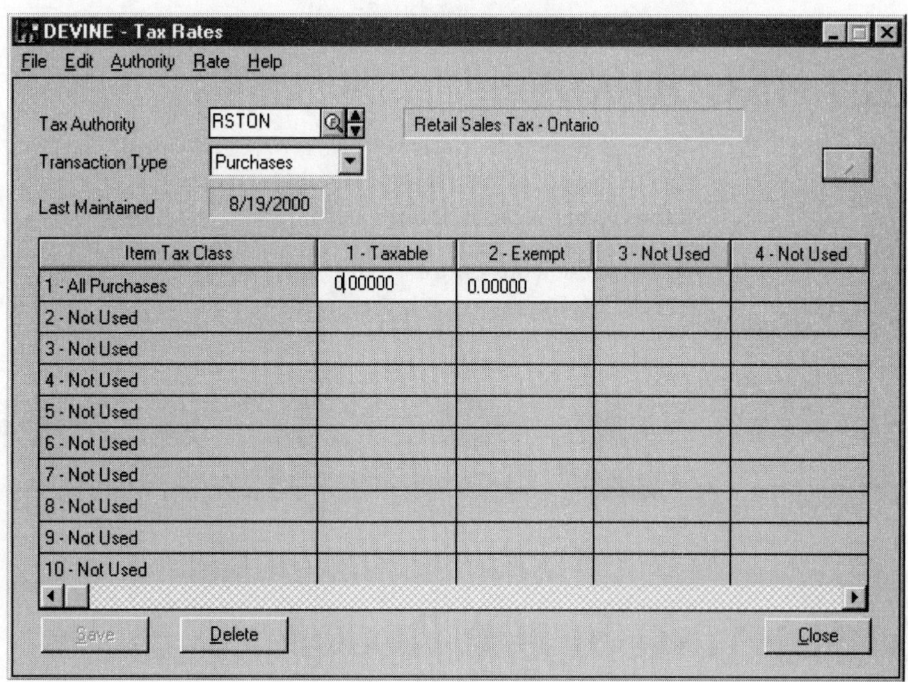

Figure 24-5
Tax Rates Window

The Tax Rates window will appear as shown in Figure 24-5. Note that the Item Tax Classes you added appear as the row and column headings. There are four active cells in which you can enter tax rates.

- ❑ Click: the **Taxable** cell
- ❑ Type: **8**
- ❑ Press: **Enter**
- ❑ Click: **Save** Save

Once you have added this Tax Rate, you can proceed with the addition of invoices in Chapter 26.

- ❑ Close: the **Tax Rates** window

Adding Setup records

This section will guide you through the process of adding the records and codes that you assign when adding vendor accounts or entering transactions in ACCPAC Accounts Payable. The information that you will add in this section reduces the time required to record transactions in Accounts Payable.

Getting Ready

- ❑ Open: the **Accounts Payable** window
- ❑ Open: the **A/P Setup** Window

Each of the icons on the A/P Setup window (Figure 24-6) enables you to add, modify, or delete information that is used when you record vendor or transaction information.

FIGURE 24-6
A/P Setup Icons

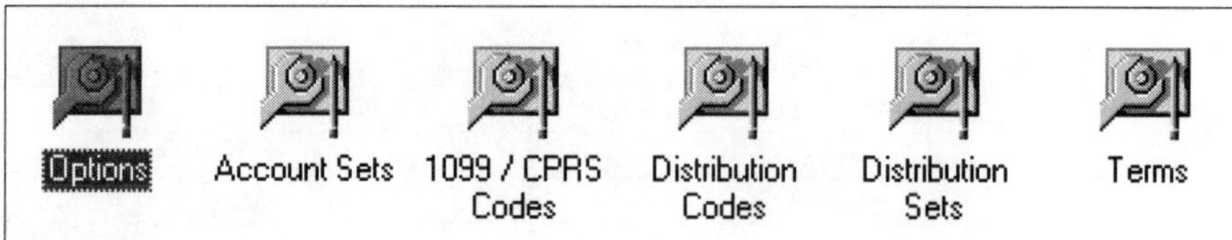

Modifying Setup Records

You can modify and delete the records you set up in this chapter as needed. To modify a record, select the code that identifies it (for example the Account Set Code), then make your changes and save them. In most records, you can change everything except for the identifying code or number. To change a code or number, you must first add a record with the code or number you want to use, then delete the record you do not want.

Adding Account Sets

Account Sets allow you to specify the General Ledger accounts to be used when Accounts Payable transaction information is posted to the General Ledger. You must define at least one Account Set before adding vendors. Each Account Set consists of Payables Control account, a Purchase Discounts account, and a Prepayment account.

Devine Designs Inc. has a simple set of books and will create only one Account Set.

- ❑ DClick: the **Account Sets** icon [Account Sets] on the A/P Setup window to get the window shown in Figure 24-7

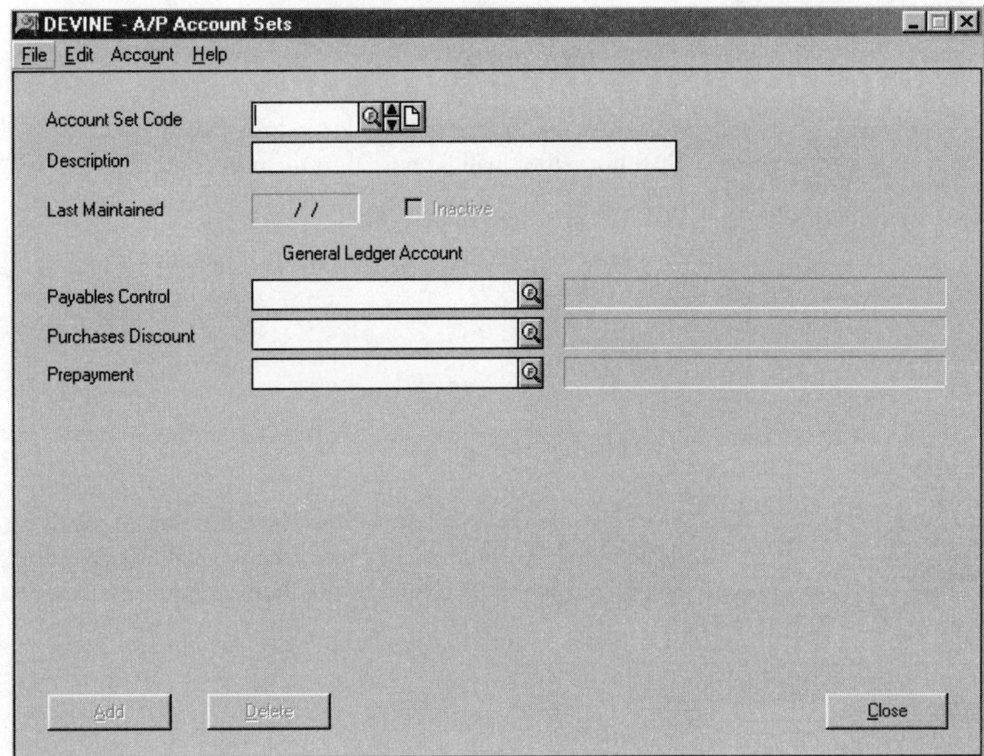

FIGURE 24-7
A/P Account Sets Window

ACCOUNT SET CODE

You enter a unique name or number, up to six characters long, to identify each Account Set.

- ❑ Type: **1**
- ❑ Press: **Tab** [Tab]

Description

- ❑ Type: **Accounts Payable - General** in the Description text box
- ❑ Press: **Tab** [Tab]

Inactive

You do not want to designate this code as inactive.

- ❑ Press: **Tab** [Tab]

Payables Control

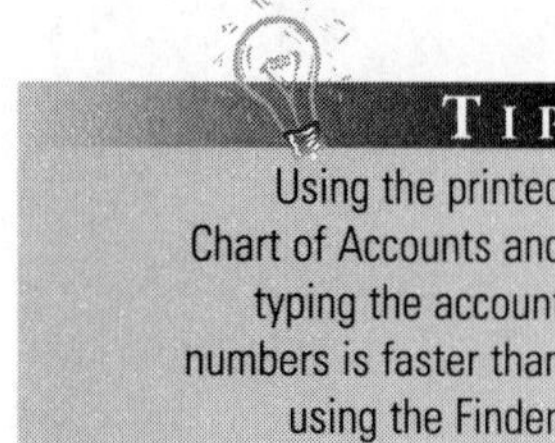

You enter the Accounts Payable Control account code from the General Ledger so that the information will be posted to the proper account.

- ❑ Click: the **Finder**
- ❑ Select: **2020** Accounts Payable, Control

The account description, Accounts Payable, Control, will be displayed to the right of the text box.

Purchases Discount

Since Devine Designs Inc. will purchase little or no goods for resale, the company has decided that it would not be beneficial to track merchandise purchase discounts separately. Discounts will be posted to the Prompt Payments Disc. Earned account.

- ❑ Enter: **6400** in the Purchases Discount text box

Prepayment

TIP
Use Print on the File menu.

- ❑ Enter: **1400** in the Prepayment text box
- ❑ Click: **Add** [Add]
- ❑ Print: the **A/P Accounts Sets Report**

Compare your printout to that shown in Figure 24-8 and verify that it is correct and complete.

- ❑ Close: the **A/P Account Sets Report** window
- ❑ Close: the **A/P Account Sets** window

FIGURE 24-8
A/P Accounts Sets Report

Date: Saturday, August 19, 2000 5:08PM **DDI Student Name** **Page 1**
A/P Account Sets (APACCT1Z)

From Account Set [ ] To [ZZZZZZ]

Account Set	Description	Account Number	Last Maintained/ Account Desc.	Inactive On
1	Accounts Payable - General		8/19/2000	
	Payables Control:	2020	Accounts Payable, Control	
	Purchases Discount:	6400	Prompt Payment Disc. Earned	
	Prepayment:	1400	Prepaid Expenses	

1 account set printed

ADDING DISTRIBUTION CODES

Distribution Codes identify the General Ledger accounts to which you post data from purchase transactions. You must add at least one Distribution Code before you can add vendor records. This function allows you to enter and maintain General Ledger distribution codes to speed up the entry of invoices, payments, and adjustments.

Rather than trying to memorize account numbers, you can use these codes or look them up using the finder on the Distribution Information page of the Invoice Entry notebook. Devine Designs Inc. will create seven Distribution Codes.

❑ DClick: the **Distribution Codes** icon on the A/P Setup window

The A/P Distribution Codes window will appear as shown in Figure 24-9.

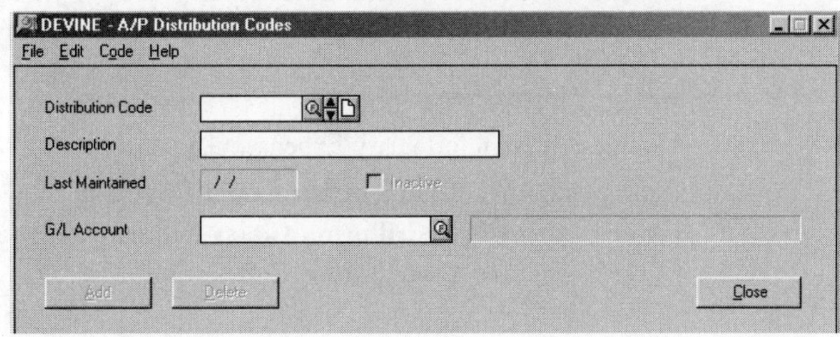

FIGURE 24-9
A/P Distribution Codes Window

Distribution Code

The cursor should be displayed in the Distribution Code text box. When creating a distribution code, use a name or short form that is easy to remember. The distribution code can be up to six characters long.

❑ Type: **OFFSUP**
❑ Press: **Tab** [Tab]

Description

❑ Type: **Office Supplies Purchase** in the Description text box
❑ Press: **Tab** [Tab]

Inactive

Do *not* select the Inactive box.

General Ledger Accounts

TIP
Use your printed Chart of Accounts and type the account numbers in the text boxes.

ACCPAC requires that you add an account in the G/L Account text box.

❑ Click: the **Finder** for the G/L Account text box
❑ Select: **1300** Office Supplies
❑ Click: **Add** [Add]

YOUR TURN

Devine Designs Inc. has decided to create Distribution Codes for the following expenditures. Add them to your Distribution Sets

❑ **Add** the following Distribution Codes:
- Code ADV for Advertising Expenses, G/L account 6000
- Code COMM for Communication Expenses, G/L account 6060
- Code COMPRT for Computer Rental, G/L account 6080
- Code ISP for Internet Services Expenses, G/L account 6140
- Code OFRENT for Office Rent, G/L account 6160
- Code SALARY for Salary Expense, G/L account 6180

❑ Print: the **A/P Distributions Codes Report** as shown in Figure 24-10
❑ Close: the **A/P Distribution Codes Report** dialog box
❑ Close: the **A/P Distribution Codes** window

FIGURE 24-10
A/P Distribution Codes Report

Date: Saturday, August 19, 2000 6:31PM **DDI Student Name** Page 1
A/P Distribution Codes (APDSTC1Z)

From Distribution Code [] To [ZZZZZZ]

Dist. Code	Description	Account Number	Account Description	Last Maintained	Inactive On
ADV	Advertising Expenses	6000	Advertising Expense	8/19/2000	
COMM	Communication Expenses	6060	Communication Expense	8/19/2000	
COMPRT	Computer Rental	6080	Computer Rent	8/19/2000	
ISP	Internet Service Expenses	6140	Internet Services Expense	8/19/2000	
OFFSUP	Office Supplies	1300	Office Supplies	8/19/2000	
OFRENT	Office Rent	6160	Office Rent Expense	8/19/2000	
SALARY	Salary Expenses	6180	Salary Expense	8/19/2000	

7 distribution codes printed

ADDING DISTRIBUTION SETS

You may find that you tend to make the same purchases for the same items repeatedly from a vendor. If this is the case, you may enter the distribution codes individually for the purchase, or you can establish a Distribution Set to automatically present the proper distribution codes or General Ledger account numbers. In effect, a distribution set is a group of distribution codes representing a standard group of distributions made while entering vendor transactions. You are not required to add distribution sets, but they provide you with a greater data entry efficiency than single distribution codes.

- ❑ DClick: the **Distribution Sets** [Distribution Sets] icon in the Setup window

FIGURE 24-11
A/P Distribution Sets

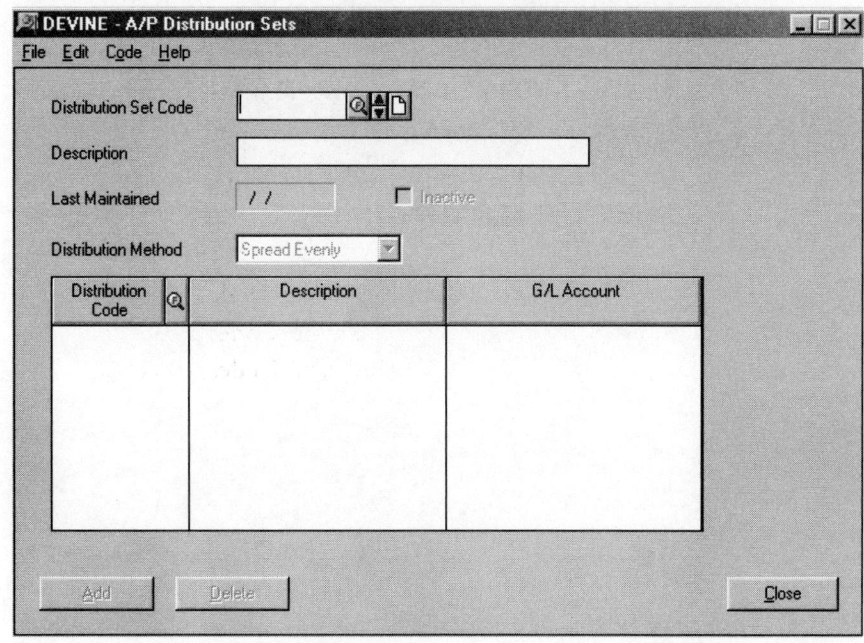

The A/P Distribution Sets window will appear as shown in Figure 24-11.

Devine Designs Inc. will create one Distribution Set for recording invoices from its Internet service provider. These invoices have two components: a charge for Internet connection and storage space, and a charge for banner advertising in the I.S.P.'s site.

- ❑ Click: the **New Document** icon to the right of the Distribution Set Code field
- ❑ Type: **ISPADV** in the Distribution Set Code field
- ❑ Press: **Tab** [Tab] to move to the Description field
- ❑ Type: **I.S.P. Services & Advertising**
- ❑ Press: **Tab** [Tab] twice to move to the Distribution Method field

This field is used to choose the method you will use to allocate the amount of the invoice between the accounts in the distribution set. If necessary, this default setting can be overridden when you add an invoice. There are three different methods for distributing the invoice:

Spread Evenly: This method allocates the invoice amount evenly across all the distribution codes in the distribution set. You can edit the result as required.

Fixed Percentage: This method allows you to specify the total invoice percentage to allocate to each distribution code.

Manual: This method gives no amount allocation; it simply enters the distribution codes and lets you enter the amounts of the distribution.

- ❑ Click: the **list tool** to the right of the Distribution Method field
- ❑ Select: **Manual**
- ❑ Press: **Tab** [Tab] to move to the Distribution Code field

You must select a code for this type of purchase.

- ❑ Click: the **Finder** for Distribution Code
- ❑ Select: **ADV** - Advertising Expenses
- ❑ Press: **Tab** [Tab] three times to move to create a second entry line
- ❑ Click: the **Finder** for Distribution Code
- ❑ Select: ISP-Internet Service Expenses
- ❑ Click: **Add** [Add]

The completed A/P Distribution Sets screen appears as shown in Figure 24-12.

FIGURE 24-12
A/P Distribution Sets

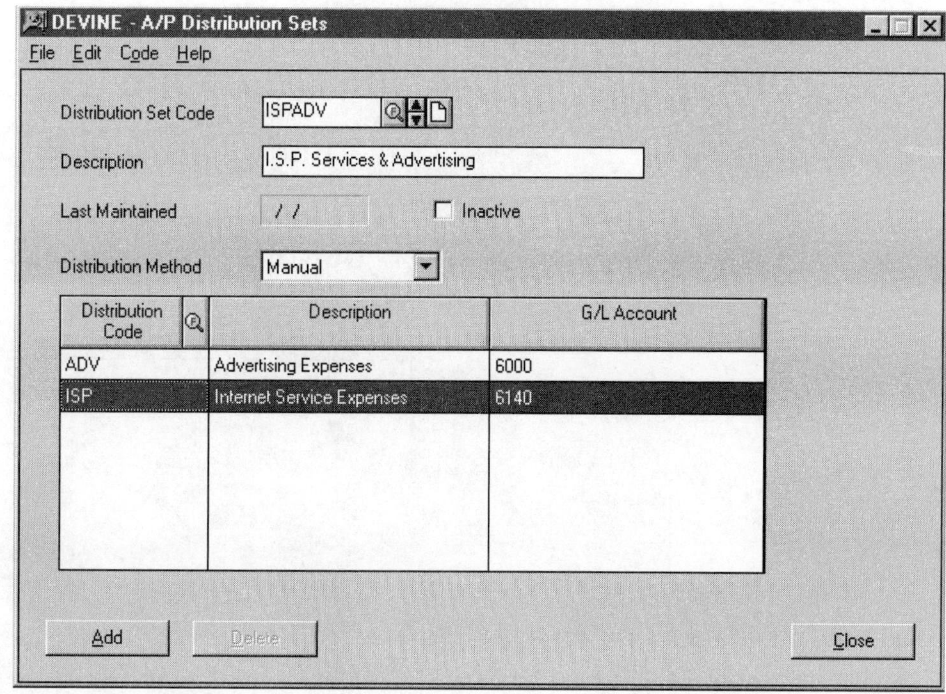

- ❑ Print: the **A/P Distribution Sets** report

Review your printout for accuracy. Once you are satisfied

- ❑ Close: the **A/P Distribution Report** dialog box
- ❑ Close: the **Distribution Sets** window

ADDING TERMS

ACCPAC Accounts Payable allows you to set up Payment Terms to use in calculating invoice due dates, discount dates, and discount amounts. At least one set of Terms must be defined before vendor accounts can be added. Devine Design Inc.'s vendors offer terms of either net 30, or 2/10, n/30.

- ❑ DClick: the **Terms** Terms icon in the A/P Setup window

The A/P Terms Codes window will appear as shown in Figure 24-13.

FIGURE 24-13
A/P Terms Codes Window

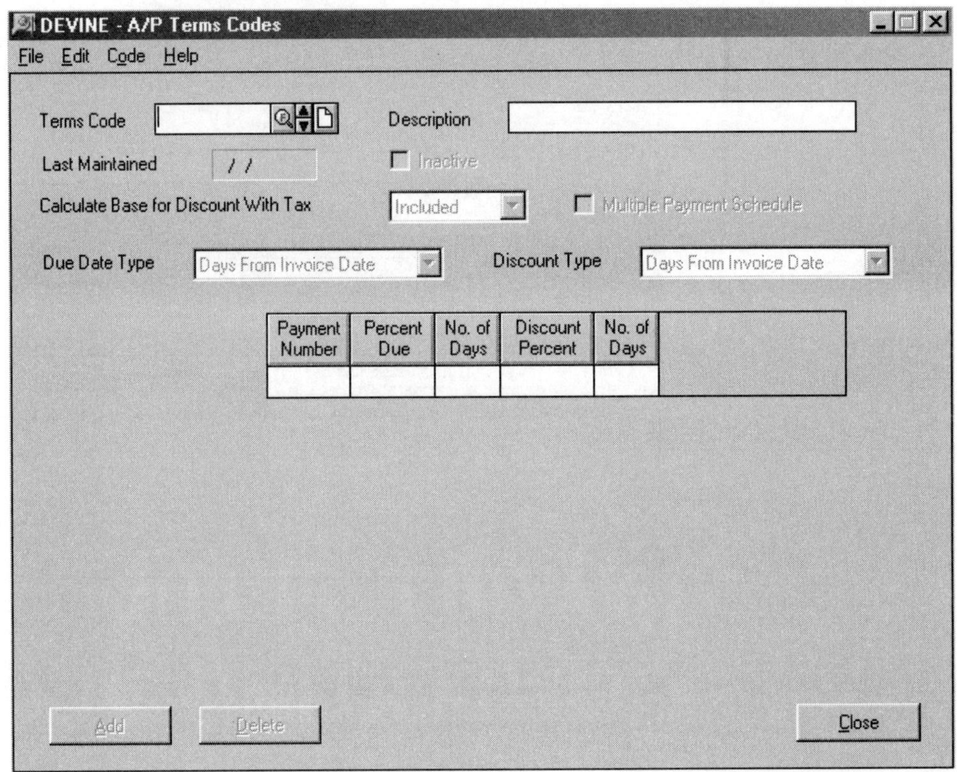

The first term that Devine Designs Inc. will add is for those invoices on which vendors allow a 2-percent discount if you pay invoiced amounts within 10 days of the invoice date. Otherwise the full amount of the invoice is due within 30 days of the invoice date.

Terms Code

Each Terms Code is identified by a unique alphanumeric name in the Terms Code text box.

- ❑ Type: **DISC** in the blank Terms Code text box
- ❑ Press: **Tab** Tab

Description

The description that you enter should describe the terms offered by the vendor.

- ❑ Type: **2/10, n/30** in the Description text box
- ❑ Press: **Tab** Tab

Inactive

This **Terms Code** should be active. If there is a tick mark in the Inactive check box, click it.

❑ Press: **Tab** [Tab]

Calculate Base for Discount

The **Calculate Base for Discount With Tax** list box is used to specify how tax amounts are calculated. You would select Included to allow a discount on taxes, and Excluded if discounts are not allowed on taxes. Devine Designs Inc. is not allowed discounts on taxes.

❑ Select: **Excluded** using the list tool
❑ Press: **Tab** [Tab]

Multiple Payment Schedule

The Multiple Payment Schedule check box is selected if vendors allow you to pay by installments. This field will be left inactive for this Terms Code. If there is a tick mark in this check box, you should click it to make the Multiple Payment Schedule inactive.

❑ Press: **Tab** [Tab]

Due Date Type

The Due Date Type list box allows you to select one of five different methods by which you determine invoice due dates.

- **Days from Invoice Date** is selected when invoices come due in a specific number of days after the invoice date. You would then type the number of days in the Number of Days column that appears.
- **End of Next Month** is used if the invoices are due on the last day of the next month. You must add the terms code after selecting this option.
- **Day of Next Month** is used if invoices are due on a specific day in the next month. After selecting this option, you must type the number representing the due date in the Day Of Month column.
- **Days From Day of Next Month** is selected if invoices are due a standard number of days after a specific day in the next month. You must then type the number of days and the number that represents the day of the month.
- **Due Date Table** is selected if you use standard due dates for invoices entered within specific ranges of days.

2/10, n/30 terms mean that the full amount of the invoice is due 30 days from the invoice date.

- ❑ Select: **Days from Invoice Date** using the list tool
- ❑ Press: **Tab**

Discount Type

The Discount Type list box allows you to select the method used to calculate the last day on which vendors allow you to take a discount. The options are similar to those for Due Date type.

- ❑ Select: **Days from Invoice Date** using the list tool
- ❑ Press: **Tab**

Data Table

The data table should now be active. ACCPAC enters 1 in the Payment Number cell and 100 in the Percent Due cell because the Multiple Payment Schedule option was not selected. You must enter the data for the other three cells.

- ❑ Click: the first **No. of Days** cell

In this cell, enter the number of days from the invoice date that the full payment of the invoice is due.

- ❑ Type: **30**
- ❑ Press: **Tab**

In the Discount Percent cell, enter the percent discount that is granted for early payment of invoices.

- ❑ Type: **2.0** in the Discount Percent cell
- ❑ Press: **Tab**

In the second No. Of Days cell, enter the number of days from the invoice date that the discount is offered.

- ❑ Type: **10** in the second No. Of Days cell
- ❑ Press: **Tab**
- ❑ Click: **Add**

YOUR TURN

Add the following Terms records. In all cases, the Calculate Base for Discount With Tax field should be Excluded.

- ❑ Add: the term **CASH** for Cash Purchases
- ❑ Add: the term **NODISC** for credit sales due in 30 days but with no discount

ADDING A MULTIPLE PAYMENT SCHEDULE

Devine Designs Inc. needs a Terms Code with a Multiple Payment schedule. This Terms Code will be used for projects that take a month to complete. Many vendors agree to accept 40 percent of the fee at the start of the contract, 30 percent when the project is delivered 30 days later, and the final 30 percent after 60 days. Devine Designs Inc. will issue the check for the first payment at the start of the contract.

- ❑ Click: the **New Document** icon in the Terms Code field
- ❑ Type: **PROJ** in the Terms Code text box
- ❑ Press: **Tab** [Tab]
- ❑ Type: **30 day projects** in the Description text box
- ❑ Press: **Tab** [Tab] twice
- ❑ Select: **Calculate Base for Discount With Tax Excluded**
- ❑ Press: **Tab** [Tab]
- ❑ Click: the **Multiple Payment Schedule** check box
- ❑ Press: **Tab** [Tab]

ACCPAC opens an expanded Number of Payments section in the lower portion of the screen.

- ❑ Select: **Days From Invoice Date** in the Due Date Type list box
- ❑ Press: **Tab** [Tab]
- ❑ Select: **Days from Invoice Date** in the Discount Type list box
- ❑ Press: **Tab** [Tab]
- ❑ Type: **40.0** on the Percent Due field
- ❑ Press: **Tab** [Tab] to move to the No. of Days cell
- ❑ Type: **0**

No discounts will be offered when a payment schedule has been arranged.

- ❑ Press: **Tab** [Tab] three times to create a new line
- ❑ Enter: **30** in the Percent Due cell
- ❑ Press: **Tab** [Tab]
- ❑ Enter: **30** in the No. of Days cell
- ❑ Press: **Tab** [Tab] three times
- ❑ Enter: **30** in the third Percent Due cell
- ❑ Press: **Tab** [Tab]
- ❑ Enter: **60** in the No. Of Days cell
- ❑ Press: **Tab** [Tab]
- ❑ Click: **Add** [Add]

Printing the A/P Terms Codes Report

☐ Print: the **A/P Terms Codes** report including Multiple Payment Schedules

FIGURE 24-14
Terms Report

Date: Saturday, August 19, 2000 9:29PM
A/P Terms (APTERM01)

DDI Student Name

Page 1

From Terms Code [ ] To [ZZZZZZ]
Report Format [Profile and Multipayment Schedules]

Terms Code	Description	
CASH	Cash	Last Maintained: 8/19/2000

Due Date
Type: Days From Invoice Date
Number of Days: 0
Day of Month: 0

Discount Date
Type: Days From Invoice Date
Number of Days: 0
Day of Month: 0
Calculate Base For Discount With Tax: Include
Discount %: 0.00000

Terms Code	Description	
DISC	2/10, n/30	Last Maintained: 8/19/2000

Due Date
Type: Days From Invoice Date
Number of Days: 30
Day of Month: 0

Discount Date
Type: Days From Invoice Date
Number of Days: 10
Day of Month: 0
Calculate Base For Discount With Tax: Exclude
Discount %: 2.00000

Terms Code	Description	
NODISC	n/30	Last Maintained: 8/19/2000

Due Date
Type: Days From Invoice Date
Number of Days: 30
Day of Month: 0

Discount Date
Type: Days From Invoice Date
Number of Days: 0
Day of Month: 0
Calculate Base For Discount With Tax: Include
Discount %: 0.00000

Date: Saturday, August 19, 2000 9:29PM
A/P Terms (APTERM01)

DDI Student Name

Page 2

Terms Code	Description		
PROJ	30 day projects	Last Maintained: 8/19/2000	Use Multiple Payments: Yes

Due Date
Type: Days From Invoice Date

Discount Date
Type: Days From Invoice Date
Calculate Base For Discount With Tax: Exclude

	Payment			Discount		
Payment Number	**Percent Due**	**No. of Days**	**Day of Month**	**Percent**	**No. of Days**	**Day of Month**
1	40.00000 %	0	0	0.00000 %	0	0
2	30.00000 %	30	0	0.00000 %	0	0
3	30.00000 %	60	0	0.00000 %	0	0

4 terms printed

Review the printout (Figure 24-14) to verify that the Terms are correct and complete. Make any necessary corrections and print the report again.

- ❑ Close: the **A/P Terms Code Report** window
- ❑ Close: the **A/P Terms Codes** window
- ❑ Exit: **ACCPAC**

REVIEW QUESTIONS

1. What is a Check Stock Code?
2. What is the purpose of the Account Sets option?
3. What is the purpose of the Distribution Codes option?
4. What are A/P Distribution Codes?
5. What is the purpose of the Multiple Payment Schedule?
6. What is the purpose of the Terms option?

EXERCISE

Sign on to your company as the system administrator using 05/01/10 as the Session Date.

TIP
Use the Setup Reports icon on the Accounts Payable window.

- ❑ Add: the Bank and Tax Services modifications that you made for Devine Designs Inc. to your Accounts Payable. Use the same setup and rates as that of Devine Designs Inc.
- ❑ Add: a Combined Check and Advice to your Accounts Payable. Use the same setup as that in Devine Designs Inc.
- ❑ Add : **Account Set** 1 as shown in Figure 24-8
- ❑ Add: the **Distribution Codes** as shown in Figure 24-10
- ❑ Add: the **Distribution Sets** as shown in Figure 24-11
- ❑ Add: the **Terms Codes** as shown in Figure 24-14
- ❑ Print: the reports necessary to document your additions
- ❑ Exit: **ACCPAC**

CHAPTER 25

VENDOR RECORDS

ACCPAC Accounts Payable allows you to keep very detailed records about your purchases from vendors, and provides several options with which you can customize the records for your business requirements. This chapter takes you through the process of adding vendor records to ACCPAC Accounts Payable and deciding on the options that will let you process vendor information and transactions to suit your company's requirements.

GETTING STARTED

- Sign on to Devine Designs Inc. as the system administrator using 05/01/10 as the Session Date.
- Open: the **Accounts Payable** window
- DClick: the **A/P Vendors** icon

FIGURE 25-1
A/P Vendors Icons

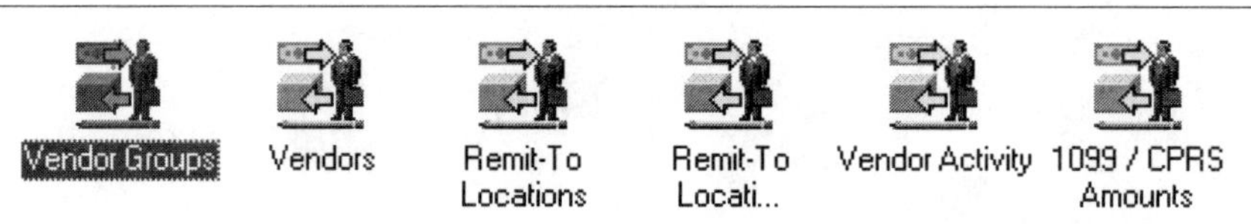

Each of the icons on the A/P Vendors window (Figure 25-1) enables you to add, modify, or delete vendor information.

ADDING A VENDOR GROUP

Use Vendor Groups to classify the vendor records into groups that share similar characteristics; for example, regional locations or industry types. Some of the information that you enter in the vendor group will become the default information for vendor accounts within the group. You must add at least one vendor group before you can add individual vendor records. Additional vendor groups can be added when necessary.

Devine Designs Inc. has decided to use one vendor group for all sales.

❑ DClick: the **Vendor Groups** icon 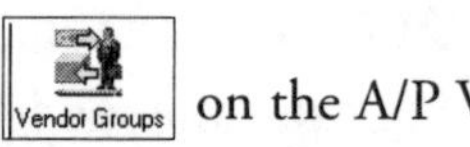 on the A/P Vendors window

FIGURE 25-2
A/P Vendor Groups Notebook

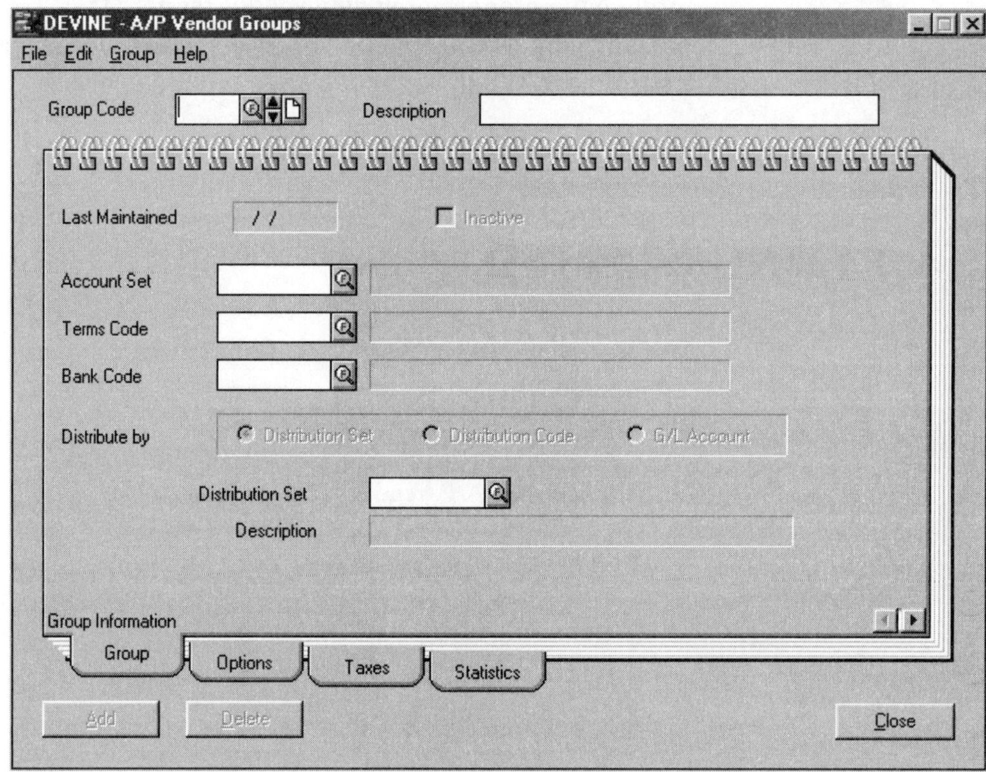

The Vendor Groups notebook (Figure 25-2) consists of four pages with two identifying text boxes displayed in the header above each notebook page.

Group Code

The Group Code may be up to three characters long. Devine Designs Inc. has decided to assign the Group Code, APM (Accounts Payable Master), to the initial account group.

- ❑ Type: **APM** in the Group Code text box
- ❑ Press: **Tab** [Tab]

If you must change a Group Code, first create the new vendor group and then reassign all the vendors from the old group to the new group. Then delete the old vendor group code.

Description

- ❑ Type: **Domestic Purchases** in the Description field
- ❑ Press: **Tab** [Tab]

GROUP INFORMATION PAGE

Inactive

Select Inactive only if you are preparing to delete a vendor group and want to ensure that no further transactions are posted to vendors assigned to the group. Devine Designs Inc. will not select this option when setting up the initial vendor group.

Account Sets

You have already created an Account Set, Terms Codes, and Bank Codes.

- ❑ Click: the **Finder** to the right of the Account Set field
- ❑ Select: **1 - Accounts Payable - General**

Terms Code

Select the Terms Code that you are assigned by most of the vendors in the group. When you add vendors, you can change this default Terms Code for individual vendors. You can also change the default Terms Code for individual purchases. Most of Devine Design Inc.'s suppliers offer terms of 2/10, n/30.

Print the README file and tape a copy of it in your manual. A second copy of the printout can be cut up and taped to the related pages in your manuals.

❑ Click: the **Finder** to the right of the Terms Code field

❑ Select: **DISC**

Bank Code

The Bank Code allows you to choose which bank account is used to pay the invoices for this vendor group.

❑ Click: the **Finder** to the right of the Bank Code field

❑ Select: **1STBK**

Distribute By

You select the method you want to use to distribute invoices to the General Ledger from the **Distribute By** menu. ACCPAC Accounts Payable allows you the three following methods for this allocation. You can change the method for individual vendors and specific invoices.

Distribution Set: Select Distribution Set when you want to use a group of distribution codes that have been defined as a set. The program will list the distribution codes by default when you add an invoice.

Distribution Code: This option is chosen when you want to distribute a single G/L account represented by a code.

G/L Account: Select the G/L account, then specify the account number if you want to distribute to a particular account. You do not use a distribution code.

❑ Click: the **Distribution Code** option button

Note that the name of the next field changes based on the option you choose in the **Distribute by** box.

❑ Press: **Tab** [Tab]

❑ Click: the **Finder** to the right of the **Distribution Code** field

❑ Select: **OFFSUP - Office Supplies**

Devine Designs Inc. will change this information for individual vendors or vendor transactions as required.

Group Options

❑ Click: the **Options** tab at the bottom of the A/P Vendor Groups notebook

The Group Options page will appear as shown in Figure 25-3.

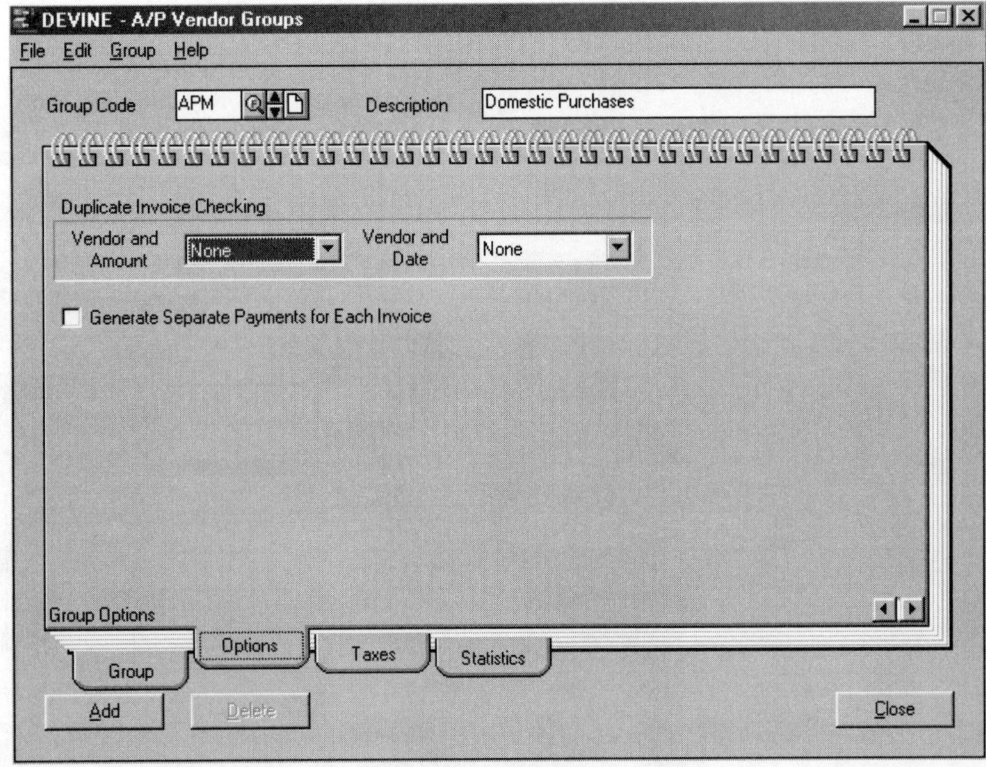

FIGURE 25-3
Group Options Page

Duplicate Invoice Checking

You have to decide how you want ACCPAC Accounts Payable to review the database for duplicate purchase invoices. You can have the system ignore, warn, or stop you from posting invoices that are duplicates according to two different criteria.

- The invoices are from the same vendor and amount.
- The invoices are from the same vendor and date.

❑ Click: the **list tool** to the right of the Vendor and Amount field
❑ Select: **Warning**
❑ Click: the **list tool** to the right of the Vendor and Date field
❑ Select: **Warning**

Generate Separate Payments for Each Invoice

If you want the ACCPAC Accounts Payable to generate separate checks for each invoice when you process payments, select the Generate Payments for Each Invoice option. If you do not select this option, the program will group the due invoices and create a single payment for each vendor.

Devine Designs Inc. plans to make payments for multiple invoices on each check whenever feasible, so make sure this option is not active.

Tax Information

❑ Click: the **Taxes** tab at the bottom of the A/P Vendor Groups notebook

The Tax Information page of the A/P Vendor Groups notebook will appear as shown in Figure 25-4.

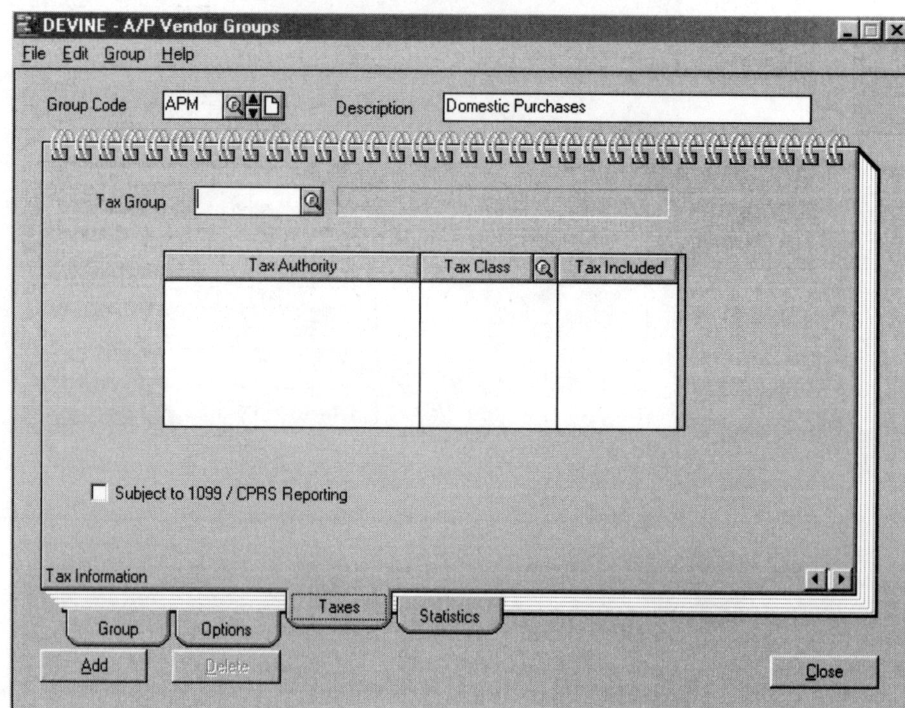

FIGURE 25-4
Tax Information Page

The Tax Information page allows you to select the Tax Group that will be used most commonly with the Vendor Group. You can change the default Tax Group for individual purchases. All of Devine Design Inc.'s suppliers belong in the DOMPUR - Domestic Purchases group.

❑ Click: the **list tool** to the right of the Tax Group field
❑ Select: **DOMPUR**

The Federal Goods and Services and Retail Sales Tax Authorities appear.

❑ Select: **Tax Class 1** for both tax authorities

For merchandise purchases for resale that are not subject to retail sales tax, Devine Designs Inc. will change the Tax Class as invoices are entered.

None of your vendors is subject to 1099 reporting, so ensure that the check box for Subject to 1099/CPRS Reporting is not selected.

❑ Click: the **Statistics** tab at the bottom of the A/P Vendor Groups notebook

Group Statistics Page

The Group Statistics page of the A/P Vendor Groups notebook will appear as shown in Figure 25-5.

FIGURE 25-5
Group Statistics Page

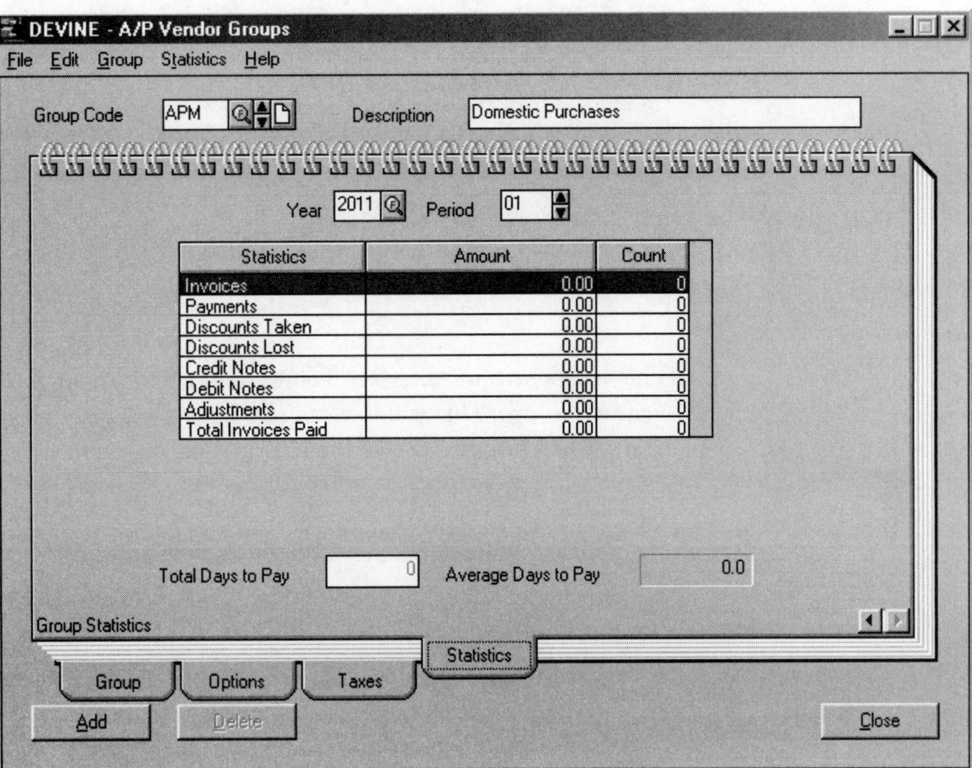

ACCPAC keeps track of the year-to-date amounts. It also keeps track of the payments, credit and debit notes, discounts taken, discounts lost, and adjustments posted to the vendor's account. The total invoices paid, total days to pay, and average number of days to pay for the Vendor Group are also calculated.

Devine Designs Inc. has decided not to add information about the previous fiscal year. ACCPAC will accumulate statistics on the fiscal year that has just begun.

❑ Click: **Add** Add

PRINTING THE A/P VENDOR GROUP REPORT

❑ Select: **Print** from the A/P Vendor Groups File menu

FIGURE 25-6
A/P Vendor Groups Report Dialog Box

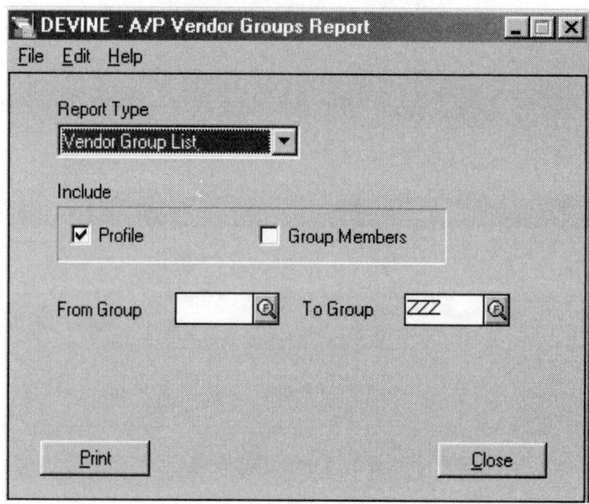

The default settings shown in Figure 25-6 will print a report listing the profiles of all Vendor Groups. This window can also be used to print group statistics. Enter any changes necessary to display the information shown in Figure 25-6.

- ❑ Click: **Print** [Print] on the A/P Vendor Groups Report dialog box
- ❑ Click: **OK** [OK] on the Print dialog box

Compare your printout to that shown in Figure 25-7. Make any necessary changes and print the report again. You can edit the information in a Vendor Group by selecting the notebook for that Vendor group, entering the changes that you wish to make, then saving the Vendor Group.

You cannot change the Group Code.

- ❑ Close: the **A/P Vendor Group Report** dialog box
- ❑ Close: the **A/P Vendor Groups** window

FIGURE 25-7
A/P Vendor Groups Report

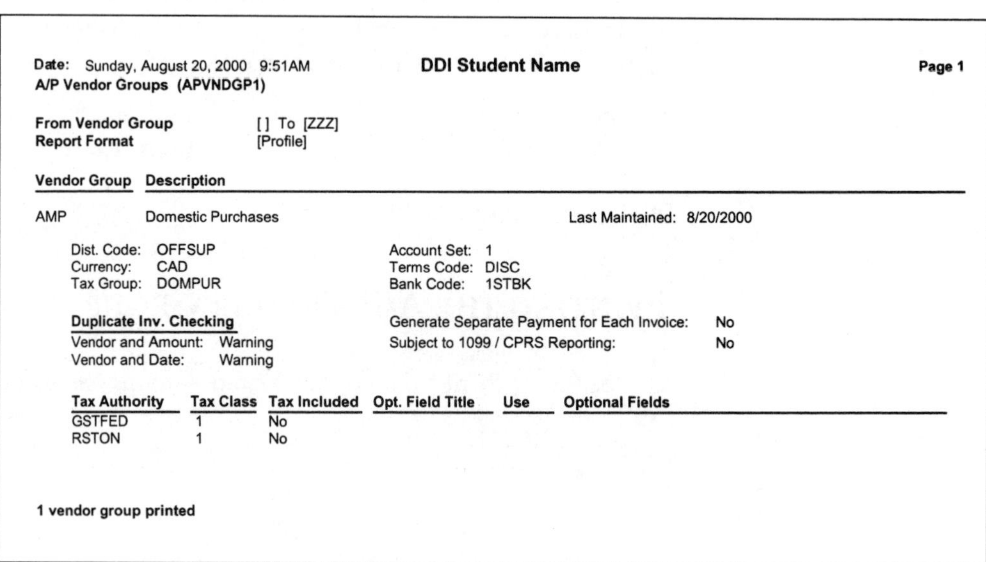

Date: Sunday, August 20, 2000 9:51AM **DDI Student Name** **Page 1**
A/P Vendor Groups (APVNDGP1)

From Vendor Group [] To [ZZZ]
Report Format [Profile]

Vendor Group	Description	
AMP	Domestic Purchases	Last Maintained: 8/20/2000

Dist. Code: OFFSUP Account Set: 1
Currency: CAD Terms Code: DISC
Tax Group: DOMPUR Bank Code: 1STBK

Duplicate Inv. Checking
Vendor and Amount: Warning
Vendor and Date: Warning

Generate Separate Payment for Each Invoice: No
Subject to 1099 / CPRS Reporting: No

Tax Authority	Tax Class	Tax Included	Opt. Field Title	Use	Optional Fields
GSTFED	1	No			
RSTON	1	No			

1 vendor group printed

Deleting a Vendor Group

You cannot delete a Vendor Group that is assigned to an individual vendor account.

To delete a Vendor Group, first assign the vendor accounts to another Vendor Group. Then select the notebook for the Vendor Group and click Delete.

Adding Vendors

Individual Vendor records must be added before you can enter and process transactions in Accounts Payable. The first vendor that Devine Designs Inc. adds is As-Tech Computers.

❑ DClick: the **Vendors** icon [Vendors] on the A/P Vendors window

The A/P Vendor notebook (Figure 25-8) contains six pages with two common fields displayed in a header above the pages.

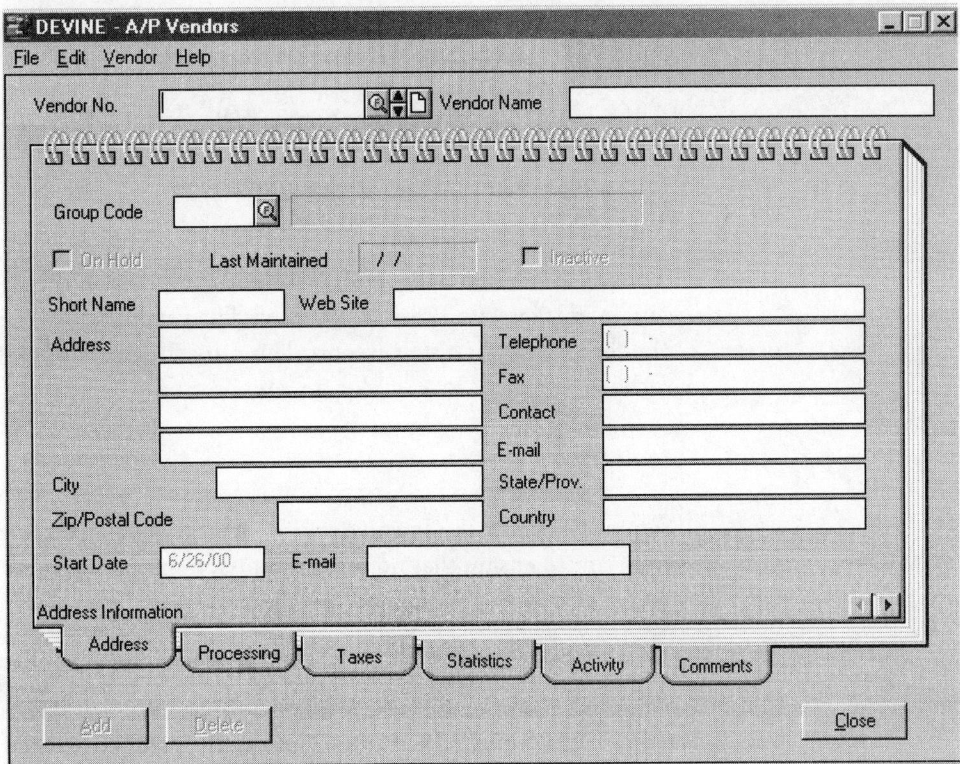

FIGURE 25-8
A/P Vendors Notebook

Vendor Number

ACCPAC will accept any combination of up to twelve characters or digits as a vendor number. Use at least four characters to allow for an increase in the number of vendors. You cannot change a vendor's number after you have created the vendor account record.

Devine Designs Inc. will use a simple sequential numbering method using four numbers.

- ❑ Type: **1001** in the Vendor No. text box
- ❑ Press: **Tab** [Tab]

Name

The Vendor Name may have up to 30 letters and/or digits. Enter it exactly as you want it to appear on statements and reports.

- ❑ Type: **AsTech Computers** in the Name text box
- ❑ Press: **Tab** [Tab]

ADDRESS INFORMATION PAGE

Group Code

All of Devine Design's suppliers are domestic accounts.

- ❑ Select: **APM** using the Finder

On Hold

If you place a vendor On Hold, a warning appears on the A/P invoice entry screen when you enter transactions for that vendor. The vendor is also flagged as On Hold on the Vendor List and Statistics Report. You can activate this check box later if you want to withhold payment to a vendor for some reason.

Inactive

You would select the Inactive option only if you are preparing to delete a vendor record and want to ensure that no further transactions are posted to the account.

Short Name

This field is used to create a nickname for the vendor. The name may be composed of as many as ten letters. Companies commonly enter the first ten letters of the name. For several reports, you can sort the vendor accounts according to this short name. If you wished to change it, you would type the new name over the current one and press the Tab key. Alternatively, you can leave this field blank.

Devine Designs Inc. will create short names for each vendor.

- ❑ Highlight: the **Short Name** field
- ❑ Enter: **AsTech** in the Short Name text box
- ❑ Press: **Tab** [Tab]

Web Site

If the vendor has a Web site, you can record it in this field.

- ❑ Type: **www.astech.com**
- ❑ Press: **Tab** [Tab]

Address Information

TIP
Be careful! Checks prints the address information entered here.

- ❑ Enter: **286 Main Street**
  Unit 20
  Georgetown, ON
  L7G 1A2

Telephone

- ❑ Enter: **905 555 5342**

Fax

Devine Designs Inc. will not use faxes; documents will be sent by e-mail.

Contact

Barb Edwards is the Supervisor, Accounts Payable, at As-Tech Computers.

- ❑ Enter: **Barb Edwards** in the Contact text box
- ❑ Press: **Tab** [Tab]

E-mail

The e-mail field is used to record the e-mail address of the contact person.

- ❑ Type: **barbe@sympatico.ca**
- ❑ Press: **Tab** [Tab]

Start Date

This text box allows you to enter the date on which you started doing business with this vendor. The default displayed is the Windows 95/98 system date, not the Session Date. As-Tech Computers signed the contract with Devine Designs Inc. on April 12, 2010.

- ❑ Enter: **04/12/10** in the Start Date text box
- ❑ Press: **Tab** [Tab]

E-mail

This second e-mail address field is used to record the e-mail address for the company.

- ❑ Type: **astech@sympatico.ca**
- ❑ Press: **Tab** [Tab]

PROCESSING INFORMATION PAGE

- ❑ Click: the **Processing** tab at the bottom of the A/P Vendors notebook

Most of the text boxes on the Processing Options page (Figure 25-9) display default information entered when vendor groups were created. The Account Set, Terms Code, and Bank Code defaults can be changed for individual vendors.

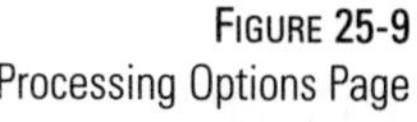

FIGURE 25-9
Processing Options Page

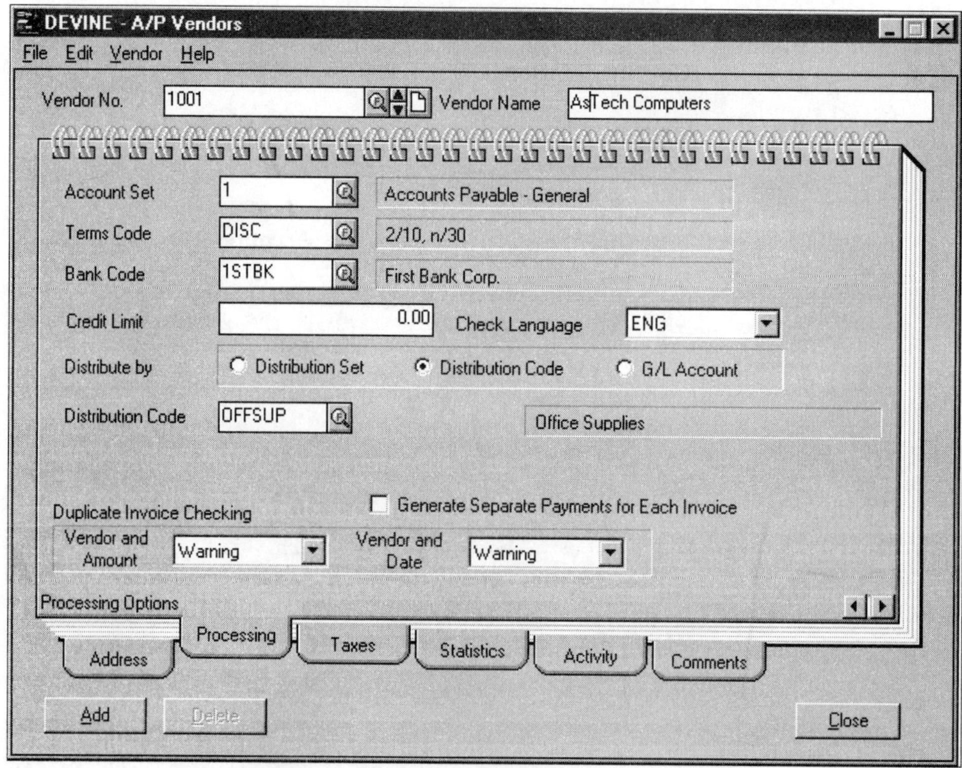

Account Set

The default displayed in the Account Set text box is 1, the code assigned to the vendor group. As Devine Designs Inc. has only created one Account Set, no changes are necessary.

Terms Code

The default terms code DISC was assigned to the vendor group, APM. You can change the code for individual vendors. As-Tech Computers allows a discount for early payment.

Bank Code

The default Bank Code, 1STBK, was assigned to the vendor group APM. Devine Designs Inc. will use the 1STBK as the default for all vendors. If necessary, changes will be entered on individual transaction documents.

Credit Limit

As-Tech Computers has set the credit limit at $500 for Devine Designs Inc.

❑ Click: on the **Credit Limit** field
❑ Type: **500.00** in the Credit Limit text box
❑ Press: **Tab** [Tab]

Check Language

You can select the language used to print checks for a vendor. The default is English.

❑ Press: **Tab** [Tab] to leave the default unchanged.

Distribute By

You can choose the method you want to use to distribute invoice amounts to the General Ledger. The method can be changed for individual invoices. AsTech is the I.S.P. used by Devine Designs Inc.

❑ Select: the **Distribution Set** option button

Note that the next field reads Distribution Set.

❑ Click: the **Finder** to the right of the Distribution Set button
❑ Select: **ISPADV**

Generate Separate Payments for Each Invoice

Activate this option if you want the program to create separate checks for each invoice. Devine Designs Inc. will combine invoices whenever possible, so make sure this option is not active.

When the Address and Processing pages have been completed, ACCPAC will allow you to add the vendor account.

❑ Click: **Add** [Add]

Tax Information

❑ Click: the **Taxes** tab at the bottom of the A/P Vendors notebook to get the Tax Information page shown in Figure 25-10

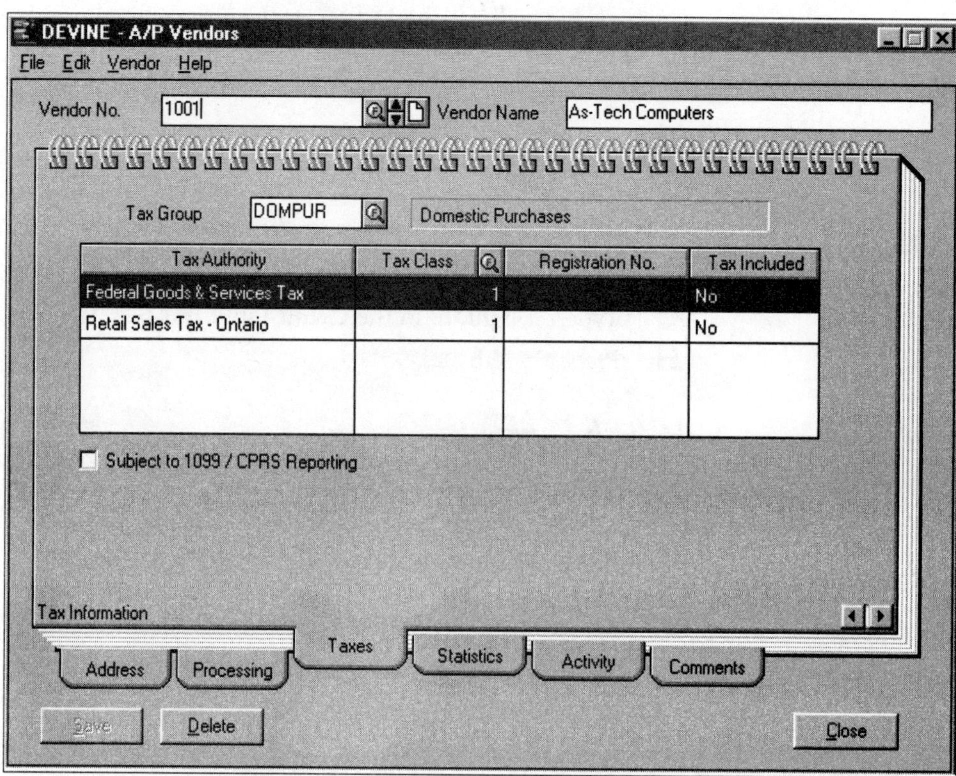

FIGURE 25-10
Tax Information Page

Choose the Tax Group Code for the tax group applicable to this vendor. The Tax Authorities in the group appear on the screen so you can enter tax classes for each authority. DOMPUR (Domestic Purchases) is the only Tax Group you have created. As-Tech Computers charges both GST and RST, so no changes are necessary.

Statistics Page

❑ Click: the **Statistics** tab at the bottom of the A/P Vendors notebook

The Vendor Statistics page (Figure 25-11) shows statistics calculated by ACCPAC for each vendor. As Devine Designs Inc. has not processed any transactions in Accounts Payable, the amounts displayed for period 1, fiscal year 2011, should be zeros. As transactions are processed in Accounts Payable, the statistics on the page will be updated.

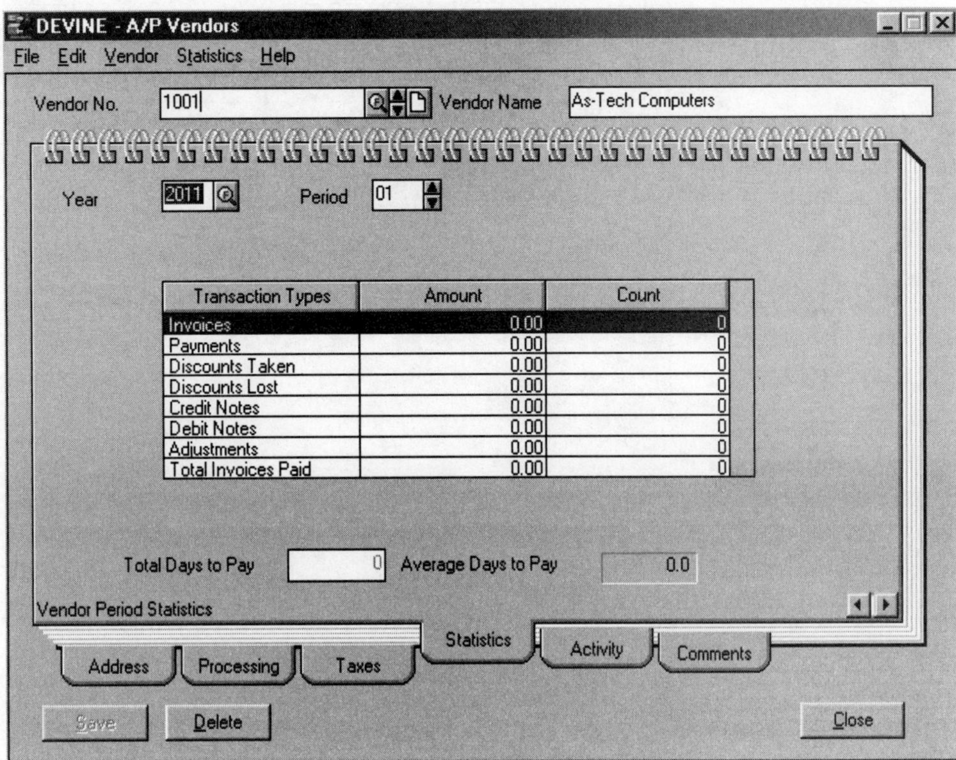

Transaction Types	Amount	Count
Invoices	0.00	0
Payments	0.00	0
Discounts Taken	0.00	0
Discounts Lost	0.00	0
Credit Notes	0.00	0
Debit Notes	0.00	0
Adjustments	0.00	0
Total Invoices Paid	0.00	0

FIGURE 25-11
Vendor Statistics Page

Vendor Activity Page

❑ Click: the **Activity** tab at the bottom of the A/P Vendors notebook

The Vendor Activity page (Figure 25-12) shows statistics calculated by ACCPAC for the current year and last year. As Devine Designs Inc. has not processed any transactions in Accounts Payable, the amounts displayed should be zeros. As transactions are processed in Accounts Payable, the statistics on the page will be updated.

FIGURE 25-12
Vendor Activity Page

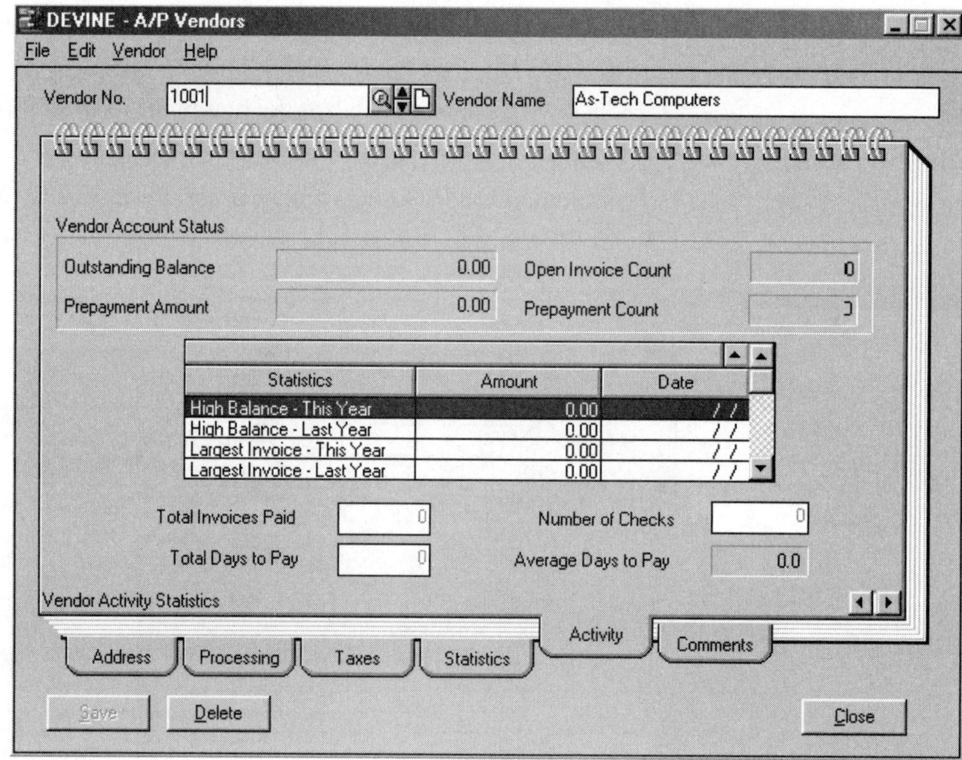

VENDOR COMMENTS PAGE

❑ Click: the **Comments** tab at the bottom of the A/P Vendors notebook

The Vendor Comments page (Figure 25-13) allows comments to be recorded in a vendor's account.

Date Entered

The Date Entered text box is used to record the date on which the comment was entered. The default displayed is the Session Date.

Follow-Up Date

The Follow-Up Date text box is used to record the date on which you want to follow up on your comment.

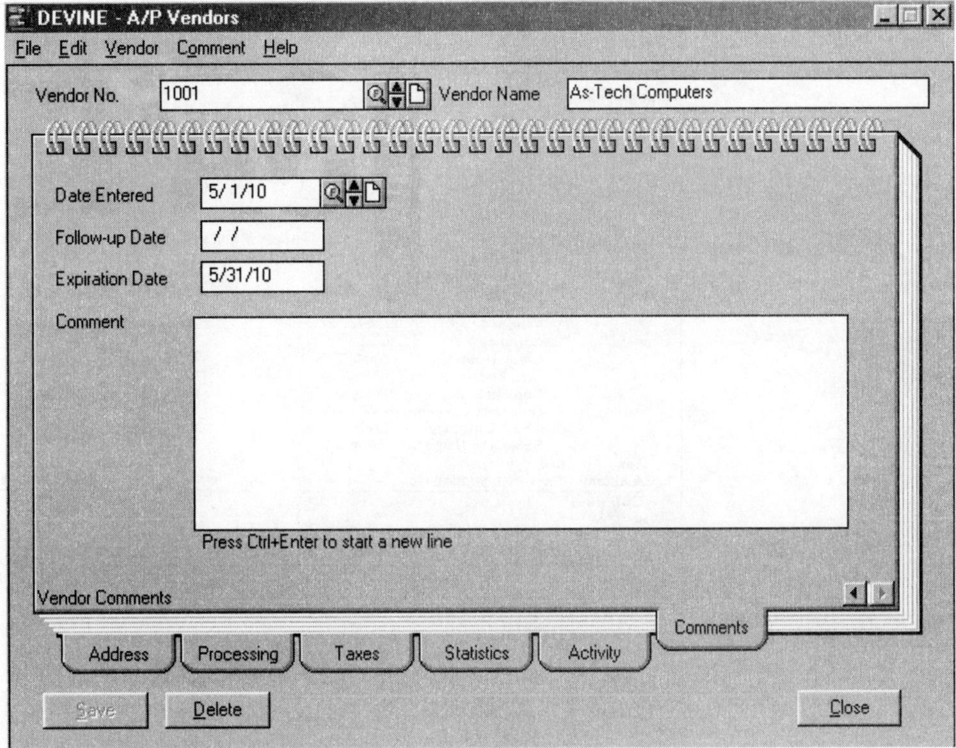

FIGURE 25-13
Vendor Comments Page

Expiration Date

The Expiration Date text box is used to record the date on which you want to delete your comment. ACCPAC will display the date that is the same number of days later than the Date Entered date that you specified for the Default Number Of Days To Keep Comments option in the Options notebook.

Comment

The comment text box holds up to 250 characters. You may type your comment in one single long line, or in several shorter lines. Press the Ctrl and Enter keys together whenever you want to start a new line.

Devine Designs Inc. will not enter any comments at this time.

YOUR TURN

You will now add seven new vendors for Devine Designs Inc.

- ❑ Click: the **New Document** icon for Vendor No.
- ❑ Add the seven new vendors using the information shown in Figure 25-14.

Figure 25-14
A/P Vendor List

Date: Sunday, August 20, 2000 10:54AM **DDI Student Name** **Page 1**
A/P Vendor List (APVNDLT1)

Report Format [Profile, Address]

Vendor No. **Description**
1001 **Start Date:** 4/12/2010 **Last Maintained:** 8/20/2000
Name: AsTech Computers
Address: 286 Main St Georgetown, ON
Unit 20 L7G 1A2

Short Name: AsTech **Phone:** (905)555 -5342
E-mail: astech@sympatico.ca
Web Site: www.astech.com
Contact: Barb Edwards **E-mail:** barbe@sympatico.ca

Vendor Group: AMP **Account Set:** 1
Currency: CAD **Terms Code:** DISC
Credit Limit: 500.000 **Bank Code:** 1STBK
Dist. Set: ISPADV **Print Sep. Check:** No
Dup. Amt. Checking: Warning **Primary Remit to:**
Dup. Date Checking: Warning **Tax Group:** DOMPUR
Check Language: ENG **Rate Type:** SP
Subject to 1099 / CPRS Reporting: No

Tax Authority	Tax Class	Registration No.	Tax Incl.	Opt. Field Title	Use	Optional Field
GSTFED	1		No			
RSTON	1		No			

Vendor No. **Description**
1100 **Start Date:** 5/1/2010 **Last Maintained:** 8/20/2000
Name: Kenin's Kopy Service
Address: 286 Main Street Georgetown, ON
Unit 6 L7G 1A2

Short Name: Kenin's KS **Phone:** (905)555 -9760
E-mail:
Web Site:
Contact: Kevin Williams **E-mail:**

Vendor Group: AMP **Account Set:** 1
Currency: CAD **Terms Code:** NODISC
Credit Limit: 1,500.000 **Bank Code:** 1STBK
Dist. Code: OFFSUP **Print Sep. Check:** No
Dup. Amt. Checking: Warning **Primary Remit to:**
Dup. Date Checking: Warning **Tax Group:** DOMPUR
Check Language: ENG **Rate Type:** SP
Subject to 1099 / CPRS Reporting: No

Tax Authority	Tax Class	Registration No.	Tax Incl.	Opt. Field Title	Use	Optional Field
GSTFED	1		No			
RSTON	1		No			

Vendor No. **Description**
1150 **Start Date:** 5/1/2010 **Last Maintained:** 8/20/2000
Name: Prestonia Office Products
Address: 229 Spadina Rd. Toronto, ON
L7B 9H5

Short Name: Prestonia **Phone:** (416)555 -1167
E-mail:
Web Site:
Contact: Ginnette Laframboise **E-mail:** gl.prestonia@gtn-bus.net

Vendor Group: AMP **Account Set:** 1
Currency: CAD **Terms Code:** DISC
Credit Limit: 5,000.000 **Bank Code:** 1STBK
Dist. Code: OFFSUP **Print Sep. Check:** No
Dup. Amt. Checking: Warning **Primary Remit to:**
Dup. Date Checking: Warning **Tax Group:** DOMPUR
Check Language: ENG **Rate Type:** SP
Subject to 1099 / CPRS Reporting: No

Tax Authority	Tax Class	Registration No.	Tax Incl.	Opt. Field Title	Use	Optional Field
GSTFED	1		No			
RSTON	1		No			

Date: Sunday, August 20, 2000 10:54AM **DDI Student Name** **Page 2**
A/P Vendor List (APVNDLT1)

Vendor No.	Description			
1180		**Start Date:** 5/10/2010	**Last Maintained:** 8/20/2000	
Name:	Software Depot			
Address:	6930 HayGlass Street		Oakville, ON L6H 5G9	
Short Name:	Software D	**Phone:**	(905)555 -5632	
E-mail:				
Web Site:				
Contact:	Ian Glaser		**E-mail:**	

Vendor Group:	AMP	**Account Set:**	1
Currency:	CAD	**Terms Code:**	DISC
Credit Limit:	0.000	**Bank Code:**	1STBK
G/L Account:	1540	**Print Sep. Check:**	No
Dup. Amt. Checking:	Warning	**Primary Remit to:**	
Dup. Date Checking:	Warning	**Tax Group:**	DOMPUR
Check Language:	ENG	**Rate Type:**	SP
Subject to 1099 / CPRS Reporting:	No		

Tax Authority	Tax Class	Registration No.	Tax Incl.	Opt. Field Title	Use	Optional Field
GSTFED	1		No			
RSTON	1		No			

Vendor No.	Description			
1200		**Start Date:** 5/1/2010	**Last Maintained:** 8/20/2000	
Name:	Prestige Properties			
Address:	80 Bloor St. W.		Toronto, ON L8H B5F	
Short Name:	Prestige P	**Phone:**	(416)555 -4497	
E-mail:				
Web Site:				
Contact:	Joseph Stern		**E-mail:**	

Vendor Group:	AMP	**Account Set:**	1
Currency:	CAD	**Terms Code:**	CASH
Credit Limit:	2,000.000	**Bank Code:**	1STBK
Dist. Code:	OFRENT	**Print Sep. Check:**	No
Dup. Amt. Checking:	Warning	**Primary Remit to:**	
Dup. Date Checking:	Warning	**Tax Group:**	DOMPUR
Check Language:	ENG	**Rate Type:**	SP
Subject to 1099 / CPRS Reporting:	No		

Tax Authority	Tax Class	Registration No.	Tax Incl.	Opt. Field Title	Use	Optional Field
GSTFED	1		No			
RSTON	1		No			

Vendor No.	Description			
1220		**Start Date:** 5/1/2010	**Last Maintained:** 8/20/2000	
Name:	MicroWare Ltd.			
Address:	1784 Seabreeze Ave.		Mississaga, ON L5G 7N9	
Short Name:	MicroWare	**Phone:**	(905)555 -7462	
E-mail:				
Web Site:				
Contact:	Larry Ward		**E-mail:**	

Vendor Group:	AMP	**Account Set:**	1
Currency:	CAD	**Terms Code:**	DISC
Credit Limit:	5,000.000	**Bank Code:**	1STBK
G/L Account:	1540	**Print Sep. Check:**	No
Dup. Amt. Checking:	Warning	**Primary Remit to:**	
Dup. Date Checking:	Warning	**Tax Group:**	DOMPUR
Check Language:	ENG	**Rate Type:**	SP
Subject to 1099 / CPRS Reporting:	No		

Tax Authority	Tax Class	Registration No.	Tax Incl.	Opt. Field Title	Use	Optional Field
GSTFED	1		No			
RSTON	1		No			

Date: Sunday, August 20, 2000 10:54AM
A/P Vendor List (APVNDLT1)

DDI Student Name

Page 3

Vendor No.	Description		
1250	Start Date: 5/1/2010	Last Maintained: 8/20/2000	
Name:	Summit Peak Computers		
Address:	1150 Stockwell Ave.	Georgetown, ON H8N 3S2	
Short Name:	Summit Pea	Phone:	(905)555 -7485
E-mail:			
Web Site:			
Contact:	Joe Day	E-mail:	

Vendor Group:	AMP	Account Set:	1
Currency:	CAD	Terms Code:	DISC
Credit Limit:	5,000.000	Bank Code:	1STBK
Dist. Code:	COMPRT	Print Sep. Check:	No
Dup. Amt. Checking:	Warning	Primary Remit to:	
Dup. Date Checking:	Warning	Tax Group:	DOMPUR
Check Language:	ENG	Rate Type:	SP
Subject to 1099 / CPRS Reporting:	No		

Tax Authority	Tax Class	Registration No.	Tax Incl.	Opt. Field Title	Use	Optional Field
GSTFED	1		No			
RSTON	1		No			

7 vendors printed

Remember to add each new vendor and then use the New Document icon to clear the window for a new vendor.

Printing The Vendor List

- ❑ Click: **File** on the menu bar of the A/P Vendors window
- ❑ Click: **Print** on the File Menu

The A/P Vendors Report window (Figure 25-15) has five entry areas that allow you to control the format and content of the printed report.

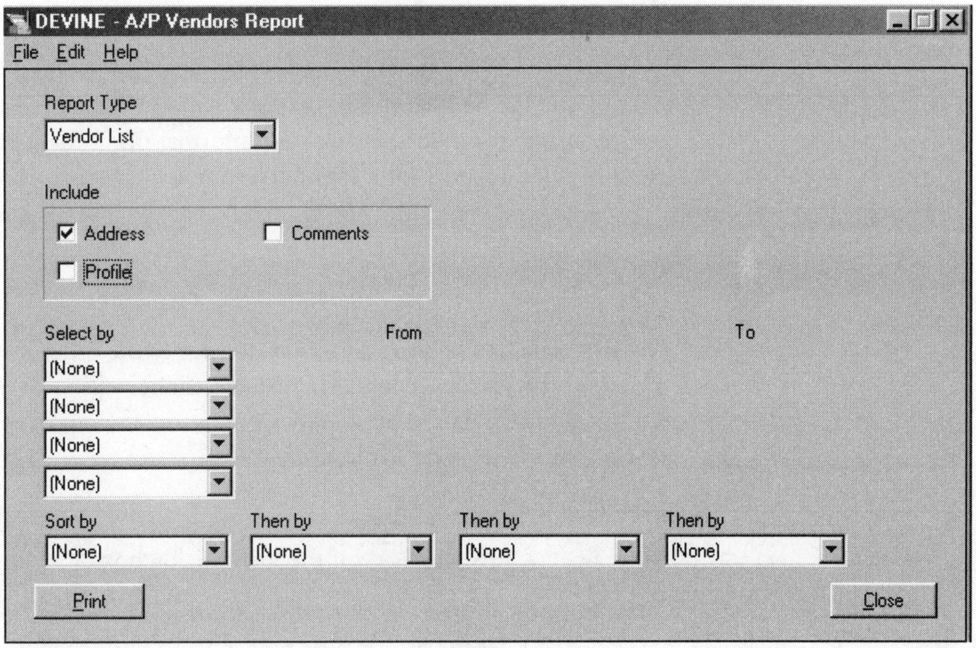

FIGURE 25-15
A/P Vendors Report Window

Report Type

The Report Type list box allows you to print three types of reports: a Vendor List, a Vendor Activity Statistics report, or a Vendor Period Statistics report. Devine Designs Inc. wants to print a Vendor List.

❑ Select: **Vendor List** using the list tool

Include

The Include area consists of three check boxes that allow you to select the information from the Vendor Account record that will be included in the report. The default is to print only the vendor address. Devine Designs Inc. will include the vendor profile in this report. Devine Designs Inc. has not yet added Comments, so this option will not be activated.

❑ Click: the **Profile** check box

Select by

The four **Select by** list boxes allow you to specify which vendor accounts will be included in the report. There are five possible selections. The default, None, includes all vendor accounts. If you use the list tool to select specific accounts, From and To text boxes with Finders will open beside the active list box. Devine Designs Inc. will print a report for all vendors but will use the first list box to specify all vendors.

❑ Select: **Vendor No.** in the first list box using the list tool

From and To text boxes will open beside the active list box. The defaults of a blank From text box and ZZZZZ in the To text box will include all vendors. If you want to print a specific group of vendors, change the information in these text boxes. Devine Designs Inc. will print a report for all vendors, so no changes are necessary.

Sort by

The four Sort by list boxes allow you to specify the order in which vendor accounts will appear on the printed report. The default, None, will print the report in order by vendor account number. As Devine Designs Inc. wants the report in order of vendor account number, no changes are necessary.

❑ Click: **Print** Print

❑ Click: **OK** OK on the Print dialog box.

WARNING
Check Distributions and Terms Carefully.

Compare your printed report to that shown in Figure 25-14 and make any needed corrections. If necessary, print the report again to document your changes.

❑ Close: the **A/P Vendors Report** window

❑ Close: the **A/P Vendors** window

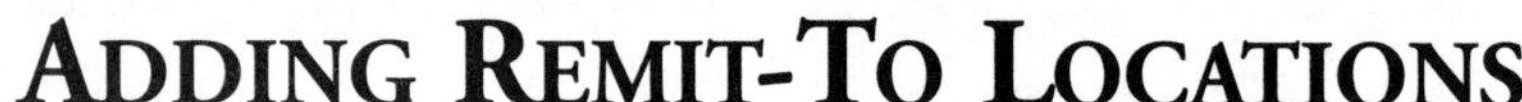

ADDING REMIT-TO LOCATIONS

ACCPAC for Windows allows you to add Remit-To Locations, which are the addresses to which vendors want payments sent. You use the Remit-To Locations notebook to add Remit-To addresses for your vendors when they are different from those in the vendor record. If you identify a Remit-To Location as the primary location, the program will use this location as the default address on vendor checks. The system can keep a nearly unlimited number of Remit-To Locations for the vendors, allowing you to choose the location when you are entering payments.

❑ DClick: the **Remit-To Locations** Remit-To Locations icon on the A/P Vendors window

The A/P Remit-to Locations window will appear as shown in Figure 25-16.

FIGURE 25-16
A/P Remit-To Locations Window

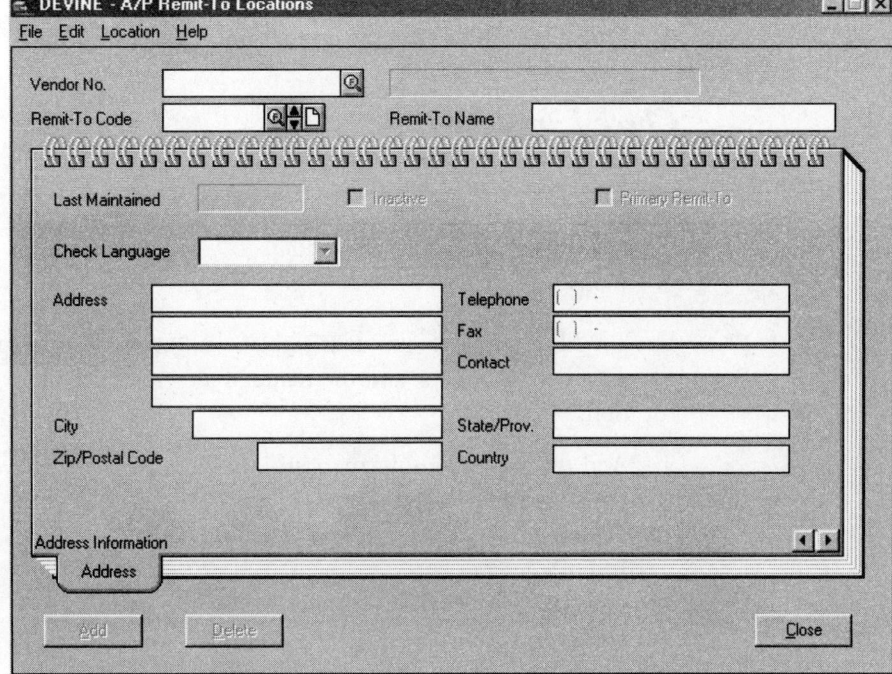

TIP

To change the vendor number, set up a new vendor record with a new number, then delete the record you no longer want.

- ❑ Click: the **Finder** to the right of the Vendor No. field
- ❑ Select: **1180 Software Depot**

Remit-To Code

The **Remit-To Location** code is a unique, six-character code that you use to identify the Remit-To Location.

- ❑ Type: **SOFDE2**
- ❑ Press: **Tab** [Tab]

Remit-To Name

The Description field is used to give a name or description of the Remit-To Location, for example, "Western Office."

- ❑ Type: **Software Depot**
- ❑ Press: **Tab** [Tab]

Primary Remit-To

If you want the Accounts Payable program to use the **Remit-To Location** address for the address on the checks printed to this vendor, check this selection box.

- ❑ Click: the **Primary Remit-To** check box to activate it
- ❑ Press: **Tab** [Tab]

Check Language

You can select the language to be used when writing a check to any individual vendor.

- ❑ Select: **ENG** using the Finder
- ❑ Press: **Tab** [Tab]

ACCPAC for Windows provides eight fields for the Remit-To address, as well as telephone and fax numbers, and the name of a contact person or position at the Remit-To Location.

- ❑ Add the following information:
  1900 Airport Drive
  Toronto, ON
  L5F 4V2
  Tel: 416 555 7846
  Contact: Chris Kanski

Review your entries. Once you are satisfied they are correct,

- ❑ Click: **Add** [Add]

YOUR TURN

- ❑ Add: the following Remit-To Location for account 1001, As-Tech Computers:

Remit-To Code	AT2
Remit-To Name	AsTech Ltd

- ❑ Click: the **Primary Remit-To** check box

The Check language will be English.

125 Erin Mills Parkway
Mississauga, ON
L5L 6C3
Tel: 905 555 3356
Contact: George Dibdin

Review your entries. Once you are satisfied that they are correct,

- ❑ Click: **Add** [Add]
- ❑ Print: the **Remit-To Locations** report icon. Include the Profile.

Once you have finished printing,

- ❑ Close: the **A/P Remit-To Report** dialog box
- ❑ Close: the **A/P Remit-To Locations** window

Modifying Remit-To Locations

You can change or delete a **Remit-To Location** whenever necessary. To change information, select the vendor number and Remit-To Location code for the record you want to change, then select or type the new information in the fields you want changed. You can change all the information in a record except the Remit-To code. To change the code, you must first add another record using a new code, then delete the record you no longer want.

To delete a Remit-To code, select the vendor number and Remit-To code for the record, then select Delete. Once you have finished modifying or deleting a record, remember to choose Save to record your changes.

- ❑ Exit: **ACCPAC**
- ❑ Back up your data.

REVIEW QUESTIONS

1. What is the purpose of Vendor Records?
2. What is the purpose of Vendor Groups?
3. Why should you set a credit limit from a vendor?
4. Group Statistics keeps track of what information?
5. What constraints are there on the deletion of Vendor Groups?
6. How long can a vendor number be?
7. Why should you leave a certain amount of space between the vendor numbers you assign?
8. How long can a vendor name be?
9. What will happen if you place a vendor On Hold then attempt to record an invoice?

EXERCISE

- ❑ Sign on to your company as the system administrator using 05/30/10 as the Session Date.

1. Add the Vendor Groups shown in Figure 25-17.

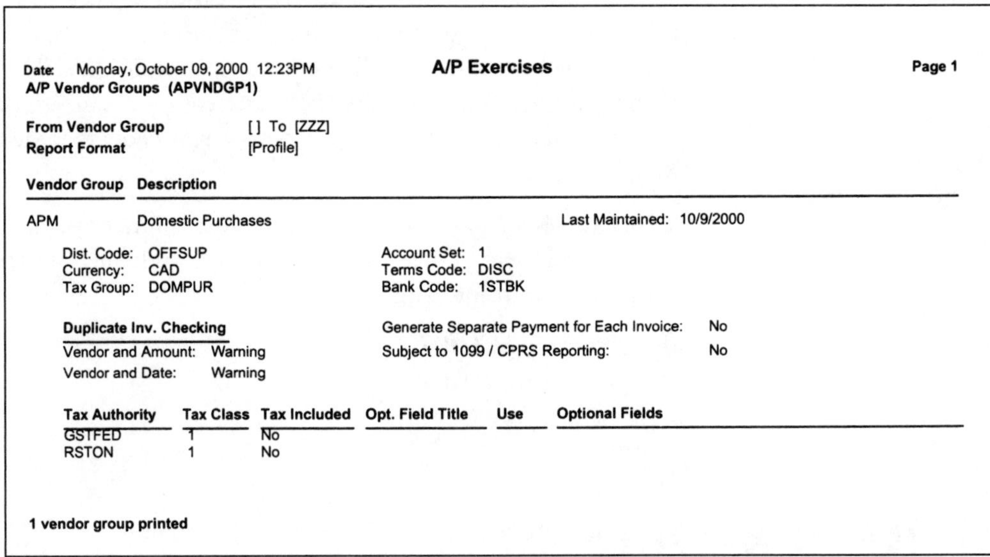

Date: Monday, October 09, 2000 12:23PM — **A/P Exercises** — **Page 1**

A/P Vendor Groups (APVNDGP1)

From Vendor Group [] To [ZZZ]
Report Format [Profile]

Vendor Group	Description		
APM	Domestic Purchases	Last Maintained:	10/9/2000

Dist. Code: OFFSUP — Account Set: 1
Currency: CAD — Terms Code: DISC
Tax Group: DOMPUR — Bank Code: 1STBK

Duplicate Inv. Checking
Vendor and Amount: Warning
Vendor and Date: Warning

Generate Separate Payment for Each Invoice: No
Subject to 1099 / CPRS Reporting: No

Tax Authority	Tax Class	Tax Included	Opt. Field Title	Use	Optional Fields
GSTFED	1	No			
RSTON	1	No			

1 vendor group printed

FIGURE 25-17
A/P Vendor Group

2. Print: the **A/P Vendor Group** report
3. Add the vendors shown in Figure 25-18. None of the vendors has a separate Remit-To Location.
4. Print: the **A/P Vendor List**

- ❑ Exit: **ACCPAC**

Figure 25-18
A/P Vendor List

Date: Monday, October 09, 2000 1:00PM **A/P Exercises** **Page 1**
A/P Vendor List (APVNDLT1)

From Vendor No. [ ] To [ZZZZZZZZZZZZ]
Report Format [Profile, Address]

Vendor No. **Description**

1005 **Start Date:** 4/30/2010 **Last Maintained:** 10/9/2000
Name: Ainsworth Stationary
Address: Unit 3
7245 Montivedeo Drive
Mississauga, Ontario
L6G 6D2

Short Name: Ainsworth **Phone:** (905)555 -4678 **Fax:** (905)555-4666
E-mail:
Web Site:
Contact: Roger Young **E-mail:**

Vendor Group: APM **Account Set:** 1
Currency: CAD **Terms Code:** DISC
Credit Limit: 5,000.000 **Bank Code:** 1STBK
Dist. Code: OFFSUP **Print Sep. Check:** No
Dup. Amt. Checking: Warning **Primary Remit to:**
Dup. Date Checking: Warning **Tax Group:** DOMPUR
Check Language: ENG **Rate Type:** SP
Subject to 1099 / CPRS Reporting: No

Tax Authority	Tax Class	Registration No.	Tax Incl.	Opt. Field Title	Use	Optional Field
GSTFED	1		No			
RSTON	1		No			

Vendor No. **Description**

1010 **Start Date:** 4/30/2010 **Last Maintained:** 10/9/2000
Name: Citabria Interconnect
Address: 170 Torbram Road
Brampton, Ontario
H8K 4C7

Short Name: Citabria **Phone:** (905)555 -7531 **Fax:** (905)555-7745
E-mail:
Web Site:
Contact: **E-mail:**

Vendor Group: APM **Account Set:** 1
Currency: CAD **Terms Code:** DISC
Credit Limit: 15,000.000 **Bank Code:** 1STBK
Dist. Code: ISP **Print Sep. Check:** No
Dup. Amt. Checking: Warning **Primary Remit to:**
Dup. Date Checking: Warning **Tax Group:** DOMPUR
Check Language: ENG **Rate Type:** SP
Subject to 1099 / CPRS Reporting: No

Tax Authority	Tax Class	Registration No.	Tax Incl.	Opt. Field Title	Use	Optional Field
GSTFED	1		No			
RSTON	1		No			

Vendor No. **Description**

1020 **Start Date:** 4/30/2010 **Last Maintained:** 10/9/2000
Name: Currys Ltd.
Address: 1330 Blondell Drive
Brampton, Ontario
J9K 5D3

Short Name: Currys Ltd **Phone:** (905)555 -5123 **Fax:** (905)555-5133
E-mail:
Web Site:
Contact: Joycelyn **E-mail:**

Vendor Group: APM **Account Set:** 1
Currency: CAD **Terms Code:** DISC
Credit Limit: 5,000.000 **Bank Code:** 1STBK
Dist. Code: COMPRT **Print Sep. Check:** No
Dup. Amt. Checking: Warning **Primary Remit to:**
Dup. Date Checking: Warning **Tax Group:** DOMPUR
Check Language: ENG **Rate Type:** SP
Subject to 1099 / CPRS Reporting: No

Tax Authority	Tax Class	Registration No.	Tax Incl.	Opt. Field Title	Use	Optional Field

Date: Monday, October 09, 2000 1:00PM **A/P Exercises** **Page 2**
A/P Vendor List (APVNDLT1)

GSTFED	1		No
RSTON	1		No

Vendor No. **Description**
1130 **Start Date:** 4/30/2010 **Last Maintained:** 10/9/2000
Name: Niemi Properies
Address: 700 Dundas St. E. Woodbridge, Ontario J9M 6F3

Short Name: Niemi Prop **Phone:** (905)555 -7914 **Fax:** (905)555-7764
E-mail:
Web Site:
Contact: Joe Niemi **E-mail:**

Vendor Group:	APM	**Account Set:**	1
Currency:	CAD	**Terms Code:**	NODISC
Credit Limit:	5,000.000	**Bank Code:**	1STBK
Dist. Code:	OFRENT	**Print Sep. Check:**	No
Dup. Amt. Checking:	Warning	**Primary Remit to:**	
Dup. Date Checking:	Warning	**Tax Group:**	DOMPUR
Check Language:	ENG	**Rate Type:**	SP

Subject to 1099 / CPRS Reporting: No

Tax Authority	Tax Class	Registration No.	Tax Incl.	Opt. Field Title	Use	Optional Field
GSTFED	2		No			
RSTON	2		No			

Vendor No. **Description**
1190 **Start Date:** 4/30/2010 **Last Maintained:** 10/9/2000
Name: Torchia Ltd.
Address: 240 Eglington Ave. E. Toronto, Ontario L7G 4C0

Short Name: Torchia **Phone:** (416)555 -3622 **Fax:** (416)555-3623
E-mail:
Web Site:
Contact: Frank **E-mail:**

Vendor Group:	APM	**Account Set:**	1
Currency:	CAD	**Terms Code:**	DISC
Credit Limit:	4,000.000	**Bank Code:**	1STBK
Dist. Code:	ADV	**Print Sep. Check:**	No
Dup. Amt. Checking:	Warning	**Primary Remit to:**	
Dup. Date Checking:	Warning	**Tax Group:**	DOMPUR
Check Language:	ENG	**Rate Type:**	SP

Subject to 1099 / CPRS Reporting: No

Tax Authority	Tax Class	Registration No.	Tax Incl.	Opt. Field Title	Use	Optional Field
GSTFED	1		No			
RSTON	1		No			

Vendor No. **Description**
1200 **Start Date:** 4/30/2010 **Last Maintained:** 10/9/2000
Name: Bell Telephone
Address: 1663 Runeymeade Rd. Etobicoke, Ontario K9H 5F4

Short Name: Bell **Phone:** (416)555 -1673 **Fax:** (416)555-1333
E-mail:
Web Site:
Contact: **E-mail:**

Vendor Group:	APM	**Account Set:**	1
Currency:	CAD	**Terms Code:**	NODISC
Credit Limit:	1,000.000	**Bank Code:**	1STBK
Dist. Code:	COMM	**Print Sep. Check:**	No
Dup. Amt. Checking:	Warning	**Primary Remit to:**	
Dup. Date Checking:	Warning	**Tax Group:**	DOMPUR
Check Language:	ENG	**Rate Type:**	SP

Subject to 1099 / CPRS Reporting: No

Tax Authority	Tax Class	Registration No.	Tax Incl.	Opt. Field Title	Use	Optional Field

Date: Monday, October 09, 2000 1:00PM **A/P Exercises** Page 3
A/P Vendor List (APVNDLT1)

GSTFED	1	No
RSTON	1	No

6 vendors printed

CHAPTER 26

INVOICE ENTRY

Before entering an invoice, you have to create at least one Payment Selection Code if you want the ACCPAC for Windows Accounts Payable system to automatically generate payments for invoices. If you intend to manually enter all payments to a batch, you do not have to create Payment Selection Codes.

GETTING STARTED

- ❑ Sign on to Devine Designs Inc. as the system administrator using 05/30/10 as the Session Date.
- ❑ Open: the **Accounts Payable** main window
- ❑ DClick: the **A/P Payments** icon [A/P Payments]

The A/P Payments window will appear as shown in Figure 26-1.

FIGURE 26-1
A/P Payments Icons

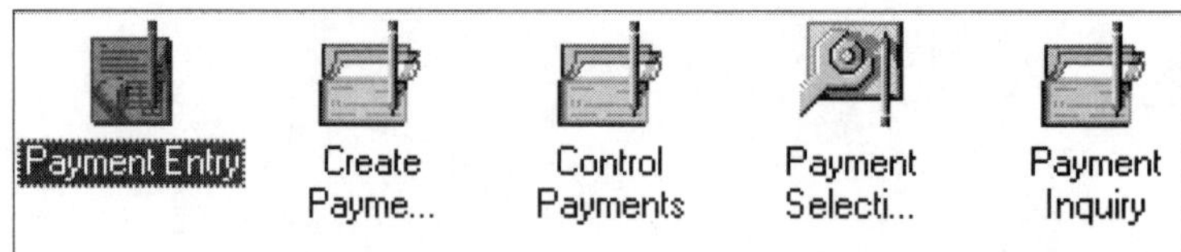

ADDING PAYMENT SELECTION CODES

You have to enter a Payment Selection Code to identify the criteria for selecting the invoices to be paid. In this case, you will be creating two codes to select all of the invoices that are due.

❑ DClick: the **Payment Selection Codes** icon .

The Bank and Currency Selection Criteria page of the A/P Payment Selection Codes notebook will appear as shown in Figure 26-2.

FIGURE 26-2
Bank and Currency Selection Criteria Page

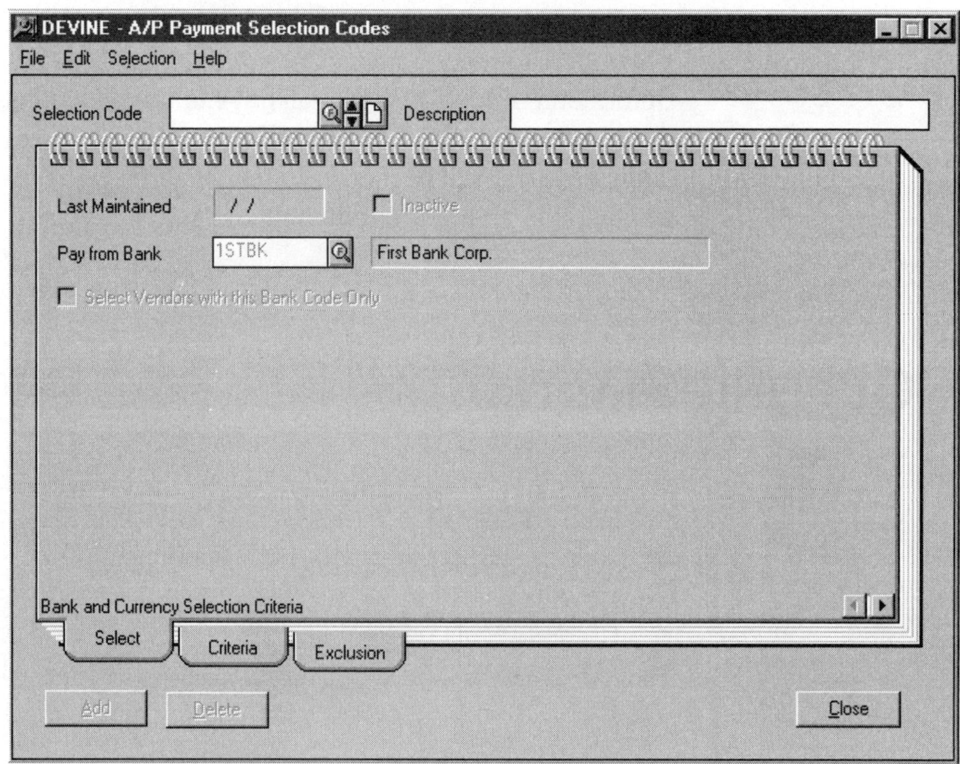

Make sure that the cursor is active in the Selection Code field.

❑ Type: **DUE**
❑ Press: **Tab** [Tab]
❑ Type: **All due invoices**
❑ Press: **Tab** [Tab]

Inactive

Select Inactive only if you are preparing to delete an A/P Selection Code and want to ensure that no further transactions use it. Devine Designs Inc. will not select this option when setting up the initial selection codes.

- ❑ Click: the **Finder** for the **Pay from Bank** field
- ❑ Select: **1STBK**

The Select Vendors with this Bank Code Only option confines the selection to vendors that have this bank specified in their vendor record. The majority of your transactions will be routed through this bank account. The remaining transactions will go through the EBANK account.

- ❑ Click: the **Select Vendors with this Bank Code Only** check box to activate it

Vendor and Date Selection Criteria

- ❑ Click: the **Criteria** tab at the bottom of the A/P Payment Selection Codes notebook

The Vendor and Date Selection Criteria page will appear as shown in Figure 26-3. This page allows you to decide if you will take discounts by making early payments. You have the following choices:

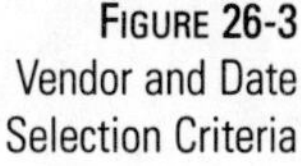

FIGURE 26-3
Vendor and Date
Selection Criteria

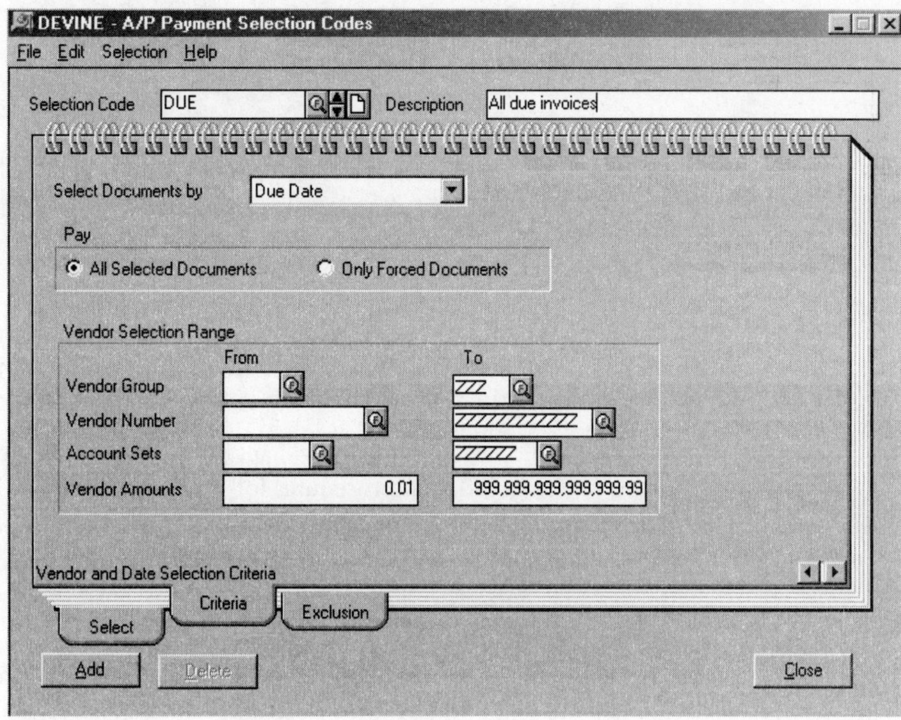

Due Date: You may select documents that are due on or before the ending date specified when you create a payment batch. The program will not choose invoices for payment based on the discount date, but will take any discounts that are available.

Discount Date: The program will select invoices that are eligible for a discount if paid on or before the end date you specify.

Due Date and Discount Date: The program will select invoices that are due on or before the date you specify, or that have a discount available if paid on or before the date specified.

The due date entered when creating a check batch is the latest date up to which you want transactions included. When creating a batch, you must also enter a date indicating how far back you want to take discounts. The program will ignore discounts that stopped being available before the date you enter.

- ❑ Click: the **list tool** for the Select Documents by field
- ❑ Select: **Due Date and Disc. Date**
- ❑ Press: **Tab** [Tab]

Pay

You may decide to pay all the documents in the selection, or only the transactions that have a Forced status.

- ❑ Select: the **All Selected Documents** option button is active
- ❑ Press: **Tab** [Tab]

Vendor Selection Range

You have to select the range of vendor groups, vendor numbers, account sets, and check amounts. The default is to select all Vendor Groups, Vendor Numbers, Account Sets, and Vendor Amounts. Devine Designs Inc. has decided to leave the defaults unchanged.

Vendor Exclusion List

Click: the **Exclusion** tab at the bottom of the A/P Payment Selection Codes notebook

The Vendor Exclusion List page will appear as shown in Figure 26-4. This page allows you to maintain different procedures for smaller checks. The Vendor Exclusion List page allows you to list vendors that you want to exclude from the check run. You do not have any vendors that you want to exclude from the payment selection.

- ❑ Click: **Add** [Add]

You have to create a second Payment Selection Code for payments made to those companies that are set up to deal with electronic banking.

FIGURE 26-4
Vendor Exclusion List Page

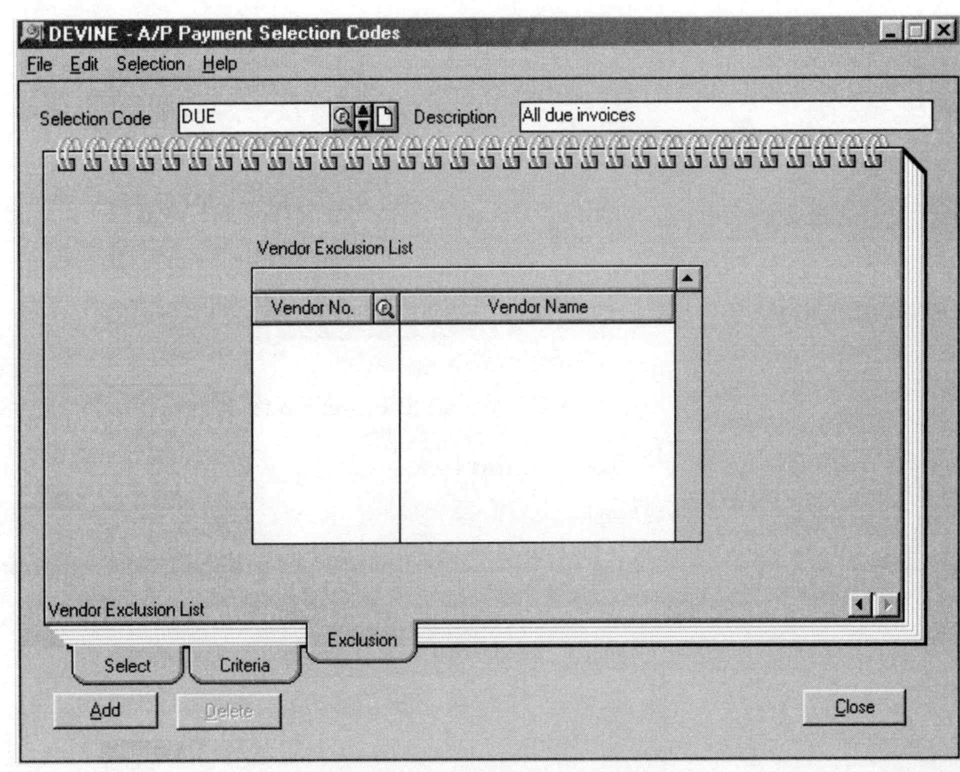

- ❑ Click: the **Select** tab at the bottom of the A/P Payment Selection Codes notebook
- ❑ Click: the **New Document** icon for the Selection Code field

Add the following information:

Selection Code: **EBANK**
Description: **Invoices Payable by E Banking**
Pay from Bank: **EBANK**

- ❑ Activate: **Select Vendors with this Bank Code Only**
- ❑ Click: **Add** [Add]
- ❑ Click: the **Criteria** tab at the bottom of the A/P Payment Selection Codes page
- ❑ Select: **Due Date and Disc. Date**
- ❑ Press: **Tab** [Tab]
- ❑ Select: the **All Selected Documents**
- ❑ Click: **Save** [Save]
- ❑ Click: **Close** to return to the A/P Payments window
- ❑ Open: the **Accounts Payable** main window
- ❑ DClick: the **A/P Setup Reports** icon
- ❑ DClick: the **Payment Selection Codes** icon [Payment Selecti...]

The A/P Payment Selection Codes Report window appears as shown in Figure 26-5.

FIGURE 26-5
A/P Payment Selection Codes Report

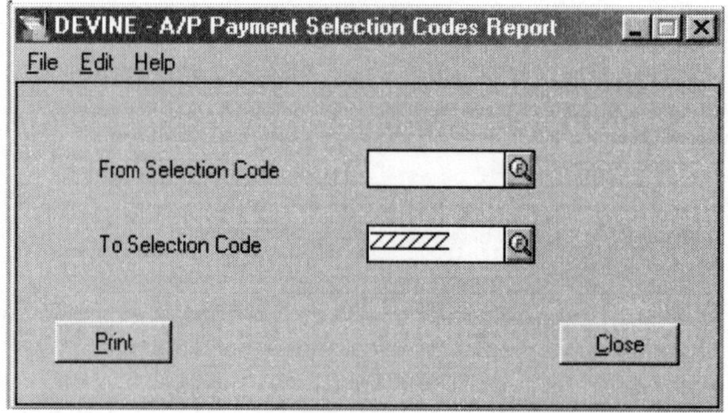

When the A/P Payment Selection Codes Report window appears,

- ❑ Click: **Print**
- ❑ Click: **OK**

Once the A/P Payment Selection Codes Report has been printed:

- ❑ Close: the **A/P Payment Selection Codes Report** dialog box
- ❑ Open: the **Accounts Payable** main window

Your ACCPAC for Windows Accounts Payable system is now ready to record invoices and transactions.

INVOICE ENTRY

In this section, you will initiate the Devine Designs Inc. data files for the ACCPAC Small Business Series Accounts Payable module. Devine Designs Inc. is already using the System Manager, General Ledger, and Accounts Receivable modules.

Remember that you can learn more about data entry options by utilizing the F1(Help) key as demonstrated by the following steps:

- ❑ DClick: the **A/P Invoices** icon 

The A/P Invoices window will appear as shown in Figure 26-6.

FIGURE 26-6
A/P Invoices Icons

❑ DClick: the **Invoice Entry** icon 

The A/P Invoice Entry notebook will appear as shown in Figure 26-7.

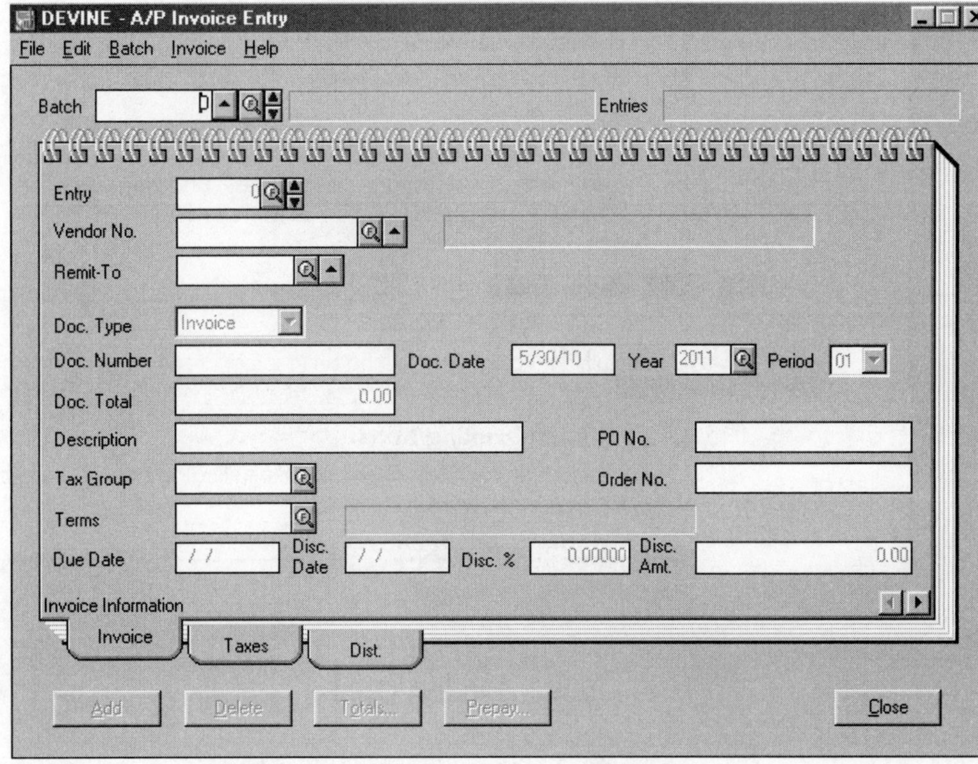

FIGURE 26-7
A/P Invoice Entry Notebook

WARNING

If you press the F1 key when a window containing icons for ACCPAC Plus for Windows is active, you will get help for the System Manager, not the Accounts Payable.

Once you arrive at a data entry, report, or enquiry window, you can press the F1 key to obtain help for a window.

The entry point should be active in the Batch field.

❑ Press: the **F1** key

The ACCPAC Accounts Payable Helper will appear as shown in Figure 26-8.

Help text provides you with assistance in determining the type of information you should enter into various fields.

Once you have reviewed the information in the Help window,

❑ Close: the **Accounts Payable Help** window

FIGURE 26-8
ACCPAC Accounts Payable Helper

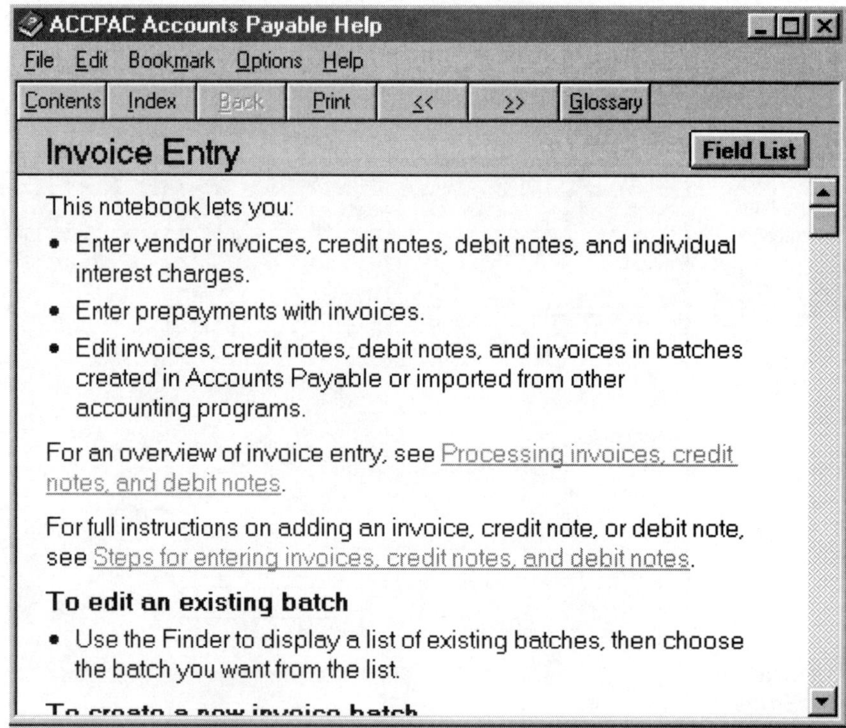

ENTERING AN INVOICE

The purpose of this section is to show you how to create a new batch, how to add an invoice, and how to enter tax amounts.

Devine Designs Inc. paid all of the outstanding invoices at the end of April 2010, so you do not have to add outstanding invoices to the accounts payable then balance it to the General Ledger. The following invoices represent transactions that occurred in May 2010.

The company made a purchase from Prestonia Office Products. The purchase transaction consisted of stationery supplies and furniture for use by the business, plus GST (VAT) Recoverable and RST.

CREATING A NEW BATCH

The Batch Field

The Batch field is used to select an existing batch, open the batch header in order to create a new one, or modify header information. In this case, you will create a new batch.

TIP

Whenever the window contains a Popup window, the Popup icon is an upward-pointing arrowhead.

When you create a batch, the Accounts Payable program assigns a new batch number that is part of the audit trail. You cannot assign the number to another invoice batch. If you delete a batch you have created, the batch number cannot be reused until after you have processed the year-end. The batch number appears with each transaction on the posting journal.

❑ Click: the **Batch Zoom** icon

The Batch Header window will appear as shown in Figure 26-9.

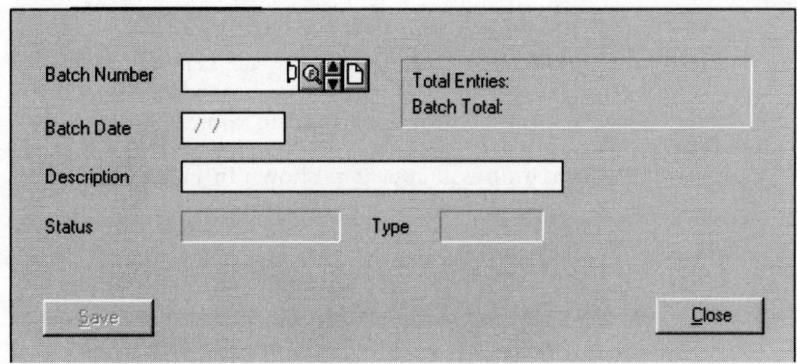

FIGURE 26-9
Batch Header Window

Batch Header

The Batch Header window is used to record the identifying characteristics of the batch.

❑ Click: the **New Document** icon on the right side of the Batch Number field

The next batch number in sequence is created by the program and appears in the Batch Number field.

When you create a new batch number, the session date appears in the Batch Date field.

❑ Press: **Tab** [Tab] to move to the Description field

The Batch Description forms part of the information that is displayed in the Batch List window. You do not have to enter a description for every batch, but it is a valuable tool that helps you keep track of your batches. If more than one person enters transactions for your company, you may also want to include the operator's initials in each batch description.

❑ Type: **May Purchases**

❑ Press: **Tab** [Tab]

❑ Click: **Save** [Save]

❑ Click: **Close** [Close]

WARNING

If a message appears inquiring whether you want to save the changes to the Batch Header, you have probably forgotten to save the Batch Header information. Make sure that your entries are correct, then select Yes.

Entry

The Entry field is used to create a new entry or select an existing entry. The Entry number is assigned automatically by Accounts Payable. You do not type in this field when creating a new batch.

❑ Click: the **Finder** to the right of the Vendor No. field
❑ Select: **1150 - Prestonia Office Products**

As soon as you select the vendor, the remaining fields on the Invoice Information page will display the information that was entered for the vendor in the Vendors notebook. To verify the vendor's name and address in the vendor record;

❑ Click: the **Vendor Information** zoom icon

Vendor Information will appear as shown in Figure 26-10.

FIGURE 26-10
Vendor Information

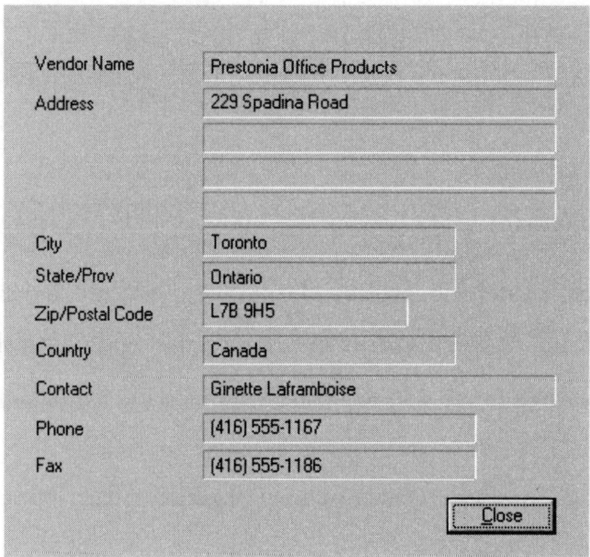

Once you are satisfied that the correct vendor is displayed,

❑ Click: **Close**

Remit-To

The Remit-To code identifies the address to which you will send payments for Prestonia Office Products. You use Remit-To locations for vendors when you send their payments to more than one address, or when you send payments to a Remit-To address and purchase orders to another.

❑ Click: the **Finder** to the right of the Remit-To field

Prestonia does not have a separate Remit-To address, so the Remit-To Locations window contains no information.

- ❑ Click: **Cancel** Cancel
- ❑ Press: **Tab** Tab

Document Type

This field shows Invoice as the default.

- ❑ Press: **Tab** Tab

Document Number

Enter the vendor's invoice number in the **Doc. Number** field. You may not use the same invoice number twice in the Accounts Payable program. Also, you cannot use duplicate numbers for other types of Accounts Payable documents, such as credit and debit notes. Transactions that duplicate a previously posted document number are placed in an error batch during posting.

- ❑ Type: **POP9889**
- ❑ Press: **Tab** Tab to move to the Document Date field
- ❑ Type: **051210**

The program will automatically display the current year and period from the company's fiscal calendar. Make sure that the year and period display Period 1, 2011. If you have to change the year, click on the Finder next to the Year field, then select one that is defined in your company's calendar. To change the period, click on the list tool next to the Period field, then select the desired period.

- ❑ Press: **Tab** Tab three times to move to the Doc. Total field

Document Total

The invoice consisted of five lines, for a total of $1092.50. The first two, for $150 and $300, were for office supplies, and the third line was for a pair of chairs for the reception room, $500. The fourth line, $76.00, was for Retail Sales Tax, and the last line, $66.50, was for GST. Retail Sales Tax is not recoverable; consequently, it is not accounted for separately. The Retail Sales Tax is included as part of the cost of the office supplies and furniture.

- ❑ Type: **1092.50** as the total amount payable in the Doc. Total field
- ❑ Press: **Tab** Tab to move to the Description field

This field is used to create a brief description for each invoice.

- ❑ Type: **Furniture and Supplies**
- ❑ Press: **Tab** Tab to move to the PO No. field

- ❑ Type: **DD0004**
- ❑ Press: **Tab** [Tab] to move to the Tax Group field
- ❑ Press: **Tab** [Tab] to leave the Tax Group field unchanged

Order Number

The Order No. field is used to record the vendor's order number if one was created upon receipt of the buyer's purchase order.

- ❑ Type: **ORD-1354**
- ❑ Press: **Tab** [Tab] to move to the Terms field
- ❑ Click: the **Finder** to the right of the Terms field
- ❑ Select: **NODISC**

When you select the terms for the invoice, the program will determine the due date. Net 30 does not allow for a discount, so the Discount Date field remains blank, and the Disc. % and Disc. Amt. fields display zeros. Had the vendor allowed a discount on this invoice, discount amounts and percentage would have appeared.

Review your entry. Once you are satisfied that it is correct,

- ❑ Click: the **Taxes** tab at the bottom of the A/P Invoice Entry notebook

ENTERING INVOICE TAX INFORMATION

The Vendor Taxes page will appear as shown in Figure 26-11.

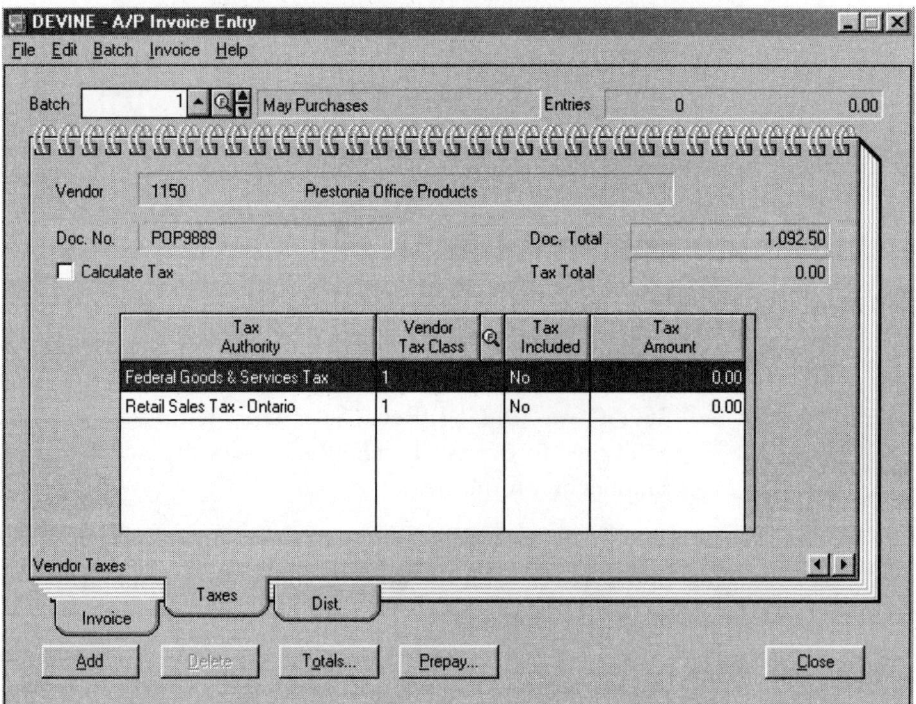

FIGURE 26-11
Vendor Taxes

This page displays the tax authorities for RST and GST. The tax authorities and tax classes for each authority are determined by the tax group assigned to the vendor record. You can change the tax class by entering a new class in the middle column, or by selecting it from the Finder.

- ❑ Click: the **Calculate Tax** check box
- ❑ Click: the **Dist.** tab at the bottom of the A/P Invoice Entry notebook

The Distribution Information page will be appear as shown in Figure 26-12.

FIGURE 26-12 Distribution Information Page

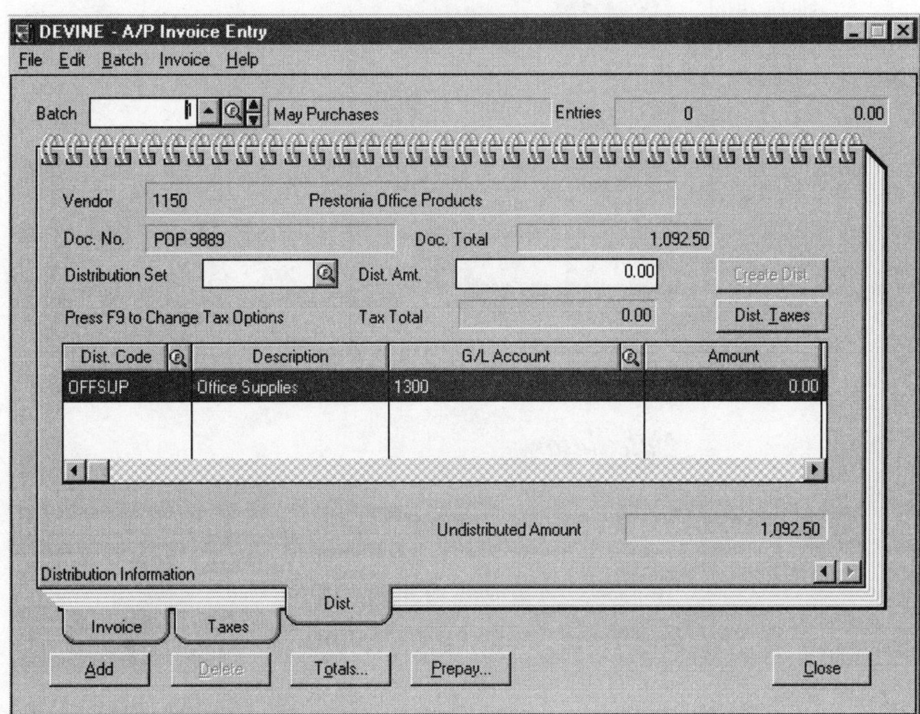

Distributing Invoice and Tax Amounts

The purpose of the Distribution Information page is to distribute the dollar amounts of purchases to the different General Ledger accounts. The invoice from Prestonia Office Products is for office supplies and furniture that will be put into use for the company.

The Vendor Record for Prestonia Office Products presents the default distribution code for an office supplies inventory purchase.

Adjusting Column Widths

You can change the width of the columns. Position the cursor on the vertical line between the Description and G/L Account titles.

Note that when it is in the correct position, the cursor changes to a "+". Click and hold the left mouse button, then drag the column boundary to the left, until you can see the entire Amount column.

- ❑ Click: the **Amount** cell for the OFFSUP line
- ❑ Press: the + key on the numeric keypad to activate the calculator

A calculator will appear as shown in Figure 26-13.

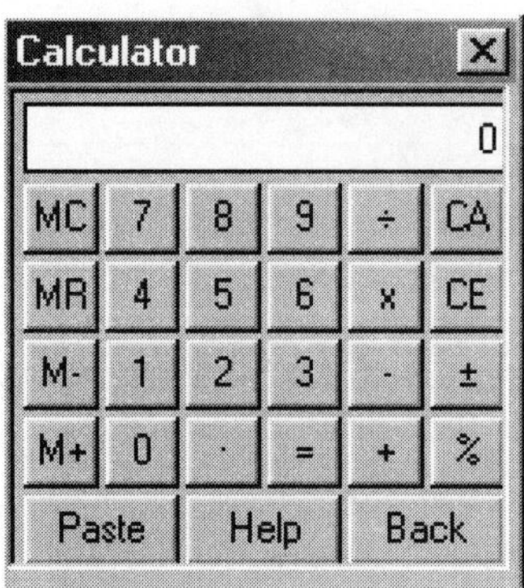

FIGURE 26-13
Calculator

Calculator

You can use the numeric keypad to add items on an invoice, or you can click on the numbers and symbols of the keypad directly. There were two different amounts listed on the Prestonia invoice as office supplies.

- ❑ Type: **300.00 + 150.00**
- ❑ Press: **Enter**
- ❑ Click: the **Paste** button at the bottom of the calculator

When you click on the Paste button, the amount shown in the calculator is transferred to the Amount field on the Invoice Entry screen.

- ❑ Press: **Tab** [Tab]
- ❑ Press: the **Insert** key to create a new distribution line
- ❑ Click: the **G/L Account** field on the second line

The next distribution is to the Furniture and Fixtures account. Since no distribution code is defined for it, you must enter the General Ledger account number. Search for the account using the Finder.

- ❑ Click: the **Finder** to the right of G/L Account title
- ❑ Select: **Account 1520 - Furniture & Fixtures**
- ❑ Click: the **Amount** field
- ❑ Type: **500.00**
- ❑ Press: **Tab** [Tab]
- ❑ Click: **Add** [Add]

The Distribution Details page is shown in Figure 26-14.

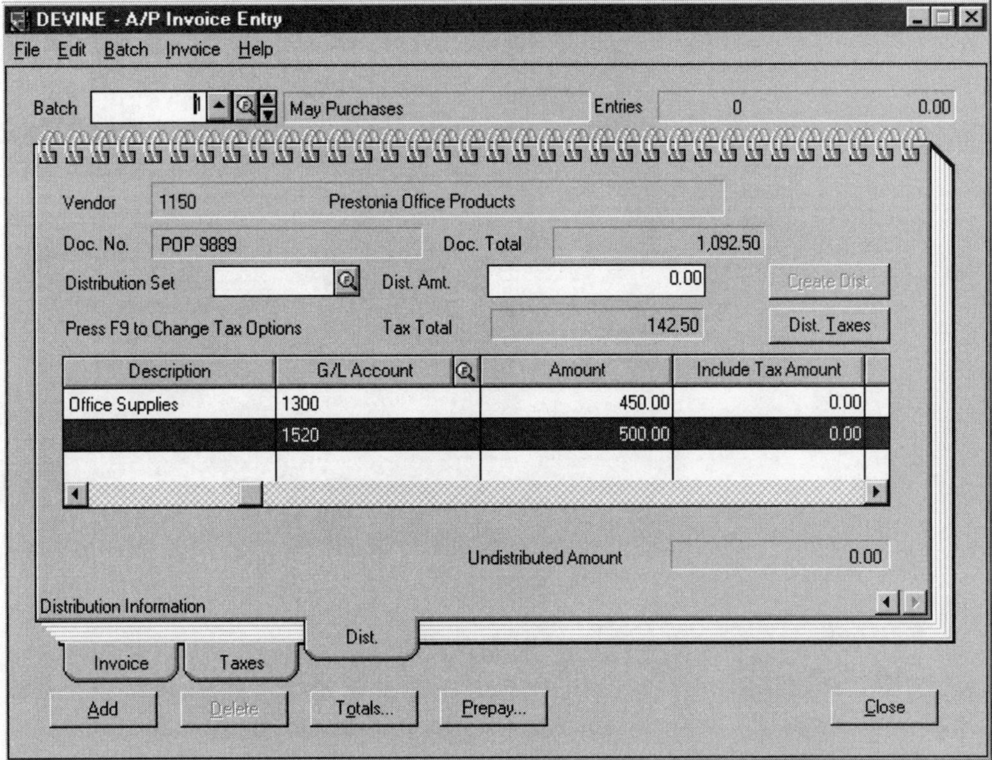

FIGURE 26-14
Distribution Details

Distribution Details

You may have to scroll the Distribution fields to the right to see the Distribution details that appear in the Amount, Allocated Tax, and G/L Distribution Amount columns. The Undistributed Amount field is zero. You have now finished distributing the invoice and tax amounts. Normally you would review the distribution amounts in this window, then add the invoice. For the purposes of this chapter, you will also review the invoice totals in the Totals window.

❑ Click: the **Totals...** [Totals...] button at the bottom of the A/P Invoice Entry notebook

The Invoice Totals window will appear as shown in Figure 26-15.

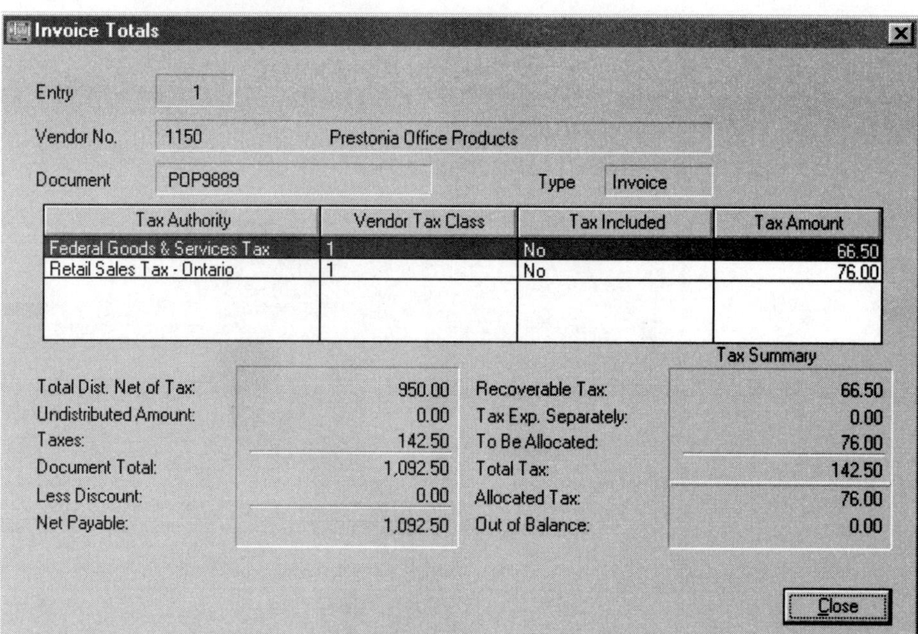

FIGURE 26-15
Invoice Totals

WARNING
You cannot change any of the information on the Invoice Totals information screen. Review the information and compare it to Figure 26-15.

Reviewing Invoice Totals

Review the totals of your invoice and compare them to the amounts on the sample invoice to verify that you have entered everything correctly.

The Invoice Totals window is available from any page in the Invoice Entry notebook when you click on the Totals button.

- ❑ Click: **Close**

YOUR TURN

Entry 2

On May 20, 2010, Kevin's Kopy Service invoiced Devine Designs Inc. for $450.00 in stationery supplies. Invoice KKS 0175 totaled $517.50. Devine Design's purchase order number was DD0005.

- ❑ Click: the **Invoice** tab at the bottom of the A/P Invoice Entry notebook
- ❑ Click: the **New Document** icon for the Entry field
- ❑ Select: **Account 1100 Kevin's Kopy Service**
- ❑ Type: **KKS 0175** in the Document Number field
- ❑ Press: **Tab** [Tab]
- ❑ Type: **052010** in the Date field
- ❑ Press: **Tab** [Tab] three times
- ❑ Type: **517.50** in the Doc. Total field

- ❑ Press: **Tab** [Tab]
- ❑ Type: **Stationery Supplies** in the Description field
- ❑ Press: **Tab** [Tab]
- ❑ Type: **DD0005** in the Purchase Order field
- ❑ Press: **Tab** [Tab]
- ❑ Click: the **Taxes** tab at the bottom of the A/P Invoice Entry notebook
- ❑ Click: the **Calculate Tax** check box to activate it
- ❑ Click: the **Dist.** Tab at the bottom of the A/P Invoice Entry notebook

The default Distribution Code for Kevin's Kopy Service is OFFSUP. If necessary, select OFFSUP in the Dist. Code cell.

- ❑ Click: the **Amount** field
- ❑ Type: **450.00** (the amount of the invoice before taxes)
- ❑ Press: **Enter**
- ❑ Click: the **Dist. Taxes** button [Dist. Taxes]
- ❑ Click: **Totals...** [Totals...]

Review the entry for accuracy. You should see recoverable tax of $31.50 and $36.00 in taxes to be allocated. The balance in the Undistributed Amount field should be zero.

- ❑ Close: the **Invoice Totals** window
- ❑ Click: **Add** [Add]

Add the following invoices. Some will be distributed using General Ledger accounts, while others can be distributed using distribution codes.

Entry 3

Devine Designs Inc. received Software Depot invoice SD-35820, dated May 20, 2010 for a total of $1144.25 ($995.00 plus taxes). Purchase order DD0006 was for operating system software. Software Depot offers 2/10, n/30 terms.

Entry 4

On May 25, 2010 Devine Designs Inc. purchased 100 blank CD disks on purchase order DD0001 from Summit Peak Computers. The CDs will be used for storage and delivery of Web pages designed for customers, and will be considered office supplies. The invoice, SP-8746, dated May 25, 2010 totaled $230.00 ($200.00 plus tax) and offered 2/10, n/30 terms.

Entry 5

On May 9, 2010 Devine Designs Inc. delivered purchase order DD0008 to MicroWare Ltd., for the development of interactive software to be used on Devine Design's Web site, and for B2B sales of images, animation, and Java applets. The agreed contract price was

$8000 plus taxes and would be confirmed on MicroWare's invoice MW0188 the next morning. Use the DISC terms code.

The batch total in the upper right corner of the notebook is a hash total, which means that it is a total of all invoices in the batch. The total amount of the invoices should be $12,184.25.

PRINTING THE A/P BATCH REPORT

❑ Select: **Print** from the A/P Invoice Entry File menu

FIGURE 26-16
A/P Batch Listing Report Dialog Box

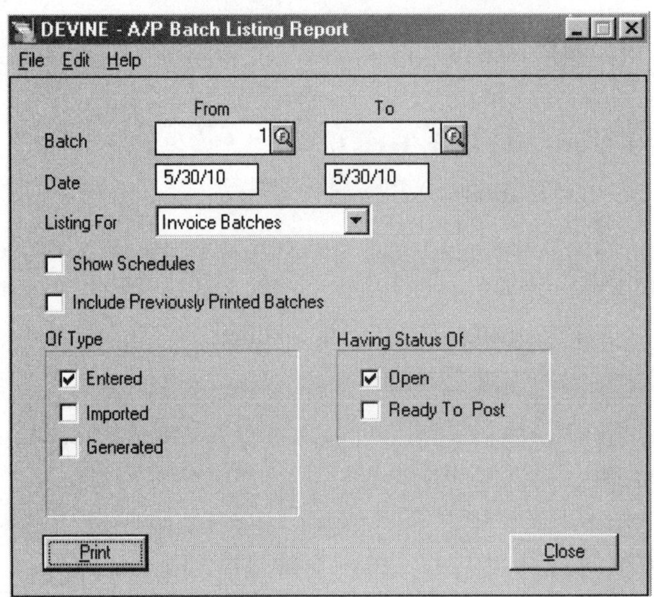

The default settings shown in Figure 26-16 will print a listing of all the entries in the batch.

❑ Select: the **Entered** check box
❑ Select: the **Open** check box
❑ Click: **Print** Print
❑ Click: **OK** OK on the Print dialog box
❑ Close: the **A/P Batch Listing Report** dialog box
❑ Close: the **A/P Invoice Entry** window
❑ Exit: **ACCPAC**

Compare your printout to that shown in Figure 26-17.

❑ Note any errors on your prinout.

If you need to make corrections, do so after completing the Editing an Invoice section in Chapter 27.

Figure 26-17
A/P Batch Listing - Invoice Report

Date: Sunday, August 20, 2000 2:28PM
A/P Batch Listing - Invoice (APIBTCLZ)

DDI Student Name

Page 1

From Batch Number	[1] To [1]
From Batch Date	[5/30/2010] To [5/30/2010]
Listing For	[Invoice Batches]
Of Type	[Entered]
Having Status Of	[Open]
Show Schedules	[N]

Batch Number:	1	**Description:**	May Purchases	**Total:**	12,184.250
Batch Date:	5/30/2010	**Type:**	Entered	**Status:**	Open

Entry: 1 **Doc. No.:** POP 9889 **Type:** IN **Vendor:** 1150 Prestonia Office Products **Document Date:** 5/12/2010

Description:	Furniture and Supplies	**PO Number:**	DD0004	**Year:** 2011	**Period:** 01
Tax Group:	DOMPUR	**Order Number:**	ORD-1354		
Due Date:	6/11/2010	**Terms:**	NODISC T		

Dist. Code	Description	G/L Account	Account Description	Tax Authority	Net Dist. Amt.	Allocated Tax Amt.
OFFSUP	Office Supplies	1300	Office Supplies		450.00	36.00
		1520	Fixtures & Furniture		500.00	40.00
				GSTFED	66.50	
				RSTON	76.00	
				Total:	1,092.50	76.00

Entry: 2 **Doc. No.:** KKS 0175 **Type:** IN **Vendor:** 1100 Kenin's Kopy Service **Document Date:** 5/20/2010

Description:	Stationary Supplies	**PO Number:**	DD0005	**Year:** 2011	**Period:** 01
Tax Group:	DOMPUR	**Order Number:**			
Due Date:	6/19/2010	**Terms:**	NODISC		

Dist. Code	Description	G/L Account	Account Description	Tax Authority	Net Dist. Amt.	Allocated Tax Amt.
OFFSUP	Office Supplies	1300	Office Supplies		450.00	36.00
				GSTFED	31.50	
				RSTON	36.00	
				Total:	517.50	36.00

Entry: 3 **Doc. No.:** SD-35820 **Type:** IN **Vendor:** 1180 Software Depot **Document Date:** 5/20/2010

Description:	Operating System Software	**PO Number:**	DD0006	**Year:** 2011	**Period:** 01
Tax Group:	DOMPUR	**Order Number:**			
Due Date:	6/19/2010	**Terms:**	DISC		
Discount Date:	5/30/2010	**Total Disc. Amt.:**	19.90	**Discount Pct:**	2.00%
Remit-To:	SOFDE2 Western Office				

Dist. Code	Description	G/L Account	Account Description	Tax Authority	Net Dist. Amt.	Allocated Tax Amt.
		1540	Software		995.00	79.60
				GSTFED	69.65	
				RSTON	79.60	
				Total:	1,144.25	79.60

Entry: 4 **Doc. No.:** SP-9746 **Type:** IN **Vendor:** 1250 Summit Peak Computers **Document Date:** 5/25/2010

Description:	writeable CD's	**PO Number:**	DD0007	**Year:** 2011	**Period:** 01
Tax Group:	DOMPUR	**Order Number:**			

Date: Sunday, August 20, 2000 2:28PM
A/P Batch Listing - Invoice (APIBTCLZ)

DDI Student Name

Page 2

Due Date:	6/24/2010	**Terms:**	DISC		
Discount Date:	6/4/2010	**Total Disc. Amt.:**	4.00	**Discount Pct:**	2.00%

Dist. Code	Description	G/L Account	Account Description	Tax Authority	Net Dist. Amt.	Allocated Tax Amt.
	writeable CD's	1300	Office Supplies		200.00	16.00
				GSTFED	14.00	
				RSTON	16.00	
				Total:	230.00	16.00

Entry: 5 **Doc. No.:** MW0188 **Type:** IN **Vendor:** 1220 MicroWare Ltd. **Document Date:** 5/29/2010

Description:	B2B software development	**PO Number:**	DD0008	**Year:** 2011	**Period:** 01
Tax Group:	DOMPUR	**Order Number:**			
Due Date:	6/28/2010	**Terms:**	DISC		
Discount Date:	6/8/2010	**Total Disc. Amt.:**	160.00	**Discount Pct:**	2.00%

Dist. Code	Description	G/L Account	Account Description	Tax Authority	Net Dist. Amt.	Allocated Tax Amt.
		1540	Software		8,000.00	640.00
				GSTFED	560.00	
				RSTON	640.00	
				Total:	9,200.00	640.00

--- Batch Summary by Currency ---

CAD	Total Invoices	12,184.25
	Total Credit Notes	0.00
	Total Debit Notes	0.00
	Total Interest	0.00
	Total:	12,184.25

T: Terms have been edited

5 entries printed
1 batch printed

REVIEW QUESTIONS

1. What is the purpose of Payment Selection Codes?
2. When you are entering Accounts Payable data files, you can activate the calculator. What keystroke activates the calculator, and what does the Paste function do?
3. What control on the sequence of Batch Numbers does the program have?
4. What happens if you try to enter a Vendor Number that has not been assigned?
5. What happens if you fail to enter a Document Number when recording an invoice?
6. Why is it important to complete the Reference field when entering an invoice?
7. How do you correct a typing error before you have accepted the information?
8. If you have already accepted incorrect information in recording an invoice, how do you correct the error?
9. What is the purpose of Open Payables?

EXERCISE

Sign on to your company as the system administrator using 05/30/10 as the Session Date.

Add a Payment Selection Code to your company. Use the same "DUE" Payment Selection Code that you created for Devine Designs Inc.

❑ Print: the **A/P Selection Codes** list

Add the invoices shown on Figure 26-18 to a new Invoice batch, then print the A/P Batch Listing.

FIGURE 26-18
A/P Batch Listing - Invoice Report

Date: Monday, October 09, 2000 2:45PM
A/P Batch Listing - Invoice (APIBTCL)

A/P Exercises

Page 1

From Batch Number	[1] To [1]
From Batch Date	[5/30/2010] To [5/30/2010]
Listing For	[Invoice Batches]
Of Type	[Entered]
Having Status Of	[Open]
Show Schedules	[N]

Batch Number: 1 **Batch Date:** 5/30/2010 **Description:** May 2010 Purchases **Type:** Entered **Total:** 16.016.250 **Status:** Open

Entry: 1 **Doc. No.:** AS3426 **Type:** IN **Vendor:** 1005 Ainsworth Stationary **Document Date:** 5/5/2010
Description: Letterhead Supplies **PO Number:** 10-101 **Year:** 2011 **Period:** 01
Tax Group: DOMPUR **Order Number:**
Due Date: 6/4/2010 **Terms:** DISC
Discount Date: 5/15/2010 **Total Disc. Amt.:** 8.00 **Discount Pct:** 2.00%

Dist. Code	Description	G/L Account	Tax Authority	Net Dist. Amt.	Allocated Tax Amt.
OFFSUP	Office Supplies Purchase	1300		400.00	32.00
			GSTFED	28.00	
			RSTON	32.00	
			Total:	460.00	32.00

Entry: 2 **Doc. No.:** CIT- 10988 **Type:** IN **Vendor:** 1010 Citabria Interconnect **Document Date:** 5/10/2010
Description: Internet Set Up Charge **PO Number:** 10-102 **Year:** 2011 **Period:** 01
Tax Group: DOMPUR **Order Number:**
Due Date: 6/9/2010 **Terms:** DISC
Discount Date: 5/20/2010 **Total Disc. Amt.:** 10.00 **Discount Pct:** 2.00%

Dist. Code	Description	G/L Account	Tax Authority	Net Dist. Amt.	Allocated Tax Amt.
ISP	Internet Services Expenses	6140		500.00	40.00
			GSTFED	35.00	
			RSTON	40.00	
			Total:	575.00	40.00

Entry: 3 **Doc. No.:** CIT - 10988 **Type:** IN **Vendor:** 1010 Citabria Interconnect **Document Date:** 5/15/2010
Description: Internet Service Charge **PO Number:** 10-103 **Year:** 2011 **Period:** 01
Tax Group: DOMPUR **Order Number:**
Due Date: 6/14/2010 **Terms:** DISC
Discount Date: 5/25/2010 **Total Disc. Amt.:** 30.00 **Discount Pct:** 2.00%

Dist. Code	Description	G/L Account	Tax Authority	Net Dist. Amt.	Allocated Tax Amt.
ISP	Internet Services Expenses	6140		1.500.00	120.00
			GSTFED	105.00	
			RSTON	120.00	
			Total:	1.725.00	120.00

Date: Monday, October 09, 2000 2:45PM
A/P Batch Listing - Invoice (APIBTCL)

A/P Exercises

Page 2

Entry: 4 **Doc. No.:** CUR234 **Type:** IN **Vendor:** 1020 Currys Ltd. **Document Date:** 5/20/2010
Description: Equipment Rental - May **PO Number:** 10-104 **Year:** 2011 **Period:** 01
Tax Group: DOMPUR **Order Number:**
Due Date: 6/19/2010 **Terms:** DISC
Discount Date: 5/30/2010 **Total Disc. Amt.:** 50.00 **Discount Pct:** 2.00%

Dist. Code	Description	G/L Account	Tax Authority	Net Dist. Amt.	Allocated Tax Amt.
COMPRT	Computer Rental	6080		2,500.00	200.00
			GSTFED	175.00	
			RSTON	200.00	
			Total:	2,875.00	200.00

Entry: 5 **Doc. No.:** JUNE RENT **Type:** IN **Vendor:** 1130 Niemi Properies **Document Date:** 5/30/2010
Description: **PO Number:** **Year:** 2011 **Period:** 01
Tax Group: DOMPUR **Order Number:**
Due Date: 6/29/2010 **Terms:** NODISC

Dist. Code	Description	G/L Account	Tax Authority	Net Dist. Amt.	Allocated Tax Amt.
OFRENT	Office Rent	6160		750.00	
			GSTFED		
			RSTON		
			Total:	750.00	

Entry: 6 **Doc. No.:** TOR9754 **Type:** IN **Vendor:** 1190 Torchia Ltd. **Document Date:** 5/30/2010
Description: Set up costs for marketing pro **PO Number:** 10-105 **Year:** 2011 **Period:** 01
Tax Group: DOMPUR **Order Number:**
Due Date: 6/29/2010 **Terms:** DISC
Discount Date: 6/9/2010 **Total Disc. Amt.:** 60.00 **Discount Pct:** 2.00%

Dist. Code	Description	G/L Account	Tax Authority	Net Dist. Amt.	Allocated Tax Amt.
ADV	Advertising Expense	6000		3,000.00	240.00
			GSTFED	210.00	
			RSTON	240.00	
			Total:	3,450.00	240.00

Entry: 7 **Doc. No.:** TOR9765 **Type:** IN **Vendor:** 1190 Torchia Ltd. **Document Date:** 5/30/2010
Description: Advertising placements - June **PO Number:** 10-106 **Year:** 2011 **Period:** 01
Tax Group: DOMPUR **Order Number:**
Due Date: 6/29/2010 **Terms:** DISC
Discount Date: 6/9/2010 **Total Disc. Amt.:** 100.00 **Discount Pct:** 2.00%

Dist. Code	Description	G/L Account	Tax Authority	Net Dist. Amt.	Allocated Tax Amt.
ADV	Advertising Expense	6000		5,000.00	400.00
			GSTFED	350.00	

Date: Monday, October 09, 2000 2:45PM
A/P Batch Listing - Invoice (APIBTCL)

A/P Exercises

Page 3

Tax Authority	Net Dist. Amt.	Allocated Tax Amt.
RSTON	400.00	
Total:	5,750.00	400.00

Entry: 8 **Doc. No.:** 05312010 **Type:** IN **Vendor:** 1200 Bell Telephone **Document Date:** 5/31/2010
Description: May phone charges **PO Number:** **Year:** 2011 **Period:** 01
Tax Group: DOMPUR **Order Number:**
Due Date: 6/30/2010 **Terms:** NODISC

Dist. Code	Description	G/L Account	Tax Authority	Net Dist. Amt.	Allocated Tax Amt.
COMM	Communications Expense	6060		375.00	30.00
			GSTFED	26.25	
			RSTON	30.00	
			Total:	431.25	30.00

--- Batch Summary by Currency ---

CAD	Total Invoices	16,016.25
	Total Credit Notes	0.00
	Total Debit Notes	0.00
	Total Interest	0.00
	Total:	16,016.25

8 entries printed
1 batch printed

- ❑ Print: the **A/P Batch Listing**
- ❑ Exit: **ACCPAC**

CHAPTER 27

INVOICE PROCESSING

In this chapter, you will edit the invoice entered in Chapter 26, print the batch again, and post it. You will then add a credit note and post the batch.

GETTING READY

❑ Sign on to Devine Designs Inc. as the system administrator using 05/30/10 as the Session Date.

❑ Open: the **Accounts Payable** main window

❑ DClick: the **A/P Invoices** icon 

❑ DClick: the **Invoice Entry** icon 

EDITING AN INVOICE

After receiving MicroWare's invoice (MW0188), Eric realized there was an error in the terms code. The correct terms code is PROJ.

❑ Click: the **Finder** to the right of the Batch field

❑ Select: **Batch 1** **May Purchases**

The invoice you have to modify should be in entry number 5. To reopen an existing invoice, type its number in the Entry field, or choose the entry number using the Finder.

❑ Click: the **Finder** for the Entry field
❑ Select: **Entry number 5**

The details for entry 5 will appear on your screen as shown in Figure 27-1.

FIGURE 27-1
A/P Invoice Entry Page

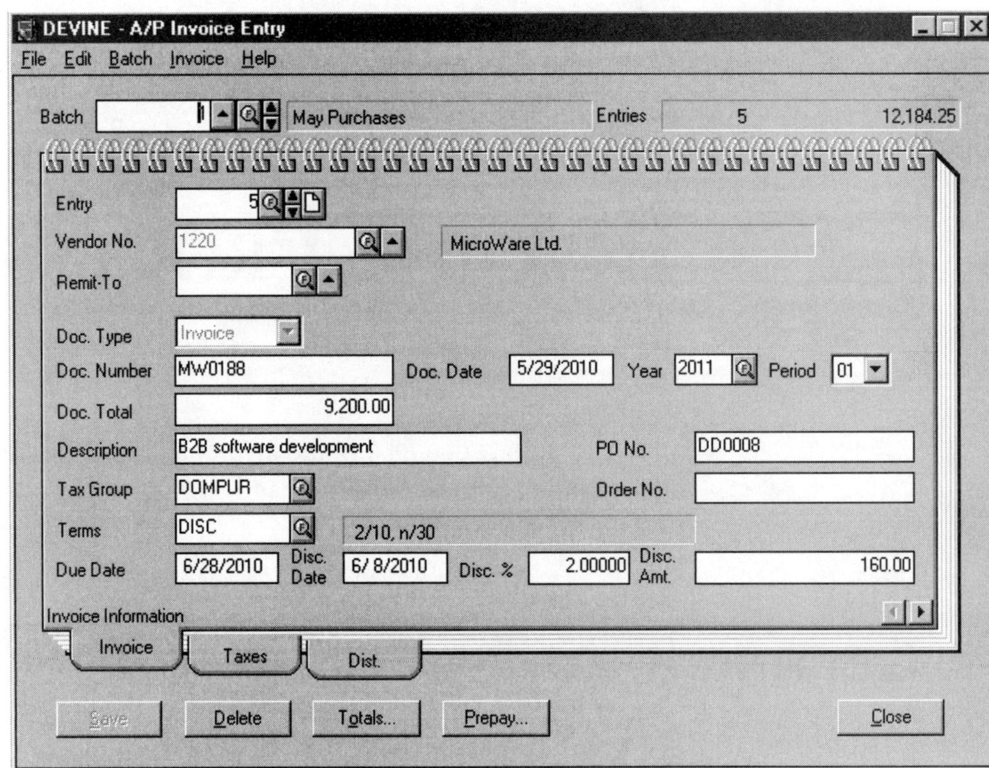

This invoice is to be paid over 60 days, with a payment schedule of three payments.

❑ Click: the **Finder** for the Terms field
❑ Select: **PROJ** **30 day projects**

Payment Schedule Page

When you selected the Payment Schedule option, a tab named Schedule appeared at the bottom of the notebook. This page is available only if you are entering an invoice and have selected a terms code that uses the Multiple Payment Schedule option.

❑ Click: the **Schedule** tab at the bottom of the A/P Invoice Entry notebook

The Payment Schedule page will appear as shown in Figure 27-2.

FIGURE 27-2
Payment Schedule Page

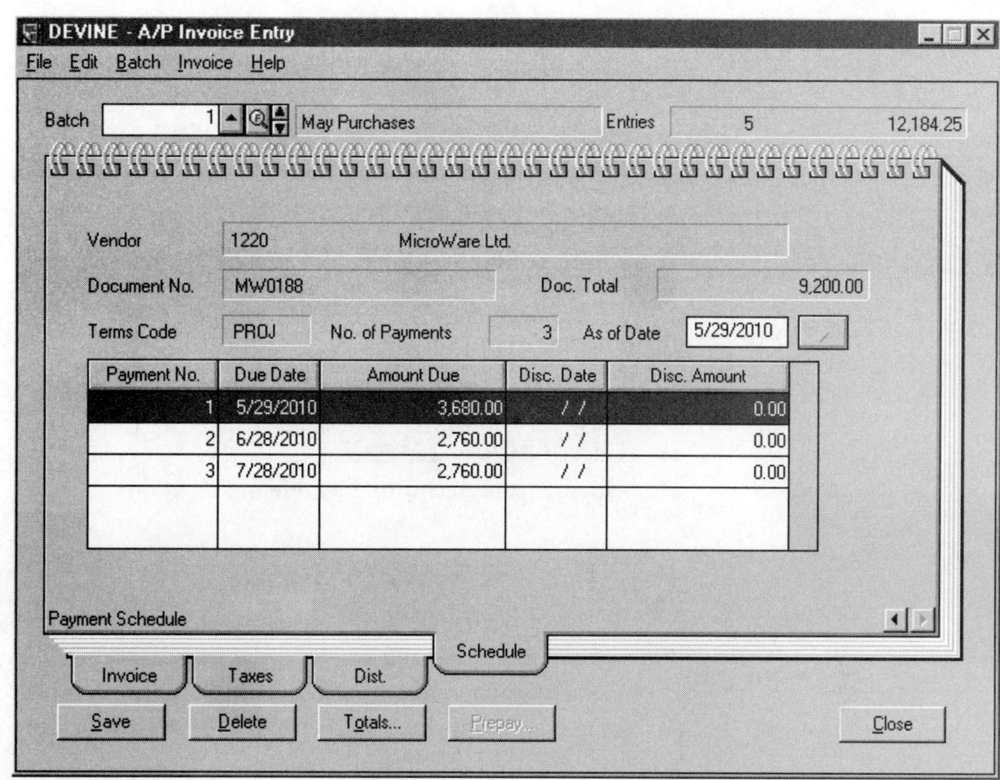

The Payment Schedule page is used to edit multiple payment schedules for invoices.

MicroWare's invoice indicates that the first payment is due on May 31, 2010.

- ❑ Enter: **05/31/10** in the As of Date text box
- ❑ Click: the **Go** button to recalculate the payment schedule

ACCPAC displays a warning that a payment schedule already exists.

- ❑ Click: **Yes** to recalculate the schedule

If necessary, you can change the due dates and amounts of payments by double-clicking the proper cell and entering new data.

- ❑ Click: **Save**
- ❑ Make (and save) any corrections you noted in Chapter 26.
- ❑ Close: the **A/P Invoice Entry** window

PRINTING AN INVOICE BATCH

- ❑ Open: the **Accounts Payable** main window
- ❑ DClick: the **Invoice Batch List** icon 

The A/P Invoice Batch List window is similar to the A/R Invoice Batch List window.

- ❑ Click: **Print** Print
- ❑ Click: the **Show Schedules** check box
- ❑ Click: **Print** Print on the A/P Batch Listing Report window
- ❑ Click: **OK** OK
- ❑ Close: the **A/P Batch Listing Report** window

Verify that the print schedule has been added to the entry for Invoice MW0188 and that any other corrections have been printed.

- ❑ Click: **Save** Save
- ❑ Click: **Close** Close
- ❑ Open: the **Accounts Payable** main window

POSTING AN INVOICE BATCH

After you have printed and reviewed the revised Accounts Payable Invoice Batch List and corrected any entry errors, you may post the batch to the Accounts Payable. You can post invoice batches from the Invoice Batch List window or from the Post Invoice Batch window.

Ready to Post

You have to manually identify a batch as Ready to Post before the program will allow you to post it. This allows you to create batches that you want to hold until a later time before they are posted.

- ❑ Open: the **Accounts Payable** main window
- ❑ Open: the **Invoice Batch** window
- ❑ Click: the **Line For Batch 1** to activate it
- ❑ Scroll to the right and verify that the batch has been printed.
- ❑ DClick: the **Ready to Post** cell to display Yes
- ❑ Click: **Post** Post

An information dialog box will appear as shown in Figure 27-3.

FIGURE 27-3
A/P Post Invoice Batch

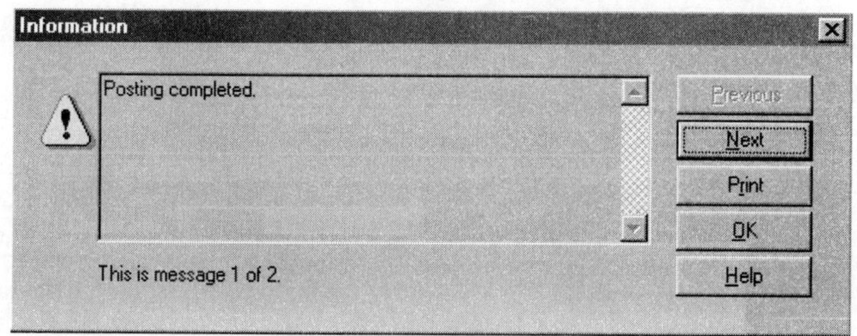

- ❑ Click: **Next** [Next >] to display the second message
- ❑ Click: **OK** [OK] to clear the messages

If you see an error message informing you that an error batch has been created, you have to open the batch, make corrections, print it, set it Ready to Post, and then post the error batch.

- ❑ Close: the **A/P Post Invoice Batch** window

PRINTING THE POSTING JOURNAL

It is a good idea to print the Posting Journal immediately after posting batches to compare the posting journal to the batch listing. Make sure that you file the Posting Journal sequentially with the other posting journals since it constitutes the audit trail of the posted entries.

- ❑ DClick: the **Processing Reports** [A/P Processi...] icon.

The A/P Processing Reports window will appear as shown in Figure 27-4.

FIGURE 27-4
A/P Processing
Reports Icons

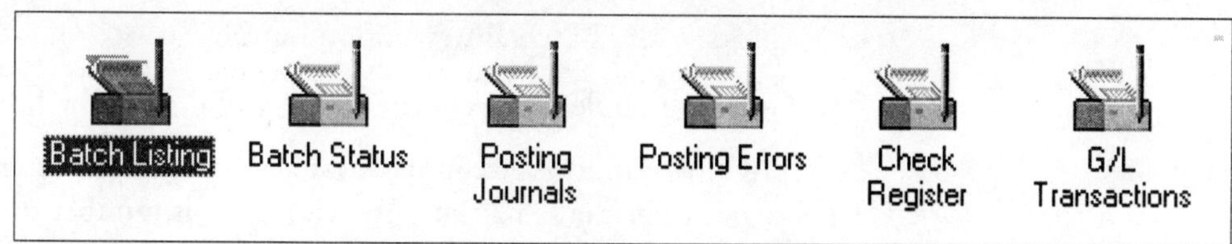

- ❑ DClick: the **Posting Journals** [Posting Journals] icon

The Posting Journal Report window will appear as shown in Figure 27-5.

FIGURE 27-5
A/P Posting Journal Report Window

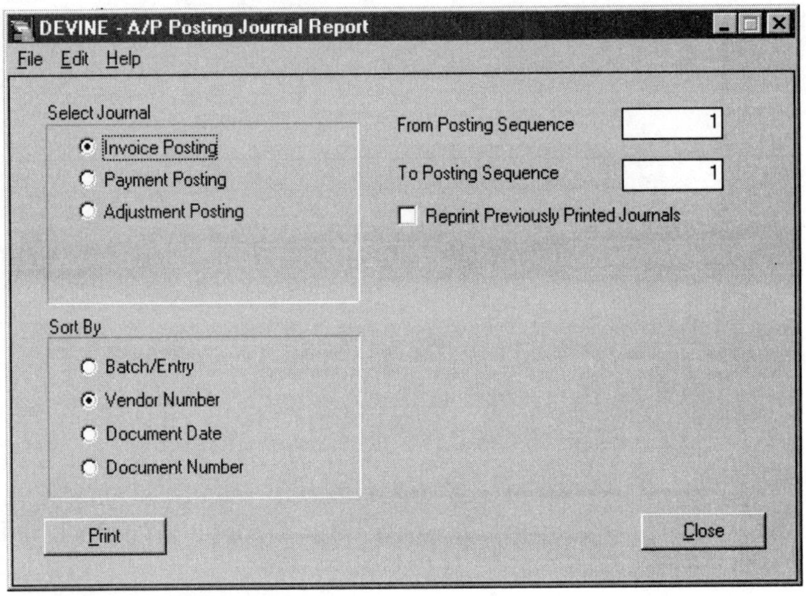

Posting Journal Report

The Invoice Posting Journal lists the invoices that you have posted. You can print the A/P Posting Journal at any time, but you must print it to a printer or file before you can process the year-end.

In the Select Journal area,

❑ Click: the **Invoice Posting** option button

You want to print the journal in the same order as the batch listing so the two can be easily compared. The Batch/Entry option allows this.

In the Sort By area,

❑ Click: the **Batch/Entry** option button

The From and To Posting Sequence fields will display the full range of batches available.

ACCPAC for Windows Accounts Payable assigns a posting sequence number to all batches posted at the same time. You can use this number to track the details from the G/L Transactions report back to the source documents, provided you did not choose to consolidate details during posting. When you consolidate details, the posting sequence portion of the entry number is lost, since details from more than one posting sequence can be included in a single consolidated transaction.

When you print journals for a range of posting sequences, ACCPAC Accounts Payable omits journals that have already been printed. If you want to reprint all the journals in the range of posting sequence numbers, you have to select the Reprint Previously Printed Journals option.

❑ Print: the **A/P Invoice Posting Journal**

Adding a Credit Note

One of the chairs you received in the shipment from Prestonia Office Products was damaged when it arrived. After the chair was returned, Prestonia issued a credit note.

- ❑ Open: the **Accounts payable** main window
- ❑ DClick: the **A/P Invoices** icon
- ❑ DClick: the **Invoice Entry** icon
- ❑ Click: the **Zoom** buttom for the Batch
- ❑ Click: the **New Document** icon for the Batch Number field
- ❑ Press: **Tab** to accept the Batch Date
- ❑ Type: **May Credit Note** in the Description text box
- ❑ Press: **Tab**
- ❑ Click: **Save**
- ❑ Click: **Close**
- ❑ Select: vendor **1150 - Prestonia Office Products** in the Vendor No. text box
- ❑ Select: **Credit Note** in the Doc. Type list box

The Invoice Information page will appear as shown in Figure 27-6.

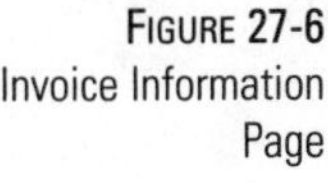

FIGURE 27-6
Invoice Information
Page

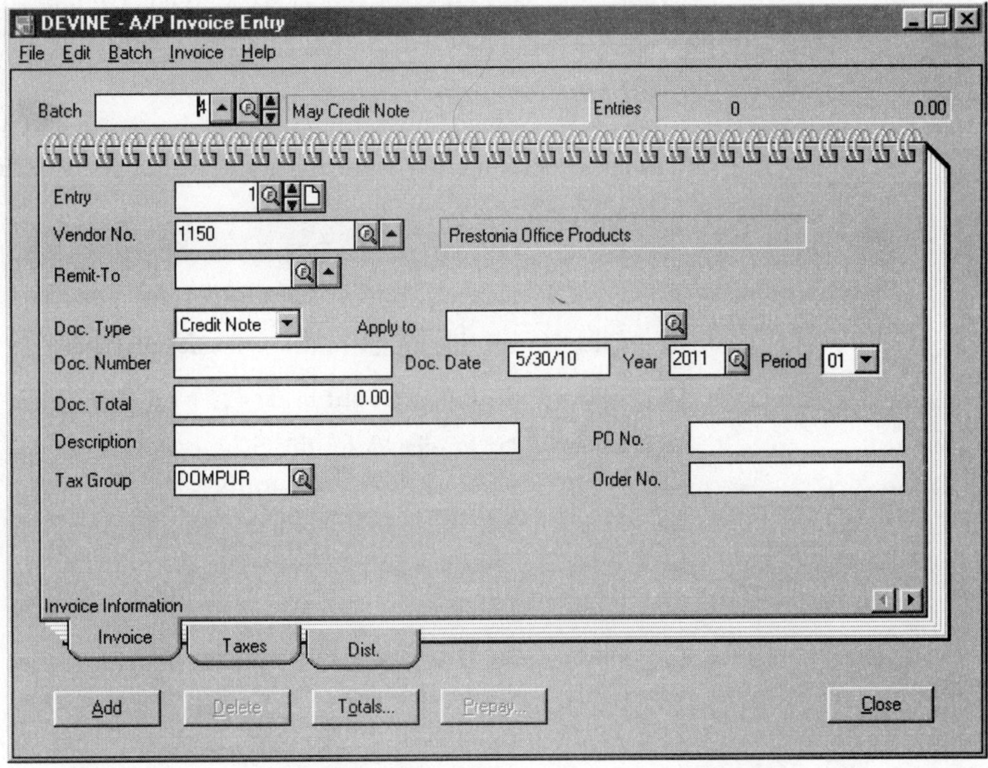

The Apply To field is to be left blank. You may select only posted documents in the Apply To field.

- ❑ Select: **Document Number POP9889** in the Apply To the field using the finder

The Prestonia Office Products credit note number is CR0056.

- ❑ Click: the **Doc. Number** field
- ❑ Type: **CR0056**
- ❑ Press: **Tab** Tab

Document Date

The program uses the document date to age credit and debit notes. The date of this credit note is May 30, 2010. Make sure that the year is 2011 and the period number is 1. This is the year and period information to which the credit note will be posted. The credit note was for $287.50, which includes GST and RST.

- ❑ Click: on the **Doc. Total** field
- ❑ Type: **287.50** in the Doc. Total field
- ❑ Press: **Tab** Tab
- ❑ Click: the **Description** field
- ❑ Type: **Inv. POP9889 - chair damaged**
- ❑ Click: the **Taxes** tab of the bottom of the A/P Invoice Entry notebook
- ❑ Click: the **Calculate Tax** check box to activate it
- ❑ Click: the **Dist.** tab at the bottom of the A/P Invoice Entry notebook

Distribution Information

The chairs portion of the original invoice was charged to General Ledger account 1520 rather than to a distribution code.

- ❑ Click: **OFFSUP** in the Dist. Code cell
- ❑ Press: **Delete** Delete
- ❑ Click: **Yes** Yes to delete the default detail
- ❑ Click: the **G/L Account** field
- ❑ Click: the **Finder** for the G/L Account field
- ❑ Select: **1520 - Fixtures & Furniture**
- ❑ Press: **Tab** Tab to move to the Amount field
- ❑ Type: **250.00** as the amount of the distribution
- ❑ Press: **Tab** Tab
- ❑ Click: the **Dist. Taxes** Dist. Taxes button.
- ❑ Click: the **Totals...** tab

Review the summary of the credit note. Note that the RST amount is shown as an amount to be allocated and the GST is listed as recoverable.

- ❑ Click: **Close** Close
- ❑ Click: **Add** Add

When you add a credit note, the program updates the number of entries and the batch total shown at the top right corner of the notebook. You should review the Distribution Information page to verify that the Undistributed Amount is now zero.

YOUR TURN

Occasionally, a credit note is received without sufficient information to apply it to a specific invoice, or the invoice has been entered but the batch has not been posted. In these cases, you enter the credit note and, after posting, use Payment Entry notebook to apply the credit note to the proper invoice. To show how this works, you will enter an invoice and a credit note, and in Chapter 28, apply the credit note to the invoice.

- ❑ Enter the following invoice:

Invoice SP-9801, dated May 28, 2010 from Summit Peak Computers for a scanner ordered on DD0009. The invoice total was $689.99 ($599.99 plus taxes).

- ❑ Enter the following credit note:

SP-C-9801 dated May 29, 2010 from Summit Peak Computers for a total of $57.50. The credit note was for an overcharge on the scanner of $50.

Do not apply the credit note to the invoice.

- ❑ Print: the **Batch Listing**
- ❑ Set the batch as **Ready to Post.**
- ❑ Post: the **Batch**
- ❑ Print: the **Posting Journal**
- ❑ Exit: **ACCPAC**

REVIEW QUESTIONS

1. What modifications can you make to a batch before it has been posted?
2. What do the Terms codes, n/30, 2/10, n/30, and PROJ indicate?
3. What is the purpose of the Payment Schedule page in the Invoice Entry notebook?
4. Why is it a good idea to select the Force Listing of Batches option on the Vendor Options page?

5. What are the two ways to open the Batch Listing Report window?
6. Why is it important to make regular backups of your data files before posting them?
7. What does the Posting Journal show?

EXERCISE

- ❑ Sign on to your company as the system administrator using 05/30/10 as the session date.

The invoice from Ainsworth Stationery included some letterhead with the wrong name at the top. They have accepted the return and issued you a credit note number CR7142 dated May 30 for $143.75 ($125.00 plus taxes).

- ❑ Create a new batch for the credit note.
- ❑ Print the new batch.
- ❑ Set the batches Ready to Post.
- ❑ Post the Invoice Batches.
- ❑ Print the Invoice Posting Journal sorted by Batch/Entry.
- ❑ Exit: ACCPAC

CHAPTER 28

Recording Payments and Prepayments

In this chapter, you will use the Prepayment notebook to issue a check to a vendor, apply a credit note to an invoice, record a prepayment, and process a miscellaneous payment.

Getting Ready

- ❑ Sign on to Devine Designs Inc. as the system administrator using 05/30/10 as the Session Date.
- ❑ Open: the **Accounts Payable** main menu

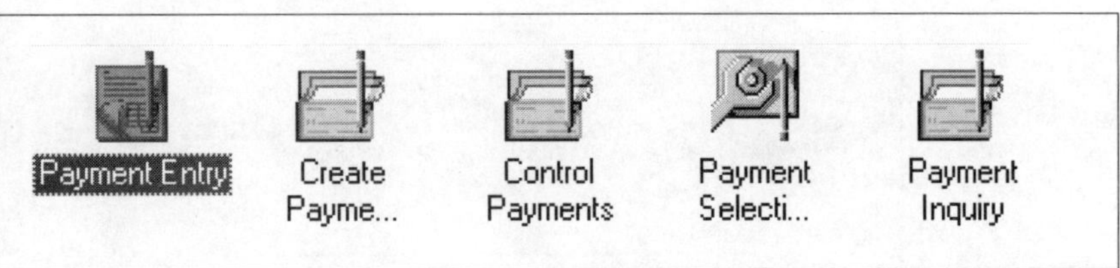

FIGURE 28-1
A/P Payments Icons

ACCPAC Accounts Payable provides two ways to create payment entries:

- The Payment Entry notebook allows you to enter and print single checks for vendors.
- The Create Payment Batch notebook allows you to generate payments according to criteria you specify. You can then print batches of checks from the Payment Batch List.

Creating a New Payment Batch

❑ DClick: the **A/P Payments** icon

The A/P Payments window will appear as shown in Figure 28-1.

Issuing a Check

Eric has decided to issue a check for the first payment due to MicroWare Ltd. for the development of B2B software. The payment will be in the amount of $3680 on Invoice MW0188.

❑ DClick: the **Payment Entry** icon

The A/P Payment Entry notebook will appear as displayed in Figure 28-2.

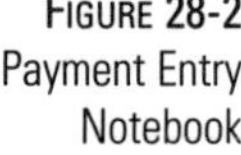

FIGURE 28-2
Payment Entry Notebook

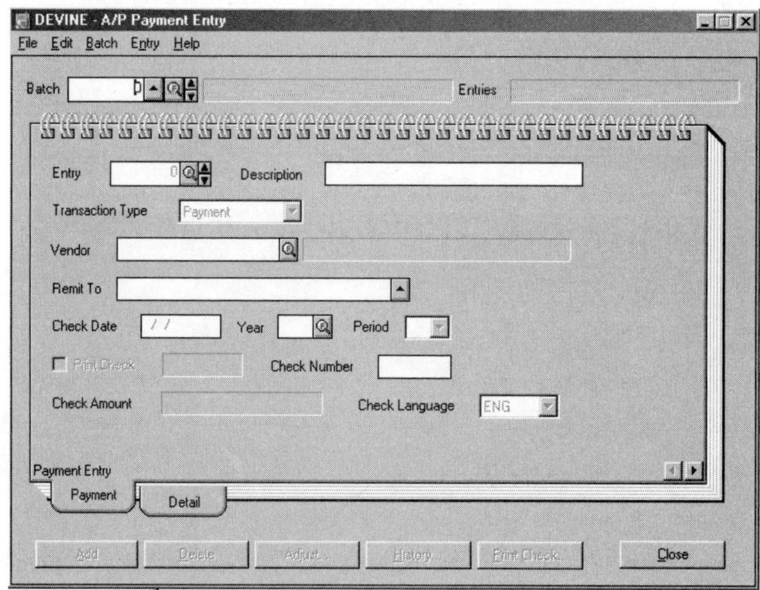

NOTEBOOK HEADER

❑ Click: the **Zoom** button for Batch

The Batch Header page of the Payment Entry window will appear as shown in Figure 28-3.

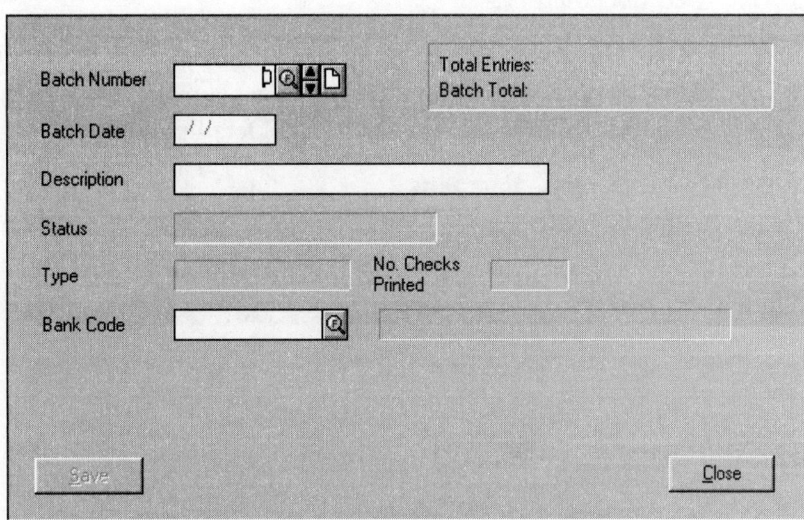

FIGURE 28-3
Batch Header Window

❑ Click: **New Document** icon to create a new batch
❑ Press: **Tab** to accept the default date and move to the Description field
❑ Type: **Payments - May 2010**
❑ Press: **Tab** to move to the Bank Code field
❑ Select: **1STBK** as the bank code, using the Finder
❑ Click: **Save**
❑ Click: **Close** to return to the Payment Entry page of the A/P Payment Entry notebook.

PAYMENT ENTRY PAGE

❑ Click: the **Description** field to activate it
❑ Type: **May 30 payments**
❑ Press: **Tab**

Transaction Type

You can record four different types of payment transactions in the Payment Entry notebook:

Payment: This option is chosen when you want to send a check to vendors to pay specific invoices.

Prepayment: This represents the deposit paid on an invoice you have not yet received or posted.

Apply Document: This is a transaction that applies a posted payment to a posted document.

Miscellaneous Payment: In this case, a check is made out to a payee who is not set up in the Accounts Payable ledger. The payment is distributed to the General Ledger accounts on the Payments Detail page.

- ❑ Select: **Payment**
- ❑ Press: **Tab** [Tab]
- ❑ Click: the **Finder** for the Vendor field
- ❑ Select: **1220 - MicroWare Ltd.**

Remit To

ACCPAC will display Microware Ltd. in the Remit To text box.

- ❑ Click: the **Zoom** button for Remit To

The information that you entered when creating the vendor account will be displayed.

- ❑ Click: **Close** [Close] to return to the Payment Entry Page

Check Date

- ❑ Press: **Tab** [Tab]

The default date shown in the Check Date field is the Session Date. This date will appear on the check.

- ❑ Press: **Tab** [Tab] to accept the default date and move to the Year field

Ensure that 2011 is displayed in the Year field and that 1 appears as the Period number.

- ❑ Press: **Tab** [Tab] twice to move to the Print Check option

Print Check

Ensure that the Print Check option is active so you can print the check. If necessary,

❑ Click: the **Print Check** box to activate it

If you had already issued a manual check and are simply recording it here, you would not have to select Print Check. You use the Check Number field to record the number of a check that has been already issued.

❑ Press: **Tab** [Tab] to move to the Check Language field

The Check Language option determines the language used when the amount is written on the check. You will leave this as ENG (English).

Payment Detail Page

❑ Click: the **Detail** tab at the bottom of the A/P Entry notebook

The Payment Detail page of the A/P Payment Entry notebook will appear as displayed in Figure 28-4.

FIGURE 28-4
Payment Detail Page

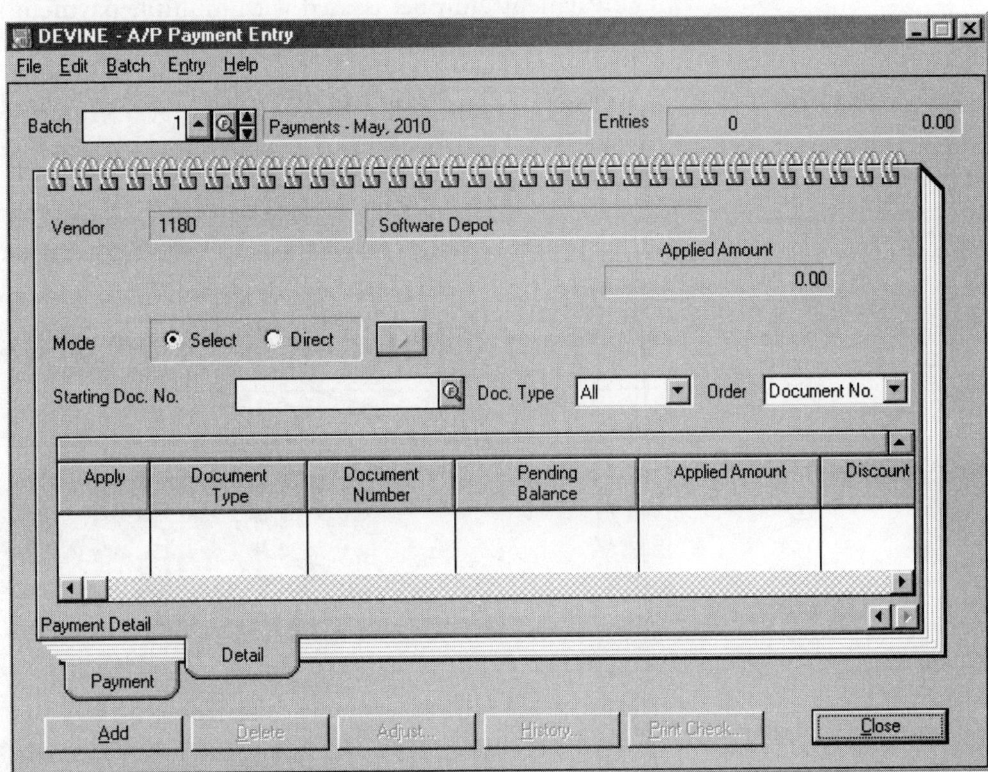

You use the Payment Detail page to choose the documents you will pay.

MODE

You use the Direct method when you know the number of the document to which you are applying the invoice, or when you have so many vendor documents tshat it is faster to look them up with the Finder than to scroll through them at the bottom of the screen.

- ❑ Click: the **Direct Mode** option button
- ❑ Press: **Tab** [Tab]

PAYMENT DETAIL

- ❑ Click: the **Finder** for the Document Number field
- ❑ Select: **MW0188 payment number 1**
- ❑ Press: **Tab** [Tab] to move to the Payment Number column

The Payment Number is used with multiple payment schedules. For single payment terms, the number is always 1.

- ❑ Press: **Tab** [Tab] to accept 1 as the Payment Number
- ❑ Click: **Add** [Add]

The Payment Detail page of the Payment Entry notebook now appears as shown in Figure 28-5. You may have to scroll the Payment Detail area to view all the columns.

FIGURE 28-5
Payment Detail Page

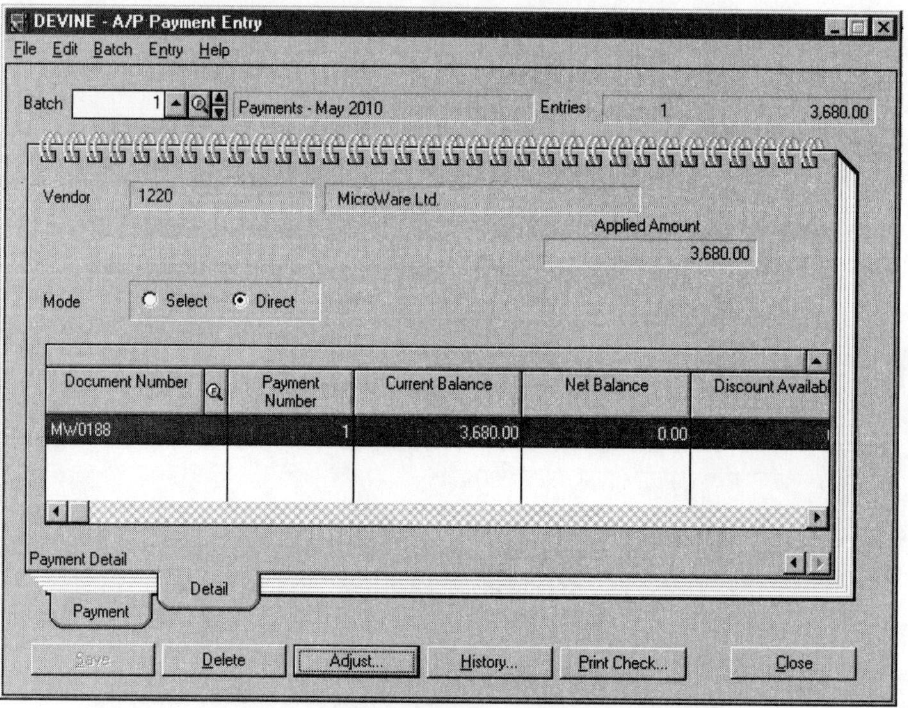

You can print checks individually as they are entered or you can print them when the batch is completed. Devine Designs Inc. will print checks later when the batch is complete.

Applying a Credit Note

Devine Designs Inc. will now apply the credit note to Summit Peak Computers' Invoice SP-980.

Payment Entry Page

❑ Click: the **Payment** tab at the bottom of the A/P Payment notebook
❑ Click: the **New Document** icon beside the Entry field

When you click on the New Document icon, the program inserts a new entry number, and the cursor moves to the Description field.

Add the following information:

❑ Type: **Applying Summit Peak credit**
❑ Click: the **List** icon beside the Transaction Type field
❑ Select: **Apply Document**
❑ Select: **1250 - Summit Peak Computers**

Ensure that 2011 is displayed as the year and 1 is shown as the period.

Payment Detail Page

❑ Click: the **Detail** tab at the bottom of the A/P Payment Entry notebook

You must first identify the credit note that you are going to apply.

❑ Click: the **Finder** for Document No.
❑ Select: **SP-C-9801**

The Select Mode

The Select mode lists vendor documents in a table at the bottom of the window in an order you specify. The Select mode presents more information about the vendor's documents than the Direct mode, adding information from any unposted payments that you have already applied.

You should know the number of the invoice against which you will apply the credit note; however, this mode allows you to verify that a payment has not been entered for this invoice.

❑ Click: the **Select** button found in the Mode box

❑ Click: **Go**

When you click Go, the program displays all the posted documents for the vendor account as displayed by Figure 28-6.

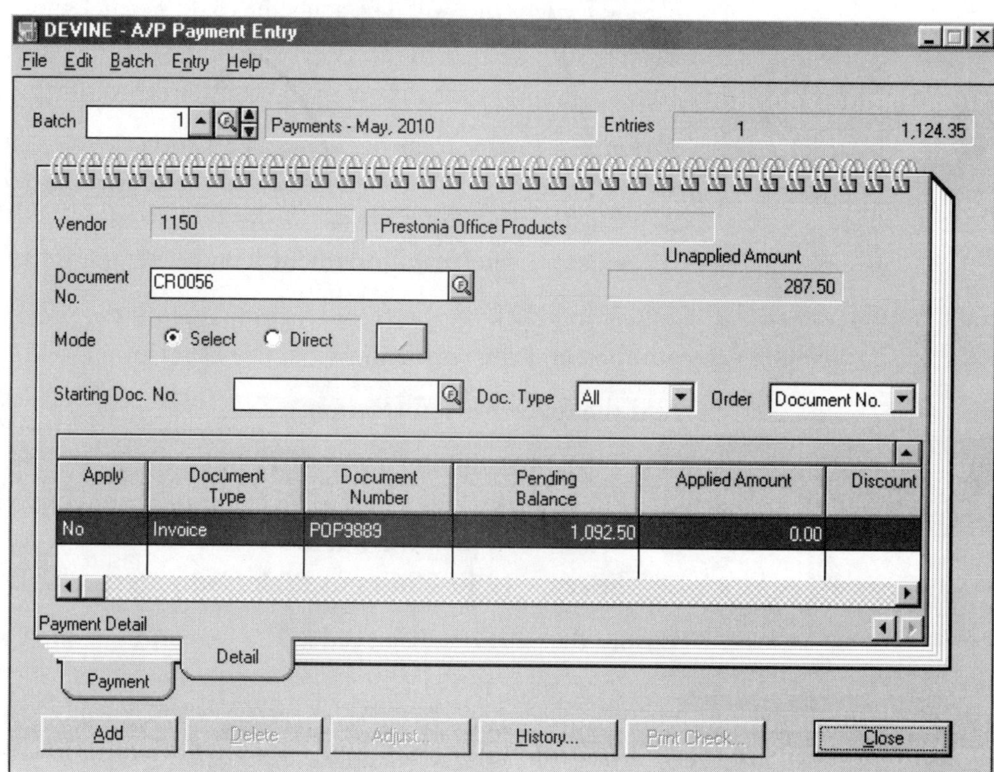

FIGURE 28-6 Completed Payment Detail Page

❑ Select: **Invoice SP-9801**

❑ DClick: the **Apply** cell to display Yes

The program will apply the full amount against the invoice, and will also take any available discount, unless specified otherwise.

❑ Click: **Add**

ENTERING PREPAYMENTS

Prepayments are payments made in advance to vendors for such items as insurance or rent. An invoice has not been received, and is therefore not recorded. When you add a prepayment, you must identify the document against which the payment applies, using an invoice number, purchase order number, or sales order number.

When the invoice is posted at a later date, the program will match the invoice to the prepayment by using the number you have entered. If the program cannot match the prepayment, you can use Apply Document Transaction to apply the prepayment.

As-Tech Computers is offering a ten percent discount to customers who pay for six months of Internet connection. Devine Designs Inc. is currently paying $125 plus taxes per month for this service. Paying for six months would represent a savings of $86.25 ($862.50 – 776.25). Devine Designs Inc. will issue purchase order DD0010 to As-Tech for six months of connection.

ADDING A PREPAYMENT

- ❑ Click: the **Payment** tab at the bottom of the A/P Payment Entry notebook
- ❑ Click: the **New Document** icon for Entry
- ❑ Type: **Prepay 6 months I.S.P.**
- ❑ Press: **Tab** [Tab]
- ❑ Click: the **list tool** beside the Transaction Type field
- ❑ Select: **Prepayment**
- ❑ Press: **Tab** [Tab]
- ❑ Select: **1001-AsTech**
- ❑ Press: **Tab** [Tab] to leave the Remit-To information
- ❑ Press: **Tab** [Tab] to accept the default date displayed in the Check Date field
- ❑ Press: **Tab** [Tab] twice to accept 2011 as the year and 1 as the period number
- ❑ Select: the **Print Check** check box.
- ❑ Click: the **Detail** tab at the bottom of the A/P Payment Entry notebook
- ❑ Click: the **list tool** to the right of the Document Type field

A drop-down list will appear as shown in Figure 28-7.

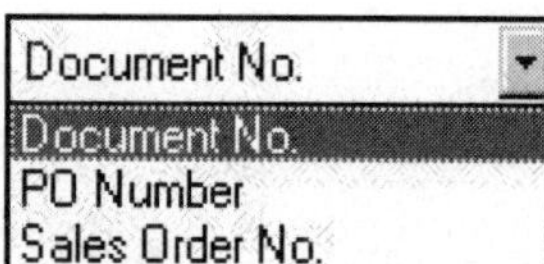

FIGURE 28-7
Drop-Down List

You can specify that the prepayment is for an invoice or debit note, or you can choose to apply it using your PO number or the sales order number. The program will try to match the prepayment to any invoices that you post in the future using the number you specify. The program will also try to match the prepayment to a posted document when it is posted, in case you post the invoice batch before you post payments.

- ❑ Select: **PO Number** as the document type
- ❑ Press: **Tab** [Tab]
- ❑ Type: **DD0010** in the PO Number field
- ❑ Press: **Tab** [Tab]
- ❑ Type: **776.25** in the Prepayment Amount field
- ❑ Press: **Tab** [Tab]

The Activation Date is the date on which the program will start to include the prepayment to offset current payables when it creates payments from the Create Payment Batch window.

- ❑ Press: **Tab** [Tab]
- ❑ Click: **Add** [Add]

When you add the transaction, the program assigns a prepayment document number, using the prepayment prefix and next sequence number that was specified in the Options notebook. The number is displayed in the Prepayment Number field.

- ❑ Click: the **Payment** tab to move back to the Payment Entry notebook page

Note that 776.25 is now displayed in the check amount field and that the check has not been printed. You will print the check later.

ADDING A MISCELLANEOUS PAYMENT WITH THE PAYMENT ENTRY NOTEBOOK

Miscellaneous payments are those made to companies or individuals who do not have vendor accounts in the Accounts Payable ledger. When you add a miscellaneous payment, you must distribute the payment amount in the same way that you distribute the amount of an invoice in the Invoice Entry notebook.

Leslie has decided to buy high-quality colour transparencies for the laser printer. They will be used as backup for company presentations to clients. The vendor, Seaforth Office Supplies, insists on payment when the transparencies are picked up. Eric will prepare a miscellaneous check for $115 and assign purchase order number DD0011 to the transaction.

- ❑ Click: the **New Document** icon for Entry
- ❑ Type: **Colour transparencies** in the Description text box
- ❑ Press: **Tab** [Tab] to move to the Transaction Type field
- ❑ Select: **Misc. Payment**
- ❑ Click: the **Zoom** button beside the Remit-to field

A Vendor Information page will appear as shown in Figure 28-8.

FIGURE 28-8
Vendor Information

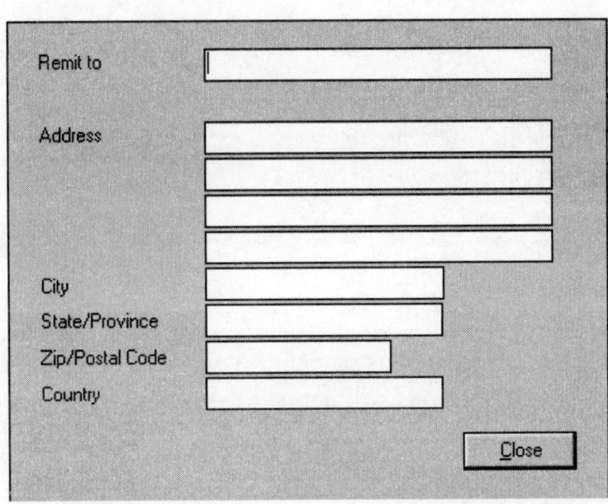

- ❑ Enter the following remittance information;

Remit to: **Seaforth Office Supplies**
Address: **3030 Speedy Rd.**
Mississauga
Ontario
L4Y 2Z6

Once you have entered the payee information,

- ❑ Click: **Close** [Close] to return to the Payment Entry page

The name of the payee that you just entered now appears in the Remit To field.

- ❑ Click: the **Detail** tab at the bottom of the A/P Payment Entry notebook

FIGURE 28-9
Payment Detail Page

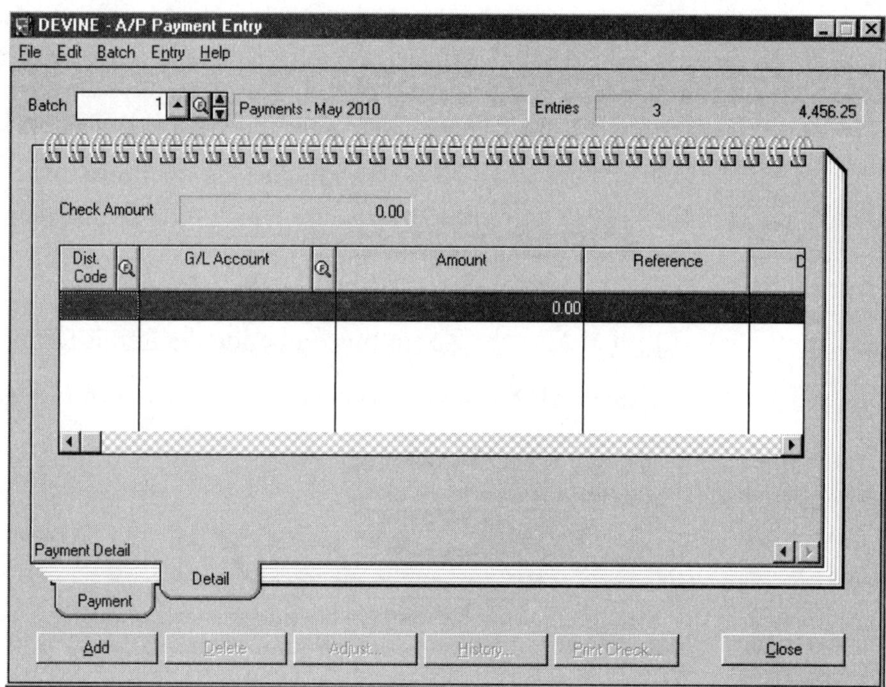

When adding a miscellaneous payment, you must enter the distribution details of the purchase. The distributions will debit the general ledger accounts you specify and ACCPAC will credit the bank account.

In this case, the price of the transparencies is $100 plus taxes. You enter distributions to debit Office Supplies $108 ($100 plus $8 Retail Sales Tax) and to debit GST Recoverable $7.

- ❑ Click: the **Finder** for Dist. Code
- ❑ Select: **OFFSUP**
- ❑ Press: **Tab** [Tab] twice
- ❑ Type: **108.00** in the Amount cell
- ❑ Press: **Tab** [Tab]
- ❑ Type: **DDOO11** in the Reference cell
- ❑ Press: **Tab** [Tab]
- ❑ Press: **Insert** to add a second distribution
- ❑ Select: **2205 G.S.T. Recoverable** using the G/L Account finder
- ❑ Enter: **7.00** in the Amount cell
- ❑ Enter: **DD0011** in the Reference cell
- ❑ Click: **Add** [Add]
- ❑ Click: the **Payment** tab

The Check Amount should now display 115.00.

Printing the Batch Listing

Before you print checks you should print the batch listing and verify that the transaction information has been entered correctly.

❑ Print: the **Batch Listing Report**

FIGURE 28-10
A/R Batch Listing – Payment

Date: Tuesday, August 22, 2000 2:16PM **DDI Student Name** Page 1
A/P Batch Listing - Payment (APCBTCLZ)

From Batch Number	[1] To [1]
From Batch Date	[5/30/2010] To [5/30/2010]
Listing For	[Payment Batches]
Of Type	[Entered]
Having Status Of	[Open]
Include Previously Printed Batches	[No]

Batch Number: 1 **Description:** Payments - May 2010 **Bank:** 1STBK **Total:** 4,571.25
Batch Date: 5/30/2010 **Type:** Entered **Status:** Open

Entry: 1 **Vendor:** 1220 MicroWare Ltd. **Check:** 0 **Check Date:** 5/30/2010 **Check Amount:** 3,680.00
Year: 2011 **Period:** 01 **Account Set:** 1 **Description:** !st Payment on B2B software

Type	Doc. No.-Sched. No.		Adjustment	Discount	Amount
PY	MW0188-1		0.00	0.00	3,680.00
		Total :	0.00	0.00	3,680.00

Entry: 2 **Vendor:** 1250 Summit Peak Computers **Check:** ** Apply Doc. ** **Check Date:** 5/29/2010 **Check Amount:** ** Apply Doc. **
Year: 2011 **Period:** 01 **Account Set:** 1 **Description:** Appying Summit Peak credit
Orig. Document: SP-C-9801

Type	Doc. No.-Sched. No.		Adjustment	Discount	Amount
PY	SP-980-1		0.00	0.00	57.50
		Total :	0.00	0.00	57.50

Entry: 3 **Vendor:** 1001 AsTech Computers **Check:** 0 **Check Date:** 5/30/2010 **Check Amount:** 776.25
Year: 2011 **Period:** 01 **Account Set:** 1 **Description:** Prepay 6 months I.S.P.
Activation Date: 5/30/2010 **Prepayment ID:** PP000000001

Type	Doc. No./PO No./SO No.		Adjustment	Discount	Amount
PI	DD0010		0.00	0.00	776.25
		Total :	0.00	0.00	776.25

Entry: 4 **Vendor:** *** Misc. *** Seaforth Office Supplies **Check:** 0 **Check Date:** 5/30/2010 **Check Amount:** 115.00
Year: 2011 **Period:** 01 **Description:** colour transparencies

Type	Account No.	Description / Reference for Misc. Payment	Adjustment	Discount	Amount
PY	1300	DD0011	0.00	0.00	108.00
PY	1000	DD0011	0.00	0.00	7.00
		Total :	0.00	0.00	115.00

----Summary----	Adjustment	Discount	Amount
Total for Batch 1	0.00	0.00	4,628.75

Compare your printout to Figure 28-10 and make any necessary corrections. Print the batch listing again.

It is good practice to print checks in entry number order.

❑ Use: the **Finder** to select Entry number **1**

Print Checks Window

- [ ] Click: the **Print Check** [Print Check...] button

The Print Checks window will appear as shown in Figure 28-11.

FIGURE 28-11
Print Checks Window

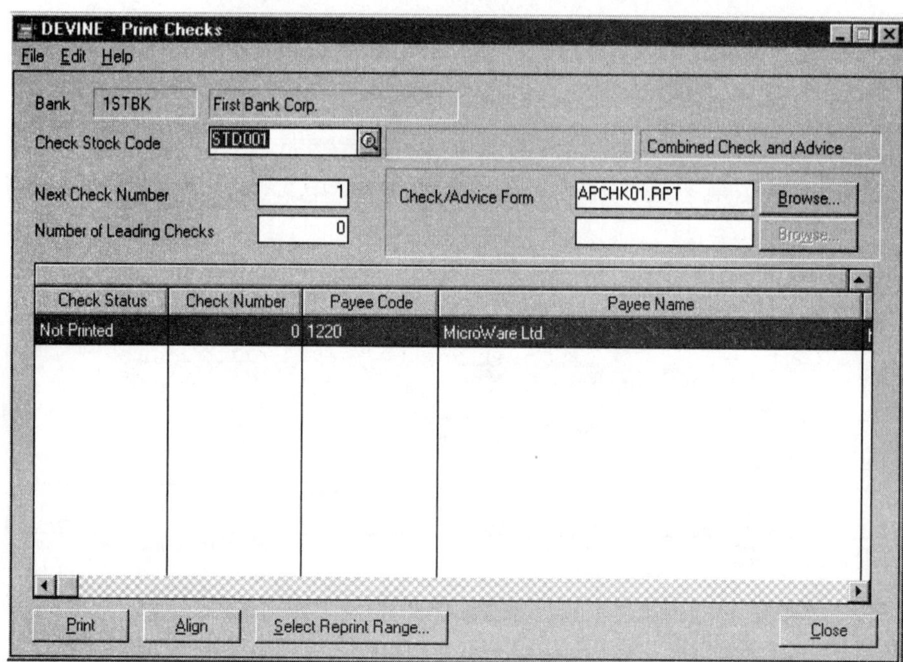

The default Check Stock Code, Next Check Number, Number of Leading Checks, and Check/Advice form to use for printing checks was set in Bank Services. The Print Status and Check Number assigned are updated once the check has been printed. You can print an alignment check to make sure that the check forms are aligned properly. If the check is not printed properly, you can reprint by answering No to the question that inquires whether all checks were printed successfully, then select the reprint range, or double-click the check status column to set the status to Not Printed.

If the name of a Check/Advice form does not appear, you can use the browse button to select one.

- APCHK01.RPT prints a combined check and advice for laser printers, and
- APCHK02.RPT prints a combined check and advice for dot matrix printers.

- [ ] Click: **Print** [Print]
- [ ] Click: **OK** [OK] when the Print dialog box appears

You should see a confirmation on your screen inquiring if all checks were printed successfully.

You should always review the checks that have been printed before you select Yes to ensure that they are acceptable. If they are not, you can reset the printer status to Not Printed by clicking in the Check Status column or using the Select Reprint Range button, then reprint the check.

- ❑ Select: **Yes** [Yes]

Once finished, the screen will return to the Payment Entry page of the A/P Payment Entry notebook.

- ❑ Print: **Checks** for entries **3** and **4**
- ❑ Close: the **A/P Payment Entry** window

POSTING THE PAYMENTS BATCH

It is good practice to post payments batches immediately.

- ❑ Open: the Accounts Payable main window
- ❑ DClick: Payment Batch List [Payment Batch List]

FIGURE 28-12
A/P Payment Batch List Window

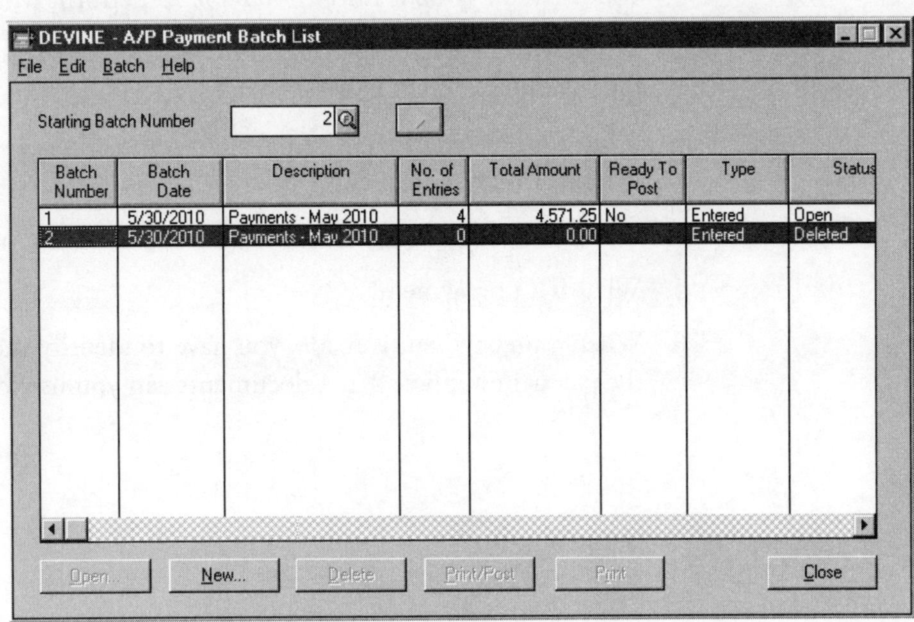

Note that batch 2, which was entered in error, has been deleted.

- ❑ Scroll: **right** to the Printed column

Batch 1 should have been printed.

- ❑ DClick: the **Ready to Post** cell to display Yes
- ❑ Click: the **Print/Post** button

After the batch has been posted, clear the information messages.

- ❑ Close: the **A/P Payment Batch List** window
- ❑ Exit: ACCPAC

VOIDING PRINTED CHECKS

If, after leaving the Print Checks window, you discover that the check is incorrect, you have to delete the payment entry to void the check from Bank Services, then create a new entry.

- ❑ Exit: **ACCPAC**

REVIEW QUESTIONS

1. You use the Payment Entry notebook to perform which tasks?
2. Which two windows does ACCPAC for Windows Accounts Payable provide for creating payment entries?
3. What four different types of payment transactions are available from the Payment Entry notebook?
4. Describe the Select and Direct modes to record the payment of an invoice.
5. What is a prepayment?
6. When a prepayment is made, you have to identify the document against which the payment applies. What documents can you use for this purpose?

EXERCISE

- ❑ Sign on to your company as the system administrator using 05/30/10 as the session date.
- ❑ Create a new payment batch to record the following payments.
- ❑ Record a payment transaction to Niemi Properties for the June office rent invoice in the amount of $750 and print check number 1. Use the Direct Method to make the payment. The date of the payment is May 30, 2010.

- ❑ Prepare and print a Miscellaneous check to Quick Transport for the delivery of advertising materials from Torchia Ltd. The payment is charged to G/L account 6000 in the amount of $25. Quick Transport's invoice number is 1309756. Quick Transport is not a regular vendor to your company.
- ❑ Record a Prepayment to Curry's Inc. for specialized software. The Sales Order number is CUR098. The amount of the prepayment is $500. The date of the prepayment is May 30, 2010. Use account 1540.
- ❑ Print the checks for Quick Transport and Curry's Inc.
- ❑ Print the A/P Payment Batch Listing.

CHAPTER 29

GENERATING, PRINTING, AND POSTING A BATCH OF CHECKS

This chapter will show you how to set the payment criteria in the Create Payment Batch notebook, print the Pre-Check Register, generate a payment batch using Create Payment Batch, print the checks, then post the Payment batch.

CREATING A PAYMENT BATCH

On May 30, 2010. Devine Designs Inc. will print checks to all vendors for amounts due on or before June 15, 2010. Devine Designs Inc. will also take advantage of any discounts available form May 30 to June 15.

- ❑ Sign on to Devine Designs Inc. as the system administrator using 05/30/10 as the Session Date.
- ❑ Open: the **Accounts Payable main** window
- ❑ DClick: the **A/P Payments** [A/P Payments] icon

WARNING

You can produce only one system-generated Payment batch at a time. If you want to use the Create Payment Batch to produce two separate batches, you must print all the checks from the first batch, then post the transactions before you produce the second batch. If you try to create a batch, or print the Pre-Check register while a previous system-generated batch is unposted, the program will display an error message. You will have to post or delete the first batch before you can continue.

❑ DClick: the **Create Payment Batch** Create Payme... icon

Bank and Currency Selection Criteria

The Bank and Currency Selection Criteria page of the A/P Create Payment Batch notebook will appear as shown in Figure 29-1.

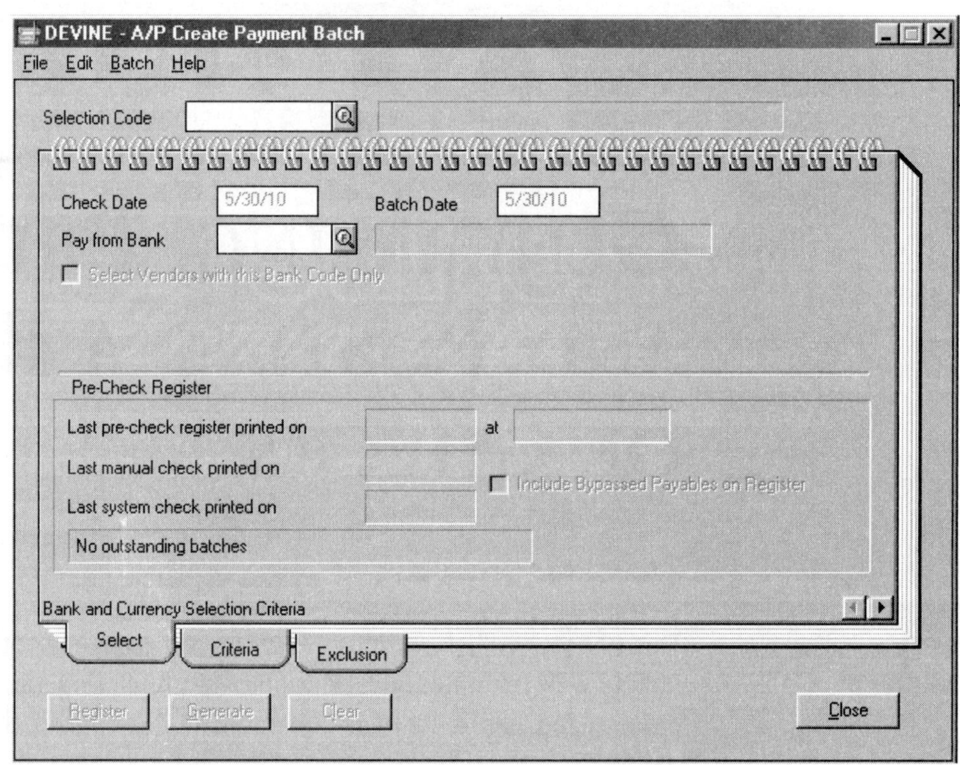

FIGURE 29-1
Bank and Currency Selection Criteria Page

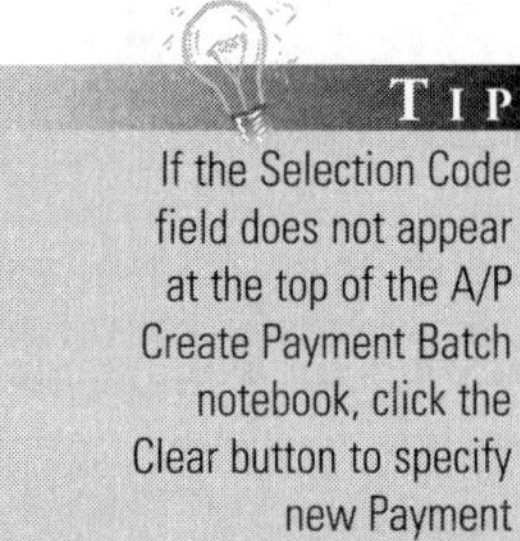

TIP

If the Selection Code field does not appear at the top of the A/P Create Payment Batch notebook, click the Clear button to specify new Payment Selection criteria.

You must select the Payment Selection code to use for the payment selection criteria. You can create as many codes as you need.

❑ Click: the **Finder** for the Selection Code field

The Finder - Selection Criteria Header will appear as shown in Figure 29-2.

FIGURE 29-2
Finder - Selection Criteria Header

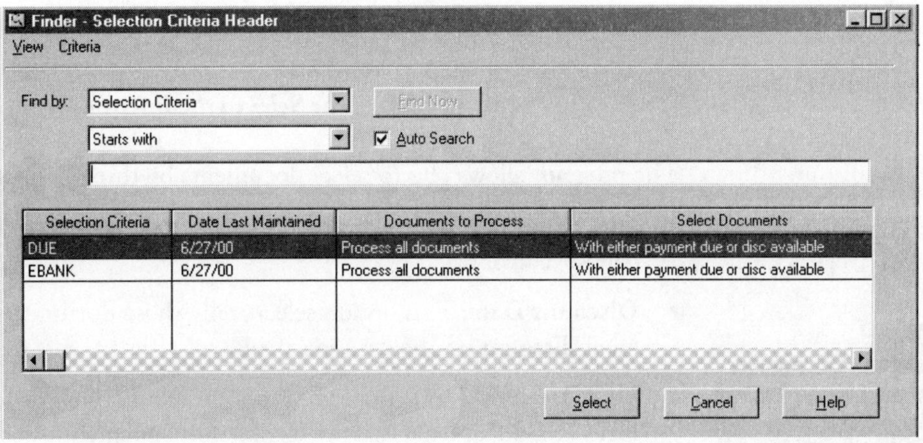

❑ Select: **DUE**

When you choose DUE as the Selection Code, the defaults created earlier for this Selection Code appear. The checks, dated May 30, 2010, will be paid from 1STBK, and the Select Vendors with this Bank Code Only option is active.

In the lower half of the screen, information on the Pre-Check Register is displayed. You cannot change any of the fields because they show historical information regarding the manual and system checks printed, and the date of the printing of the last Pre-Check register.

VENDOR AND DATE SELECTION CRITERIA

FIGURE 29-3
Vendor and Date Selection Criteria Page

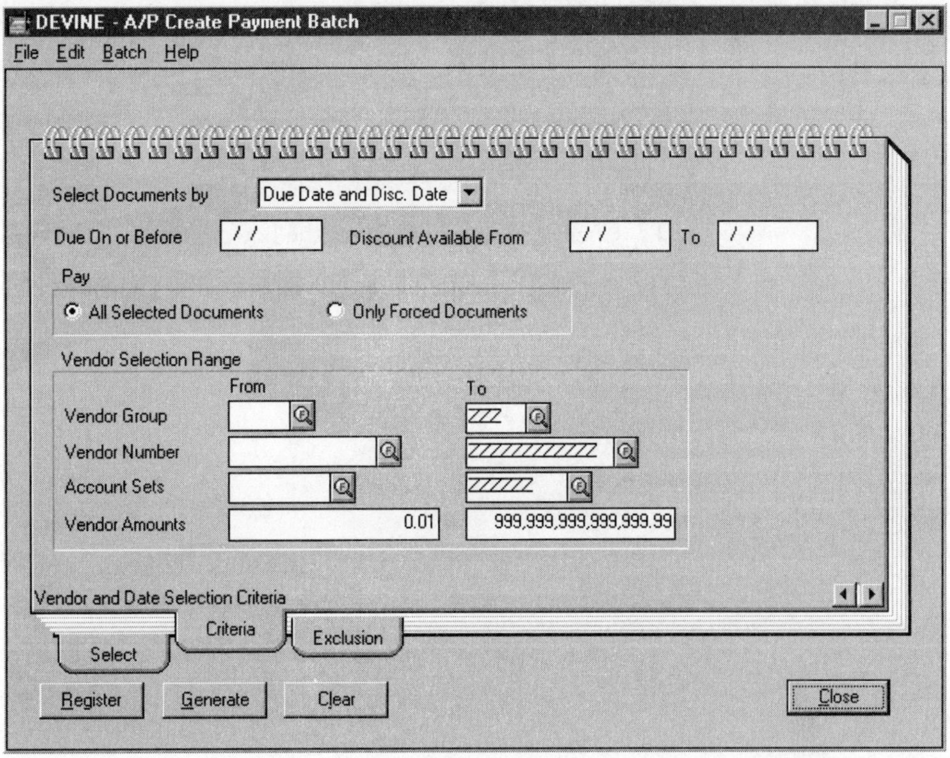

- ❑ Click: the **Criteria** tab at the bottom of the A/P Create Payment Batch notebook
- ❑ Click: the list tool for **Select Document by**

The program allows you to select documents by three different criteria:

- **Due Date:** This option selects only those documents that are due for payment on the date specified.
- **Discount Date:** This option selects only those documents that are eligible for a payment discount on the date specified.
- **Due Date and Disc. Date:** This option selects those documents that are due for payment and documents that are eligible for a payment discount on the date specified.

WARNING

If you were to select Only Forced Documents, the program would pay only those documents that are assigned a Forced Document status in the Control Payments window and meet the criteria specified on the first page of the A/P Create Payment Batch notebook.

- ❑ Select: **Due Date and Disc. Date**
- ❑ Press: **Tab** [Tab] to move to the **Due On or Before** field
- ❑ Type : **061510**
- ❑ Press: **Tab** [Tab]
- ❑ Type: **053010** in the **Discount Available from** field
- ❑ Press: **Tab** [Tab]
- ❑ Type: **061510** in the **Discount Available to** field

Ensure that the **All Selected Documents** option button is active so you will pay all the documents that fall within the selection criteria specified.

- ❑ Press: **Tab** [Tab] to move to the Vendor Selection Range fields

The program default is set so that all Vendors, Vendor Groups, Account Sets, and Amounts will be printed. There is no need to change any of the settings for the current Pre-Check Register.

Vendor Exclusion List Page

- ❑ Click: **Exclusion** tab at the bottom of the A/P Create Payment Batch notebook

The Vendor Exclusion List page will appear as shown in Figure 29-4.

FIGURE 29-4
Vendor Exclusion List Page

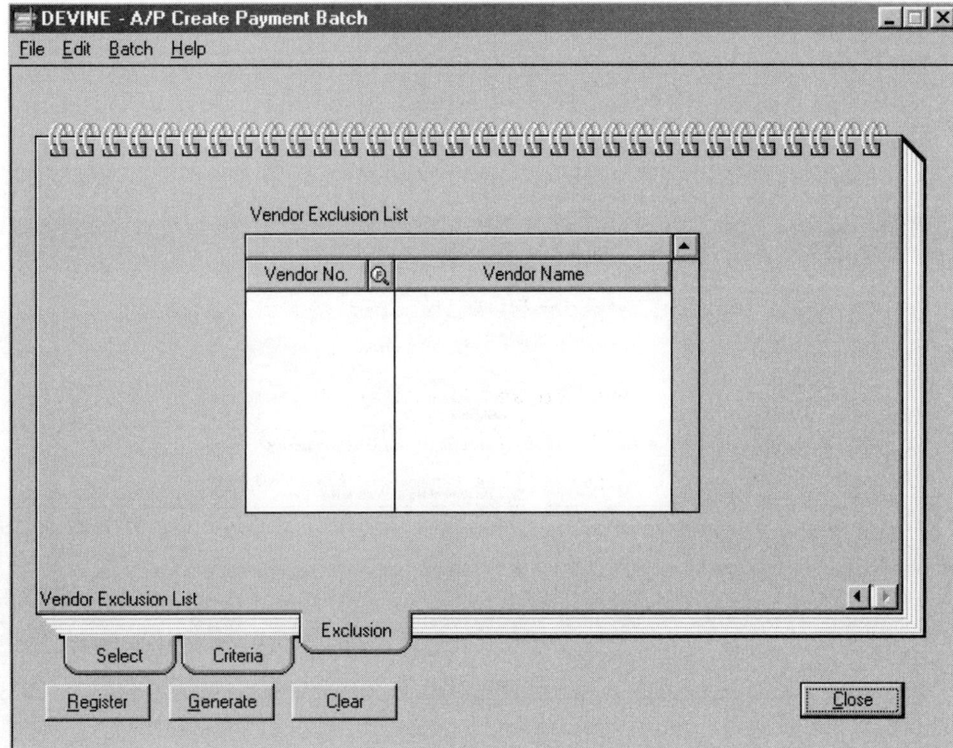

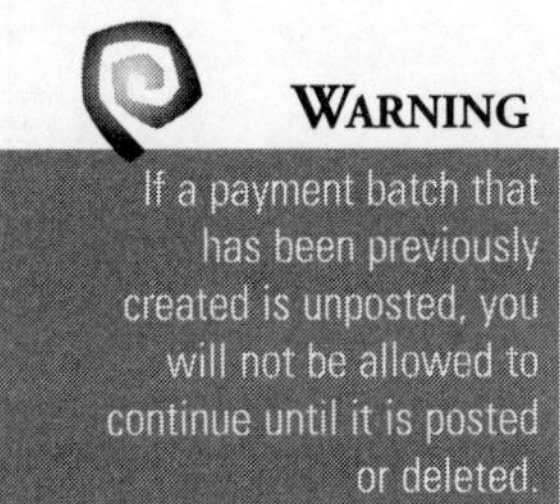

WARNING

If a payment batch that has been previously created is unposted, you will not be allowed to continue until it is posted or deleted.

This page allows you to choose the vendors you want excluded from the check run. You can add vendors to the exclusion list by selecting the list, pressing the Insert key, then typing a vendor number or selecting one from the Finder. You can delete vendors from the list by highlighting the vendor number and pressing Delete. The DUE code does not exclude any vendors.

PRINTING THE PRE-CHECK REGISTER

You print the Pre-Check register before generating a check run to review the payment batch being created.

❑ Click: the **Register** [Register] button

If any error messages appear indicating that you have missed some fields in the notebook, choose OK, complete the required information, then click the Register button again.

When the Print dialog box appears:

❑ Click: **OK** [OK]

The Pre-Check register, as shown in Figure 29-5, shows the payments that will be made if you generate checks using the Selection and Exclusion criteria specified. You can also print a list of transactions or vendor accounts that have been placed on hold.

Figure 29-5
Pre-Check Register

Date: Wednesday, October 04, 2000 2:09PM
A/P Pre-Check Register (APPCHREG)

DDI Student Name

Page 1

Check Date	[5/30/2010]
Batch Date	[5/30/2010]
Bank Code	[1STBK]
Bank Currency	[CAD]
Vendor Currency	[CAD]
Vendor Rate	[1.0]
Select Vendors With This Bank Code Only	[Y]
Report Excludes Vendors	[N]
Select Document By	[Due Date and Disc. Date]
Due On or Before	[6/15/2010]
Discount Available From	[5/30/2010] To [6/15/2010]
Pay All Selected Documents	
From Vendor Group	[ ] To [ZZZ]
From Vendor Number	[ ] To [ZZZZZZZZZZZZ]
From Account Set	[ ] To [ZZZZZZ]
From Vendor Amounts	[0.01] To [999999999999999.99]

CODES: S - Special discount amount; **F - Force payment; D - Transaction selected based on discount**

Seq. No.	Vendor Number	Payee Name	Ty.	Document No.-Schedule No.	Discount Date	Active/ Due Date	Orig. Amount	Curr. Payable	Discount	Net Payment	
1	1150	Prestonia Office Products	IN	POP 9889-1		6/11/2010	1,092.50	805.00	0.00	805.00	
								805.00	0.00	805.00	
2	1180	Western Office	IN	SD-35820-1	5/30/2010	6/19/2010	1.144.25	1,144.25	19.90	1.124.35	D
								1,144.25	19.90	1.124.35	
3	1250	Summit Peak Computers	IN	SP-9746-1	6/4/2010	6/24/2010	230.00	230.00	4.00	226.00	D
			IN	SP-980-1	6/7/2010	6/27/2010	689.99	632.49	12.00	620.49	D
								862.49	16.00	846.49	

Date: Wednesday, October 04, 2000 2:09PM
A/P Pre-Check Register (APPCHREG)

DDI Student Name

Page 2

---Pre-Check Register Summary---

	Current Payable	Discount	Net Payment
Total payable:	2,811.74	35.90	2,775.84
Total withheld:	0.00	0.00	0.00

Codes that show why transactions are selected, or why the payment amount differs from the net amount payable, are printed beside the Net Payment column.

S - The discount amount was changed for the transaction.
F - The invoice will be paid whether or not it meets the criteria set for the check run.
D - The transaction has been included in the check run because it is eligible for a discount. Note the three discounts taken by Devine Designs Inc.

A summary of the total amount of checks that will be paid in the check run and the total amount of checks that will be withheld because the transaction or vendor is on hold is also printed.

GENERATING A PAYMENT BATCH

- ❑ Click: the **Generate** button at the bottom of the A/P Create Payment Batch notebook

An Information box similar to Figure 29-6 will appear once the batch generation is finished.

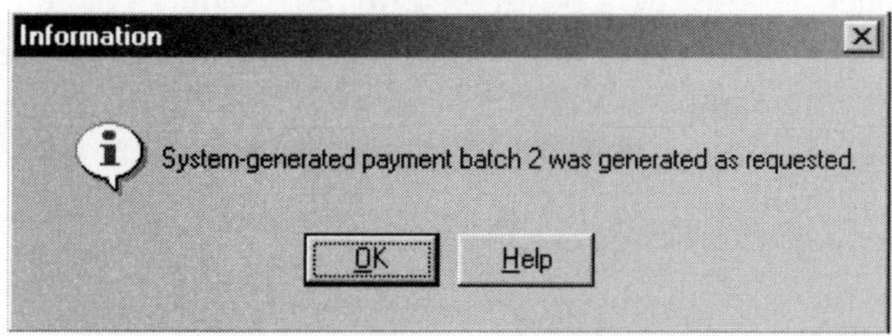

FIGURE 29-6 Information Dialog Box

- ❑ Click: **OK**
- ❑ Close: the **A/P Create Payment Batch** notebook

PRINTING THE BATCH LISTING, PRINTING AND POSTING THE CHECKS

Once the payment batch has been created, it has the same characteristics as the batch of payments you created with the Payment Entry notebook. You cannot edit or add to the system-generated batch unless you selected the Allow Edit of System Generated Batches option in the Options notebook.

Devine Designs Inc. has activated the Allow Edit of System Generated Batches option, so you can use Payment Entry to change, add, or delete entries to the batch, and print individual checks before printing the rest of the batch.

You would normally print the Payment Batch Listing report, review the listing, make any corrections or deletions of payment entries as necessary, then print the checks and post the batch. If you have selected the Force Listings Of Batches option in the Options notebook, you must print the batch listings before posting them.

PRINTING A BATCH LISTING

- ❑ Open: the **A/P Processing Reports** window
- ❑ DClick: the **Batch Listing** icon

❑ Click: the **Finder** for the Listing For field
❑ Select: **Payment Batches**

You want to ensure that all the payment batches created, including the one from Chapter 28, have been printed and are ready to be posted, so you will select a wide range of batches to print. The defaults for the Batch From and To fields are to print all the batches. In the Of Type box,

❑ Click: the check boxes for **Entered, Generated**, and **System**
❑ Click: the check boxes for **Open**, and **Ready to Post** in the Having Status Of area
❑ Print: the **A/P Batch Listing** report

Once you have reviewed the list,

❑ Close: the **A/P Batch Listing Report** window

Printing Checks and Posting the Payment Batch

❑ Open: the **Accounts Payable** main window

❑ DClick: the **A/P Payment Batch List** [Payment Batch List] icon

The A/P Payment Batch List window will appear as shown in Figure 29-7.

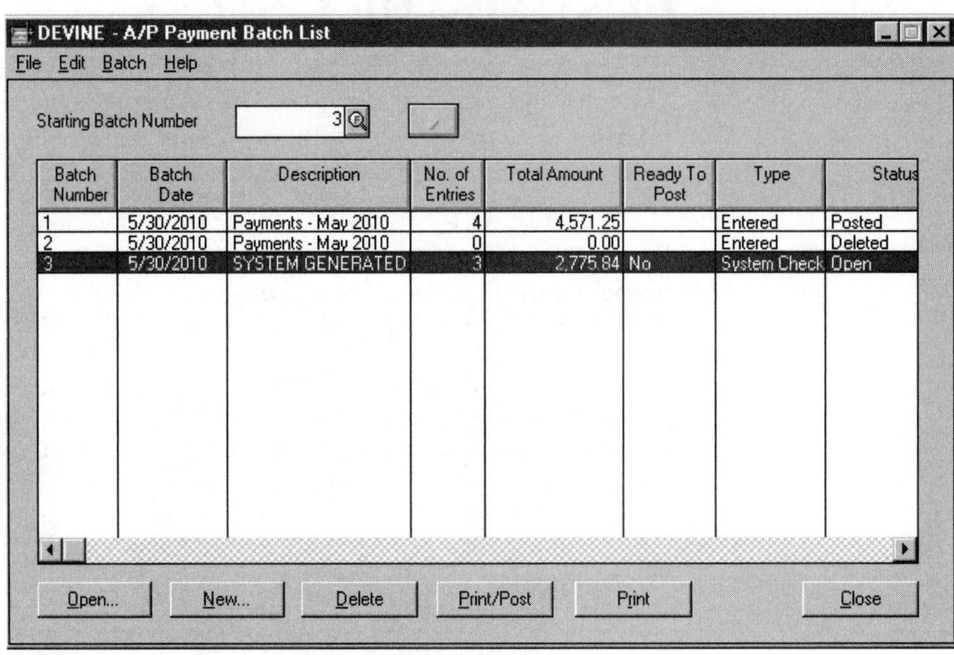

Figure 29-7 A/P Payment Batch List Window

You will print the checks for System Generated batch number 2.

- ❑ Select: the **System Generated** batch
- ❑ Click: the **Print/Post** button

A warning message will appear as shown in Figure 29-8.

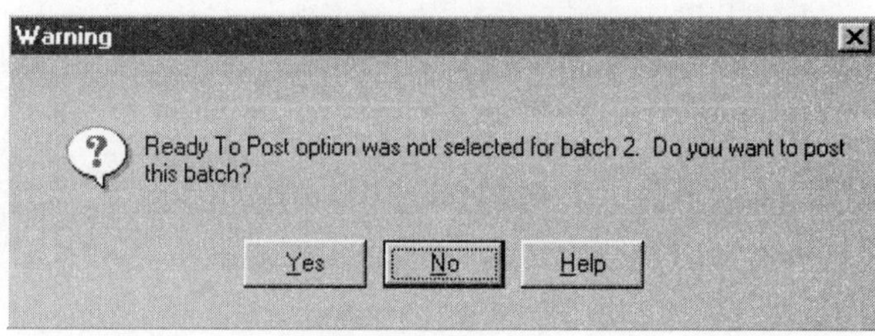

FIGURE 29-8
Warning Message

- ❑ Click: **Yes** [Yes]
- ❑ Click: **Print** [Print]
- ❑ Click: **OK** [OK]

When a message inquiring if the checks were printed successfully appears,

- ❑ Click: **Yes** [Yes]

When the information screen appears informing you that posting is complete,

- ❑ Click: **OK** [OK]
- ❑ Close: the **A/P Payment Batch List** window

PRINTING THE PAYMENT POSTING JOURNAL AND CHECK REGISTER

- ❑ Open: the **A/P Processing Reports** windows

You can reject the checks and advices and reprint them if necessary. If you have experienced a disruption in printing, so that a restart record exists, the program will complete the previous operation before it prints and posts the batches selected. If, for example, you started to print check batch 5 using the Payment Entry notebook, then cancelled the procedure, later returning to print and post the batch, the program will:

- Inform you that a restart record exists and inquire whether you want to proceed.
- Open the Print Checks window and let you print the checks that were not printed earlier.
- Post the check information to Bank Services.

PRINTING THE POSTING JOURNAL

The final step in the check processing cycle is to print the payment audit reports, which include the payment posting journal and the check register. You can print Posting Journals for invoice, payment, and adjustment batches.

You should print posting journals after each posting, then file them with your other audit trail records. You must print all outstanding posting journals before you can process the Clear History window or use the Year-End window to process the year-end.

❑ Open: the **A/P Processing Reports** window

❑ DClick: on the **Posting Journals** [Posting Journals] icon

The A/P Posting Journal Report window will appear as shown in Figure 29-9.

FIGURE 29-9
A/P Posting Journal Report Window

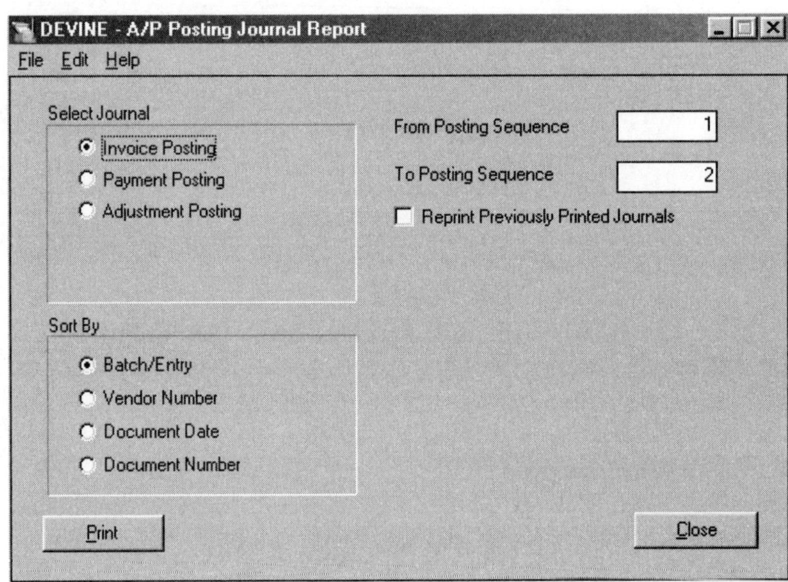

❑ Click: the **Payment Posting** option button in the Select Journal area

❑ Press: **Tab** [Tab] to move to the From Posting Sequence field

In the From and To Posting Sequence fields, enter the lowest and highest numbers of the journals you want. A unique posting sequence number is assigned each time you post batches. The default is to include all posting sequences.

❑ Press: **Tab** [Tab] for both the From Posting and To Posting sequences

You can reprint previously printed journals if desired. In this case, it is not necessary.

❑ Press: **Tab** [Tab] to move to the Sort By area

Sort By

You can specify the order in which you will list the transactions on the posting journal. You can sort by Batch/Entry, Vendor Number, Document Date, or Check Number. Devine Designs Inc. wants the information printed by check number.

❑ Select: **Batch/Entry**
❑ Print: the **A/P Posting Journal** report

Once printing is complete, review the Posting Journal and compare it to the batch listing printed earlier. Ensure that all transactions are posted.

❑ Click: **Close** to return to the A/P Processing Reports window

PRINTING THE CHECK REGISTER

❑ DClick: the **Check Register** Check Register icon

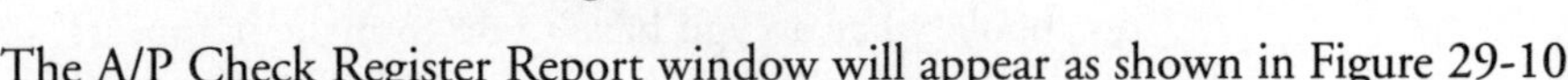

The A/P Check Register Report window will appear as shown in Figure 29-10.

FIGURE 29-10
Check Register Report Window

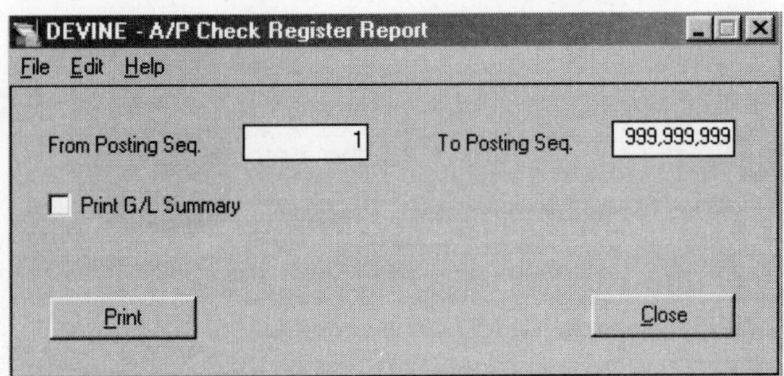

The Check Register Report lists the details of checks that are produced and posted to vendor accounts during a check run. The Check Register Report can also list the General Ledger distributions. You should print this report after posting a check run as part of your audit trail of payments made during a check run.

❑ Click: the **Print G/L Summary** check box to obtain a General Ledger distribution
❑ Print: the **A/P Check Register** report

The Check Register prints all valid checks, but does not list alignment or voided checks. If you need information on all the checks printed by the program, you can print the Checks Status Report from Bank Services.

Review your printout. Once you are satisfied it is correct,

❑ Click: **Close** Close

Posting the Accounts Payable Batches to the General Ledger

Once you have completed the month's Accounts Payable transactions, you have to transfer the information to the General Ledger. General Ledger batches were created automatically as you created the various Accounts Payable entries. If you cannot remember how to post the Accounts Payable transactions, refer back to the General Ledger portion of the book for instructions.

Review Questions

1. How many system-generated batches can you produce at any one time?
2. If the Selection Code does not appear at the top of the A/P Create Payment Batch notebook, what do you have to do to make it appear?
3. What is the purpose of the Vendor Exclusion List Page?
4. What is included on the Pre-Check Register?
5. If you are not satisfied with the printing of a check, can you reprint it?
6. What is the final step in the check processing cycle?
7. When should you print the Posting Journals?
8. In what orders can you sort transactions on the Posting Journal?
9. What does the Check Register contain?

Exercise

- ❑ Sign on to your company as the system administrator using 06/15/10 as the Session Date.
- ❑ Prepare to process the system checks by creating a payment batch for amounts due on or before 06/20/10 and discounts available from 06/10/10 to 06/20/10.
- ❑ Print the Pre-Check Register.
- ❑ Generate a Payment batch.
- ❑ Print the Batch Listing.
- ❑ Print the checks and post both Payment batches.
- ❑ Print the Posting Journal.
- ❑ Print the A/P Check Register Report.

CHAPTER 30

ANALYTICAL REPORTS AND PERIODIC PROCEDURES

In this chapter, you will print three Accounts Payable analytical reports: Vendor Transactions, Aged Payables, and Aged Cash Requirements. Paid transactions will then be cleared and transferred to the history file.

PRINTING THE VENDOR TRANSACTIONS REPORT

The Vendor Transactions report lists the transactions that have been posted to vendor accounts during the period you specify when printing the report. You can print the report whenever you want to see the current status of the vendor accounts.

- ❑ Sign on to Devine Designs Inc. as the system administrator using 06/30/10 as the Session Date.
- ❑ Open: the **A/P Analytical Reports** window

The A/P Analytical Reports icons will appear as shown in Figure 30-1.

FIGURE 30-1
A/P Analytical Reports Icons

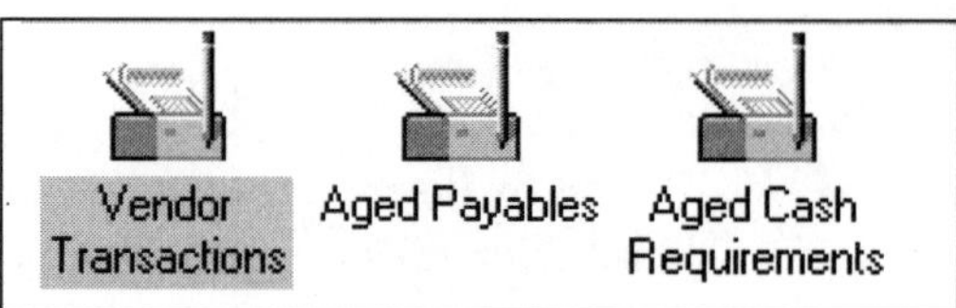

❑ DClick: **Vendor Transactions** 

The A/P Vendor Transactions Report window will appear as shown in Figure 30-2.

FIGURE 30-2
A/P Vendor Transactions Report Window

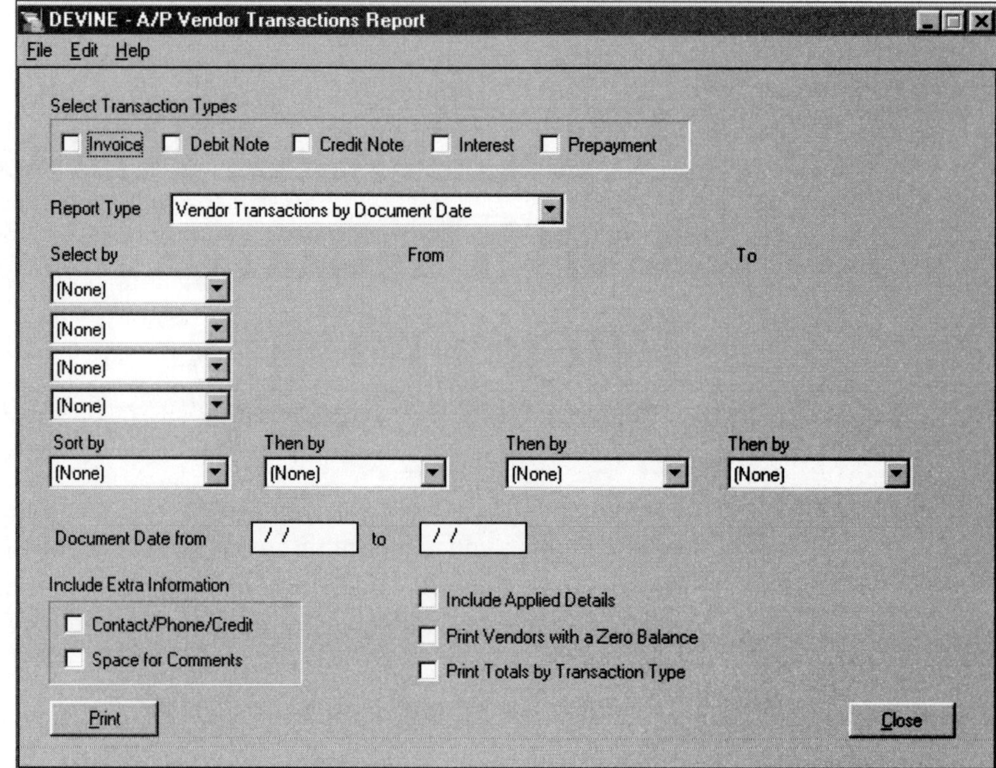

Select Transaction Types

❑ Locate: the **Select Transaction Types** selection area
❑ Click: each check box (a total of five times) to select all transaction types
❑ Press: **Tab** [Tab]

Report Type

You can print this report in order by document date, document number, or fiscal year and period. This report will be printed by document number.

- ❑ Click: the **list tool** to the right of the Report Type field
- ❑ Select: **Vendor Transactions by Fiscal Year and Period**
- ❑ Press: **Tab** [Tab]

Select by

- ❑ Click: the **list tool** to the right of the first Select by field
- ❑ Select: **Vendor No.**
- ❑ Press: **Tab** [Tab]
- ❑ Press: **Tab** [Tab] in the From field
- ❑ Press: **Tab** [Tab] in the To field

This will identify the entire range of vendors for the A/P Vendor Transactions Report.

WARNING

If a payment batch that has been previously created is unposted, you will not be allowed to continue until it is posted or deleted.

- ❑ Click: the **Include Applied Details** check box near the bottom of the screen
- ❑ Click: the **Print Vendors with a Zero Balance** check box
- ❑ Click: **Print** [Print]
- ❑ Click: **OK** [OK] when the Print File window appears

Once the report has been printed,

- ❑ Close: the **A/P Vendor Transactions Report** window

FIGURE 30-3
Vendor Transactions Report

Date: Sunday, October 08, 2000 10:11AM
A/P Vendor Transactions (APVTRN01)

DDI Student Name

Pa

From Vendor No.	[ ] To [ZZZZZZZZZZZZ]
Include Documents Through Year/Pd.	[2011-02]
Report Format	[Vendor Transactions by Fiscal Year and Period]
Transaction Types	[Invoice, Debit Note, Credit Note, Interest, Prepayment]
Contact/Phone/Credit	[N]
Space For Comments	[N]
Include Applied Detail	[Y]
Print Zero-Balance Vendors	[Y]
Print Transaction Type Totals	[N]

Vendor No./ Doc. Number	Vendor Name	Ty.	Order Number/ 1099/CPRS Code/Amount	PO Number/ Check Number	Year-Pd.	Due Date/ Applied Number	Batch-Entry/ Appl. Type	Days Over	Original Amount	Cu Am
1001	AsTech Computers									
PP000000001		PI		DD0010	2011-01	5/30/2010	1-3	31	-776.25	-77
						Vendor Total :			-776.25	-77
1100	Kenin's Kopy Service									
KKS 0175		IN		DD0005	2011-01	6/19/2010	1-2	11	517.50	51
						Vendor Total :			517.50	51
1150	Prestonia Office Products									
CROO56		CR			2011-01	5/30/2010	2-1	0	-287.50	
CROO56-1					2011-01	POP 9889	CF		287.50	
POP 9889		IN	ORD-1354	DD0004	2011-01	6/11/2010	1-1	0	1.092.50	
POP 9889-1					2011-01	CROO56	CT		-287.50	
POP 9889-1				5	2011-01		PY		-805.00	
						Vendor Total :			805.00	
1180	Software Depot									
SD-35820		IN		DD0006	2011-01	6/19/2010	1-3	11	1.144.25	
SD-35820-1				6	2011-01		PY		-1.124.35	
SD-35820-1				6	2011-01		ED		-19.90	
						Vendor Total :			1.144.25	
1220	MicroWare Ltd.									
MW0188		IN		DD0008	2011-01	6/30/2010	1-5	0	9.200.00	5.52
MW0188-1				1	2011-01		PY		-3.680.00	

Date: Sunday, October 08, 2000 10:11AM
A/P Vendor Transactions (APVTRN01)

DDI Student Name

Page 2

Vendor No./ Doc. Number	Vendor Name	Ty.	Order Number/ 1099/CPRS Code/Amount	PO Number/ Check Number	Year-Pd.	Due Date/ Applied Number	Batch-Entry/ Appl. Type	Days Over	Original Amount	Current Amount
						Vendor Total :			9.200.00	5.520.00
1250	Summit Peak Computers									
SP-9746		IN		DD0007	2011-01	6/24/2010	1-4	0	230.00	0.00
SP-9746-1				8	2011-01		PY		-226.00	
SP-9746-1				8	2011-01		ED		-4.00	
SP-980		IN		DD0009	2011-01	6/27/2010	3-1	0	689.99	0.00
SP-980-1					2011-01	SP-C-9801	CT		-57.50	
SP-980-1				8	2011-01		PY		-620.49	
SP-980-1				8	2011-01		ED		-12.00	
SP-C-9801		CR		DD0009	2011-01	5/29/2010	3-2	0	-57.50	0.00
SP-C-9801-1					2011-01	SP-980	CF		57.50	
						Vendor Total :			862.49	0.00
						Report Total:			11.752.99	5.261.25

CR: Credit Note | *DB: Debit Note* | *IN: Invoice* | *IT: Interest Charge* | *PI: Prepayment*
AD: Adjustment | *CF: Applied Credit (from)* | *CT: Applied Credit (to)* | *DF: Applied Debit (from)* | *DT: Applied Debit (to)*
ED: Earned Discount Taken | *GL: Gain or Loss (multicurrency ledgers)* | *PY: Payment*

6 vendors printed

On the Vendor Transactions Report, note the unapplied prepayment to As-Tech Computers and the zero balance accounts resulting from the checks issued in Chapter 29.

PRINTING THE AGED PAYABLES REPORT

You use the A/P Aged Payables Report to review and analyze overdue accounts payable. The report lists the total current payables for each vendor. You print the report whenever you need a listing of the status of your payables on a given date, for example, at the end of a fiscal period or year, or when you want to identify documents or balances you will write off.

❑ DClick: the **Aged Payables** icon

The A/P Aged Payables report window will appear as shown in Figure 30-4.

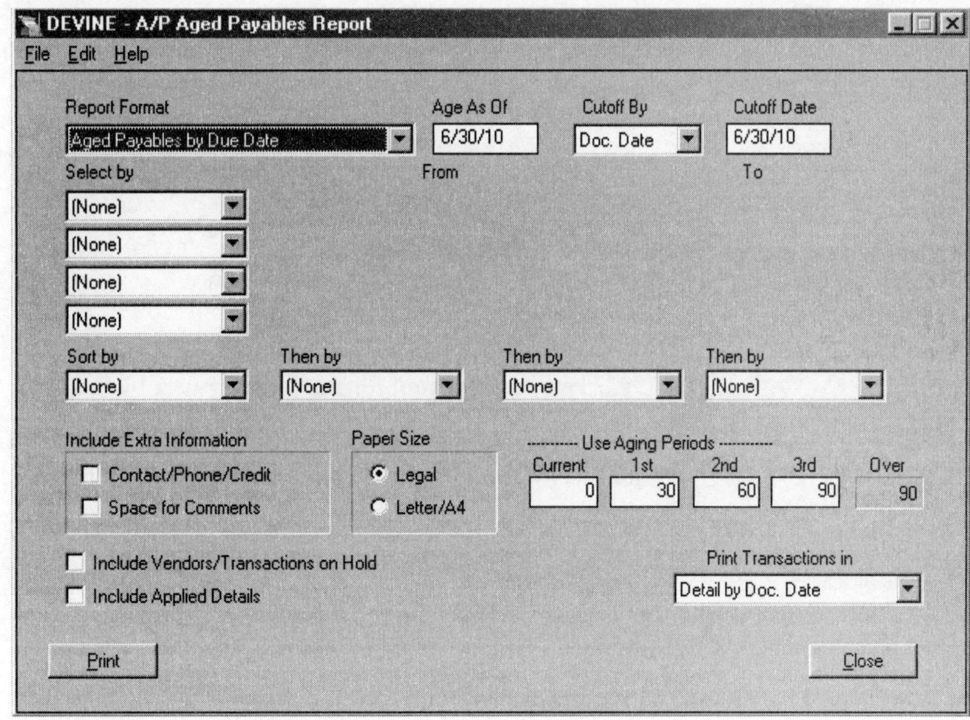

FIGURE 30-4
A/P Aged Payables Report Window

You can age the outstanding or overdue documents or balances by their due dates or document dates.

❑ Click: the **list tool** for the Report Format field
❑ Select: **Aged Payables by Due Date**
❑ Press: **Tab** [Tab]

The Age As Of field is used to identify the date you want to use to report the payables. The program will use this date to assign transactions to aging periods.

- ❑ Type: **063010** in the **Age As Of** text box
- ❑ Press: **Tab** [Tab]

The report will include only those transactions that have a document date that is on or before the cutoff date you specify. There are two methods of selecting a cutoff date:

Document Date: You choose this option if you want to include documents based on their document date.

Year/Period: Use this method if you want to include all transactions up to the end of a fiscal period.

- ❑ Select: **Doc. Date** in the **Cutoff By** text box
- ❑ Type: **063010** in the **Cutoff Date** text box
- ❑ Press: **Tab** [Tab]

Select By

You can choose up to four criteria to select the vendor accounts to list on the report.

- ❑ Click: the **list tool** for the first Select by field

You have four choices: None, Vendor No., Vendor Group, and Short Name.

- ❑ Select: **Vendor No.**
- ❑ Press: **Tab** [Tab]

Leaving the From field blank and the z's in the To field will ensure that all vendors are included in the report.

- ❑ Click: the **list tool** for the second Select by field

As you can see, there is a greater variety of choice in the remaining Select by fields. If you do not specify any criteria, the report will include all the vendor records that meet the criteria you selected earlier in this window.

- ❑ Select: **(None)**

Sort By

You have as many as four orders in which you can sort records for the report. If you do not specify sorting criteria, the report will order the records by vendor number.

Contact/Phone/Credit

You choose this option if you want to list the vendor's contact person and phone number, and the credit limit assigned to you by the vendor.

Space for Comments

You choose this option if you want to leave a blank space at the end of each vendor record for notes.

Include Vendors/Transactions on Hold

You choose this option if you want to include transactions that you have placed on hold in the Control Payments window.

- ❑ Click: the **Include Vendors/Transactions on Hold** check box

Include Applied Details

You select this option if you want to include all the documents, such as payments and credit notes, that were applied to each invoice. If you choose not to select this option, the report will show only the balance owing for each outstanding document.

- ❑ Click: the **Include Applied Details** check box

Use Aging Periods

The aging periods you entered in the Options notebook are displayed on the screen. You can assign different periods for individual reports if necessary. No change is necessary at present.

Print Transactions In

You can print the report in either summary or detail format. The detailed report can be printed by Document Date or by Document Number. The detail versions of the report can be printed on legal-sized ($8^1/_2 \times 14$ inch) or letter-sized ($8^1/_2 \times 11$ inch) paper. The summary report prints on letter-sized paper.

- ❑ Click: the **list tool** for the Print Transaction In field
- ❑ Select: **Detail by Document**

When you select either of the detailed reports, a Paper Size selection area is displayed on the screen.

- ❑ Select: **Letter/A4** as the paper size
- ❑ Print: the **A/P Aged Payables by Due Date** report

Compare your report with Figure 30-5.

Figure 30-5
A/P Aged Payables by Due Date

Date: Sunday, October 08, 2000 10:55AM
A/P Aged Payables by Due Date (APAPAY11)

DDI Student Name

Page 1

From Vendor No.	[] To [ZZZZZZZZZZZZ]
Age Transactions As of	[6/30/2010]
Cutoff By Doc. Date	[6/30/2010]
Print Transactions In	[Detail by Document]
Contact/Phone/Credit	[N]
Space For Comments	[N]
Include Applied Details	[Y]
Include Transations on Hold	[Y]

Doc. Date / Appl. Date	Ty.	Doc. Number / Applied No./App. Type	Due Date	Current	1 to 30 Days	31 to 60 Days	61 to 90 Days	Over 90 Days	Total Overdue	Total Payables
Vendor Number: 1001				Vendor Name:	AsTech Computers					
5/30/2010	PI	PP000000001	5/30/2010			-776.25			-776.25	-776.25
		Vendor Total :		0.00	0.00	-776.25	0.00	0.00	-776.25	-776.25
Vendor Number: 1100				Vendor Name:	Kenin's Kopy Service					
5/20/2010	IN	KKS 0175	6/19/2010		517.50				517.50	517.50
		Vendor Total :		0.00	517.50	0.00	0.00	0.00	517.50	517.50
Vendor Number: 1220				Vendor Name:	MicroWare Ltd.					
5/29/2010	IN	MW0188	6/30/2010	5,520.00	3,680.00				3,680.00	9,200.00
5/30/2010		PY			-3,680.00				-3,680.00	-3,680.00
		Vendor Total :		5,520.00	0.00	0.00	0.00	0.00	0.00	5,520.00
		Report Total:		5,520.00	517.50	-776.25	0.00	0.00	-258.75	5,261.25
				104.92%	9.84%	-14.75%	0.00%	0.00%	-4.92%	100.00%

AD: Adjustment CF: Applied Credit (from) CT: Applied Credit (to) DF: Applied Debit (from) DT: Applied Debit (to)
ED: Earned Discount Taken GL: Gain or Loss (multicurrency ledgers) PI: Prepayment PY: Payment

3 vendors printed

Note the detail for each vendor. If you had selected Summary in the Print Transactions selection box, only totals would be printed for each vendor.

❑ Close: the **A/P Aged Payables Report** window

Printing the Aged Cash Requirements

The Aged Cash Requirements Report focuses on the amount of cash that is required to meet all obligations as they become due. This report is used for cash flow analysis and projections.

❑ DClick: the **Aged Cash Requirements** icon 

The A/P Aged Cash Requirements Report dialog box in Figure 30-6 is very similar to the A/P Aged Payables dialog box.

FIGURE 30-6
A/P Aged Cash Requirements Dialog Box

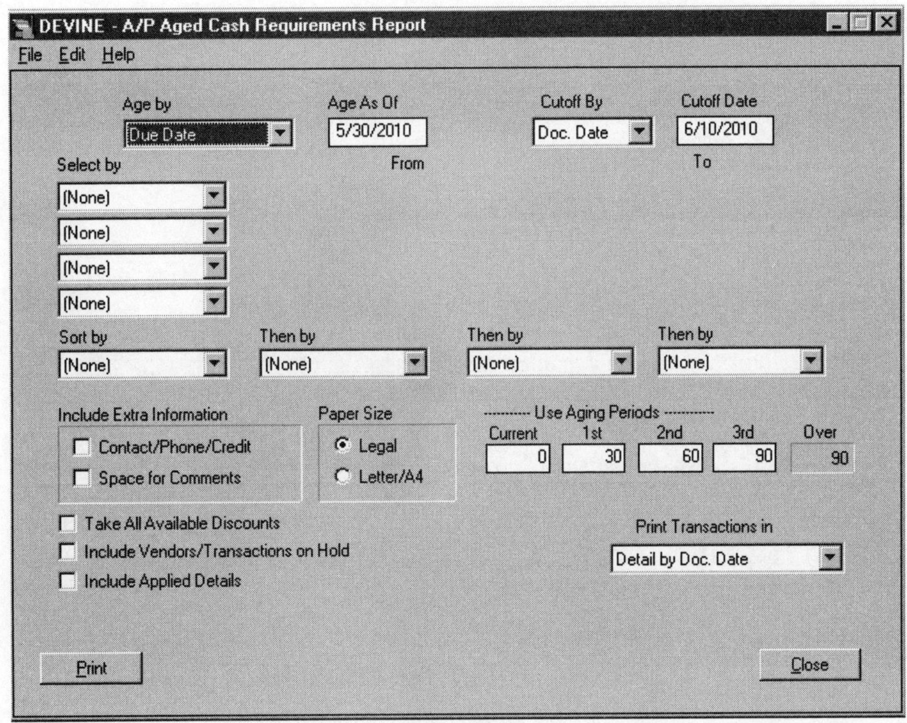

- ❑ Select: **Due Date** in the **Age by** selection box
- ❑ Type: **063010** in the **Age As Of** text box
- ❑ Select: **Doc. Date** in the **Cutoff By** selection box
- ❑ Type: **093010** in the **Cutoff Date** text box
- ❑ Select: **Vendor No.** in the first **Select by** selection box
- ❑ Select: **1001 AsTech Computers** using the Finder for the **From** text box
- ❑ Select: **1250 Summit Peak Computers** using the Finder for the **To** text box
- ❑ Click: the **Take All Available Discounts** selection box
- ❑ Select: **Summary** in the **Print Transaction in** list box
- ❑ Print: the report

FIGURE 30-7
Aged Cash Requirements Report

Date: Sunday, October 08, 2000 11:31AM
A/P Aged Cash Requirements by Due Date (APCREQSY)

DDI Student Name

Page 1

From Vendor No.	[1001] To [1250]
Age Transactions As of	[6/30/2010]
Cutoff By Doc. Date	[9/30/2010]
Print Transactions In	[Summary]
Contact/Phone/Credit	[N]
Space For Comments	[N]
Take All Available Discounts	[Y]
Include Transactions on Hold	[N]

Vendor Number	Vendor Name	Overdue	Current	1 to 30 Days	31 to 60 Days	61 to 90 Days	Over 90 Days	Total Payables
1001	AsTech Computers	-776.25	0.00	0.00	0.00	0.00	0.00	-776.25
1100	Kenin's Kopy Service	517.50	0.00	0.00	0.00	0.00	0.00	517.50
1220	MicroWare Ltd.	0.00	2,760.00	2,760.00	0.00	0.00	0.00	5.520.00
	Report Total:	-258.75	2,760.00	2,760.00	0.00	0.00	0.00	5.261.25
		-4.92%	52.46%	52.46%	0.00%	0.00%	0.00%	100.00%

3 vendors printed

❑ Close: the **A/P Aged Cash Requirements** dialog box

PERIODIC PROCESSING

Periodic Processing enables you to complete the types of processing you do at specified times such as month end, period end, or year end. You can also clear out obsolete records and data.

❑ Open: the **A/P Periodic Processing** window

The A/P Periodic Processing icons will appear as shown in Figure 30-8.

FIGURE 30-8
A/P Periodic Processing Icons

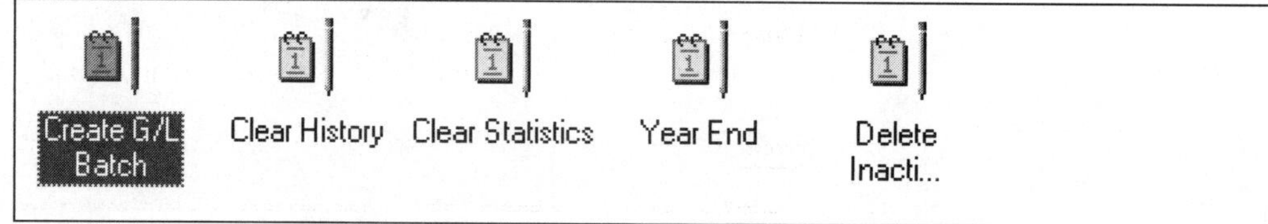

CREATING GENERAL LEDGER BATCHES

On the Integration page of the A/P Options notebook, you selected the Create G/L Transactions During Posting option, so there is no need for you to create General Ledger batches. This procedure is for those times when the On Request Using Create G/L Batch Icon option has been selected.

You use the Create G/L Batch window to produce batches of General Ledger transactions from the invoice, payment, and adjustment batches posted in accounts payable; however, you can use this window to create batches only if you did not select the Create General Ledger Batches During Posting option. You must create all outstanding General Ledger batches before you can clear posting journals or use the Year-End function.

CLEARING HISTORY

You use the Clear History window to remove outdated data from the Accounts Payable system. You can clear fully paid documents, vendor comments, vendor period statistics, vendor group statistics, vendor 1099/CPRS summaries, and printed and posted journals. Before clearing History, you must ensure that you have posted all outstanding batches that could affect the records you want cleared, determined the dates through which transactions and comments are to be cleared, ascertained the fiscal year and period through which you will clear the statistics, identified the highest posting sequence number to clear, and printed reports of the data you want to clear.

❑ DClick: the **Clear History** icon

FIGURE 30-9
A/P Clear History
Dialog Box

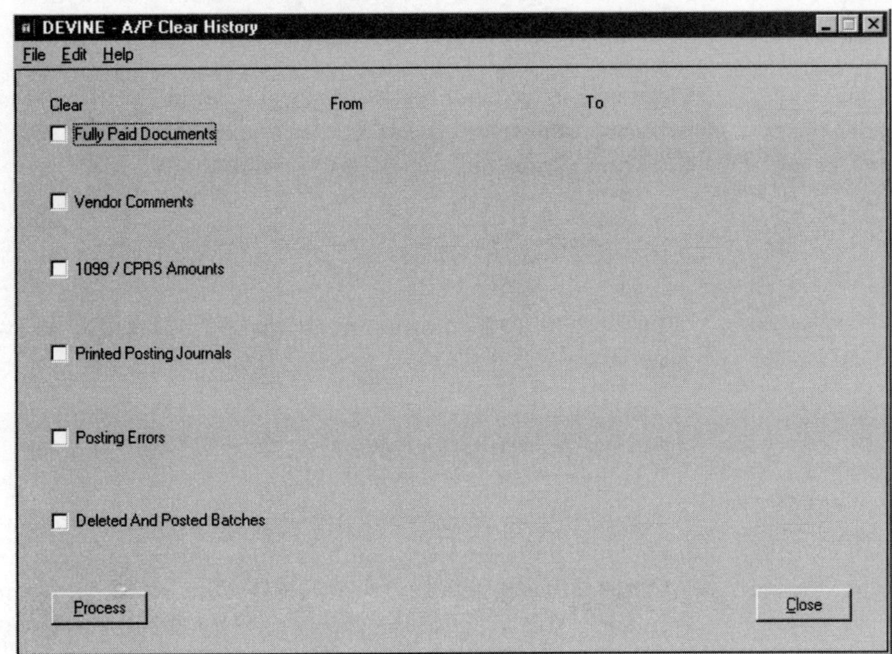

The A/P Clear History dialog box allows you to select the information that you wish to clear. As each item is selected, additional data entry areas appear on the screen.

Fully Paid Documents

❑ Click: the **Fully Paid Documents** check box

The new data entry areas are shown in Figure 30-10.

FIGURE 30-10
Additional Data Entry

The initial defaults show the From field as blank and the To field as containing a row of z's. These defaults clear fully paid documents for all vendors. You can also use the Finders to clear fully paid documents for a range of vendors. The session date is the default in the Through text box. You could enter any earlier date as required.

Devine Designs Inc. will accept the defaults to clear fully paid documents through to June 30, 2010.

Vendor Comments

Devine Designs Inc. has not used vendor comments. If you had entered vendor comments you would click this check box, select a range of vendors, and enter a date in the Through text box.

1099/CPRS Amounts

This selection works the same as above. Devine Designs Inc. will not clear 1099/CPRS Amounts.

Printed Posting Journals

As Devine Designs Inc. prints and files each posting journal while transactions are posted, the printed posting journals can be cleared. You can only clear one type of posting journal at a time. Devine Designs Inc. will clear the Invoice Posting Journals first. Later, you will clear the Payments and Adjustments Posting Journals.

❑ Click: the **Printed Posting Journals** check box
❑ Select: the **Invoices** radio button

Posting Errors

If you have made posting errors, you should activate this check box and select the transaction type for those errors.

Deleted and Posted Batches

This option works in the same way as the Printed Posting Journals option. Devine Designs Inc. will clear deleted and posted invoice batches now. Later, you can clear the payments and adjustment batches that have been deleted or posted.

- ❑ Click: the **Deleted and Posted Batches** check box
- ❑ Activate: the **Invoices** radio button
- ❑ Click: the **Process** button

After reading the three Information messages,

- ❑ Click: **OK**
- ❑ Clear: the **Payments** and **Adjustments** batches
- ❑ Close: the **A/P Clear History** dialog box

Clearing Statistics

The Clear Statistics option clears period statistics up to and including the period you specify. Activity statistics are retained and can be cleared by the Year End option, with the current year statistics becoming the previous year statistics.

- ❑ DClick: the **Clear Statistics** icon
- ❑ Click: the **Vendor Statistics** check box
- ❑ Click: the **Vendor Group Statistics** check box

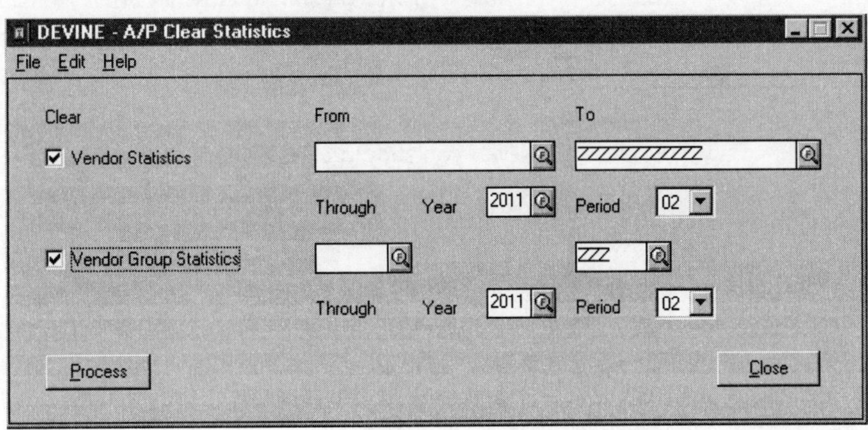

FIGURE 30-11
A/P Clear Statistics Dialog Box

To clear period statistics, you would select the range of vendors or vendor groups and the year and fiscal period. Devine Designs Inc. will not clear statistics at this time.

- ❑ Close: the **A/P Clear Statistics** check box

Deleting Inactive Records

The Delete Inactive Records window is used to eliminate obsolete vendor, vendor group, and remit-to records from the Accounts Payable program. The records can be removed only if they have an inactive status and have been set to inactive within the range of dates you specify.

Before deleting active records, you have to pay or clear all invoices and credit notes, clear all of the vendor's fully paid documents in the Clear History window, delete the Remit-To locations for the vendor, print the accounts payable reports, update the files, and assign an Inactive status to the records you want to delete. None of the Devine Designs Inc. vendors can be classed as inactive.

Year End Processing

The Year End function resets the batch numbers so that the next batch number you create will be number 1. It moves the vendor activity statistics for the current year to the prior year, and reduces the totals for the new year to zero. It resets to zero the Total Invoices Paid and Number Of Checks fields in the Vendors notebook, and the Total Days To pay fields in the Vendors and Vendor Groups notebooks.

Before you start the Year End processing, you should post all outstanding batches, print all unprinted posting journals, then use the Clear History window to clear the data for the posting journals. You should also create all outstanding General Ledger batches (if you did not activate the option to create the batches during posting), then print the G/L Transactions report. Finally you should close all other ACCPAC for Windows Accounts Payable windows and if you are on a network, ensure that no one else is using the accounts payable program.

You can use the Year End function at any time of the year if you need to reset batch numbers; however, you should clear activity statistics and the Total Invoices Paid and Total Days To Pay totals only at the end of the fiscal year.

❑ DClick: the **Year End** Year End icon

The A/P Year End window will appear as displayed by Figure 30-12.

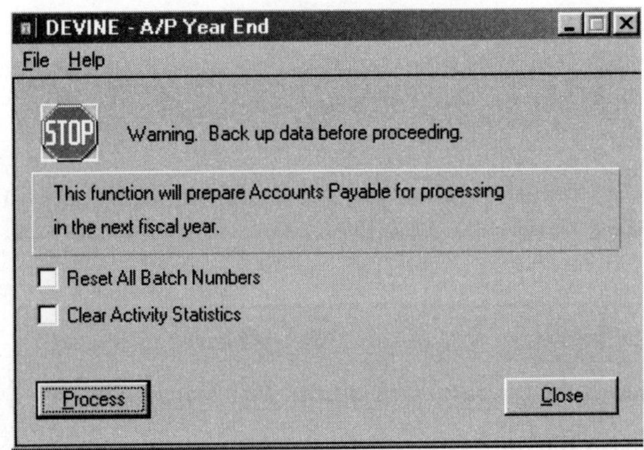

FIGURE 30-12
A/P Year End Window

Reset All Batch Numbers

You select this option when you want to reset the batch numbers to 1 again.

❑ Click: the **Reset All Batch Numbers** check box

Clear Activity Statistics

When you activate this option, the program will enter zeros in the current-year fields on the Vendor Activity page in the Vendors notebook, and transfer current-year statistical information to the corresponding fields for the prior year. Since this is not the actual year-end for Devine Designs Inc., you will not clear the activity statistics.

Leave the Clear Activity Statistics check box unselected.

Note that if you had activated the Clear Activity Statistics check box, a new field, Clear Invoices Paid and Days to Pay Counter, would have appeared.

Clear Invoices Paid and Days to Pay Counter

This option is used to enter zeros in the Total Invoices Paid and the Number of Checks fields in the Vendors notebook, and in the Total Days To Pay fields in the Vendors and Vendor Groups notebooks. You do not use this option if you want to include prior-year documents in the numbers you use to calculate the entry in the Average Days To Pay field for vendor accounts. Devine Designs Inc. will *not* use the Year End Function now.

❑ Click: **Close** [Close]

❑ Exit: **ACCPAC**

Review Questions

1. What are the purposes of the Period End function?
2. What kind of statistics can be cleared from the Clear History window? What kind of statistics cannot be cleared?
3. When are the Activity Statistics cleared?
4. What is the purpose of the A/P Aged Payables Report?
5. What is the purpose of the Create G/L Batch window? What restrictions are present?
6. What is the purpose of the Delete Inactive Records window?
7. What restrictions must be satisfied before you can delete inactive records?
8. What is the purpose of the Year End processing?
9. What restrictions must be satisfied before you can complete the Year End processing?
10. When can you use the Year End function? What restriction should be observed?

Exercise

- ❑ Sign on to your company as the system administrator using 06/30/10 as the Session Date.
- ❑ Print: the **A/P Vendor Transactions** report for all transactions between 05/01/10 and 06/30/10
- ❑ Print: the **Aged Accounts Payable** report
- ❑ Print: the **Aged Cash Requirements**
- ❑ Clear: **Fully Paid Documents**, **Printed Posting Journals**, and **Deleted and Posted Batches**

CASE 4

MURPHBALLS & CO. ACCOUNTS PAYABLE

This case continues from the Murphballs & Co. cases presented earlier in the text. After Murphballs & Co.'s first month of operations, Ruff Tuff McDuff decided to add the ACCPAC for Windows Small Business Series Accounts Payable module to the computerized accounting system.

After completing this case, organize and submit Murphballs & Co.'s printouts. Each printout *must* contain your initials, followed by the company name. If you are given no instructions regarding a field, leave the defaults unchanged.

Sign on to Murphballs & Co. as the system administrator using August 31, 2010 as the Session Date.

Follow the steps and procedures in the Accounts Payable chapters to complete the required tasks.

ACTIVATE ACCOUNTS PAYABLE

❑ Activate: **Accounts Payable 4.1A**

1. CREATE THE FOLLOWING OPTIONS

SETUP OPTIONS

Contact Name:	Your own name
Force Listing of Batches:	Select
Keep History:	Select
Allow Edit of Statistics:	De-select
Include Tax in Statistics:	De-select

INVOICING OPTIONS

Use 1099/CPRS Reporting:	De-select
Allow Edit of Imported Batches:	De-select

PAYMENT PROCESSING OPTIONS

Default Bank Code:	Buried Bone Bank
Aging Periods:	Leave unchanged
Default Order of Open Documents:	Document Number
Allow Adjustments in Payment Batch:	Activate
Allow Edit of System Generated Batches:	De-activate

Leave the Prefix for the generated document numbers unchanged

Age Credit and Debit Notes:	By Date
Age Prepayments:	By Date

INTEGRATION OPTIONS

Create G/L Transactions:	During Posting
Append G/L Transactions to Existing Batch:	Select
Consolidate G/L Batches:	Do Not Consolidate
G/L Reference:	Vendor Number
G/L Description:	Document Number

❑ Print: the A/P Options Report

2. Modify the Following Bank Records

Use Common Services to complete the following:

Bank: Buried Bone Bank
Check Stock Code: STD001
Description: Standard Forms
Next Check Number: 107
Stock Type: Combined Check and Advice
Select Report: APCHK01.RPT

❑ Print: the Banks Report

3. Create Tax Classes

All of the Tax Classes should have been defined when you added them for the Accounts Receivable. Ensure that you have set up Tax Classes for RSTON and GSTFED. You should have Purchases and Vendors, as well as Sales and Customers, set up with Class 1 - Taxable, and Class 2 - Exempt.

The Tax Rates were created when you did the Accounts Receivable case. Ensure that you have created rates for all Tax Classes.

Create Tax Group

Tax Group: PURCH
Transaction Type: Purchases
Description: Purchases on Account
Tax Calculation Method: Calculate Tax by Detail
Authority: GSTFED and RSTON

❑ Taxable: set both authorities to No

❑ Print: the Purchases Tax Groups Report

4. Create Account Sets

Account Set Code:	1
Description:	Accounts Payable - General
Payables Control:	2101
Purchases Discounts:	1450
Prepayment Liability:	2115

❑ Print: the A/P Account Sets Report

5. Create Distribution Codes

❑ Create: the following Distribution Codes

Distribution Code:	OFFSUP
Description:	Office Supplies Purchase
G/L Account:	1301
Distribution Code:	GSTPAY
Description:	GST Payable
G/L Account:	2110
Distribution Code:	PYRL
Description.:	Payroll
G/L Account:	6060

❑ Print: the A/P Distribution Codes Report

6. Create Distribution Sets

❑ Create: the following Distribution Set

Distribution Set Code:	OFFSUP
Description:	Office Supplies
Distribution Method:	Fixed Percentage
Distribution Code:	OFFSUP
Distribution Percent:	93.4579
Distribution Code:	GSTPAY
Distribution Percent:	6.5421

❑ Print: the A/P Distribution Sets Report

7. Create Terms

Murphballs & Co. will have only two Terms Sets.

❑ Add: the following specifications.

Terms Code:	n/30
Description:	Net 30
Calculate Base for Discount With Tax:	Excluded
Due Date Type:	Days from Invoice Date
Discount Type:	Days from Invoice Date
First No. of Days cell:	30
Discount Percent cell:	0

Terms Code:	DISC
Description:	2/10, n/30
Calculate Base for Discount With Tax:	Excluded
Due Date Type:	Days from Invoice Date
Discount Type:	Days from Invoice Date
First No. of Days cell:	30
Discount Percent cell:	2
Second No. of Days cell:	10

❑ Print: the A/P Terms Report

8. Create Vendor Records

During July, you made purchases from three vendors, Dogs' World News, Dog Chow Supplies Ltd, and Dog Catchers Insurance. The full profiles for all three vendors plus two new vendors follow. Create the vendor records for all five. No comments or references will be added to the vendor profiles. Murphballs & Co. will create only one Vendor group for all of its vendors.

Add the Vendor Group

Vendor Group:

Group Code:	APM
Description:	Accounts Payable Master
Account Sets:	1 (Accounts Payable - General)
Terms Code:	n/30
Bank Code:	BBB
Distribute By:	Distribution Set
Distribution Set:	OFFSUP

Group Options

Duplicate Invoice Checking:
Vendor and Amount: Warning
Vendor and Date: Warning
Generate Separate Payments for Each Invoice: De-select

Taxes

Tax Group PURCH

❑ Print: the A/P Vendor Group Report

9. Add Vendor Accounts

Vendor Number:	1010
Vendor Name:	Boneworks Restaurant (Their motto is: "We gnaw to please!")
Group Code:	APM
Short Name:	Boneworks
Address:	100 Chewable Bone Way Muttsville Junction BOW WOW
Telephone:	555-555-9293
Fax:	555-555-9291
Contact:	Rambaran
Start Date:	August 1, 2010

Processing Information:

Credit Limit:	$500
Distribute By:	G/L Account Number 6030

Generate Separate Payments for each Invoice: De-select

Tax Information:

Both GST and RST will apply to purchases made from this vendor.

Vendor Number	1020
Vendor Name	Dog Catchers Insurance (Their motto is: "Protection against unlawful incarceration!")
Group Code:	APM
Short Name:	Dog Catch
Address:	125 Dog Pound Way Muttsville Junction BOW WOW
Telephone:	555-555-9246

Fax: 555-555-9245
Contact: Arjumand
Start Date: July 1, 2010

Processing Information:
Credit Limit: $500
Distribute By: G/L Account Number 1401
Generate Separate Payments for each Invoice: De-select

Tax Information:

Only the RST is applicable for this vendor. GST is not charged.

Vendor Number: 1030
Vendor Name: Dog Chow Supplies
(Their motto is: "Finger Lickin' Good!")
Group Code: APM
Short Name: Dog Chow
Address: 34 Kibble Ave.
Muttsville Junction
BOW WOW
Telephone: 555-555-8795
Fax: 555-555-8796
Contact: Bedarka
Start Date: July 31, 2010

Processing Information:
Credit Limit: $500
Distribute By: OFFSUP
Generate Separate Payments for each Invoice: De-select

Tax Information

Only GST applies to purchases made from this vendor.

Vendor Number: 1050
Vendor Name: Dogs' World News
(Their motto is; "All the news that's fit to cover the floor!")
Address: 110 Fleet St.
Muttsville Junction
BOW WOW
Telephone: 555-555-7567
Fax: 555-555-7568
Contact: Carlspur
Start Date: July 10, 2010

Processing Information:
Credit Limit: $500
Distribute By: G/L Account Number 6000
Generate Separate Payments for each Invoice: De-select

Tax Information

Both GST and RST apply to purchases made from this vendor.

Vendor Number:	1070
Vendor Name:	Doghouse Rentals (Their motto: "When you're in the doghouse, stay here!")
Group Code:	APM
Short Name:	Doghouse
Address:	74 Sleeping Dog Way Muttsville Junction BOW WOW
Telephone:	555-555-9789
Fax:	555-555-9788
Contact:	Partagas
Start Date:	August 1, 2010

Processing Information

Credit Limit:	$750
Distribute By:	G/L Account Number 6070
Generate Separate Payments for each Invoice:	De-select

Tax Information

GST is exempt for office rentals but RST applies

❑ Print: the A/P Vendor List including the Address and Profile

10. Add Payment Selection Codes

Selection Code:	DUE
Description:	All due invoices
Pay from Bank:	BBB
Select Vendors with this Bank Code Only:	Select
Select Documents By:	Due Date and Disc. Date
All Selected Documents:	Active

❑ Print: the A/P Payment Selection Codes Report

11. ENTER THE AUGUST TRANSACTIONS

Ensure that the session date is August 31, 2010. Create a new batch to record the following invoices. The Description for the Batch Header will be "August Transactions".

August 1: Purchased a one-year freedom insurance policy from Dog Catchers Insurance. P.O. number M001. The cost of the policy is $120.00 plus RST.

August 5: Since the first advertisement had been so successful, Murphballs & Co. placed another advertisement in Dogs' World News advertising their service. Purchase Order number M002. The invoice, DW 8345 was for $35 plus RST and GST.

August 9: Murphballs & Co. received a shipment of Doggie Treats from Dog Chow Supplies. The invoice, DC 234, was for $32 plus GST. Murphballs considers the Dog Treats to be Office Supplies. Purchase Order number M003.

August 16: Invoice 10-453 from Boneworks Restaurant for the howling good time the company had celebrating the first month of operations. The Purchase Order number was M004, and the invoice was for $20 plus GST and RST.

August 25: Monthly invoice from Doghouse Rentals for the September office rent. $30 plus RST.

August 30: Since Murphballs was running low on office supplies, made an emergency purchase of Doggie Treats from Dog Chow Supplies. The invoice (number DC 302) was for $30 plus GST. Purchase Order number M005.

- ❑ Print: the A/P Invoice Batch Listing - Invoice
- ❑ Post: the batch to the Accounts Payable ledger
- ❑ Print: the Invoice Posting Journal sorted by Vendor Number
- ❑ Print: the A/P Aged Payables Report on letter-sized paper, aged by Due Date

12. ADJUSTMENTS

It has come to your attention that the invoice from Dog Chow Supplies, invoice DC 234, was incorrectly recorded as $32 plus GST. The invoice amount should have been $23 plus sales taxes. The amount of the debit note is $9.00 plus GST.

- ❑ Create: a new batch for Debit Note DN-001 dated August 31, 2010
- ❑ Print: the new batch

- ❑ Post: the new batch to the Accounts Payable ledger
- ❑ Print: the Invoice Posting Journal sorted by Vendor Number
- ❑ Reprint: the Aged Payables Report on letter-sized paper, aged by Due Date

13. Record Prepayments

- ❑ Create: a new Payment Batch to record the following prepayment

Murphballs & Co. has decided to place an ongoing ad in the Dogs' World News for September 2010 through February 2011. The total cost of the ad is $207 (including sales taxes). Because Murphballs is a relatively new client, Dogs' World News requires a check for the six months along with the order. The Murphballs & Co. Purchase Order number is M006.

Description: Prepayment on P.O. M006
Transaction Type: Prepayment
Check Date: August 30, 2010

The check you are going to create will be manually **paw**duced rather than being computer-generated.

Print Check: De-select
Check Number: 107
Apply to Document Type: PO Number
Apply to PO Number: M006
Prepayment Amount: $238.05
Activation Date: September 30, 2010

- ❑ Print: the A/P Batch Listing Report

14. Record a Miscellaneous Payment

The emergency Dog Chow Supplies delivery was made by Grizzly Express on manual August 31, 2010. The delivery charge of $5 including taxes was paid upon delivery with manual check number 108. (The employees of the company were not about to argue with the delivery bear about the price.) Record the payment of $5.75 made to Grizzly Express as a miscellaneous payment. Charge the disbursement to Office Supplies. Grizzly Express's address is

17 Great White North Way
Deepforest
ROA MNG

❑ Print and Post the Payment Batch.

15. Generating, Printing and Posting a Batch of Checks

❑ Exit: from ACCPAC Small Business Series for Windows

❑ Restart: the Accounts Payable module for Murphballs & Co.

❑ Set: the date to September 30, 2010

All of the August invoices are due for payment. Select the documents by Due Date. The Due Date is September 30, 2010. Use the Create Payment Batch notebook to print all of the DUE invoices using the defaults created earlier.

❑ Print: the A/P Pre-Check register

❑ Generate: the Payment batch

❑ Print: the A/P Payment Batches Listing Report

❑ Print: the checks

❑ Print: and post the Payment batch

❑ Print: the A/P Posting Journal report sorted by Vendor Number

❑ Print: the A/P Check Register report

16. Periodic Processing

❑ Print: the Vendor Transactions report for all Transaction Types, sorted by Vendor No.

❑ Print: the Accounts Payable Aged Trial Balance aged by Due Date. The aging date is September 30, 2010. Print the report on letter-size paper. Include the applied details and print vendors with a zero balance.

❑ Print: the A/P Batch Status report

❑ Post: the Accounts Receivable transactions to the General Ledger

❑ Print: the General Ledger G/L Transactions Listing sorted by Account Number